Soldier of Peace

Also by Dan Kurzman

Blood and Water:
Sabotaging Hitler's Bomb

Left to Die: The Tragedy
of the USS Juneau

Fatal Voyage: The Sinking
of the USS Indianapolis

A Killing Wind: Inside Union Carbide
and the Bhopal Catastrophe

Day of the Bomb:
Countdown to Hiroshima

Ben-Gurion: Prophet of Fire

Miracle of November:
Madrid's Epic Stand, 1936

The Bravest Battle: The 28 Days
of the Warsaw Ghetto Uprising

The Race for Rome

Genesis 1948: The First Arab–Israeli War

Santo Domingo: Revolt of the Damned

Subversion of the Innocents

Kishi and Japan: The Search for the Sun

Soldier of ——Peace——

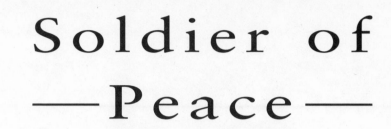

The Life of

YITZHAK RABIN

—— 1922–1995 ——

DAN KURZMAN

HarperCollins*Publishers*

HarperCollins books may be purchased for educational, business, or sales promotional use. For information please write: Special Markets Department, HarperCollins Publishers, Inc., 10 East 53rd Street, New York, NY 10022.

FIRST EDITION

Designed by Gloria Adelson/Lulu Graphics

Library of Congress Cataloging-in-Publication Data

Kurzman, Dan.
   Soldier of peace : the life of Yitzhak Rabin / Dan Kurzman.
     p. cm.
   Includes index.
   ISBN 0-06-018684-4
   1. Rabin, Yitzhak, 1922–. Prime ministers—Israel—Forces—Biography. 3. Generals—Israel—Biography. 4. Israel—Armed Forces—Biography. I. Title.
DS126.6.R32K87   1998
956.9405'092—dc21
[B]   97-51898

---

98 99 00 01 02 ❖/RRD 10 9 8 7 6 5 4 3 2 1

For my dear wife, Florence—whose gentle,
generous nature is as soothing
as a song of peace

Contents

Photographs follow pages 174 and 430.

Preface

I first met Yitzhak Rabin while covering the Six-Day War for the *Washington Post* and conducting research for my book *Genesis 1948: The First Arab–Israeli War.* Rabin had led the Israeli army to one of the most remarkable victories in history, but when I interviewed him for the first time, he did not greatly impress me. He was shy, dry, and uncomfortable, with suspicious eyes, a dour expression, and red cheeks that almost suggested embarrassment as he answered questions with staccato brevity. Rabin did not fit the image of the heroic, tough-minded, self-asserting general of military lore. He was certainly no Moshe Dayan, whose charismatic presence and intimidating sardonic smile were legendary.

But as I got to know Rabin over the years, I realized how mistaken my first impression had been. Shy, yes, but by no means dry. In fact, his shyness, apparently fed by an inbred insecurity, cloaked a warm, sensitive nature and an iron will that would change the course of history.

When I called his secretary to request a meeting shortly before he became prime minister in 1992, he got on the phone himself and welcomed me back to Israel. After our meeting, he offered to write an introduction to a new edition of *Genesis 1948,* though he was haggard from the pace of his campaign schedule. At the same time, though, he did not hesitate to snap at me when I dared to ask him to repeat an answer or questioned the validity of some statement. He could not waste a second with the future of Israel and the Middle East at stake—especially because he wasn't at all sure that the public would support him in the coming election. Still, as head of the Labor Party, he hoped to be the next prime minister. He made clear that he knew how to achieve peace. As I was leaving, he stood up and said, "You can write that if we win I'll make peace within nine months after taking office."

I stared at Yitzhak Rabin in disbelief and saw reflected in his eyes a burning resolve—almost an obsession with peace that I could never have imagined would one day lead to his brutal murder.

This book, a study in perseverance, courage, and vision, traces Rabin's life from birth to the moment the assassin's bullets ended his long, tortuous journey to Oslo, the symbol of the peace he so passionately pursued. In piecing together his biography, I interviewed more than two hundred people who had known or dealt with him at some point in his life. I also perused many documents found in Israel, the United States, and Europe, and read countless published and unpublished accounts of events in Rabin's life, including books and magazine and newspaper articles.

All quotations, thoughts, and feelings presented in this book appear precisely as the interviewees expressed them to me or as they were recorded in their diaries, memoirs, or letters. Nothing, I must stress, is fictionalized. The sources of quotations and important facts not indicated in the text can be found in the Notes, and all persons who granted me interviews or otherwise helped me are listed in the Acknowledgments.

Dan Kurzman
December 1997
New York

Acknowledgments

I am especially indebted to my wife, Florence, for her brilliant collaboration on this book. She helped conduct interviews and edited every page, rewriting and brightening many passages. Sometimes she irritated me with her criticism, but after some resistance, having recovered from the insult, I almost always found that she was right and made the suggested change.

I also wish to warmly thank Gladys Justin Carr, vice president of HarperCollins, for her editing, support, and friendship. I'm grateful to editors Elissa Altman and Cynthia Barrett and to Deirdre O'Brien for their work on my behalf. And I greatly appreciate the editorial advice and encouragement given me by my agent, Julian Bach.

I have only praise for the skill of Orit Cohen in translating countless books, articles, and documents from Hebrew to English. Haia and Ellis Hayeem also did fine translation work. Marilyn Mazur, a HarperCollins attorney, vetted this book with great care. And production editor Jane Hardick and copy editor Eleanor Mikucki deserve my thanks for a job well done.

Others who were kind enough to facilitate my research include David Bedein; Jenny Koren and Moshe Fogel of Israel's Government

Press Office; Nina Keren-David, Elaine Moshe, and Doreen Ravona of
the *Jerusalem Post* archives; Richard Skorza, spokesman of the U.S.
Embassy, Tel Aviv; Shoshana Gabbay; George Griffin; Marty Griffin; Ben
Hayeem; Masha Kaplan; Claire Knopf; Fred Knopf; and Ceremia Padan.

The following people graciously agreed to interviews for this book:

Edward Abington—chief, U.S. mission, Jerusalem
Shulamit Aloni—Israeli minister of communications
Tsion Amir—attorney for Dror Adani
Meir Amit—Israel Defense Forces (IDF) general, childhood
    friend of Rabin
Morrie Amitai—director, American–Israel Public Affairs
    Committee
Maen Areikat—spokesman, Orient House, East Jerusalem
Chaim Asa—Rabin aide
Shlomo Avineri—Israeli foreign ministry official
Colette Avital—Israeli consul-general, New York
Yehuda Avner—Rabin aide
Uri Avneri—Israeli journalist, Knesset member
James A. Baker—U.S. secretary of state
Eliahu Bakshi-Doron—Sephardic chief rabbi of Israel
Gabi Barabash—director, Ichilov Hospital
Ehud Barak—IDF chief of staff (later, leader of Labor Party)
Uzi Baram—Israeli minister of tourism
David Bar-Ilan—editor, *Jerusalem Post*
Meir Bar-Ilan—professor, Bar-Ilan University, Israel
Mohammed Bassiouny—Egyptian ambassador to Israel
Yona Baumel—father of Israeli soldier missing in action
Yossi Beilin—Israeli deputy foreign minister
Oded Ben-Ami—Rabin media aide
Avi Benayahu—IDF media officer
Binyamin Ben-Eliezer—Israeli minister of housing
Yehuda Ben-Meir—Knesset religious supporter of Rabin
Yoel Ben-Nun—Israeli rabbi, supporter of Rabin
Yeshaya Ben-Porat—Israeli journalist
Meron Benvenisti—Israeli politician and writer
Israel Ben-Yaacov—Israeli water expert
Norman Bernstein—U.S. businessman, friend of Rabin

Shaul Biber—childhood friend of Rabin

Gabi Bin-Nun—husband of Tsibia Bin-Nun

Tsibia Bin-Nun—schoolmate of Rabin

Menachem Brinker—professor, Hebrew University

Edgar Bronfman Sr.—president, World Jewish Congress

Amos Chorev—IDF officer

Nir Cohen—physician, Ichilov Hospital

Sheldon Cohen—U.S. commissioner of internal revenue

Menachem Damti—driver for Rabin

Uri Dan—Israeli journalist and adviser to Sharon

Marit Danon—secretary to Rabin

Aboulwahab Darawshe—Arab Knesset member

Arnaud de Borchgrave—editor, *Newsweek, Washington Times*

Thomas Dine—U.S. leader of Jewish lobby (AIPAC)

Simcha Dinitz—Israeli ambassador to the United States

Uri Dromi—Rabin spokesman

Lawrence Eagleburger—U.S. secretary of state

Abba Eban—Israeli foreign minister

Jacqueline Efrati—official, prime minister's office

Giora Eini—mediator between Rabin and Peres

Amos Eiran—Israeli diplomat

Binyamin Elon—Israeli right-wing rabbi and politician

Walter Eytan—Israeli diplomat

Shmuel Fleishman—attorney for Yigal Amir

Arnold Forster—general counsel, Anti-Defamation League

Yitzhak Frankenthal—father of murdered Israeli

Yehuda Friedlander—rector, Bar-Ilan University, Israel

Menachem Friedman—professor, Bar-Ilan University, Israel

Mordechai Gazit—Israeli diplomat

Kalman Geyer—Rabin aide

Amos Gilad—IDF spokesman

Joseph Gildenhorn—U.S. businessman, friend of Rabin

Carmi Gillon—chief, Shin Bet

Yossi Ginosar—Rabin's secret link to Palestine Liberation
  Organization

Dore Gold—Netanyahu's spokesman, then ambassador to the
  United Nations

Ruth Goldmuntz—friend of the Rabins

Dov Goldstein—Israeli journalist and Rabin intimate

Hirsh Goodman—editor and publisher, *Jerusalem Report*
Aliza Goren—media aide to Rabin, then to Peres
Amos Goren—Rabin bodyguard and security expert
Haim Gurie—Israeli poet and Rabin childhood friend
Mordechai Gutman—surgeon, Ichilov Hospital
Richard Haass—Middle East expert, Brookings Institution
Eitan Haber—Rabin aide
Alexander Haig—U.S. secretary of state
Jamil Hamami—Hamas official
Micha Harish—Israeli minister of trade and industry
David Hartman—Israeli professor and philosopher
Hayim Hefer—Israeli poet and Rabin army comrade
Ya'acov Heifetz—friend of Rabin
Rahama Hermon—Rabin aide, later Israeli consul in Atlanta
Chaim Herzog—president of Israel
Ya'ir Hirschfeld—Israeli Oslo negotiator
Yitzhak Hoffi—Mossad chief
Faisal Husseini—Palestinian leader
Martin Indyk—U.S. ambassador to Israel
Avraham Infeld—Israeli religious scholar
David Ivry—IDF general
Aharon Katz—professor, Bar-Ilan University, Israel
Noah Kinarti—Israeli water expert
Henry Kissinger—U.S. secretary of state
David Klayman—official, American Jewish Committee, Israel
Yoram Kluger—surgeon, Ichilov Hospital
Teddy Kollek—mayor of Jerusalem
Rivka Kramer—schoolmate of Rabin
Shlomo Lahat—mayor of Tel Aviv
Niva Lanir—aide to Rabin
Terje Larsen—Norwegian peace negotiator
Gabriel Last—Tel Aviv police chief
Israel Lau—Ashkenazi chief rabbi of Israel
Dov Lautman—Israeli businessman
Yehiel Leiter—Israeli settlement leader
Samuel Lewis—U.S. ambassador to Israel
Charles Liebman—professor, Bar-Ilan University, Israel
Sol Linowitz—U.S. peace negotiator
Amnon Lipkin-Shahak—IDF chief of staff
Dan Margolit—Israeli journalist

Abu Mazen—deputy to Yasir Arafat

Carmela Menachi—Israeli journalist

Ariel Merari—professor, Tel Aviv University

Ron Milo—mayor of Tel Aviv

Uri Milstein—Israeli right-wing writer

Uzi Narkiss—IDF commander

Gad Navon—IDF chief rabbi

Yitzhak Navon—president of Israel

Jacques Neriya—Rabin aide

Moshe Netzer—childhood friend of Rabin

Francis Ofner—Israeli journalist

Meir Pa'il—IDF colonel and leading dove

Dan Pattir—Rabin media aide

Dahlia Pelossof—daughter of Rabin

Shimon Peres—Israeli prime minister, foreign minister

Abe Pollin—friend of Rabin, owner of Washington Bullets

Irene Pollin—sociologist, author, friend of Rabin

Ron Pundak—Israeli Oslo negotiator

Leah Rabin—wife of Yitzhak Rabin

Rachel Rabin—sister of Yitzhak Rabin

Yuval Rabin—son of Yitzhak Rabin

Itamar Rabinovich—Israeli ambassador to the United States

Nahum Rabinovich—Israeli right-wing rabbi

Stanley Rabinowitz—Washington rabbi, friend of Rabin

Chaim Ramon—Histadrut chief, Labor Party politician

Moshe Raziel—rabbi and professor, Bar-Ilan University, Israel

Chagai Regev—Shin Bet officer

Uri Regev—Israeli reform rabbi

Ogden Reid—U.S. ambassador to Israel

Omar Rifai—Jordanian ambassador to Israel

Avraham Rivlin—Israeli yeshiva rabbi

Chana Rivlin—sister of Haim Gurie

William Rogers—U.S. secretary of state

Susan Hattis Rolef—Israeli journalist

Dennis Ross—U.S. Middle East mediator

Amnon Rubinstein—Israeli minister of energy

Elyakim Rubinstein—Israeli peace negotiator and judge

Yossi Sarid—Israeli politician

Harold Saunders—deputy U.S. secretary of state

Uri Savir—Israeli Oslo negotiator

Ze'ev Schiff—military correspondent, *Ha'aretz*

Brent Scowcroft—U.S. national defense adviser

Avraham Shafir—childhood friend of Rabin

Moshe Shahal—Israeli minister of police

Avraham Shahat—Israeli minister of finance

Yitzhak Shamir—prime minister of Israel

Yehezkel Sharabi—driver for Rabin

Ariel Sharon—IDF general, defense minister

Shimon Sheves—Rabin aide

Joel Singer—Israeli Oslo negotiator

Hana Siniora—Palestinian newspaper editor

Joseph Sisco—U.S. undersecretary of state

Ohad Skornick—friend of Yigal Amir

Yehuda Skornick—father of Ohad

Ephraim Sneh—Israeli minister of health

Abraham Sofer—U.S. diplomat

Ehud Sprinzak—professor, Hebrew University

Yehuda Z. Stern—dean, law faculty, Bar-Ilan University, Israel

Israel Tal—IDF general

Aida Tamir—childhood classmate of Rabin

Ahmad Tibi—Palestinian physician and adviser to Arafat

Dov Tsamir—Rabin aide

Cyrus Vance—secretary of state

Hillel Weiss—professor, Bar-Ilan University, Israel

Lally Weymouth—*Washington Post* columnist

Gad Yaacobi—Israeli ambassador to United Nations

Ehud Ya'ari—Israeli television commentator and author

Danny Yatom—military adviser to Rabin, Mossad chief

Haim Yavin—Israeli television anchorman

Haim Zadok—Israeli minister of justice

Zvi Zamir—Mossad chief and Rabin childhood friend

Eliahu Zeira—IDF general

Interviews conducted in the past relating to this book:

Yigal Allon—Israeli foreign minister

Samuel Ariel—Irgun official in Paris

Hanan Ashrawi—Palestinian official

Majid Aslan—Lebanese minister of defense

Ehud Avriel—Israeli arms procurer in Europe

Abdul Rahman Azzam Pasha—secretary-general, Arab League

Menachem Begin—prime minister of Israel

Leah Ben-Dor—editor, *Jerusalem Post*

David Ben-Gurion—founder and prime minister of Israel

Alexander Broida—aide to Colonel "Mickey" Marcus

Nigel Bromage—British officer, Arab Legion

Mullah Cohen—IDF brigade commander

Yeroham Cohen—Palmach officer

Sir Alan Cunningham—British high commissioner in Palestine

Ezra Danin—Israeli specialist in Arab affairs

Moshe Dayan—Israeli defense minister

Ya'akov Dori—IDF chief of staff

Monroe Fein—U.S. captain of Altalena

Israel Galili—Hagana commander, cabinet member

Simon Garfeh—cleric in Lydda (Lod)

John Bagot Glubb Pasha—commander, Jordan Arab Legion

Shlomo Goren—chief rabbi of Israel

David Hacohen—Mapai Party leader

Yehoshafat Harkabi—IDF officer

Haj Amin el-Husseini (Grand Mufti)—Palestinian Arab leader

Haim Israeli—defense ministry official

Dov Joseph—military governor, Jerusalem (New City)

Masha Kaplan—heroic nurse, Old City

Moshe Kelman—IDF officer

Hafez Abu Kuwaik—mukhtar, northern Lydda

Chaim Laskov—IDF officer

Naphtalie Lavie—aide to Dayan and Peres

Ted Lurie—editor, *Jerusalem Post*

Mordechai Makleff—IDF brigade commander

Gordon McMillan—commander, British forces in Palestine

Golda Meir—prime minister of Israel

Ya'acov Meridor—Likud leader

Said Mufti—aide to King Abdullah

Captain Zakaraya Muhieddin—colleague of Egyptian
president Nasser

Abdullah Omari—aide to Abd el-Kader el-Husseini

Amitai Paglin—Irgun chief of operations

Mattiyahu Peled—IDF officer

Mordechai Raanan—Irgun Jerusalem commander

Moshe Rousnak—Hagana commander, Old City Jewish
Quarter

Fuad Sadek—commander, Egyptian forces (1948 war)

Nahum Sarig—IDF commander

David Shaltiel—Hagana Jerusalem commander

Shlomo Shamir—IDF officer

Moshe Sharett—prime minister of Israel

Adib Shishekly—president of Syria

Moshe Sneh—Hagana commander

Rudolf Sonnenborn—U.S. industrialist and arms procurer

Yosef Tabenkin—IDF brigade commander

Abdullah Tel—Jordanian military governor, Old City

Yigael Yadin—IDF acting chief of staff

Nathan Yellin-Mor—commander, Stern Gang

Rehavam Ze'evi—IDF officer, later right-wing political leader

Prologue

The morning loomed balmy and blue, a typical fall day in Tel Aviv. But November 4, 1995, would not be a typical day for Prime Minister Yitzhak Rabin. For that evening, Rabin would preside at a huge rally in Malchei Yisrael (Kings of Israel) Square to celebrate the Oslo accords that pointed the way to a final historic peace between the Israelis and Palestinians.

The prime minister had decided to attend the event only a few days earlier, fearing that a low turnout might embarrass him and weaken the fragile peace process, already under serious attack from political rightists and religious extremists. They were threatening violence, staging hate-filled demonstrations, plastering posters on every pole and wall, charging him with murder and treason, and picturing him in Arab headdress. Some rabbis cited biblical passages that they thought would sanction his murder, and at least one placed a curse on him. His supporters, on the other hand, were displaying little passion and had been holding few demonstrations to counter the hatred.

Rabin thus had little reason to welcome the call of his wife, Leah: "Yitzhak, get up! It's 8 o'clock."

The prime minister could hardly greet with joy a day that might expose him as the leader of a failed peace movement he viewed as crucial to Israel's future security. The burden weighing upon him had probably not been as great since 1967, when he feared possible disaster just before sending his troops into battle in the Six-Day War. Deepening his depressed mood was news that on the previous day nine Israeli soldiers had been killed in Lebanon. He wouldn't let a single event influence his peace policy, but when would the killing end? He could only hope his people would be as patient as he.

The prime minister opened his grayish-blue eyes, if with difficulty, and acknowledged Leah's call with a low moan:

"There's something wrong with my eye. Something is irritating it."

Leah examined the affected eye but could not find the irritant, though she noted a slight redness. They could not take a chance, she said. Nothing must mar the majesty of this great day, which had to dispel all notions that the peace process was collapsing, perhaps along with her husband's glorious role in history.

"I'll call the doctor," Leah told her husband.

"Where will we find one this early on the Sabbath?" he asked.

She knew one and called him, saying: "I don't think it's serious, but he wants to be perfect. Please come and examine him."

Leah then dressed in her tennis garb, grabbed her racket, and prepared to leave for the Ramat Aviv Country Club, where she would play tennis with friends. Normally on the Sabbath, Rabin, who, like Leah, was a nonobservant Jew, would join his wife on the court for a doubles match. But he had too many appointments on this day to take time off for tennis, a sport the couple had learned when Rabin had served as ambassador to the United States almost thirty years earlier. Besides, he could hardly play when his eye was bothering him.

She would call the doctor later from the court, Leah told her husband, and arrange for a pharmacist to bring him medicine if necessary. Meanwhile, he should not exert himself.

Leah regretted having to go without him; in fact, she would very seldom leave him alone, whether at home or away. With the world perched precariously on his shoulders, someone had to take care of him, drink with him, and make sure he dressed appropriately, covered himself with a blanket on plane trips, and befriended the right people. Her husband to her was still the "gorgeous," dashing young officer in the underground Palmach who helped to lead the Israelis to victory in the 1948 War of Independence. She seemed hardly to notice that his once-thick, strawberry-blond hair had been reduced to streaks of white and his stern, pinkish face had become somewhat jowly, with his pouty, sensual lips well-furrowed at the edges.

Though a tough soldier and taskmaster, Rabin did not mind being pampered by his wife, a handsome, blue-eyed woman with a wreath of dark brown hair framing an oblong face often lit with a wide smile that could reflect either radiance or wrath. The prime minister perhaps welcomed the attention because his politically active mother, who died when he was a boy, had not often been around to care for him. But he wished he did not need pampering this morning. He looked forward to the Saturday matches, which helped keep him fit for the week of grinding work ahead and permitted him to sublimate his aggressive tendencies.

But Rabin would make the most of the morning in his elegant apartment in Ramat Aviv, an upper-crust district of Tel Aviv, where Persian carpets and an eclectic mix of furniture adorned with mementos from exotic places lent a Mediterranean atmosphere conducive to relaxed conversation. Usually, Giora Eini, a long-haired trade union lawyer and intellectual, visited Rabin each Saturday afternoon after tennis, but today he arrived at the prime minister's home at 9 A.M.

However busy or indisposed, Rabin would seldom miss a meeting with Eini, though the man was virtually unknown to the public. For Eini had a special secret assignment: to mediate between Rabin and Foreign Minister Shimon Peres, who had been feuding for more than twenty years, so that their personal animosity would not seriously damage their Labor Party. Each man had finally agreed to sign an unusual document, drawn up by Eini, that spelled out the rules for his mediation.

Now Eini was seeking to smooth out any lingering ruffled feathers that might threaten unity in the pursuit of peace. Trusted completely by both men, who saw him together as well as individually, he was delighted by the prospect that his work would finally bear fruit that night when their once-rocky relations would gel into a truly tight partnership amid the acclaim of thousands. Rabin, however, a pessimist by nature, was skeptical about the acclaim. How many people would show up to applaud anyway?

In the midst of their conversation, the doctor arrived and, after examining Rabin's affected eye, put drops into it. The prime minister, casually dressed in slacks and T-shirt, went back to talking, his eye no longer fluttering.

After little more than an hour, Eini left, and a financial expert arrived to advise Rabin on how to reinforce the economy that had been flourishing because of the peace process.

Shortly, Leah returned from the tennis court, and the couple headed for the wealthy Tel Aviv suburb of Herzylia Petuach, where they lunched on the lawn with friends, including some from the moderate opposition. Rabin seemed relaxed and reflective as he sat with the other guests in the garden, silently ignoring the small talk, but remarking on what the rally might bring. Would it help to turn people against the extremists' threats of violence and toward the peace option? No one could be sure.

"Their offensive remarks about Leah especially worry me," Rabin told Eli Landau, the Likud mayor of the town.

The couple departed at about 2:30 P.M., and on arriving home, the prime minister lay down for a nap to be well rested for the big event. Meanwhile, Leah prepared for the trip back to Jerusalem, where they would head that night following the rally and a party afterward given by friends. Since Rabin was both prime minister and defense minister, he spent four days of the week in Jerusalem, the capital, living in the prime minister's residence, and three days in Tel Aviv, where he presided over the defense ministry.

Rabin awoke at about 5 P.M., sat on the edge of the bed shining his old but comfortable shoes, and went to greet a personal friend. His final visitor was Chaim Ramon, formerly a leader of the Labor Party, who had left it to head the Histadrut, Israel's powerful trade union movement. Rabin urged him to return to the party fold and help him plan the campaign for the crucial elections scheduled for the coming year. Ramon, a very savvy politician, was needed to help stem the rightist tide.

But Rabin didn't press too hard now, as his mind was on the rally. Would people come? he asked Ramon. With Arab terrorists brandishing their bombs and Jewish extremists threatening riots, were not many Israelis afraid to attend pro-Oslo demonstrations? Even superstar Barbra Streisand, a good friend who had been invited in the hope of drumming up popular interest, had declined to come.

But Ramon offered little encouragement. Too many supporters, he acknowledged, were passive and overconfident, leaving the streets to the opposition.

At 7 P.M., Shlomo Lahat, the former mayor of Tel Aviv and chief organizer of the rally, telephoned Rabin to remind him that the event would start in forty-five minutes, at 7:45 P.M.

"Chich," the prime minister asked again, referring to Lahat by his nickname, "do you think people will come?"

He needed someone to reassure him.

Lahat, a white-haired, charismatic political master who headed a group of forty-two generals supporting Rabin, had done his best to make sure the rally would succeed. He had arranged for about five hundred buses to bring more than 100,000 supporters to the event from all over the country. The Labor Party, he lamented, had failed to go into the towns and villages to stir enthusiasm for the peace process, dealing with the people bureaucratically, while the rightists were meeting everywhere and crying that the Rabin government was selling out Israel. This rally, he hoped, would trigger a nationwide emotional response to this charge.

"Yitzhak," Lahat said to the prime minister, trying to relieve his anxiety, "I am an expert on mob psychology, and I know the atmosphere. Everybody will be there. We'll have a great time."

After a pause, Rabin muttered: "Okay, seven forty-five."

He quickly dressed in a dark suit laid out for him by Leah, swallowed some white cheese, and, with his wife and a bodyguard, Yoram Rubin, went down in the elevator to the front door, where they were greeted by his relief driver, Menachem Damti. He had already loaded a few bags with their personal belongings into the trunk so they could head directly for Jerusalem after the postrally party.

"Shalom, how are you?" Rabin said to Damti.

"Fine, sir," Damti replied, a thin smile on his dark Yemenite face.

Damti couldn't remember when his boss did not greet him with a cheerful word. How fortunate he was to drive for so great a man, so wonderful a human being. Before thinking about himself, Rabin would think of him, making sure Damti had eaten enough before reporting for work, asking his driver whether he wanted to stop for something to drink. It was hard for Damti to believe that this man was prime minister, this simple, unpretentious man who sometimes sat in front with him asking about his family, who visited him at his home and attended his son's bar mitzvah and bris (circumcision ceremony). He knew this was an important night for the prime minister and reveled in the excitement.

The Rabins climbed into the rear of the bullet-proof silver Cadillac parked outside, the bodyguard into the front seat beside the driver. Rabin seldom used this $300,000 car, preferring an old automobile the government had previously provided for him. He didn't need such a majestic car, he told security officials. He was not a king. Nor did he wish the people to think he was squandering their tax money on such luxuries, as some newspapers were charging.

But Rabin finally struck a deal with Carmi Gillon, head of the General Security Service, known as the Shabak or Shin Bet, which was mainly responsible for the prime minister's security.

Gillon constantly argued with Rabin about enhancing his security when he went to a restaurant, the tennis court, or other public places, but Rabin was adamant: He would not be intimidated. He must have contact with the public. The two men finally agreed that the prime minister would use the Cadillac when traveling in the West Bank and Gaza, and when driving to and from publicized events such as this one.

Gillon had warned Rabin that Jewish as well as Arab extremists had threatened violence against him, but Rabin shrugged off the Jewish threat. He refused even to wear a bullet-proof vest. The Shin Bet had offered him an old, bulky model, apparently seeing little reason to order the new lightweight American kind that he might have found more acceptable.

"A Jew would not kill another Jew," he said, "however much he might hate him."

Damti also had supreme confidence that the Shin Bet would protect his boss. Yet he had nagging fears. He had seen the venomous looks on the faces of demonstrators and heard their cries of "traitor," "Nazi," "murderer." They certainly wouldn't kill, but . . . who knew what might happen? Though his elder daughter, seventeen, insisted on going to the rally, the chauffeur left his younger one, fourteen, at home.

"I was afraid for her," he told me.

And he felt he had good reason to be afraid, especially when Yoram Rubin, a Shin Bet agent, turned in his seat and told Rabin that an Arab suicide bomber might try to infiltrate the rally. The information didn't seem to faze the prime minister, who was sure his security forces could frustrate any terrorist plot. Anyway, his mind was on the rally. What if few people showed up? Leah was less sanguine about the warning.

"The words . . . sent a shiver down my spine," she would say later, "though I tried not to let it show. God forbid this should happen now, I thought. Not tonight. Especially not tonight. . . . You're going to a peace rally, you have a fleeting vision of what could happen, and then you file it away."

In about twenty minutes, Damti, who had been followed by a Shin Bet car, lurched to a halt on a small side street bordering the square of the Municipality Building and the huge Malchei Yisrael Square just beyond, where the rally would take place. As the Rabins stepped out, surrounded by security men, they were greeted by Tel Aviv Police Chief Gabriel Last. Apparently with some apprehension, Rabin asked him:

"Are there many people here?"

"Over 100,000," Last replied.

"Really?" Rabin exclaimed, beaming.

Last was happy to relate the good news, though he showed signs of exhaustion. Two weeks earlier, Shlomo Lahat had called him and said:

"We're going to hold a rally on November 4, and we expect about 100,000 people. Can you give us adequate protection?"

"You bring the people," Last replied, "and I'll bring the security."

Last knew, however, that he did not have ultimate control of security; Shin Bet did, being responsible for protecting the prime minister. And it alone could arrest people who were not common criminals. Even more troubling, sometimes it did not share vital information with the police. Still, Last was determined to prevent right-wing disturbances, though he, like Rabin himself, could not conceive of an assassination attempt by Jews. And he would thwart any Arab terrorist effort, which he especially feared because a Palestinian terrorist leader had been killed in Malta only a few days earlier, presumably by the Israelis. Reports, in fact, indicated that a terrorist on a mission of revenge was on his way there from Gaza. Last had thus taken unprecedented security measures, and he was confident that the prime minister was safe.

Shlomo Lahat guided the Rabins up a cement staircase leading to the Municipality Building, and from a terrace in the sprawling structure they gazed down upon the adjoining square. A mass of humanity stretched before them as far as the eye could see in the soft glow emanating from street lamps.

"Didn't I tell you?" Lahat chirped with a smile.

"Unbelievable!" Rabin exclaimed, his normally stern face flushed with excitement.

Then, as if trying to hide the embarrassment of this uncharacteristic spark of emotion, he sought refuge in an attempt at self-deprecating humor.

"Are these people waiting to get into the movie house?" he asked, referring to a nearby theater.

Rabin's dark mood had suddenly brightened. His worst fear—that he would be repudiated by a low turnout—had been unfounded. And, as often in the past, he reveled in the good news that dispelled unnecessary alarm. The people supported the peace after all. His enormous Oslo gamble, it seemed for the moment at least, had a good chance of reaping dividends.

A great chant burst forth as another rally organizer, Jean Frydman, a French industrialist close to Rabin, led the prime minister to the front of the stage, where he joined Leah, who was already there mingling with cabinet ministers and other associates and notables:

"Rabin! Rabin! Rabin!"

The prime minister's pink cheeks stretched into a rare smile as he stood before the huge, wildly cheering audience and expressed in inelegant Hebrew his gratitude to them for having dissipated his doubts.

This vast crowd, he said, "proves the majority of the people really want peace, and is willing to take a risk for peace." And he added: "Violence undermines democracy and must be denounced and isolated." He thanked the Egyptian, Jordanian, and Moroccan diplomats for their presence and praised the Palestine Authority for rejecting terrorism and seeking peace. He saw "the pain of the families of the soldiers of the Israel Defense Forces," and said, "it is for the sake of our children and grandchildren that I hope this government will exhaust every possibility to advance and achieve a comprehensive peace."

Rabin's speech sent his listeners into a paroxysm of ecstasy; they cried his name, clapped, cheered, wept, waved banners, and shouted their devotion to this great peacemaker. The reaction, it was evident, profoundly moved Rabin, and some thought he was desperately trying to suppress tears in a display of emotion rarely manifested during his life.

Among those seated on the stage was Aliza Goren, an attractive media aide to Rabin, who saw this as the perfect moment to make heady headlines. Vivaciously aggressive, she went over to Shimon Peres, Rabin's nemesis before Oslo. Though the two men had grown closer in recent months, in the public's perception there was still a substantial gulf between the two politicians that could threaten the unity of the peace movement. And now was the time to fill the gap.

"Go and stand by him," Aliza whispered to Peres.

And in a moment the once-bitter foes were not only standing together but Rabin hugged Peres—a move all the more remarkable considering that Rabin seldom touched anyone or let anyone touch him.

"He embraced me as he would a woman," Peres told me afterward as if still experiencing shock.

The cries and cheers from the crowd rose to a new crescendo. No one present could now believe that the surging wave of peace could possibly recede.

Aliza then asked Lahat to call to the platform all VIPs not already there to join Miri Aloni, a popular vocalist, in singing the "Song for Peace," the anthem of the peace movement. Aliza then passed out a sheet of lyrics to each of them. Rabin, who had had no warning that he would be expected to sing, shrank back. Self-conscious about his low, uneven voice, he hadn't sung in public since he was a young officer sitting around a campfire with his men, though he sometimes mouthed the national anthem, "Hatikvah," at public ceremonies.

"He always sang off-tune," one of these men told me. "He would joke about his singing voice."

Once, in the United States, when a television entertainer insisted that Rabin sing a few lines of a particular song, he finally agreed simply to recite them.

Now, at this moment of triumph, his red face and body language reflected the sudden dread of a likely blow to his dignity.

But Rabin could hardly refuse to accept the lyric sheet when everyone around him, including Peres, seemed prepared to risk such a blow. And so, with Miri Aloni sandwiched between him and Peres, Rabin joined in the hymn to peace:

> Let the sun rise, and give the morning light
>
> The purest prayer will not bring back
>
> The one whose candle was snuffed out . . .
>
> So sing only for peace,
>
> Don't whisper a prayer,
>
> It's better to sing a song for peace
>
> With a great shout . . .

As the hysteria grew, Rabin's face continued to flush, but now, it seemed, more from excitement than from embarrassment.

Another famous singer, Aviv Geffin, once a foe of Rabin, then performed and found himself clasped in Rabin's arms. The prime minister, it seemed, had finally found the key to the openness he had suppressed all his life. His soul, for so long chained to a rigid pioneer tradition, was free at last.

Shortly, after several more speeches, the crowd wailed forth the strains of "Hatikvah" and the rally was over. The event had ended, and no terrorist had stained the glory.

Where was he heading? Peres asked.

"Home," replied Rabin, who appeared exhausted.

And he turned to his wife and said: "Let's go directly to Jerusalem."

But Leah urged: "Yitzhak, shouldn't we first go to the party for a while and celebrate the moment?"

With a shrug of resignation, her husband agreed, and the couple, together with Peres, walked toward the stairway at the rear entrance, which led to their parked cars, stopping occasionally to chat with friends. Suddenly, Leah said:

"Yitzhak, we haven't said good-bye to Chich and Jean."

Leaving Peres behind, they turned around and went back to Lahat and Frydman.

"How stupid I am," Rabin said to them. "I didn't thank you. I'll never forget what you've done for me."

Lahat's wife then emerged from the throng and cried: "Yitzhak, go with Shimon and mix with the people. They love you. Listen to them."

But the security men surrounding the group vetoed the idea— especially in light of the report about a possible Arab terrorist attack. Rabin then hugged Lahat and Frydman and strode again toward the stairway, with Leah trailing slightly behind and guards fending off people who were shouting Rabin's name and their loving support. Someone cried out:

"Leah, take care of him!"

"I'll do my best," Leah replied.

As they started down the stairs, they stopped to thank Police Chief Last for so efficiently keeping order. Last was delighted. He had already been congratulated by the officer in charge of the Shin Bet guards—though Last still resented that agency for keeping its own security plans secret from him. It had also neglected to "sterilize" the garage area under the Municipality Building to make sure that no unauthorized person was loitering there. That was the responsibility of the Shin Bet, not of the police.

With a broad smile, Leah took Last's hand and said, calling him by his nickname: "Gaby, it was so good . . . "

Even as she spoke, a young man stood in the shadowy light of the garage entrance just below them, leaning against a car—the chauffeur, it seemed. He watched the people waiting near Rabin's bullet-proof vehicle parked on the narrow street only several yards from him to cheer the prime minister once more. But this man was not one of them. He was calm and seemed utterly detached from the scene. Yet he eagerly embraced the statement they were making:

This night could help to decide the destiny of Israel.

1

The Ingredients of Destiny

The November 4 rally clearly seemed to Yitzhak Rabin the climax of an almost three-decade struggle to divert Israel's destiny from the path of war to the path of peace. In the process, he helped to alter the map of the Middle East and, just as important, the psychology of its people. Though the peace process has been plagued by serious setbacks, and there are bound to be more, Rabin—and Peres—creaked open the door to Israeli-Arab coexistence with the Oslo agreements, and no one may be able to slam it shut.

The agreements call on Israel to gradually give autonomous status to Arab-inhabited territory it has occupied, in return for peace, with final negotiations to determine final borders and the degree of independence the Palestinians would enjoy. Without Rabin, there probably would have been no accords, for however important Peres's role, the country was not prepared to follow him into the frightening unknown. After David Ben-Gurion, the founder of Israel, Rabin may well be judged the greatest leader in Israel's history and one of the greatest soldier-statesmen of our time.

His story, in a sense, traces the story of Israel from its inception as a British-controlled Jewish homeland to Oslo. He was born in Jerusalem in 1922, the same year the British separated Transjordan from Palestine and placed the Hashemite dynasty on its throne, thereby setting the stage for the birth of a Jewish state in the remaining part of Palestine. His pioneering life as a child, his military career, and his political role coincided with the development of a besieged, largely desert wilderness into a prosperous modern nation nearing full acceptance by its neighbors.

In many respects, Rabin, the first native-born Israeli, or sabra, to become prime minister, was indeed a mirror of Israel's complex character, with all its virtues, flaws—and contradictions.

He made some of the most daring decisions in Israel's history, yet hesitated before reaching even minor ones.

He was raised as an ideological socialist but sought to emulate American capitalism, inducing some Israelis to lament that their people had become more American than the Americans.

He was shy, pessimistic, honest, yet avidly pursued politics, a profession that required ingratiating oneself with thousands of strangers, exuding optimism, and stretching the truth.

He intimidated some people with his often brusque manner but treated his employees and friends with great kindness, sensitivity, and compassion.

He was a poor speaker and failed to resonate in the soul of the people—at least until he died—yet he exuded a certain natural magnetism that generated in people an instinctive trust.

Most dramatically, he had a hawkish reputation but, with Oslo, would prove that he had the heart and spirit of a dove.

It is often thought that Rabin's campaign for peace seriously began only in the late 1980s, when, as minister of defense, he found that no military force could suppress the Intifada, the Palestinian popular uprising that drained Israel of so much blood, money, and confidence. Yet, while often camouflaged by tough security measures and macho talk, his dream of a compromise peace actually crystallized in his early days as an officer in the 1948 War of Independence, which left him guilt-ridden and haunted with the memories of men he had sent to their deaths in impossible battles.

Rabin's search for peace became compulsive with victory in the Six-Day War. Though the main architect of this amazing triumph, Rabin had not been at all sure that Israel would survive the war. Thus, when he marched into Jerusalem and unified that holy city under Israeli rule, he elatedly vowed to devote himself completely to one central goal: making sure that Israel would never again stare into the abyss.

But while Rabin became obsessed with security, he hitched this obsession to a rigid pragmatism. Land, he decided, was not the important thing; peace with the Arabs was. For only peace with Israel's equally vulnerable neighbors could guarantee that the Third Temple would not fall, especially with Moslem fundamentalists frantically seeking nuclear and other unconventional weaponry. And there could never be peace as long as the Jews dominated another people and didn't give them their own homeland. While this view may have sprung originally from a rationale based almost solely on security grounds, Rabin gradually came to see the question of domination as a moral issue as well. It was simply immoral to keep the Palestinians under the thumb of the Jews, who had themselves suffered so greatly under foreign control.

Nor ultimately, Rabin believed, could there be a democratic Jewish state without such compromise. Not with almost 20 percent of the inhabitants already Arab and the Arab birth rate greatly outstripping that of the Jews. If all residents of the territories were given the vote, an Arab prime minister and an Arab-dominated parliament might rule one day. The alternative to a democratic state, on the other hand, would be a system of apartheid that Rabin so feared would assure perpetual war and violate the Jewish ethos.

Most members of the Labor Party also supported the land-for-peace principle, but few embraced it with the intensity of Rabin, who, as army chief of staff, had been most intimately exposed to the threatening winds of catastrophe: catastrophe fanned by a massive fifth column of hostile Arabs.

With the end of the Cold War, Rabin was ready to move, for the Arabs could no longer rely on the Russians to fill their arsenals. At the same time, Yasir Arafat, critically weakened by setbacks in the Lebanon and Persian Gulf wars, desperately needed peace with Israel to save himself and his Palestine Liberation Organization from political oblivion. And finally, the great tenacity and courage the Palestinians displayed in the Intifada dispelled any doubts Rabin had that they, like his own people, had the heart and cohesion of a viable nation and should be separated from Israel within some form of state.

Yet before Oslo the public considered Rabin a hawk, and he was—tactically. Israel, he felt, had to negotiate peace from a position of maximum strength, and that meant crushing Arab terrorism and aggression. But, less obvious to the public, he was in fact a dove strategically, viewing peace as his underlying goal. Nor did Rabin try to stress his dovish intentions, knowing that most Israelis, conditioned by decades of Arab violence, feared the price of peace even more than the prospect of war.

Those Israelis who called him a "traitor" for pursuing Oslo when the opportunity for peace arose, as if he had suddenly changed course, never perceived what even some Arabs did. Mahmoud Abbas—known as Abu Mazen—chief deputy to Yasir Arafat, who had become president of the Palestinian Authority, told me over Turkish coffee in his well-guarded Ramallah office that he realized in the early 1970s that Rabin, for all his toughness ("Isn't any general tough?" he asked), was a man the Arabs could deal with.

In fact, Abu Mazen had been secretly dealing with Rabin, if indirectly, since the mid-1980s. As defense minister, Rabin clandestinely appointed a security official his "ambassador" to the PLO, and the official met regularly with PLO representatives, though such contacts were forbidden at the time by Israeli law.

When Rabin, who had served as prime minister from 1974 to 1977, returned to the post in 1992 and promised to make peace within nine months, most Israelis, as he had envisioned, were finally prepared to cede a substantial amount of land to the Arabs. For was not Rabin "Mr. Security"? And they had good reason to trust him. Suspicious and pessimistic, Rabin was so cautious in reaching decisions, achieved only after minute examination of every detail involved, that his closest colleagues sometimes threw up their hands in exasperation. But the people knew that once he made a decision, he carried it out meticulously, driven, it seemed, by some irresistible inner force.

Though Rabin fully recognized his intellectual gifts, this force was apparently an extraordinary resolve to overcome a lifelong affliction of insecurity, outwardly suggested by his extreme shyness and disposition to blush, especially when meeting strangers. It was an affliction perhaps nurtured by parental neglect in his childhood.

Rabin's greatness, it seems, stemmed in part from this resolve, which pushed him almost obsessively to overcompensate with bold initiatives. Once he reached a decision, he would run roughshod over diplomatic and political convention in advancing toward his goal, even as he wallowed in worry that his people might not follow him.

It was in part to ease his angst that Rabin would meticulously analyze every issue. He could not afford to fail. And his unrelenting suspicion of plots being hatched against him fed his craving for ever more data.

"The more you mistrust," Amos Chorev, an old friend of his, would explain, "the more you want to know."

Rabin would integrate the details into a comprehensive aggregate that he would impart to others masterfully, if not inspirationally. As Ehud Barak, an army comrade who would become chief of staff and then Labor Party leader, would say:

"Sometimes Yitzhak would show up at a meeting with a paper on which he had written only three words. He would develop a whole analysis based on these words, including dates, illustrations, and a complete perspective of a given subject. His plan would reflect an extraordinarily comprehensive strategic approach."

After deciding on an issue, Rabin would listen to those who opposed him, but their arguments would have to be cogent and logical.

"Yitzhak," Barak would relate, "quickly lost patience with visitors who wasted his time with excess verbiage. You could see this by the way he looked at his watch and rubbed the palm of his hand. Still, he would give everybody a chance to speak. When it was my turn, Rabin would wink at me, as if to say, 'Come on, don't make a big deal out of it. After all, the answer is 'no.'" And as Haim Israeli, a venerable defense ministry official, said of Rabin, he "wasn't the sort of man who would regret anything."

Still, Rabin, a determined pragmatist, did not hesitate to change his mind about an issue if circumstances suggested the change would better serve his purpose. But he would not change his purpose, especially the paramount purpose of peace; and he would take full responsibility for every decision he made. As one aide told me:

"If you explained your disagreement with him patiently and logically, you could convince him to change his mind. He was by no means inflexible, except on his strategic goals."

Thus, before becoming prime minister in 1992, Rabin assured the public that he would not return to Syria the Golan Heights, which Israel had conquered in 1967, then, after taking office, decided to give back most or all of it if Syria made "real peace." And while he originally envisioned handing over most of the West Bank and Gaza to Jordan, he tried, when this became impossible, to negotiate with the local Palestinian community. Finally, this effort, too, failed, and he secretly dealt with the Tunis-based PLO—though he told me in 1991 that he would never sit at the peace table with Yasir Arafat.

A more dovish reputation might have doomed Oslo from the start—a likelihood suggested by the 1996 elections in which the reputedly dovish Shimon Peres, after succeeding the murdered Rabin as prime minister, lost to Benjamin Netanyahu and his hawkish right-wing Likud Party and its religious allies. On the other hand, Rabin's hawkish image, which he carefully cultivated, had paid dividends, paradoxically turning almost his whole career into a road map leading inevitably to Oslo.

But not only Rabin's tough tactics and attention to detail won him the trust of the people, particularly many young sabras, who saw him as a mirror image of themselves—a sensitive core encased in a prickly shell. They also perceived an honesty rare among politicians, in Israel or elsewhere. As one of Rabin's former aides, Yehuda Avner, told me:

"Authenticity encapsulated the man. From his childhood days when he studied farming to his rise to the premiership, he has been authentic. He had an almost ruthless compulsion to tell the truth even if unnecessary."

Actually, on rare occasions Rabin did lie, but only to shield secrets involving national security, peace plans, or personal matters that could cause his family worry or pain. And, without lying, he sometimes misled people or was less than candid with them when dealing with these bedrock interests. He thus led the public to believe he was more hawkish than he was and kept Oslo secret until agreement was reached. As he told one adviser who was unaware of the talks while they were in progress:

"Until I find a way to make peace, I don't intend to tell anyone what I think."

Such infrequent resort to falsehood and evasion, understandable to most Israelis, did not affect Rabin's reputation for probity. Indeed, his usual forthrightness, devoid of ambiguity, was legendary.

When Rabin first became ambassador to the United States in 1968, he seemed awkward and even a little "ridiculous" (according to Avner) at diplomatic cocktails as he desperately tried to overcome his shyness and join in the small talk despite knowing little English at that time. But he was soon himself, startling American officials with his diplomatically naked demands, though winning their admiration, grudging at times, for his brilliantly analytical arguments, especially in seeking large-scale aid.

In part because of his refreshing directness, Rabin's fellow ambassadors to the United States, who would not themselves dare to deviate similarly from the diplomatic norm, voted him the best ambassador in Washington. And six former secretaries of state— Henry Kissinger, James A. Baker, Lawrence Eagleburger, Alexander Haig, William Rogers, and Cyrus Vance—described him to me as one of the greatest national leaders they had ever dealt with. Kissinger would write in his memoirs:

> Rabin possessed few of the attributes commonly associated with diplomacy. Repetitious people bored him and the commonplace offended him. . . . He hated ambiguity, which is the stuff of diplomacy. . . . His integrity and his analytical brilliance in cutting to the core of a problem were awesome. . . . [But while] Rabin had many extraordinary qualities, . . . the gift of human relations was not one of them. If he had been handed the entire United States Strategic Air Command as a free gift he would have (a) affected the attitude that at last Israel was getting its due, and (b) found some technical shortcoming in the airplanes that made his accepting them a reluctant concession to us.

Secretary of State Warren Christopher would sum up: "Rabin was one of the towering figures of the century."

Still, a few other American leaders were less impressed with

him. At a White House dinner meeting with President Jimmy
Carter, Rabin did not hide his feelings when Carter made a proposal he strongly took issue with. After dinner, when the President
asked his guest whether he would like to hear his daughter, Amy,
play the piano, the reply was succinct:

"No!"

In another, perhaps unintentional, affront to the President,
Rabin ground a cigarette stub into the carpet.

Rabin's curtness was often unintentional. An American diplomat
once introduced his aunt to Rabin at a reception, and she gushed:

"Mr. Ambassador, I've always wanted to meet you."

Rabin stared at her and responded stonily:

"So, now you have met me."

The prime minister was far more severe with anyone who disagreed with him or did not come to the point quickly in a conversation. With a sharp backhanded wave of his hand, he would let
the person know the discussion was over. This body language
became a staple at government meetings, sometimes even stopping ministers in mid-sentence.

"Rabin wasn't a politician," Uzi Narkiss, who had been a military commander under him, told me. "He didn't know how to
maneuver people."

Even after Narkiss left the army and became head of the
Jewish Agency in New York, Rabin, according to Narkiss, sought
to impose his authority on him. As ambassador to the United
States, Rabin dressed down his former officer for agreeing to be
interviewed together with Henry Kissinger for a *Life* magazine
article without Rabin's permission.

"I was no longer under him," Narkiss said, "but he still was
suspicious. What was I cooking up? He wanted control."

Yet, paradoxically, Ambassador Rabin infuriated his own
superior, Foreign Minister Abba Eban, by conducting diplomacy
without feeling the need to confer with him.

According to Dov Tsamir, an aide to Rabin in the 1970s, Rabin,
while no politician, understood politics, as well as diplomacy and
international relations, "but not relations with individuals." When
Tsamir once told Rabin this, calling him "autistic," Rabin asked:

"What's that?"

Unsocial behavior, Tsamir replied.

Rabin reflected for a moment, then said: "Yes, you're right."

How could he deny the truth?

And in fact, most people did not hold Rabin's often abrupt manner against him, precisely because it was rare for a politician to consistently tell the truth, especially with his sometimes shocking bluntness. Nor did they mind that he was not a charismatic speaker. Indeed, they were often charmed and amused by the way he mangled his unsophisticated Hebrew and introduced quaint, sometimes inexplicable expressions that had them laughing and reaching for the dictionary. At one press conference, in ridiculing a decision to keep settlements in the Gaza Strip, he grunted, "They are useless *kugelager*," mysteriously meaning "moving parts" in German.

Some of Rabin's gems suggested a certain macho attitude. When the French, whom he distrusted, sought to play a role in the peace process, he charged their effort was "ball-stretching" (*bablat* in Hebrew). And while he never complained about "accurate" news reports even if they reflected negatively on him, he would call an "inaccurate" story "a load of balls." Other notable phrases include *kishkush* ("nonsense"), "a stinking trick," and "good-for-nothing losers." Perhaps his most famous one was reserved for Yossi Beilin, a protégé of Shimon Peres: "Peres's poodle." Many of his expressions were selected from the unique slang vocabulary he learned while a student at the workers' elite Kadouri Agricultural School he attended as a child.

In any case, authenticity prevailed over autism in the minds of most Israelis, who would probably agree with Leah's comment to me that "while Yitzhak didn't kiss babies, people knew he cared about them."

One such person was a reporter who was visiting Rabin when his editor suddenly arrived. Rabin seldom embraced anyone, especially journalists, but he suddenly put his arm around the reporter's shoulder to impress the editor with the young man's valuable relationship with the prime minister.

Hayim Hefer, a well-known Israeli songwriter and a member of Rabin's military unit in the 1948 War of Independence, also learned that Rabin cared, despite his laid-back and often sullen manner. When Hefer produced a musical revue for the troops, Rabin came to him after the show and, with a small smile, uttered a single, unembellished word:

"Nice."

"I was delighted," Hefer told me. "Coming from him, this was a tremendous compliment."

Occasionally, Rabin was more expressive, especially when he was dealing with an attractive young woman. He always enjoyed meeting Carmela Menashe, a beautiful Israeli journalist, never failing to kiss her on the cheek. And he wasn't upset when Carmela complained once that because he kept her running after him all day and evening, she didn't have an opportunity to get married. In fact, Rabin introduced her to a visiting foreign leader with the remark:

"This young woman can't get married because of me."

The dignitary was startled. Was this the shy, serious prime minister he thought he knew?

This was, in any case, the prime minister Carmela knew—and liked—she told me. But she refused to take his advice that she marry someone who could keep her company while she ran after him—perhaps "an IDF officer or a terrorist."

This playful relationship, however, was not typical of Rabin's rapport with people, even with many who greatly admired him. Nor was his normally frank, unembroidered talk an impediment to his career. It was, in fact, one of his greatest strengths. Yet it was also, perhaps, one of his greatest weaknesses, and may have contributed, if peripherally, to the atmosphere that would spark his assassination. Once he decided to back Oslo, he made little effort to sell it to the West Bank settlers and other right-wingers who opposed the agreements, while answering their vicious attacks, understandably if undiplomatically, with contemptuous replies of his own.

"Let them spin like propellers!" he rasped, squelching and seemingly delegitimizing them.

Actually, Rabin and his attackers were acting in the best—or worst—Israeli tradition. As Israeli philosopher David Hartman told me:

"Israelis are generally unaccustomed to civilized discourse— as anyone attending the Knesset can attest—and seldom talk to those who disagree with them."

Rabin's most venal assailants were the religious extremists.

Still, some of the devout admired him even though he tended to be agnostic and supported a peace process they may have opposed. Ashkenazi Chief Rabbi Israel Lau, a good friend, spoke with him about spiritual and other matters for an hour every week, and Sephardic Chief Rabbi Eliahu Bakshi-Doron also had warm relations with him. Rabin, Bakshi-Doron told me approvingly, had a "strong feeling" for religion despite his limited knowledge of the Bible and Jewish tradition. He made sure at Oslo that the most important Jewish holy places in Palestinian areas would stay under Israeli control. He gave the rabbinate, which had been a department of the Ministry of Religious Affairs, autonomous status. He banned the import of nonkosher meat into the country.

Another religious leader, Gad Navon, chief rabbi of the Israeli army, effusively praised Rabin for assuring—ever since the 1948 war—that the troops ate kosher food and could practice all religious rituals while on duty. As one of the prime minister's aides explained:

"Rabin wanted to smooth the way to peace with the minimum difficulty, and so he was ready to let the religious people have almost anything they wished—except to expand their settlements."

But if Rabin found religious concessions a bearable price to pay for a degree of rabbinical cooperation in the struggle for peace, his military background with its autocratic and hierarchical principles sometimes intruded into this struggle. For example, he expressed envy of Egyptian President Hosni Mubarak, who, unlike himself, didn't have to accept the decisions of a high court.

"Rabin had contempt for democratic mechanics," an aide told me, "but he treasured democratic values."

Regardless, he always managed to suppress whatever authoritarian impulses he had.

Probably not too easily, however, in the case of Shimon Peres. He would clearly have liked to ban Peres from the government forever. His contempt for the man until the last months of his life was rooted in a gnawing suspicion that Peres was nefariously plotting to steal his office, a suspicion that his wife and advisers did little to discourage.

Nevertheless, the two men had always shared the same basic

vision of peace, differing only on timing, tactics, and scope. Rabin, viewing peace through a strictly pragmatic lens, was wedded to a step-by-step solution that would nurture mutual trust, and refused to set publicly a final goal in advance. Peres wanted to leap precipitously to what he saw as the ultimate solution—a Palestinian state that would be integrated economically into a Benelux-type Middle East bloc.

Rabin wasn't at all sure that such a bloc was possible in view of the vast cultural differences between Arab and Jew and the great discrepancy in the rate of their economic and technological progress; Egypt had already expressed fear of Israeli economic dominance in the Middle East. But he did not oppose such a future development in principle if one day it could prove workable. For the immediate future, however, he pragmatically wanted cooperation, not integration.

At the same time, Rabin suggested in private that he was resigned to the eventual establishment of a demilitarized Palestinian state, though he hoped it would be linked in a federation with Jordan. When Simcha Dinitz, who followed Rabin as ambassador to the United States, advised the prime minister to simply fix the frontier lines and reach a two-entity solution, letting the Palestinians call their entity a state if they wished, Rabin replied:

"I can't agree to a Palestinian state now as it is a negotiating point."

In other words, the final talks would apparently produce such a state.

Meanwhile, it was in the interest of Israel that the Palestinians enjoy full autonomy, and he would arrange for the World Bank to siphon $100 million in aid into the autonomous areas for the development of industrial parks. Only better living standards would convince the Palestinians that peace was worth having.

But before Rabin would agree publicly to any final peace arrangement, he had to be certain that Arafat would do his best to assure Israel's security—and that the Israeli public would not rebel at the speed of the process. Once Oslo made Rabin and Peres realize they needed each other in the common struggle, personal antagonisms gradually dissolved in the national interest and climaxed in one of the country's most dramatic moments when they embraced in public. The two men, according to Dinitz, now fused into the equivalent of one great man, David Ben-Gurion, who was both a tough pragmatist and a bold dreamer.

In Oslo, Rabin thus found his own peace.

Constantly preoccupied with achieving his aims, Rabin had not often experienced such peace during his career. Even the parties and receptions that he was required to attend as ambassador and prime minister did little to relax him, though he did like debating politics with reporters, who, unlike the diplomats and politicians he often found boring, did not hesitate to argue vociferously with him.

The only affairs Rabin really enjoyed were the occasional military reunions he attended, being essentially a soldier in statesman's clothing. His soul was rooted in the Israel Defense Forces (IDF) he had helped to create and lead, an almost sacred organization he saw as the answer to any threat of a new Holocaust. And he viewed every soldier he met, it seemed, as a fresh embodiment of someone who had died under his command.

It was during such meetings that one could best perceive that Rabin's abnormally controlled personality hid a deep reservoir of emotion. And he met many soldiers, visiting them often during training, looking them in the eye, and asking them about their families, ambitions, and feelings—paradoxically, personal questions, however well meant, that he himself would have thought intrusive if directed to him.

Rabin suffered greatly with every casualty and personally visited the loved ones of those who died, "pushing his feelings deep into himself," one fellow general, Danny Yatom, told me. Every time Rabin ordered a unit to attack, his commanders could almost feel vicariously the pain he felt knowing that the next day some of his beloved men would join the dead of past wars.

When another general, David Ivry, lost his son in an air force accident, Rabin tried to console him but needed consoling himself. He excused himself, Ivry told me, and went into another room to weep.

Nor did Rabin shrink from assuming full responsibility for every military action, even if disastrous. In fact, he reacted to his own blunders in a way that few commanders would have. During the Six-Day War, on a visit to a unit that had been decimated by the enemy, he told the commander:

"I want you to promise that you'll tell those who survived that I apologize to them for what happened. I sent 300 men into a battle against 5,000 Egyptians, basing my decision on faulty information."

Rabin, moreover, found it almost impossible to take action against old army comrades who may have violated orders, even the military code. When Major General Shlomo Goren, who had been chief rabbi of the IDF, called on soldiers to disobey any orders issued under the Oslo program for the forcible evacuation of Gaza–West Bank settlements, Rabin refused even to reduce his rank.

At the reunions, Rabin suddenly found himself free of tension as he listened rapturously to stories of past battles and to gossip about old comrades. He laughed at jokes (though he rarely told them) and relived moments of glory, managing to break loose from his emotional straitjacket for a few precious hours. As a young military instructor, one comrade said, he would, however reluctantly, appear at masquerade parties on the holiday of Purim. But he "didn't dance to the music of *Swan Lake* in long underwear like others; he wore an Arab sheikh's disguise. That character enabled him to act in a restrained manner."

Still, some remembered that Rabin had not always been generous with his compliments for his men's battle heroics, for he expected them to act heroically. When, in 1957, Rabin, then northern commander, called for help during a Syrian attack, a battalion raced to the scene and liberated him and his men from a trap. But he greeted the commander of the rescue unit with little sign of appreciation: Why had it taken him three hours to arrive? It was only in 1995 that, on a visit to the scene, he belatedly thanked the rescuers. What were words? Didn't they realize he loved and admired them?

But if Rabin cherished his soldiers and comrades-in-arms, who had fought so courageously to protect this land of the Jews, he held in contempt those Israelis who had fled to another country, especially the United States. Branding them "draft-dodgers" and "chicken dropouts," he demanded that they at least send their children to live in Israel.

Actually, as he rose to the top, Rabin seemed even more attached to young soldiers he did not know personally than to old friends who had fought beside him but seldom heard from him between reunions. At the same time, apparently influenced by society-conscious Leah, he mingled mostly with eminent political figures and wealthy businessmen—for whom Leah personally cooked exquisite meals served on the roof of their penthouse apartment.

Nor did the social mix change when at least one aide warned Rabin that such close association with the rich and powerful could damage his reputation as a son of pioneers and a man of the masses. In the view of Yeshaya Ben-Porat, a highly respected Israeli journalist, these business friends "influenced Rabin's economic policies."

To the people who worked for him, Rabin was indeed a man of the masses. His principal driver, Yehezkel Sharabi, like his relief, Menachem Damti, worshipped him. When Sharabi began driving for Rabin, then chief of staff, he was "under a lot of stress," Sharabi told me. What could he say to the commander of the army? But Rabin immediately put him at ease, speaking "as though there was no difference between us." In fact, Rabin asked to be addressed as "Yitzhak." When he later served as ambassador to the United States and returned home on visits, he would reject the foreign ministry's offer of an air-conditioned limousine, jump into the front seat of Sharabi's small, steaming car, remove his tie, and chatter freely as he seldom did with his peers, often about his hopes for peace.

As with Damti, who drove him to the scene of his murder, the prime minister attended Sharabi's family celebrations and was careful not to overwork him. Often, in the evening, he would send Sharabi home and get behind the wheel himself or enlist Leah for the job. Once, when Rabin learned that Sharabi had suffered an allergic reaction, he raced to the hospital at 2:30 in the morning.

"I came to see how you were doing," he explained. "Besides, I want to encourage the doctors to treat you better. I want them to know who cares about you."

On another occasion, when Sharabi was stricken with a heart attack, Rabin even promised to take care of his family for life if he didn't survive. And when the driver's son fell ill, he phoned the youth in the hospital every day. He also abandoned an important meeting to walk in the funeral procession for Sharabi's mother.

"I loved everything about him," Sharabi told me.

Another employee who idolized Rabin was his secretary, Marit Danon.

"Sometimes he gave me the impression of a child," she would say, "like asking if I would bring him some chocolate. I felt I wanted to protect him. He would talk with the secretaries and ask us about our families. After a meeting he would often collect the coffee cups himself. He said he was used to it from home."

Marit and other members of Rabin's staff received a book and a card on their birthdays as a token of appreciation for their work. And he was warm to them, Marit told me, even when he was exhausted and under great pressure. This was often, since he remained at his desk on many days from 7:30 A.M. until late in the evening, often in shirtsleeves, reading cables; meeting with cabinet members, politicians, and other visitors; analyzing economic statistics; dispatching no-nonsense memos to aides that told them, like a chief of staff giving orders to his generals, what they must do that day. Since Rabin chain-smoked about five packs of cigarettes a day, those who entered his office, which, in Leah's words, "smelled like a chimney," sometimes couldn't wait to leave.

On most days Rabin allowed himself hardly a half-hour for a weight-watcher's lunch. When he first took office in 1992, he called in Marit and asked her if she could perhaps bring him a special delicacy he craved. What exotic dish did he want, she wondered—perhaps caviar or some rare species of bird? No, he would like some *leben* (a kind of yogurt) and cucumbers, a common Israeli dish. Sometimes he had an omelet, cheese, and bagel instead.

Anything to drink? Sometimes empty wine or whiskey bottles could be found in his desk. Usually, at about 5 or 6 P.M., he would imbibe a half-glass of whiskey. He enjoyed beer, too, especially the crate sent to him by German Chancellor Helmut Kohl. No one had ever seen him intoxicated in or out of the office, but, one aide would say, a half-hour after the afternoon refreshment, there would be "another Rabin"—almost optimistic.

Yet Rabin was deeply concerned about the opposition's attempt to portray him as a drunkard, and so was his staff. When one reporter, during an interview, asked Rabin's secretary for a glass of whiskey, the young woman, fearing bad publicity, snapped:

"We keep no such beverages around!"

Later, Rabin personally poured the reporter a whiskey. He happened to trust that one.

So humble could Rabin be that when he walked into the office of an aide once and found him talking with a visitor, he exclaimed apologetically: "Oh, I'm sorry. I didn't mean to disturb you. I'll wait outside."

And his aide Shimon Sheves would say: "He cared about everything. He knew everything about people who worked with him, including their family affairs and problems. For example, when I had a leg problem, he made me tell him which doctors I had seen and what kind of treatment I received."

Still, Rabin, who did not hesitate to admit his own errors in public, could be tough on his political aides when they erred. His occasional impatience with them contrasted with the almost unlimited forbearance that characterized his relations with his secretaries and drivers, who were among the few people he regarded as unreservedly loyal and pure-hearted. While seldom raising his voice, he scolded the erring aides or peremptorily dismissed them from the room with a dreaded shake of his hand if they did not reply to his searching questions clearly, briefly, and logically. He would thus metamorphose into the hard-nosed authoritarian he had been as a general, refusing to tolerate inefficiency, ineptitude, or indiscipline, and viewing all decisions through a military prism.

In the process, he might either retain the almost worshipful love of disciples ready to accept, Moses-like, the admonitions of a god, or arouse deep resentment in others, sometimes expressed in crude, whispered expletives. Rabin, for his part, would claim, not without justification, that he knew "how to get the best out of people working for me."

If Rabin could be hard on his subordinates, he seldom had the heart to fire anyone, hoping the unwanted or unneeded person would take the hint and quit. And he would stand up firmly for his assistants whenever they were attacked or even treated disrespectfully. During one visit to the United States, at a breakfast for American journalists, an Israeli official introduced Rabin and his entourage but neglected to mention his spokesman, Uri Dromi. Suddenly, Rabin cut off the speaker with a gruff order:

"Introduce Dromi!"

Cabinet ministers were no more spared Rabin's intemperate reaction to failure and incompetence than were his lesser subordinates. Since he fully trusted only himself, he sheared from their respective ministries all responsibilities relating to peace and personally shouldered these tasks.

It was the placid, kind, almost childlike aspect of Rabin's personality that was manifested at home in the little time he spent there. On Saturdays and holidays he would slouch in a chair and, to relieve his tension, watch an action drama or a sports event on television; he could rattle off the names of the ten top tennis players in the world or of the best soccer players in Europe. At other times he would tinker with his camera, which he loved to use on his vacations, or with other mechanical objects. Once, when a reporter who was interviewing him could not make her tape recorder work, he startled her by volunteering:

"Don't worry. I'll fix it."

And he took the recorder apart, carefully checking each part as he might the words in a battle order, and repaired it on the spot. When the interview resumed, Rabin's tense demeanor had softened into relaxed casualness.

Rabin might also pick a book from his bookshelf and peruse it. Usually it was a detective story or, if he wasn't too fatigued, a volume dealing with his field of interest—politics, history, biography—but seldom other subjects. Though he had a brilliant mind, he saw no need to broaden the scope of his reading, according to one former aide. Still, he had dreamed of studying in the United States, and in fact his enrollment was approved at various times by the University of California and Harvard, though a war always intervened. He wanted a practical education for careers he contemplated: irrigation engineering and political science.

In any event, he did not think there was much that scholars could teach politicians since politics was not a science. Scholars, he felt, were too abstract; they couldn't deal with day-to-day governance but could only analyze history. Nor did art particularly move him, though the walls of his living room were covered with paintings by well-known Israeli artists. Rabin didn't know them all, but he would tell guests:

"See Leah about that. She's the expert."

On weekdays, Rabin was seldom at home to enjoy the luxury of leisure, though he and Leah would dine together every Thursday at the Olympia Restaurant in Tel Aviv. Usually arriving home between 10 P.M. and midnight, he would first light up a cigarette and then feast on a supper of cornflakes or low-fat cheese and coffee, followed by a whiskey or two, often sipped with Leah after he poured the same for her. These were moments of salvation for Rabin—a cigarette finally puffed at leisure, a drink that momentarily dissolved his pessimism, and a few words from Leah about the children or his successes. How bright was the day—late at night.

They would then go to bed, but Rabin would not sleep until he inhaled another cigarette despite Leah's protests that he might fall asleep and set the bed on fire. She tolerated his addiction, however, since he had failed several times to break the habit; besides, doctors said smoking had not affected his health so far. About the only time a cigarette did not dangle from his lips was when he drove in his car with Yehezkel Sharabi. After the driver suffered a heart attack, Rabin vowed he would never smoke again when driving with him, and he kept his promise.

Leah awakened her husband at about 6 A.M., when he would puff on still another cigarette before breakfasting on half a grapefruit, a roll with low-fat cheese, coffee, and vitamin pills. He consumed the meal while reading the morning newspapers, especially articles that Leah had read earlier and would bring to his attention. Then he left for the office, careful not to be late, since promptness was almost a religious obligation to him. Once, when he appeared at the office about fifteen minutes later than usual, he apologized profusely to his staff; his wife had awakened him late. Another time, while serving as ambassador to Washington, he showed up at a friend's house hours before a dinner party was to start, explaining that he would be coming without his driver and wanted to make sure he knew the route in advance so he wouldn't be late.

Rabin and Leah were, in a way, an odd couple. He came from a pioneering working-class family with roots in Russia, she from a wealthy middle-class family that had fled Nazi Germany. He was an introvert with few close friends, she an extrovert with a coterie of them. He was taciturn, speaking only when he had something to say; she seldom was without something to say.

But they formed a symbiotic relationship, and their mutual need for each other, psychological and pragmatic, was powerful. Leah needed the heady cultural and social milieu to which her husband's position gave her entree. She was never happier than when she could chat with artists, writers, diplomats, and political leaders whom she met at receptions, aglow in a designer gown and gold bangles that ringed a forearm.

"Fortunately," Leah told a reporter in 1993, "I had an opportunity to learn from past mistakes and correct them. People may say now that I show a lot of warmth. . . . Now, I realize, for instance, how important it is to stand at the door, welcome our guests and let them know how glad I am to see them. . . . I don't have to make a huge effort in order to turn their visit into a memorable experience. . . . When diplomats arrive, I speak with every one of them, discussing with the Brazilian or Pole something about art in their countries or talking with the Czech about literature in his."

On the other hand, Rabin needed a wife like Leah who would free him to spend virtually all his time running the nation, as Leah did. She not only presided over social events, but dealt with personal financial matters and household problems. Nor did he seem to mind when Leah, who was more dovish than he, offered her own strong views on political and other issues, though, according to friends, he was not influenced by them. Occasionally, however, when she sharply criticized his political foes in front of others, he would snap:

"Leah, stop it!"

But Rabin felt comfortable with his wife. He admired her caring, compassionate nature, reflected in her significant work for autistic children. As chairman of the Israeli Autistic Society, she has built a village for them in several cities to save them from being institutionalized. And she was extremely loyal to her friends, as long as they didn't criticize her or disagree too sharply with her husband's policies. As one of them, Naomi Heifetz, would comment:

"She was with me while I was mourning my mother and sister, who both died from cancer. If you tell her you've got a newborn grandchild with some physical problem, she will soon get you the best doctor possible."

At the same time, Rabin apparently enjoyed being coddled and flattered by Leah. Even so, their marriage, according to friends, was in trouble more than once. But they always succeeded in overcoming their problems.

Leah's intense devotion to her husband made her very selective in her choice of guests or hosts; she refused to dispense her considerable charm on those who strongly opposed her husband's views, even as she reserved the right to oppose them herself. When one television commentator spoke ill of him, she reacted in much the way President Harry Truman did when a reviewer panned his daughter's debut as a concert vocalist. Leah called up the commentator and protested in rage—only to be admonished for daring to tell a pundit what to say on his own program. Nor would she speak to any other journalist who wrote strongly critical articles about her husband or herself.

And Leah's unbending attitude did not change following her husband's death. When an old friend called at the Rabin home to express his condolences, she refused to let him in the door because he had opposed one of her husband's policies. Not surprisingly, she was taken aback when, during an interview, I happened to refer to some right-wing friends of mine.

"You have right-wing friends?" she exclaimed. "I would never have such friends. They were Yitzhak's enemies."

Leah's strong will is also reflected in the firmness of her hold on her children, especially her daughter, Dahlia, who has always been very close to her and seldom makes a significant move without her approval. Leah's son, Yuval, friends say, has been more resistant to the authority of her iron-tinged personality.

If the prime minister, for his part, found little time to spend with his wife, he found even less for his children and grandchildren. And this was one of his deepest regrets, since, he would say, he didn't want them to "feel the way I did in my childhood," when his parents were seldom home. But his children and their own brood understood his duty to the nation, and found some compensation in the honor he was bringing to the family. Rabin saw them mainly on Friday nights, when they all gathered for a Sabbath-eve meal in his home. These were hours of intense enjoyment for the prime minister, who finally could relax after a week of unrelenting tension. Usually present were Dahlia and her second husband and two children, and Yuval, also divorced, and his son. Rabin embraced the family guests and listened to their problems as intently, it seemed, as he might listen to a report of some crucial battle.

Dahlia, a pretty, soft-spoken lawyer, had particularly loving remembrances of her father, who, she would say, "never told me what to do. He just analyzed all the possibilities and let me choose the best." Born with a defective heart, she recalls how he would sleep in her bed when she was a child so that Leah would not have to rush to her in the middle of the night should she need help.

Rabin was proud of Dahlia for becoming a leading lawyer in Tel Aviv, and bragged to his friends about her ingenuity, especially after she once crossed the border into the Israeli-occupied zone in southern Lebanon to speak about an urgent matter with a client on army duty there—even though women were banned from this dangerous area. Showing friends a photo of her in Lebanon dressed in helmet and flak jacket, he asked, his face radiant:

"Would you like to see something really sweet?"

Rabin was also proud of Yuval, who became an army tank commander in the early 1970s. He entered the tank corps on the advice of his father, who felt it would increase Yuval's technical knowledge—which, in fact, he expanded when he left the army; he would eventually become an executive in a computer software firm. Hoping to help keep his father's flame of peace alive, he may enter politics.

As for Rabin's grandchildren, they worshipped him as a kind of family god—a feeling projected by granddaughter Noa when she made international headlines with a moving tribute to Rabin at his funeral. Rabin acted like a father to them after Dahlia's first husband was disabled in an accident when they were children, spoon-feeding them, putting them to bed, telling them stories.

Once, his friend and ghostwriter, Dov Goldstein, asked Rabin over dinner what event had brought him the greatest happiness in his life. Was it perhaps his conquest of Jerusalem, his appointment as chief of staff, his election as prime minister?

"No," Rabin replied, "it was when my grandson, Jonathan, sat on my knees and said, 'Grandpa, if it weren't for you and grandma, we would be miserable kids, but you make us a little bit happier.'"

His eyes teary, Rabin got up, embraced Goldstein, and kissed him on the cheek, spurring one shocked observer to exclaim, "Is Yitzhak nuts?" Who could believe that anything could wring such emotion from this introverted, seemingly alienated man?

When Jonathan turned eighteen and joined the paratroops, Rabin, at the swearing-in ceremony, kissed his grandson on the lips, his eyes shining with pride. Yet friends sensed a hidden anxiety behind his show of joy. His son had survived in the army, but now—a new terrible risk. And as a general who had sent many youths to their death, he could not afford to display even a hint of special concern for his grandson. The experience further personalized his resolve to bring peace to Israel. Even in his last speech, Rabin would make this point:

"The path of peace is better than that of war. I say this as someone who was an army officer and defense minister. I have seen the agony of families of IDF soldiers. For them, for our own sons—or grandsons, as in my case—I want this government to seize every opportunity to promote and achieve a comprehensive peace."

Rabin was also extremely close to Noa, viewing her as the perfect paragon of Israel's new generation—strong, proud, unflappable. And he admired her intelligence, listening to her political opinions more patiently sometimes than to the ideas of some of his official advisers, though, like Leah, she was more aggressively dovish than he. Her grandfather, Noa would say, was involved in her personal life in particular, but took an interest in young people's lives in general. He wanted to know "what they study, do, wear, read, and talk about."

For all the love, respect, and admiration showered on Rabin by his employees, subordinates, friends, and family, he was a lonely man. One political colleague would observe:

"Rabin was in the army for thirty-five years, yet he couldn't name one man he could call for advice."

Actually, there were a few people he would listen to, although even they knew they were suspect. Eitan Haber first met Rabin when, as a young newsman, he covered Rabin's northern command in 1958. He probably grew as close to Rabin as any person did, and, after serving as a top editor on *Yediot Aharonot*, one of

Israel's leading newspapers, became one of Rabin's chief advisers in the 1980s and 1990s, together with Shimon Sheves. But how close was he?

"Yitzhak knew me since I was eighteen years old," Haber told me. "I was like his son. But even after thirty-seven years, I don't think he trusted me 100 percent. I never could reach the depth of his thoughts. And I doubt that even his wife could. He was extremely suspicious and didn't trust anyone. He had a kind of paranoia."

Sometimes Rabin tried to relieve his loneliness by calling for an aide, who rushed in ready to perform some vital mission, only to learn, to his astonishment, that Rabin simply wanted him to sit down for a chat.

"Come and have tea with me," he asked one aide.

And then they would talk about subjects ranging from morality in politics to the next day's schedule. Once, while dealing with nutrition, Rabin nostalgically drifted back to childhood and spoke of his mother's porridge. With a barely perceptible smile, he revealed a little of his upbringing:

"She said it was healthy and forced me to eat it."

His mother's porridge and other memories of his past evoked by these ad hoc conversations helped to ease his tension and loneliness. It was somehow soothing to turn, however briefly, to those pioneering days when life was so magnificently uncomplicated, when everybody dreamed of building a perfect society and trusted everybody else . . . and when his mother made him eat his porridge . . .

2

Red Rosa

Porridge had a special meaning to Yitzhak Rabin, not because he liked it, but because his mother served it for breakfast. And this was often the only time he got to see his parents until the next morning. Rosa Cohen loved children, and she spent much of the family earnings on feeding, clothing, and educating those from poor families. But that didn't leave her much time to care for her own children—Yitzhak and his younger sister, Rachel. Their father, too, was seldom home; during the day he worked at the electric company, and at night he often presided at union meetings.

And so young Yitzhak had to care not only for himself but for his sister. Still, they never went hungry, for Rosa, the dominant parent, took in boarders and moved near friendly neighbors whom she knew would cook for them. Yes, her children were important, but so was her mission. She had to save the world, or at least any part of it within reach. And she had to do it urgently, for she had a serious heart condition and couldn't be sure how long her enormous energy, or her life, would last.

Rosa's austere, authoritarian personality seemed to fit her role as probably the most activist female in the Yishuv (the Jewish community in Palestine) in the 1920s and 1930s. Tall and statuesque, endowed with a swanlike grace, she had large, intelligent blue eyes set deeply in a thin, delicate face. Her dark hair drawn tightly over a high forehead into a large bun lent her a severe appearance. When Rosa arrived in Palestine, a local journalist wrote that "her face couldn't hide her emotions, which were a sign of her Jewish heart." She looked like an aristocratic princess, the journalist added, but she didn't act like one or expect any special treatment, since she was soon found at the kitchen sink washing the dishes.

Rosa was, in fact, "beautiful," a childhood friend of Rabin told me, "but she judged people only by their inner beauty and tried her best to make herself look plain."

The young woman usually wore a somber, even painful expression and clothes that accentuated her plain appearance—a blue dress with white buttons during the week, and the reverse, a white dress with blue buttons, on weekends.

The dress was intended as a kind of uniform, the uniform of the revolutionary. And Rosa was a revolutionary to the core, ever since she had been a young girl in White Russia. Born in 1890 in the Dneiper River town of Mohilov, she rebelled at an early age against the traditional religious strictures imposed on her family by her father, Yitzhak Cohen, a black-bearded Orthodox rabbi who ruled the household imperiously. Rosa was devoted to him and was proud of her heritage, with both her parents coming from families rich in rabbinical scholarship. But she was interested more in fighting the system than in feeding the soul.

Riding the wave of liberalism that swept through Russia in the late nineteenth century, Rosa, influenced by her two idealistic elder brothers, saw herself as a kind of Joan of Arc who would help to free the serfs starving and writhing under the whip of Czar Nicholas II, who succeeded the equally cruel Alexander III in 1894. As her future son Yitzhak Rabin would say:

"My mother was very radical and never hesitated to say out loud what she thought. She had very clear views on matters. Her world of concepts consisted of very strict rules of what was forbidden and what was allowed, like black and white. I suppose this trait of character made people think of her as an inconsiderate person."

But though the strong-willed young girl, defying her father, turned to socialism and viewed a communist revolution as the only answer to Russia's feudalistic misery, her dedication to the cause was agonizingly ambiguous. For the very impoverished serfs she wanted to liberate supported the murderous anti-Semitic pogroms that perniciously eased their own pain—and took the pressure off the czar, who conveniently let the blood flow, and even sent his soldiers to make sure it did.

The flow was especially great in the Bessarabian town of Kishinev, where, in 1903, eighty-five Jewish men, women, and children were massacred, with hundreds more beaten and raped. The czar was motivated by more than the need to divert peasant fury from himself. He was determined to root out the revolutionaries, and many of their leaders, he was sure, were Jews.

Some Jews now fled to Palestine, but to Rosa's relief her father was anti-Zionist, as were most Orthodox, and refused to follow them with his children (Rosa's mother died in 1896). Though only thirteen, Rosa was an avid reader of socialist literature, especially that of the Bund, a left-wing, anti-Zionist Jewish party, and thus fell easy prey to propagandists who preached that the Jews of Palestine were bourgeois adventurers from the capitalistic West. The Jews, she felt, should stay in Russia and seek autonomy, not leave for a false paradise.

Even so, the revolution now took on, for her, a new dimension; it would be fought in parallel with a defensive stand, in part, ironically, against the mobs she was counting on to revolt. And this new dimension was tested perilously close to home in 1905 when a pogrom bloodied the Jewish community of Homel, where the Cohens had gone to live after Rosa's mother died. While nursing the victims of the assault, she helped to form a local Jewish defense group. Each subsequent pogrom further strengthened her Jewish consciousness and nourished her ethnic pride, but without diminishing her ideological commitment—a commitment to a more egalitarian socialist society. Rosa would not, however, accept any particular political label for fear of compromising her independence.

Her father was not appeased. His two sons had already broken his heart with their secular communist activities. He had even struck the elder son at a Saturday night meal because the youth had refused to eat one of the traditional Sabbath desserts to show his contempt for religious custom. And now one of his two daughters was following the same path. Actually, he admired her devotion to the poor. He also cared about them. Indeed, every Friday he would return home from the ritual bath without a shirt on his back. It had been given, together with other garments, to the more impoverished people in the pool. Charity was the way, not revolution. How could she disgrace him like that? Already when she went to visit her mother's family in Bialystok, where the Cohens had lived for a while, the door had been slammed in her face. Didn't she know she came from a family of famous religious scholars?

Rosa also came from a family that had grown wealthy in the timber and real estate businesses. Even Princess Ktsenia Alexandrovna, the czar's sister, consulted Rabbi Cohen on real estate matters, despite her brother's anti-Semitic policies. And she so respected him that she refrained from telephoning him on the Jewish Sabbath and hid all Christian symbols when he visited her at her palace. Did Rosa want to ruin his business and his dealings with the royal family?

The daughter's relations with her father did not improve when she insisted on attending the local high school for girls, the best school in town. A Christian school? The rabbi was aghast. What kind of things would they teach her there? And she would have to attend class on the Sabbath!

No, he would not give her one penny for tuition.

So Rosa earned the money by tutoring and secretly went to class, sleeping at a friend's house on Friday nights so her father, who agreed to this arrangement, wouldn't see her leave for school on Saturday morning. After graduating, Rosa added to her father's fury by meeting with the poor people working on a forest estate he managed for the czar's brother-in-law; she sat with them around a bonfire at night and extolled the benefits of socialism.

Rosa shortly moved to Petrograd, where she became the only female—and Jew—to study engineering at a technical institute. Then, when the communists took over Russia in 1917, she left her studies to work in the city as a bookkeeper in a military factory and was soon promoted to manager. She won the hearts of her workers, even though she made no secret of her Jewish identity, by sharing her pay with the poorest of them.

The communist leaders were less moved. Like their royal predecessors, they persecuted the Jews, Zionists and anti-Zionists alike, and Jewish communists were forbidden to read the Bible, speak Hebrew, or even read modern Jewish literature. Outraged by this pressure to deny her Jewish roots, Rosa refused to register as a member of the Communist Party, though managers of large military plants were required to do so. When the government tried to transfer her to a small mill in southern Russia, the factory workers, in solidarity with her, went on strike. Moscow then stopped sending materials to the plant, and it eventually closed.

Harassed constantly by the police, utterly disillusioned with a Soviet system that tried to crush the individual spirit, Rosa, fearing arrest, dressed as a nurse, boarded a Red Cross train, and managed to reach Odessa on the Black Sea. She intended to sail to Sweden, where she would stay with friends, but the only vessel waiting at the pier was bound for Palestine—the first to leave Russia for that country following World War I. Should she take it? She had always opposed Zionism, feeling it was simply a Jewish bourgeois device for escaping the inevitable revolution, though revolution alone, she was sure, could end anti-Semitism. But the revolution had failed her, and she did have an uncle who had immigrated to Palestine and lived in Jerusalem. She could visit with him and then sail to Sweden. This was better than being caught by the police and left to rot in a Soviet jail.

And so, because of a ship-scheduling dilemma, Rosa made the fateful decision to set out for Palestine, a decision that she could not have imagined would ultimately help steer the Jewish community of Palestine toward its destiny.

This destiny was first glimpsed by a tall, handsome Austrian Jew with a long black beard that made some Jews wonder whether he was the long-awaited Messiah. As a reporter for an Austrian newspaper, Theodor Herzl had covered the treason trial of Alfred Dreyfus, a Jewish army officer, in Paris, and was so appalled by the anti-Semitism underlying the charge that he wrote a political booklet, "The Jewish State," urging the Jews to set up a country of their own.

Although the idea was not new, the repercussions were explosive, for unlike earlier Zionists with their penny-ante fund-raising campaigns and gradualist *aliya* ("immigration") schemes, Herzl would grandly negotiate with the great powers of the world to provide a Jewish home and finance it with millions of dollars from a Jewish international bank. His visionary plan swept the Jewish world with its dazzling detail and audacity. Yes, the Messiah had come!

A year later, in 1897, Herzl imperiously summoned the First Zionist Congress in Basel, Switzerland, and, like a monarch dealing with his mesmerized subjects, masterminded the conversion of his idea into a political resolution: The aim of the new Zionist movement was "a publicly recognized and legally secured Jewish home in Palestine."

Finally, in 1905, the Seventh Zionist Congress declared that a Jewish homeland must be set up in Palestine and not, as some wanted, in the colony of Uganda that the British had offered the Jews. And though leaders of the Ottoman Empire, which embraced Palestine, opposed the idea, the persecuted Jews in Russia and other east European countries continued to trickle into the country, where, gradually, they would build cities on sand, settlements in swampland.

Only days after arriving in Palestine in 1919, Rosa Cohen was among those steeped in swampland. Discovering swiftly that the country was no repository of bourgeois malcontents as she had supposed, she found herself in the new collective settlement of Kvutzat Kinneret on the shores of the Sea of Galilee in northern Palestine. Here she planted cedar trees amid a swirl of mosquitoes buzzing in the scorching sun, work so rigorous that even the serfs she had wanted to liberate in Russia, it seemed, might have rebelled against it. Rosa didn't, even though she had a heart problem.

Actually, she was, in a sense, acting out a fantasy that had long possessed her. She was doing the work of the people she had wanted to liberate, doing it with her own hands—while finding time at night to study Hebrew. Only now could she begin to understand the kind of life that so many millions of poor in Russia and elsewhere were compelled to do until they died. Yet the workers laboring beside her, all men, seemed actually to be enjoying the work. For they were pioneers building their own cooperative settlement, building their own nation. Incredible. No whip-wielding boss standing over them. They were like the revolutionaries she had imagined would take over Russia before the Bolsheviks cracked down on the people they had vowed to liberate. Like the son she would eventually have, Rosa was a pragmatist who could change her views as circumstances changed. And so Zionism began to replace in her mind the broken ideal of communism.

The first hint that Palestine did not conform to her vision of the country came aboard the ship carrying her there. On deck she met several young people who were heading for the Kinneret settlement to help build it, and they told her about the wonders of the place and the beauty of life there. But this life, they stressed, was hard and not suited for everyone.

Rosa found it difficult to believe this utter repudiation of her long-held view of the Zionist endeavor. She was, however, intrigued. The work was hard? How else could she fulfill her fantasy? And this she did, but at a price. After a few months she was stricken with malaria and had to leave for a healthier, more hospitable part of the country, especially because of her heart problem. Passover was approaching, so it seemed a good time to visit her uncle in Jerusalem, though that fabled city, while surely fascinating, did not seem likely to offer the challenges she craved.

Mordechai Ben Hillel Hacohen and his family welcomed Rosa into their Arab-style twenty-room mansion as if she were a daughter more than a niece. Her father had been close to his brother and had even moved with his family to Homel so he could be near him. But they had one strong disagreement; Hacohen was a Zionist and Rabbi Cohen was not. They were soon separated again when the Hacohens and their seven children left for Palestine in 1897 and settled in Jerusalem, where Hacohen, a well-known writer, soon became a leader of the Yishuv. And now Rosa was renewing the link between the two brothers.

Hacohen, a generous, good-natured man himself, would never tire of telling Rosa about the virtues of her Great-Grandfather Hershl, and her Grandfather Hillel. Hershl, who had started the family timber business, once went to jail after taking responsibility for a white-collar crime that a friend committed.

As for Grandfather Hillel, when some ultra-religious relative wrote him that he should discipline Mordechai for associating with secular intellectuals, Hillel, a more tolerant religious man, angrily told the relative to mind his own business and instead wrote his son an affectionate letter. And Hillel cared for the poor, too. He would pay the poor owner of the local ritual bath far more than the required fee and would not accept any change.

Yes, kindness and generosity ran in the family. But shouldn't these qualities, Rosa wondered, have been reflected in their attitude toward the whole world?

Rosa's stay in Jerusalem was a welcome hiatus in her hectic, heart-thumping life, for she needed to recover from her past traumas, starting with her struggle to retain her post at the Soviet military factory and ending with her backbreaking work at the Kinneret settlement. Jerusalem had a calming effect on her, and she now seemed hesitant to take on any new immediate challenge.

In fact, Rosa still wasn't sure, despite her changing view of Zionism, whether to stay in Palestine or continue on to Sweden as she had originally planned. Could she make a lifetime commitment to a new cause, one that she had only recently rejected, after so little orientation? Should she risk disillusionment again? While she contemplated her decision, she would recover from her fever and simply enjoy the excitement of Passover and the placid atmosphere of Jerusalem that was blemished only by the anti-Jewish cries of a few Arab fanatics emanating from the Old City nearby.

But even as Rosa eagerly awaited the Passover seder, the calm of Jerusalem, as the crackle of Arab anger hinted, cloaked a brewing storm.

Actually, the storm had started more than two years earlier, on November 2, 1917, when the British government, revealing the Middle East policy it would pursue after World War I ended and the Ottoman Empire fell, made public a letter that Foreign Minister Arthur Balfour had sent to Lord Rothschild, head of the British branch of that illustrious Jewish family. It read:

"His Majesty's Government view with favour the establishment in Palestine of a national home for the Jewish People, and will use their best endeavours to facilitate the achievement of this objective."

While Zionists everywhere rejoiced, the Arab population of Palestine wailed. Jew and Arab had been living in relative peace up to then, since, under Turkish domination, neither saw much opportunity of gaining independence soon. But the Balfour Declaration, as the letter became known, ignited the nationalist impulses of both Palestinian peoples. The Jews pointed to the British promise of a "national home" for the Jews, interpreting this to mean a Jewish state. And the Arabs pointed to another statement in the declaration pledging to hand over former Turkish lands in the Middle East to them, with no exceptions mentioned. And so the scene was set for a momentous clash of destinies.

No one looked forward to the clash more fervently than a twenty-seven-year-old Arab leader in Jerusalem, Haj Amin el-Husseini, a man of striking appearance with his reddish beard and shrewd blue eyes. Haj Amin was a fierce Arab nationalist who had vowed to "throw the Jews into the sea" before they grew strong enough to take over Palestine. The British may have issued the Balfour Declaration, but up to then they hadn't challenged the Arab sword. The way, it seemed, was now clear. He would strike at the Jews in the very heart of Zionism: Jerusalem.

Passover would be a suitable time. It coincided with an Arab religious holiday, and a procession of worshippers could easily be turned into a bloodthirsty mob, especially if they thought the Jews planned to seize the Moslem holy places. And he would make sure that was what they thought.

Jewish leaders in Jerusalem feared that the Arabs would launch such an attack, and they doubted that British forces would try to protect the Jews, though they were virtually defenseless. One of the leaders, Rachel Yanait, a pioneer who had helped in the defense of several settlements and now lived in Jerusalem, chilled to the Arab street cries that didn't greatly concern Rosa Cohen, who still failed to realize fully how powerful Arab resistance to Zionism was: *"Itbah il Yahud!"* ("Massacre the Jews!"); *"Yahud kabna!"* ("The Jews are our dogs!"); *"Al dola ma'ana!"* ("The government is with us!")

Rachel thus confronted a member of the Zionist Commission, which represented the World Zionist Organization in Palestine. The Jews, she demanded, must form an underground army immediately from young settlement fighters and former members of the Jewish Legion. This was a Jewish armed force that the British,

toward the end of World War I, had formed in the United States
from alien Jews who could not be drafted in Allied armed forces.
The Legion was to fight the Turks in the Middle East, but before it
could enter combat the war ended, and many members would
remain in Palestine.

Now, Rachel said, these trained soldiers could help to defend
Jerusalem. The WZO representative agreed and put Vladimir
Jabotinsky, leader of the right-wing Zionist Revisionists and the
chief organizer of the Jewish Legion, in command of a defense
committee that would now organize a Jewish armed force. And
thus was born the Hagana, which almost thirty years later would
burgeon into the army of Israel—the army that Yitzhak Rabin
would lead to victory in the 1967 Six-Day War.

Among the former Legionnaires who joined this underground
group was Nehemiah Rabin, a good-looking young man with
thick, wavy dark hair, close-set eyes, and a strong cleft chin. His
original name was Robichov, but he had shortened it in the hope
of being accepted in the Legion after his first effort to enlist in the
United States under his original name failed because of a physical
ailment—a hint of the strong will that fueled his Zionist idealism
and seemed to conflict with his laid-back, pipe-smoking, soft-spoken persona. Born in 1886 in a village near Kiev, Russia, Nehemiah
suffered the brutal pangs of poverty as a child, especially after his
father died. To help his mother make ends meet, he worked in a
bakery on and off from the age of ten.

Poverty made Nehemiah an easy target for socialist proselytiz-
ers, and he took part in a strike led by the noncommunist Social
Democrats, who formed underground cells that included fifteen-
and sixteen-year-old boys. The czar's police were soon harassing
him, and in 1905, when it appeared they might arrest or kill him
during a pogrom, he fled from town to town and finally clam-
bered aboard a steamer headed for the United States. Like the one
and a half million other Jews who chose America instead of
Palestine by the end of the nineteenth century, he had little inclination at that time to join the few thousand Zionists who preferred to
develop their own homeland.

Arriving in New York lonely, destitute, and unable to communicate in English, Nehemiah worked in a bakery to earn some
money, then left for Chicago, where he had heard he could take

special courses at the University of Chicago once he learned enough English. Once there, he got a job selling newspapers while studying English, then started working as a tailor. At the same time, he registered at the University of Chicago, where he attended class at night.

Nehemiah also found time to play an active role in the Jewish Tailors' Union, and this activity opened up a new world to him—the world of Zionism, which he had shrugged off in Russia as an insignificant fringe movement. Many immigrant members of the socialist-Zionist Poelei Zion Party belonged to the union, and in their cheap, dingy rented rooms, warmed only by their camaraderie, they persuaded him after passionate debate that Palestine was the only practical answer to anti-Semitism. He joined the party, apparently wondering why he hadn't chosen to take a boat to the Holy Land instead of to the United States.

Yet Nehemiah, it seems, found himself caught in a strange dilemma. While he began to feel that Palestine was his real home, he had come to love the United States with an intensity that few native-born Americans might have matched. As Yitzhak Rabin, Nehemiah's future son, would one day remark:

"His stories about America used to fascinate me, and he might well have settled there."

But if Nehemiah would ultimately choose not to, he nevertheless felt deeply grateful to the United States for giving him the opportunity to acquire an education, to learn the meaning of democracy, and to enjoy complete freedom—something he was unaccustomed to after enduring so many years under the czar's brutal thumb. He felt he had awakened from a nightmare. The stories about America that would fascinate his son decades later would help to set the stage for the intimate relations that would develop between the United States and Israel after the Six-Day War.

Nehemiah's new commitment to Zionism was to be tested shortly after the Balfour Declaration, which promised the Jews a "national home" after World War I. Vladimir Jabotinsky had been pleading with the British since the beginning of World War I to form a Jewish Legion. It would fight the Turks in Palestine, who were allied with the Germans. Now, in February 1918, the British, knowing that General Edmund Allenby's imminent capture of southern Palestine would bring the war to an end, finally agreed to set up offices in the United States to recruit Legionnaires. It seemed a cheap way to pacify the Jews in Palestine and elsewhere, and ease Jewish pressure on both the British and U.S. governments.

Nehemiah needed no prodding from his Zionist friends to jump at this chance to fight for a Jewish "national home." It was then that some legion recruiters rejected him because of a physical ailment, while others accepted him after he had changed his name to Rabin so they wouldn't realize he had already been examined. Shortly, he was sent to Canada for training, and from there to Britain, where he joined the 38th Battalion, made up largely of American volunteers but including exiled Palestinian Jews, among them David Ben-Gurion, who was one day to establish the State of Israel, and Yitzhak Ben-Zvi, who would serve as president of that state.

The battalion was now sent to Egypt, where Nehemiah took lessons in Hebrew from Jabotinsky while languishing under a scorching desert sun until orders came to attack the Turks in Palestine. He finally reached Palestine, but, perhaps as the British planned, the war was ending by then. After all, how could a unit of Jews contribute much to victory? And so, to the dismay of Nehemiah and his comrades, they were never blessed with the honor of fighting the enemy in their promised homeland.

But Nehemiah had achieved one goal; he had come to Eretz Yisrael. And if he had not come with the Legion, he might never have come at all, for he lacked the money and the motivation to leave his relatively good life in America. Nor did he intend to go back to the United States when the war ended.

When Jabotinsky formed the defense committee that Rachel Yanai had so fervently fought for, he chose Nehemiah as a member since he was a first-class gunsmith and could train people for a Jewish army. But when the British learned that the Jews were planning to confront the Arabs if they should launch a pogrom, they ordered the Legionnaires to Jericho, about twenty-five miles from Jerusalem. Only the British must be allowed to keep the peace.

Nehemiah was disappointed, but awakened on the morning of April 4 in good spirits. It was Passover, and he and his men would hold a seder in remembrance of the terror that the Egyptian pharaoh had unleashed on his ancestors thousands of years earlier, a day to remember the horrors of the past.

He could not know that at that moment, in the Dome of the

Rock in Jerusalem, an Arab leader was whipping the crowds celebrating a religious holiday into a frenzy. The Jews, he cried, were
planning to destroy the Arab holy places. It was time for the Jews
to suffer new horrors.

Rosa Cohen, like Nehemiah, awoke on this morning with the
pleasant thought that she would be celebrating Passover at a seder
that night with the loving family of her Uncle Mordechai. But suddenly she heard shots in the distance. And then more.

She looked out the window and saw people running down the
street toward the Old City. A pogrom—in Jerusalem? She must
have thought she was back in Homel on that terrible day when
mad crowds poured through the town, killing, wrecking, raping.
She had run out then and given first aid to the victims. Now,
though still weak from malaria, she ran out again, wearing nurse's
clothing so no one would stop her from reaching the wounded.

British soldiers, in fact, were blocking the gates leading into
the Old City, keeping everyone out—except doctors and nurses.
They were urgently needed. For wild-eyed throngs of men wielding guns, knives, and sticks had swept through the Jewish Quarter
murdering and looting. And the narrow streets were strewn with
eight dead and more than two hundred wounded sprawled amid
the broken glass, fluttering mattress feathers, and other debris of
unleashed madness. Yes, another Homel.

As Rosa stopped to give first aid to the wounded, other Jews
who had survived or somehow managed to enter the Old City
sped past like shadows, seeking to salvage what they could of the
human wreckage. Rachel Yanait had dressed in her mother's most
elegant dress and a ribbon-decorated hat and, with pistol in purse,
tried to help after entering the Old City pretending she was an
"English lady." David Ben-Gurion and Yitzhak Ben-Zvi carried a
victim on a stretcher. And there was Nehemiah, disguised in a
medical orderly's uniform he had stolen from Hadassah Hospital.

When he saw Rosa, he was shocked that a young woman would
be roaming around alone in blood-drenched streets littered with
debris from attacks. Why wasn't she taking shelter? he wanted to
know, apparently not realizing she was a "nurse." But she saw no
reason to answer a medical orderly. They became involved in a passionate argument and had to be separated by a British soldier. The

couple then went off, each caring for victims. Nehemiah led one family, which had survived the burning of their house, to Nablus Gate, only to be surrounded by a group of Arabs. He was about to hurl a hand grenade when British soldiers intervened and chased the attackers off. Later, he was arrested by the British and dumped into jail for illegal possession of arms, but was freed after three days.

Shortly released from the Jewish Legion, Nehemiah went to work for the Palestine Electric Corporation, which was situated in Haifa. There he ran across a familiar figure—the young woman he had argued with in the Old City right after the massacre, several months earlier. A British soldier had separated the two strangers then. This time no one could have. Rosa, thirty, and Nehemiah, thirty-four, were married in 1921.

The wedding of the couple sealed the decision of both to remain in the country permanently, a decision that had budded during the Old City massacre, which accentuated their identity as Jews fighting for their homeland. In a sense, Palestine to them had become a kind of social hothouse where they could carry on the revolutionary struggle they had begun in Russia with such sad results, while at the same time building a safe national home for Jews that they were convinced would eventually become an independent state.

The couple sprang from contrasting cultures, with Rosa coming from a wealthy merchant family and Nehemiah from poor working-class parentage. And their characters were a study in diversity. Nehemiah had a pleasant, easygoing, oft-smiling personality, while Rosa was aggressive, compulsive, and humorless. But their differences seemed to complement each other and meld into their struggle toward a common goal. A local journalist wrote at the time:

> If Rosa would have found here bourgeois settlers who wore straw hats and sang all day, she wouldn't have hesitated to leave this country. It was the poverty and suffering of her people here that led her to decide to stay, feeling that it was a challenge she had to meet and that she was needed here. This feeling of being on a mission attracted her to this country until her last day.

Rosa, and also Nehemiah, pursued this mission relentlessly, though Rosa, as she had in Russia, refused to label herself ideologically for fear, as usual, of compromising her independence. In fact, she even insisted on using her maiden name, Cohen, so the world would harbor no doubt she was acting as an individual. When she protested a British decision not to permit ships full of Jewish pioneers to anchor off Palestine, people would ask her cynically: Why did she invest so much effort in saving those settlers when she didn't call herself a Zionist?

She replied simply that they were needed to work in the settlements.

Rosa, who now worked as an accountant for a Haifa timber firm owned by relatives, spent much of her time trying to improve the conditions of the company's workers, often enraging her relatives as she had earlier enraged her father when she urged the workers of the czar's son-in-law to join in a revolution.

The company refused to employ Jews, rather than Arabs, to carry heavy cargo? Discrimination! she cried. Go on strike!

Rosa also helped to establish a workers' medical cooperative, and forced the railway system, postal service, and police force to hire Jews. Most important of all, she helped to organize a Hagana force in Haifa to defend against a possible Arab attack like the one that had terrorized Jerusalem. If any recruit dared to disobey an order, she would slap him in the face, remove his weapon, and dismiss him from the defense force. To pay for the force, she solicited funds by trekking from door to door. Not many would refuse; she was an intimidating figure as she rode down the sandy streets atop a strutting horse, about the only woman in town who owned one. ("I guess she looked pretty weird," her son would comment many years later.)

But Rosa was by no means trigger-happy. Once, when a Jew was found murdered and many people urged revenge attacks on the Arabs, she insisted that it was unethical to kill just any innocent Arab. Eventually, the guilty man was caught, and the population was grateful to her for preventing an unjustified assault.

No one now doubted that Rosa was a true Zionist, however firmly she resisted labeling. Had she not spent all her free time serving and protecting the community? Actually, not all her free time, her colleagues learned with raised eyebrows. In 1921, a few months after her marriage, she managed to use a little of it to become pregnant.

3

Going It Alone

Rosa must have known that her child would want to be born in Jerusalem, which would be the scene of his greatest military and political triumphs. At any rate, about a month before the event, Rosa decided that she would give birth in the Holy City and finally left her job with a warm good-bye to the workers she had been championing. Having a baby was inconvenient, but she would try to make up for lost time. She would be staying once again with the Hacohens, whom she knew would take good care of her. There was one fleeting concern. This time, in her condition, she could hardly run out into the street to help victims in the event of another pogrom.

Nehemiah took Rosa to Jerusalem and left her in the care of her twenty-six-year-old cousin Hannah. But despite Hannah's warm attentiveness, Rosa could hardly wait to have her baby so she could get back to work. The people in Haifa needed her, and who else could find the funds and talent necessary to build an effective local Hagana defense force?

Finally, on March 1, 1922, the day came, and the Hacohens rushed Rosa to Sha'are Zedek Hospital, where she gave birth to a healthy boy. When Nehemiah arrived from Haifa, the happy parents decided to name him Yitzhak in honor of Rosa's father, who had recently died. It was a way to keep his memory alive despite the conflicts that had strained relations between father and daughter.

Yitzhak, the couple were determined, would be brought up to believe in genuine human values, devoid of the materialism and pretensions of bourgeois society. Nehemiah still had fond memories of his twelve years in the capitalist United States. Life was good there and he never went hungry. But something was missing. Here he had found food for the soul. So had Rosa. And so would Yitzhak. He would be honest, caring, strong in character. He would reject hypocrisy and fight for what was right, whatever the odds. He would be the prototype of the kind of human being they felt society should produce.

Rosa wanted to leave immediately for Haifa to resume her work there, but Nehemiah and the Hacohens insisted that she stay in Jerusalem for a few weeks to recuperate. She still had a heart condition, they reminded her. Finally, Rosa agreed, silently acknowledging that she felt weak and fatigued. And when she did return to Haifa after about a month, she felt refreshed and strong. She had to, for she divided her time between her infant and her army.

Nor did her burden grow lighter when she formally became the force's first commander in 1923. Remarkably, this frail, rather sickly woman, a newcomer who could speak only elementary Hebrew, had risen to one of the top military posts in the Yishuv and was giving orders to tough, macho pioneers who seldom took orders from anyone. While relying heavily on the advice of military experts, she prepared training schedules and worked on defense plans with great aplomb. Then she ran home to nurse and care for little Yitzhak, whom she had left with friends. The future would almost suggest that the child had absorbed the genius of command with his mother's milk.

But Rosa did not long hold the reins of military power in Haifa. The following year, in 1924, Nehemiah was offered a job in the Tel Aviv branch of the Palestine Electric Corporation, and so the family moved there, renting an apartment on Shadel Street, a sandy, unpaved road furrowed by carriage tracks. The move did not slow up Rosa's furious pace. She got a job with Solel Boneh, a construction company owned by the Histadrut trade union federation, where another prominent labor organizer, Golda Meyerson (later Meir), also worked. When Rabin many years later mentioned to Meyerson that his mother had served as a cashier in the company, she replied:

"No, I was the cashier. Your mother was the accountant."

Again Rosa combined this job with her usual activities on behalf of the workers, though she refused to have anything to do with the Working Women's Council; female workers, she averred, were as strong as men physically and mentally and so should not seek special treatment. She also continued her activity in Hagana headquarters, resigning, however, after a quarrel with other leaders. Since she was seldom at home to care for Yitzhak, and a second baby, Rachel, was born in 1925, she and Nehemiah chose to live near neighbors they knew well so these friends could care for the children when necessary. In fact, the whole family was at the dinner table only on Friday night.

"This was simply the only opportunity we had to sit together during the week," Rabin would recall wistfully. "We even used to sing, although I don't believe I am a great singer and I have almost never sung since. . . . Each member of the family would use [the opportunity] to talk about his or her experiences [during the week]. Our parents would recall bits of their past and we children would listen more than be heard."

They would also continue to eat, for one of Rosa's strictest rules was that not a morsel of food could be left on the plate.

"Whatever a person chooses not to eat at breakfast," she proclaimed, "he must eat for supper. You must never throw away food leftovers."

Even so, what a wonderful night—Friday.

But while that night was the beginning of the Jewish Sabbath, no candles were lit, no prayers mumbled. For Rosa no longer had to please her Orthodox father and was still a rebel against tradition, while Nehemiah came from an unreligious family and knew little about Jewish ceremony. Yitzhak's only exposure to religion came when, out of curiosity, he visited a synagogue across the street and got to know its rabbi well.

"Just living by a synagogue," he would later say, "was enough to develop within me a sense of religious tradition."

Still, he was part of a generation that believed basically in the religion of labor.

Often, out-of-town friends and relatives stayed at the Rabin home, though Nehemiah might be absent at night, either working or attending meetings of the Metal Workers' Association, the largest labor union in Tel Aviv. Sometimes, however, the leaders met at his home. There was plenty of room for such meetings because there was so little furniture; no one minded sitting on the floor if the chairs and beds were occupied. As Yitzhak grew older he would stay in one room and listen through the open door to chatter in the next room about Labor Party politics, workers' rights, salary disputes, prospects of a strike, and other problems.

Sometimes the local Hagana leaders would also meet in the house, despite their quarrel with Rosa, but then the door was closed and the boy, to his disappointment, could hear nothing. Were the Jews going to fight the Arabs? Would he and his sister be left alone in the house?

The lack of furniture also drew the neighborhood children, who felt comfortable playing games in a place where they couldn't cause damage. Besides, the candy bowl there was always full.

The Rabins' two-room house was, indeed, almost bare. In one room there was a table, chairs, two narrow backless beds, and a bookshelf containing mainly books on left-wing social subjects and history. In the other room were two more beds, two cabinets, and a desk. There was also a small kitchen. No pictures graced the walls, no carpets covered the floors, which, however, were designed with mosaic patterns, the "in" style of the day and the only concession to decorative embellishment aside from a plant-laden terrace.

The Rabins' ascetic tastes were not due to lack of money. Nehemiah, one of the most respected activists in the union, earned a good salary and could have earned more if he had not refused a promotion to an executive job for ideological reasons; he wished to remain a worker. And Rosa earned more than her husband, but spent the money on projects to help the poor. She was enraged when Nehemiah bought an electric refrigerator for $80.

"How can we spend money on such a luxury," she cried, "when there are children who haven't got enough to eat?"

The argument personalized their intramural political and social differences. Nehemiah supported the less ideological right wing of the Labor Party, and Rosa, who, her son would say, "served as a private welfare bureau," backed the extreme left wing. Normally, however, they never discussed money. As the future prime minister would explain:

"One did not work merely to satisfy material needs; work was valuable in itself. Public activity was not a way of furthering personal interests; it was a duty owed to the community." And so the Rabins "lived under a Spartan regime, in the best sense of the term. The family fostered respect for property, and no form of waste was ever tolerated. My parents lived with a sense of mission that permeated the atmosphere at home."

Outside the home, too. Even when Rosa managed to find the time to take the children shopping or simply for a walk, their joy was diluted by constant encounters with friends and colleagues of their mother, who rapped with her on labor and personal problems, ignoring the children as they tugged at her dress.

The dress itself reflected Rosa's missionary zeal; often pinned to it were notes reminding her, for example, to help a poor working mother get a kindergarten tuition discount for her son; a poor widow to obtain a license for opening a store; a poor worker to pay his medical bills with money she contributed herself; a poor delinquent youth to get professional training for an honest job; or a poor policeman, resented by many fellow Jews for "evading hard physical labor," to get a higher salary or medical insurance.

At one Purim festival, Rosa did not need to pin on her dress any reminder that she must protest against what she considered a social outrage. A group of Jewish employers from Petah Tikva who had hired underpaid Arabs instead of Jews were scheduled to lead a traditional costume parade, and Rosa, infuriated by the profit-driven discrimination, was determined to stop them in their tracks—literally. As the employers approached on horses, she rose from her honorary seat, caught the first rider's bridle, and cried:

"Those who ban Jewish manpower cannot lead our parade!"

A riot broke out, and finally Rosa grabbed her children and went home.

Rosa also became the nemesis of Vladimir Jabotinsky's right-wing Zionist Revisionists—who called her "Red Rosa"—even though Nehemiah had once served under Jabotinsky in the Jewish Legion. In 1934, when the Revisionists marched in Tel Aviv during a dispute with labor groups, Rosa sent a team of toughs to beat up the marchers with sticks—an action that her son decades later no doubt wished he could emulate when Jabotinsky's Likud political descendants did little to halt the vitriolic rightist campaign that would culminate in his murder.

Yitzhak was proud of his mother. Like some kind of god, she loved many people and many loved her. And he loved her, too, of course, though in later years he could not recall when she ever kissed him. In any case, a god could only be loved from a distance. Not like his father, whom he loved in a different way. Nehemiah would agree to almost anything the children asked—at least when his gaze was fixed on his next move in a chess game. And he took Yitzhak to soccer games. He was like—a father.

His parents had a special technique for helping their children make decisions. They would simply give their own opinions on some problem and leave the final decision to the children, except in unusual cases.

"The way they respected our thoughts," Yitzhak would say, "made us consider their point of view with much more care, since we were more aware that we were responsible for the consequences of our own decisions."

Rosa's sense of mission assumed a new dimension when she won a seat on the Tel Aviv City Council, enabling her to intensify her struggle to help the working class. Typically, she told her fellow city leaders with a passion they had seldom encountered before:

"It's a shame that the working class has to pay all the taxes to city hall but benefits less than the higher classes from the budget. . . . [The biggest poor neighborhood] still hasn't been connected to the electricity system and is completely dark at night. There is only one gas lantern in the entire neighborhood."

This situation soon improved.

Rosa also demanded that the workers be permitted to attend their own schools so they could learn how to work the land and speed the pace of developing the country. Finally, the local government agreed, and in 1924, labor groups set up Beit Hachuch, the School for Workers' Children. It was a bare wooden barracks standing in a deserted area adjacent to a park, where students could learn how to grow vegetables that they would cook in the school kitchen and eat for lunch. In a sense, the school was an elite institution. Only twenty-five out of some two hundred applicants were accepted, and about one-fourth of these were the children of labor leaders and viewed as the future leaders of the coming Jewish state.

Rosa was elated, especially because her own children could now attend a school that would inculcate in them the values that really counted in life. The school would do what she had little time to do.

Yet when Yitzhak enrolled in the school at the age of six, his mother was too busy to take him there or to introduce him to the teacher. As Rabin would later say:

"Mother had no time to ease me through those first days of school, or perhaps she believed it was better for me to find my own way. At any rate, I found myself standing there confused and on the brink of tears."

His feeling of loneliness and abandonment at this critical stage in his young life may have nurtured the sense of insecurity that would dog him until the day he died, despite his great achievements. Once again, Rosa appeared to express a greater interest in the universality of her dream than in the personal welfare of her own child. She may have left him on his own at the school, but she embraced to her bosom the other children, as well as their teachers.

Rosa visited the school often, trying to improve everything. She inspected the carpentry shop, the kitchen, the vegetable garden, offering advice to the teachers and criticizing their faults. More important, she raised funds from every possible source, especially the rich, and spent her own money to buy food for the children so they would be well nourished. She also obtained a new electric oven for the kitchen to replace a wood-burning stove that constantly spewed choking smoke. At the same time, she arranged for impoverished girls who had only summer dresses to wear in the winter to come to school in woolen clothes. She made appointments with medical specialists for students who needed them. And she even brought milk to one pupil's father who suffered from pneumonia.

Eventually, Rosa would persuade her Uncle Mordechai to

finance the construction of a new sturdy school building by having him talk with the pupils, who, he found to his satisfaction, were receiving a noncommunist education and were familiar with the Bible and Jewish traditions. She also expanded her activities to all other schools in Tel Aviv.

Meanwhile, Yitzhak, despite his initial doubts, found his own way in school—with the help of his teacher, Eliezer Smoli, who opened up a whole new world to him. Smoli, Rabin would say many years later, was "an extraordinary educator whose wonderful lessons had tremendous influence on me and all of my friends. The many things I learned from him are instilled in me even to this day."

Smoli instructed them in botany, zoology, geography, the Hebrew language, world history, and the Bible, but from a cultural rather than a religious point of view; the parting of the Red Sea was explained as the result of natural causes. Smoli also took the children on field trips and taught them about the country's history, the Jews' history in particular. And he took them to villages where Arabs lived and asked the children to accept their existence as part of the life of the nation.

The teacher also imparted to Yitzhak a "feel for the land . . . and proved to us that nature was a living, breathing, talking thing. He taught us how to look at it and how to understand it. Why a certain plant grew only in a certain place and not in another, and why a different plant thrived on the slope of one hill while another sought a shady place in order to hide from the hot sun in the summer. These lessons left an enormous impression on me. They imparted to me a strong affinity to open spaces, for the love of the landscape and everything connected with our country."

Yitzhak's love of the landscape and the open spaces was especially intense because of conditions in the original school building. He would later write of the school:

> It was . . . sweltering hot in the summer and cold and wet in the winter. But we loved . . . its special atmosphere and enjoyed studying in it. That is, to study when it was possible to be there. For the conditions in it were not conducive to learning. . . . During the winter the school was flooded and inundated with rain water. If the water level was a few centimeters high on the floor, we continued with the lesson, but when the water rose to an impossible level, it

was exceedingly difficult to study, so we all went to the dining hall and sat there, and . . . Smoli would read to us from a notebook a chapter from the book he was writing at the time—the part where the torrential rain forced the watchman and his family to seek refuge in the cave.

The School for Workers' Children was notable for more than its washed-out classrooms. There were no examinations, no grades, no homework, no schedule, no bell. Students, who called their teachers by their first names, could stay in class as long as they wished, or not show up at all. And they chose what they wanted to study. A children's assembly would judge any conflicts, but no one would be punished. The purpose of the school was not to saturate students with information they would learn by heart, but to help them grow as individuals, to give them a sense of belonging and togetherness and to discourage them from selfishly competing with each other.

In the workshop Yitzhak learned how to mend shoes and make chairs for the class. In the garden he learned how to grow crops and care for animals. Discipline, the students were taught, could not be imposed but had to spring from the individual's will, a libertarian philosophy that permitted pupils to call the teachers by their first names. English was not taught even though Palestine was a British mandate—precisely because the mandate was British. Yitzhak, in particular, despised the soldiers who were "occupying" his country, so why should he learn their language? Besides, the students were being trained to work in a kibbutz, to be pioneers, then considered the elite of the nation. Who needed English—or algebra, for that matter? Eliezer Smoli himself did not know algebra.

Yitzhak only grew familiar with great Jewish literature and other important works during summer vacations when he would visit Uncle Mordechai, who, wishing to enhance the boy's education, asked him to arrange the books in his library. A scholarly boarder was available to answer all his questions, and Yitzhak found himself reading adventure books like those by Jules Verne and works about the history of the Jewish people, though he would never become an avid reader of literature.

Was Yitzhak a good student? He himself would say that until he entered the third grade he "wasn't really into schoolwork" and that he was more interested in playing games and going on field trips. But his priorities would change shortly before he entered the fourth grade, when his mother noted that his Hebrew skills were below par. She scolded him even though she and Nehemiah were partly responsible. They still thought and counted in Russian and, speaking poor Hebrew themselves, corrupted their son's.

Practice until you can do it perfectly, she told him.

And he did. But nobody could really tell how much he learned in school since there were no tests. He was especially enigmatic since he seldom asked questions or offered answers during class discussions. Perhaps he simply wasn't smart. Later, they understood his silence: He was, in fact, smarter than they, but too shy to show off his knowledge.

Nor did Yitzhak ever display emotion—except when he was caring for Dionea, a scruffy little gray donkey, which was used to carry supplies from market and to haul earth to the sandy school garden. There the children planted beets, radishes, carrots, and other vegetables, as well as flowers. The boy helped to build a special stall for Dionea made of thin boards, and in winter he would run from home every morning directly to the animal "to see how she was doing, to make sure she was alive and not drowning in the heavy rain." One morning he barely arrived in time to lead her out of the stall as she was about to perish in a flood. He was shattered every time the animal gave birth and the offspring died. When Dionea was about to give birth for the third time, he slept with the donkey all night and helped deliver the offspring, vowing that this time the offspring would survive. And to his joy, it did.

Yitzhak's fellow students, fifteen girls and nine boys, felt ambivalently toward him. He was not part of the crowd, usually remaining alone while the others gathered together, laughing, gossiping, telling jokes. At a dance party in which the children intermittently chose a partner on the sidelines, Yitzhak would refuse to be pulled in by a girl who might approach him, ducking under her arm. His only friend seemed to be Moshe Netzer, the son of famous politicians who came from Russia on the same ship that brought Rosa. Netzer's extroverted character contrasted sharply with his own introverted personality.

"Yitzhak didn't talk very much," he told me. "He was as closed as I was open. He wasn't friendly with anyone but me. He wanted to learn and had no time for friends."

In fact, the other students often teased Yitzhak, in part because his shyness made him seem aloof. They would tell him that he would never be a worker but would own the factory, implying that he might betray his class. More often, they teased him because of his reddish hair and tendency to blush, calling him "Burik," meaning "beet" in Yiddish, or "Antotzion," a chemical reaction that produced a red substance. He might then display a rare sign of emotion otherwise reserved for the donkey, hitting the tormentor if she was a girl, or throwing sand at her. He seemed to be especially self-conscious in relating to girls, perhaps because he always feared rejection by his mother.

At any rate, Yitzhak's reaction suggested that, while he had handsome features, his ginger hair and reddish, freckled complexion, together with his small, thin stature, further added to his feeling of insecurity; he even resorted to smearing *leben* on his face when someone told him that it would get rid of freckles. He apparently sought to counter rejection, or the prospect of it, by rejecting others. As one classmate would say: "It was the only way he could communicate."

One time Yitzhak threw not sand but rocks at other children— Arabs. He was retaliating for an attack they had launched against him and some companions. Finally the two sides withdrew in a stalemate. The boy never told his parents about this incident, for the emotion that generated the action somehow seemed too personal to share even with them.

"I generally maintained a close relationship with my parents," he would say, "though my family was never very sentimental and each of us used to keep a certain portion of his mind private. . . . [The stone-throwing incident] was one of those things that I would keep to myself and not share with my parents."

The incident apparently stirred a nascent thought in his mind. He remembered what his teacher, Eliezer Smoli, had told him: Jews and Arabs had to learn to live together. For the first time, the problem of finding a way to stop the two groups from throwing rocks at each other had a serious impact on him.

As the pressures on him at home and in school grew, Yitzhak found one way to relieve the tension: He hid himself in the lavatory at school and puffed on a cigarette. When he came out, he remarked to a classmate:

"Not bad."

And except for brief periods of abstinence, he would continue smoking day and night for the rest of his life.

For all his appeal as a target for teasers, for all his aloofness (perhaps in part because of it), Yitzhak was one of the most respected students in the school. He was, after all, the son of the students' fairy godmother, Rosa Cohen, who was always checking on their welfare, making sure they had enough food, and trying to improve conditions at the school. According to one classmate, when her son walked down the street, other children often followed him "as if he were the Pied Piper."

At the same time, Yitzhak was admired for his proficiency in sports, though students were taught to admire the group, or team, not individuals. There were no heroes at the school. But he was unbeatable at marbles because, a classmate said, he had short fingers, and was one of the most aggressive soccer players. He loved the sport and looked forward to the weekends when his father would take him to a soccer game. On the school grounds, he was constantly bouncing the ball. Sports, after all, didn't require one to talk. Extremely competitive, he always played his heart out, refusing to concede defeat until the game was over.

When the boy grew older, he would also play chess, and sometimes beat his father, who was an excellent chess player but not always a gracious winner. When he beat Yitzhak, he would cluck that his son was a *kaliker*, or "invalid," deeply wounding the boy and hardening his determination to win the next time. Whatever his positive qualities, Yitzhak's fellow students did not regard him as a great future leader of a Jewish state.

"We felt Moshe Netzer could be," one classmate would say, "but we couldn't imagine Yitzhak as the leader of our army or nation. We would have bet a million dollars on that."

Although Yitzhak, however respected, was unloved by his fellow students, who, like him, were sabras, he was the essence of the sabra, if perhaps in purer form than most of the others. He was, and would remain until the end of his days, tough and sentimental, rude and kind. Most typically of all, he was reluctant to reveal his feelings, or even to show that he had any, suppressing tears, usually restricting laughter to a half-smile. The pioneer could not yield to emotions that might suggest weakness and reflect on his machismo. And someone who was raised by a stoic, ideologically obsessive parent like Rosa Cohen and who had to compensate for a feeling of insecurity would find it especially hard to do so.

After school, at about 4 P.M., Yitzhak would take a half-hour walk home and do the chores he had been taught were almost a sacred responsibility—making beds, sweeping floors, caring for his little sister, working until one of his parents came home, usually his father, who would do his share of the housework, as would Rosa when possible. If neither came home at a reasonable time, the two children might go to a neighbor's house to play with friends and perhaps eat there. But in general, according to Yitzhak, his parents "made us feel part of the house and responsible for it, too, by counting us as family members who shared the responsibility of maintaining it and keeping it clean. Both adults and children equally took turns in carrying out larger cleaning assignments."

But he and Rachel were left alone a good part of the time and, he would sadly recall, he "didn't really like that situation at all." The children suffered through their most difficult days in 1929 during a period of Arab attacks.

In Jerusalem, at 11 A.M., August 23, Haj Amin el-Husseini, now the mufti, or Moslem religious leader of that city, who had instigated the 1920 massacre that brought Rosa and Nehemiah together, greeted his guest with an Oriental majesty vividly embellished by his pointed red beard and white flat-topped turban. The British police chief, "nervous and worried," wasted no words: Why had a huge screaming crowd armed with knives and daggers gathered in the Old City again?

Only to protect themselves in case the Jews attacked, His Eminence calmly replied.

And the Jews would attack, Haj Amin had been predicting for months. They flocked to the Wailing Wall for prayer, he charged, because they yearned to seize the Dome of the Rock nearby; they wanted to destroy it and rebuild the Temple that 2,000 years earlier had rested on the same spot. Mohammed's magic horse was tied to the Wall when the prophet, according to legend, rose to heaven from the site of the mosque; so what right did the Jews have to claim the Wall as their own?

The Arab press echoed these arguments and called for *Jihad*, while Jabotinsky's rightist Revisionists demonstrated feverishly at the Wall, screaming "The Wall is ours!" In response, thousands of Arabs from all over the region had swarmed into Jerusalem on this Moslem religious day to pray in the mosque—armed with deadly weapons.

Haj Amin's studied reply did not seem to ease the anxieties of the police chief as he stared into the mufti's cool blue eyes. The Arab leader had every reason to be cool—and confident. For never were his people more insecure, and insecurity bred violence. They were worried about the mosque, about Jewish restrictions on Arab labor, about the waves of Jewish immigration that might soon flood the land. It was time to strike, too, because the tattered economy had sent Jewish morale plunging, and violence could further stem the flow of Jewish investment money into the country. And since the British forces resented the Jews, they would most likely stand by and do nothing, as they had in 1920. Yes, the Arabs must attack soon, before the whole Jewish population drained into the Hagana. And so the Arabs surged like a raging sea through Jerusalem's Old City, stabbing Jews to death.

The mufti struck a far more brutal blow than he had in 1920. And over the next few days, the murder spree would spread like a biblical plague from Jerusalem to Hebron, Haifa, Safed, and dozens of Jewish settlements. More than 130 Jews and about 100 Arabs would hug in death the ground they had so uncompromisingly claimed in life, many of the Arabs felled by British soldiers who were finally ordered to end the fighting.

But before they did, the Jews of Hebron suffered horrors that burn deeply in the Israeli psyche even today. The massacre there had begun when Arabs in the countryside who were in debt to the Jewish merchants decided to wipe out the Jews and the debts simultaneously. A mob chased a group of Jews to an inn, broke down an upstairs door, and, finding twenty-three men, women, and children cowering inside, stabbed them all with daggers and then chopped them to pieces with axes. When British police arrived, they saw blood flowing down the stairs to form a large pool on the ground floor, and more dripping from the dining room ceiling onto a table below like rainwater after a storm. Mingled with the blood in many houses and offices were the ashes of promissory notes.

Though Yitzhak was only seven and Rachel four at the time, they found themselves terrifyingly alone for weeks, since their parents were busy working with the Hagana, helping once again to assist the survivors of this new massacre. Dependent on their neighbors for all their basic needs, the two children could not even use their shower because it was full of ammunition, and had to wash themselves outside with buckets of water. Yet, even as a child, Yitzhak felt "strange" because he was "forced to be passive" while some of his people were being killed.

When their parents finally returned home, the joy of reunion was soured by even more devastating news. The whole Zionist movement was now in grave danger. Two British commissions of inquiry had taken tea with select Arabs and Jews and decided that the promised national home should remain a Jewish dream rather than an Arab nightmare. And in October 1930, Colonial Secretary Lord Passfield framed this sentiment in a White Paper: Henceforth only a limited number of Jews could set foot on Palestinian land, and only a limited amount of this land could be sold to Jews.

The Rabins were shocked. The Arabs now outnumbered the Jews 800,000 to 150,000. Were the Jews forever to be a persecuted minority in their own land?

But once the shock dissipated and the Rabins took heart that the Jews would somehow overcome this obstacle, legally or illegally, they suddenly began to realize that they had exposed their children to a terrible trial. They could not permit this to happen again. And so, eventually, in 1931, they moved to an apartment at 5A Hamagid Street, sharing it with the landlord and his wife and grandson. The Rabins rented two of the five rooms, and both families used the kitchen. Thus, whenever Rosa and Nehemiah were away, the landlord's wife would take care of their children, while the grandson, Avraham Shafir, who was one year older than Yitzhak, would sometimes keep him company and exchange with him dreams about pursuing their studies one day at the elite British-sponsored Kadouri Agricultural School in northern Palestine. With his parents seldom at home, these conversations would help to relieve Yitzhak's loneliness.

As for Rachel, her brother deeply loved her and she worshipped him, but she was too young to talk with him about anything. And he didn't relish the role of surrogate parent and often tried to avoid her. She forgave him even if he sometimes treated her with an older sibling's arrogance. Once when their father bought them each an ice cream, Yitzhak consumed his quickly, then asked Rachel for hers.

"But you ate yours," she said.

"Yes, but I haven't got it now," he replied with a sly logic.

She gave him her ice cream.

Yes, Rachel loved him, even if she did bother him all the time. No one ever heard her make fun of him. Why couldn't the other girls be like her?

All the ice cream in the world could not have brought Yitzhak real joy as he grew older and became aware that his mother was living on borrowed time.

"I was dogged by the fear that [her heart ailment] would bring her to her grave," he would say. "Whenever she had a heart attack, I would run as fast as I could to call the doctor, terrified that I would return to find her dead. Rachel and I lived in the shadow of this dread throughout our childhood, and we were very careful not to upset her."

Nehemiah contracted large debts seeking a cure, or at least a medicine to alleviate her suffering, but Rosa continued to pursue her activities as if she were in perfect health. In 1935, when Yitzhak was thirteen and about to graduate from the School for Workers' Children, she began to worry about her son's future. Students whose families lived in the country would go back home and work in their settlement, but those from the city, like Yitzhak, might go to a conventional high school and then to a bourgeois university, which would most likely prepare him for a capitalistic career, as in the United States. Eight years of socialist agricultural training was not enough, she felt. There was the Kadouri school, but it was only for advanced students. There was no high school of that nature.

Rosa herself therefore opened such a school in Kibbutz Givat Hashlosha near Tel Aviv, but apparently with more in mind than education. Fondly recalling the days she spent on a new kibbutz when she first arrived in Palestine, Rosa planned to move eventually to such a settlement. As a friend would write, Rosa sent

Yitzhak, and later Rachel, into the country hoping they would stay there and later give her reason to move there herself.

"Her activity in the city," the writer said, "was only preparation for the culmination of her dream—to live on the land."

That, after all, was the habitat of the true, unswervingly dedicated Zionist pioneer, a description that now fit Rosa so well.

But was there time?

4

The Plow or the Sword?

Yitzhak Rabin enrolled in his mother's school at Kibbutz Givat Hashlosha in 1935, fairly certain now, at age thirteen, how his career would evolve. His teacher in elementary school, Eliezer Smoli, had taught him to love the land. So while he had earlier shown little enthusiasm for farm work, he now could hardly wait to plant seeds that would sprout life, affirming the validity of the Zionist claim.

"As a city boy," he would say, "I had never really developed a private passion for agriculture. But the return to the soil—and especially the establishment of collectives—was something of a national passion in those days, especially for youngsters who had been raised on the principles of the labor movement. It was our way of laying claim to the land in the most literal fashion possible."

One joke Yitzhak heard so often that he almost believed it was about a nurse who fainted after delivering a baby who clutched a farming tool in one hand and a pistol in the other. Indeed, the plow and the sword were the two legs on which the Jews would stand in the struggle for revival. This joke would lead to another: A boy who received a pen from his father for his bar mitzvah returned it when he graduated high school, saying, "I don't need it anymore." It was more important to work with the hands than with the mind.

So zealous was Yitzhak in his studies now that while students here still didn't have to take examinations, or even show up for class, no one at the school wondered any longer how good a student Yitzhak was. Moshe Netzer, who followed him to the school and never doubted his brilliance, would say that his friend "spent all his time studying." And the school principal, too, was impressed, reporting that Yitzhak "was a good student in the important subjects, industrious in his work and well-behaved."

Too industrious even to seek a seat on the autonomous student council, and, in Netzer's view, too disinterested as well.

"He didn't show any signs of striving for leadership even by the time he was in high school," Netzer told me.

Perhaps because Yitzhak had suffered under someone who did have such a passion. While he admired his mother for her idealistic zeal, she did not serve as a role model for him. He also wanted to help the poor and promote economic equality, feelings reinforced by the debates on socioeconomic problems at meetings of his youth movement, Noar Ha'oved, or Working Youth. But he was not inclined to lead a revolutionary crusade at the expense of his family and perhaps his life—though he would, of course, actively help to defend his people if they were threatened.

Perhaps, also, Yitzhak avoided a leadership role because he feared rejection by his fellow students. It was difficult for him to accept failure in any activity he undertook, one reason that he studied so hard. Once he tried to build a radio and told a classmate that it worked.

"No, it doesn't," the classmate said after putting on earphones. "I don't hear a thing."

"Sit down and raise your legs off the floor," Yitzhak said. "Then you'll hear it."

His friend obeyed but still couldn't hear anything.

"Well, I hear it," he assured the stunned classmate.

Yitzhak was not known to lie, so was he fooling himself? It was hard to accept failure, even when it was obvious. It was hard to risk the ridicule of his fellows.

In any case, young Yitzhak had limited ambition. He contemplated living comfortably and quietly in a kibbutz, doing his best to help build up the country in preparation for the inevitable Jewish state. He would go to the Kadouri Agricultural School and then to college, possibly abroad, for studies in some scientific field that would benefit agriculture. His work would earn him little public recognition but a great deal of satisfaction. Which was fine with him. He was essentially a loner, not, like Moshe Netzer, someone who enjoyed playing the politician.

Yitzhak felt confident that his future had been set. What could divert him from his chosen course? He could not know that the mufti, Haj Amin el-Husseini, whose bloody machinations had brought his parents together in 1920, would tinker with their son's destiny sixteen years later.

The first Arab bullets tore through the night of April 15, 1936, ripping into two Jews on the Tulkarm-Nablus road and setting off a chain reaction of violence in the dark, twisting alleys of several towns. Four days later, Arab bands thundering over the cobblestones of Jaffa wantonly knifed and shot sixteen Jews to death. Were these attacks simply a spate of common Arab street crimes? Though many Jewish leaders thought they were, others were doubtful. The mufti and his men would surely exploit them to spark others. The crimes had made the Palestine Arabs look odious to the world anyway, so why not seize this opportunity to detonate a full-scale rebellion?

They seized it. The mufti called a general strike on April 22 and formed a Supreme Arab Committee, which vowed to close down shops, factories, and ports until the British stopped Jewish immigration, banned land sales to Jews, and formed an Arab-majority government. The aim of the strike was to fuel new violence, and it did. Palestine exploded into a battleground with Arabs, daggers raised, guns drawn, attacking Jews and Britons alike and even uprooting trees the Jews had planted on barren land.

In desperation, High Commissioner Sir Arthur Wauchope wanted to give the Arabs almost everything they demanded. He would cut down Jewish immigration and land purchases and set up a legislative council with an Arab majority.

The Hagana was now emerging as a far stronger guerrilla army than it had been. It was a national force, embracing men who wore not only the working clothes of the farmer and laborer, but the baggy suits of the new middle class. All Jewish fighters obeyed its orders, at least until 1937, when some formed Irgun Zvai Leumi.

The Jewish defense network had come a long way since the first armed group, Bar-Giora, was launched in 1907 by ten men at a clandestine candlelight ceremony in Jaffa. Named after the last Jewish defender of Jerusalem in A.D. 70, it was a secret underground watchmen's organization whose members took the oath, "In blood and fire Judea fell and in blood and fire Judea shall arise!" With their few rifles, they resolutely defended Jewish settlers against Arab raids with the help of paid Arab watchmen.

Two years later, in 1909, Bar-Giora members created a larger organization called Hashomer, The Watchman, which expanded its defense screen to more settlements, this time without the help of hired Arabs, who had often collaborated with the attackers. Both Bar-Giora and Hashomer, like Hagana, which stemmed from them, were led largely by socialist pioneers who combined settlement of the land with military training.

Actually, the Yishuv did not have to rely entirely on the Hagana for its strength to resist. The Arabs were inadvertently helping it not only by pushing the British into Jewish arms, but by spurring the Jewish economy with their strikes. For the jobs they vacated could be filled by Jews climbing off the ships anchored in the murky waters of the Mediterranean. Had not the British tied immigration quotas to available jobs? Soon, with the Jaffa docks shut down, the Jews were carrying timber on their backs to build new docks in Tel Aviv, and Jewish rather than Arab stevedores were hauling freight.

Now it was the Arab leaders who grew desperate. They accelerated their attacks, promising not to cease until the British shut off the flow of Jews streaming in, at least temporarily, and the British began to quake. Reluctant to stir the wrath of the whole Moslem world—especially while Adolf Hitler and Benito Mussolini threatened war—mandate officials avoided cracking down on the mufti and his lieutenants even though Britons as well as Jews were their victims.

The Arab attacks had a powerful impact on Yitzhak. Jews were dying every day. There was no security. But he wouldn't let the growing tragedy interfere with his plan for the future. As an agricultural specialist he could help shape the future—his people's as well as his own—whatever the Arabs did. So he plunged into study for the Kadouri school entrance examinations, confident that he would pass, though only 25 of 350 candidates would be accepted. And he passed, but only conditionally. He would have to take a further examination. Yitzhak was disconsolate, his pride shattered. What would his parents think? More important, in a sense, what would his fellow students think? Was he less intelligent than the others? Many years later, he would say:

"This shock of failing the first exam actually gave me a push that affected my whole life. The feeling, 'How could I have failed?' motivated me more than anything else. . . . I decided to invest all my efforts in proving myself something different."

Yitzhak found that he was especially weak in mathematics, since it had not been stressed in school so far. Desperate now to save his reputation—and his career—he was determined to master the subject, and persuaded a neighbor, an engineer, to tutor him in it. Suddenly he was "captivated by the logic of mathematical structures." The awakening was dramatic: If only he had been forced to study the subject in the free-thinking schools he attended! The second time around, in summer 1937, he scored high grades. With his ego restored, he elatedly prepared to resume his march toward the goal he had set for himself.

Nestled at the foot of Mount Tabor in the Galilee, Kadouri Agricultural School, isolated and remote, was understandably called "The Monastery." The bus that carried Yitzhak from Tel Aviv to Afula rumbled dangerously over unpaved roads that twisted through open fields in Arab-inhabited territory. From Afula, he climbed into a local coach operated by a tough, money-minded man named Ari Kimmel. Yitzhak and other students, when they occasionally went home, often had to sleep on benches in the station because of Bedouin terror attacks along the way to the school. And when the antiquated bus did finally leave, Yitzhak and the other passengers would sometimes have to get out and push it up a hill or pull it out of the mud. And the ticket price was high, too—

5 shillings—at least until the students revolted. They began to walk the three rugged miles to Kadouri, followed by Kimmel in his coach waiting for them to break down and mount the vehicle. They did not, and the price went down.

Yitzhak discovered that Kadouri, founded by the British in 1934, had little in common with the two earlier schools he had attended. He was no longer given complete freedom to study what he wished or even to stay away from class. There was firm discipline here—examinations, rules, punishment. And he couldn't go home in the afternoon after class, but lived in a second-story dormitory in a three-floor, white stone building. His family could visit him only twice a year.

A British-sponsored school, Kadouri was run in the same tight manner as schools in Britain. Awakened at 5:15 A.M. in the summer, a half-hour later in winter, he had to shower in cold water and wasn't permitted to enter the dining room wearing a sleeveless shirt or to start eating without saying *"B'teyavon"* ("Good appetite"). He was also at the mercy of upperclassmen, who would occasionally storm his dormitory room, drag the twenty-five new students out of bed, beat them, and turn their beds upside down. One night they were forced to climb Mount Tabor, lie down while their tormentors stomped on them, and, at dawn, humiliate themselves by praying to the sun.

But despite the tyranny and the tricks, Yitzhak flourished in the autocratic atmosphere. He was perfectly willing to take orders as long as he could concentrate on his studies without distraction. And since no women could enroll there, he didn't have to worry about silly girls making fun of his ginger hair and blushing cheeks. However, as he moved into his teens he began to miss the feminine presence. He looked forward to the Sabbath, when he would walk to the town of Kfar Tabor to watch the girls parade by—"just to see what they looked like," one schoolmate would say. And he apparently missed being able to show off his soccer skills to the girls as he had done in the earlier schools. He still starred on the soccer team, though it wasn't as exciting now.

"No one could break through Yitzhak's defense," one teammate would say. "He used his mind as well as his feet."

Yitzhak was a superstar in the classroom, especially after his first year. Though he had done poorly in mathematics in his initial entrance examination, he now proved himself a near master of the subject, and also of science. The students hated their chemistry teacher because of his exacting standards, and even chalked on the blackboard that he was a "devil" (he replied that it was better to be a devil than a *shmata*, or "dishrag"). But the teacher embraced and kissed Yitzhak after one chemical experiment, marveling:

"You'll be a great figure in science."

Still, his freshman year was not his best, though he scored an A not only in chemistry but in zoology, farm work, plant nursery, and the raising of cattle, sheep, poultry, and bees, as well as in leadership. In addition, he received an A- in botany and anatomy, a B+ in physics and general agriculture, and a B in plant reproduction, agricultural arithmetic, and vegetable gardening. But he earned only a B- in the cultivation of fruit trees and plantation work, and a C+ in agricultural measurement.

Yitzhak especially enjoyed farm work, though he had to do it with his head wrapped in an Arab *kheffiah* to ward off swarms of mosquitolike insects that attacked his ears, nose, and eyes. One subject Rabin refused to study was English, "the language of our enemy." His hostility toward the British led him to play with an extraordinary ferocity in soccer games against British soldiers, who knew that whenever Rabin had the ball, they had no chance to win.

Yitzhak also took part in a plot to embarrass the high commissioner when he was to visit the school. The principal had brought a special chef from Tiberias to prepare a chicken meal, but, on checking the oven, the chef found only bones. The students had enjoyed the best meal they ever had at the school. The principal nearly had a heart attack when he learned of this, though, to his relief, the high commissioner canceled his trip at the last minute.

Yitzhak did not study the humanities either; they were not taught there since the purpose of the school was to turn out a "different kind of Jew." Haim Gurie, a fellow student who would become a famous poet years later, would explain:

"The feeling of the socialist Zionists at that time was that the Jews knew too much about history, philosophy, literature, and other humanities. They wanted to create pioneers, Jews of the soil."

Yitzhak tried to play down his status as the smartest student in the school, remaining silent during class discussions and pretending to study, though he had already learned the lessons assigned him in about one-fourth the time it took the other students. He didn't want to feel "different."

"Whenever the teachers used to ask something requiring some knowledge," a classmate would say, "he didn't raise his hand, because it didn't fit his character. Still, all the teachers knew that he was aware of the correct answer, so when they lost hope of getting a full answer from the other students, they would turn to him. That's how he acquired a unique status in our class."

Yitzhak was so respected that during examinations fellow students tried to peer over his shoulder at his answers, though he would shield his work by raising the cover of his notebook. Testing took place under the honor system, with no teacher present, and Yitzhak would not dishonor himself by helping anyone else cheat. But he would tutor his fellow students, including Haim Gurie, whose poetic inclinations were stifled by the perfumes of the laboratory and the stable. Yitzhak earned the nickname "Shafshif," or "Wear Out," suggesting that he wore out his study material as well as his chair with his intensive work.

Just as Yitzhak was beginning to enjoy his success and the respect of his peers, earned not for his family connections but for his own abilities, he was struck a horrific blow. In November 1937, David Hacohen, the son of Rosa's uncle Mordechai, drove up to Yitzhak's dormitory and rushed in to see him. Yitzhak took one look at David's tense face and knew why he had come.

The visitor confirmed the worst: Rosa was dying and he had come to take him home.

Yitzhak was shocked despite his dire expectations. He knew his mother had a bad heart, and he had been living in dread that she might die. Yet part of him said that it could not happen.

Being away from home, he didn't know that she had calmly told friends that she knew the end was near. In minutes, Yitzhak, desperately controlling his tears, was heading toward Tel Aviv. After greeting his shattered father at home, the boy rushed to Tel Aviv's Hadassah Hospital, "praying," he would recall, "that I would find my mother conscious and able to recognize me so that I could bid her farewell. I think she did recognize me, though she did not speak. I wanted to believe that she knew I was on my way and had called up her last ounce of strength to hold on. Her eyes were open, but she remained silent. I did not want to cry in front of her but I just couldn't help myself, and all my grief flooded out."

It seemed ironic. His mother's heart had held out. She died of cancer at the age of forty-seven.

Few people in the Yishuv's history were missed so deeply. Over 1,000 people attended Rosa's funeral—city and labor officials, bureaucrats, students; all the hundreds of people she had helped to feed, clothe, educate; all those whose lives she had enriched with her struggle to instill in them transcendent human values.

As the eulogies poured forth, Yitzhak, with his hand on Rachel's shoulder, stared with glassy eyes at his mother, whose serene face was exposed in the coffin. Normally the coffin would be closed, but Nehemiah wanted all those who loved Rosa to view her one last time. A young girl who had been a classmate of Yitzhak's in elementary school would say, speaking of herself and her friends:

"We stood watching Yitzhak with his tortured look and wondered how we could help him and his sister. But we didn't dare cross the border of his loneliness. We were afraid to soothe him. We were educated not to show our feelings with words. We were taught that it was shameful to cry. It was the spirit of the times. Sentimentality was not in vogue. Only the bourgeois could be sentimental. Only they could cry. And so we did nothing."

But Yitzhak, who had wiped away the tears he had shed when he was alone with his mother as she lay dying, broke away from the crowd as soon as the services were over and, in some private little world, convulsively wept again. How could he ever be worthy of his mother? A letter of condolence from the principal of Kadouri suggested an answer:

> Your mother was one of the great women in the Yishuv whose names are associated with the lofty idealism of the nation. . . . May you find comfort in studying for your chosen profession, for your own good and for that of the people your mother loved so much and to which she gave so much of her time in her short life.

Yitzhak took the advice to heart. "After the seven days of mourning," he would recall, "I returned to Kadouri with the feeling that I had crossed over the threshold to manhood. Part of my home no longer existed, and I had to strike out on my own path. I became withdrawn again and dedicated myself almost exclusively to work and lessons, finishing my first year as the top student in the class."

But before the year ended, his dedication to study was not that exclusive.

Shortly after Yitzhak Rabin returned to Kadouri, the first shots there echoed across the fields. The Arabs were firing at the school, and there were no British troops in the area to protect the students. The attacks that Haj Amin el-Husseini had instigated the previous year had spread to northern Palestine, and the school was in danger. Rabin and his fellows were faced with a chilling reality: They would have to defend themselves without outside help. A defense system was organized, with the upperclassmen in charge of the school's handful of rifles—obtained illegally since the British banned Jewish possession of arms—and Rabin and the other lowerclassmen serving as guards or messengers.

His mother's death and the threat to the school left Rabin in an emotional quandary. He was determined to graduate at the top of his class in homage to his mother's memory, even though he had to spend much of his time rushing from one defense post to another with messages and peering into the distance waiting for another Arab attack. But while he knew he must help in the school's defense, he felt his fellow students were better soldiers, for most of them came from the settlements and were experienced warding off Arab marauders with firearms. He was a city boy who had never used a weapon or learned defense tactics. And he hated to engage in an activity in which he did not excel.

He had already suffered embarrassment when one of his instructors, testing the vigilance of the students, dressed like an Arab and feigned an attack. The students all fled in terror, but Yitzhak was caught and forced to walk around the school naked as a mark of his disgrace.

Yet he felt he must learn how to survive the storm and return a few lightning bolts of his own. He was thus delighted when the "King of Galilee" visited the school. Yigal Allon, sandy-haired, blue-eyed, thin-lipped, with a warm, congenial nature, was a well-known and highly respected figure at Kadouri, having been a member of the first graduating class three years earlier. He had since become a heroic, even legendary Hagana leader, molded by perhaps the greatest warrior in the Yishuv's history—a young gentile British intelligence officer named Orde Wingate.

Wingate was no Zionist when he first walked down the gangplank into Haifa one day in 1937 to be greeted by silent people who glanced at him with distrustful eyes. He believed, as did many Britons, despite the anti-British Arab revolt, that only their country stood between these "exploiting" Jews and the "backward, unprotected" Arabs. Yet, within three months, he was to become a mystical Zionist as extreme as any Jew, and far more aggressive than most Jews at the time in asserting Zionist rights.

"When I was at school," Wingate later explained to a friend, "I was looked down on, and made to feel that I was a failure and not wanted in the world. When I came to Palestine I found a whole people who had been treated like that through scores of generations, and yet at the end of it they were undefeated, were a great power in the world, building their country anew. I felt I belonged to such people."

A biblical scholar of ascetic appearance, with deep-set, penetrating blue eyes, Wingate had informed Jewish leaders in impassioned terms that he wanted to devote his life to their cause.

"This is the cause of your survival," he said. "I count it as my privilege to help you fight your battle."

And he helped—first of all, by burning the concept of *havlaga* from the Jewish soldier's consciousness. *Havlaga* meant "self-restraint." No Jew was to let the smell of blood go to his head. The Jew would be the purest fighter in the world, killing only those individuals who killed and no one else. Wingate argued—successfully—that an enemy could not be defeated with such a philosophy.

"I have seen Jewish youth in the kibbutzim," he wrote his uncle, Sir Reginald Wingate, "and I assure you that the Jews will produce soldiers better than ours."

Soldiers who would attack, not simply defend. Soldiers who would overcome what he regarded as an inner lack of confidence in their soldierly ability, a complex rooted in *havlaga*.

In 1938, shortly before Yigal Allon visited Kadouri, Wingate persuaded his superiors to recruit members of Hagana for Special Night Squads that would strike at the Arabs in a counterguerrilla war. Taking the initiative for the first time, Jewish fighters, dressed in blue police shirts, linen trousers, and broad-brimmed Australian army hats, helped to protect the pipeline from Kirkuk, Iraq, to Haifa, and to clear Arab forces from Galilee. In these squads were trained the officers who would become the Jews' best soldiers, including perhaps the best of all—Yigal Allon.

Now based nearby at Kibbutz Ginossar, which stretched along the western bank of Lake Kinneret, Allon would teach the students how to use their weapons and strengthen their defense. Perhaps now, thought Rabin, who viewed Allon with awe, he would learn the rudiments of defense that had absorbed the energies of his parents at times. Everyone at Kadouri knew that Allon had been fighting the Arabs since he was thirteen.

Whatever doubts Rabin may have had about his military prowess, he tried his best to please Allon. And Rabin did impress the visiting hero with his extraordinary analytical skills and his authenticity. He would keep asking questions until he thoroughly dissected a problem. Rabin clearly had a future in the Hagana, Allon felt, though he still didn't know how to shoot a gun.

But before Rabin's potential could be exploited, the Arabs fired several more times on the school. And since the British couldn't spare enough men to defend it and feared to give the students arms that could be used against them, they closed down the school. Rabin was furious. It almost seemed a plot against him. He had the highest marks in his class but now he might never complete the two-year course. Perhaps worse, at this time of emergency he would no longer be taking lessons from Allon on how to grapple with the attackers.

But Allon did not forget his zealous pupil. To Rabin's joy, he asked him to come to Kibbutz Ginossar, and there Rabin worked the fields, served on guard duty, and learned how to set ambushes and use rifles, pistols, and hand grenades.

"They taught us how to throw stones from a distance at a target circle," a fellow student would recall, "but Rabin was the only one among us who managed to hit the target. And while we all fooled around and had affairs, Yitzhak was responsible and serious and stuck to his goals."

Finally, Rabin was sworn in as an auxiliary policeman, his first military post. After about six months, he was sent to Kibbutz

Hasharon in the heart of the Jezreel Valley, where he was shortly notified that Kadouri would reopen in October 1939.

Rabin's elation was tempered by the outbreak of World War II a month before he returned to school. One more year and he would graduate. But it was hard for him to concentrate on studies with the world exploding into war. Still, he managed to remain at the head of his class, barely beating out his friend, Moshe Netzer.

At the graduation ceremony in August 1940, he sullenly accepted his diploma from the high commissioner, who, he recalled, no doubt with regret, had never been served the chicken bones that had been left for him when he had earlier planned to visit the school. Rabin won a prize of seven and a half Palestinian pounds, to be given him if he purchased a cow for the school. But he wasn't given the money to buy the cow, though the British ambassador presented him with the money years later when the Jewish state was born. He was no longer required to buy a cow.

Rabin now had to decide on his future: Should he continue his studies at a university as he had long dreamed of doing, or should he join the armed struggle in Palestine? And the dilemma grew more painful after his father, on the advice of the school principal, sought a scholarship for him at the University of California at Berkeley. Yitzhak, the principal said, would probably be accepted for the study of irrigation engineering because of his mastery of mathematics and science.

Rabin was thrilled by the possibility. Water was the most important resource in the area. And he would be studying in the United States. He thought of the stories his father had told him of the wonderful life there, though he recalled also that his mother had often criticized that country for its materialistic values. What was it like to be overwhelmed with the evils of the good life? And since the war had not yet touched America, he could study in peace.

What was the alternative? Join the Hagana? He was not impetuous like his mother, who would compulsively leap into crises. He carefully analyzed each one, weighed the options, and decided on action based on long-range considerations and common sense. Was it realistic for him to rush into battle when he had so little training and may not have been cut out to be a soldier anyway, however much Yigal Allon encouraged him? Could he really serve the cause best with a rifle and a hand grenade?

On the other hand, the Yishuv urgently needed agricultural specialists who could make the desert bloom in preparation for a Jewish state. A kind of "division of labor" based on one's capabilities, it seemed to him, was the best way to strengthen the Yishuv's long-term security, which was his chief concern.

When he had the opportunity, Rabin visited various regions in Israel studying the land and its history, recalling what he had learned on the field trips of his childhood. Later, while on marches with his fellow soldiers, he would describe to them almost all the geographic features they passed, even naming the wadis and water holes. And so, as a student, he could visualize himself cultivating the land more than he could killing Arabs. He chose to be an irrigation engineer.

While waiting to learn if Berkeley would accept him, Rabin moved to Kibbutz Ramat Yohanan, north of Haifa, where he joined graduates of the labor youth movement who were training to set up a new kibbutz of their own.

"I was fond of my companions and the kibbutz way of life," he would say, "but under the circumstances I chafed within the confines of a life of work, nocturnal discussions, and kibbutz entertainment."

Yes, he was still a city boy, but he would get used to the kibbutz. And he couldn't imagine a career that would offer him a finer opportunity to help his country. After all, what would he be better at?

5

Training for
Survival

"Do you know how to fire a rifle?"

"Yes."

"Have you ever thrown a hand grenade?"

"Yes."

"Do you know how to operate a machine gun?"

"No."

"Can you drive?"

"No."

"Can you ride a motorcycle?"

"No."

"You'll do."

And thus in 1941 did Yitzhak Rabin's destiny suddenly take a U-turn. He might never be a good soldier, but he couldn't argue with Moshe Dayan, who fired the questions with almost the speed of machine-gun bullets. Rabin would stay in Palestine and fight. With Orde Wingate whisked back to Britain in 1939 (he would be killed while fighting the Japanese in Burma during World War II),

Dayan and Allon, his field commanders, were now helping to form within the Hagana a new special commando unit, the Palmach. And the British were backing it, realizing that a Jewish force could help them prevent disaster in the Middle East.

German Field Marshal Erwin Rommel's divisions were already grinding toward Egypt, and the British were packing their equipment for transfer to a defense line farther north. The Palmach would cut Nazi communications and, if the enemy invaded Palestine, use guerrilla tactics against them and their Arab supporters.

Rabin had been at supper in the Ramat Yohanan dining hall one evening when fate turned his future around. The local Hagana commander walked up to him and asked if he would like to join a new commando unit.

"I will never know what prompted him to approach me that evening in the kibbutz dining hall," Rabin would later say, "but . . . the invitation to join the Palmach changed the course of my life."

What prompted the local commander was apparently an order by Yigal Allon, who felt that Rabin had the right ingredients of character to perform the most dangerous military tasks—even if he was a city boy. Rabin, in his shock, didn't ask any questions, but he realized that his dream of a university education had suddenly evaporated. He knew how he could best serve his country, even if he wasn't the best.

Yes, he would accept the invitation, he told the Hagana commander, trying to hide his elation.

As one officer who served under him would say, "This decision was a milestone in Rabin's way of thinking. Regardless of his personal interests and the difficulties he might face, he would support unreservedly what he thought was important and necessary and stick to his decision." And after a few weeks' wait, the same commander took Rabin to his room, where he found Moshe Dayan waiting to question him as a meaningless formality.

Rabin thus joined fewer than 1,000 men, almost all from the agricultural collectives, who were chosen to fight with the Palmach. In a sense, it was a thankless honor. Since the Palmach was an underground group, members wore the shabby clothes of the farmer and worker, and so most people didn't know they were risking their lives for the Yishuv. On the other hand, about 30,000 Jews had joined the British army and strutted around in elegant uniforms, smart berets, and shiny shoes, drawing glances of admiration when they walked down the street.

But Rabin, though admitting he was tempted by the glamour, would not be sidetracked from reality. The security of the Yishuv was his only concern. What if the Germans took over Palestine? And if they didn't, what if the British tightened their stranglehold on the Yishuv after the war and helped the Arabs fight the Jews? Only a home-grown army of guerrillas could effectively fight back. And the Palmach, as the hand-picked, ideologically driven spearhead force of the Hagana, would be needed to lead the struggle. Besides, he could not imagine fighting in the "anti-Jewish" British army, even though the British and the Jews had a common enemy, one that was growing more dangerous each day as it crept toward Palestine. The Balkans fell, then Crete. A pro-Nazi regime took over in Iraq, backed by the mufti, and the French Vichy regime clamped a grip on Syria. More ominous yet, Rommel's tanks were slithering eastward across the North African desert toward neighboring Egypt.

Meanwhile, with a grotesque persistence, the Jewish political parties were squabbling in a struggle for power. David Ben-Gurion, head of the Jewish Agency, the Yishuv's shadow government, met with the Hagana commanders to seek a way to save the Yishuv despite itself. Ben-Gurion, only five feet, three inches tall, looked dwarfish, but the odd proportions of his stubby torso, topped with a great round head from which sprouted tufts of frothy white hair on either side of a shiny pate, conveyed the impression of a giant in miniature. And indeed, he was a giant, politically and intellectually, a stature desperately needed in this life-and-death emergency.

If the British withdrew, Ben-Gurion told the commanders, his leathery lion's face taut with resolve, all Jewish soldiers serving in the British army would desert wholesale with their arms and remain behind. Most of the other Jewish fighters would join them on Mount Carmel in Haifa, where the Yishuv would fortify itself against a Nazi assault and fight to the death as Jewish zealots did at Masada in A.D. 70. And the survivors, what would happen to them? a colleague asked. They would work for the Germans until they were liberated, Ben-Gurion replied. The Nazis would need workers and technicians. And as Rommel inched closer, party leaders finally agreed in June 1941 to stop bickering and build barricades.

The time had come for a Palmach strike.

Shortly, Rabin and other carefully selected young men were in Kibbutz Hanita, on the Lebanese border. And waiting for them in the kibbutz reading room were top leaders of the Hagana.

Rabin listened with pounding heart as Chief of Staff Ya'akov Dori explained their mission. The British, Dori said, would soon invade Greater Syria, including Lebanon, to prevent Axis forces from using the region as a springboard for invading Palestine from both the north and the south. And the Palmach would help the British in their campaign.

Despite his excitement, Rabin had mixed feelings. Help the British? Men who were letting the Arabs slaughter the Jews of Palestine while keeping the Jews of Europe out? But Rabin was a pragmatist. With the security of the Yishuv at stake, he would cooperate with the devil. He might even learn his language if necessary. The important thing was to engage in action that could save the Jews from certain death.

"I was elated," he would say. "At last I was about to take part in a battle on a global scale."

But it soon became clear "that fantasy was a gross exaggeration." The Palmach force had been divided into two companies, one commanded by Yigal Allon and the other by Moshe Dayan. The force would cross into Lebanon in advance of the Australian forces fighting there and cut the telephone lines so the Vichy French could not send reinforcements to their troops. Rabin's elation was restrained.

"Not exactly battlefield high drama," he would later lament. "Furthermore, we drew scant encouragement from a string of warnings." One of them:

"You men are not soldiers, and if you're taken prisoner you won't fall under the protection of the Geneva Convention. But you don't have to worry about that because the forces in this sector are Senegalese [who were backing the Axis], and they don't take prisoners."

Rabin and his comrades were also told to keep "away from the Australians' line of advance, because they're in the habit of shooting first and asking questions later."

And to think he might at this moment be listening in comfort to some world-renowned expert lecturing to him in California on how to grow a better crop!

In several groups of twos and threes, the men, dressed in civilian clothing, slipped across the border that night, with Rabin and two others marching fifteen miles to telephone lines connecting Zur and Sidon. They finally reached the village of Binai, where the lines were to be cut. Who would climb the poles? Since Rabin, at nineteen, was the youngest man, and presumably the nimblest, he was chosen. But he had received his climbing irons only that day and hadn't had time to practice using them. Now, when he tried to climb the pole with his irons, he was unable to. He had never been confident that he would be a good soldier. And this situation did not dispel his doubts. Here he was behind enemy lines, with many lives at stake, including his own, and he didn't know how to use a pair of climbing irons!

In desperation, Rabin removed his boots and shinned up the pole barefoot, as he had climbed trees in his childhood. When he reached the top, he took out his pliers and cut the first wire. Suddenly, the pole started to sway, and Rabin realized that it had been held upright by the tension of the wires. He fell to the ground like a stone. Miraculously unhurt but severely shaken, he could leave it to a comrade to complete the job. But should he? This was his first mission, and if he failed now he might never again be able to climb a pole, or achieve any military objective.

Rabin shinned up the swaying pole again and cut the second wire. He then severed the wires on another pole, and the mission was accomplished. Rabin was euphoric. But shortly, when he had returned to base, his euphoria turned to shock. Moshe Dayan, who had been leading another group that night, had, he learned, been less lucky. He had lost his eye in a battle with a Vichy French force. All groups, however, had achieved their objectives, seriously disrupting Axis communications.

In a sense, Rabin's personal triumph had, ironically, contributed in a small way to the early demise of the Palmach, or at least to its forced transformation. As Rabin would say:

"Even the meager glory derived through association with the British was short-lived."

For with Syria and Lebanon in Allied hands and Rommel's tanks smashed by British Field Marshal Bernard Montgomery at El Alamein in late 1942, the British saw little reason to cooperate any longer with the organization. In fact, its success actually frightened London. The Palmach, if it survived the war, could cause Britain serious problems after the conflict. Why keep alive a possible Frankenstein monster? And so the British closed the Palmach training camps, confiscated the weapons they found, and once more began arresting Palmach and other Hagana members for possessing arms.

Adding to the fighters' problems, many Jews, with another Masada no longer imminent, viewed the war less seriously than they had. In fact, the atmosphere in Palestine soon changed drastically as more and more Allied troops poured in and 2,000 war-supply factories spouted pollution into the sky, turning a depression into a zooming prosperity. There was excitement and even a certain gaiety in the air as foreign soldiers tarried in the cafes with their Jewish girlfriends and people packed the shops casually dispensing their pounds.

Without British cooperation, the Hagana leaders, who had themselves tried to disband the Palmach shortly after the incursion into Lebanon, now wondered once more if the Palmach should survive. They had their own fears; not only was the Palmach too costly to keep, but it was basically an instrument of the leftist, kibbutz-oriented Mapam Party, and Ben-Gurion's more moderately socialist Mapai Party, which controlled the Hagana, was not eager to see Mapam reinforced after the war with an armed force of its own.

But Palmach leaders argued that it was essential to preserve a standing Jewish force that could fight the Germans in the war and, if necessary, the Arabs, or even the British, after the war. And since many of Hagana's men came from the kibbutzim, which backed the Palmach, the Hagana leaders finally compromised. They would place graduates of the kibbutz youth movement in Palmach units that would be based in the kibbutzim. A little more than half their time would be spent on training and the rest on farm work, which would defray about 80 percent of the organization's expenses. The Palmach thus became a true workers' army.

This arrangement infuriated some Palmach members, who

now preferred to join the more glamorous British army. Why do hard farm work when they didn't have to? Anyway, it was disgraceful, they thought, that the Hagana did not prop up the Palmach with funds so they wouldn't have to work for the honor of defending their people.

But Rabin, who had been training and helping to train others for more than a year in various camps, was pleased, for he would now meld his agricultural aspirations with his military obligations and serve his country in both realms. He resented the attitude of those who turned in their overalls and work shoes for the more fashionable British garb. Didn't they understand the postwar dangers that the Yishuv would face if the British backed the Arabs after the war and the Jews had to rely on their own strength to survive?

"Only deep faith and inner conviction kept the Palmach together," he would say.

Rabin was shortly promoted to platoon commander, based in Kibbutz Kfar Giladi near the Lebanese border, where he trained his men in modern military tactics when they weren't working the land. As he tried to overcome the unit's impoverishment by scrounging for every bullet and shell, his zeal on one occasion nearly brought his military career to a startling end.

In the fall of 1943, during a fire display before some Hagana senior officers at a kibbutz near Haifa, a mortar shell failed to fire. It was placed aside, and after the display Rabin, who had mortars for his platoon but no shells, decided to expropriate it—secretly, since Hagana leaders had issued strict orders that no one was to carry weapons openly for fear they might be found by the British, jeopardizing the entire organization.

Rabin led his platoon to Haifa on foot, lugging the mortar shell in his shoulder bag, and in Haifa sent his men back to their base by train. Then he took a bus so that if the British caught him with the shell, he alone and not other members of his platoon would be blamed. He arrived safely, but a week later was summoned by the company commander.

"There's a shell missing," he grunted. "Did you take it?"

Rabin would later remark in a statement that would remain valid throughout his life: "Like . . . George Washington faced with the evidence of his cherry-tree crime, I could not tell a lie."

He was reprimanded and then, a few days later, notified that he would be court-martialed. Rabin was devastated. He had hardly begun to fight and he was already in disgrace. For days he "walked around in a trance and couldn't sleep at night." What would his father think of him? Was this how he was honoring his mother's memory?

At his court-martial in a clandestine Hagana office in Haifa, he confessed his crime once more and then explained his motives with the kind of reasoned detail that would help to catapult him to the top in later years.

Wait outside, please, Rabin was ordered. And as he waited, "the minutes ticked past like an eternity." His destiny was about to be set. Finally, he was called into the room. The sentence: No promotion for at least a year.

As Rabin departed, he heaved a sigh of relief. At least he was still in the Palmach. But he would just have to live with the fact that he would never get very far as a soldier.

Adding to Rabin's dejection was a failed love affair. The frail, freckle-faced child subject to cruel teasing had grown into a well-built handsome man with great appeal to women. But he was still so shy that he never pursued them, while those wishing to meet him, intimidated by what they interpreted as aloofness, were afraid to approach him. One of the braver young women stood outside his tent and played the flute, hoping he would come out and talk to her. She played and played, and when she finally stopped, conceding failure, he suddenly emerged and said:

"That was very nice. Please keep playing."

And he reentered the tent.

Still, according to one comrade, he did meet with some women, though very discreetly. As he would conceal some personal matters in his childhood even from his parents, so he kept his personal life secret in later years. According to one source close to him, he had a serious relationship with one particular woman he met while in the Palmach, but the couple broke up for unknown reasons. Shortly afterward, in 1944, he met someone else who was determined not to let this prize get away.

It was a hot day in Tel Aviv, and Rabin, who had come home on leave, strode into Whitman's ice cream parlor on Allenby Street for an ice cream cone. Suddenly, he caught the eye of a pretty brunette who was also waiting for a cone.

"There he was," sixteen-year-old Leah Shlossberg Rabin would wistfully recall. "Just like the description of King David: 'Chestnut hair and beautiful eyes.' Our eyes met. And they met again near home. . . . Something about him—his appearance, his walk—captured my heart. He seemed different."

She guessed that he was from the Palmach, Leah told me, and she was sure she would see him on that street again. Preparing for the "inevitable" meeting, she described the handsome stranger to some of her friends and asked if they knew who he was. Most people on the block knew everybody else.

"That must be Yitzhak Rabin," one friend said. "He's very special. Everybody wants to meet him."

A few days later, Leah, now more eager than ever to do so, succeeded—as they passed each other on the street. Gathering her nerve, she stopped him and asked:

"Are you Yitzhak Rabin?"

"Yes, I am," he replied.

"And I'm Leah."

"Finally we had met," Leah would say years later, "and we walked on together—till this day."

Rabin confirmed that he belonged to the Palmach and told her about some of his activities. After that meeting, Leah would relate, "I bumped into him a few times, and then the encounters stopped being coincidence. We started to look for each other. He vanished for a few weeks, then was back again." She was attracted by his shyness, his intelligence, his sharp perceptions of people, his devotion to his work. And he was "gorgeous."

Rabin was captivated by Leah's vivacious smile and open personality, which so contrasted with his own withdrawn nature. He needed someone who had the "chutzpah" to walk up to a stranger and introduce herself, something that he, a tough soldier, found it extremely difficult to do. And Leah's extroversion relieved the tension of the blushing introvert.

If Rabin and Leah had disparate characters, they were molded in environments having almost nothing in common. Rabin was raised in a rigidly austere, egalitarian society that even frowned upon pictures on the wall. As a child he was left alone much of the time, and he often ate irregularly and came to school carelessly dressed.

Leah, on the other hand, was the daughter of a wealthy upper-middle-class industrialist from Koenigsberg, Germany, where she had lived in relative luxury, attended from birth by a nursemaid. She was required to curtsy to adults, to eat with her elbows tucked inward, to chew with her mouth closed. And her nursemaid measured the temperature of her bath with a thermometer. When, at the age of five, she fled with her family to Palestine in 1933 to escape Hitler's grasp, the family lived less comfortably in Tel Aviv, where Leah's father, having lost his estate, worked as a clerk.

Still, the family, infused with the Zionist pioneering spirit, soon turned socialist, and Leah, while in high school, joined the radically leftist Hashomer Hatzair youth movement. Shortly after she met Rabin, she decided to go a step farther in her journey from one world to another; she had become disillusioned anyway with the Bolshevik-like restrictions on personal liberty.

"As my relationship with Yitzhak, which had begun in sixth grade, grew stronger," Leah would say, "so did my resolve to join the Palmach after graduation. His tales of the Palmach fired my imagination. I had to go."

The Palmach also continued to fire Rabin's imagination despite his court-martial and the penalty imposed on him. Actually, Rabin had not suffered excessively from the penalty, for success to him didn't necessarily mean high rank. It meant achieving security for his people by whatever means. Of course, the generals determined military policy, but lower-ranking officers could provide the ideas and influence them. And Rabin had innovative ideas and remarkable influence.

Since the British no longer used the Palmach and, indeed, tried to disband it, Rabin and his men would fight no battles. So he had plenty of time to study and analyze the everyday military problems faced by the settlement commanders. Starting with little knowledge of military strategy, Rabin had, within four years, become one of the Palmach's leading experts on guerrilla warfare. He gave short shrift to conventional military theories, since he saw the Palmach's role in postwar Palestine in iconoclastic terms. If it had to fight the Arabs, and perhaps the British, only a strike force using surprise and stealth might be able to win, or at least hold the enemy at bay.

Rabin's brilliance did not go unnoticed by Yigal Allon and the Palmach's founder and commander-in-chief, white-bearded Yitzhak Sadeh, a master theorist himself. So, early in 1945, when the Palmach was reorganized in battalion formations, Rabin was appointed second-in-command of the First Battalion, which was responsible for security in the northern region of Palestine, and placed in charge of instruction. He did not start on the job, however, until he recovered from a bout with typhus. Shortly thereafter, he was given command of a national section leaders' course, which trained noncommissioned officers to take over from their superiors if necessary. He stressed in his lectures three vital rules. The men must:

- Stick relentlessly to an objective.
- Improvise plans until one succeeded.
- Attack the enemy by indirect means and
  never break one's head against a wall.

"He had a special, persuasive voice," recalled one former pupil who would later become a general. "He spoke to us directly with irrefutable logic, point by point, expressing himself clearly. We never had any doubts about what he thought."

Neither did Leah. Rabin thought it was unfortunate that they had to be separated for long periods. She agreed.

Why shouldn't she join the Palmach, too? Then they could spend more time together.

Life would be very rough in the Palmach, and very dangerous.

The whole nation was in danger, she replied. She would join.

When Leah told her father, he pleaded with her to change her mind.

But she wouldn't.

So hardly had Leah graduated from high school in 1945 when she reported to a national recruiting center and, "as preplanned with Yitzhak," requested assignment to the First Battalion. To no one's surprise, Rabin, its deputy commander, did not object. Especially since Leah would not be joining until September, and Germany had surrendered in May. She would be safe—at least until the eventual struggle with the Arabs, and perhaps the British, when virtually the whole population would be fighting for survival anyway.

Amid screaming banners and fluttering flags, the people in Allied countries swirled through the streets, singing, cheering, shouting in rapturous response to the news. Peace at last! Except for the Yishuv. The British would be leaving Palestine soon, Ben-Gurion predicted, and the Arab armies would then try to butcher the Jews. The Hagana had enough men and arms to hold off local Palestinian gangs, but not regular Arab armies. And though most of the Jewish soldiers would stream in from the refugee camps in Europe, the required weapons—and the dollars to buy them— could come only from the United States.

Ben-Gurion thus went there and on July 1, 1945, met with a group of seventeen wealthy American Jews whom he implored to mobilize money, arms, machinery, technology, everything needed to fight a war of survival.

"On that memorable day," philanthropist Rudolf Sonnenborn, at whose New York home they met, would write in a confidential memorandum, "we were asked to form ourselves into an ... American arm of . . . Hagana. We were given no clue as to what we might be called upon to accomplish, when the call might come or who would call us."

But all agreed to answer the call. Shortly, Sonnenborn would tell his colleagues over the phone:

"The time has come!"

He formed his group of millionaires into a secret Sonnenborn Institute, which cooperated with Hagana agents in setting up dummy companies to buy tons of government-surplus arms and ships from any source it could find, including the Mafia. Jewish-American war veterans left souvenir firearms at "gun drops." Gambling casinos gave a percentage of each pot to the cause. Even Hitler's victims helped, contributing their gold teeth, which the American army had found in the death camps and sold cheaply.

The arms collected would be used against the British if they didn't scuttle the White Paper, or against the Arabs if they tried to scuttle the state that Ben-Gurion was determined to create. Ships, packed with immigrants, would run the blockade of Palestine. Meanwhile, the Jews would fight the British with the wile and weapons they had.

On October 1, Ben-Gurion rushed off a letter to Moshe Sneh,

the Hagana chief in Palestine, ordering what amounted to an armed uprising: Begin *Aliya Gimel* (the third wave of immigration)! Land refugees in Zion at the point of a gun. Set up a central command in Paris to direct and finance this operation. Sabotage and retaliate—without killing people indiscriminately. And make a deal with the two dissident terrorist groups, the Irgun Zvai Leumi and the Stern Gang, for unified action under the Hagana command—though until now he had been trying to destroy them. Circumstances had changed. And the British Labor Party, which had just come into power, might change its pro-Zionist policies.

In early October, the Hagana, the Irgun, and the Stern Gang, now linked in an unholy alliance called the Hebrew Resistance Movement, were ready to launch a series of daring operations. The first would be at the Atlith detention camp, on the Mediterranean shore eight miles south of Haifa.

One day, Yitzhak Rabin was called to First Battalion headquarters for an urgent meeting. The Yishuv leadership, his commander, Nahum Sarig, told him, had approved the first operation in the "linked campaign" against the British. The Hagana had learned that the British planned to deport about two hundred immigrants who had entered Palestine from Syria on foot and were detained in the Atlith camp.

The First Battalion, Sarig said, had to force its way into the camp and liberate the immigrants. They would be taken to a nearby kibbutz, from where they would be dispersed throughout the country. As deputy commander of the operation, Rabin was to lead a two-hundred-man assault force on the mission.

"We accepted the plan with considerable apprehension," Rabin would say. "These people were survivors of the Holocaust, the few snatched from the conflagration. We would never be able to forgive ourselves if any harm were to befall them."

The night before the operation, Rabin expressed this sentiment to Leah at her camp in Kibbutz Tel Yosef, where she was stationed, meeting in the dining hall that had become their permanent rendezvous. She was surprised to see him, for it was the middle of the week, and usually he would zoom in on his motorcycle on Saturdays. He would then, she would recall, send her "to the platoon commander for permission to join him on a short outing, not very enthusiastically, because these were already days of restricted leave in the Palmach." The commander would agree, mumbling, apparently with a degree of sarcasm:

"After all, it's an order."

It is not surprising that Rabin lacked enthusiasm for requesting favors; his whole career would bear this out. He was always reluctant to use his high position to advance his own personal interests or those of his friends, however minor the request. But Leah was already exerting an important influence on him. And so she would climb on the rear of his motorcycle and they would ride into Afula for coffee, then "continue through the green expanses of the Jezreel Valley, or up onto the slopes of the Nazareth hills. A few moments of happiness, good weather, beautiful valleys, and the two of us together."

But this time Rabin did not send her to the platoon commander, and there would be no leisurely ride through paradise. As they sat nibbling on a bar of chocolate, Rabin "revealed his secret." As he related the details of his mission, "he sounded a little worried and tense." And their parting, to Leah, was pure drama, with "my soldier going off to battle." But she wouldn't let herself believe that anything would happen to him.

Rabin's plan was to have a group of his men infiltrate into the camp to organize the immigrants and overpower the Arab police guards, but how would he do this? Finally, he thought of a way. He sent them to the camp posing as welfare workers and teachers.

Then, on the moonless night of October 10, Rabin led his assault force to a spot about one hundred yards from the fence of the camp. In the glare of bright light emanating from the camp, someone cut the wire and the others approached a second inner fence. There they met one of the "teachers." The infiltrators, he reported, had managed to break the firing pins in the rifles of the Arab policemen.

As the attackers moved forward, the policemen, alerted, pulled their triggers, but no bullets popped out of the barrels. Rabin and his men raced to the British billets to make sure the men were sleeping so the intruders would not be greeted by gunfire. But the only noise they heard were their snores. The immigrants then started rushing out of the building toward trucks lined up almost two miles away along the Haifa–Tel Aviv road. But many were slowed down by the weight of burdensome bundles they had refused to leave behind, though some, under orders from Rabin, finally dropped them on the roadside as they ran. Parents with children in their arms also found it difficult keeping up with the others.

When Rabin, running ahead, reached the trucks, Sarig, who was waiting to take the survivors to safety, made a daring decision. He would leave for nearby Kibbutz Yagur with those refugees who had already reached the trucks, and Rabin would stay behind and wait for the latecomers, whom he would take to Kibbutz Bet Oren on Mount Carmel in Haifa.

Suddenly, a truck with British soldiers came roaring down the road and opened fire on the refugees. The Palmach men fired back and killed a British sergeant, while the truck raced on. Would the firing wake up the soldiers inside the headquarters? In desperation, Sarig decided on a duplicitous move. He would mislead the British by sending the trucks off empty in one direction and leading his immigrants by foot in another.

Meanwhile, Rabin gathered the hundred or so latecomers as they trickled to the assembly point and, along with about sixty of his men, trudged toward Mount Carmel in Haifa. It was a strange procession that plodded up the steep winding hill, with the fighters carrying the terrified children on their shoulders. Rabin himself picked up a child so petrified that the tot could not control his bladder.

"As my shoulders bore the hopes of the Jewish people," he would recall, "I suddenly felt a warm, damp sensation down my back. Under the circumstances, I could hardly halt."

The survivors finally reached Bet Oren after dawn, and Rabin, ordering everyone to hide in the woods nearby, sent two of his men to reconnoiter the area. They returned with frightening news. The British had encircled the settlement.

Rabin was dismayed. These refugees had survived the greatest crime against humanity in history. Were they now to return to the murder scene and live amid the ashes of their loved ones?

Could the survivors get through?

They had found a gap, the scouts said. Maybe it was possible.

Rabin breathed more easily. There was nothing to lose. They had to try, even though the British could easily detect them in daylight. If necessary, his men would engage in battle with them.

In small groups, the survivors edged to the perimeter of the kibbutz, following the two scouts. As Rabin herded them forward, he prayed that none of the children would cry. The seconds seemed like minutes, the minutes like hours.

Rabin, like most people who had not endured the horrors of the Holocaust, had never really comprehended it. He had heard reports of the massive slaughter, but the numbers were too overwhelming to translate into a realistic perception of the brutality. But now he had come face-to-face with the Holocaust. In the morning light, he saw in every pair of eyes a gleam of madness, a mirror of unspeakable memories reflecting terror, resignation, and death. He had to save them.

And he did. The survivors filtered through the British cordon and dispersed while Rabin's men buried their weapons in prepared caches. The British, now aware of the infiltration, brought up reinforcements and tried to smash through the kibbutz gate. But they were stymied, for thousands of people from Haifa surged up the hill toward Bet Oren and the nearby kibbutz where the battalion commander had taken his batch of immigrants and fanned out throughout the area, ignoring the roadblocks and daring the British to shoot. Meanwhile, the immigrants streamed into the kibbutz and mingled with the survivors, who couldn't be distinguished from the residents. The British were forced to scrap their deportation plans.

Rabin was ecstatic. He couldn't imagine a more satisfying victory. And now he could change his wet clothes.

Later that day, Leah was serving tables in the dining hall of her kibbutz when word spread that the Atlith operation had succeeded. The kibbutz security officer then came over, shook her hand, and said:

"My compliments to Yitzhak."

"I think," Leah would recall, "that I must have been the proudest human being in the entire Jezreel Valley at that moment."

She was especially proud that her comrades realized that Yitzhak belonged to her.

Following the successful Atlith operation, the newly formed Hebrew Resistance Movement, including the Hagana and Palmach, undertook other daring missions. On November 1 it sabotaged the railroad in Palestine and blew up British coast guard vessels. The British were shocked. And this shock was reflected in a speech that British Foreign Secretary Ernest Bevin made in Parliament. Sarcastically dismissing "the view that the Jews should be driven out of Europe," Bevin proposed setting up a joint Anglo-American Commission of Inquiry to investigate where the refugees should lay down their pitiful bundles once and for all. But Britain would feel bound by the recommendations only if the commission agreed to them unanimously, an unlikely prospect.

So, in March 1946, a group of distinguished Americans and Britons went to Palestine and investigated, then issued a report calling for a United Nations trusteeship, an end to the White Paper and Land Regulations, and the immediate entry of 100,000 refugees into the country. And they agreed on these measures unanimously, meeting Bevin's condition. But the foreign secretary wriggled out of his promise. For the sake of racial harmony, he explained, he had to turn down the commission's proposals. This was more important than keeping a promise.

Ben-Gurion was furious. Step up the operations against the British! he ordered. There must be more Atliths.

The order trickled down to the First Battalion, and Rabin was handed a new assignment. He would lead an assault against one of the British police stations headquartering the Police Mobile Force, the most repressive unit in Palestine. Preparing for the attack, Rabin put on the overalls of an electrician and, equipped with a set of screwdrivers, managed to enter the station and sketch the locations of switches, fuses, and emergency batteries. He now had all the information he needed to launch a successful attack.

Rabin jumped on his motorcycle and headed for his headquarters in Alonim, near Haifa, to report his findings to Nahum Sarig. But he never arrived. As he was "cheerfully roaring along," he noticed a truck from the Nesher cement factory suddenly making a sharp left turn into the factory entrance, cutting right in front of him.

"I knew that I would not have time to brake," he would recall.

And he was right. Knocked unconscious, he awakened in the hospital to hear from a friend that "we found your left ankle. It was just by your knee." Not quite that bad. But he had broken his

leg and would have to follow Palmach operations from an armchair at home, the leg in a cast. Rabin was devastated, and so was
Leah. She learned of the accident that evening at roll call when
"the platoon commander—with, for some strange reason, a broad
grin on his face—asked" Leah if she knew what had happened to
Yitzhak.

Now the commander wouldn't have to give her any more
leaves. Her soldier had been training for years, and suddenly
when the battle against the British was at its height, he was a helpless invalid. Rabin was frustrated and miserable. He would write
his sister, Rachel, on January 17, 1946:

> ... in the area where the breakage was, there appeared to be a crack
> in the cast, but more accurately, the cast became more flexible and
> started to bend in all directions. Of course, this caused Dad some
> excitement and worry. ... Besides this, there is nothing new under
> the sun, or to be more accurate, under the ceiling of my room. I'm
> just going nuts from boredom.

Then, with tongue in cheek, Rabin added, unwittingly fore-
casting in a sense his own role in history: "Well, this is probably
what a genius suffers; he isn't recognized in his generation and
only when he's not present do people feel his absence."

The struggle against the British reached a climax some months after
Rabin's accident when Black Saturday dawned on June 29, 1946.
Tanks and armored cars slithered through kibbutzim and city
streets hushed by a general curfew, people screamed into phones
that were dead, and anyone trying to leave the country was greeted
by cocked guns at the border. The British had launched a drive to
intimidate the Yishuv and destroy the Hagana along with its
Palmach. All over Palestine, troops broke into homes, ripped open
floors and walls looking for arms, and dragged out Jews by the
hair, locking them in cages, then dumping them into detention
camps, where some were beaten, tortured, even killed. The British
arrested almost all the Jewish political leaders, though Ben-Gurion
was outside the country and was one of the few who remained free.

Nor were the Hagana and Palmach commanders ignored.
Senior officers, including Moshe Sneh, Yitzhak Sadeh, and Yigal
Allon, had been warned in time by spies in the British administra-

tion and had gone into hiding. But no one had warned Rabin that he was on the wanted list, though Leah had strangely felt that something terrible would happen to him.

The feeling came after something terrible had almost happened to her. A few days earlier, she was sent on a reconnaissance mission with several other Palmach soldiers to scout the Arab villages nestled in the Gilboa mountain range. The Arabs in one village sighted the soldiers, who were disguised as innocent hikers, and ran toward them brandishing clubs and screaming threats. Leah and her comrades, though burdened with heavy packs, sprinted in fright toward another village where moderate Arab inhabitants arrived just before the angry mob caught up with them. The moderate Arabs held off the militant ones and called the British police, who shortly arrived and dragged the Jews to the police station for interrogation, which, in this period of crisis, usually meant jail for an indefinite period.

Identity card! the interrogator demanded.

He examined it, and a smile broke the tension.

"I met a man called Shlossberg in Netanya. Could that be your father?"

Yes, Leah replied, her father had worked there.

"A good, honest man, your father."

And the Briton picked up the phone and said: "I think this bunch is all right. Let them go."

Shortly after Leah returned to her base, she attended a big wedding there, and "while everyone danced and sang into the wee hours," Leah, still shaken by the terrifying experience, would say:

"I was filled with a strange premonition. Something bothered me. I couldn't put my finger on it, but I knew it had to do with Yitzhak. . . . I knew that something bad was about to happen."

The next morning, June 29, as Leah was driving with several comrades to another base, they were flagged down by the British police, who arrested the passengers on the wanted list. As the others sped on, they could see from a hilltop that the settlements in the Jezreel Valley had been encircled with barbed wire and that armored cars were crawling all around them. When Leah arrived back at her home base she found that not a single man was there. They had all been arrested. It now seemed clear that her father unknowingly had saved her and her comrades from a similar fate.

"The kibbutz dining hall," she would recall, "was deserted that evening. Everyone was walking as if on tiptoe and talking in whispers. Nobody had yet completely grasped the sudden storm that had left the kibbutz without its menfolk. Dinner was served to women and old people alone. The works organizer was tearing his hair out trying to solve tomorrow's problems on the farm without 270 of his labor force."

What had happened to Yitzhak? she desperately wondered. He wasn't at home and there was no way to contact him. With dread, she remembered her premonition.

Leah had good reason for alarm. And so did Rabin when he awakened at dawn that Saturday to the roar of vehicles on the street. Minutes later, a bang on the door sent Nehemiah to open it, and when he did a British paratroop captain said:

"Rabin?"

Nehemiah nodded. Yes, he was.

Three squads of paratroopers then rushed in waving their Brens and machine guns while another group surrounded the house with barbed wire.

"This was an imposing military operation!" Rabin would later comment.

The British soldiers, unsure whether it was father or son who was on the wanted list, grabbed both of them, as well as a guest, and dragged them out to a waiting truck, which rumbled on to local British headquarters. An armored car then delivered them to a tent camp in Latrun, and two days later to a large warehouse in Rafah at the southern tip of the Gaza Strip, where they would remain in detention, along with 1,600 to 2,000 other arrested Jews.

Rabin was shocked by this massive roundup of almost all Jewish leaders, and could better understand the suffering of his parents during the pogroms in Russia, however more terrifying they were. His hostility toward the British, intense since childhood, escalated until he could barely wait for his leg to heal so he could fight them again. They were now not simply occupiers but anti-Semitic oppressors. Hadn't the Jews suffered enough under Hitler? Actually, the British treated their prisoners quite well. They gave Rabin good medical attention, sending him to the military

hospital in Gaza. On the way there in a tender with British policemen aiming their machine guns at him, he scornfully remarked:

"What are you scared of? You can see that I can't move."

But he soon could, since physiotherapy greatly improved the
condition of his leg. Rabin was, in fact, more concerned about his
father than himself, especially since Nehemiah had been hauled
off from home before he could find his dental plates and thus had
a hard time eating. Adding to Yitzhak's depression was his inability to speak with Leah since the telephone was not working. But
after about two weeks, the British released the father, and shortly
afterward the guest who had been invited on the wrong weekend.
But when a Jewish Agency doctor asked a British intelligence official to release the younger Rabin as well, the official replied:

"He'll remain in detention even if he breaks both legs."

About a month later, Rabin's cast was removed, and to his
shock he found his leg "misshapen and lifeless." A British doctor
gave him more intensive treatment, but the patient could not
shake his depression. All his dreams were unraveling. His leg, he
thought (erroneously, it turned out), would never function properly and he would be a semicripple. Nor was his depression
relieved when he heard reports that his comrades would launch
an attack on the camp and free the victims. How could he run with
a crippled leg? He remembered how the slow movement of some
survivors during the Atlith escape almost doomed everybody. He
was not unhappy when the reports proved unfounded.

Rabin felt that after his release he would have to change his life
if he was not to waste it. World War II was over and he was in no
condition to fight the British or the Arabs, if this became necessary.
Now he could do what he had dreamed of doing before Hitler
threatened the future. His application to the University of
California had been approved, so he would study to be an irrigation engineer after all. He asked his father to send him a stack of
textbooks and brushed up on what he had learned years earlier.
Perhaps he was fated to realize his dream. He wrote Rachel on
October 17, 1946:

> The number of books . . . that everyone receives from home allows
> a better use of our time, but there is a certain laziness here, since the
> noise and crowded conditions are still great, although compared to
> how it was, it is ideal here now. . . . I have started with math and I

hope to continue with English and political economy. . . . I will not
describe in detail Dad's first visit. . . . It was not a happy scene,
watching how people approached one another from both sides of
the metal fence, serious and talking rapidly, afraid they wouldn't
have enough time to finish what they wanted to say after a long
separation.

A few weeks later, in November 1946, the separation ended for
Rabin. After eight months of detention, the British released him,
and he returned home limping on a cane and helped along by
Leah. His leg was improving every day, it seemed, and although it
was a bit shorter than his good one, he could move around quite
well. So now he had to make a crucial decision. Should he still go
to Berkeley to study or should he remain in the Palmach?

He went to see Yigal Allon, who had emerged from hiding. For
who knew better than Allon if a "semicripple" was really needed
in the struggle for security, or if he could better serve the national
interest by finding ways to quench the thirst of the desert soil. And
Allon wasted no time answering this question. Go to school? He
seemed shocked.

"Out of the question!" he exclaimed. "The world war has
ended, but our war is only just beginning."

Rabin realized now that the time was approaching for a Jewish
state to be proclaimed. In May 1942, Ben-Gurion had presided at an
American Zionist conference in New York's Biltmore Hotel where
the delegates approved a program calling for the establishment of
a "Jewish commonwealth." And Rabin knew that the Yishuv
would eventually fight for this goal, but he hadn't given it much
thought till now, believing that it could only be achieved gradually—unify the nation, build up an arsenal, make life miserable for
the British, bring in the immigrants, win American support. All
this, he had thought, would take time and might permit him to
leave for Berkeley without making him feel he was abandoning his
people at a moment of crisis.

But Allon convinced Rabin that there was no time. The United
Nations was making partition proposals. The British were thinking of leaving Palestine. The Arabs, aware of this, were preparing
to attack the Jews. The survival of the Yishuv was at stake. Yes, it
had been his dream to continue his education, and he had already
relinquished one opportunity to realize it. He would now do so a

second time, though he knew this meant the end of the dream.

And a week later, Rabin took command of the Palmach's Second Battalion.

Early in 1947, Ben-Gurion summoned Rabin and all other Hagana officers from battalion commander upward to a secret meeting that would set the stage for the momentous future.

They must prepare, Ben-Gurion said, for war on a scale never before envisaged. The main mission of Hagana had changed, he said, and so must the character of Hagana. It would have to fight not British forces bound by conscience but regular Arab armies bent on carnage. Thus, it must urgently build its own regular army. It was a startling announcement. Rabin and the other commanders could envisage guerrilla warfare with the British and local Arabs, but a clash with the Arab states?

Later, at a briefing for top commanders, Ben-Gurion asked Yigal Allon whether Jewish forces could, in fact, repel an invasion by Arab armies. Allon replied:

"We have the basis. If the present nucleus grows by substantial numbers and if we get suitable equipment, we could indeed face the Arab armies."

But could they get the equipment? And even if they could, would there be enough Jewish fighters to hold back a sea of soldiers closing in from every direction? Ben-Gurion was alarmed. With the arms promised by the Sonnenborn Institute just starting to dribble in, the Jews had only about 10,000 rifles and a few hundred light machine guns. They had no heavy equipment. The Arab states, on the other hand, were equipped with tanks and artillery. Moreover, the British blockade kept thousands of potential Jewish fighters from reaching Palestinian shores, while those who did filter through were largely untrained, though most of the Palestinian Arabs were, too; only about 6,000 out of a million Palestinian Arabs had some training.

Furthermore, the Yishuv was again plagued by disunity following the bombing of the King David Hotel, the British military headquarters in Jerusalem. The Hagana, with Ben-Gurion's approval, and the Irgun, under Menachem Begin, had originally agreed on the attack, but when the Hagana withdrew from the operation, the Irgun went ahead alone. Scores of people died in the explosion, though they had been warned a half-hour earlier that a bomb would go off. Ben-Gurion was furious at the Irgun for this act of terrorism—though he originally supported the attack—and the Hebrew Resistance Movement crumbled. Again, though, the Arabs helped to reduce the damage with their own tendency to compete with, and even plot against, one another for power and influence in the Arab world. Even so, the Arabs had the strategic advantage, ensconced in the mountainous areas while the Jews were concentrated mainly in the lowlands.

Yigal Allon, Ben-Gurion knew, was brilliant, but he was linked to the prime minister's leftist political enemies and was trained to fight only guerrilla wars; the next war would be fought against armies that would rumble into Palestine with tanks and artillery. Ben-Gurion had to seek the views of someone trained as an officer in the British army. And so he called in Chaim Laskov, who had fought with the British-sponsored Jewish Brigade.

"This meeting must be strictly confidential," Ben-Gurion mumbled, staring into Laskov's slightly Oriental eyes. "Do you know what keeping a secret means?"

He did, replied Laskov, wondering why this talk in Ben-Gurion's home was clandestine.

Whatever the United Nations decided, Ben-Gurion said, the British would soon march out and the Arabs, in. The Yishuv's life was on the line, and a real Jewish army must spring forth urgently.

"What must we do to build a force?" he asked. "What do we need to hold out?"

The question tormented Ben-Gurion, who now started educating himself overnight in defense matters. The time for "night squads" was over, he realized. The homegrown Hagana commanders, though brave and able guerrilla fighters, could not stand up to regular armies. Besides, the best guerrilla fighters belonged to the Palmach, which was dominated by the Mapam Party he feared might try to take over power. Already Yitzhak Sadeh, the Palmach founder and commander, was threatening to become a legend. And one legend was enough for the country.

What was needed? Laskov replied: Twelve infantry brigade groups, one to three armored brigades, as many aircraft as possible, 120,000 rifles. . . .

The top commanders, Ben-Gurion said, must be trained to operate regular army units.

No time, Laskov responded. First train the corporals and sergeants, because their men would be in the front line.

Ben-Gurion agreed, and Laskov immediately began designing the army that had to save the Yishuv—an army that would absorb the Palmach.

When word trickled down to Rabin that the Palmach was not likely to play an independent role in the coming war, he was exasperated.

"My feelings about Ben-Gurion," he would say, "could only be described as ambivalent. Though I respected his breadth of vision, I could not help objecting to his attitude toward the Palmach. . . . He gave preference to British army veterans over 'homegrown' commanders."

But if Rabin was bitter, his bitterness was tempered by the bold statement Ben-Gurion made when, in June 1947, a United Nations Special Committee on Palestine (UNSCOP) flew to the Holy Land to finally sort out the tangled claims of Arab and Jew.

"Who is willing and capable of guaranteeing that what happened to us in Europe will not recur? Can the conscience of humanity . . . absolve itself of all responsibility for that Holocaust? There is only one security guarantee: a homeland and a state."

The committee searched its collective soul and saw sense in this argument. And the British helped in their own way. While members looked on in horror, British troops wielding gun and club stopped the refugee ship *Exodus* from disgorging its pathetic load, which was finally sent back to the graveyards of Europe. On September 3, UNSCOP issued a historic report: The Palestine mandate should dissolve into two sovereign states, with Jerusalem internationalized. The United Nations General Assembly would now consider this recommendation.

Yet even a victory for partition would not assure a state—or the Yishuv's survival. For the Arabs bitterly rejected the plan, guaranteeing that war would explode, and the British wouldn't be around to save the Jews from possible annihilation. But Ben-Gurion was ready to gamble that the Jews, however disadvantaged, would win. He would explain the meaning of destiny to the one Arab leader who might understand, for this man, too, had a dream. Ben-Gurion sent Golda Meir, then a Jewish Agency leader, and another colleague to visit the man with a plea for mutual fulfillment.

The two emissaries stole into Amman and there, in the royal palace, found King Abdullah of Jordan in a cooperative mood. He told them jokes and then, over Turkish coffee, what they wanted to hear. With merry eyes, he said that if the Jews let him swallow up the projected Palestinian Arab state, he would make sure no Arab army would pass over Transjordan territory to attack the Jews.

Abdullah's guests agreed, and Ben-Gurion, indeed, hoped the king would take over the West Bank immediately, before the mufti could. He did not wish Israel to absorb this Arab-populated region and risk losing either its Jewish or its democratic character. It was an argument that would be echoed by Yitzhak Rabin almost fifty years later.

On the cold, clear night of November 29, 1947, Ben-Gurion went to bed early, one of the few Israelis who could sleep at all in those historic hours. He and his wife, Paula, were seeking to escape the tension at home as they waited for word from the UN General Assembly: Would it agree to a Jewish state?

Hardly had Ben-Gurion fallen asleep when the door swung open and a man burst in, ignoring Paula's shrill protests. He was a comrade from the Jewish Agency, and he had just come from Jerusalem. "Mazel tov!" he cried. "We won!"

The partitionists had gained the necessary two-thirds majority. Ben-Gurion stared up at him with joy. A state at last! He slowly rose and, slipping on his robe, shuffled to a table, picked up his blue Parker pen, and began writing a declaration. When he ran out of paper, he asked for more and scribbled the last words on a sheet of brown toilet tissue:

> ... The Jewish people, which has never given way to despair, even at the darkest moments of its history, and which has never once lost its faith in itself and in the conscience of humanity, will not fall short at this great hour of the opportunity and the historic responsibility that have been given to it. The restored Judea will take an honorable place in the United Nations as a force for peace, prosperity and progress in the Holy Land, the Near East and the world at large.

The Yishuv exploded in an orgy of joy with the news. Rabin, who had just been appointed deputy commander of the Palmach, joined the jubilant throngs in Tel Aviv. And the following evening he met with Leah, who had just returned from a vacation with her parents, "to celebrate this very special moment," as Leah would say, "but he was not in the mood for partying. He was already deeply concerned about 'tomorrow,' . . . the inevitable hard and bloody war. Despite Palmach awareness, and its years of preparation, it was clear that we were not ready or properly equipped to face the dangers that threatened the 600,000 population of our tiny country, surrounded as it was by an ocean of hostility."

Indeed, Rabin would concede, he "harbored few illusions. The irony of it all was that the success of our political struggle left us more vulnerable than ever to destruction. We would now have to protect our political gains by force of arms."

6

Birth and Death

Ben-Gurion brooded over his small arsenal. He needed time for the Sonnenborn Institute to deliver enough weapons to make an important difference. And while he had been counting on arms from the Soviet Union and its satellites, they had attached strings to their aid, demanding to know the political views of the Hagana.

None of their business, Ben-Gurion replied.

But the price of pride was high. He would now have to rely on his own agents in Europe to purchase weapons from wherever and whomever they could. And also on Golda Meir, whom he sent to the United States to solicit money from the Jewish community there to pay for the arms. Stout and striking with black hair knotted in the back and eyes that perpetually reflected an inner sadness, she had migrated with her parents from Kiev, Russia, to Milwaukee as a young girl before moving to Palestine in the 1920s. She learned English well enough to work as a teacher, and she knew how to deal with American Jewry.

The urgency of these missions struck with greater impact each day as howling Arab mobs attacked in Jerusalem and elsewhere. On December 2, 1947, they broke into Jewish shops in west Jerusalem and set them ablaze—while British policemen passively looked on. The Arabs, with British help, would try to make it clear to the world that partition would not work. In the Jewish Quarter of the Old City, they tried to break into the Warsaw Synagogue, which the British finally saved by flashing their bayonets. But Arab snipers on the rooftops forced shops and schools to close and turned the quarter into a silent maze of death.

Then, on January 14, 1948, a thousand Arab villagers stormed the Etzion Bloc of settlements perched atop the rolling hills between Jerusalem and Hebron, surging up the rocky gray slopes wave upon wave. The Jews managed to push them back, but when a Hagana force of thirty-five tried to reach Etzion with arms and food, it was ambushed and, after a dramatic battle from rock to rock, wiped out.

Uzi Narkiss, the short, slight, brilliant commander of the area, was outraged. One more attack, he feared, and the Etzion Bloc would be overrun, for his desperate pleas for more weapons had been rejected. And in fact, several months later, after the Jewish state was proclaimed, the Jordanian Arab Legion would overrun the kibbutz. He thus set off for Palmach headquarters in Tel Aviv and barged into the office of Yitzhak Rabin, the chief of operations.

"Yitzhak," he urged, "you must help me. If the bloc doesn't get arms immediately, we'll lose it. You must help. Come with me and see for yourself."

Rabin stared at Narkiss with tormented eyes and groaned: "Uzi, you know I'd help you if I could. We're getting calls for help from everywhere."

But he agreed to accompany Narkiss to the bloc to view the situation. They arrived there just after another attack and many Jews had been killed.

"Okay, Yitzhak," Narkiss said after a tour of the area, "you've seen the situation. Now will you help me?"

Rabin again addressed Narkiss with his eyes, which squinted with controlled grief. "I'm sorry," he said, "but I still can't help you. We have nothing anywhere."

Narkiss was crushed. But he was not angry. Indeed, he had never admired the man more.

"Yitzhak could have evaded the visit since he knew he could not help," Narkiss told me. "But he thought it was his duty to come and had the courage to say 'no.' Other commanders would have stalled."

Despite the severe shortage of arms in the settlements, the Arabs in the first months after the UN vote were unable to smash through the bitterly defended barricades. And so they began ambushing convoys along the main roads, cutting communications everywhere, slicing up Jewish Palestine into isolated pockets and sealing off Jerusalem, which was swiftly running out of ammunition, food, and water. But Ben-Gurion ordered the Jews to defend every colony, every town, whatever the odds. Each one abandoned could mean that much smaller a state. It was time for Plan D.

This plan called on the Jews to strike back remorselessly and consume all areas granted to them under the partition scheme—and any Arab sectors within them—especially the enemy-infested highlands overlooking the Tel Aviv–Jerusalem road, a deadly gauntlet of fire and lead. The death toll among troops escorting food and arms convoys was especially high since, unlike the drivers and passengers, who were protected by armor plating, they could only hide behind sacks of provisions to cover themselves from Arab fire. And when the Jews finally manufactured armored cars, the Arabs attacked with their own homemade armor-piercing bullets.

By March 1948, the convoy system proved untenable, leaving the Jews trapped in Jerusalem on the verge of starvation and possibly annihilation. Operation Nachshon, which was part of Plan D, would, it was hoped, ease this disastrous situation. And Yitzhak Rabin, who would head this operation, would lead the largest concentration of Hagana forces ever gathered under a single command. His challenge was to gain control of Arab areas paralleling the road to Jerusalem in order to prevent attacks on the convoys.

Thus, for the first time, the Jews would seize and hold Arab villages, though the surviving inhabitants—those who had not fled—would be allowed to remain in their little stone houses if they didn't revolt against Jewish military control.

On April 1, Rabin and other Hagana and Palmach chiefs met with Ben-Gurion, who ordered them to rustle up 2,000 rifles so they could storm strongholds along the road, mainly the village of

Kastel, the last hilltop bastion overlooking the road to Jerusalem. If the Jews could take the fortress there, the road would be open.

Rabin agreed with Ben-Gurion that whatever happened to any other Jewish areas, the Holy City must be saved, for it was the soul of the Jewish people. The prime minister had agreed that it be internationalized as a temporary concession. But an Arab flag over Jerusalem? Not for a minute! And the next day, 1,500 men, drawn from settlements and battle lines around the country, were ready to launch Operation Nachshon, named after the first Israelite to leap into the Red Sea during the exodus from Egypt.

On the morning of April 3, 1948, Uzi Narkiss, whom Rabin chose to attack the highland village of Kastel, calmly briefed his men. Kastel! After all these centuries, still a monstrous sentinel blocking the way to Jerusalem, dominating the region for miles. But now the Jews, armed with brand-new Czech rifles miraculously flown in the night before, seized Kastel in a quick thrust at dawn. Shortly afterward, the Arabs stormed the height and recaptured it, but the Jews took it back again. Rabin's men scored a greater victory than they realized.

The most feared of all the Arab fighters was a handsome, charismatic warrior named Abd el-Kader el-Husseini, a relative of the mufti, who inspired the mobs to fight to the death. In one battle, Arab fighters had clawed their way up to the crest of the hill, laughing and shouting, embracing each other, arguing excitedly over who killed how many Jews. Then someone yelled:

"We found him! Abd el-Kader . . . He's dead!"

The madness stopped abruptly. "Where is he? Where is he?" went the cry, and men surged toward the house that had been Hagana headquarters. In front lay a corpse in a leather jacket. A great silence descended over Kastel as fierce fighting men sobbed gently. Several men lifted the body and began to carry it down the hill toward the main road, and the crowd followed. The Arabs had fought an intensely personal battle—mainly to please and protect Abd el-Kader. Now their hero was dead. Some would go with him to Jerusalem to stay until he was buried. Others drifted off in all directions to their villages, having no more stomach for battle. With little trouble, the Jews recaptured Kastel, while breaking the spirit of the Palestinian Arab forces.

Rabin's link with Abd el-Kader's death would have a curious corollary almost fifty years later. Abd el-Kader's son, Faisal Husseini, the resident leader of the Palestinians, would realize that his people would best be served by a peace agreement with a Jewish state led by Rabin, whose troops had killed his father.

In any case, the dust of death hovering over the road to Jerusalem suddenly vanished in the sunlight. Shortly afterward, the Arabs stormed the height and recaptured it, but the Jews took it back again. And within hours Jerusalemites deliriously welcomed three supply-crammed convoys, leaping onto running boards, crawling over every vehicle, screaming and weeping and throwing kisses.

Rabin, almost always pessimistic about future events, was ecstatic as he watched these scenes, proving once again that his pessimism had been unwarranted. He was especially happy when Yigal Allon placed him in command of the Harel Brigade, one of three newly formed Palmach brigades; until their creation on April 15, the Palmach had been a single force. Harel was to wipe out Arab bases along the Tel Aviv–Jerusalem road. But Rabin's joy began to dim when headquarters insisted that he send three more convoys to Jerusalem before he had time to clean up the flanking villages. One of them, scheduled to leave Tel Aviv on April 20, would be composed of about three hundred trucks and would stretch out over a length of fifteen miles, carrying flour, sugar, margarine, and other basic foods.

Delay the convoy, Rabin pleaded. However, reports—later proved false—circulated that the British planned to evacuate the key strategic positions they held in Jerusalem before the mandate ended on May 15. Ben-Gurion jumped at the apparent opportunity to fill the vacuum before the Arabs could.

Move the Harel Brigade to Jerusalem, he ordered Rabin, and prepare a plan for taking over the city.

But Rabin objected. If he sent his troops to Jerusalem, he replied, he would be leaving control of the road to the enemy. Besides, it was wrong to think that the British would leave Jerusalem before the end of the mandate.

Obey instructions! Ben-Gurion responded. And he added that he and Yitzhak Sadeh, the Palmach commander, would be joining the April 20 convoy and would take command of the operations in Jerusalem.

On the evening of April 19, Rabin received his final instructions, repeating what he had already been told, but in greater detail: Move brigade headquarters and the attached battalion to Jerusalem with the convoy on the following day.

The convoy left Tel Aviv at dawn with Ben-Gurion and Sadeh seated in an armored bus that trailed behind the escorting battalion, followed by the food-packed trucks. The battalion and the bus got through without trouble, but then hundreds of Arabs began attacking from the hills along the road all the way from Latrun to Bab el-Wad, and the convoy was forced to grind to a halt.

Rabin, who had been riding in a white, open jeep up and down the line of vehicles, was aghast. His worst fears had materialized. Had he not warned headquarters that the hills should be cleaned out before it sent the convoy? He ordered his reserve armored company forward to stop the Arabs from reaching the road, but they were sweeping the vehicles with fire, and even those still capable of advancing were blocked by those who were not. Nor could he concentrate a large force to fight back since the troops were scattered among the trucks, "sitting targets on top of the cargo," as he would say.

Rabin thus had to make a fateful decision. The convoy could be rescued only by an outside force, and reinforcements, he knew, were available in the nearby Jewish village of Kiryat Anavim. But should he send someone else for them and remain with the convoy to direct its defense, or should he risk breaking through the Arab gauntlet himself? He decided to go himself since he could best organize a rescue mission. As he raced past the trucks, his jeep came under heavy fire, but miraculously he was not hit.

Rabin roared into Kiryat Anavim and found Uzi Narkiss in one of the tents.

"Uzi, the convoy is under attack!" he cried. "Go out with a relief force in the two armored cars."

The vehicles had been stolen from the British, but it was time to take them out of hiding.

And after a prolonged battle, the Jews managed to extricate all except twenty of the vehicles, but only after more than twenty men lay dead and many more wounded. Nor was the road open any longer. Rabin's whole brigade was now trapped in Jerusalem, though the top brass could fly to Tel Aviv in small, rickety planes.

But as long as their supplies held out they could fight for the city, and they did—ferociously. Ben-Gurion now personally ordered Rabin to capture the northern and southern parts of the city. And his men were to engage in some of the bitterest fighting of the war.

Ben-Gurion was adamant; Operation Jebusi had to succeed or Jerusalem could be lost. And Rabin's Harel Brigade would play the major role. Rabin would have three major objectives:

- Capture the Arab hilltop village of Nebi Samuel, which blocked the route to the enemy-surrounded kibbutz of Nevi Yaakov northwest of Jerusalem.
- Take the Sheikh Jarrah area, which isolated Hadassah Hospital and Hebrew University on Mount Scopus to the north.
- Seize Katamon in Jewish Jerusalem, the missing link that connected the southern quarters of Mekor Hayim, Talpiot, and others to the rest of West Jerusalem.

Rabin would have preferred to attack from Jerusalem and seize the main strong points dominating the Jerusalem–Tel Aviv route; and also to sever the Jerusalem-Ramallah road so the Arabs could not be supplied from Ramallah. Without supplies, the Arabs could not fight. Why risk heavy losses with direct attacks inside Jerusalem, at least while the British still controlled most strategic points and might intervene on the side of the Arabs? That was conventional military thinking, not the logic he had learned, and taught, in the Palmach. The best way to save lives, he thought, was to circumvent the enemy, not confront him directly.

But David Shaltiel, the stern-faced, bespectacled Hagana commander in Jerusalem, a conventional soldier, disagreed. No, he argued, this was not logical. Certainly not when hundreds of Jews were trapped in the Old City and were pleading for rescue before they were slaughtered. Rabin, Shaltiel felt, should urgently attack within Jerusalem and save the civilians, but instead, Shaltiel lamented, his main objective was to protect his troops.

The Hagana High Command agreed to a compromise—Operation Jebusi. The Jews would seek to cut the Ramallah supply line while smashing into the northern and southern sections of Jerusalem.

The assault on the Arab village of Nebi Samuel, launched on April 26, ended in disaster when Rabin's troops neared the top of the hill at dawn only to find themselves ensnared in a murderous ambush that struck down many men as they retreated. The deputy company commander, though wounded himself, crawled down with his more seriously wounded commander in his arms. The commander died on the way, one of forty fatalities in the battle, and his deputy, after being hit again, was about to blow himself up with a grenade when a medical orderly rescued him.

The attack on the Sheikh Jarrah Quarter the same night fared better, as Jewish troops, in room-to-room fighting, dislodged Arab irregulars entrenched there—that is, all but a few snipers who, trapped on the roof of a house, kept lobbing grenades down the staircase. A British officer then intervened and negotiated their evacuation with an attractive Jewish female squad commander. Intrigued by the girl, the officer kept talking for hours, and at one point, apparently to win her favor, even declared that of course he had nothing but contempt for the Arabs.

Meanwhile, higher British authorities had more pressing matters than romance on their minds. They ordered Rabin's forces to leave Sheikh Jarrah since it was to be the British evacuation route, promising to maintain control of the quarter themselves and not return it to the Arabs. When Rabin refused, the British forces opened fire on the house. Rabin then agreed to retreat, having failed to call the British bluff. As things turned out, the British would keep their part of the bargain, and the Jews would be able to reoccupy the quarter as soon as they departed.

But though Rabin could not know this when he had to order a retreat, he was not too depressed to think about home. On April 26, after the withdrawal, he wrote to his father not to worry about him, offering the impression that he was not really in danger:

> I am now in Jerusalem in connection with an assignment I was given. I am well and living in a nice pension . . . , and things are going well. . . . It is important that I know how you are getting along, and what you know about my little sister. . . . I can imagine that you are very worried, but I am optimistic about our chances in the near future, although in this area things might escalate.

And they escalated.

While two of Rabin's columns had been halted, if for different reasons, the third stabbed southward into Katamon, a quarter replete with luxurious Arab homes, and up a steep hill toward the massive Greek Orthodox monastery of Saint Simon, where an Iraqi unit dominated southern Jerusalem. The column piled through the monastery's iron gate and peppered its walls and courtyard with bullets, toppling men off the roof and drowning out the cries of others already in flight. They smashed into the building, blindly spraying every room. And the battle was over.

Or so it appeared. At dawn the Iraqis counterattacked, and seemed about to succeed when Palmach fighters climbed to the roof and dropped grenades on them.

In Amman, King Abdullah was deeply worried by the attack on Katamon but, despite the pleas of Palestinian leaders, refused to send in his Arab Legionnaires camped nearby and risk full-scale war with the Jews. But the king's commander in Jerusalem, Abdullah Tel, acted on his own. He supplied the Palestinians with three armored cars and a number of soldiers dressed as civilians, and one of the cars spearheaded a new counterattack on the monastery.

By then, about half the Jewish force had been killed or wounded, but the rest resolutely held on, encouraged by news that the Arabs were beginning to abandon the quarter. Jewish reinforcements finally arrived, and within hours all of Katamon had fallen. As the Jews tramped from house to abandoned house, they stared in amazement at the rich furnishings, the closets full of finery, the jewels, and the artwork. Amos Chorev, whom Rabin had sent to take over command of the Jewish forces, saw the glitter in his men's eyes and ordered the homes to be blown up and burned. It was a pity to destroy such luxury, but it would be worse by far to see his disciplined soldiers break down and start looting.

Rabin had been devastated by his failure to take over Nebi Samuel and Sheikh Jarrah, and even victory at Katamon could not lift his spirits. So many men lost, men only slightly younger than he, the youngest brigade commander in the Hagana. The weight of his responsibility was crushing. Could he have saved some of them with different orders? Yet, in the end, they had succeeded. As he would say:

"The sheer stubbornness of our men despite a harrowing toll of casualties largely settled the city's fate."

Not quite. Early in May, Rabin flew to Tel Aviv in a light plane, which barely lifted off the end of an improvised airstrip while the pilot mumbled prayers. The Harel commander had been summoned for consultations with the general staff. His troops had secured part of the road to Jerusalem, but Latrun, a dominating height, was still in Arab hands. And the troops and supplies that had reached Jerusalem were now insufficient to hold Jerusalem against future Arab attacks, especially with the Arab states poised to invade Palestine in little more than a week, when the British would be leaving.

He must open up the road to Jerusalem once and for all, his superiors told him. Did he have a plan?

His plan, he said, was still to seize the main strong points dominating the Jerusalem–Tel Aviv route and finish the job he had started before the attacks in Jerusalem. This time, he tried to assure himself, he would not fail.

But Rabin was deeply troubled. Since moving to Jerusalem, his brigade had suffered over one hundred dead and over four hundred wounded. He now had to reinforce one of his two battalions with a platoon of youth detachments, fifteen- and sixteen-year-olds, though he was terrified by the thought of having to face parents whose children were struck down.

At the same time, however, the constant horror to which he had to subject his troops spurred him to suppress his feelings and seal himself in a shell that seemed to harden with every casualty. He had to dull his senses, to render himself immune to tragedy, even heartless. He could not afford to be soft—or let his superiors think he was. When he decided to attack Bet Mahzir, an Arab base of operations near the Jerusalem road, Yosef Tabenkin, a battalion commander, and his deputy, Uzi Narkiss, visited him in his tent in Ma'aleh Hahamishah. It was May 11, the day before the scheduled attack.

They were not ready yet for the attack, the two visitors said. A month ago the battalion had a thousand men. Now, only six hundred were left. They needed more time to rest.

"No," Rabin replied, "we'll attack on schedule."

Just twenty-four hours more.

Rabin glowered at them. "I said no!" he shouted, banging on the table. "Get out! You have an order. Obey it!"

The two commanders left, swearing under their breath.

"We hated him," Narkiss told me years later. "How could he refuse? How could he not understand? . . . But now I realize that he was right once again."

Rabin's troops attacked as scheduled. It would be the last battle fought under the British mandate.

The following day, May 12, as the assault was in progress, Ben-Gurion strode into a Jewish Agency conference room in Tel Aviv, his face haggard and grim. He solemnly greeted fellow members of the National Council of Thirteen, a body that had replaced the Jewish Agency Executive as the supreme Jewish ruling group and would become the provisional government when the mandate ended.

On paper, Ben-Gurion felt, the Jews seemed to be holding their own. They occupied almost solidly the coastal strip of Palestine from Tel Aviv north to Haifa, eastern and western Galilee, and the Beisan Valley. They controlled much of the Negev network of roads that linked twenty-seven dispersed settlements, and they were standing fast in Jewish Jerusalem despite renewed Arab attempts to strangle this hungry besieged city.

Yet something of a miracle was still needed. Arabs entrenched in the hills less than ten miles from the coast could sweep down and slice the Jewish state in two. The twin Arab towns of Ramle and Lydda were deadly arrows aimed at Tel Aviv, only twenty minutes away. Arab guerrillas dotted the heights twisting from Jerusalem to Hebron to Beersheba, and once more blocked the Tel Aviv–Jerusalem road. And while Arab arsenals bulged, the Jews were still looking out to sea for their precious ships to come in. At the same time, the Jewish command was almost as splintered as the Arab leadership, with the Mapam-dominated Palmach determined to remain a semiautonomous force.

Ben-Gurion called the council to order and posed the most important question they would ever have to answer. Two days later, on May 14, the British would leave Palestine. Should the council accept an American compromise proposal calling for the Jews and Arabs to peacefully rule their own communities without either declaring a state? If the majority replied "no," Ben-Gurion would proclaim a state. If "yes" . . . He shuddered to think of that happening. Gazing at the faces around the table, Ben-Gurion found them even more anxious than his own. At least a third of his own party was leaning against a state. He tried to remain calm, to appear confident.

But the mood grew more morose by the minute as speaker after speaker pessimistically analyzed the danger. Finally, Ben-Gurion called on Yigael Yadin, the Hagana chief of operations, feeling he would surely support him. But Yadin was less than optimistic.

He could not offer an opinion, he said, since the responsibility was too great. After a heavy silence, he went on: A concerted invasion would give the Arab armies a "distinct edge." A truce would help, for at least the army could obtain more arms.

And what were the chances for victory now?

Perhaps fifty–fifty.

Only a fifty–fifty chance to survive? A chill wind of desperation swept through the room.

Set up a "government" instead of a state, one council member cried.

Accept the truce, demanded another.

Ben-Gurion tried to calm the storm. They must understand.

"Do we envisage any realistic possibility of resisting invasion?" he said. "My reply is . . . given our moral values, and on condition that our manpower is wisely used and equipment is increased, then we have every prospect of success. . . . The outcome depends on our wiping out most of the Arab Legion."

Wipe out the Arab Legion, King Abdullah's powerful British-led army? The council members were appalled by Ben-Gurion's impudence, enthralled by his pluck.

"And now we shall vote on whether to accept the truce proposal," Ben-Gurion declared calmly.

He announced the results with controlled casualness: For the truce, four votes; against, six.

Two days later, as the British marched out of Palestine, Ben-Gurion would proclaim the rebirth of the Jewish state.

"Considering the mood, there was a mixed flavor to the tidings of May 14, 1948," Yitzhak Rabin would recall about the moment he and some of his men heard the incredible sounds of redemption emanating from the Tel Aviv Museum.

They were listening to an ancient radio in Kibbutz Ma'aleh Hahamishah during a pause in the battle for Bet Mahzir nearby.

It was difficult indeed to mix the joy that was exploding in Tel Aviv on this historic day with the despair of the warriors fighting and dying in an obscure Arab village. Tel Aviv was another world to these men who had seen their comrades blown to pieces. The only real world was one of death and horror. Yet they listened, if almost with dazed indifference, to what was happening in the other world. . . .

Ben-Gurion stood before a battery of microphones as he waited to make his proclamation. Beside him sat members of his first government and, just below the dais, those of the first Knesset, or parliament. On the wall behind him a portrait of Theodor Herzl hung between two blue-and-white Zionist flags, benignly contemplating the sacred moment he had prophesied more than fifty years earlier.

The windows, draped with black cloth, were wide open, and the mirthful rhythms of celebration in the street filtered in, blending with the restless chatter of the guests, the click and grind of cameras, and the whining complaints of those who had arrived late and couldn't find a seat. Gradually, the sounds from outside rose in jubilant cacophony as thousands of people clad in light-colored summer clothes gathered under a hazy blue sky in front of the building on Rothschild Boulevard, waving flags, shouting, singing, humming in cadence with youngsters in shorts and sandals who linked arms and hopped around in circles to the quick beat of the hora. Automobiles honked with blasts of raucous revelry as they threaded their way through the exultant throngs that surged toward the museum from every direction. Young boys and girls standing in army trucks en route to the front waved greetings, holding old rifles aloft.

Inside the museum, Ben-Gurion picked up a gavel, rapped it on the table, and in his small monotone voice, began reading the Declaration of Independence:

It is . . . the self-evident right of the Jewish people to be a nation, as all other nations, in its own Sovereign State. Accordingly, We . . .

meet together in solemn assembly today ... and by virtue of the natural and historic right of the Jewish people and of the Resolution of the General Assembly of the United Nations,

Hereby proclaim the establishment of the Jewish State in Palestine, to be called the State of Israel.

Ben-Gurion then declared that British regulations limiting Jewish immigration were annulled, and the audience, rising, wildly applauded in acclamation, while the sad notes of "Hatikvah," the Jewish national anthem, drifted down from a balcony....

In Ma'aleh Hahamishah, one exhausted soldier who had been trying to sleep in a corner opened his bleary eyes and cried: "Hey guys, turn it off. I'm dying for some sleep. We can hear the nice words tomorrow."

Someone got up and turned off the radio, and a heavy silence pervaded the room.

"I was mute, stifling my own mixture of emotions," Rabin would say. "None of us had ever dreamed that this was how we would greet the birth of our state, but we were filled with an even stronger sense of determination now that the state existed."

The next day, Bet Mahzir fell to the Jews, and at least part of the Jerusalem–Tel Aviv road was open to Jewish traffic.

Though exhausted, Rabin's men would have almost no rest. For David Shaltiel, the commander of Jerusalem, phoned Rabin almost immediately at his new base in Bab el-Wad, a few miles from Jerusalem.

He had decided, Shaltiel said, to attack the Old City in order to save the fifteen hundred inhabitants of the Jewish Quarter there. Would Rabin please lend him a company or two for the operation?

Rabin was skeptical. He had little respect for Shaltiel's military skill. Why should he have to sacrifice more of his men to carry out the plan of an "incompetent" commander? Anyway, army headquarters had not ordered him to go to Shaltiel's aid. ... But how could he refuse so urgent a request?

Very well, he replied, but he was sending Itiel Amitai, his operations officer, to Shaltiel's headquarters to be briefed on details of the plan.

About two hours later, Rabin's phone rang again. Amitai was speaking from Shaltiel's headquarters.

"Yitzhak, it's a disaster," he cried. "You must come to Jerusalem immediately!"

Shortly, Rabin was sitting with Shaltiel studying his plan; Shaltiel's Etzioni Brigade would break into the Old City through Jaffa Gate and fight its way into the Jewish Quarter. The men had even prepared a Zionist flag they would plant on David's Tower.

And what would Rabin's soldiers do?

They would make a diversionary attack toward Mount Zion with the help of an Irgun force.

Rabin was appalled, feeling that this plan was doomed to disaster. It was tactically flawed, he thought, because the main thrust should be made through Zion Gate, which was closer to the Jewish Quarter than Jaffa Gate. Nor did he like the diversionary role reserved for his crack troops while less seasoned forces were assigned the main task.

"Don't go charging headfirst right into a wall," he warned Shaltiel. "I'll place the whole of the Harel Brigade under your command, but there must be a different plan."

What was Rabin's plan?

He would close in on the Old City from areas under Jewish control in order to isolate it from the Arab forces, and then try to break in through Zion Gate.

No, said Shaltiel. He would implement only his own plan.

This plan, Rabin snapped, was "idiotic and bound to fail."

Yet, Rabin had no choice. He couldn't let Shaltiel attack alone. With the Jewish Quarter about to fall, any action was better than none.

All right, he bitterly agreed, his troops would carry out the diversionary attack.

The coordinated assault was to start shortly after midnight on May 18. But it never got off the ground because of a breakdown in Etzioni communications. And instead of the Irgun force being sent to its scheduled takeoff point for the attack, it was driven in armored buses to the Tanus Building some distance away and simply told to remain in the buses until further orders.

Ironically, only the diversionary attack by Rabin's men on Mount

Zion succeeded. They climbed the steepest slope and surprised the irregular Arab forces.

Uzi Narkiss, deputy commander of the successful battalion, radioed Shaltiel before dawn on May 18 and asked, referring to a pledge Shaltiel had made before the attack: "Where are the replacements you promised?"

"Don't worry," Shaltiel replied, "they'll come."

A little later, Shaltiel called and asked Narkiss to attack Zion Gate that night and make contact with the Jewish Quarter, simultaneously with the delayed attack by the Etzioni force on Jaffa Gate.

He would speak to his superiors, Narkiss replied, smiling at having forced Shaltiel to ask him to play a major role in the operation after all. But he thought they would agree only on condition that his men were replaced as soon as they reached the Jewish Quarter.

"We are not garrison troops," Narkiss said, "and we're certainly not going to hold both Mount Zion and the Jewish Quarter when we're needed desperately elsewhere."

When Rabin heard of Shaltiel's request, he quickly returned to Jerusalem, his "rage beyond restraint."

"Where are all the troops?" he demanded. "Are the eighty exhausted Palmachniks I lent you the only force that the Jewish people can muster for the liberation of its capital?"

But again Rabin realized he couldn't afford to spend time arguing, especially after he read some of the desperate messages received from the Jewish Quarter:

"They are bombing the Jewish Quarter."

"Our situation is lost. Our last request. Send help."

"We urge you please bomb the quarter heavily so we can hold on. It is [a] matter of minutes for us."

"Send help immediately, immediately, immediately."

Yes, Rabin agreed, he would send help.

At about midnight that same night, the sky over Mount Zion shone with the glow of embers and hot bricks as Arabs in the Old City fired a steady, rhythmic barrage into the zone occupied by Rabin's troops, hoping to stave off an attack through Zion Gate. But Uzi Narkiss's men were not discouraged as they lay in the shadows of trees on the hallowed slopes of the hill. They were about thirty yards from the Dometian Church, waiting for the signal to attack, and could hear the radio operator announcing:

"Zero hour is beginning!"

At 2 A.M., May 19, light machine guns opened fire on Arabs on the wall, covering a heavy machine-gun team that scrambled down the hill and set up the gun near Zion Gate. At 3:15 A.M., two young sappers with dynamite on their backs crawled to Zion Gate, and while enemy fire poured down from the wall above, placed the explosives against the sandbags and concrete blocking the gate and quickly retreated. At 3:25 A.M., a great explosion blasted a hole in the great wooden gate.

The Arabs in the area, shocked by the force of the blast, held their fire just long enough for the assaulting platoon to scramble through the breach.

Meanwhile, Uzi Narkiss was waiting nervously in his headquarters at the church when the commander of the attack strode in and breathlessly reported: "We have carried out the great task and have reached the Jews of the Old City . . . seventeen hundred souls have been saved."

Thus, contrary to the original plan, Rabin's force, which was to play only a diversionary role in the attack, managed to break into the Old City at least in part because the Arabs had been diverted by the Etzioni Brigade's abortive assault on Jaffa Gate—the brigade earlier earmarked for the main breakthrough.

But the liberators did not remain in the Old City long. Apparently with Rabin's approval, Uzi Narkiss, pointing to the loss of about one-third of his fighters in the battle, pulled his men out after demanding that Shaltiel replace them with reserves. Though Shaltiel had few reserves available, Narkiss's troops withdrew anyway, to Shaltiel's shock. Shock turned to desperation when an aide rushed into his headquarters and told him:

"The Legion has entered the Old City and shut down Zion Gate. It looks like we'll have to fight our way in again."

Assuming that Rabin agreed to the withdrawal, the decision, though clearly intended to save the precious lives of his surviving fighters, was perhaps the biggest and most dramatic mistake he made in the war. And if Rabin was really unaware of the withdrawal plan, he was still responsible for the failure, since he was the brigade commander.

Actually, in the chaos of this war between two largely untrained, amateur fighting forces, such costly blunders, stemming more from emotion and whim than from calculated risk, were commonplace. The Jews had captured Kastel after the Arabs abandoned it in their despair over the death of their beloved leader, Abd el-Kader el-Husseini, and now the Arabs were penetrating the Old City after the Jews abandoned it, also for emotional reasons.

Even so, the fighters in the Jewish Quarter miraculously managed to push back repeated enemy attacks. And that night Rabin ordered his men to try once more to break through Zion Gate to help them, possibly moved by conscience. But they were, ironically, thrown back with heavy casualties. Jordan's Arab Legionnaires, who had taken over from the irregular Palestinian force, deceived the Israelis by letting them pass through the gate, then opening concentrated fire that converted the gateway into a death trap. Two more attempts to break through from the north also failed.

On May 28, Rabin went up to Mount Zion, where, in his words, he "witnessed a shattering scene. A delegation was emerging from the Jewish Quarter bearing white flags. I was horrified to learn that it consisted of rabbis and other residents on their way to hear the Legion's terms for their capitulation. That same night the Jewish Quarter surrendered to the Arab Legion."

The horror Rabin felt burrowed deeply into his soul, it seems, perhaps more deeply than any event since his mother's death thirteen years earlier. The sight of bedraggled civilians stumbling along under the gaze of enemy soldiers clearly shocked him. He had removed his soldiers from Mount Zion because he cared about them. After their terrible ordeal in Bet Mahzir and elsewhere, he could not bear to see them suffer further, especially since Hagana headquarters had not ordered him to assist in the attempt to free the residents of the Jewish Quarter. That was, after all, Shaltiel's responsibility, not his.

But Rabin may have suspected, as he viewed the pitiful line of civilians, that his love for his troops, as Shaltiel felt, may have blinded him somewhat to the suffering of the civilians, whose plight could not have been easily imagined until seen with his own eyes. Anyway, he would assert, the few survivors in his force could not have stood up to the large enemy force facing them, though, in the end, ironically, he would make two more attempts to win back the same objective he had voluntarily abandoned. Attempts that would fail at huge cost.

Ironic, too, was the attitude of at least some of his men toward him, those who did not reciprocate his love. They mistakenly viewed his gruff, blunt, sometimes arrogant manner as reflecting a certain indifference toward their fate—an error that almost five decades later would help fuel the atmosphere that would trigger his murder. Rabin's youth, to some extent, seemed to undermine the authoritative image of a senior commander. He was twenty-six, only a few years older than most of his men.

But if Rabin would later refuse to let personal feelings block the way to peace, so would he now refuse to let them influence his conduct of war. As he watched the wretched residents of the Jewish Quarter pass before him—about three hundred would be taken prisoner, the rest released—he would thus sublimate his agony and coolly analyze the defeat in the larger, impersonal context of the struggle for national survival. And he would do so without the knowledge that of the 3,000 Palmach fighters, 1,100 already lay dead on the lush fields, in the windy deserts, and in the narrow alleys of an almost weaponless infant state.

Wasted Blood

W hile Rabin's brigade and other Israeli troops desperately defended every square foot of Jewish-held territory in Jerusalem's New and Old Cities, top army leaders grew alarmed at the prospect of losing both sections to the Arabs.

Rabin and most of the other top commanders were determined to save Jerusalem within an overall national defense plan, though some argued that they could most easily save it by more vigorously defending the rest of the country. An Egyptian armored column had crawled to within twenty-five miles of Tel Aviv; other Egyptian forces were attacking Beersheba, the largest town in the Negev; Arab Legionnaires and Iraqis were thrusting toward the sea; and other Arab fighters were assaulting settlements everywhere.

Though advocating divergent tactics, all agreed that Jerusalem was vitally important from a military as well as from a spiritual point of view; for if large Arab Legion and Egyptian forces linked up there, they could launch a concerted attack on Tel Aviv. It was now necessary to liberate the Old City before the Legion could storm into the New City.

But first, they decided, they had to open the Tel Aviv–Jerusalem road so that convoys carrying fighters, equipment, and food, which now could make the trip only at terrible risk, might safely reach the New City. The first Israeli target would thus be the hills surrounding the ancient Arab village of Latrun. No one knew, however, where the weapons for this ambitious strike would come from.

But then, on May 23, an aide burst into Ben-Gurion's office with the news that Messerschmitts had arrived from Czechoslovakia. In joy, the prime minister ordered that the planes be assembled immediately and sent to the fronts.

Then more good news: A ship was nearing Tel Aviv loaded with almost 50 cannons and 5,000 rifles.

"That will mean the turning point!" Ben-Gurion jotted in his diary.

Now he could save Jerusalem—after first taking Latrun.

Latrun was a cluster of stony hills overlooking the Tel Aviv–Jerusalem road, a pinkish-brown mass dominated by a police fortress that reached into the sky like a gnarled claw.

Hit this stronghold head-on, Ben-Gurion ordered, then push down the branch road to Ramallah skirting these hills and strike at the Old City from the rear, trapping the occupying Arab Legion forces within its walls. The key to victory was speed.

But his men were not ready yet, Yadin protested, supported by Yigal Allon and Rabin. Anyway, a head-on attack would leave the hills littered with bodies. They should outflank the fortress.

There was no time for that, Ben-Gurion replied. They would have to improvise. And he wasn't interested in the obstacles. It was their job to overcome them.

A direct attack would be suicide, Yadin insisted. And he pleaded with the prime minister to postpone the attack for just one week.

Not for a day.

But Ben-Gurion finally relented. All right, one day. Twenty-four hours.

At dawn, May 25, the Israelis, mainly untrained refugees from Europe just off the boat, stumbled through a wheat field toward the forbidding heights until greeted by a stream of shells and bullets that sent the survivors staggering toward the rear. Officers shouted for them to halt, but everyone, it seemed, spoke a different language and would not listen to reason anyway as they frantically fled their Tower of Babel. The bodies of about 140 of them were shortly scattered across the landscape.

Ben-Gurion persisted; his men must attack still again. And he appointed Colonel David "Mickey" Marcus, a jovial, potbellied American Jew, who had just arrived from the United States to help organize the budding Israeli army. He would be Israel's first *aluf* ("general"), since Judas Maccabees held the rank 2,000 years earlier. But the new attack failed, too, after a unit had reached the fortress—then took too much time trying to blow open what it didn't realize was an unlocked door!

Even before the first battle, Rabin churned with fury and frustration. Why didn't Ben-Gurion understand that direct attacks were futile—a lesson that he himself had learned from his own traumatic experience? How many more hundreds of men would have to die needlessly? Rabin felt a compassion for his fighters that spilled over into personal matters. Amos Chorev, one of his officers, discovered this when he came to Rabin and asked for a favor. Could he have a few days' leave in Tel Aviv to visit his wife and baby, whom he hadn't seen for weeks? Some convoys, Chorev pointed out, were still getting through.

"Okay," Rabin replied, "but you'll have to go and return at your own risk."

Chorev thus left for Tel Aviv from the Harel camp, rejoiced with his family, and started back to camp. But en route, his truck stopped in a kibbutz and he learned that the Arab Legion had taken the Latrun fortress and had cut the road completely. He then met Mickey Marcus, who was in the area preparing for his attack on Latrun.

"Amos, don't worry," Marcus said. "We'll attack again. We've got to get you to Jerusalem."

"Well, if you don't," Chorev replied, "I think I know of a way of getting myself there, and maybe everyone else, too."

He then drew a map on a sheet of paper showing how the Israelis already controlled part of an alternative dirt-path route to Jerusalem. He penciled in a three-mile extension of this path, showing it would bypass Latrun to the south.

"Can we forge a path for vehicles through these hills?" Marcus asked.

"I think we can," Chorev replied.

Marcus slapped Chorev on the back and said: "Okay, Amos, get yourself a couple of boys and try to make it across those hills in a jeep. If you get through in one piece, maybe we all can."

The jeep made it across the hills, and the next night, ten jeeps piled high with military supplies made the same trip with Chorev in the first vehicle, and all but one reached Jerusalem.

Marcus was ecstatic. But the road would not be ready until a UN-sponsored truce, scheduled in a few days, was over, and the Arab Legion might assault the road before the truce took place. Meanwhile, Ben-Gurion demanded that his troops attack again immediately to improve Israel's position. And a battalion of Rabin's Harel Brigade was to take part in the assault.

Rabin and his superior, Yigal Allon, protested again and hoped to stall off this attack until the truce took effect. If Ben-Gurion agreed to build the road, perhaps he would agree that a new frontal thrust was unnecessary. Marcus wanted to attack regardless but decided to let Rabin solicit Ben-Gurion's approval of the road.

The prime minister responded to Rabin's proposal with anger.

"Is it or is it not possible to attack Latrun tonight?" he barked.

"It's possible," Rabin replied, "but the chances of success are close to zero."

"Why wasn't I notified yesterday that you had no intention of attacking Latrun?" Ben-Gurion demanded.

"I don't know. I have been charged with submitting the proposal on behalf of Allon and Stone [Marcus's pseudonym]. Latrun is not sacred. The purpose of taking it is to safeguard our link with Jerusalem. If that purpose can be gained by other means, why must we shed our blood over Latrun?"

Unfazed by this irrefutable logic, Ben-Gurion persisted:

"Why didn't Allon tell me that he doesn't intend to attack Latrun?" Then he shouted: "Yigal Allon should be shot!"

Rabin was "astounded, barely able to mumble" a reply.

"Ben-Gurion, what are you saying?"

"Yes, you heard me correctly!"

Finally, after a two-hour tirade against those who would dare oppose his orders, Ben-Gurion conceded: "You have left me with no choice. I approve."

A "Burma Road" would be built. But it was apparently up to Marcus to decide whether a third attack would be made on Latrun.

"I left general staff headquarters tense and exhausted," Rabin would later say.

Yet he felt a surge of pride. He had stood up to Ben-Gurion as few people had ever done. And he had won. Now it was up to Allon to convince Marcus he should call off the new attack. And Allon tried his best. But Marcus would not budge.

"I know your men are tired, Yigal," he said, "but so are the enemy. You have one mission, only one: Latrun. And don't forget it!"

"Mickey, it's unnecessary to hit Latrun," Allon persisted. "Look what happened in the last two attacks. Let's bypass Latrun and take Ramallah, and from there we can surround the Old City. Once isolated from its supply lines, Latrun will fall automatically."

Marcus looked at Allon with fiery brown eyes devoid of their usual good humor.

"The decision has been made, Yigal," he said. "You are a soldier. Your job is to fight. You will attack in four hours."

He did. And this time the Israelis attacked the wrong hill in the dark and were mowed down again, with Rabin losing half his battalion. He was sick. Another unnecessary slaughter. If only they had waited for the road.

The following day, June 11, the guns finally stopped firing as the truce took hold.

The decision to build a "Burma Road" symbolized a turning point in the war and the end of the bloodiest, most critical period in Israel's history. The debacles at Latrun and in the Old City were only the latest Arab victories. Egypt had captured Beersheba and was only a few miles from Rehovot. The Arab Legion had seized Ramle and Lydda. The Syrians had crossed the Jordan River and were attacking settlements in Upper Galilee.

Now, with the truce, the wounded, weakened nation finally had a chance to count its casualties, bury its dead, and draw up new plans for survival. The road Rabin had "sold" to Ben-Gurion could be built, assuring that food and arms from Europe and the United States would finally flow into Jerusalem. And refugees from

Europe could be trained and integrated into experienced units. These units would become part of the new Israel Defense Forces (IDF), which would embrace the Hagana, Irgun, and Stern Gang.

With the battlefields silent, Ben-Gurion met at general headquarters with his commanders, who, haggard and mud-stained, swapped horror stories of impossible struggles. The troops, Rabin and the others agreed, had fought to the breaking point and were near collapse. But Ben-Gurion looked at the broader picture. No reason for pessimism. The Israelis, after all, had held out against the regular Arab armies in almost every settlement within the territory that the UN had allocated to Israel. The big problem for him was not the suffering of the individual, but the individualism that caused the suffering. Israel must have a single disciplined national army embracing all armed groups.

Ben-Gurion's obsession with "one army" even overshadowed his hunger for arms, as the tragic odyssey of the *LST Altalena*, in which Rabin would play an important role, would demonstrate. The ship sailed from a French port crammed with almost 1,000 Jews and a huge cargo of weapons secretly delivered by a French army convoy—a token of France's sympathy for Israel in the midst of its own battle against Arab guerrillas in North Africa.

The problem was that the vessel, and the Jews aboard, belonged not to the Israeli government but to the nationalist Irgun Zvai Leumi. On the morning of June 12, Irgun chief Menachem Begin announced dramatically to government officials:

"The *Altalena* is carrying men and iron to Israel that can win the war for us. She's carrying enough arms to equip ten battalions. She will arrive in five days."

It seemed only fair, Begin said, that the Irgun keep 20 percent for its own fighters in Jerusalem.

When Ben-Gurion learned of this announcement, he was enraged. Begin had already agreed to integrate his units into the army and turn over all their arms to it. And the prime minister wasn't impressed by Begin's argument that since Jerusalem was, under the partition plan, to be outside the Jewish state, his men there could operate independently of the army and equip themselves with their own weapons.

Ben-Gurion was convinced that Begin planned to use the arms to seize the government by force—a charge that the Irgun leader denied, though some of his extremist followers were, in fact, plotting a coup, apparently without his knowledge. Amitai Paglin, who was then Begin's chief of operations and would eventually head an antiterrorist unit in the Begin government, admitted to me that during the *Altalena* incident, he and another Irgun leader, Bezalel Stolnitzky, conspired to overthrow the Ben-Gurion government. And they were prepared, Paglin said, to "wipe out" Ben-Gurion and his cabinet if necessary. But before they could round up an Irgun "commando force" for the operation, Paglin was arrested and the plot fell through.

In any case, Ben-Gurion ordered his commanders to let the *Altalena* come. All the weapons, however, would go to the army. Israel Galili, Ben-Gurion's military aide, then told Begin that the ship could land.

"What about the arms for Jerusalem?" Begin asked.

"We'll work that out," Galili replied. "I think 20 percent can go to Jerusalem."

Begin was delighted. Apparently he hadn't listened very carefully. Galili had not specified who in Jerusalem would be getting the 20 percent. At any rate, the two men clashed when Begin insisted on storing the arms in an Irgun warehouse.

In fury, Galili sent an urgent note to Ben-Gurion: The Irgun was challenging the authority of the state, and the prime minister should take "swift and clear action" to meet this "internal threat to Israel."

Ben-Gurion agreed, and he had a good excuse for the world. The Irgun was trying to smuggle in soldiers and arms in violation of the cease-fire—though he was engaged in such activity himself. He would destroy an "internal threat," procure a shipload of arms, and win the sympathy of the world all at once.

On the afternoon of June 20, Ben-Gurion called a secret meeting of the cabinet and persuaded it to make a grave decision. The army would seize the weapons by force if necessary.

The *Altalena* anchored that night at Kfar Vitkin on Israel's northern coast, and the men and women aboard immediately began unloading their precious cargo into motor launches and rowboats that carried them to shore. When Begin was warned by a Hagana officer who met the ship that he must turn over all the arms to the army, Begin refused. And within an hour a hail of bullets sprayed the beach.

As Irgunists toppled to earth, several men grabbed Begin, who was imploring everyone to stay and fight, and dragged him kicking and cursing to a motor launch that sped to the *Altalena*. With most of the Irgunists and arms aboard—those people still ashore surrendered—the ship raced southward toward Tel Aviv and possible civil war.

A few hours later, on the morning of June 22, Ben-Gurion sat with his cabinet, his eyes inflamed from sleeplessness, his hair in even wilder disarray than usual. Solemnly, he exclaimed that not only were the Irgunists endangering the war effort, but they were threatening the existence of the state. A state, he asserted, could not exist without its government exercising control over a single army. The dissidents were, he charged, trying to kill the state.

After the meeting, Ben-Gurion telephoned Yigal Allon at Palmach headquarters in the Ritz Hotel, which stretched along the beach within sight of the *Altalena*, now anchored offshore. The prime minister would use the Palmach to "abolish" the Irgun before he abolished the Palmach. Allon, who had succeeded Yitzhak Sadeh as Palmach commander, was to take command of the Tel Aviv area—a tough assignment, for he might have to kill Jews. Perhaps many, for the ubiquitous Irgunists were marching on the city from all directions, while there were few army troops around. Allon should start firing, he was ordered, only if the Irgunists fired first—or tried to unload the arms.

While Ben-Gurion addressed his cabinet, Begin addressed the local population through a loudspeaker rigged on the ship:

"People of Tel Aviv, we of the Irgun have brought you arms to fight the enemy, but the government is denying them to you. . . ." Then, directing his appeal to the army, he shouted: "Use your heads. Help us unload these arms, which are for the common defense. If there are differences among us, let us reason later. . . . "

On the veranda of the Kaete Dan Hotel, due west of the ship, a group of UN observers listened in astonishment over breakfast. At press headquarters in a nearby building, correspondents scribbled notes as Begin spoke. And at Palmach headquarters in the Ritz Hotel, Yitzhak Rabin, now deputy Palmach commander, handed out grenades to his men.

That morning, Rabin was to take Leah on a tour of Harel Brigade battlefield sites and had gone to the hotel, where she worked in the promotion department, to pick her up. He had seen little of Leah since independence.

"I occasionally wrote him short notes," she would say. "We never telephoned. There was no way to do so. But we had known each other for three years, and the ties were very strong. Yitzhak was at war. And I waited. He would be gone for weeks, then, all of a sudden, he would appear. . . . He looked for me at my parents' home [in Tel Aviv] or at Palmach headquarters, where I would be drafting copy for the next edition of our newspaper."

With the truce, Rabin had appeared again and was looking forward to spending a peaceful day with Leah. As he approached the hotel, he saw a landing craft sailing from the ship with uniformed, helmeted men aboard. A Palmach officer he met then explained what was happening.

Those were Irgun people, he said. And they were trying to take over the beach so they could unload their weapons.

Weapons for what?

Rumors were rampant. Some said they want to take over the city, others, the whole state.

Rabin ran into the hotel, up to the third floor, and telephoned Allon, who was then at home.

Should he attack with the forty soldiers based in the building? he asked.

"Respond if you're fired on," Allon replied. "I'm leaving for the Ritz now."

Rabin rushed to Leah and told her to leave the building at once. They would not be visiting the battlegrounds this day. The hotel itself might become a battleground. He also ordered all other noncombatants out of the hotel.

Allon then arrived, but was immediately summoned to the meeting in Ben-Gurion's office, where he was given command of the Tel Aviv area.

The tension grew as Irgunists who had been integrated into the army defected from the front lines and joined their fellows on the beach. Rabin ordered his men to fill sandbags and place them by windows and doors. Some government troops nearby, realizing that Jews were about to fire on Jews, abandoned their weapons and left. But others cleared the beach of civilians as a motor launch carrying arms chugged from the *Altalena* to shore, delivered its contents to waiting sympathizers, and returned for more.

Then, at about 1 P.M., the launch approached shore once again. With each chug of the motor, Rabin and the hundreds of spectators—soldiers, sailors, diplomats, United Nations observers, politicians, and others who just happened to be in the area—felt they were about to witness a spectacular moment in history. And some were reminded of the fate of the Second Temple almost 2,000 years before, when, within the sacred walls of Jerusalem, Jew slew Jew. In the next three years, tens of thousands lay dead or dying in the narrow, twisting alleys, their bodies pierced by arrows or split by the sword. . . . History, it seemed, might be about to repeat itself.

A machine gun sputtered a murderous welcome, and within seconds the antagonists on shore and aboard ship raked each other with gunfire. At the same time, Irgunists—many of them new recruits who had deserted from the army—began storming the beach from the city, and all along the waterfront and on nearby streets Jews shot at Jews, sometimes mistakenly at friends, since all wore the same uniform.

Soon the larger Irgun forces, it seemed, had won control of Tel Aviv.

As Irgunists fired at the Palmach building, Rabin ordered his men to respond. He then ran up to the roof and threw grenades toward the units on the beach, stopping only when these units raised a white flag and requested a pause to evacuate the wounded. Rabin called for ambulances, but the shooting soon resumed and continued for several hours.

Ben-Gurion remained icily calm in the face of this perceived threat to his rule and his state. In fact, when one official rushed into his office with news of the battle, the prime minister was calculating with a colleague how to fit out the army with more pants, undershorts, and shoes.

"What shall we do?" the official cried desperately.

Ben-Gurion thought for a moment and replied: "There's no other way. We must shell her."

Rabin would later write: "I was told of a decision to shell the ship. The third shell hit it. An ancient cannon, unequipped with sights and offering a very slim chance for a direct hit—and what a hit! . . . This was a shelling to hit. It was not . . . to frighten the people on the ship. Without destroying the ship the affair would not have ended."

With the *Altalena* aflame, the survivors jumped into the sea to be picked up by Irgunist boys in small boats, leaving the dead to go down with the ship. Begin, who had wanted to be the last man off, was hurled overboard by his men, picked up in the water, and safely carried ashore. Pondering his losses—almost one hundred casualties—he broke into tears as he defiantly cried over the secret Irgun radio that evening:

"Irgun soldiers will not be a party to fratricidal warfare, but neither will they accept the discipline of Ben-Gurion's army any longer."

Ben-Gurion contemptuously replied: "Blessed be the gun that set the ship on fire—that gun will have its place in Israel's war museum."

The Palmach then arrested all the Irgunists it could find, but Begin slipped through the dragnet. The arms were to rot at the bottom of the sea. A shame, Ben-Gurion felt. They might have fired the decisive volleys in the struggle to save the state. But what was a state without authority—plagued, and perhaps seized, by parochial men like Begin with no sense of *havlaga*, social justice, or universal mission, and lacking even the majesty of their late spiritual mentor, Jabotinsky?

Rabin could only say "amen." But he was torn by conflict. He had never dreamed this was possible—Jew killing Jew. Had he personally killed one? He couldn't be sure. But he would make any sacrifice in support of the principles for which his parents had so fiercely struggled. He would even endure the agony of killing fellow Jews and seeing the soldiers he loved killed by them, though, if destiny so dictated, he himself might die at the hands of a Jew.

Red Streaks, White Stockings, and a Bracelet

After the tragedy of the *Altalena*, with all its moral and political implications, Rabin was almost relieved when the truce ended on July 8 and Operation Dani was launched. At least he would be fighting the enemy. And now he and his comrades had weapons to fight with.

The aim of the operation, named after Dani Mass, leader of the thirty-five students killed earlier near Kfar Etzion, was to eliminate the Arab Lydda-Ramle wedge pointed toward Tel Aviv, and then to open the route to Jerusalem by capturing Latrun and Ramallah.

But Rabin and his superior, Yigal Allon, had to "grapple with a troublesome problem." After attacking Lydda (later called Lod) and then Ramle, what would they do with the 50,000 civilians living in the two cities?

"Not even Ben-Gurion could offer any solution," Rabin would later say, "and during the discussions at operational headquarters, he remained silent, as was his habit in such situations. Clearly, we could not leave [Lydda's] hostile and armed populace in our rear, where it could endanger the supply route to [our troops who were] advancing eastward."

Ben-Gurion would only repeat the question: "What is to be done with the population?, waving his hand "in a gesture which said: 'Drive them out!'"

Allon consulted with Rabin, who "agreed that it was essential to drive the inhabitants out." But agreement came with a heavy heart.

"'Driving out' is a term with a harsh ring," Rabin would say. "Psychologically, this was one of the most difficult actions we undertook."

Actually, the Arabs themselves had conveniently given the Israelis a good excuse for driving them out. It grew out of the attack on Lydda. Moshe Kelman, commanding the attack force, would describe to me years later the details of what happened in that town:

Late on the morning of July 10, Kelman stood in a hillside village about a mile east of the town, and scanned the outskirts. To his surprise, he could see no trace of Arab Legion forces. So far, he thought, lowering his binoculars, everything had gone well. Since starting toward Lydda the night before, two battalions attacking from the south had captured several Arab villages. And by evening of this day they had captured most of Lydda.

As Kelman drove through the town in a jeep, he stopped when he saw a black-bearded, black-robed figure standing by the door of an apartment house.

"I would like to speak to your commander," the man said.

"I am the commander," Kelman replied, jumping from his jeep.

The Greek Orthodox priest, Simon Garfeh, surveyed the blond Israeli indifferently.

"I am the Archmandrite of Lydda," he announced. "I hope you have come to seek peace."

"If it is the desire of the people of this town to live with us in peace," Kelman assured him, "we shall be very happy. They may open their shops and renew normal life. Can you arrange for the surrender?"

"I shall try," the prelate answered. "I shall ask the leaders of the Moslem and Christian communities to meet with us immediately in my apartment upstairs."

He then instructed an aide to run to the Big Mosque to fetch the Moslem leaders, and sent another to his own church to bring the Christian leaders taking refuge there.

About an hour later, a dozen Arab notables were sitting in Garfeh's living room sipping coffee and chatting with the clergyman, Kelman, and other Israeli officers. Finally, Kelman put down his coffee and addressed them:

"Gentlemen, the city has been conquered, and we want your cooperation. We suggest that you find the citizens who have been operating the utilities so that your people can have water and electricity without delay. But first, you must accept our terms for peace: Surrender of all fighting personnel and of all arms within twenty-four hours. If these conditions are not met, we shall have to take action."

"We agree," one of the Arabs said with quiet resignation. "May the inhabitants stay here if they wish?"

"Yes, they may," Kelman replied, "if they live here peacefully."

Toward noon the next day, July 11, an Arab Legion patrol composed of one tank and two armored cars crawled through the western unoccupied part of the town to assess Israeli strength. When the patrol found itself trapped, it blasted its way through the streets and managed to escape.

One of the last buildings the vehicles passed during their angry exit was the small Dahmash Mosque. Hardly had they roared past when a boy emerged from the mosque, which was packed with refugees, and threw a grenade into a group of Israeli guards stationed outside. This was the signal for an Arab mob, rushing from the mosque and from nearby houses, to materialize within seconds. They killed the surviving Israelis and mutilated the bodies.

The Arabs were certain that the patrol was the spearhead of the long-awaited Arab Legion effort to save them. And as this rumor spread throughout the city, Arabs began firing from almost every window and door in a massive flash revolt against their conquerors.

After helplessly watching the Legion patrol smash through the town, Moshe Kelman descended to his office from the roof of his headquarters building and opened a creaking shutter. The world seemed to be exploding before his eyes. His great victory was apparently about to crumble. Aside from the 7,000 Arabs jammed into the Big Mosque and its compound, about 30,000 had remained in their homes, each of which had suddenly turned into a fortress. And he had only about five hundred men, scattered in patrols throughout the city, to quash the revolt.

"This is all against all," Kelman said to an aide as he turned away from the window. "Get the word to our men somehow. Order them to shoot at any target that moves, understand?"

That was about as severe an order as the army could give, the aide said.

"I know," Kelman replied, "but we're finished unless we take this action. This is not a conventional battle. This is a revolt by people who have already surrendered."

Within the next hour, some two hundred Arabs were killed, according to Israeli estimates (far more, according to the Arabs), as Israelis, crawling stealthily from doorway to doorway, tossed grenades into windows and broke into houses to silence snipers. The severity of the Israeli counteraction turned threatened defeat into final victory as firing began to cease throughout the city— except around Dahmash Mosque, which, according to the Israelis, had been converted into an armed stronghold.

About seventy armed men, firing from the windows and tower, continued to hold out there, apparently fearful of retribution for killing the Israeli guards and encouraged by the sight of Legion armored cars approaching along the road from Beit Nabala. The cars were in fact halted by intense Israeli fire outside the town and forced to retreat, but the defenders in the mosque were able to keep the Israelis at a distance. Kelman ordered his officers, he told me:

"There's only one thing we can do. We've got to pierce those walls."

"But they're a yard or a yard and a half thick," an officer pointed out. "And we haven't got any artillery."

"We've got a Piat."

Within half an hour, two Israeli soldiers made their way through the bullet-swept approaches to the mosque, entered a building adjacent to it, and ran upstairs to a window facing the side wall of the stronghold. One of the men aimed the Piat and fired.

An Israeli platoon, Kelman said, immediately rushed the

mosque and smashed through the front door with guns blazing. But they soon saw that they were wasting bullets and stood there in silence contemplating what an explosion could do in a small enclosed space. The Persian rugs covering the floor were soaked with blood from bodies strewn everywhere, and some corpses and bits of flesh were stuck to the crimson-streaked walls from the force of the blast. Even hardened Israeli veterans quickly looked away, and some felt like vomiting.

Moshe Kelman then drove up to inspect the scene.

"Get fifteen or twenty Arabs from the other mosque to carry the bodies to the cemetery," he ordered an aide. "And have them clean up in here."

Within two or three hours, Kelman revealed to me, all the remains had been transported on horse-driven carts to the cemetery about a mile away and buried in a long trench dug by the bearers—witnesses who would never be seen again.

Rabin and Allon were shocked when they learned what happened and were furious with Kelman, who insisted that drastic measures had to be taken to put down the revolt. In their rush to the scene, the two men almost joined the dead. Their car hit a land mine and both men were thrown out. Miraculously, neither was seriously hurt. But they were compensated now with a rational excuse for evacuating the whole population of the city, as Ben-Gurion wished.

"The inhabitants must leave for Transjordan within three hours," an Israeli officer informed the Moslem leaders and Archmandrite Garfeh.

And shortly, individual Arabs, under Israeli orders, were slowly moving down the streets shouting: "O people of Lydda, you must leave the town immediately on the road to Ramallah!"

As Rabin would write years after the war:

The population of [Lydda] did not leave willingly. There was no way of avoiding the use of force and warning shots in order to make the inhabitants march the 10 to 15 miles to the point where they met up with the Legion.

The inhabitants of Ramle watched, and learned the lesson: Their leaders agreed to be evacuated voluntarily, on condition that the evacuation was carried out by vehicles. Buses took them to Latrun, and from there they were evacuated by the Legion.

Great suffering was inflicted upon the men taking part in the eviction action. Soldiers ... included youth movement graduates who had been inculcated with values such as international fraternity and humaneness. The eviction action went beyond the concepts they were used to. There were some fellows who refused to take part in the expulsion action. Prolonged propaganda activities were required after the action to remove the bitterness of these youth movement groups, and explain why we were obliged to undertake such a harsh and cruel action.

These paragraphs from the manuscript of Rabin's memoirs never appeared in the published version, for Allon was determined to keep events in Lydda and Ramle secret from the public and prevailed on the Israeli cabinet to censor the account. Nothing, he felt, must blemish the reputation of Israel or its army. But Rabin was a realist who was compulsively honest, as he thought his country must be.

As devastating as the expulsion was to his own self-esteem, Rabin wanted to reveal the incident, it seems, not only for therapeutic relief, but for history, to show how war, especially a war of survival, could push people to act in savage ways. It was the revelation of a man with a disturbed conscience who was bent on achieving a peace that would preclude future Lyddas.

Yet even Rabin could not bring himself to report what happened in the mosque and the cemetery.

Ten days after the truce, a second one took effect. And now the Israelis were in a commanding position. They had not only captured Lydda and Ramle, but had occupied Nazareth in the central Galilee, blocked the Egyptian offensive in the south, and torn a hole in the Egyptian line that had sealed the Negev off from the north. Meanwhile, the Arabs were running low on equipment—and morale—while the IDF built up its strength. Not only with arms trickling in from Europe and the United States, but with a reorganized army designed to crush the enemy in the next offensive. In the shakeup, Yigal Allon moved south to head the southern front, and was followed by many Palmach men, including Rabin, who would continue as Allon's deputy.

But before he left for his new assignment, Rabin, in his words, "underwent personal reorganization." On August 23, trembling as he seldom did on the front line, he strode with an uncertain gait into Beit Shalom Hall in Tel Aviv and stood, with Leah at his side, under a wedding canopy.

"Yitzhak was embarrassed by the ceremony," Leah would recall, "and planned for it to take place just among the close family," with his comrades coming later so they "wouldn't witness his 'misconduct.'" But they all arrived before the rabbi did, and Rabin was now more nervous than ever.

"I can still recall the excitement and jitters, aggravated by the fact that the rabbi was late," he would say. "All the guests had arrived, everything was prepared, and no rabbi."

In his frustration, he muttered half-seriously: "This is the last time I'm getting married."

But the rabbi finally arrived and, as Rabin lovingly gazed at his bride, he seemed to calm down and the guests were certain that it would indeed be the last time. Leah wore a white dress, white sandals, and white stockings that she put on only for the benefit of the rabbi. She had bought Greek sandals with crossover thongs halfway up to the knee, but her Aunt Nettie insisted that the rabbi wouldn't conduct the marriage if she didn't wear stockings.

The rabbi, however, did not even glance at Leah's white-clad legs as he performed the ceremony with the required warmth and passion. Once the bond was sealed, Rabin felt almost as relieved as he did after winning a battle. However, just when the price of victory was farthest from his mind, he was called back to the battlefield. The newlyweds had moved in with Leah's parents and were about to leave on a honeymoon when the unsentimental High Command asked the groom to help plan a strategy for breaking the Egyptian line and liberating the Negev.

When the second truce ended, the Jews, Ben-Gurion decided, must seize almost all of Arab-held Palestine. Where would they strike first? Ben-Gurion stood for hours by his wall map, and his roving finger always came to rest on Jerusalem.

The Israelis, he told the High Command, must attack the whole West Bank from the Judean hills in the north to the heights south of the Holy City.

This military decision clashed with his political goal, which was to let King Abdullah absorb this area, but he apparently felt that he could eventually trade territory for peace. And on September 26, he presented the plan to his cabinet, expecting a quick "amen." It didn't come.

Take over the West Bank, the "Arab state"? What would the United Nations say—especially after the Stern Gang assassinated UN mediator Count Folke Bernadotte for proposing that the Negev be given to the Arabs under the projected partition plan? The UN might even send troops to stop Israel. And Ben-Gurion lost by a single vote. He was dismayed. His own cabinet? His own party? They were cowards. He went home and with a tremulous hand raged in his diary:

"The plan has been dropped. Fortunately for us, most of the offensives we've launched this year were not put to the vote of that lot!"

Yadin, with the support of Allon and Rabin, now called for a drive against the Egyptians, arguing that "Egypt . . . is our principal enemy" since it "controls the Negev." At Negev headquarters, the prime minister listened to them describe the battle plan that Rabin had helped to draw up. Once the Egyptians were crushed, those entrenched in the Hebron hills would flee, clearing the way for an all-out assault on the West Bank.

Ben-Gurion's eyes gleamed. He would have the Negev and the West Bank, too! That night, he wrote in his diary: "We have just made the gravest decision since the proclamation of the state."

Rabin was delighted by this decision, but his jubilation was soon curdled with depressing news. On September 14, Ben-Gurion summoned him and other leaders of the Palmach to a meeting and showered "praise upon the Palmach for the outstanding role it had played in the country's defense and for its unique values, which deserved to be adopted throughout the IDF."

Rabin could hardly believe what he heard. Ben-Gurion praising the Palmach, which he had always criticized as an unprofessional political tool of the Mapam Party? Then—a "but . . ."

"What a painful 'but' that was for us," he would say. "The existence of a separate Palmach command had lost its relevance."

The Palmach would no longer be a separate force, but would be integrated into a unified army. It would thus be directly controlled by the area commanders and the general staff. Either accept this order, Ben-Gurion warned, or risk destruction of the state.

Rabin remained silent. He felt "somewhat ambivalent" about the order. He realized there was no place for a separate command— "Yet the state's leadership, and the IDF command, were now dominated by men who had a vested interest in diminishing the stature and contribution of the Palmach." If Ben-Gurion really intended to preserve the Palmach's values, why not maintain the command and charge it with some special task? In a sense, this decision desecrated the dream of his socialist-Zionist parents, his teachers, his classmates. Would he be fighting now only for geography?

Mapam yelped and threatened to form an underground inside the army.

Ben-Gurion cried back: Mapam was "a danger to the integrity of the state."

With the army on the verge of disintegration, the Palmach command, though seething with bitterness, dissolved itself. Allon was no longer Palmach commander but simply commander of the southern front, with Rabin still his deputy.

Ben-Gurion was joyous. The armed forces of Israel were unified at last—under him.

The prime minister now sat down with his commanders to prepare for the coming campaign. All the Israelis needed was a pretext to attack and break the UN-sponsored truce. And they soon had one: The Egyptians violated the truce agreement by refusing to let Israeli trucks drive through the lines to supply the besieged settlements. So, on October 15, the Israelis decided to send a supply convoy through as a deliberate act of provocation, hoping that the Egyptians wouldn't let this one through.

"As the convoy covered every additional mile unmolested," Rabin would say, "our nerves were stretched to the breaking point. The excuse for our attack was slipping out of our grasp. In the end, with the aid of a random shot here, another there, we had our pretext."

The Israeli army rumbled across the dusty red earth of the Negev to detonate Operation Yoav, or Ten Plagues, a reference to the horrors that God had inflicted on the ancient Egyptians—and to those the Israelis hoped to inflict on their descendants. His spirited troops smashed open the road to the Negev and, in a surprise attack, even seized Beersheba.

On October 22, after stalling the United Nations for a week, Ben-Gurion had to give the cease-fire order to his commanders. He had largely won the race against time. The Egyptians still held part of the Negev, but, he felt confident, not for long.

In a pocket of one area controlled by the Israelis, Egyptian soldiers, comprising about one-fourth of the Egyptian force in Palestine, refused to surrender even though they were surrounded by Israeli forces. The men trapped in the Faluja pocket, southeast of the port of Ashdod, ignored an ominous warning on a leaflet dropped from an Israeli plane:

> If you just looked at the map you would see that the Israelis surround you as a bracelet does a wrist. You have to choose: if you prefer life, you must yield and surrender. . . . Your leaders . . . expect medals and rewards and never think of hundreds and thousands of their soldiers dying. They get medals and you death. . . . Everyone that comes with this leaflet in hand will get security and we promise him a safe return home. . . . Keep in mind that this is an ultimatum.

Major Abdul Gamal Nasser was enraged as he read one of the leaflets—partly because he felt the Jews had correctly estimated the Egyptian leaders, partly because he was sure they vastly underestimated the tenacity of the Egyptian fighters. The Egyptian soldier, he conceded, might not be sufficiently aggressive in attack, lacking proper military training, confidence in his weapons, education, and, because of primitive social conditions in Egypt, a personal stake in victory. But he could be very stubborn in defense—if his leaders supported him—fighting as if for his own home.

As the leaflets with their pleas and threats continued to float down, however, Nasser and his fellows began to enjoy them, even waiting for them as they might for the evening newspaper—though they were never sure when bombs might fall instead. For fighting in the Negev continued despite the "truce" ending Operation Ten Plagues, each side still trying to improve its positions.

"How can I surrender when I still have ammunition, equipment, and soldiers?" Colonel Sayed Taha, the commander of the pocket, asked his officers with a smile, referring to the leaflets.

A stocky man with a black face and a gentle manner, Taha was a tough, courageous soldier, like most of the fighters of Sudanese descent in the Egyptian army. But as the Israelis tightened the bracelet around Faluja and he found himself cut off from reinforcements, he wondered how long he could hold out.

So did Rabin and Allon as they contemplated the situation in their desert hut headquarters. Allon called for his aide Yeroham Cohen, a short, swarthy man.

"The messages we've intercepted," he told Cohen, "indicate their commander might want to negotiate. Have you found the right man to go to them yet?"

"Yes, Yigal."

"Who is it?"

"Me," Cohen replied with a smile.

Allon quietly conferred with Rabin. Yeroham was certainly qualified, and there was no man they trusted more. A Yemenite Jew, Cohen had served in Orde Wingate's "night squads" in the late 1930s, in the Allied intelligence service disguised as an Arab during World War II, and as the Palmach's chief intelligence officer after the war. Perhaps it wasn't right to protect Yeroham's life more than they might some other man's.

"All right, you win," Allon said, trying to withhold a smile. "Go to see them tomorrow. We'll cease firing at eight in the morning. Maybe they'll be in the mood to talk business."

About 10 A.M. the next morning, November 10, Major Nasser was in his headquarters when a sergeant burst in and cried:

"Sir, an enemy armored car with a white flag is waiting outside our lines. The loudspeaker is saying 'An Israeli officer wants to meet an Egyptian officer.'"

Nasser dashed outside and heard the call repeated in Arabic and English. What had he to lose? Maybe he could learn something of Israeli intentions. Cohen soon realized that he was up against a stone wall of Arab pride. He would have to chip away at it.

"You people fought very well," Cohen observed, "but that is the luck of war."

And shortly, Nasser, warming up to his guest, arranged for Colonel Taha to meet with Allon and Rabin. When Cohen returned to his camp, he reported to the two commanders.

"Yigal," he told Allon, "come with Yitzhak to Kibbutz Gat at three-thirty this afternoon."

"Why?"

"They're coming."

"Who's coming?"

"The Egyptian commander and other officers."

"Are you crazy?"

"Come and find out for yourself."

"Then they must be crazy, risking a trap like that!"

In a few hours, Cohen greeted the Egyptians as their three jeeps, each with a white flag, halted at the kibbutz and introduced them to Rabin, who was waiting for them outside the building where they would talk. It was a moment Rabin would not forget. He had apparently never met with an Arab before, certainly not with an Arab leader. He knew them only from a distance; in his childhood, it was the distance that a stone could be thrown. And later, in the military, he had come into contact with them only on the battlefield. Thus, while he wished for conciliation and genuine peace, he still found it hard imagining Arabs who did not throw stones, wield a knife, or fire a gun. They simply wanted to kill all the Jews.

Now, here saluting him was an Arab colonel and his officers.

Would they listen to reason? Somehow, it seemed, this meeting, though only a tiny fragment of the war, could hint at the shape of Israel's future place in the Middle East.

Entering the conference room, the visitors found Allon at the head of the table, which was adorned with a vase of flowers. After being introduced by Cohen as "General Yeshaya Bergstein," in line with Israel's policy of keeping the names of commanders secret, Allon opened the meeting, with Cohen interpreting his Hebrew into English.

"Colonel," he said, "allow me to extend to you my compliments on your soldiers' courage."

Taha: Thank you, sir, and I must say that the tenacity of your forces astonished me and put me in a very difficult position.

Allon: Is it not tragic for two sides, who actually have no reason to fight, to set upon each other mercilessly?

Taha: A real tragedy, but that is the way of the world. Fate is fate, and there is no avoiding it.

Allon: You must understand, Colonel, that the situation at the
front has been settled. Your brigade is now besieged on all
sides, and has no hope of breaking out. . . . What purpose
would be served by your desperate stand?

Taha was silent for a moment, then replied: "Yes, sir, I see. But
as long as I have soldiers and ammunition there is no reason why I
should stop fighting."

Rabin listened raptly as the two men exchanged comments in
a more civil way than many officers he knew did in internal Israeli
disputes. Would he not have given the same answer if he had been
in Taha's predicament? And Allon put into words what he was
thinking:

"I greatly admire your courage, Colonel, but do you not agree
that the lives of men are precious, and that there is no logic in sacri-
ficing your men fighting a nation that does not consider itself your
enemy, and which has only good intentions toward you? I am not
advising you to surrender dishonorably, but with full respect and
military honor, with the possibility of an immediate return home.
Think about it. Let us save the blood of our soldiers and cease fighting. I cannot cease firing as long as foreign armies are on our soil. But
you do not fight on your soil. Try to understand that I am right."

A tense silence gripped the gathering as Taha hesitated. Rabin
and the other Israelis looked at him expectantly, seeing in his dark
eyes the torment of a man torn between logic and pride. Nasser
and the other Egyptians watched him anxiously, wondering why
he hesitated when only one reply was possible. Finally, Taha gave
it. In a quiet voice charged with suppressed emotion, he said, staring directly at Allon:

"Sir, there is no doubt that your position is much better than
mine. The planning of your operation and the performance of
your soldiers have been admirable. You have broken through our
strongest lines, and you have put to shame the Egyptian army,
which had never before tasted defeat. I do not flatter myself by
thinking that I can possibly change the existing situation to our
advantage. But there is one thing that I can save—the honor of the
Egyptian army. And that is why I shall fight until the last bullet
and the last soldier, unless I receive different orders from my government."

There was another brief silence, and Rabin and the other Israelis looked as moved as the Egyptians. Allon then urged with a smile:

"May I ask you to give your government and your commanders a description of the real situation and to request their consent to your surrender?"

"I will send a full report to them."

With the tension eased, Allon said: "Gentlemen, help yourselves to refreshments."

After nibbling on cookies and sandwiches, the Egyptians climbed into their jeeps, saluted, and sped off. Like the other Israelis, Rabin was exhilarated by a feeling of deep respect, even affection, for the Faluja leaders. And like them, he suddenly felt depressed. For it was still his duty to try and kill them. Even so, the real peace that had seemed almost impossible now appeared a little less so.

And Taha shared Rabin's sentiments. As his jeep drove off, he told Nasser, who would be running Egypt in a few years:

"Gamal, we were guests at that settlement. Let's not shell it anymore."

9

The Final Thrust

The second truce came to an explosive end. There was no bomb thrown, but the UN Security Council passed a resolution that shook both the Israelis and the Egyptians: Both sides would have to return to the boundaries they shared before the last Israeli offensive.

Not an inch back! Ben-Gurion exclaimed.

Ralph Bunche, the thoughtful black American who had replaced Count Bernadotte as UN mediator after his assassination, suggested a compromise. Mobile Israeli troops would evacuate the Negev, but those in the settlements could stay. Most of the Negev would still be in Jewish hands.

Ben-Gurion agreed.

Now, with the United Nations pacified, it was time for a new Israeli thrust, one that would finally win the whole Negev. But since the operation would put the Israelis on King Abdullah's border, Ben-Gurion feared that the Arab Legion might try to block the way. Better to make peace with the king, who now had what he wanted. On December 1, Abdullah had fused Transjordan with the

West Bank, which was to have been the heart of the new Palestinian Arab state, to form the Kingdom of Jordan—as the Israelis had suggested before the war. Moshe Dayan, the new commander of Jewish Jerusalem, approached his Arab counterpart in the Old City and shortly was sipping Turkish coffee with Abdullah in his palace.

The upshot was that the king did not protest when the Israelis, on December 22, hit the Egyptians in a new offensive, Operation Horev. After all, Egypt's King Farouk had backed the mufti and condemned Abdullah's seizure of Arab Palestine.

And so by the end of the month, Allon's troops had not only swallowed up almost the entire Negev, but were grinding over the trackless Egyptian Sinai Peninsula toward El Arish on the Mediterranean coast, threatening to encircle the Gaza Strip and the remnants of the Egyptian army.

Ben-Gurion was aghast. Allon had no orders to advance that far! America would never stand for an invasion of Egyptian-held territory. And the British might even attack.

Rabin had made the swift advance possible by exploring an ancient Roman road that led from Beersheba to El Auja in the central Negev, and determining that trucks and tanks could use it despite the craggy surface. After bursting into El Auja, the Israeli convoy ground toward Abu Ageila farther south and, on capturing it, barreled across the sands of the Sinai desert toward El Arish on December 29. Two hours later, when they had seized deserted El Arish airport, about twelve miles from the town, a jeep raced up from the rear and a soldier jumped out with a message for Allon. Yeroham Cohen took it and handed it to Allon, who was sitting with Rabin in their jeep on the side of the road. Allon smiled as he put the cable down and reported:

"GHQ says they've heard from the Egyptian radio and our pilots that we're heading for El Arish. . . . Send back a message, Yeroham. This is not an operation. We're simply chasing the enemy in self-defense. They won't stop firing at us!"

Rabin, too, managed to smile. Three days earlier, he had driven to Tel Aviv, he would later relate, "to obtain Yigael Yadin's approval [for the thrust toward El Arish]. Yadin heard me out and gave his consent, but I had neglected to specify our entire plan and confined myself to the capture of Abu Ageila [a village just inside

Egypt on the way to El Arish]. I had reason to believe that if I were to reveal the whole plan, including the capture of El Arish, the general staff might suspect we had gone mad."

Now, the convoy, in all its madness, continued to advance in the face of sporadic fire, including strafings by Israeli planes, which believed that any convoy racing through the Sinai must be Egyptian. When Rabin saw a soldier firing back at one of these planes, he asked the man:

"Can't you see that they're ours?"

"Sure I can see," the soldier replied. "Our planes are a hundred times more dangerous!"

When the convoy had advanced to within about three miles of El Arish, Egyptian planes began to strafe, and the Israelis were ordered to halt.

A few minutes earlier, a jeep coming from the rear had roared to a stop and, as before, a soldier ran to deliver a message to Cohen for Allon, who, with Rabin, had been watching the action from a sand dune off the road. The tight flesh on Allon's youthful face quivered slightly as he read and reread the message, which was from Yadin:

"1. I have been informed that our units are moving toward El Arish.

"2. You are hereby ordered to halt any movement without my previous consent."

Allon consulted with Rabin, then ordered Cohen:

"Yeroham, call for a Piper Cub . . . I'm flying to Tel Aviv tonight to see Ben-Gurion."

Rabin doubted that Allon would succeed in his mission. Ben-Gurion wasn't satisfied with dissolving the Palmach; he couldn't bear seeing its fighters win any glory. But how could he order a retreat when the whole Egyptian army was about to collapse in Israel's arms?

Allon failed to see Ben-Gurion, who was in Tiberias, but the prime minister told him through a cabinet member that he would not change his mind. Allon returned to his Negev base and reluctantly ordered his troops to retreat, but he would not give up. He was back in Tel Aviv to greet Ben-Gurion when the prime minister returned from Tiberias on January 2, 1949.

"All of our troops are out of Egypt," Allon reported, "but I implore you once more to let us go back and attack El Arish."

"Offer any alternative plan you want," Ben-Gurion replied, "but I promised the Americans we would withdraw from Egypt by today and the stakes are too high to go back on that promise."

Finally realizing that an attack on El Arish was precluded, Allon offered an alternative plan. Why not attack down the road to Rafa? True, it ran mainly in Egyptian territory, and Rafa itself was located there, but it was closer to the Israeli border than El Arish. He could thus still bottle up the Egyptian army.

There was a glimmer of interest in Ben-Gurion's eyes. Struggling to decide, the prime minister stared at Allon, unable to suppress his admiration for this steel-willed young man, however politically innocent; this magnificent product of Zionism, strong, dedicated, confident—and uncomfortably persuasive.

"Very well, Yigal," he said in a quiet voice. "When do you think you can start the attack? The Security Council may order a truce at any moment."

"By tomorrow night," Allon replied when he had recovered from shock.

The next night, Israeli tanks streamed toward Egypt, and after bitter fighting, Allon's men captured the last of six hills before Rafa.

"Now the armored brigade has only to roll into Rafa," a battalion commander rejoiced.

But then a sandstorm howled through the desert and the men could see only seventy or eighty yards in front of them. Although the untimely phenomenon worried the commanders, they were cheered when, in the early morning, they heard the roar of an armored column that was grinding toward them.

"The Eighth Armored [Brigade]—they're coming!" an officer shouted gleefully as dozens of men left their positions and raced to greet the tanks, cheering and waving blindly in the thick sweep of dust.

Meanwhile, at the height of the storm, Rabin heard the hum of aircraft engines and thought he saw a mirage in the sky.

"To my astonishment," he would recall, "I saw parachutes opening as a number of unidentified airmen drifted down to earth."

Who were they? The British? Were they attacking his troops?

To find out, he jumped into his jeep and drove toward the para-chutists. He chilled when he realized they were indeed British. Perhaps Ben-Gurion's fear had been justified after all. But, to his relief, he found they were not attacking.

"I drove toward what turned into a bizarre encounter with a British air force officer whose expression betrayed a mixture of fury and astonishment at the behavior of the Jewish 'natives.'"

Israeli aircraft had shot down five British planes in a dogfight, while no Israeli aircraft were hit.

"What a humiliation!" Rabin would gloat. "I picked up the pilots one by one and drove them to the safety of one of our kib-butzim, lending a sympathetic—and somewhat amused—ear to explanations that ranged from apology to complaint."

But however proud Rabin was of the incredible Israeli feat, his joy was short-lived. For as his men rushed in delight along the road adjacent to the hill toward the tanks emerging ghostlike through the wispy sand clouds, a voice cried from the peak:

"Oh, no! It can't be!"

"But it is!" someone else groaned in dismay. "Those are enemy tanks!"

At that moment, the tanks opened fire on the surprised Israelis, and they withdrew in disorder from the hill. Hardly had a counter-attack failed when Allon, in his headquarters, received a message from Yadin:

"All signs are this might be last night of fighting stop I'll inform you later final decision stop take this into consideration."

Allon showed the message to Rabin and they looked out the win-dow at the raging brown blizzard that swept the desert like a biblical curse. Too late now, anyway, with another truce about to be called. It seemed almost hilarious in a way. Tel Aviv pressing them to attack.

"If El Arish had fallen into our hands," Rabin would lament, "the Egyptian army in the Gaza Strip would have been cut off; the major part of the Sinai would have been ours; and the subsequent military history of Israel would have taken a different course. . . . As it was, we attempted to cut off the Egyptian contingents in the Gaza Strip by taking the crossroads south of Rafa. But another—and final—cease-fire came into effect and the Gaza Strip remained in Egyptian hands."

Prime Minister Ben-Gurion struggled to reach one of the most important decisions of his life. Which way should he go? The Egyptians agreed to sit down with the Israelis at an armistice conference, but only if Israeli troops withdrew from the Rafa area. However, Allon and Rabin, while failing to take the city, had captured most of the heights around it and were close to cutting off the Egyptian army. Were they right in keeping the Egyptians penned up and under constant attack—at the risk of British intervention? Or should he, Ben-Gurion, gamble that the Egyptians would agree to a reasonable peace and make it worthwhile for his troops to withdraw after all the sacrifice in blood? A true leader had to know how far to push his adversaries and when to fire the last shot. The question was: Had he pushed them far enough?

Late into the night, Ben-Gurion pondered over his reports and gradually the crucial decision crystallized in his mind. And Allon and Rabin could not change it.

On the morning of January 9, Yeroham Cohen handed Allon a radio message.

"Yigal," he said, "a cable from Yadin. You won't like it."

Allon raged inwardly as he read:

ALL OUR FORCES SHOULD BE EVACUATED FROM BEYOND THE BORDER INCLUDING THE POSITION ON THE AUJA-AGELLA ROAD STOP COMPLETE EVACUATION BY MONDAY, JANUARY 10 STOP CARRY OUT WITHOUT RESERVATION STOP A MESSENGER HAS BEEN SENT TO YOU WITH A LETTER STOP START EVACUATION IMMEDIATELY.

Allon conferred with Rabin, who was equally incensed.

"We've got to answer right away," Cohen said.

He would answer, all right, Allon fumed. And, pacing the floor, he dictated to Cohen:

I CONFIRM RECEIPT OF ORDER TO EVACUATE POSITIONS BEYOND BORDER STOP SHALL EXECUTE ACCORDINGLY STOP I AM SHOCKED BY THIS ORDER AS WE ARE LOSING ONE OF OUR TACTICAL ADVANTAGES AGAINST THE ENEMY STOP THIS SECOND TIME IN THIS OPERATION THAT WE ARE LETTING OPPORTUNITY GO BY AND LOSING DEFINITE POSSIBILITY OF INFLICTING FINAL DEFEAT ON EGYPTIAN ENEMY.

Rabin agreed with the harsh tone of the cable and with Allon's decision to see Ben-Gurion again. They could not let the prime minister fritter away Israel's future.

"Yigal Allon?" Ben-Gurion barked to an aide. "I knew he'd be coming. Did you see this cable he sent?"

Allon entered the prime minister's office and saluted with a cold formality foreign to his character.

Ben-Gurion walked over to him with a smile, embraced him, and said: "Yigal, when will you learn to be a good soldier?"

"Am I not? I'm doing my best."

"Yes, you're good when you're advancing, but bad in retreat. You must obey orders. . . . Don't you understand the importance of the first official conference with an Arab country? . . . Yigal, I will present you Gaza on a silver platter. . . . You're a brilliant commander, maybe the greatest in this war, but you are not yet a mature politician."

"Maybe that is to my advantage."

Ben-Gurion rose, strode over to Allon and, laying a hand on his shoulder, said like a father admonishing his child: "Commanders must obey orders even if they don't like them."

Allon knew then that, once more, Ben-Gurion would not change his mind. He walked to the door and left. With heavy heart he returned to his headquarters in Beersheba and ordered a withdrawal from the Rafa area.

"There is no room for any appeal or delay in carrying out the order, however harsh it may be," read the radio message to Rabin for dissemination to his commanders.

Rabin was equally heartsick. After all the sacrifice . . . Yet he could understand and even sympathize with Ben-Gurion's view.

"Egypt had declared its willingness to conduct separate armistice negotiations even before the operation," he would say. "Now, however, we enjoyed undisputed military superiority. The Faluja pocket had not been eliminated, but that only gave Israel a further advantage because its existence irked Egypt's military and political leaders more than anything else. Their eagerness to avoid a further setback and to rescue the trapped force spurred the Egyptians toward the negotiating table."

In other words, Israel's military strength may have convinced the Arabs that peace would be to their advantage—a thought that would underlie Rabin's future peace philosophy. But the Israelis must be tough at the peace table and keep what it could. At least enough to assure its future security, its victory in any new war.

To his surprise, Rabin himself would have the opportunity to press for this kind of peace. For on January 7, Egypt agreed to attend armistice talks on the Greek island of Rhodes, and Rabin would be one of Israel's representatives. Not that he wanted to be. He was a soldier, not a diplomat. He was trained to give and take orders, not to argue and negotiate, having neither the patience nor the temperament for that.

Nor the wardrobe. He had never worn a suit in his life, and certainly not a ceremonial uniform. Yet he had to wear one at the conference, even though he viewed it as a "dreadful nuisance." Finally, he was given a used American World War II uniform that had been purchased at a Tel Aviv secondhand clothing store and used at other diplomatic meetings. If the sleeves were a bit short, so was his temper when Allon had informed him of his new assignment.

Why him? he wondered. What did he know about diplomacy? Allon, on the other hand, had displayed his diplomatic talent at the meeting with General Taha.

But though the High Command had, in fact, asked Allon to attend, he refused, still sizzling with fury at Ben-Gurion's order for a retreat from the Sinai. He should be advancing, not retreating. If he wouldn't go, the High Command had replied, then he would have to send someone else, and Rabin knew more about the military situation on the southern front than anyone except Allon himself.

"See to it," Allon told his deputy, "that no agreement is reached which is less than peace. And don't agree to anything which gives us less than Gaza."

What Allon couldn't get from Ben-Gurion, he could perhaps get from the Egyptians themselves. But he would not give up on Ben-Gurion. If the Old Man feared to attack in Gaza because the British might intervene, perhaps he would agree to an attack elsewhere. Allon thus sent a new message to Ben-Gurion: Before the war ended, let him take over the West Bank. After all, the prime minister himself had wanted to do this earlier in the war. And the British wouldn't intervene; his men had intercepted a British message to Abdullah saying that he should not expect their help unless the Israelis attacked Jordan itself.

But Ben-Gurion now rejected the idea. Circumstances had

changed, and just as peace with Egypt was more important than Sinai territory, peace with Jordan was more important than West Bank territory. Indeed, the closer he came to peace, the less ambitious he became. He wanted to sign armistice agreements with the bordering Arab states, but not to rule over Arab-inhabited land. So he wouldn't win everything—nor was he in a hurry to.

"I do not know any generation in Jewish history," he would write, "that completed its task." And he quoted from the Book of Joshua, Chapter 13: "Now Joshua was old and stricken in years; and the Lord said unto him, 'Thou art old and stricken in years, and there remaineth yet very much land to be possessed.'"

Biblical philosophy, however, could not console Yigal Allon— or Yitzhak Rabin. He wanted precisely what Allon wanted: real peace and real security. Rabin wasn't brought up to regard territory as sacred, whatever God may have told Joshua. But Israel must insist on having what was necessary to guarantee its security. And now it was necessary to take over Gaza—at least until the Egyptians proved they were serious about peace.

But while he may have been good at fighting them, would he be good at haggling with them?

On January 13, 1949, on the lovely Greek island of Rhodes, armistice talks with Egypt began in the Hotel des Roses within view of majestic Greek ruins and whitewashed huts that graced green hillsides alive with peasants riding their donkeys. Rabin was overwhelmed by this first trip outside Israel.

"My first challenge," Rabin would recall, "was getting used to a complete change of environment: peace, and quiet, and the fantastic comfort of the hotel.... I was immediately impelled to inquire, 'what's the Greek word for "more?"' 'Encore,' I was told. So, seated in the dining room, I repeatedly uttered, 'Encore,' and the kitchen disgorged a series of thick steaks."

Remembering the encounter with Colonel Taha, Rabin wondered if the Egyptian representatives at the conference would be as warm and friendly. At first, they were not. In fact, when an Egyptian encountered an Israeli in the corridor, he eyed him contemptuously and then looked away, though sometimes, unable to quell his curiosity, glancing back.

When the Egyptians initially refused to meet with the Israelis at all, Ralph Bunche, the UN mediator, told them brusquely but diplomatically: "It was my understanding that we had come here to negotiate, and to do this, gentlemen, one side must talk to the other."

Finally, the Egyptians agreed to a meeting in Bunche's sitting room, with the mediator himself presiding from the sofa and the two delegations grouped on either side of him. Egyptian efforts to address all their remarks to Bunche, as if the Israelis were not present, soon broke down, and the two contending parties began arguing with each other in English and French. Argument led to understanding, at least on the personal level, and eventually to friendliness as the days stretched into weeks.

Rabin and other members of the two delegations even competed in billiard contests, complete with cheering sections. And when Abdul Moheim Mustafa, the chief Egyptian political adviser, fell ill, Israeli delegates sat at his bedside and comforted him.

Rabin's most immediate problem was not convincing his newfound Egyptian friends that they should leave Gaza to Israel. It was learning how to wear a necktie. Before coming to Rhodes, he had never worn one, and he didn't take one with him. When Walter Eytan, Israel's chief delegate, told his colleagues that they must wear ties for dinner and on visits to the governor-general's palace, Rabin alone bridled.

"I have no tie," he said.

"All right, Yitzhak," Eytan replied, "I'll lend you one of mine."

His cheeks turning red with embarrassment, Rabin mumbled: "But I don't know how to tie it."

"Don't worry," Eytan said consolingly, as if to a child, "a secretary can do it."

Rabin reluctantly agreed, but when a girl started to put the tie around his neck, he panicked and struggled to get away.

"We had to hold him while the tie was being tied," Eytan told me. "But this unsophisticated young man finally came to dinner looking like a gentleman."

Rabin could take apart almost any gadget and put it together again, but he somehow couldn't master the technique of knotting a tie even after taking lessons from his driver.

"One day," he would later report, "I walked into the hotel barbershop and who should I find sprawled in one of the chairs if not

my friend, [General] Sif el-Din [the chief Egyptian delegate]. The
barber was hostile enough to ask me to remove my tie, so, pulling
at the knot, I yanked it up over my head. As I did so, I could see
the Egyptian officer staring at me in amazement, and I'm sure he
must have been thinking, 'What kind of savages am I dealing with
here?'"

The Egyptians would soon learn what kind when, at one meeting, they demanded that the Israelis return Beersheba to them.

"Otherwise," one Egyptian explained, "the Egyptian public
will think that we permitted you to take it."

Israeli fury was aroused at this logic, and Yadin, a top Israeli
delegate, burst out: "Before we give Beersheba back to you, we'll
give back the sun and the stars!"

As Yadin shouted angrily, he banged on the conference table
and the pencil in his hand flew into the air, hitting Sif el-Din
squarely on the forehead.

There was an appalled silence. The flight of the wayward pencil, it seemed, could put an end to the armistice talks. Then an
Egyptian delegate looked at Yadin and asked:

"Why don't you give us back the moon also?"

The tension broke amid the laughter. But even as Rabin joined
in, he was concerned. He knew that his colleagues were under
great pressure from Ben-Gurion to make the best deal they could.
What if the Egyptians refused to budge? Would his fellow delegates cave in? He had pleaded with them not to, but he wasn't
sure they had listened.

The Egyptians clung to their demand for a concession on
Beersheba and finally argued that the Israelis should at least permit an Egyptian governor to rule in that town.

"But that is absurd," Eytan replied. "Israel controls Beersheba!"

An Egyptian delegate came up with a new idea: "Will you
agree to the appointment of an Egyptian military governor at Bir
Asluj?"

Rabin and the other Israelis were astonished, and somewhat
amused, by this suggestion, since Bir Asluj was little more than a
cluster of mud huts on the road from Beersheba to El Auja and
hardly warranted the presence of a military governor.

"Of course we cannot agree," Eytan said, his usually puckish face now deadly serious. "And it is surprising that you should make this request since such an appointment would simply make Egypt a laughingstock in the eyes of people who know what Bir Asluj is."

The Egyptians then asked for the appointment of an Egyptian military governor in El Auja. The Israelis again refused.

Bunche, feeling that the Egyptian need to save face was genuine, however awkward, then suggested: "Well, perhaps both sides would agree simply not to keep troops in El Auja, which would then become a demilitarized area."

Rabin and his colleagues protested but finally agreed to this compromise. When other questions proved even more insurmountable, Bunche, sensing when to be gentle and when firm, used another tactic. He ordered two sets of decorated ceramic plates from a local manufacturer and had inscribed on them, "Rhodes Armistice Talks 1949." Then he called the delegates into his room and opened a chest of drawers.

"Have a look at these lovely plates!" he said, his face alight. "If you reach agreement, each of you will get one to take home. If you don't, I'll break them over your heads!"

Shortly afterward, Israel agreed that the Egyptian brigade locked in the Faluja pocket could depart for Egypt when an armistice was signed, and that it could meanwhile be supplied with food and medicines. With Rabin vigorously dissenting, both sides then agreed that they would hold the areas they occupied at the time of the cease-fire. Egypt would thus retain the coastal area, which was to be known as the Gaza Strip—at least until a more permanent peace arrangement was reached.

On February 24, the two delegations signed an armistice agreement and attended a joyful party in the evening. But conspicuously absent was Yitzhak Rabin, who had refused to sign the accord, arguing heatedly against giving the Gaza area to Egypt. Years later, he would comment:

"Then, at least, I was hardly enraptured by the charms of diplomatic 'give and take.'"

Before leaving for home, he asked his colleagues:

"Why should Egypt get a slice of Palestine? Why are we giving up so meekly after we fought so hard at Rafa?"

How many of his men had died there? Should they be betrayed?

Before giving up territory, he felt, the Arabs had to prove they wanted real peace. Then he would give up land.

But Eytan replied, reflecting Ben-Gurion's decision: "An armistice with Egypt is worth the Gaza area. And besides, this is only a temporary military armistice. When we have full-scale peace talks, then we can press for better boundaries."

Speechless with anger, Rabin shrugged contemptuously and flew home. Curiously, he would later say, "I derived some satisfaction from the fact that our delegation's attitude on demarcation lines was largely influenced by my views and recommendations." Rabin was characteristically reluctant to admit that sometimes people didn't listen to him. He wasn't secure enough for that.

Rabin would at least get a consolation prize before the war ended. Allon, supported by his deputy, pleaded with Ben-Gurion for one last military thrust. Could he take the southern wedge of the Negev leading to Eilat on the Gulf of Aqaba, which still lay out of Israel's reach? At least let them grab this enticing triangle.

Send a patrol, Ben-Gurion agreed. See if the Israeli troops could seize it without a battle that would threaten the truce accord with Egypt and the one that had just been reached with Jordan, perhaps sparking a British assault.

Thus, on March 10, following a plan largely designed by Rabin, not a patrol but two brigades, the Negev and Golani, engaged in a race southward over the sun-baked sands—until the Golani sighted a group of Arab Legionnaires in the distant glare.

Not an inch farther! Tel Aviv ordered.

And Allon's men complied—in a sense. They didn't move an inch farther; they moved, bypassing the opposition, all the way to the sea! (The Negev Brigade won the race by an hour or so.) After planting an Israeli flag in the sand and tearing off their clothes, they dived into the welcoming glassy bay where Solomon's ship had once sailed laden with gold from Ophir. Ben-Gurion exulted, but in silence. Allon and Rabin had disobeyed orders again—and seized the whole Negev!

The war was over and Israel had triumphed. But to Rabin, the victory was bittersweet. The Palmach, which had not been just a military force but a way of life, had been demolished—by his own government. And the Arabs, with their hundreds of thousands of troops, were in a position to strike again at Israel as soon as they could rearm. After all the indescribable suffering, with one out of ten Israelis dead, how could he rest while his people remained in danger of annihilation, without even the Palmach to protect them?

"I had been under arms for six years," Rabin would muse, "and along the way, without making a conscious decision about the matter, had become a commander in the Israel Defense Forces. But since all endings are simultaneously beginnings of something else, I could no longer allow myself to be swept along by events. For the first time since leaving the Kadouri school, I had to make a choice about my future."

10

Struggle
to the Top

"**S**tanding now at a crossroads in my personal life," Rabin would assert after the War of Independence, "I felt a profound sense of moral responsibility, a kind of debt of honor toward the men whose courage and whose very bodies had blocked the Arab advance. It was to these soldiers that I swore an oath of loyalty."

Rabin would dedicate his life to "ensuring that the State of Israel would never again be unprepared to meet aggression." Security thus became an obsession. And it was fed not only by a sense of loyalty to those who died, but, apparently, by a sense of guilt for causing their deaths. How many of his boys had he sent into unwinnable battles, however necessary they might have been? How many of them might be alive now if he had issued different commands? The horrors of that war must never be repeated. Security must be achieved through peace, not war, if at all possible. And the only rational way to preserve peace was to build a mighty army, an invincible army that no enemy would dare challenge. He would remain a military man, but now precisely in order to keep the peace.

Rabin thus made a grave decision, for it meant abandoning his dream of studying irrigation engineering. But it was a timely decision; even after Egypt, then Lebanon, Jordan, and Syria signed armistice accords, they refused to move toward real peace, blockading the country economically, isolating it diplomatically, even fomenting terrorism. Israel would need a strong army.

However eager to serve, Rabin didn't find life in the postwar IDF easy, especially as a former leader of the Palmach. In June 1949, the Palmach brigades went the way of the Palmach command months earlier. Many Palmachniks soon left the army because of the bias against them, with almost every command given to British army veterans. Ben-Gurion was adamant. Those trained in the Palmach were good guerrilla fighters, he conceded, but they were undisciplined and knew little about fighting in a regular army. Besides, he was still worried that the Mapam Party might use them to serve as its own army.

Ben-Gurion reserved much of his enmity for Yigal Allon. Yes, he was a great field commander. But he couldn't take orders. He saw, in the prime minister's view, only the immediate military situation and could not see the political ramifications of military action. Besides, he was a very popular leader—too popular. So, despite Allon's formidable accomplishments, he mustn't play a role in Israel's new defense force. And he didn't. When the French army invited Allon to visit France, Ben-Gurion took advantage of his absence by replacing him with Moshe Dayan in the southern command post and appointing Yigael Yadin chief of staff; he had been acting chief of staff during Ya'akov Dori's sick leave.

Left without a job and incensed at what he regarded as a deliberate slap in the face, Allon resigned from the army and remained in Europe.

Ben-Gurion's next target, some thought, was Rabin. Other Palmach officers had decided to hold a large rally of Palmachniks as a kind of farewell party, since they were either leaving the army or had been assigned to non-Palmach units. But Ben-Gurion saw in this projected rally a threat to army discipline. Chief of Staff Dori, before leaving office, thus issued a stern order:

Anyone still serving in uniform was forbidden to attend the rally.

Rabin struggled with his dilemma. On the one hand, an officer did not disobey a direct order. On the other, he felt an obligation to his comrades-in-arms and a deep personal need to attend the rally. Yes, he was obligated to his men, but what if he attended and then was punished and lost whatever influence he might exert in the creation of a strong army? Would he be violating his vow to the men who had died? He left the question to his conscience, and decided he couldn't let his comrades down. He would attend. Certainly he would be punished, but somehow he would blot out the stain on his record.

Ben-Gurion apparently learned of Rabin's decision and, shortly before the rally, asked Dori to summon him to his home.

When Rabin arrived, he found the prime minister in a friendly, expansive mood. He asked his visitor a few questions about some shooting incidents that had taken place in the south and asked his opinion of various senior officers. Meanwhile, Rabin kept glancing at his watch, noting that it was almost time for the rally. Finally, he said:

"Ben-Gurion, may I ask you a question, openly and frankly?"

"Of course."

"Why did the chief of staff—certainly with your knowledge, if not on your instructions—forbid attendance at the Palmach rally? Why should those of us who remained in the army be placed in the embarrassing position of having to choose between our duty to maintain discipline and our duty to comrades-in-arms with whom we have come such a long way?"

There was a long, tense silence, broken only when Ben-Gurion asked: "Would you join me for dinner?"

Rabin was startled. Ben-Gurion normally did not invite his commanders, especially Palmach commanders, to dinner. He was clearly trying to keep Rabin there until the rally was over. Glancing at his watch once more, Rabin stood up, thanked his host, and strode out the door. He rushed home, changed into civilian clothes to soften his defiance of the government, and left with Leah for the rally. His tardiness was not greatly appreciated.

"The glances flung in my direction," he would recall, "indicated what would have happened had Ben-Gurion succeeded in tempting me to join him for dinner."

In a further bow to the government, Rabin did not address the meeting. But the next day, having little choice, he nervously marched in a Palmach parade. Ben-Gurion was now furious, and might have banished him from the army if Rabin belonged to an ideological party, projected the threatening charisma of Allon, or did not arouse fond memories of Rosa Cohen. But his fury was perhaps reflected in the ceremony, or lack of it, when, as acting southern commander, Rabin had to transfer the command to Dayan, a close ally of Ben-Gurion. It was a difficult task.

"Everyone was silent and expressionless when [Dayan] arrived," Rabin would recall, "and Dayan may have felt ill at ease in the company of all those Palmach men. I transferred the command without any ceremony, and the feeling that Dayan would prefer to be rid of me as well was strengthened by our first talk. He was cold, reserved, and laconic. Moreover, he was frank.

"'Thank you,' he said, 'I don't need you any longer.'"

Dayan, who had served with the Palmach only in World War II, was the same icy, curt person he had been when he questioned Rabin in machine-gun bursts before enlisting him in the organization. Now, eight years later, Rabin was its highest officer, if one of the few Palmachniks remaining in the IDF. He was in a quandary, especially when he received Dori's answer to a letter he had sent him expressing his resentment at the dissolution of the brigades. Rabin understood the need to put them under a unified command, but why couldn't they remain intact under this command to preserve their esprit de corps?

The army had to be reorganized, Dori wrote, but there was no deliberate campaign to reduce the influence of the Palmach.

"In any case," he added, "you would not have been able to remain in command of a brigade, since you are the first candidate to study abroad."

Clearly, it seemed to Rabin, the army leaders wanted him to quit, especially since he had declined Ben-Gurion's political invitation to dinner. They were trying to force him out as they had done to Allon. Did honor now require him to resign as his mentor had? Perhaps this was an opportune time to fulfill his dream of studying abroad. But then he remembered his vow of loyalty to those who had died under his command. What happened to them must never happen to others in the future. Would it not be more honorable to swallow the humiliation and remain in the army and possibly scratch his way into a position of influence?

As Rabin painfully pondered his future, an unlikely person helped set him on his road to destiny. Chaim Laskov, a British army veteran who had pushed Ben-Gurion to disband the Palmach and now headed the Training Command, approached him with a surprising offer.

Would he like to take over the battalion commanders' course? Laskov asked. In fact, he could "bring in all the Palmach officers. I'll make sure that any of them who are willing to remain in the army will be posted there, either as an instructor or as a participant."

Rabin was stunned. "I could hardly believe my ears," he would exclaim.

Apparently, while opposing separate Palmach units, which could threaten the army's unity, Laskov deeply respected the spirit and ability of the Palmach fighters.

Of course he would accept, Rabin replied. And he was promoted to the rank of full colonel.

But hardly had he taken up his new post when he was summoned to a court-martial for having attended the Palmach rally. He recalled his court-martial during World War II and agonized even more now, as did Leah, the day of the court-martial. She was frantic when her brother-in-law, a high officer, came over looking pale and reported: "They were all thrown out of the army!"

"I froze," Leah would say. "Mother was shocked. She knew how devoted Yitzhak was to the army. . . . And now it was all over, and for what . . . ? We sat all afternoon discussing Yitzhak's future, and the options open to him. I was in early pregnancy with Dahlia, and that of course made the feeling no easier."

But Rabin arrived home in the evening in good spirits. Thrown out? No, he assured Leah, he "got a reprimand from the chief of staff." Dori had simply lectured him on the need for discipline and said that he had committed a "grave misdeed." Didn't Rabin understand that the army had to be reorganized and that it would not embrace any semi-independent elite unit? The Palmach was history, and he should accept that.

Actually, reason had already conquered emotion, and Rabin now did accept that. However strong his loyalty to the Palmach, he realized that a single, unified army had to be built. And he used his position as instructor to lay the foundation for such an army. He institutionalized a new military doctrine, based on the principles of perseverance, improvisation, and resourcefulness, and fused the lessons learned in the Palmach, other Hagana units, and the British army. The Palmach emphasis on speed and surprise, with an out-flanking strategy replacing the Latrun-type head-on attack, was integrated into the conventional large-unit operations run by a general staff. And the officers he taught were to teach these principles to their men. Even the lowest private must feel responsible and accountable and be able to take over command of his unit at any time. Actually, more important than the technical ability of a soldier, Rabin felt, was his spirit, something he had learned in battle.

"Rabin was a tough commander and instructor," recalled General Meir Amit, who was one of his students. "He was remarkably logical and systematic in his thinking. And deadly serious. He would not tolerate any nonsense. When one officer set fire to paper in an ashtray, he suspended him from class. And anyone who talked was also thrown out. He didn't compliment anyone either."

Utterly driven, Rabin had patience only for his plan to achieve security by making war too costly for the enemy. He had little time even to spend at home, though Leah was pregnant and had to care for her mother, who was suffering from cancer and would die in December 1949. He was torn between his family and his job, but how could he not devote himself completely to a cause that could mean life or death for his country? That could mean his own redemption by the ghosts of the fallen?

His dilemma was especially painful, it seems, when he thought of his mother, whose fervent devotion to a cause had so often left him hungry and lonely. He could better understand what drove her now, but also what distressed Leah and would certainly disturb his child while she was growing up with a part-time father. He did his best to reduce Leah's stress, agreeing to all her wishes—even when, feeling the need for exercise, she insisted on walking to the hospital shortly before the birth. He followed along in his car, checking every footstep.

The child, Dahlia, was born in March 1950, and was adored by Rabin, who never lost an opportunity to hold and coddle her—but the opportunities were few, stoking his feeling of guilt.

He was not alone in this feeling.

"I was thrust into the running of a household and cooking,"

Leah would recall. "I very much wanted to ease Father's distress and I thought that if I performed exactly as [Mother] had, he would suffer less from her absence. And so, overnight and with immense determination, I learned to cook." She thus found herself "torn between loyalty and care for Father and loyalty to Yitzhak and his needs. Yitzhak was working hard. His hours at home were few, and I constantly felt guilty that I was not doing enough to look after him."

Rabin, for his part, sought to drown his own sense of guilt in his work, which amounted to creating, in the most basic sense, the powerful army he had vowed to build. He was teaching the best soldiers in Israel how to make war ever less likely and, if war came, how to win it at the least cost. Every time he told a student how to kill a man, he was apparently thinking of how to keep that man alive. For without war, he would not be killed.

Rabin was especially excited when he and Laskov began preparing a brigade commanders' course. He would now teach his students how to apply the new army principles to brigade-size units. During the 1948 war, he himself, as a brigade leader, was not fully knowledgeable about how to use his Palmach training in the deployment of so large a force. Now he would pass on to others what he had personally learned, sometimes at great cost.

But this was not to happen. In late 1950, Yigael Yadin called him in and praised his work. It was so good that Yadin was appointing him to head the general staff's Operations Division.

Rabin was chagrined. The general staff? Operations, current security, mobilizing reserves? But he was a creator, a builder, a teacher, not a general staff man who would take orders from men who did not really understand the principles he had so painstakingly nurtured to fruition. In the Palmach there had been no general staff, and while he had merged Palmach concepts with the bureaucracy of the British army, he was still a Palmachnik at heart and did not covet a personal niche in the bureaucracy.

With Laskov's support, Rabin appealed to Yadin to have the transfer annulled. Yes, the new job could be taken as a promotion, but, he claimed, he could best serve the army by continuing to train its officers. The answer, however, was "no." He must accept the promotion, whether he wanted it or not.

Yitzhak Rabin (1922–1995)

First Lady Leah Rabin

Yitzhak, aged five, with his sister, Rachel; his mother, Rosa; and his father, Nehemiah. Rosa fled from the Soviet Union to Palestine and became the most important female Zionist leader of her era. She had little time to care for her children, and Yitzhak never fully recovered from the neglect he suffered.

Rachel, Rosa, and Yitzhak at age five.

Yitzhak's class in the School for Workers' Children. Yitzhak is in the front row *(third from left)*. In this elite socialist-Zionist school, the students studied mainly farming and took no examinations, learning only what they wished to learn.

Yitzhak in his early teens.

Yitzhak *(standing, third from right)* was a star on his soccer team at Kadouri Agricultural School, where he was also first in his class.

Yitzhak at eighteen, in his last year at Kadouri Agricultural School. After graduating, he joined the Jewish guerrilla force, Palmach, to help the British defend Palestine against the German army.

Rachel, Nehemiah, and Yitzhak at age twenty.

Acting Chief of Staff Yigael Yadin, Southern Commander Yigal Allon,
and Rabin confer during the 1948 War of Independence. Allon was
the greatest commander of the war, and Rabin was his deputy.

Israeli Prime Minister David Ben-Gurion *(to the right of center, with white hair)* visits the troops during the 1948 war. Rabin is behind Ben-Gurion to his right.

Rabin confers during the 1948 war with Egyptian colonel Sayed Taha, commander of an encircled force, at a desert meeting where Allon pleaded in vain with Taha to surrender. Rabin is to Taha's right.

Rabin and Leah shortly after they were married, during the 1948 war. Both were in the Palmach, Israel's elite fighting force.

Rabin holds his firstborn, Dahlia, in 1952.

Rabin shows his affection
for his grandchild Jonathan
in 1977, the year he resigned
from his first premiership.

Chief of Staff Rabin *(right)* walks with Jerusalem liberator
Uzi Narkiss *(left)* and Defense Minister Moshe Dayan
after they conquered Jerusalem in the 1967 Six-Day War.

Shimon Peres, Yigal Allon, and Rabin relax after a political meeting.

Rabin *(center)* visits a unit commanded by Ariel "Arik" Sharon *(left)*.
Rabin opposed Sharon's hard-line military and political
views but remained friendly with him.

Rabin with Golda Meir, whom he succeeded as prime minister when Meir's cabinet was forced to quit after the nearly disastrous Yom Kippur War in 1973.

Rabin visits the Bergen-Belsen concentration camp during his first premiership. He was so moved that he could barely deliver his scheduled speech.

Rabin meets with President Richard Nixon, whom he regarded as a good friend to Israel. Nixon never forgot that Rabin had treated him royally during a visit to Israel after the former vice president had lost the race for governor of California and was being largely ignored by other Israeli leaders.

Rabin grew very close to Henry Kissinger during peace negotiations between Israel and Egypt.

Rabin meets with President Gerald Ford, who considered Rabin unreasonable at first but proved to be a good friend.

Rabin is welcomed to Morocco by King Hassan, who had been
conducting a secret dialogue with Israeli leaders for years. Rabin's adviser
Shimon Sheves is the bearded man to the king's right, and adviser
Eitan Haber *(with white hair)* stands to the right of Rabin.

Rabin removes his shoes as he enters a mosque in Morocco.

Rabin took over his new post as 1950 ended, and within months he helped to improve the combat units and organize the reserves. And he did this while spending much of his time on a nonmilitary operation—the modern-day Ingathering of the Exiles. Thousands of poor, mostly uneducated refugees from Moslem countries were being brought into Israel and deposited in tent cities with their pitiful bundles. And it was Rabin's job to run the camps. Soon he had soldiers serving as teachers and even social workers in a massive effort to absorb these people into modern Israeli society before they succumbed to bitterness and frustration.

At first, Rabin was startled by this new assignment. He was a military man, not a nursemaid for poor refugees. Ben-Gurion's decision to bring to Israel simultaneously all Jews who wished to come—hunched carpet weavers from Iran, swaggering street urchins from Morocco, powerful porters from the Kurdish mountains—defied logic, it seemed. How could Israel afford so enormous a project? asked the economic experts in the cabinet, Eliezer Kaplan, Pinhas Sapir, and Levi Eshkol.

Immigration must be gradual, they said. Israel had been devastated by war and was virtually bankrupt. And it cost $2,500 to transport a Jew there, keep him in a reception camp, build him a home, find him work, and assimilate him into the life of the state. To settle a million people in five years, as Ben-Gurion wanted to do, would cost $2.5 billion. Where would Israel get that kind of money, even with aid from abroad? He must be practical.

What was more practical, snapped Ben-Gurion, than assuring the security of his people? The state needed as many soldiers as possible to face the countless millions of Arabs surrounding it; the Diaspora needed to come home before new Holocausts struck. Was not the Ingathering the very essence of the state?

Go to the Jews in the Diaspora and ask them for the money, Ben-Gurion admonished the skeptics. If they didn't give enough, every family in Israel would have to take in an immigrant family. But they would come! And in one of the most extraordinary epics of migration in history, they did.

It was now Rabin's lot to play a role in this epic.

"Placing the army in charge of the camps may have been unprecedented in military history," he would say, "but it was characteristic of Ben-Gurion, who regarded the army as the 'nation's emissary' for any and every task."

Despite harboring bitter memories of the Palmach reunion episode, the more Rabin dealt with the camps, the more he respected Ben-Gurion for his decision. The Ingathering was indeed the essence of Israel, something worth fighting and dying for. And he soon realized how vital his role was in it. Without the army's help, it was clear, the suffering of the newcomers would have been unbearable.

"During the bitter winter of 1951–52," Rabin would point out, "when heavy rains and snowstorms brought the tents down and heavy flooding threatened to inundate the camps, IDF engineering units were sent into action and other units were called out to repitch the tents. No other agency or body in the country would have been capable of responding to this challenge, and alongside the IDF's other operations, this nonmartial 'battle of the transit camps' will be recorded as one of its most splendid victories."

Meanwhile, in the fall of 1952, Rabin scored a personal victory that he had long been anticipating. He moved with his family into their own home in the new Tel Aviv suburb of Zahala, which became a village for army officers. Leah no longer had to serve as her father's nurse since he had "linked up" with a woman who "loved him dearly and looked after him devotedly until the day he died, ten years later."

"Oh, how we rejoiced on the day we entered our house in Zahala," Leah would recall. "It had three and a half rooms, and was simply furnished, yet to us it was a veritable palace. Finally we were in a home of our own."

Rabin relished gazing out at the freshly planted garden and the tiny trees that would soon shoot skyward. Everything was fresh and green, an appropriate place to start a new life with his wife and baby, if only he could find more time to enjoy them. Perhaps on weekends he might even have time to exchange war stories with his uniformed neighbors, many of them old friends.

Hardly had the family settled into their home when Rabin was offered an opportunity to study at a foreign military school. And in December 1952, with Leah and Dahlia in tow, he was off to England, where he would spend a year attending classes at the

Royal Staff College in Camberley, about thirty miles from London. They moved into a small, pleasant flat and settled down once more.

Rabin had mixed feelings about coming to England. He was thrilled to be visiting Europe, to feel what it was like living in a country with tall buildings, fully stocked stores, magnificent palaces and museums, a unique architecture, and the energy of a great power. But he did not get off to an auspicious start on arriving in London, especially with the smothering welcomes to which he and Leah were submitted.

"I passed all seven stages of hell while going to festive dinners in the homes of the attaché and the ambassador and all sorts of Jews who felt obligated to invite us, and we couldn't refuse."

The real "hell" burned in memories of the bitter days of the British mandate—the pro-Arab attitude, the White Paper, Black Saturday, when Rabin himself had been thrown into jail. Now he was in the homeland of those who had oppressed him and his people. He wrote Rachel:

"Although the kindness of the English can impress one from the outside, it doesn't have much value in my eyes, and therefore I'm not especially impressed."

Rabin was impressed least of all by the commandant of the college. He turned out to be the commander of the battalion that had arrested him! And being an avid duck hunter, the man taunted Rabin with his own recollections of how, as a target of Jewish terrorists, he, the commandant, had been the hunted duck in Palestine.

Nor did Rabin, with his action-accented Palmach training, enjoy many of the courses he had to take, especially those dealing with technical staff work.

"I was charged with working out a transportation timetable for an entire division," he would later recall. "It was boring, and bizarre into the bargain. Since when did the IDF contain any formation as large as a division?"

But he liked analyzing a situation and preparing an operational plan, even though he had to do it according to British military thinking, which he didn't believe could, or should, be applied in a small country like Israel.

Nor were the British greatly impressed by the thinking of the man they had once arrested. After the course, they reported to his superiors that Rabin was suitable as an officer in the quartermaster corps—providing troops with clothes and food!

But though the family lived in a cold apartment that was difficult to heat, especially when the temperature plummeted to zero degrees, Rabin enjoyed life in England when he could forget he was a guest of his former jailkeepers. He could at least, for the first time, spend substantial time with Leah and Dahlia.

"Yitzhak devoted a few hours every day to learning English," Leah would say. "The rest of the time, we simply enjoyed the peace and quiet, the new surroundings and the different life style. We had come from austerity in Israel and threw ourselves upon the apples, chocolate, ice cream, and cheeses. In no time at all we had each put on a few pounds."

They visited southern England during the summer break and London several times to see the shows and shop, and, once, to attend a reception for the queen at Buckingham Palace. And they made friends with many people of different nationalities, including an Iraqi diplomat. A wonderful hiatus from the pressures and austerity of a hectic, insular life back home.

Yet Rabin was delighted when he received word from the new chief of staff, Mordechai Makleff, that on his return to Israel he would be appointed chief of operations in place of Moshe Dayan, who was no friend of Makleff. Rabin would be in a position of real power. Now he could build up his army with little interference from the top. And perhaps he would be at the top when Makleff's term was up.

But shortly he received another message: Dayan had fought back—and won. Makleff had been forced to resign, and Dayan would replace him.

Rabin was crushed. The Palmach reunion episode, it seemed, would forever plague him. Clearly, Ben-Gurion would never appoint him chief of staff. And remembering the way Dayan, Ben-Gurion's protégé, treated him on taking over as southern commander, he was sure Dayan would never appoint him chief of operations or offer him any position that would enable him to shape army policy. Rabin had little incentive now for a swift return to Israel.

"Under the circumstances," he would say, "I requested permission to remain in England for another year in order to study at the London School of Economics."

His successor would have to decide, Makleff wrote back.

Another disappointment. Dayan, Rabin felt, would never agree. But when Dayan shortly visited London, Rabin made the request to him anyway.

"What are your instructions from the chief of staff?" Dayan responded.

"My standing instructions were to return to Israel at the end of my year of study."

"Well, then, return to Israel at the end of your year of study."

Rabin would later caustically comment: "Short and sweet."

And so, when the year was up in late 1953, Rabin and Leah sent Dahlia home with a friend, then toured Europe before returning home. Rabin was glum about his future, and was not optimistic when Dayan invited him to his office for a talk, especially since Dayan had read the Camberley report declaring him fit only for the quartermaster corps. Dayan had sent him a note saying: "I hope you won't take what they wrote too seriously."

But Rabin didn't take Dayan's note too seriously.

The chief of staff, however, was apparently sincere. When Rabin reported to him, Dayan asked him how he would like to head a new autonomous training branch at GHQ. Until then, the training department had been a division of the general staff. With the job would come a promotion—from colonel to major general.

Rabin was jubilant—and surprised. He wouldn't be chief of operations, but he would be able to continue the work he had started as a battalion commanders instructor. He would become a major general and be in charge of all army training.

Dayan realized, it was clear, that the army was top-heavy with British-trained officers and that an injection of Palmach blood was needed: the kind of blood he had been looking for when he signed up Rabin more than ten years earlier.

Yes, said Rabin, he would gladly accept the offer.

Rabin's initial effort was to set up a command staff school, and he threw himself "into the task of formulating combat concepts, staff work, logistics, and instructional methods of the highest standards." At times he almost pined for the leisure hours he had left behind in England, for it was back to the old grind, sometimes eighteen-hour days. And the pressure mounted when Leah became pregnant again.

"In the early stages of pregnancy," Leah would recall, "I was ordered to lie down, and Yitzhak came to the rescue. We had a woman who came in three times a week to see to everything, but the other days were a problem. Yitzhak would run in from the general staff, warm the food, serve me in bed, and sit down to eat with Dahlia. That took about half an hour, then he was on his way back to work. Sometimes he found an extra moment or two to water the flowers in the garden."

Then Dahlia fell ill with a serious ailment that persisted for eight months and was in the hospital at the same time Leah was in a different hospital giving birth to a son, Yuval. The harried father thus found himself racing back and forth between the two hospitals, while thumbing through staff reports on the way.

"I still shudder at the memory of that period," Leah would recall.

But there was one experience that Rabin would not wish to forget—his first trip to the United States in the summer of 1954. He accompanied Dayan on a tour of U.S. Army military schools and installations to acquaint himself with American instruction methods and organization. The buildings, he marveled, were even taller than those in London, and the people were warmer. And the "mighty American army" was, in some ways, a blown-up version of the kind of army he hoped to build.

"That was a truly instructive visit," he would comment, "and much of what we saw and heard was subsequently applied to IDF training techniques—given the restrictions of our far more limited resources."

One thing they applied to the IDF was the requirement that every combat officer take a parachute or commando course on completing his training. After returning to Israel shortly before Yuval's birth, Rabin, with Dayan's approval, decided to put the entire general staff, including themselves, through the parachute course. But with Leah pregnant, Rabin decided not to tell her that he would be jumping. However, when he set the alarm clock for 4 A.M. one day, she sat up in bed and told her husband:

"I've had a strange dream. I dreamed that I said to you, 'why don't you tell me where you're going?' Are you hiding something from me?"

Rabin denied he was and offered some excuse for the early rising. He had never lied to his wife before. Was he doing the right thing? When he had jumped several times and had completed the course, a friend she met at the supermarket ran up to her and said:

"Congratulations! I hear that Yitzhak has completed parachute school. Dayan dislocated his hand but Yitzhak sailed through."

Leah almost gave birth then and there. She couldn't believe the story.

"We live in the same house don't we?" she snapped. "Where did you get that story?"

Later, Rabin confirmed the story. He was delighted with his achievement. And he had lied for a good cause. But he was apparently a bit disturbed. He was no longer George Washington. By lying about the parachute course, he had cut down the cherry tree while denying that he had. He was now simply Yitzhak Rabin, plain human being.

By spring 1956, Rabin, now a major general, had helped to set in motion a training program that would finally turn the IDF into one of the best armies, man for man, in the world, though the world did not yet realize this. So, as Dayan had done before, he made it clear to Rabin that he didn't need him anymore, at least in a top command post. In fact, the job of chief of operations was open again, but Dayan chose someone else. So Rabin would take over the northern command, about as distant from GHQ in Tel Aviv and the principal crisis area in the south as possible.

Many years later, Shimon Peres, who at that time was deputy minister of defense, would explain that Dayan "was reluctant to acknowledge" that Rabin was a good military man. . . . Before the Sinai campaign, Dayan appointed him O/C Northern Command, 'where he won't get in our way.' We planned to fight in the south and expected possible action in the east, too, but we assumed the northern front against Syria and Lebanon would stay quiet."

Rabin would later claim that "it was an exciting and refreshing change after years of staff duties," especially since he knew the northern region well from his early service in the Palmach. But he was, in fact, embittered by the change. For not only was he far removed from the center of power, where the army-building process was taking place, but the main crisis areas, as Dayan well knew, bordered on Jordan and the Egyptian-controlled Gaza Strip, from where terrorists launched ever more murderous raids, posing a growing threat to Israel's security.

The Syrians also threatened in the north, but only with minor shooting and artillery attacks in the demilitarized zones along the border; there was no major confrontation. But if this was mainly a war of nerves, Rabin demanded that Israel win this war. Even if a conflict erupted over possession of a tiny parcel of land not worth dying for, Rabin would order his men to fight to the death. The enemy must understand that only through peace negotiations could it have Israeli-occupied land.

Meanwhile, in mid-1956, the situation in the south deteriorated rapidly as Egyptian President Nasser, whom Rabin had admired at the desert meeting with the Faluja leaders in the 1948 war, fomented ever more terrorist raids that killed and maimed hundreds of Israelis. Finally, Nasser closed the Straits of Tiran to Israeli shipping and threatened to send across the border divisions armed with newly purchased weapons from Czechoslovakia.

One day in fall 1956, as tensions soared, Rabin and all other senior IDF commanders were summoned to GHQ for a super-secret meeting.

Reprisal raids, Dayan announced, had failed to end the terrorism, and since Nasser supported the terrorists, Israel might be forced to attack Egypt soon. The attack would be coordinated with British and French forces. And since Syria and Jordan were not likely to join in the fighting, Rabin and his counterpart in the central command must transfer part of their forces to the southern front and deploy for defense in case they did attack.

Rabin felt frustrated and even resentful. He had done so much to help create the army that would now attack, and he would play no role in that attack. Dayan had sidelined him to a secondary command, preventing him from tasting the first fruit of his work. Ben-Gurion, through Dayan, was getting his revenge.

"We were living in Haifa when the war broke out on October 29," Leah would say, "and the war was far away in Sinai. When it began, Yitzhak 'dug in' at northern command headquarters and didn't come home while the war lasted."

Even before the war began, Leah seldom saw her husband. Border incidents "were Yitzhak's daily fare. There wasn't a week without some serious flare-up and gunfire from Golan on the villages of the northern valley was a daily occurrence. Yitzhak knew neither day nor night, and sometimes neither Sabbath nor holiday. He would arrive home exhausted, then often he was called in the middle of the night [to] return to headquarters in Nazareth."

Leah was always anxious, and with good reason. Once, during an inspection of a border area, the Syrians opened fire on her husband and his party, and they spent two hours crawling out of the field of fire. Another time, Rabin's horse fell on him when it slipped on wet rock while climbing Mount Meron on patrol. It took several days for his injuries to heal, and then he was back to work.

Nor did Leah enjoy living in an undeveloped area on Mount Carmel in Haifa, usually alone with her two children. She "felt social and cultural strangulation, despite the natural beauty of the city and the mountain above the sea." And she was "stuck with a one-year-old baby," she would recall, while "Dahlia had to struggle up the mountain slope in the heat of day, for her class took place . . . in the afternoons. A private car was out of the question in those days. Nowadays parents wouldn't dream of letting a six-year-old walk that distance from a remote area alone." Despite the hardships, Leah persevered, conquering them with grit and determination and creating an atmosphere at home that made her husband forget the rigors of his job when he finally returned home at night.

At the same time, however, the Sinai War increased Leah's anxieties, for though her husband was not in the fighting zone, her brother-in-law, Avraham Yoffe was, as commander of the Ninth Brigade, which was advancing across the desert to the Straits of Tiran. Her sister, Aviva, and her two children moved in with Leah, and, Leah would say, "I think that I devoted all my spiritual energies to supporting Aviva, to convincing her that Avraham wasn't dead yet."

And he wasn't. He would return home a hero after taking part in a lightning thrust that opened the straits. Rabin was happy that at least one member of the family did, and that the army, his army, had won so great a victory, using the highly refined strategies that he had so painstakingly honed.

The end of the Sinai campaign on November 5 did not signal the end of tension on the northern front. In fact, it escalated as the

Syrians shelled Israeli settlements from the top of the Golan ridge that overlooked them. Israelis constantly had to leap into shelters, running from their homes, schools, and public buildings. Rabin even had to order his men to use armored tractors to cultivate the land and mount raids on Syrian fishing vessels and their military protectors to stop them from exploiting Israeli-controlled waters.

During one Syrian attack, Rabin left the scene of battle so he could visit Dahlia in a hospital after she had been injured in an automobile accident. While she was undergoing minor surgery, Rabin's jeep skidded to a halt in front of the hospital, its radio blasting away. The anxious father leaped out and stood by during the operation—while controlling the battle by radio.

He would not let a personal emergency keep him from preventing a national one.

Rabin was frustrated dealing with dozens of small incidents, especially after having missed the thrill and honor of sharing in the great victory in the south, a victory that he had helped make possible. And he was not very hopeful that his situation would change for the better when Chief of Staff Dayan summoned him and several other commanders to a meeting as his term was about to expire. Still, one of the commanders would replace Dayan in the top military position, and a miracle was always possible. And as Dayan listed the qualities he expected in his successor, Rabin was still hoping. Then the chief of staff suggested that some senior officers should take study leave. And among those who should, he said, was Yitzhak Rabin.

"When he raised my name as a candidate . . . ," Rabin would lament, "it seemed evident to me that Dayan was hinting that my usefulness to the army had run its course and I should therefore terminate my service."

The sudden realization that his army career was about to end left Rabin in shock. How would he now be able to repay his debt to the men who had died under his command? How would he be able to continue building the mighty force that could bring permanent peace to Israel? Resignation, however, gradually set in. Yes, he would take study leave. But he no longer thought of being an irrigation engineer. He wanted to influence national policy. If he couldn't do it in the army, he would do it in civilian public service.

He agreed to take study leave, Rabin told Dayan, and would like to study public administration at Harvard.

Dayan shook his head. No, he said, he was opposed to study abroad at present. It was too expensive. He himself planned to study in Jerusalem after leaving the army. Why shouldn't Rabin do the same?

Rabin replied, knowing he would never be promoted again: If he couldn't study at Harvard, he would remain in the army.

Some days later, fate played a hand. Ben-Gurion vetoed Dayan's choice of a successor, and Chaim Laskov became the next chief of staff. Rabin was delighted, remembering how Laskov had appointed him training chief a few years earlier. Ben-Gurion would surely still block his advancement in the army, but maybe now he could at least go to Harvard.

Harvard? exclaimed Laskov. Sure, he could go.

Shortly, the university approved Rabin's application, and he was set to leave for the United States in the summer of 1959. But suddenly an odd twist of destiny once more blocked the path to school while opening the way to a greater fulfillment. It happened when military leaders called a public mobilization exercise that people didn't realize was an exercise.

"Dramatic radio announcements in dozens of languages galvanized the IDF reserves," Rabin would relate, "as though we faced a grave state of emergency. That evening I attended a festive concert at Tel Aviv's Mann Auditorium and, as the hall filled with music, frantic messengers called the chief of staff to step outside. He was followed by a train of senior officers. Were we at war?"

Ben-Gurion was forced to dismiss the chief of operations and the chief of military intelligence. And Laskov chose Rabin as chief of operations. But would Ben-Gurion approve the choice? Rabin had his doubts. The prime minister had a long memory, and he surely remembered the Palmach reunion. Once more, Rabin waited with foreboding to learn what the future held.

This time his pessimism was unwarranted. Ben-Gurion finally agreed to catapult him into the army's second-highest position.

"I saw," Rabin would say, "that we sometimes move ahead not only by virtue of our own powers but in the wake of errors committed by others."

Now, at last, at the age of thirty-seven, he would have an "opportunity to tackle problems that embraced every facet of the defense forces." And he was only one step from the top.

Rabin took over as chief of operations in 1959 at a fiercely challenging time, with the Middle East bubbling in turmoil and simmering toward new explosion. Nasser had joined with Syria to form the United Arab Republic, a revolution was ripping through Iraq, and the Soviet Union was pouring arms into all the radical Arab countries. Rabin was alarmed. His theory now seemed more valid than ever: Israel had to build up its strength sufficiently to deter the enemy from attacking. But Soviet arms and Arab unity, however fragile, were gradually gnawing away at Israel's military advantage, at least in Arab eyes.

Until then, Israel had depended almost entirely on the French for arms, an arrangement stemming from French cooperation with Israel in the 1956 Sinai War. But Rabin did not see France as Israel's natural ally. As the Holocaust had decimated the Jewish community in France, it could exert little clout on the government, and President Charles de Gaulle had no particular love for Israel despite his friendship with Ben-Gurion. An ultra-nationalist, he would probably cut off aid as soon as French interest did not require it. Besides, why rely on one source, especially since France did not produce weapons in massive quantity?

Rabin thus pressed Ben-Gurion to try to switch most of Israel's arms business to the United States, even though the prime minister still harbored bitterness toward Washington for forcing him to withdraw from Sinai areas Israel had captured during the 1956 war.

The United States, Rabin argued, could provide Israel with more and probably newer weapons, and would be under pressure from American Jewry not to sever such aid even if Washington was disposed to do so. The United States, he pointed out, was reluctant to sell offensive weapons to Israel but was willing to sell Israel defensive ones, and what Israel needed most, to thwart any surprise Arab attack, was a modern early-warning system.

Rabin had fallen in love with the United States during several trips there and enjoyed the comradeship of his American counterparts, while Europe still smelled to him of either Middle East imperialism or wartime collaboration.

Opposing this view, in perhaps the first serious conflict between the two men, was Deputy Defense Minister Shimon Peres, a man of dramatic presence with a high forehead, promi-

nent nose, cleft chin, and probing, sharply lidded eyes. He had
arranged for French arms aid before the 1956 war and had become
close friends with French leaders. An intellectual steeped in
European culture, he had emigrated from Poland as a teenager,
and thus felt more at home with the cultivated French elite than
with the more rough-hewn Americans. At the same time, he
shared the attributes of many politicians brought up in the tumultuous politics of manipulation and ambiguity common in the East
European shtetl. Peres was supported in his European orientation
by Air Force Chief Ezer Weizman, who had also worked closely
with the French and trusted them. Neither man forgot America's
tough treatment of Israel after the Sinai War.

Rabin was delighted when Ben-Gurion, though close to Peres,
backed what he considered Rabin's more pragmatic view and left for
the United States with a long laundry list of arms he would request,
headed by the early-warning system. Ben-Gurion shortly returned
with a U.S. promise to sell this system—but not quite in time.

Shortly, at the beginning of 1960, after a shooting incident on
the Syrian border, Israeli troops were sent to the area, giving rise to
suspicions that they were about to attack Syria. And these suspicions were fed by a Soviet report to Nasser that an attack seemed
imminent. Soon, Egyptian forces were massed in the Sinai near the
Israeli border without Israel's knowledge.

When a reconnaissance plane finally spotted these enemy
troops, Rabin, realizing that there were only twenty or thirty
Israeli tanks in the area, scribbled a note to Air Force Chief
Weizman:

"We've been caught with our pants down. For the next 24
hours, everything depends on the air force."

Rabin was nearly desperate. "Clearly," he would later relate,
"if the Egyptians intended to go to war, we would need at least
twenty-four hours to get our armored forces to the front; till then
only the air force could block an offensive."

Within minutes, 100 to 130 tanks were crawling southward.

And within twenty-four hours the two armies faced each other
in a state of alert. Rabin, in a cold sweat, held his breath. He had
barely been on the job, and Israel's very existence was being threatened. How could he have been unaware of the Egyptian military
movements?

But no one fired a cannon, and the threat dissipated. Eventually the Egyptians retreated across the Suez Canal, with Nasser crowing that he had prevented an Israeli attack on Syria.

But Rabin's mind remained awhirl with anxiety. This must never happen again. The next time, Israel could disappear.

Rabin's anxiety was not eased when he returned home to Zahala late each night. For he was burdened with worry not only by the danger to Israel but by the damage to his children that might result from their parents' absence much of the time. Except for weekends, Rabin would see them only for breakfast, which Leah called a "holy business." And Leah, on returning from Haifa in the summer of 1958, began teaching English each day in a school situated about forty minutes away, feeling "glad to get out of the house."

Leah insisted on keeping her job even though her husband, remembering the "holy business" of his own childhood that was always followed by what seemed like abandonment, urged her to quit and stay home with the children.

"He had undoubtedly suffered from the absence of his own mother," Leah would later say, "and I sensed that if anything compensated for his own childhood, and for the immense effort invested in what he did, it was the security of knowing that I was at home on 'a full-time job.'"

Finally, after two years, Leah agreed to his entreaties and left the school to remain home and take care of the children. Rabin felt a deep sense of relief. A radio interviewer would remark:

"Because of their public activities, your parents often left you and your sister alone at home, and you suffered for it. And here you are, away from home most days and nights, and your children are small."

"But my children," Rabin replied, "have their mother at home with them."

However much he neglected his children because of his demanding job, at least he was comforted in knowing that they would not have to endure what he did as a child. They would not feel lonely or abandoned. And this lifted an enormous burden from his shoulders. At the same time, however, the burden on Leah's grew heavier. She not only had to care for the children, but she alone had to solve all the minute problems that filled her day.

"I learned the hard way," she would recall, "that the garden, the children, the desperate battle of the budget, which never supplied all the wants and needs, were in my exclusive domain where I could expect very little help from Yitzhak. Furthermore, he was to be bothered as little as possible."

Sometimes, however, when the problem got out of hand, Leah would, in desperation, call her husband at the office. Once, a mouse invaded the house, and Leah became hysterical and cried over the phone to him:

"You must come home immediately. There are mice in the house!"

After a pause, Rabin replied: "There's no way I can come now."

In other words, Leah would muse to herself, she must solve the problem herself. "The mouse wasn't on his mind."

She phoned her father, who worked for a company that sold agricultural products, and sobbed: "Father, save me! Come with your poisons. There's a mouse here!"

Shortly, the mouse disappeared but not her myriad problems.

One problem Rabin would not ignore, however, was that of his family's health.

"Yitzhak was one of the worrying-type parents," Leah would say, "and if one of the children was ill, there was full partnership. Telephone calls throughout the day, and shared chores at night if there were fevers or other troubles. 'Call the doctor, I'm uneasy,' he would say. When I tried to protect the poor doctor's slumber, Yitzhak said: 'When they need me, they call me at night. Now I need him.'"

At the same time, the children needed their father.

At sundown on Friday, little Yuval would go to the entrance to Zahala and wait for his father. If Rabin was late, Yuval would return and lament:

"All the fathers are already home; only my father is not."

"I felt sorry for the child," Leah would say, "and it wasn't always easy to explain why his father hadn't yet come home. But Saturday was devoted to time with the children. In summer we continued, from time to time, to go to the beach, and in winter we arranged occasional picnics in the Jerusalem hills with other families. And there were Saturdays of work in the garden or relaxation at home."

But there was no relaxation at the office.

"As chief of operations," Rabin would say, "I cannot deny that I regarded myself as a worthy candidate for the post of chief of staff upon Laskov's retirement."

And indeed, Rabin was reputed as perhaps the best staff officer in the army. No one could match the accumulation of facts filling a mind that worked like a computer, facts gathered to a large extent during visits to American and European military bases.

The problem was that Shimon Peres wanted to get rid of Laskov and replace him with Laskov's deputy, Zvi Zur. And Ben-Gurion agreed. Rabin was shattered, once again frustrated by someone who, in his view, didn't appreciate his independent stance on military policy. At a GHQ meeting, Ben-Gurion asked him to remain behind.

"Are you offended that Zur has been appointed chief of staff?" he asked Rabin.

"It's not a question of being offended," Rabin replied, surprised by the question. "I presume you had your reasons for the choice, and there's no need to explain them to me."

"But I want to tell you why I decided on Zur," Ben-Gurion insisted. "True, on one occasion you did disobey orders. And you are cautious [Rabin thought he meant overcautious]. But these considerations did not affect my decision. Zur is simply ahead of you in the military hierarchy. If I had appointed you, he would have resigned, and I could not ask him to remain in the army."

Rabin was angered by Ben-Gurion's remark about his disobeying orders, obviously referring to the Palmach reunion. He retorted:

"I didn't ask for explanations, Ben-Gurion. But as long as we're on the subject, let me ask you a question. I am serving in the army out of a sense of duty. But if you think I should leave, I'll do it quietly. I don't want to hang on by my fingernails."

Ben-Gurion interrupted, obviously disturbed: "Wherever did you get that idea? I want you to remain in the army. It's imperative that you stay! What can I do to convince you of that?"

Well, Rabin replied, in addition to being chief of operations, he would like to be deputy chief of staff.

"There's no problem about that," said Ben-Gurion. "You'll be deputy chief of staff."

Only if Zur approved, Rabin replied.

Ben-Gurion merely shrugged with a wave of his hand, as if to say this wasn't important.

When Zur became chief of staff, he said, sure, Rabin could be his deputy. But he stalled on the appointment until Ben-Gurion intervened and anointed Rabin deputy chief. And though Rabin claimed he followed his superior's instructions, relations between them deteriorated.

This antagonism was reflected, for example, in an argument over which service branch should control a batch of Hawk missiles that had just arrived from the United States. Ezer Weizman, as air force chief, wanted his branch to control them, while Rabin favored the ground forces. Zur supported Weizman, though he agreed to transfer some ground forces to the air force to take charge of the missiles.

There was also a conflict over creating a second regular brigade. Zur overruled Rabin, who preferred to strengthen the battalions within Israel's only regular brigade (it had two reserve brigades) rather than create a second regular brigade. For there were not yet enough tanks and other equipment for such a brigade.

Whatever other differences fed their mutual animosity, Rabin blamed Peres, a supporter of Zur, for inflaming the chief of staff's feelings toward him.

"Peres," he would claim, "fomented personal conflicts to place his adversaries under pressure"—a charge that Peres would deny.

Finally, when Rabin showed no inclination to resign, Zur invited him to his home and candidly told him:

"I've decided that I want a different chief of operations, and I want you to know that I've asked Ben-Gurion to replace you. Let's wind things up in a dignified manner. As chief of staff, it's my prerogative to work with a different chief of operations, and I intend to insist on that."

"Please permit me to talk with Ben-Gurion," Rabin replied. "If he accepts your view, I'll go."

Early in March, Rabin visited Ben-Gurion in his Jerusalem office, and the prime minister told him:

"Yitzhak, I promised that you'd be chief of staff, and you are going to be the next chief of staff."

Rabin was shocked. Ben-Gurion had never made such a promise. The prime minister went on:

"The intention is for Zur to remain at his post for another year. You wanted to study, and this is a good opportunity. But if you decide that you'd prefer to continue your service now and forgo your studies, that's up to you."

Rabin was deeply moved. But why was Ben-Gurion supporting him when he had avoided naming him chief of staff in the past and clearly had not forgotten the Palmach reunion episode? Was it a matter of conscience? Was it because the leftist group Rabin had been peripherally linked to, Yigal Allon's Ahdut Avodah, broke in the 1950s with Mapam, the party Ben-Gurion so mistrusted?

Whatever the reason, Rabin thanked Ben-Gurion, but said that in view of current security problems, he preferred to remain in the army. He apparently also worried that if he took a leave, it would be easier for Ben-Gurion to change his mind.

"Inform the chief of staff of your decision," Ben-Gurion responded. "I'll see to it that his assistant is informed of the conclusion we've arrived at."

Two days later, Rabin went on a trip to Europe and in Paris met with Peres, who was also there. According to Rabin, Peres said:

"Well, I understand you had a talk with Ben-Gurion. How did it go?"

"Very well."

"What happened?"

"Ben-Gurion told me that I'm going to be the next chief of staff."

Rabin would say that Peres "paled" and asked, "Did he say it in so many words?"

"In just so many words."

Peres would deny he asked Rabin what Ben-Gurion told him, since Ben-Gurion had told him the same thing before speaking with Rabin. Peres would claim he supported the choice.

Rabin thought he must wait a year to take over, but then the unexpected happened and his future was once more thrust into doubt. For in June 1963, Ben-Gurion decided to resign as prime minister and defense minister.

"The news left everyone dumbfounded," Rabin would recall.

And no one more than himself. Every step up the ladder, it seemed, depended on someone else falling off it. Without Ben-Gurion in power, would he still reach the top rung? Since current Chief of Staff Zur was in Paris for an air show, Rabin would use his post as acting chief of staff to plead personally with Ben-Gurion on behalf of the army to remain in power.

So, together with the chief of intelligence, he left for Sde Boker, Ben-Gurion's kibbutz in the Negev. Yitzhak Navon, Ben-Gurion's aide, was surprised by the visit. After all, Rabin had never been close to Ben-Gurion, and it was unusual for military leaders to involve themselves in politics.

After being welcomed by Ben-Gurion, Rabin, in his usual direct manner, came right to the point.

He and his colleague, he said, were dismayed by the prime minister's decision to retire and hoped he would not for the army's sake.

Rabin then described the dangerous military situation. France, he said, was moving away from Israel, and the Arabs were growing stronger. Was this the time for the prime minister, "who was unique and unrivaled in the eyes of the army, to leave the helm and abandon the IDF?"

"Nothing means more to me than the army," Ben-Gurion replied, "but for reasons having nothing to do with the army, I must retire."

The two officers finally accepted Ben-Gurion's decision and departed. And when the prime minister emerged from his office, Navon was surprised to see tears in his eyes.

"I never saw him so moved," Navon would tell me. "There were not often tears in his eyes."

And Ben-Gurion himself would later say: "The words of Rabin touched deeply in my heart. I could hardly overcome my feelings and my tears."

But Rabin still didn't know whether, with Ben-Gurion's resignation, he would be the next chief of staff, or when it might happen. Would Ben-Gurion's successor, Levi Eshkol, a mild-mannered but master politician, honor his predecessor's promise? Rabin didn't know, but his natural pessimism dissipated somewhat two or three days before Ben-Gurion left office when the outgoing prime minister asked him to remain behind after a GHQ meeting.

"I remember my promise to you about becoming the next chief of staff and have told Eshkol of it," Ben-Gurion reassured Rabin. "I hope and believe that he will respect it. More than that I cannot do."

It was now Rabin who was very moved. Despite past differences, he realized now just how great a man Ben-Gurion was.

"My generation regarded Ben-Gurion with reverence," he would say. "He stood head and shoulders above his contemporaries and was not a man to concern himself with trifles. His spirit soared toward lofty visions and the broad sweep of statesmanship."

Rabin clearly did not perceive these "lofty visions" and "sweep of statesmanship" when Ben-Gurion forced Yigal Allon out of the army, or when he apparently tried to do the same to him by delaying his promotion to chief of staff because he attended a Palmach reunion. But this was a Ben-Gurion who wanted to leave office at peace with himself, who realized, it seemed, that he had erred and wanted to ease his conscience. A Ben-Gurion who really wanted him to be the next chief of staff!

And it soon became clear that what Ben-Gurion wanted, even out of office, he got. To make sure of it, he stood up at a party convention and stated as if he were still prime minister: A new chief of staff would be appointed. He was a sabra, a talented, honest fighter. The convention was stunned. Was not Eshkol the prime minister? Both rightists and leftists attacked him.

But Eshkol, a good-natured political pragmatist with a keen memory for detail, was not about to defy his longtime master. He decided, against his better judgment, not to extend Zur's term another year but to obey immediately. He called in Rabin and informed him in an authoritative manner that suggested he was making an independent decision:

Be ready to take over as chief of staff on January 1, 1964.

Rabin was apparently speechless. All that worry for nothing.

Now, at forty-one, with no military superior to persuade and a prime minister with little military knowledge, he could finish building an army that would pave the way to real peace. And even after his term ended, this work, he was determined, would not end.

In November 1963, before taking over as chief of staff, he went with Leah to the United States to strengthen his ties with military leaders there. Leah was thrilled by this first encounter with the country, and was, she would say, "enchanted by the beauty and splendor of Washington."

Her husband was, too. In fact, he was already thinking of coming back. When the couple left for home, he remarked to Leah:

"You know, when I finish my term as chief of staff, I'll be ready to replace [our ambassador here]."

For wasn't the United States the one guarantor of Israel's welfare, in fact, its very existence? The one nation qualified to arbitrate peace with the Arabs when the time was ripe? And he could perhaps influence its policy.

The future somehow looked brighter. But then, on their return home, the phone rang and the news suddenly cast an ominous shadow over it. President Kennedy had been assassinated.

"The shock and mourning for the young President," Leah would recall, "was for us as if we had brought the terrible news back with us directly from Dallas."

Who would want to kill a national leader? she wondered. Especially one who was serving his country, and the world, with such skill and heart. This tragedy, thank God, could never happen in Israel.

And on January 1, Rabin took over as chief of staff, the first giant step toward national leadership.

11

A Terrifying
Choice

Rabin became chief of staff on a quiet New Year's Day typical in a period uncorrupted by the reek of explosives or the rattle of gunfire. While the Syrians launched pinprick raids in the north, no large-scale enemy attack seemed imminent. But sooner or later, Rabin calculated, the Arabs might try to use the flood of Soviet arms pouring into their countries. And the trigger, he feared, could be the National Water Carrier irrigation system that would soon carry water from the Jordan River in the north to the arid land in the south.

"Our neighbors were in a full-blown uproar over the project," Rabin would say, "believing that it would enhance Israel's strength and give her an enormous economic advantage."

Actually, he would claim, the 300 million cubic meters of water that would nourish the desert was too small a quantity to have much effect on the balance of power in the Middle East. But the Arab states held a summit conference in Cairo only a few weeks after Rabin settled into his new job, and he mused about its mean-

ing. War? No, not now, he soon learned with relief, but they hud-
dled under a unified Arab command that would oversee the further buildup of their armed forces for a future clash with Israel.
Meanwhile, a newly formed Palestine Liberation Organization
would keep the region ablaze with incidents of terrorism.

While Rabin tried to convince the United States to supply
Israel with a massive arsenal of modern weapons that Europe
couldn't provide, he took drastic steps to keep the Arabs off balance until he succeeded. Apparently in cooperation with the
Mossad, Israel's Central Intelligence Agency, he directed clandestine operations—involving bombings and assassinations—behind
the lines of the countries bordering on Israel.

According to Ehud Barak, who would one day himself become
chief of staff, then head of the Labor Party, Rabin personally examined every detail of an operation, feeling an enormous responsibility for the life of every soldier.

No one was more impressed than Rahama Hermon, a stun-
ning officer who had just been assigned as an assistant to Rabin
and would become a close confidant. She would recall:

"Every time Yitzhak sent someone on a mission, he was so nervous waiting for his return that no one could talk to him."

On one occasion when Barak had set a booby trap obviously
intended to assassinate someone, Rabin, for some reason, decided
it shouldn't be used. But he wouldn't let Barak and his men return
to the scene to retrieve the trap before knowing every step that
was needed to defuse it. Barak even had to produce the people
who built the trap so they could explain with a model exactly how
it could be done.

"Everything had to be perfect," Barak would tell me. "He was
so careful to protect human life."

The attempt to defuse the booby trap failed, but Rabin could at
least find compensation in the safe return of his men.

In any event, Israeli reprisals, both clandestine and open military strikes, persuaded Jordan and Lebanon that it didn't pay to let
Palestinian guerrillas launch attacks on Israel from their territory.
But trouble escalated in the north when the Syrians began to divert
water from two tributaries of the Jordan River before it could
reach Israel.

Moshe Dayan, now minister of agriculture, advised Rabin

what to do: Seize the territory where the diversion channels were to run, even at the risk of full-scale war.

But Rabin overruled his former superior: He could stop the Syrians without taking such a risk. Hadn't enough Israeli boys died? And in November 1964, when Syrian artillery shelled two border settlements, Rabin conceived a way, he thought, to stop not only the shells but the work on the diversion canals. For the first time, Israeli planes bombed the guns on the Golan Heights. But while the artillery stopped, the work on the canals did not.

Rabin then summoned the chief of operations, the commander of his armored force, and the commander of the northern region and asked them:

"Can our tank guns hit the Syrians' heavy earth-moving equipment at a range exceeding thirteen hundred yards?"

They could, replied the armored corps commander, Major General Israel Tal.

And the next day incendiary shells smashed into the earth-movers—twice; when the original equipment was replaced, shells struck again. Finally, after the tanks hit their targets at a range of up to two and a half miles, the Syrians gave up on diverting the water, though not on trying to kill Israelis, whether with Syrian guns or Palestinian terrorism launched from Syrian soil.

And now Rabin issued a blunt warning to the Syrians. He said in an interview published in the army newspaper, *Ba'machane*, that Israel should take measures not only against those who perpetrated aggressive acts but "against the regime which supports these acts."

Shocked by this veiled threat of an armed attack against Syria, which might have triggered an Arab assault, Levi Eshkol, Ben-Gurion's successor as prime minister and defense minister, who was normally a warm, humorous man, found nothing funny in this article and severely rebuked Rabin. And, many Israelis thought, with good reason.

Rabin, undiplomatic by nature, would soon learn that in so lofty a position, what was on his mind could not always be on his tongue. He had calculated that Syria could not initiate a war without Egyptian support, and that Nasser, with his troops bogged down in a five-year war in Yemen, was not likely to push Egypt into a second conflict. On the other hand, he felt, the threat might induce Syria to stop the violence. But he now realized he might simply have escalated the tension and admitted that he had erred.

And the threat did, in fact, stir more violence. On April 7, the Syrians fired from a Golan position on an Israeli tractor working the land in the demilitarized zone.

Rabin was livid. He must respond powerfully—even at the risk of war. He went to Eshkol and urged him to approve a drastic move: Israel should respond not only with artillery, but with an air attack on Syrian positions.

Eshkol, who now felt there was no other way, reluctantly agreed. And Israeli aircraft were soon blowing up Syrian emplacements. The Syrians responded with MIG jets, and in a fierce dogfight the Israeli pilots shot down six of them and chased the rest back to Damascus.

The Arab world was enraged. This attack, it charged, was an act of war. The Syrian leaders also blasted Nasser. Why, they demanded, wasn't he striking back? Wasn't he committed to help defend Syria under a mutual defense treaty? Why did he let United Nations forces, based in the Sinai since the 1956 war, remain on Egyptian soil? To give him an excuse not to fight back? The Egyptian leader thus found himself under increasing pressure to act, though, as Rabin surmised, he apparently had no wish to tangle with Israel in a major war.

Noting the violent Arab reaction, Rabin, it seems, once more began to question a decision he made: Would the planes he sent up precipitate a war? A new bloodbath? Rabin could only be thankful that his effort to extract sophisticated arms from the U.S. arsenal had started to pay off.

When Eshkol went to Washington in June 1964, he returned with a promise of Skyhawks and Patton M-46 tanks that were far superior to the French Mirages and lighter tanks—and to the Soviet equipment going to Egypt and Syria.

"Yet," Rabin would say, "matters were not quite that simple. A string of 'buts' filtered into the picture between the time when [President] Johnson gave his consent 'in principle' and the day we could expect to conclude a formal deal."

One important "but" required Israel to agree to a linkage of arms sales to Israel and Jordan, which was also seeking weapons from the United States. For Johnson did not want Jordan to solicit arms from the Soviet Union, as Egypt and Syria had done. And with linkage, Johnson felt, Congress would not be likely to reject arms to Jordan since, for political reasons, it would not keep weapons from Israel.

When Eshkol and Rabin dismissed the idea, Johnson sent Roving Ambassador Averell Harriman and a member of the National Security Council to Israel early in 1965 to "lean" on them. After a frustrating clash in which Harriman warned that the United States might "withdraw" from the Middle East altogether, the ambassador, Rabin would relate, "changed his tactics. Abandoning his stick, he held up a juicy carrot before our noses. The United States would be prepared to ... provide Israel with planes, tanks, and artillery—offensive weapons that had been withheld till then, provided, of course, that we agreed to a few 'minor' conditions."

The conditions included not only acceptance of the linkage plan, but a promise not to initiate a preemptive strike against the Arabs, not to use force to halt the Syrian water diversion operations, and not to acquire nuclear weapons.

Rabin responded furiously: How could they ask Israel to "give in on fundamental strategic issues concerning our right to self-defense?"

But the fury was really for show. Rabin was, in fact, exhilarated, indeed, ecstatic. At last a source of sophisticated weapons in massive quantity. At last the key to enough arms to win the likely coming war—if they arrived in time—even to guarantee Israel's security forever. But he argued over every condition and finally agreed to a compromise, as he knew he would. Israel would not oppose the Jordanian arms deal. The other conditions would be ignored or overtaken by events.

"Thus 1967," Rabin would recall, "found us immersed in a mass overhaul of the Israel Defense Forces in anticipation of a presumably inevitable clash with our neighbors. But then, as if out of the blue, the inevitable was upon us. It was as if the shock waves of a dogfight over the slopes of Mount Hermon had sent a political snowball careening across the Middle East, gathering momentum with every passing day as it charged blindly and inexorably toward war."

Even so, both Rabin and Nasser desperately sought to hold off the "inevitable." Rabin, chastened by the "shock waves" he had sent across the Middle East, tried to calm colleagues who too readily accepted the inevitable. And Nasser told the Syrians:

"We will not permit the enemy to dictate the timing or circumstances of war. Don't depend on us to come to your aid because of some limited incident. As long as Israel does not perpetrate an all-out attack on Syria, we will not be drawn into war prematurely."

But what the Syrians couldn't do, the Soviet Union could. And it would, because it finally saw an opportunity for its Arab allies to use their Soviet weapons to wipe out, or at least weaken, a powerful American "base" in the strategic Middle East. Thus, in mid-May it fed the Syrians false information that about a dozen Israeli brigades had massed along the northern border and were preparing to attack Syria. The Syrians urgently passed the report to Nasser. Now he was trapped. He could not ignore this threat and remain the idolized torchbearer of the Arab world.

And on the evening of May 14, Rabin learned that his old acquaintance, Nasser, would not ignore it. While dining at a friend's house, Rabin received a phone call from an aide who read to him an intelligence report: Nasser had put his army in a state of alert.

Rabin did not seem overly worried. Nor did he the following day when a note was handed to him at an Independence Day parade in Jerusalem: Egyptian troops were marching through Cairo toward the Suez Canal. The news was troubling, but Nasser, it seemed clear, was just putting on a show, as he had a few years earlier when his troops had crossed the Suez for a while and then had withdrawn.

But Rabin immediately left the parade and returned with his family to his hotel so he could issue orders to his headquarters. Since the weather was extremely hot, he immediately removed his uniform, and, standing near the window, soon found himself unintentionally putting on a show of his own.

"Daddy," Dahlia screamed, "there are Jordanian soldiers on the wall with binoculars, and they're looking this way. They'll see you in your underpants."

Rabin could only hope that the Jordanians were too busy watching the parade to notice. The important thing now was to keep Nasser from catching him with his pants down. He alerted some of his units and ordered minefields laid along some parts of the Egyptian border. But he also ordered his officers to avoid initiating any movements that could increase the tension.

They didn't need to, for Nasser increased the tension anyway. He asked the UN to remove its forces from the Sinai border and transfer them to the Gaza Strip and Sharm el-Sheikh, which guarded the sea lane through the Straits of Tiran. Rabin was still not alarmed. Again, it seemed, Nasser might simply be trying to impress his Arab neighbors with his martial posturing, hoping that the UN would reject his demand.

"But even if the UN let him have his way," Rabin would later explain, "Nasser assumed that as long as he did not order the UN force to leave the Gaza Strip and Sharm el-Sheikh, he would not be confronting Israel with a casus belli," since he would simply be transferring the force to new positions in the area. "Instead, he would be maneuvering us into the uncomfortable position of having to deal with a potentially explosive situation that nonetheless fell short of being a clear-cut pretext for war, while he would remain free to dictate all the moves."

UN Secretary-General U Thant, however, issued a response that Nasser clearly did not expect, one that would have earth-shaking consequences: All UN troops would remain in place or all would be removed.

This response grossly violated a UN commitment made in 1957 that "in case of a request from Egypt for the withdrawal of [UN troops] . . . the matter would at once be brought before the General Assembly. . . . If they found that the task [of the force] was not completed, and Egypt all the same maintained its position and enforced the withdrawal, Egypt would be breaking the agreement with the United Nations. . . . If a difference should develop, the matter would be brought up for negotiation with the United Nations."

But there was no negotiation, and U Thant's unauthorized response did indeed shake the earth. Nasser, faced with his ultimatum, felt he had no choice.

Take them all out! he ordered.

And shortly, about half of Egypt's armed strength would stretch over the sands of the Sinai.

Now Rabin was alarmed, even though he realized that U

Thant had forced Nasser's hand by leaving him no room to save face. Rabin ordered all land, sea, and air units on top alert and mobilized additional reserves.

"Whether or not the Egyptians were bent on leading the situation to war at present," Rabin would say, "we were inevitably moving in that direction. . . . I ordered all commanding officers to make it clear to their men that we were heading for war. Without doubt we now faced the gravest situation Israel had known since the War of Independence."

What would be the casus belli that would finally trigger war? It was generally agreed: an Egyptian blockade of the Straits of Tiran, which would mean that Eilat would no longer serve as an Israeli port. Rabin thus hoped that the United States would honor a commitment it had made to Israel after the Sinai War that Israeli ships would sail freely through the straits. The Americans were talking with the Egyptians, whom they found "jumpy and confused," and were trying to avert war through a diplomatic solution.

On May 21, Rabin, "very tense, chain-smoking all the time," visited Foreign Minister Abba Eban at his Jerusalem home, though, reflecting their policy and personality differences, he would later say of him: "I am not a great admirer of Eban except for his English." When asked what the diplomatic establishment could do to help, the foreign minister replied:

"Time. We need time to reinforce the south."

Until then, most Israeli troops had been based in the north and central zones to defend against Syrian and Jordanian forces, respectively. Rabin then asked Eban:

"If Nasser should block the straits, and the government orders the IDF to attack, how much time would we have before our operations were halted by the UN or the powers?"

About twenty-four to seventy-two hours before international intervention halted operations, Eban replied.

Rabin was shocked.

"An army," he would say, "does not go to war without the fundamental conviction that it is capable of achieving its objectives. No nation—particularly not a nation as small as ours—can afford to shed its soldiers' blood with the sand running out so rapidly."

Most of Rabin's military colleagues were mentally prepared to explode into action immediately, but he was not. He remembered the hundreds of men who had died under his command in the 1948 war. In the next war, he feared, perhaps there would be as many as 50,000 casualties. And the crushing burden, the ultimate responsibility, would be his to bear.

Rabin had wanted his job, dreamed of it. But he couldn't imagine how lonely it would be at the top. Nor could he easily adapt to the ruthlessness required there in dealing with his men's lives. He was a magnificent military planner and analyst, perhaps the best Israel ever had. The nation's powerful, modernized army was largely his creation. Before the 1956 war, Israel had placed emphasis on building up the infantry, but with the great success of the armored units in that war, Rabin gave priority to strengthening them as well as the air units. He knitted together a superb striking force.

But Rabin couldn't desensitize his heart or temper his sense of personal responsibility for the fate of every soldier. His compassion, in fact, influenced his military decisions. If Israel had to attack Egypt, he favored fighting in phases to limit the scope of battle and thus the casualties. First, Israel would capture the Gaza Strip and the area just west of it. Then it would press Egypt to open the Straits of Tiran in exchange for a withdrawal from the area. Refusal would trigger the next phase: Israeli forces would grind toward the Suez Canal against the bulk of the Egyptian army, a prospect Rabin hoped to avoid.

Yes, he was confident, his forces could destroy that army, but at what cost in human life?

Some of Rabin's commanders, especially Ariel "Arik" Sharon, the gruff, paunchy, tough-minded head of a division in the Negev, opposed this piecemeal strategy, contending that Israel should demolish the Egyptian army immediately in one swift strike. At a meeting of military and political leaders in southern command headquarters, Sharon vigorously argued against fighting in phases.

"After the fighting," he said, "we would be in a position of political weakness. If the Egyptians did not meet our demands, we would already be under great pressure from the Americans as well as the Soviets. We would not be able to resist and we would become weaker by the day. With the army mobilized, the country would be at a standstill. Going by phases was asking for a disaster, and it was completely unnecessary."

In private, Eshkol, who was a financial but not a military wizard, would respond: "Arik, what you are saying is irresponsible! You are irresponsible!"

Rabin was silent at the meeting. Sharon's argument made military sense to him, but, as Eshkol felt, the IDF would suffer tremendous casualties. The two military men appeared to view differently the importance of the human element in fighting a war. To Sharon, the dead and the maimed were, unfortunately, an inevitable product of war. The idea was to win—at almost any cost.

Sharon was especially remembered for his role as a battalion commander in the 1956 war. Though his superiors ordered him not to advance to the Suez Canal through the Mitla Pass in the Sinai, feeling it unnecessary, Sharon persuaded them to let him send a patrol. The "patrol," which, in fact, resembled a mechanized brigade, was attacked in a disastrous ambush that left dozens of Israeli bodies strewn on the sands of Sinai and contributed little to victory.

Still, Rabin, though deploring Sharon's indiscipline and many of his callous actions, admired his decisiveness and some of his aggressive battle views and would, in the future, often seek his advice, which he would sometimes meld with his own military thinking. And now, with Israel in grave danger, he would not dismiss his arguments, or, for that matter, those of other colleagues, whatever he thought of them.

At another meeting, this time in the Pit, the underground operations center in Tel Aviv, Eshkol and Rabin again met with Sharon and other military commanders, and the debate over strategy resumed. At the end, Rabin would say:

"There's only one element that can stand now, and that is the army. That's why our responsibility is so grave. It all depends on us now, all of it."

Rabin was saying that the army stood alone because Eshkol, while unjustly pilloried by the public for many developments beyond his control, was lacking in the decisiveness required during a military crisis. And without firm political leadership at the helm when Israel's survival was at stake, the chief of staff had to make all the vital decisions. Perhaps Sharon and his supporters were right, Rabin felt, and he should try in one bloody blow to destroy the Egyptian army.

Yet he could not expunge from his soul the guilt he felt for those who died under his command in 1948, and now for those who might die because he may have set in motion the wheels of war with his threatening statements and retaliatory orders.

It seemed a monumental irony: He had struggled to become chief of staff so he could build a powerful army that would guarantee peace, and in that post he had instead helped to bring his nation to the threshold of war.

"Rabin thought he had unleashed events," Ehud Barak would say. "He did not have much direct command-post experience, and so felt responsible for everything. He was thus under great tension."

Rabin was, temperamentally, a warrior for peace more than for war. Living with the ghosts of the past, he could not make a combat decision without a struggle with himself. He was, in fact, repelled by the very sight of blood. When he would one day take his son, Yuval, to the dentist and watched while the boy's tooth was extracted, he returned home white-faced and snapped to Leah:

"You didn't tell me it would be so bloody!"

Now he had to make one of the most important and fateful decisions in the history of the Jewish people, with their state, as it had been 2,000 years earlier, risking massive bloodshed and possible national oblivion. And it would be fighting the entire Arab world without allies, unlike in the 1956 Sinai War, when Israel fought only one Arab country, Egypt, with the help of Britain and France.

It was thus terrifying to be alone at the top. And Rabin, feeling as Atlas might have supporting the world, would now carry the full burden of his country's future on his shoulders. For Eshkol seemed too confused to give him direction, an impression magnified when he appeared on television and stammered through a speech that did little to raise public morale. His authority, moreover, had been undermined by Ben-Gurion, who, for political reasons, bitterly attacked his successor as incompetent and demanded his ouster.

And Rabin's loneliness deepened as the seed of insecurity engendered a deep suspicion and mistrust of almost everyone around him. He yearned, at this moment of crisis, to hear words of advice and encouragement, to feel that he wasn't alone and could share, even if informally, at least the moral responsibility for the decision he must make. But military subordinates like Sharon, he knew, favored war, eager to prove their men could perform miracles. And the politicians, while relatively moderate, thought more about what was best for themselves than what was best for the country.

Still, there were a few leaders who had the integrity and honesty that would justify trust. And the most important ones, he felt, were David Ben-Gurion, the founder and first prime minister of Israel, and Moshe Dayan, one of Israel's first great warriors and the man who had recruited him as a fighter. Neither man had any power now, having been political outcasts since 1965, but they were still national icons.

Ben-Gurion had resigned as prime minister in 1963 after bitter political disputes with Eshkol and other colleagues from the ruling Mapai Party (which, in December 1967, would become part of a larger Labor Party coalition) and formed his own Rafi Party with his two disciples, Dayan and Shimon Peres.

With the nation's life on the line, Rabin decided to confer with Ben-Gurion even though the Old Man had hurt him deeply in the Palmach reunion episode, and then, several years later, lied about it.

"Yitzhak," Ben-Gurion had said at a meeting in his home, "do you remember when you came to me in 1949 and asked me why I was placing your Palmachniks in the position of having to choose between your duty to obey orders and loyalty to your former comrades-in-arms? Remember what I told you then? That if you feel that way, you can go to the Palmach rally."

Rabin was "struck dumb." "You gave me permission to attend the rally?" he exclaimed. "Then why did the chief of staff put me on trial and find me guilty of disobeying orders?"

"Really?" Ben Gurion replied in seeming amazement. "Why didn't you tell the chief of staff that I had given you permission to attend the rally?"

Rabin had wondered if Ben-Gurion was trying to "re-tailor history in order to harness me to his political chariot."

But if Ben-Gurion had his warts, he was still Ben-Gurion: the only person to have shouldered a burden as great as his—though one that other Jewish leaders shared—when the Yishuv leader had proclaimed the birth of the state while the Arabs stood, as they did today, poised to attack and liquidate the nation. Surely Ben-Gurion would understand the mental torture he was suffering and offer some inspiration. And while Dayan had also treated him shabbily in the past, he was still frank and honest and was often more cautiously thoughtful than were the other commanders.

"Troubled by the course of developments and finding the uncertainty beginning to jar on my nerves," Rabin would explain, "I felt that I needed their advice and perhaps their encouragement. I was carrying a heavy burden. Israel was facing one of the most serious situations she had ever experienced, and I sensed that in its perplexity the cabinet expected me not only to present and analyze the military options, but also to dispel any doubts by telling it which option to adopt. Needless to say, that made me feel very lonely, and I hoped that discussing the situation with Ben-Gurion and Dayan would be of help to me."

But when Rabin called on Ben-Gurion at his home on May 22, the distinguished host, after receiving him warmly, could hardly have been of less help. In fact, his words struck Rabin "like hammer blows":

"I very much doubt whether Nasser wanted to go to war, and now we are in serious trouble. . . . The army is all right; the officers are all right; you're all right. But there's no one to tell you what to do! The prime minister and the cabinet should take responsibility for deciding whether or not to go to war. That's not a matter for the army to decide. The government is not discharging its proper duties. This is no way to function in an emergency!"

Rabin was dismayed as Ben-Gurion hammered away.

"You made a mistake," Israel's founder said, regarding the mobilization of reserves.

"I recommended mobilization to make sure we were ready," Rabin replied.

"In that case, you, or whoever gave you permission to mobilize so many reservists, made a mistake," Ben-Gurion repeated. "You have led the state into a grave situation. We must not go to war. We are isolated. You bear the responsibility."

As Rabin departed, these words vibrated in his psyche. He had come for encouragement and left shattered, feeling now more than ever that "the entire burden was resting on my shoulders."

"When Yitzhak returned from his visit with Ben-Gurion,"

Rahama Hermon, the aide to Rabin, would tell me, "his shoulders drooped and his head was down, with a cigarette dangling from his lips. You could feel his suffering. I knew what he meant when he told me, 'the higher you climb, the higher the wall.'"

A few hours later, Rabin visited Dayan, though the fallen hero's somewhat contemptuous attitude toward him during many of the years they served together had contributed to his sense of insecurity. Dayan greeted Rabin with cool civility, apparently surprised by the visit. But, Rabin felt, however strained their relationship, Dayan was a great military leader and, unlike Ben-Gurion, his close ally, might be able to lift his spirits. Dayan, however, would say of their meeting:

"Yitzhak seemed not only tired, which was natural, but also unsure of himself, perplexed, nervously chain-smoking, with hardly the air of a man 'impatient for battle.' He complained that instead of being allowed to do his work in the army, he was being rushed to Jerusalem each day to take part in government consultations, and that he was not getting from Eshkol a clear political-military line or definitive instructions. . . . My principal impression of the evening was that Rabin was in a state of dejection, and if this were also apparent to his officers and men, it would be most unfortunate."

The government, Dayan told Rabin, had threatened Nasser's leadership of the Arab world by retaliating against Syria and Jordan too vigorously, and thus forcing Nasser to defend his image and prestige. Nasser would now blockade the Straits of Tiran, he predicted, and Israel would have to respond by first routing the enemy "at a location favorable to us" and then moving south toward the straits.

Rabin agreed. But he added that the most suitable place for the first clash was the Gaza Strip, for the Egyptians would probably rush troops there.

That would be a mistake, Dayan replied. The large civilian population and the many Palestinian refugee camps would get in the way of the war. Hit a purely military objective, he advised.

But if Dayan, like Ben-Gurion, blamed Rabin for mobilizing the reserves and also questioned his tactics, the chief of staff was at least grateful for a complimentary crumb Dayan threw his way: He had done a good job building up the army.

But even the crumb crumbled in importance, it seemed. Nasser, feeling, or wishing to feel, that if Israel's army acted without big-power support it couldn't conquer his own forces, threw down the gauntlet.

"We are in confrontation with Israel," he told officers of the Egyptian air base at Bir Gafgafa in Sinai, one hundred miles from Israel's southwestern border. "In contrast to what happened in 1956 when France and Britain were at her side, Israel is not supported today by any European power. . . . Henceforth the situation is in your hands. Our armed forces have occupied Sharm el-Sheikh. . . . We shall on no account allow the Israeli flag to pass through the Gulf of Aqaba. The Jews threaten to make war. I reply: 'Ahlan wa sahlan—Welcome!' We are ready for war. . . . This water is ours."

At 3:45 A.M., May 23, Rabin was awakened by a call from GHQ. Dayan's prediction had come true: Nasser had blockaded the Straits of Tiran. At the same time, the Syrians closed a key road to UN observers and were streaming onto the Golan Heights.

Rabin, Leah would say, "grabbed his trousers, put them on as he ran to the door, and got into his car." As he met with his colleagues at headquarters, Eshkol arrived with a warning from President Lyndon Johnson: Don't fire the first shot or take any action without first consulting him. And while several commanders urged an immediate preemptive attack on Egypt, Eshkol held out. If Israel ignored Johnson's plea and war broke out, it might find itself facing the Soviet Union as well as the Arabs—alone.

Rabin seemed relieved by the delay. At a noon meeting of the ministerial committee on defense, he was still undecided.

"It's not just freedom of navigation that is hanging in the balance," he said. "Israel's credibility, determination, and capacity to exercise her right of self-defense are all being put to the test."

Would a forty-eight-hour postponement decisively endanger the prospect of an Israeli preemptive strike? Rabin was asked.

No, it would not, he replied.

Abba Eban immediately took off on a tour of France, Britain, and the United States. Perhaps, Rabin prayed, they could still talk sense into Nasser. Perhaps a miracle could still happen. But after the meeting, he stayed behind to talk with a man who didn't believe in miracles—though he belonged to the National Religious Party. Interior Minister Moshe Chaim Shapira had vehemently argued against launching a preemptive attack even if Nasser refused to give in, an argument that Rabin, for all his agonized caution, could not accept, yet felt compelled to explore. For with Israel's very existence at stake, he had to understand explicitly the rationale of every argument.

Why, Rabin asked Shapira, was he so opposed to a preemptive strike?

"You're the one who owes an explanation," he cried. "Do you really believe that the Eshkol-Rabin team has to be more daring than the Ben-Gurion–Dayan team? In 1950 and 1951 the straits were closed; did Israel rush into a war? The straits remained closed up to 1956; did that endanger Israel's security? Ben-Gurion didn't go to war even though the Egyptians were backing terrorist raids against Israel.

"When did Ben-Gurion strike? Only when Israel didn't have to go it alone! France and Britain were still world powers, and they undertook to destroy the Egyptian navy and air force. Egypt's army was massed west of the Canal Zone then—not in the Sinai, as it is now. French air squadrons were posted to Israel to safeguard us from Egyptian raids. The British and French fleets defended Israel's shores. Our civilian population was protected.

"Ben-Gurion did not go to war before he was certain that the fighting would be against Egypt alone; before making certain that at least two powers would veto any anti-Israel resolution in the Security Council. Now Egypt will be fighting on a single front, but we will have to fight on at least two, perhaps three.

"Politically, we will be totally isolated, and we won't receive arms supplies if we run short during the fighting. If we're attacked, of course, we'll fight for our lives. But to take the initiative? To bring this curse down on us with our own hands? Do you want to bear the responsibility for endangering Israel? I shall resist it as long as I draw breath!"

Rabin, his confidence shaken once again, struggled to reply:

"Nasser has presented us with a grave provocation. If we don't face that challenge, the IDF's deterrent capacity will become worthless. Israel will be humiliated. Which power will support a small state that has ceased to be a military factor? Why bother with a state whose neighbors are growing stronger and subjecting it to humiliating pinpricks? We're going to war over freedom of navigation. Nasser has threatened Israel's standing; later on his army will threaten Israel's very existence. I don't want to go to war either, but there's no way out if the American political efforts fail."

"Israel's existence will be endangered if we go to war," Shapira shot back. "If we dig in we shall be strong. We'll dig in. We'll fortify ourselves. We can withstand any attack. But we won't fire the first shot!"

Rabin left for home, he would say, "in a state of mental and physical exhaustion." Didn't his accusers hear the bloodcurdling cries for revenge echoing from the Arab world? He had been determined to avoid another devastating war, to save the lives of many thousands of Israelis. Now he might have to support war for the same purpose—to save these Israelis, who could be massacred without a preemptive strike. When he arrived home at about 6 P.M., Leah was jolted by his disturbed, confused look, his restlessness as he paced the hall, puffing on a cigarette incessantly. Suddenly, he stopped and said:

"I'm leaving for Beersheba to see the southern commander."

"No," Leah responded. "You're not going anywhere. You're exhausted and need rest."

Rabin offered no resistance, as he normally would if Leah tried to make him slacken his pace. He realized she was right.

How did he get into such a state? Rabin asked himself. He would try to find an answer:

"The past few days had seemed endless. Meals were taken on the run and only when the occasion arose. I had hardly slept, and I was smoking like a steam engine. But it was more than nicotine that brought me down. The heavy sense of guilt that had been dogging me of late became unbearably strong on May 23."

And he could not forget Ben-Gurion's words, "You bear the responsibility," or Shapira's haunting charges. Though he had prepared the army for such a moment, had he failed in his duty as Eshkol's chief military adviser?

"Maybe that was why Israel now found herself in such difficult straits," he would lament.

With his guilt complex, fed by insecurity, anxiety, exhaustion, and nicotine, rubbing his nerves raw, how could he meet so challenging a responsibility? How could he risk letting history condemn him for leading his people to slaughter? He was honest with others, and now he had to be honest with himself, to summon the courage to place his whole future in jeopardy for the sake of his country. He had to accept the fact that he was, at least temporarily, unsuited for the terrible task and act accordingly.

"Never before had I even come close to feeling so depressed," he would admit, "and rarely had I allowed myself to share my deepest feelings with someone else. It's just not in my character and never has been. But this time I sensed an urgent need, and I called up Ezer Weizman, the chief of operations. We had often disagreed over various issues, but I had complete faith in his personal integrity. I wanted to pour my heart out to him."

Weizman was a handsome, dashing, hard-drinking, profane-tongued officer, who had helped found the Israeli air force and was for many years its commander. He had a history of friction with Rabin, whose introverted nature contrasted sharply with Weizman's extroverted personality. The year before, Weizman had persuaded Eshkol to appoint him chief of operations in place of Chaim Bar-Lev, though Rabin, close to Bar-Lev, strongly protested. What Rabin apparently didn't realize, despite his suspicious nature, was how determined Weizman was to succeed him—in part, ironically, because of Rabin's own encouragement. As Weizman himself would write:

> The truth is that when I had mapped out my career . . . , I thought that I would serve as head of the air force until the age of 40, and then, at the height of my powers, . . . I would leave the military for a civilian career—though I hadn't thought about exactly what it would be. But Shimon Peres, Zvi Zur and, afterwards, Yitzhak Rabin, thought otherwise, and . . . began to plant the seeds of a new ambition in my heart:
>
> "Weizman, why don't you become a future candidate for chief of staff? Who decides that the next chief of staff can't come from the ranks of the air force?"
>
> And the seeds fell on fertile soil. The stronger the suggestions, and the more diversified their sources, the more they aroused my desire to reach that top post. At first the great challenge still seemed far off, but the more I toyed with the idea, the closer it grew, as these things do, until it was almost within reach.

And it was indeed—because of Rabin's unusual show of trust, generated by his shaky physical and psychological state.

Weizman rushed to Rabin's home on receiving his phone call and "found him sitting alone. . . . Everything was silent and still. He looked broken and depressed. He sat on the edge of the couch and I sat down beside him."

Rabin immediately asked: "Am I to blame? Should I relinquish my post?"

Weizman would say that Rabin, speaking in "a weak voice," asserted: "Due to a series of mistakes, I've led Israel into an entanglement, on the eve of the greatest and hardest war the state has ever experienced. In this war, everything depends on the air force. The air force will decide the war. I believe that if a man has erred, he should go. I've erred. Will you take on the post of chief of staff?"

"I was very upset," Weizman would add. "It was so unexpected, and I paused for a moment or two to compose myself. Then I said: 'Yitzhak, you know I want to be chief of staff. But under these circumstances, I won't accept the post. If you resign, it's worth a few divisions to Nasser. In the present difficult circumstances, it will be a heavy blow to the army's morale. The government is hesitant about going to war, and this will make it hesitate even more. As for you, Yitzhak, if you resign now, you'll be finished for the rest of your life. Summon up all your strength. I promise to do the best I can to help you get through. You'll be the victorious chief of staff. You'll reach the Suez Canal and the Jordan."

Rabin would later deny that he asked Weizman to take over the post of chief of staff, claiming he asked him simply to assume his duties until he was well enough to return to work.

"I made him no such offer [of chief of staff]," he would insist, "nor was I empowered to 'bequeath' the job to him or anyone else. That is not a chief of staff's prerogative. Be that as it may, Ezer talked me out of any thought of resignation. Over and over again, he told me I would get over it. He would not hear of my resigning and assured me that I would lead the Israel Defense Forces to a great victory."

Rabin felt no better when Weizman left, and so Leah called their physician. Dr. Eliahu Gilon rushed over and confirmed that Rabin was in a severe state of exhaustion and gave him a sedative. He slept until about noon the following day.

... all that night, [Weizman would write] I couldn't shut my eyes. I didn't say a word to anyone, and the next day, at seven in the morning, I returned to Rabin. When I got there, I found his aide-de-camp, Colonel Raphael Efrat, and Dr. Gilon.

Again Rabin asked me, "Are you prepared to take the job?"

I replied, "The answer is negative, like last night."

Dr. Gilon, Efrat, and I agreed that we had to report to Eshkol. We decided to spread the story that the chief of staff had been taken ill with nicotine poisoning.

Weizman then called a meeting of the general staff and heads of regional commands, and they modified the overall plan for the campaign in Sinai. Rabin's limited scheme for a takeover of the Gaza Strip had stretched into a larger plan for a march toward the Suez Canal. And that evening, Weizman would claim, he returned to Rabin to report on the decision, and Rabin "smiled and gave his approval."

But according to Rabin, he didn't give his approval, or even know the meeting took place, until he returned to work. He might have approved the change if he had been at the meeting, but Weizman, he thought, had no right to do so in the capacity of chief of staff; Weizman should have consulted with him.

"I felt he had acted rashly," Rabin would say, understating his feelings.

On the morning of May 25, Rabin, in much better shape, was back at work. And now he felt less alone. For Chaim Bar-Lev, who had preceded Weizman as his chief of operations, had returned from a study tour in Paris and was to be named deputy chief of staff a few days later—to Weizman's shock. Weizman threatened to resign, realizing that Bar-Lev, and not he, would eventually succeed Rabin. He didn't resign, but in his bitterness he would boast, referring to Rabin:

"I had to hold his balls."

Bar-Lev, a more experienced field commander than Rabin, now took over many of Rabin's command responsibilities, relieving the pressure on his boss.

Meanwhile, Rabin went to Eshkol and said: "I had a personal problem, and I regret it. But I do consider myself fit for duty now. Yet, if you think I should relinquish my post, I shall accept your decision without protest."

"No problem," Eshkol replied.

"I stole one last, hard look at him," Rabin would say. "He, too, was under great pressure, and I wondered for a moment what he really thought. . . . Perhaps he had long known—and I had just then been forced to face—the frightening depths of a man's vulnerability."

In any case, what was important was the depth of Israel's vulnerability now that it had to decide whether to answer Nasser's explosive challenge. And it was growing more explosive by the hour as more and more Egyptians troops poured into the Sinai, many of them straight from the war in Yemen.

The total Arab strength was formidable: over 500,000 soldiers, over 5,000 tanks, and nearly 1,000 planes, as compared with Israel's 275,000 soldiers, 800 tanks, and fewer than 200 planes. And every report of troop buildups along Israel's borders boosted the weight of Rabin's burden, though he was now able to handle it, if with the agonizing resignation of an all-or-nothing gambler betting the life of his family on the number seven. He couldn't just helplessly wait for the slaughter. He thus ordered the regional commands to deploy for defense on full alert and began mobilizing all the reserves not yet called up. Rabin then held a further meeting with Eshkol and other military and political officials and told them bluntly:

"We are no longer certain who will take the initiative in commencing hostilities. Do you believe we can extract an American declaration that any attack on Israel will be regarded as an attack on the United States? And if not—since such a possibility does not appear to be likely—what is the point of waiting any longer? We've already forfeited the advantage of strategic surprise. If we continue to wait, we run the risk of losing even the advantage of tactical surprise. That would be the worst situation imaginable. What are we waiting for?"

Eshkol icily replied: "The IDF will not attack before the political options have been exhausted."

Rabin was almost relieved by Eshkol's strong stand against his view. Maybe Eshkol was right. Maybe he himself was overly influenced by his fellow officers. At any rate, he helped to write a cable to Eban, who was about to solicit President Johnson's help in a last-minute effort to avoid war:

Israel faces a grave danger of general attack by Egypt and Syria. In this situation, implementation of the American commitment is vital—

in declaration and action—immediately, repeat, immediately, meaning a declaration by the U.S. government that any attack on Israel is equivalent to an attack on the United States [and that it gives] specific orders to U.S. forces in the region that they are to combine operations with the IDF against any possible Arab attack on Israel. . . .

Now all Rabin and the others could do was wait for the haggling over Israel's destiny to end.

Meanwhile, the home front organized for civil defense. The few shelters that had been built were cleaned out, and women and children were seen everywhere digging foxholes in their gardens, crisscrossing their windows with paper tape to protect against explosions, and storing foodstuffs, since most delivery trucks had been mobilized for war.

Dahlia, now seventeen, came home from school, changed into working clothes, and went out to dig foxholes in her own garden and those of her neighbors. Could she be digging the graves of her family? she wondered.

"Out of all the people in Israel," she would tell me, "Father was responsible for saving Israel. The whole thing was on his shoulders. I was terrified."

Leah, however, was confident that her husband would make sure no enemy planes would strike civilian areas, and "looked on the foxhole in [her] garden with just a little contempt." Nor did she "bother pasting paper on all the windows." But she was glad that a detachment of military police had been assigned to protect the home of the chief of staff, and she felt "the need" to play tennis in order "to unload all my tensions." People were relieved to see her play: This meant that war hadn't broken out yet.

On May 26, however, it seemed that Leah would no longer be swinging her racket; a report on the Johnson-Eban talk had finally arrived: The United States strongly opposed Israel acting alone and would not give it any aid if it ignored this advice. Soviet Premier Kosygin and French President de Gaulle also warned Israel not to start a war.

The Israeli cabinet urgently met a few hours later, and Rabin now pressed for an immediate preemptive strike regardless of international pressure.

"Our political efforts had gained nothing," he said. If we failed
to respond to Egyptian aggression, we would only lose more
time—which was working against us—and further endanger
Israel's security."

But Abba Eban arrived at the meeting from the airport shortly
before midnight, May 27, and pressed for another postponement.
Johnson had told him, he said:

"Israel must not be the first to act! I need two or three weeks to
implement our political plans for resolving the problem."

Eban argued that it would be senseless to go to war under the
circumstances until it was clear whether Johnson could succeed in
his effort. If he failed, then the whole country would support a war
as the best, if not the only, way to avoid possible annihilation. The
meeting degenerated into shouts, accusations, pleadings, and
when Eshkol passed a note to Rabin indicating that the ministers
from the National Religious Party threatened to resign if the
nation went to war, the chief of staff could only groan:

"That was all we needed now—a cabinet crisis with nearly a
thousand tanks in the Sinai!"

Finally, on May 28, Rabin and Eshkol, who had both felt, however reluctantly, that they had no choice but to go to war, changed
their minds when Johnson and Secretary of State Dean Rusk sent
new messages to Israel: Don't go to war. Let the United States
explore all political avenues. It might still be able to persuade
Britain and France to break the blockade, by force if necessary. The
cabinet, except for one minister, now agreed; the first shot wouldn't
be fired for two to three weeks.

Though supporting this decision, Rabin was extremely uneasy,
especially when, on May 30, Jordanian forces joined those of Egypt
and Syria, forming a single military front. Every day of delay
meant many more of his men would die. And his generals, he
knew, would scream. And at a meeting of the general staff,
attended by Eshkol, they did. So did a large part of the public, nervously perplexed by the government's confusion and uncertainty.

A cry went up now for Moshe Dayan, the veteran soldier and
hero of the 1956 war, to replace Eshkol as defense minister. Eshkol
was alarmed by this potential diminution of his power and, to
relieve the pressure on him, wanted to offer Dayan the post of southern commander, which Dayan had indicated he wanted anyway.

Rabin was disturbed by this suggestion. He did not wish to

remove the current southern commander, Yishayahu Gavish, from the post, especially since the chief of staff feared the independent-minded Dayan would ignore his orders. Rabin had no desire to take orders from "Defense Minister" Dayan.

But when Eshkol insisted that Dayan become southern commander, Rabin agreed to talk with him. Better that Dayan serve under him than over him. At their meeting, he asked Dayan:

"Are you prepared to submit to my authority as chief of staff?"

Yes, he would, Dayan replied, but with reservations.

"General Maxwell Taylor is the commander of the American forces in Vietnam," he said. "Being in command of the Vietnam front, he is, of course, subject to the orders of the Joint Chiefs of Staff in Washington. I presume that our relationship will be of that nature."

Feeding Rabin's insecurity, this statement seemed to confirm in his mind that Dayan had little intention of taking orders from him. He now bluntly asked:

"Do you want to replace me as chief of staff?"

"No!" Dayan responded. "You are chief of staff, and I shall obey every order from the general staff. I merely want to take part in the war, rather than watch it from the sidelines. I understand that Eshkol supports my request."

Finally, Rabin had little choice but to agree as well, and reluctantly summoned Gavish.

He was sorry, Rabin said, but Eshkol had ordered him to appoint Dayan to the southern command.

This task was deeply painful for Rabin. But while Gavish would apparently never forgive him, feeling he hadn't tried hard enough to protect him (he refused even to discuss Rabin with me), Rabin's pain would soon vanish. For Gavish could remain at his post after all.

When a cable arrived from Washington stating that the United States had failed to assemble an international fleet to break the Egyptian blockade, it was clear that Johnson could not reverse the deteriorating situation. With war now inevitable, Eshkol, under mounting pressure, formed a National Unity government including Menachem Begin and other opposition leaders. And Eshkol could no longer ignore the public demand that Moshe Dayan be brought into the cabinet. He made Dayan an offer:

How would he like to be deputy prime minister and his military adviser?

Dayan rejected the offer. If he joined the cabinet, he said, he would agree only to be defense minister.

Eshkol was frustrated. His choice for that post was Yigal Allon, who had recently returned from a long sojourn in Europe.

As the public pressure grew, Eshkol asked Rabin whether he thought Dayan, under the circumstances, should be appointed defense minister.

"Was it merely out of politeness?" Rabin would later muse. "In any event, I knew that I could not influence domestic political developments, so I held my peace."

Some of his old Palmach comrades felt Rabin should have held his peace less resolutely and fought harder for the appointment of Allon. They suspected that the chief of staff, however much he distrusted Dayan, wasn't thrilled by the prospect of resuming a role in Allon's shadow. Sometimes, they explained, a successful person did not always like being constantly reminded that he owed his success to a parent or patron.

Eshkol offered Dayan the job, but could Dayan overcome a daunting obstacle in his path? As a member of the opposition Rafi Party, which Ben-Gurion had formed after breaking away from the governing Mapai Party he had founded, Dayan could not defy his patron. And Ben-Gurion, whose hatred of Eshkol was boundless, strongly opposed any cooperation with his government. Anyway, he disagreed with Dayan's view that a preemptive strike was now necessary. A great soldier, a great mind, but still too impetuous. Still not ripe enough to make the big decisions, to see the full picture.

But at a meeting of Rafi leaders, among them Shimon Peres, who supported Ben-Gurion's opposition to war, all but the former prime minister agreed: Dayan should accept. Only he could raise the army's slumping morale.

Ben-Gurion slowly backpedaled. All right, but if Dayan was to be defense minister, why not prime minister as well? Let Eshkol take orders from him.

Impossible! replied the others.

"Moshe," Ben-Gurion finally said, "accept!"

Dayan smiled. "I'll accept on one condition," he said. "That I'll have your advice."

Ben-Gurion was assuaged. Perhaps he could still talk Moshe into stopping a full-scale war—a wishful thought.

Dayan thus became defense minister, to the relief of the frightened, demoralized public. But not to the relief of Yitzhak Rabin. With Dayan now his boss instead of his subordinate, he almost wished he were Atlas again holding up the world alone.

On June 4, Rabin visited his airmen and told them they would probably be going to war within days.

"Yitzhak wanted to see if the men were confident and put all his cards on the table," David Ivry, an air commander who was present, told me. "He found that the men were confident indeed, and this, in turn, gave him a confidence that wasn't as strong before his visit. He and the men mutually encouraged each other."

Returning home, Rabin met Dayan at a Tel Aviv airfield. The cabinet, Dayan informed him, had finally voted for war, and the IDF would initiate action the following morning. The air force, they hoped, would demolish most Egyptian planes on the ground in a few hours, and the troops would then thrust with lightning speed to cut off the bulk of the Egyptian army in eastern Sinai and attack it from the flank and rear. His whole life, and Israel's, it seemed to Rabin, added up to tomorrow.

"I felt calm and relaxed," he would recall, "as if the enormous burden of anxiety and doubt that had weighed on me since May 15 had suddenly disintegrated. I knew that the IDF was well prepared—in its training, its deployment, and the operational plans we had drawn up. . . . For the first time in weeks, I went home to get a good night's sleep."

12

"By Morning It'll Be Okay"

"**I** have so much to say to you, I cannot find the words," Rabin told his pilots in a hoarse, emotional voice on the morning of June 5 as he stood on the airfield where the bombers were poised to launch their historic attack. So he paraphrased Winston Churchill's words:

"Never in the field of human conflict has the fate of so many depended on the skill and courage of so few. It is you who will decide the destiny of our people and our state."

And they did. Waves of Israeli planes thundered over Egypt firing cannons on enemy planes lined up on nine airfields and dropping bombs on their runways. In about three hours Egypt had lost almost two hundred supersonic and subsonic fighters, nearly sixty bombers, and more than thirty transport planes. Rabin exulted in his own air force command post and called Leah with the news:

"The Egyptian air force is completely destroyed!" he cried.

Israeli aircraft, now free to rain disaster on airfields in Syria,

Jordan, and Iraq, knocked out an additional one hundred planes or so when the three countries began to attack Israel late in the morning. A total now of about four hundred Arab aircraft!

Israel had tried to persuade Jordan's King Hussein to stay out of the war through UN and American channels, but to no avail. How could he stand by, he felt, while his Arab neighbors were under attack, even if the alternative was national suicide? In fact, there seemed to be no way now for the Arabs to effectively assault Israel, especially with their morale plummeting together with their planes.

Within hours, Israeli paratroopers captured Jerusalem's northern Arab suburbs while other fighters attacked south of the city. Finally, Israeli tanks reached the crest of the Jerusalem hills before the Jordanian armor could. In the Sinai, Israeli tanks had ground into El Arish by evening.

"The night of June 5–6 must have been a difficult one for Nasser and Hussein," Rabin would say with mock pity. "Never in their worst nightmares could they have dreamed they would be in such a harrowing position after the first day of fighting. Our forces had made a swift breakthrough in both the Sinai and the West Bank, not to mention the fact that we had totally conquered the skies."

That first evening, however, Jordanian artillery shells fired from Kalkilia in the West Bank whistled over Tel Aviv—and Zahala, Rabin's nearby village, as well. Terrified, Leah and her two children scrambled into the foxhole that she had deemed unnecessary.

"We sat close together," Leah would say, "as every few minutes a shell passed overhead with an eerie whistle and a strange tail of light. We lowered our heads each time, and prayed that this one, too, would move on elsewhere. Our twelve-year-old, Yuval, kept on murmuring:

"'I want to be where my father is.'"

When the shelling stopped, they found that a neighboring house had been hit. Stunned, they ran into their own house, and Leah telephoned her husband.

Did he know that Zahala was being shelled? she cried almost hysterically.

"'Yes,'" he replied in a voice that Leah thought was "too cool for my liking" at that moment. "'I know. By morning it'll be okay.'"

Couldn't her husband, Leah wondered, have exhibited a little more emotion? Yet her fear and shock were tempered by elation; Israel was winning the war. She then taped up more windows and lay down with her children in her double bed, with all of them sleeping in their clothes in case they had to rush again to the foxhole.

They didn't have to. In the morning—perfect quiet. So her husband was sometimes too cool. But he had good qualities, too. His word could be trusted.

With Egypt and Jordan virtually knocked out of the war, the Syrians, who provoked the war in the first place, ironically made little effort to join the battle, preferring to fight to the last Egyptian. And while the Israeli northern commander pleaded with Moshe Dayan to let him attack Syria, the defense minister refused. Early on the second day, Dayan called Rabin to his office and, with great agitation, made clear why. What if the Soviets came to the aid of their closest Middle Eastern ally? Reports, he said, were piling up about frenzied Soviet political activity aimed at halting the fighting. And it might succeed before the Straits of Tiran were opened.

"[So] what about Sharm el-Sheikh?" he snapped. "We'll find the war coming to an end before we get our hands on it! Get to Sharm and establish our presence there, irrespective of the progress of fighting in the Sinai!"

Rabin urgently planned an attack, though he felt Sharm el-Sheikh would fall automatically like ripened fruit when the Egyptians were beaten in the Sinai. And he was right. Before an operation could be launched, the Egyptian forces in the Sinai, threatened by the swiftly advancing Israelis, fled toward the Suez Canal and turned into a ragged, barefoot, panicky mob as their pursuers reached the waterway (after Dayan, who had opposed going all the way, changed his mind). And when the navy reached Sharm el-Sheikh, it reported:

"There's no one to fight!"

But then, some hours later, there was someone—not at Sharm el-Sheikh, but offshore near El Arish in the Sinai, where mysterious explosions pierced the desert air. Were the Egyptians attacking the town from the sea? Rabin rushed naval vessels and planes to the area, and when they sighted an unidentified ship, rained bullets and bombs on it. But then a second report sent chills down his

spine. His men had attacked a Soviet ship! Dayan's vision of
doom, it seemed, had crystallized. He urgently called a meeting
with Dayan, Eshkol, and the senior GHQ commanders, who, on
learning of the report, were horrified. Had all the gains been a
cruel joke?

"It was vital to make preparations," Rabin would later say,
"but no one wanted to articulate exactly for what. We did not dare
put our fears into words, but the question that hung over the room
like a giant saber was obvious:

"Are we facing massive Soviet intervention in the fighting?"

As Rabin and the others feverishly, almost incoherently, tossed
options at each other for saving Israel from annihilation, someone
rushed in with a new report: The ship was not Russian. It was
American!

The shock from the first report dissipated into a collective sigh
of relief. But now there was a new fear. At a time when Israel
needed U.S. support, at least at the UN, how could it explain to
Washington that Israeli planes and an Israeli naval vessel had
bombed and torpedoed the American ship *Liberty*, killing, they
would learn later, thirty-two and wounding many more?

The stricken vessel was to monitor the Israeli army's signals
networks so the United States would know what was happening
in the war. Washington had apparently issued an order to the
Liberty to stay away from the coast, but it never reached the ship.
So the United States accepted Israel's explanation and apology, as
well as compensation for the families of the casualties, and there
was another collective sigh.

In Washington, too. The Americans thought that the planes
attacking the *Liberty* were Soviet aircraft, and were pondering
whether to attack the Soviet fleet in the Mediterranean, perhaps
triggering World War III.

The tragedy was followed by triumph, one of the greatest in Jewish
history in Rabin's view—the capture of Jerusalem's Old City. After
a day of heavy fighting with the Arab Legion, Israeli paratroops
blasted their way through Lions' Gate on the eastern side of the Old
City wall near noon on June 7. Rabin and Dayan then flew to the
Jerusalem headquarters of Uzi Narkiss, the brave head of the central command who had fought with such distinction in the 1948

war. He had lost the Old City then, but had now seized it, and its hallowed stones would now be more than a memory for the Jewish people.

They drove to Lions' Gate, where Dayan left the jeep and asked the others to wait for him. He shortly returned with a photographer.

"I believe," Narkiss told me, "that Dayan intended to have a photo taken of himself alone at the gate for history. But then he seemed to feel that something was missing, and he said, 'Yitzhak, come,' then, 'Uzi, you, too.' And so we had our picture taken for history. Dayan really understood public relations. Rabin didn't seem to care about it."

As the three men drove through Lions' Gate past a smoldering tank, Rabin relived the terrible, heroic days of the 1948 war. In the eerie silence, broken only by occasional sniper fire, he could almost see the faces of the dead from that war as he moved through the narrow, twisting alleys that were now deserted, with every house shuttered as if hiding the ghosts that haunted him. He had dreamed of returning one day to be among them once again and reminding himself what he owed them. And now there were more ghosts, another generation of dead to repay with the peace that would finally end the cycle of death.

But there were cherished memories, too. He had been born there, and although his family had taken him away shortly afterward, he had returned often to wallow in the ancient glories of this ageless Jewish capital that gave meaning to the State of Israel he had fought to create.

And then they came to the Western, or Wailing, Wall, the very soul of the Jewish people.

Its stones [Rabin would write] have a power to speak to the hearts of Jews the world over, as if the historical memory of the Jewish people dwelled in the cracks between those ancient ashlars. For years I secretly harbored the dream that I might play a part not only in gaining Israel's independence but in restoring the Western Wall to the Jewish people. . . . Now that dream had come true, and suddenly I wondered why I, of all men, should be so privileged. I knew that never again in my life would I experience quite the same peak of elation. . . .

We stood among a tangle of rugged, battle-weary men who were unable to believe their eyes or restrain their emotions. Their eyes were moist with tears, their speech incoherent. The overwhelming desire was to cling to the Wall, to hold on to that great moment as long as possible . . . Following the ancient custom, Dayan scrawled a wish on a slip of paper and pushed it in between two of the stones. I felt truly shaken and stood there murmuring a prayer for peace.

But then it was back to the world of war. The *Liberty* tragedy had brought into focus the real threat to Israel's existence—the Soviet Union. Rabin would never forget the terror he felt when the false report came through: The Soviets were attacking! What if that should come true? Could Israel gamble that Soviet forces would not come to Syria's aid if it stormed into that country?

"No one in our political or military leadership," Rabin would say, "could promise that an all-out attack on Syria would not result in Soviet involvement, nor could anyone promise that such a dangerous development would induce the Americans to deter the Soviets."

Dayan still refused to take the gamble and order a major action against Syria, though the field commanders and the northern settlements, which had been shelled so often, begged him to order an assault, with Rabin's support.

"The Syrians are riding on our backs!" the settlers cried. "If the State of Israel is incapable of defending us, we're entitled to know it! . . . We should be told to leave our homes and flee from this nightmare!"

Rabin then pleaded with Dayan. The Syrians, he argued, had caused Israel the most trouble for the last decade, and now they would get away unscathed. But the defense minister would not budge. And the war, therefore, seemed over.

At 2 A.M. on June 8, Rabin went home for the first time since the war had begun. According to Leah, he looked thin and tired and his eyes were red with sleeplessness, since he had seldom had a chance to snatch any sleep on his cot in his office. He was in a "bad mood" despite his great victories, for there was one more victory he was denied: Syria.

"Utterly exhausted," he would say, "I exchanged a few words with Leah and the children before crumpling into bed. I think I was asleep before my head touched the pillow."

But it didn't touch the pillow for long. At 7 A.M. Ezer Weizman knocked on the door. Rabin was furious. Why was Ezer disturbing him in what seemed to him the middle of the night? He soon found out.

"Fifteen minutes ago," Weizman reported, "Dayan contacted Dado [Northern Commander David Elazar] and ordered him to attack the Syrians immediately."

Rabin rushed to the Pit and prepared for the attack. When he phoned Elazar and asked why Dayan had changed his mind, the northern commander replied that he didn't know. But Dayan had told him that "the Syrian units were crumbling and their soldiers had begun fleeing even before the IDF assault commenced."

Rabin was disturbed by this comment, which could be based on a misleading assumption.

"The Syrian army is nowhere near collapse," he warned Elazar. "You must assume that it will fight obstinately and with all its strength!"

And Rabin was right. As the Israelis fought their way up the Golan Heights, they were met with bitter resistance. Dayan called Rabin and issued an order: All military operations must cease the following morning.

But he had just ordered Elazar to send an airborne brigade into action, Rabin replied in dismay.

The order stands, Dayan replied.

But when Rabin relayed the order to Elazar, the reply was: "Sorry. Following your previous order, [the men] began to move off, and I can't stop them"—though, in fact, they were still awaiting orders.

The Syrian forces began to crumble, and Rabin's greatest enemy now was time. Not only Dayan, but the United States was demanding a cease-fire in the morning, and so Rabin had to order Elazar to forgo a plan to occupy the Golan town of Kuneitra. The Syrian radio, however, mistakenly announced that Kuneitra had fallen, and the Syrian soldiers, hearing the report, fled the city in panic. The Israelis thus walked in. And since the Syrians had fled Mount Hermon as well, a helicopter-borne force captured that bastion the next day, June 12. Since there was no firing, the cease-fire remained undisturbed.

The Six-Day War was over.

13

To Keep a Vow

"**M**other," wailed Dahlia as she lay on her bed on the evening of the cease-fire, "there's no justice. No justice at school, no justice in the [girl] scouts, none anywhere."

Leah was astonished. No justice? Hadn't Israel won one of the greatest victories in Jewish history? But Dahlia seemed inconsolable.

"All the children say that Dayan won the war, not Daddy. . . . "

Leah was touched by her daughter's fierce loyalty to Yitzhak and was sympathetic to her view. Her husband, after all, had built Israel's great army, while Dayan had become minister of defense only days before the war started and was riding on his reputation for daring and courage in past conflicts, a reputation he was adept at exploiting. But this was not the time to claim one's share of glory.

"Dahlia," Leah gently responded, "each of them made a massive contribution to this victory. . . . Now, do me a favor, don't cry. Whatever happens, your father has a historic place in it. Tomorrow they're going to inform the bereaved families of their loss. They are the ones with reason to cry."

And the next day, the tears of the grief-stricken families and friends of about eight hundred fallen soldiers dampened the great outpouring of joy that exploded in Israel as a besieged people suddenly found themselves in control of territory three times the size of the stifling state they knew only six days earlier. At the same time, as Israelis awakened in their new world, Dayan's name and not Rabin's was on most lips and in most headlines heralding Israel's victory around the world. Had not Dayan's dramatic appointment as defense minister, they asked, sparked new life into the army and raised the slumping morale of the nation at a critical moment?

Rabin was clearly hurt by this backseat treatment, even though there was an outpouring of gratitude for his role in the war.

"Our home," Leah would say, "was flooded with flowers, boxes of chocolates, and endless letters. Each letter brought the tears back again. I had never known such emotion. Bereaved parents wrote to Yitzhak that if their son was doomed to fall in war, then they were thankful that it happened while he was chief of staff, and they knew that the blood had not been spilled in vain."

Still, Rabin, with his withdrawn, taciturn personality, knew he could not compete with Dayan's charisma and flair for public relations. Nor with his tremendous ego. A week after the war, Dayan, fearing that Rabin would reap most of the credit for victory, said publicly:

"Anyone who says that I came in and found everything ready is just trying to obscure the issue."

And he rebuked Abba Eban for glorifying Rabin as a war hero in a speech to the Security Council, though Eban, too, harbored little love for the man.

Rabin was thus delighted when Hebrew University announced it would award him, rather than Dayan, an honorary doctorate in philosophy. Now he would have an opportunity to explain how the army he built and led could win so great a victory, how it could pave the way toward an even greater victory—permanent peace. It seemed ironic. He had longed to study at a university, but had always been frustrated by the need to defend his country. And now, without any higher education, he was being awarded a "doctorate" for the activities that kept him from getting it. Yet the war was a higher education for Rabin, at least in a spiritual sense.

"The Six-Day War," Chief Rabbi Israel Lau told me, "opened Rabin's eyes, ears, and heart to Israel's real traditions and heritage. As he captured town after town with a biblical name—Hebron, Beit El, the Old City of Jerusalem—he realized the true meaning of these hallowed places. Jerusalem, where he was born, had in his own words lain in his heart 'like an open wound.' Now the wound had finally healed."

And now Rabin would speak to the world from the liberated university campus on Mount Scopus.

But, insecure as usual, he was worried as he prepared his speech. He "felt far from certain that the speech was great," Leah would say. "It seemed to him somewhat lacking in sequence." So she nervously expected to listen to a "mediocre" lecture that, it seemed, would fail to rouse the audience that gathered on June 28, 1967, in the university's magnificent amphitheater facing the sun-bathed Judean Mountains.

"The air was charged with electricity," Leah would recall. "The moment arrived for Yitzhak to speak. I froze from tension and emotion. I was still waiting for a 'mediocre' speech when I noticed out of the corner of my eye a huge tear rolling down the cheek of my neighbor. . . . I looked around and could see others wiping away tears."

In a booming voice, Rabin proclaimed:

> Although [the army's] first task is the military one of maintaining security, it has numerous peacetime roles, not of destruction but of construction and of strengthening the nation's cultural and moral resources. . . . The men in the front lines saw with their own eyes not only the glory of victory, but also the price of victory—their comrades fallen beside them soaked in blood. I know, too, that the terrible price paid by our enemies also touched the hearts of many of our men. It may be that the Jewish people has never learned and never accustomed itself to feel the triumph of conquest and victory, with the result that these are accepted with mixed feelings.
>
> There has never been any hatred for the Arabs. . . . Can one fight against enemies without hatred in one's heart? Perhaps in this respect, too, we are different from many other people. I do not believe that hatred adds anything to fighting capacity. . . . We go forth to war when we are forced to, when there is no other choice.

We fight for survival, only when the other side makes war absolutely unavoidable.... We didn't celebrate the victory. There were no victory parades.... As Jews our celebration was of a different kind. Every one of us in his heart ... gave ourselves to thoughts of those who had fallen.

As Rabin ended his talk, he and Leah waited tensely for the reaction. He had never before spoken to a large audience. Everyone knew the name Rabin, of course, but not the person. Despite his title, he always remained in the background while more colorful men like Dayan and Weizman appeared in the news columns. But now, as Leah would say, "something special was happening." Mediocre speech? Everyone was standing, and applause and cheers echoed like thunder across the mountains for endless minutes.

Perhaps the proudest person of all was Rabin's father, Nehemiah. Forty-five years earlier he had listened to his son's plaintive wails in a hospital not far away; now he had listened to his son's passionate words, and the sound was just as precious. Rosa's spirit was still alive, it seemed, within the soul of their son.

Rabin himself was euphoric, as he would be almost thirty years later at a pro-Oslo rally he had feared would fail. The speech he now finished helped to make people realize that his army was not just a military force, but a spiritual and moral force that "had earned the right to feel confident in our military prowess without denigrating the virtues of our adversaries or falling into the trap of arrogance." A force for peace.

As Rabin would later say: "If there can be any recompense for the long, anxious nights, for the awful awareness of sending young men to face death, for the heavy burden of responsibility that bore down on me, I gained it at that Mount Scopus ceremony."

And the Israeli public gained a new perspective on the shaping of the victory. Who contributed most to it? In a popular poll, Rabin now surpassed Moshe Dayan, winning 45 percent of the vote to Dayan's 31 percent.

Before retiring as chief of staff, Rabin had to make an important decision. Whom should he recommend to replace him? Ezer Weizman came to him and argued that he deserved to be chosen. And when Rabin refused to commit himself, Weizman strode away in fury, slamming the door behind him. Painfully, bitterly, he realized that his dream was beyond reach; Chaim Bar-Lev would get the job. And he was right.

Rabin now pondered his own future—and that of Israel. From the moment of its birth, he had devoted himself to saving his country from destruction. As an officer in the War of Independence, he had helped to achieve a new state. As chief of staff, he had helped to build an army that once more saved Israel from possible annihilation. What must he do now to make sure Israel would survive?

Rabin favored giving back much of the conquered territory in return for a real peace, arguing: "A genuine agreement can only be achieved at a price. And the price is territory. To go to the Egyptians and say: 'We want peace, but you must agree to our new border being the Suez Canal' is a beautiful dream; in reality it's impossible."

But the Arabs rejected Israeli offers to exchange land for peace, declaring at a meeting in Khartoum in August 1967 that there would be no peace, no negotiations, no recognition of Israel. And with massive Soviet military aid cascading into Arab lands, the enemy, Rabin feared, might well bounce back. Israel therefore needed greater military muscle to defend itself. It must, in a sense, extend the Six-Day War with a struggle to keep permanently its overwhelming military edge over the Arabs. Yet, Rabin felt, he could not rely on domestic arms production.

"Yitzhak didn't trust our ability to develop our own weapons system," one of his friends would say. "He wanted to be on the safe side. Only later in his career did he overcome this lack of trust."

Israel, Rabin thought, had to forge an indestructible link with a big power that would constantly supply it with a massive amount of the latest military equipment. And the United States, the mightiest and friendliest power, the center of the world, was the logical choice as supplier. Especially since Britain would not sell weapons to Israel, and France, the country's chief source of arms for almost fifteen years, might cut off such aid because the Israelis had ignored French pleas to avoid the 1967 war.

Israel must now persuade the United States to reverse its own chilling postwar policy of suspending all arms deliveries, even spare parts, to Israel while Soviet arms flowed into the Arab countries. Only an iron link with Washington would convince the Arabs that they had to make peace if they wanted their land back.

Even before the Six-Day War, Rabin talked with Prime Minister Eshkol about his future; he had known what he wanted ever since he and Leah visited Washington in 1963.

What did he have in mind? Eshkol asked.

He would like to be ambassador to the United States.

"Hold on to me, Yitzhak, or I'll fall out of my chair!" Eshkol cried. "That's the last thing I would have expected you to want."

What he apparently expected was a request for a cabinet post. Rabin was, after all, a national hero. But finally composing himself, the prime minister replied that he would think about it.

"I have to talk to Eban, of course, but I can tell you what my initial reaction is. You're no diplomat! Are you going to stand around at tedious cocktail parties, sit through boring banquets, and play all those other diplomatic games? Are you really up to it?"

"Well," Rabin said, "I am up to what I consider to be the task of Israel's ambassador to Washington. Cocktail parties don't worry me. . . . Tightening ties with the U.S. is the sphere in which I would like to make whatever contribution I can, and I'm confident that my military and political background as chief of staff will make up for any deficiencies in diplomatic experience."

Eshkol was noncommittal, and at a second meeting told him, according to Rabin: "Eban has some reservations. We'll see."

Eban, however, would claim that he had "broached [Rabin's appointment] with Eshkol [but that] he was not enthusiastic. 'Why not one of our Hevra?' [Eshkol was referring to members of his Mapai Party, to which Rabin did not belong.] On the other hand, both Eshkol and I were impressed by the allure that the appointment of a celebrated military commander would bring to the central diplomatic post."

Even Rabin's friends tried to discourage him from pursuing the ambassadorship. Why not enter politics instead?

"I may go into politics someday," he replied, "but definitely not now. I need some time to adjust, a kind of transition period. And in Washington I can put my knowledge and abilities to good use."

While Rabin was motivated mainly by his obsession with meeting Israel's security needs, he was also influenced by his father's stories, told and retold, about the wonders of life in the United States. He apparently felt as well that after he became a seasoned diplomat he would be ready to fill a top cabinet post. Meanwhile, he turned down a highly paid job as president of the Israel Electric Corporation, the firm that had employed his father as a worker. He was interested less in money than in power, power to follow up his military victory with a final peace. And Eban, whether reluctantly or not, backed the appointment, though he worried that Rabin, with his independent mind, might forget he was no longer chief of staff and try to run his own show.

In fact, hardly had he been appointed when he shook the foreign ministry bureaucracy with his demand for clear, unambiguous thinking.

"What does the government expect Israel's ambassador to the United States to achieve?" he asked Eban and other foreign policy specialists. "What are his objectives?"

Rabin would claim: "Eyebrows shot up at my use of military terminology. Objectives? No one had any idea."

Wondering how he could succeed in his job without pursuing finely drawn objectives, Rabin drew up his own list in terse military style and presented it to the foreign ministry. Israel would, first of all, obtain arms, especially fifty Phantom jets, from the United States. It was given $150 million in arms from 1965 to 1967 and only $25 million worth in 1968, after the Six-Day War, when the United States cut off military aid to the Middle East, except for what was already moving through the pipeline.

Israel would also ask for financial aid to pay for the arms and bolster its economy. And it would seek to coordinate its peace-oriented policies with those of the United States, and elicit a U.S. promise to use force if necessary to prevent the Soviets from attacking Israel directly.

"All right, that's fine," muttered ministry officials as they slipped the list into a bureaucratic drawer.

There was more bad news when Henry Kissinger, then a Harvard professor, visited Israel and told Rabin what to expect in Washington.

Vietnam, Kissinger said, had soured the United States on any further involvement in foreign affairs. Israel, therefore, might not get the kind of commitment it wanted.

Despite the prospect of wrestling with his own foreign ministry and the U.S. State Department, Rabin was determined to succeed in his quest for a peace shielded by military strength.

When he returned, he would be better equipped to launch a
political career that would enable him to push with greater force
toward this goal—an ambition that Ezer Weizman apparently
vowed would never be realized. According to Dov Goldstein, who
worked with Rabin on his memoirs, Weizman, still embittered by
Rabin's failure to recommend him as his successor in the post of
chief of staff, told the new ambassador before he left for
Washington:

"If you intend to return from the United States and be a political figure, forget it. Because I'll tell the people about your collapse
in 1967."

Rabin was given a fonder farewell at a party in the Jerusalem
home of Haim Gurie, who had attended the Kadouri Agricultural
School with him and had since become one of Israel's most
renowned poets. Rabin's resolve was clear in his unequivocal
answers to his comrades' questions.

Do you believe that real peace is near?

"No, but exhausting every possibility should be Israel's first
priority."

What should Israel do to assure peace?

"It must maintain military superiority over all its neighbors
continuously while giving up territory."

What did he think of the Likud's movement for a Greater Israel?

"It is corrupting the correct order of Zionist priorities. The correct order is to achieve understanding and agreements with our
Arab neighbors through direct talks that will prevent war. This is
far more important than territories."

Did he consider the Greater Israel movement fascist, as some
people thought?

"No, but it is a dangerous movement, a danger to Israel's
democracy. Political settlements in the West Bank would not, as
the rightists claim, add to Israel's security. This is an anachronistic
idea."

In Washington, Rabin concluded, he would fight to lay the
foundation for permanent peace by forging close relations with
American leaders, especially the President. Israel, in his view, had

relied too long on Europe for military and economic support, even though most Europeans cared little about Israel and were still stained in some degree by wartime indifference to the Holocaust. Golda Meir was close to West Germany's Willy Brandt, and Shimon Peres embraced the French leaders. But the Europeans, Rabin was convinced, were fair-weather friends.

He would thus seek to change this erroneous orientation and win greater sympathy from the President. Until then, it had been easier for American Jewish leaders to enter the White House to argue Israeli interests. Even Israeli prime ministers seldom set foot in the Oval Office. David Ben-Gurion may have founded Israel, but he was able to see President Kennedy only in a New York hotel. Why antagonize the great, oil-rich Arab world?

Unlike his predecessors, Rabin would deal face-to-face with the President, defining the real interests of both Israel and the United States and stressing fundamental points of agreement. The logic of his arguments would presumably persuade the United States to change its Middle East policy and embrace Israel as a strategic ally.

His comrades smiled politely. Yitzhak may have reached the top of the mountain in school and in the army, and, as a superb strategic analyst, would combine the strategies of diplomacy with his military genius. But climbing a mountain was a lot easier than moving one.

In February 1968, Rabin, with Leah and Yuval in tow, flew to Europe for a short vacation, then to Washington, where the three arrived in great anticipation of enjoying a segment of their life in a superpower bursting with the dynamism spawned by individual initiative and freedom from the daily fear of annihilation that plagued their own country. Their joy was diluted only by the absence of Dahlia, who remained in Israel to finish school and serve in the army.

Rabin had visited the United States for short periods in past years and sensed the energy, optimism, and compassion that lent to its grandeur. And so he understood why memories of life there so haunted his father. But now he was looking forward to absorbing its spirit and unearthing the secrets that might ultimately turn Israel into a kind of miniature America in the Middle East—prosperous, secure, democratic in the purest sense.

Yet Rabin was not quite sure he would be wholly satisfied with the secrets he might uncover, for he was, after all, the product of a sharply different political, economic, and social culture. Like Israel itself, Rabin had his roots in the collectivism inherent in the Zionist and socialist philosophies.

His mother had instinctively placed the interests of the group above those of her own children, and if his father was more caring of them, it was apparently because his American experience had somewhat devitalized his ideology.

While Rabin was not brought up on a kibbutz, an agricultural collective society, he was immersed in an urban socialist way of life in which capitalist materialism, even a fully furnished home, was viewed as the product of an almost evil philosophy of exploitation. And in school, individualism was discouraged by a teaching system without examinations without pressure on students to compete for good grades and the admiration of their fellows. There were no budding geniuses or athletic heroes. It was the group that counted.

Since Rabin's youthful days, the practical realities of life had propelled him toward a more centrist view of society, as had happened to Israel itself, where the kibbutz, the kernel of the original Zionist concept, was vanishing as a vital social force.

But his past, if somewhat amorphously, still exerted a powerful influence on him, and its grip would be unsparingly tested during his tour as Israel's ambassador to the United States.

Actually, it was not a very propitious time to begin the test, for Rabin arrived in the United States during a period of almost unprecedented political and social upheaval. He soon learned that Henry Kissinger had grossly understated the demoralized condition of the American people and government as they sought to dig themselves out of the bloody mire of Vietnam. A measure of their desperation was their immediate interest in Rabin's view of how to achieve salvation, though he knew little about the situation there.

"I suppose they found it incomprehensible that the omnipotent United States of America," he would say, "could not overcome a guerrilla force supported by the army of a small and impoverished people when a Middle Eastern country approximately the size of Massachusetts had routed the armies of four Arab states."

And so Rabin would give the astonished U.S. establishment its first taste of his unique diplomatic style. As he told one American authority who had said the United States must eliminate the fighting power of the enemy:

"If that's the way you see the concept of winning, you'll lose the war in Vietnam. There's no way of eliminating the fighting capacity and spirit of tens of millions of people who are dedicated to the sanctity of their cause."

This was precisely the conclusion he would reach in principle almost twenty years later when the Intifada would get out of hand.

If American officials were slightly taken aback by his bluntness, they soon grew to appreciate it.

"He gave us some good advice on Vietnam," one official told me. "We took seriously everything he told us, for he always stated exactly what he believed without any ambiguity. He was a rarity in Washington—an undiplomatic diplomat."

On one occasion, congressmen and intelligence experts asked his opinion on the Soviet military threat. Russia had a fleet of heavy bombers in Aswan, Egypt, he was told, but it lacked fighter bases. It had ships in the Black Sea, but had no air cover. It could drop a nuclear bomb, but since there was no defense, why discuss it? Then one congressman asked:

"Do you think we need another aircraft carrier?"

"No," Rabin replied, "Russia needs one."

If Rabin could speak about making peace in Vietnam, he could, ironically, speak little about keeping peace in the Middle East, for few people would listen to him. The mood in the United States grew darker each day, it seemed, and amid the chaos there was little interest, as Kissinger had warned, in the needs of other countries, including a request by Rabin for fifty Phantom jets. President Johnson announced he was withdrawing from the presidential race, then Martin Luther King Jr. was murdered, setting off racial riots around the country. He was shocked by what he saw in Washington:

"I watched people looting and policemen just standing by," he would say. "No one dared do anything."

When police stopped his car during curfew hours despite his diplomatic identification, he mused with a shudder: "Suddenly I saw Haifa and Jerusalem in the days of the [British] curfew and I thought to myself: Great! Twenty years later and several thousand kilometers away, and you're back living under a curfew again."

But when a friend asked him if "soldiers" had bothered him as he drove through town, he replied rather tartly, as if surprised that the friend did not realize he was a general who had won a historic military victory:

"Soldiers don't bother me!"

Leah wrote Rabin's sister, Rachel: "We are really going through a seminar on the problems of the United States. Even though we are not involved, and feel no fear or pain, it's still very depressing to be witness to such a sad show. The riots, I think, are symptomatic of a problem whose solution is very, very far away. . . . No one knows where it will end."

It didn't end soon. Robert Kennedy was then assassinated, and street violence shortly afterward rocked a stormy Democratic Party convention in Chicago.

"Believe me," Rabin would tell Bill Seamans of the American Broadcasting Company, "I looked around and I thought—if this is the major power that the free world future is dependent on—oh, too bad."

So bad that he would lament to writer Robert Slater that in place of the "mighty giant" he had envisioned, he found "bitterness—the endless struggle, the lack of guidance, the lack of clarity of purpose, the question mark over everything." With the United States shrinking into a second-rate power, the Soviet Union stood poised to fill the world power vacuum, and its first victim could be Israel. He was thus not surprised when Soviet forces invaded Czechoslovakia on August 20, 1968—and the United States could only sit back and feebly mourn the loss of a budding democracy.

But Rabin would not give up, especially with an election pending and Republican Richard Nixon favored to beat Democrat Hubert Humphrey. For the Jewish vote grew ever more crucial in Democratic political calculations. Finally on October 9, 1968, barely three weeks before election day, Rabin's efforts bore fruit: Johnson agreed to sell the planes. But the next President would have to deliver them, and it appeared that Nixon would be the man.

Rabin was taking no chances. Even before Johnson's announcement, he had gone to see Nixon and was welcomed warmly. He had met Nixon before and had clicked with him, even though they shared few character traits. Rabin was honest, frank, and blunt almost to a shocking degree. Nixon was opportunistic and often devious and deceptive. But they were both pragmatists and perhaps sensed a common bond of insecurity.

Rabin could thus understand Nixon's discomfort when they had met in Israel two years earlier, in 1966, at a U.S. embassy dinner party for the visiting former vice president. Nixon had lost to Kennedy in the presidential race, then suffered defeat in a governor's race in California, and his political stock was at a nadir. Rabin, to his embarrassment, thus found himself the only senior government official who bothered to show up. And it was clear that Nixon felt humiliated. After his loss in the California race, he had bitterly told reporters that they would not have Dick Nixon to "kick around" anymore. Now, it seemed, even the Israelis were kicking him around, figuring that he was politically dead.

Perhaps remembering his own social isolation in his early years and sensing that this man would somehow scratch his way back to a top rung of the political ladder, Rabin conquered his taciturnity and conversed with him warmly.

"Have you enjoyed your trip to Israel?" Rabin asked.

"So-so," Nixon replied with a look of chagrin.

"When do you plan to leave?"

"Tomorrow morning."

"Could you spend another day here?"

"Perhaps—if it was worthwhile."

"I'll show you things you haven't seen. If you can stay over, I'll pick you up at 9 A.M."

Nixon smiled in gratitude. At least someone gave a damn about him!

The following morning, Rabin took Nixon on a helicopter tour of the border areas that Israel would later win in the Six-Day War, including the Golan Heights. As he stared down at the cliffs overlooking Israeli settlements, Nixon remarked that he could well understand why Israelis felt so insecure.

Now, two years later, in early 1968, Nixon was running for President of the United States, and he welcomed the man who gave a damn about him, repeatedly thanking him and adding once:

"I won't forget it in the future, either."

Did he favor selling Israel the Phantoms?

"If the people elect me as their President," Nixon said, "I promise you that I will advocate a strong Israel, and you will get your planes."

Rabin glowed, feeling that Nixon was sincere. He was even more impressed when Nixon said that Israel had a crucial role to play in the power balance between the United States and the Soviet Union, adding:

"I believe it necessary to reach an understanding with the Soviets, and I am convinced that the only language they respect is the language of force. You can't reach an agreement with them unless you do so from a position of strength."

Rabin was struck by the "uncanny" resemblance between this approach toward the Soviet Union and his own toward the Arabs.

"We, too, believe that it is vital to reach agreement with our adversaries in the Middle East," he told Nixon. "But negotiations can only begin when Israel speaks from a position of strength and has concrete backing."

Nixon replied, reinforcing his earlier commitment: "You will find considerable understanding from me in everything connected with guaranteeing Israel's strength—including your request for the Phantoms."

Rabin now could only hope that Nixon would win the presidency, even though most American Jews supported Humphrey. The Democratic nominee was very pro-Israel, but, still loyal to Johnson, had not yet said that he would give Israel the key role in Cold War geopolitics that Nixon promised. Still, there was a potential problem with Nixon. Since he would be unburdened by any debt to the Jews if he won, would he break his promise? Rabin didn't think so. Nixon was said to have anti-Semitic tendencies, and, in fact, an American official warned Rabin that Nixon was motivated more by his hatred of communism than by his love of Israel. But he was, Rabin felt, a pragmatic cold warrior who realized that Israel could be a helpful ally and seemed to identify with it as an underdog.

Anyway, the important thing was to harness and influence the center of power—the presidency. And Rabin was confident that he could do it if Nixon, who felt indebted to him, entered the White

House. As long as the mountain moved, who cared about the content of the President's character?

In fact, soon after Nixon won the election, Rabin nudged the mountain with hard-nosed diplomacy, setting President against President-elect. When the White House stalled on delivery of the promised Phantoms, he suggested to his Democratic friends that if Johnson didn't conclude the sale of Phantoms before he left office, Nixon would do so—and reap all the credit. Only several days before the inauguration, Johnson did indeed conclude the sale. Rabin was joyous, but he would soon find that it took more than a nudge to move a mountain.

Several months earlier, in April 1968, President Nasser's Soviet guns had fired across the Suez Canal, launching, with Moscow's complicity, the War of Attrition. Israeli air attacks stunned the Egyptians into silence, though a curtain of smoke soon curled skyward again and again along the banks of the canal despite every Israeli attempt to knock out the guns. Washington was not impressed by Israel's failure to meet the challenge of this Soviet-backed aggression.

Rabin wasn't impressed either. His aim, after all, was to persuade the United States that Israel could be a reliable Cold War ally.

"I continued to be dogged by a crucial question," he would say. "Did the Americans think that the United States was losing ground in the Middle East because its 'client,' Israel, was incapable of putting an end to the War of Attrition? Were they intimating that Israel's failure to alter the situation in the Middle East was costing her America's support because the United States found itself forced to adopt conciliatory positions vis-à-vis the Soviet Union?"

With the War of Attrition dragging on for months, Rabin had reason to worry, especially after speaking to Joseph Sisco, Nixon's assistant secretary of state for the Middle East and South Asia, about the kind of peace that Israel should make with Egypt and the other Arab states.

"Our interests in the Middle East do not center on Israel alone," Sisco told Rabin. "Our moral and practical commitment to Israel is by no means toward everything Israel wants or does. Let me tell you frankly: If our friendship with Israel is the only thing

the United States is left with in the Middle East, that will be a catastrophic setback for American policy. We must work for a political
solution because it's the only thing that will safeguard our own
array of interests in the region."

America's interests did not contradict Israel's, Rabin retorted.
"The sides must reach a binding agreement in which they undertake mutual commitments. In order for it to last, peace must have
substance: open frontiers, the movement of goods and people,
diplomatic relations."

"That would be wonderful," Sisco said, "and the United States
would like nothing better. But since the Arabs reject such a possibility outright, the question remains: What is the minimum necessary to put an end to the conflict? We can't force the Egyptians to
love you. As far as we're concerned, a solution that falls short of
the peace you've described would be sufficient, considering the
circumstances. We've got to be realistic!"

Rabin calculated that it was Israel's failure to put an end to the
War of Attrition that suddenly made Israel's peace demands seem
"unrealistic" to the United States. Ironically, Israeli leaders had
deliberately refrained from sending bombers over Egyptian soil
because they thought the United States might cut off military aid to
Israel for fear of spreading the war. But Rabin now, on September
19, 1968, wrote his superiors in Jerusalem:

> Continuation of Israeli military operations, including air attacks, is
> likely to lead to far-reaching results. Nasser's standing could be
> undermined, and that would in turn weaken the Soviet position in
> the region. Some sources have informed me that our military opera-
> tions are the most encouraging breath of fresh air the American
> administration has enjoyed recently. A man would have to be blind,
> deaf, and dumb not to sense how much the Administration favors
> our military operations. . . . Thus, the willingness to supply us with
> additional arms depends more on stepping up our military activity
> against Egypt than on reducing it.

Finally, on October 25, 1968, Rabin, determined to prove
Israel's Cold War credentials in order to loosen the American
purse, cabled his government that Israel should "alter the course
of the war."

"We had to undertake deep-penetration raids and strike at military targets in the Egyptian heartland," he advised. "That was the

only way to induce the Egyptians to halt the war. Moreover, delivering a sharp blow to Nasser would help to shore up America's status in the region and thus block the retreat in talks with the Soviet Union."

Rabin would later relate: "In Israel I was regarded as being 'on the brink' of losing my mind. I had never been a 'hawk,' and yet here I was calling for attacks on targets deep inside Egypt. But my proposals had nothing at all to do with 'hawkishness.' I saw where the War of Attrition was leading American policy, and I was horrified."

So was Abba Eban, but mainly because Rabin was asking Jerusalem for drastic action without even consulting him. Eban would later write:

After a daring raid against Egypt under his successor's command, a Rabin cable poured scorn on the operation as inadequately intensive and added that even the Americans expected stronger military action than our forces were taking. On one occasion, a telegram from the Washington embassy recommended for simultaneous action, (a) intensification of air attacks on Egyptian targets, (b) preparation to intervene in Jordan in the event that King Hussein was superseded, (c) actions in the air that would induce Syrian aircraft to present themselves for elimination by Israel.

Another veteran Israeli diplomat, Gideon Rafael, would share Eban's view of some of Rabin's recommendations. He would write of Rabin's conversations with Sisco:

Rabin ventured to suggest that the Israeli army might have to march on Cairo. In his report, he described Sisco's reaction—"he did not fall from his chair"—concluding from the secretary's sedentary stability that the United States was in sympathy with such far-reaching Israeli action. The assumption was received in Jerusalem with considerable skepticism.

And indeed, still fearful that an escalation of violence in Egypt might provoke rather than please Washington, Jerusalem ignored Rabin's plea. The upshot was a proposal by Secretary of State William Rogers, known as the Rogers Plan. Under this plan, the pre-1967 border between Egypt and Israel would become the "secure and recognized" frontier between the two countries required by UN General Assembly Resolution 242, which was passed on November 22, 1967, with the fate of Gaza to be negotiated.

In return, a "formal state of peace" would be established between the two parties, though its details were not delineated. Rogers would first seek support for his plan from Russia, then from Britain and France at a Big Four meeting, with Israel and the Arabs getting the final draft for their approval.

When Rabin cabled this proposal to Jerusalem in November 1969, Prime Minister Golda Meir was shocked. She sent back a blistering answer that this plan was "a disaster for Israel" and she added, "any Israeli government that would adopt and implement such a plan would be betraying its country."

Peace, Jerusalem insisted, could be achieved only through direct negotiations between Israel and each Arab state, not through a plan imposed by the big powers.

Rabin passed along this bitter response to American officials and "dredged up every conceivable argument to prove that Rogers's proposal was not the way to establish true peace. It did not define the nature of peaceful relationships, and it made no mention of open frontiers, diplomatic relations, or the free movement of people and goods."

In his conversations with Rogers, a mild-mannered, good-humored man, Rabin felt especially frustrated because he felt the secretary, however pleasant a personality, had little understanding of the Middle East and Israel's security concerns. He felt more comfortable with Assistant Secretary Sisco, who he felt empathized with Israel's view even though, in one conversation, Sisco flatly told him that the kind of peace Israel wanted "is not attainable now."

Actually, the Americans suggested that the Rogers Plan be applied to Israel's relationship with Jordan, too. Rabin was appalled, especially since the Israelis were secretly negotiating with Jordan and hoped to reach an eventual peace accord with it.

"Never, in any of its decisions, has the Israeli government consented to withdraw from the West Bank," Rabin replied, fearing that King Hussein would never compromise if he thought Israel might accept the Rogers Plan.

Rabin made a quick trip to Jerusalem and returned to Washington with approval to launch a public campaign against the Rogers Plan. In a meeting with Henry Kissinger, who was then Nixon's national security adviser, he asked:

"What is the value of our demand for true peace in exchange

for territory if you suggest that we give up all the occupied territories without it? Why should the Arabs consent to give us more than you recommend?"

And then Rabin decided to "put matters clearly on the line":

"Let me tell you in complete frankness, you are making a bad mistake," he warned. "In taking discussion of a peace settlement out of the hands of the parties and transferring it to the powers, you are fostering an imposed solution that Israel will resist with all her might. I personally shall do everything within the bounds of American law to arouse public opinion against the moves!"

Kissinger was taken aback. No other diplomat had ever talked to him like that.

"What's done is done," he said cautiously. "But under no circumstances, I beg you, under no circumstances should you attack the President! It would mean a confrontation with the United States, and that's the last thing Israel can afford. . . . I advise you again: Don't attack the President!"

It seemed strange to Rabin that he was being asked not to attack the President who had, before he took office, promised to support the very policies that he himself favored. Yet now he suspected the United States was subtly tying defense aid to Israel's compliance with policies contrary to his country's interest.

With such deception, Nixon might deserve to be attacked, but Kissinger was right: Israel couldn't afford a confrontation with the man.

Suddenly, Kissinger "sprang an incredible move" on Rabin. He announced:

"The President would like to shake hands with you. Shall we go in and see him for a few minutes?"

Rabin was astonished. The President was asking an ambassador to see him without prior notice or a request for a meeting. It was simply not done. Welcoming him with a smile, Nixon said:

"I understand this is a difficult time for us all. I believe that the Israeli government is perfectly entitled to express its feelings and views, and I regard that with complete understanding."

He then turned to Kissinger and asked: "Where do matters stand on Israel's requests for arms and equipment?"

"We are in the midst of examining Israel's needs," Kissinger replied.

"I promised that we would not only provide for Israel's defense needs, but her economic needs as well," Nixon added.

"The examination covers both spheres," Kissinger responded.

The President then turned back to Rabin and said: "I can well understand your concern. I know the difficulties you face in your campaign against terrorist operations, and I am particularly aware of your defense needs. In all matters connected with arms supplies, don't hesitate to approach . . . Kissinger."

When Rabin departed, he was confused. Why had Nixon reiterated his promises in conflict with the proposals of Secretary of State William Rogers? Was the President playing "good cop–bad cop"? It seemed likely to Rabin that his lectures against the Rogers Plan had given Nixon pause in pursuing that plan. The President was, after all, a pragmatist.

And so was Rabin; he needed a double-edged sword. While continuing his campaign against the Rogers Plan, he had to persuade his government to strike harder at Egypt. Maybe that would finally turn U.S. policy around. And this time he "got through" to Jerusalem. In the spring of 1970, Israeli planes struck deeply into the heart of Egypt.

"From then on," Rabin would say, "the American administration was gradually to shake free of the depressing feeling that it was backing the loser in the Middle East and consequently losing its own standing in the region."

Washington no longer felt it had to give way to Soviet demands in the Middle East, while the American people grew increasingly sympathetic to Israel. Just as important, Rabin, as well as the Americans, learned just how far each side could go in their demands. Perhaps Nixon would now keep his promise after all. In any case, the atmosphere finally seemed ripe for moving a mountain.

14

Molehills on the Horizon

"**L**ife in the U.S. is completely different from what I'm used to," Rabin would write Rachel, "and so is my job."

Despite his initial fears that the United States was slowly sliding into decay, Rabin began to realize that for all the immediate crises and tragedies, the United States at its core was still strong and resilient, as the Jews had been in their long history. And so he absorbed with enthusiasm the differences that set apart life in America from life in Israel.

Until now, what had been luxury to Rabin was the simple cottage he and his family inhabited in the military community of Zahala. Now he lived in a magnificent ambassadorial residence studded with elegant furnishings that would have sent egalitarian chills down his mother's back. And the friends he saw each day were not neighboring officers from backgrounds similar to his, but the rich and powerful, the politicians who determined the destiny of nations, the business magnates whose industrial empires fed, clothed, and armed the masses of the world.

Differences, yes. Heady differences.

In some ways, they were discomfiting. He seldom felt comfortable at the almost nightly cocktail receptions and formal dinner parties protocol required him to attend or host, especially before he learned enough English to carry on a meaningful conversation. His discomfort was especially great when he once greeted guests, to their amused astonishment, with a black shoe on one foot and a brown shoe on the other; and another time when he splashed whiskey on a guest's dress by plunking ice cubes in the glass she was holding.

As people sputtered gossipy "nonsense," Rabin could only be thankful that Leah intensely enjoyed these events and could charm their companions while he gazed around the room with droopy-eyed boredom, hoping to find some well-placed person who would listen to his awkwardly phrased but elegantly argued pleas for military aid.

Or Rabin might sidle off to a corner to savor a drink in silence. Sometimes he wished he could rush home and watch an action film on television while stroking his beloved German shepherd, Apollo. For he felt lonely amid all those people, especially since about two-thirds of them were Arab diplomats or their sympathizers.

"Whenever we encountered them . . . ," Leah would say, "they absolutely ignored our existence. On one occasion, a lady tried to introduce the wife of the Tunisian ambassador at a tea party, but she just stood back with her arms crossed and said, 'I can't!' It was not at all pleasant to be reminded that Israel [was] isolated among the nations."

Such reminders only hardened Rabin's conviction that it was in Israel's vital interest to make peace with the Arabs at almost any territorial cost within the bounds of an adequate security structure. And he longed for the day when he could meet with Arab colleagues socially and chat about trade, or perhaps about the World Cup.

Even when Rabin tried to fit into the Washington social scene, he found local tastes and customs perplexing. Once, at a dinner party he hosted, he shocked State Department officials when he offered them after-dinner cigars that an Israeli colleague had brought from Cuba. Havana cigars? The guests responded with dark frowns, and Rabin's suddenly red cheeks reflected a belated realization that the United States had placed an embargo on all Cuban products.

The next day, at a dinner party for high Pentagon figures, Rabin, in a rare moment of self-revelation, related to them how he had committed the faux pas with his Havana cigars. Instead of yielding more frowns, the mention of them this time brought only sly smiles.

"You've got Havanas?"

And shortly, they were happily puffing away—Rabin, not so happily. Now he was more confused than ever. Was there no coordination between the State Department and the Pentagon?

Another time he agonized when he received an invitation to a White House "white-tie" reception. White-tie? What was that? He was reminded of the time he was sent to the armistice talks in Rhodes at the end of the 1948 war and embarrassingly didn't know how to put on a tie. Who could he now ask for guidance without making a fool of himself? He finally learned what a white-tie reception was from a local tailor, who fitted him out with a complete formal outfit that felt to him like a "straitjacket" and required him to move like a "poorly oiled robot."

And there was more embarrassment to come. All diplomats and military officers were expected to show up with their chests emblazoned with medals. But Rabin, though he had led an army to victory in the Six-Day War, had never been awarded a battle decoration, since this was not the custom in Israel.

"Each time I found someone furtively looking at me as if I were naked," Rabin would recall. "I tried to explain as humbly as possible that the IDF tries to excel at winning wars and hopes that victory alone will compensate its soldiers for their bravery."

Rabin had greater appreciation for the essence of American life. Like his father before him, he marveled at the splendor of American democracy, especially with its constitutional guarantees and its system of checks and balances that prevented the President, Congress, and judiciary from ever accruing too much power. This was the country that had given his father refuge after he had fled Russia almost sixty years earlier—a point vividly recalled when Nehemiah died in 1971.

Rabin flew to Israel for the funeral, disappointed that Nehemiah had forbidden family members to inform Yitzhak of his critical condition and thus force the ambassador to leave the vital work he was doing for Israel. When his mother was dying, Rabin had at least been taken to her for a final good-bye. He was grateful, however, that his father had lived to see him appointed chief of staff and then ambassador to a country that he so loved.

Rabin's socialist instincts largely melted away as he saw the power of free enterprise yield products and services almost beyond the human imagination, with entrepreneurs making millions in the process. He found some good instructors in the art of accumulating wealth, especially rich Jewish businessmen in Washington who were proud to court this Israeli military hero. He spent weekends at their summer homes, went fishing with them, sat with them at Washington Bullets basketball games; the owner of the team, Abe Pollin, was, in fact, one of his closest friends.

Actually, Rabin preferred football because, as one of these friends who accompanied him to Washington Redskins games said, "it was like war." Perhaps remembering his days as chief of staff of a commando-style army, he was constantly demanding risky, unorthodox plays.

"Why didn't he throw a pass?" he asked when the Redskins once ran the ball with one yard to go on third down.

The Rabins had another set of friends, too—military and political officials who dealt with the ambassador daily and enjoyed his company even though he often lectured them on policy with a curt candor. He was a novelty. What other diplomat could they talk with so openly without the strain of wondering what the person was really thinking?

High military officials especially liked him, feeling that he was one of them, a soldier who had scored one of the most remarkable military victories in history. He lectured at all the military academies and, in private meetings with the top brass, explained every battle tactic and every encounter with Soviet military equipment. His expertise was solicited even on the U.S. defense budget, weapons development, and the advantages of one weapon over another.

Once, he showed that he understood the North Vietnamese military mind even better than the American generals did. He predicted

to a group of them that the communists, who were about to launch
an offensive, would attack at a certain place and "go for a flanking
movement and try to encircle you." After the offensive began, Henry
Kissinger commented, as the generals bent over maps:

"You know, the only general who forecast precisely the direction of the enemy's thrust was the Israeli ambassador to
Washington!"

But the Americans, despite their embarrassment, did not hold
Rabin's brilliance against him. In fact, so trusting were they that
they took him on a tour of the underground command post of the
Strategic Air Command and explained to him the communications
systems of nuclear submarines. They found it difficult to call
Rabin "Mr. Ambassador."

"To me," Admiral Thomas Moorer, commander of U.S. forces,
told him, "you're General Rabin, and a general is much more to
me than any ambassador. So let's be done with this 'ambassador'
bit."

Rabin was also a favorite of members of Congress. They, too,
so respected his military knowledge that they sometimes questioned him on strategic matters unrelated to Israel, and he replied,
of course, with Israel's best interests in mind. Should they establish a base for the Sixth Fleet in Greece? (Yes.) Should they build
another aircraft carrier? (Yes.) Before the carrier proposal was
approved, Senator John Stennis told Rabin:

"You know, even the navy's memorandum wasn't as convincing as yours."

Rabin made a point of cultivating the friendship of Senator
Henry Jackson, a key member of the Senate Armed Services
Committee, who had much to say about the allocation of military
aid. But the ambassador let his underlings deal mostly with
Congress, while he focused on swaying the upper echelon in the
executive branch, which initiated foreign policy.

One of Rabin's closest political friends was the man who told
him Israel couldn't at this time have the kind of peace it wanted—
Assistant Secretary of State Sisco. This highly influential diplomat
was as gregarious as Rabin was withdrawn, but they were equally
straightforward, a quality that drew the two men to each other
and made for spirited conversation over lunch twice a week.

Once, Rabin made a strange request: Could he fly in one of the

Israeli-purchased Phantoms during a ceremony marking the end of a pilot training program? Sisco agreed and so informed the air force. And for forty-five minutes, Rabin returned to his days of glory. Sisco would say of Rabin:

"His public persona was that of the gruff soldier, using words sparingly. But in reality he was a man of quiet and genuine warmth and kindliness. . . . He said it as it was—no sugar coating like many politicians. The few times we quarreled, they were like intrafamily differences, quickly forgotten."

Henry Kissinger also became more than a valuable American contact. The two men developed a close friendship, apparently based in part—though neither would admit it—on their common Jewish heritage. Unlike other U.S. Jews, of course, Kissinger could hardly embrace an Israeli leader as an ethnic brother deserving of his political support. But Rabin sensed that Israel at least had Kissinger's emotional support, however much he had to subordinate Israel's interests to America's geopolitical interests.

Nor did Rabin feel, as some observers speculated, that Kissinger would "bend over backwards" to support the Arabs so that no one could accuse him of bias stemming from his own Jewish origin. In fact, the ambassador used his remarkable analytical powers to subtly convince Kissinger that Israeli and American interests largely coincided. He found Kissinger's pragmatism akin to his own, and admired—perhaps even envied—the depth of Kissinger's academic knowledge, a knowledge that he himself had hoped to attain in higher studies before World War II dashed his dream.

Though Rabin enjoyed the company of other Jewish friends in Washington, he admitted to one of them that in general he felt more comfortable with the gentiles he knew. For one thing, many American Jews regarded him more like the modern version of a Maccabean warrior hero, a rather distant idol, than as a simple human being like themselves. They found it hard to identify with this sabra who shared none of their "Yiddishkeit," their ghetto-bred Jewishness with the ironic, self-deprecating humor, the demonstrative behavior, the synagogue-centered social life. He was a quintessential native-born Israeli but, it seemed, almost an incidental Jew.

And Rabin apparently recognized the distinction. Once, American Ambassador Averell Harriman chatted with him at a dinner party about the refusal of American Jews to support a particular U.S. government policy:

"Mr. Ambassador, you should control your people," Harriman admonished him.

Rabin replied almost resentfully: "My people? I can't control the American Jews!"

Nor did Rabin find much political capital in gefilte fish. At another party, Leah served this delicacy to her distinguished guests, feeling they would appreciate a traditional Jewish meal, though not a strictly kosher one since the Rabins never observed the Jewish dietary laws at home and did not feel compelled to do so in Washington. But not even the horseradish made the food edible for some of them.

"Teddy and Joan Kennedy," Leah would lament, "didn't even try to overcome their distaste for it. Perhaps you have to be Jewish to enjoy gefilte fish."

Rabin, who himself preferred shrimp, a nonkosher dish, wanted to be liked as a person, not worshipped as an idol. Why should American Jews feel they possessed him, using him for fundraising events and as a showpiece at their conventions, and expecting to serve as intermediaries between him and the President?

"Following a deeply ingrained pattern of Diaspora living," he would say, "some of the leaders of the American Jewish community exercised their influence by means of a *shtadlan* ["court Jew"], the traditional intermediary who had sought the favor of the ruling powers in Europe. . . . I believed that the Israeli embassy should assume the principal role of handling Israel's affairs at all political levels and that it was entitled to avail itself of the help of Jews and non-Jews alike as it saw fit."

At the same time, Rabin was disturbed by the refusal of American Jews to exchange the comforts of America for the more rigorously demanding life in Israel, as his father had done. Why should these people take the liberty of advising Israel what policies to follow? And he would ask this question even more resentfully in later years during his two stints as prime minister, antagonizing many Jewish groups in the United States.

He seldom followed the advice of his own advisers, so why

should he listen to Jewish foreigners—especially when many supported the view that Israel must not give up an inch of land for peace?

Ironically, Rabin grew more aware of his Jewishness in the United States than he had in the Jewish state. For like many Israelis, especially those raised in the agnostic atmosphere of the socialist pioneering world, he took his roots for granted and felt little need for ceremony. But in the Diaspora, Jewish awareness centered around the synagogue, and Rabin, because of his job and a newfound affinity to Jewish tradition stemming from the recent conquest of Jerusalem, developed close ties with the Adas Israel Congregation in Washington.

"Like most Jews," Leah would say, "we went to synagogue for the festivals and for bar mitzvahs, or bat mitzvahs, of embassy families or friends. The experience of sitting for hours in a synagogue was a new one for us. Yet I must admit that I liked the ceremonies and sermons."

And so did her husband. Though he himself had never entered manhood via a bar mitzvah, his son, Yuval, made the transition at the synagogue. And at the end of his tour, Rabin would tell the congregation:

"My Jewish identity began with my first breath in Jerusalem. The encounter with the synagogue has given me a different way of living a Jewish life. It was a rewarding experience."

Nevertheless, Rabin reached out to non-Jewish America more than any ambassador had before him, feeling that strong gentile support for Israel would strengthen congressional support. When he learned English well enough, he lectured around the country, especially in the Baptist South and other areas of Middle America, and granted interviews to newspapers, large and small, everywhere. And everywhere, his blunt, rough-hewn personality appealed to people who distrusted the slick, "double-talking" politicians and diplomats they usually encountered.

At one college in Maryland, a member of the welcoming committee went to the room where Rabin was staying the night to escort him to the auditorium. When he knocked on the door, the diplomat opened it wearing only his undershorts.

"Come in," he said, as if this was a perfectly normal way for an ambassador to greet a caller. "I'll be ready as soon as I put on my trousers."

While most youth appreciated Rabin's unvarnished naturalness, a small minority had no interest in evaluating his personality. Arabs and radical blacks on American college campuses were set on hating him whatever his ideas or quirks. For he represented the enemy, the enemy of Islam and the supporter of those who, in their view, were trying to exterminate the poor peasants of Vietnam. They greeted him on campuses with signs reading "Murderer!" and heckled him in the lecture hall—one time, at Stanford University, setting off the fire alarm so that no one could hear him.

They even threatened to bomb the various places where Rabin was scheduled to speak. While he was lecturing at a Catholic college for women in Chicago, police burst in warning of a bomb threat and wanted to evacuate the hall. But the sister in charge of the event refused.

"We will go on as planned," she said firmly, "and I will sit on the stage next to the ambassador."

She did and Rabin completed his lecture without incident.

This was the real America, he felt. No wonder his father had so loved this country.

But Rabin was bitterly disappointed that the young protesters were revolting "against the most cherished values of the American political tradition," that they would "pour so much energy into preventing a man from speaking his mind." He was "witnessing a self-righteous crusade based on sheer ignorance." Calling him a "murderer" and threatening to kill him! "How profoundly sad and shamed I felt for America."

Thank God this could never happen in Israel.

Rabin had never regarded making money as one of his major aims in life, especially since his mother had cultivated in him a certain contempt for materialism. But suddenly Rabin, an unsophisticated man of modest means, was thrust into the role of ambassador in the world's richest and most important capital, where the cost of mandatory luxury living, including lavish diplomatic entertainment, exceeded the budget allocated by a small, struggling government. Like other Israeli ambassadors before him, Rabin had to defray some of his own expenses, and this was made especially difficult by Leah's inclination to share the expensive tastes of her wealthy American friends.

Thus, Rabin charged a fee for many of his lectures—which Leah deposited in a Washington bank account, apparently with her husband's knowledge, though such overseas accounts were a violation of Israeli law at that time. Should an ambassador, the media asked, accept money from those he was trying to influence? Though some of Rabin's predecessors did the same without media comment, his reputation for undiluted rectitude made him the focus of public controversy.

Leah's pragmatic view that the money was needed for the Rabins to successfully play their vital roles in Washington overcame any moral qualms the ambassador may have had, and apparently fueled his own pragmatism. Anyway, why challenge his wife over so small a matter? He was too busy urging the United States to fill Israel's needs.

Rabin's job was hard enough since he not only had to haggle with his hosts but also, as he had anticipated, to fight the foreign minister. Abba Eban was rabid when he learned that Golda Meir had decided to bypass him and communicate directly with his ambassador. Rabin was by no means unhappy; after all, this arrangement enhanced his standing with American officials.

Besides, he agreed with Meir that with the United States so crucial to Israeli defense and economic interests, she needed a direct pipeline into the Israeli embassy. The Israeli ambassador to Washington thus became, to Eban's dismay, the representative of the prime minister in the United States, while the foreign minister would receive copies of their cables—sometimes.

"During his service in Washington," Eban would later write, "he had shown incomprehension of the ambassadorial role. He considered that the hierarchical principle on which he had relied in the army career was not applicable to the relations between an embassy and a foreign ministry. A study of his cables to Jerusalem showed periods of thoughtfulness and moderation interrupted by sudden outbursts of aggressiveness. These eruptions would target members of my own staff or myself or other ambassadors or, on occasion, the Israeli government or the army command, which he had recently led."

In one of Rabin's cables, Eban would cite as an example, the ambassador "suggested that Israel should close down its UN mission and effectively cease to be a member of the world organization. I replied that this was a result that our Arab enemies would have spent endless days and millions of dollars to achieve. Every year the Arabs attempted to secure our suspension from participation in the UN General Assembly. Why should we fulfill their ambition?"

Eban was especially outraged when Rabin began what became known as a "pink paper" service for feeding the press information about events happening in the Middle East and interpreting them. Rabin started the service after a meeting with Sisco to discuss a shipment of aircraft to Israel. He then sent a press release written on pink paper to the media, reporting on the negotiations and explaining Israel's position. The next morning a local editorial discussed the subject, and from then on Rabin dispensed "pink papers" every week sharply analyzing events as they occurred.

"When a reporter received a pink paper," Rabin's aide Yehuda Avner would tell me, "he knew it was hot stuff."

Too hot for Eban. His ambassador was not only communicating with the prime minister behind his back, but he dared to send out press releases without Eban's approval. He was even giving radio and television interviews criticizing Israeli policies, and telling newsmen that the foreign ministry was teaching diplomats about protocol but little about policy.

Stop dealing with the media! Eban ordered.

But Rabin ignored him and continued the practice. Finally, Avner warned him: "Yitzhak, if Golda has to choose between an ambassador and the foreign minister, she'll choose the foreign minister."

But Rabin was adamant. He would do what he thought was in Israel's best interest, and it wasn't in its best interest to let Eban decide what his ambassador should tell the world. And he wasn't worried about Meir. The last thing she wanted was to bring home a military hero who might seek her office. And she didn't.

In fact, Meir realized that Rabin was turning out to be a most valuable ambassador. For one thing, he wrote reports in the succinct, unvarnished style he had mastered as a military commander. He reported the facts, then brilliantly evaluated them. But sometimes Rabin irked Meir with cables that described a particular situation but did not, in normal diplomatic fashion, assess it or offer an opinion on how to deal with it. Simcha Dinitz, Meir's aide at the time, told me:

"Golda didn't easily make concessions and was pretty tough in her positions. When Rabin sent her Kissinger's suggestions, she would sometimes argue with him because he didn't turn them down. He bluntly told her this wasn't his job."

Once, when Meir asked him to take a certain action he opposed, Rabin wrote her a curt reply starting *"Boker tov, Eliahu"* ("Good morning, Eliahu.") This was a way of saying, an Israeli official explained, "Don't irritate me with your silly cables."

But Rabin grew more diplomatic as he dealt with the Americans, sometimes keeping Meir from committing gaffes of her own. Once, before Meir was to leave on a trip to Washington, the Israelis blew up a Libyan plane over the Sinai after it ignored warnings. When Meir heard that a *Washington Post* editorial called the attack an "act of murder," she phoned Rabin and ordered him to cancel a meeting she was to have with Katharine Graham, publisher of the *Post*.

"I want to save her the embarrassment of meeting with the head of a murderous state," she explained with bitter sarcasm.

Rabin was stunned. Why make an enemy of an important newspaper?

"Are you sure you want to do this?" he asked.

Rabin was relieved when the publisher apologized and two of the world's most influential women ended their cold war.

Meanwhile, the world's two most powerful nations were heating up their cold war. Egypt's Nasser, shocked by Israel's deep-penetration raids on his country that Rabin had pressed for, ran to Moscow with a plea for help. Moscow listened, for the attacks had already eroded Soviet influence in the Middle East, and if Nasser collapsed, so might its whole carefully built power structure in the region.

Tell Israel to stop the raids, Premier Aleksei Kosygin warned President Nixon, or the Soviet Union might ship its latest weapons to Egypt.

Tell Egypt to cease firing across the canal, Nixon responded. And it had better not acquire new modern weapons or Israel would acquire them, too—from the United States.

Rabin was delighted. "We have achieved a marked improvement

in the United States position," he cabled Jerusalem. "Continuation of that improvement depends first and foremost on keeping up our air raids in the heart of Egypt."

But then his hopes began to crumble. For Nixon delayed a decision on whether to send Israel a requested second batch of planes, twenty-five Phantoms and one hundred Skyhawks; he would keep these planes in cold storage, hoping that Moscow might be enticed to pressure Nasser into accepting a cease-fire. And columnist Joseph Alsop did not ease Rabin's apprehension when he told the ambassador to prepare himself for "bad tidings." Would Nasser win out after all?

Rabin secretly went to see Henry Kissinger in the White House and asked if the stage was really being set for such a disaster.

Not at all, Kissinger replied. True, the President would not announce a decision. No need. He would simply replace Israel's arms when they stopped functioning. That way, the United States could maintain an arms balance in the Middle East without endangering Israel. There was further good news, Kissinger implied. Moscow had proposed an undeclared cease-fire: Neither side would launch air attacks on the other, though Egypt had never launched such attacks, carrying on the war only with artillery. Incidentally, Egypt would be free to continue these artillery assaults without Israel being able to retaliate with any air raids, but—don't worry—only for a limited time.

Rabin was speechless with fury. The mountain suddenly seemed immovable. A cease-fire that would permit the enemy to continue the war unopposed? A plan that would delay indefinitely the shipment of planes to Israel and, in effect, allow Moscow to decide whether Israel would get them? When he managed to catch his breath, he snapped:

"The Russians have promised Egypt up-to-date antiaircraft missiles. What they need is time to get those weapons in place and operational. You come along and tell us, 'Give them that time.' They've made no commitment to maintain any cease-fire, and the minute their missiles are operational, they'll be able to resume the War of Attrition."

In any event, Israel soon had to stop sending its aircraft on deep-penetration attacks when some eighty SAM–3 missile sites newly manned by over 12,000 Soviet soldiers threatened to bring down its planes. Worried that the Russians, as a result, would regain the power they had before the deep raids, Rabin now accompanied Eban to a meeting with Nixon.

"In view of the Soviet involvement," the President asked, "is Israel's position still—as I once heard Ambassador Rabin say— 'Give us the tools and we'll do the job'?"

"Yes!" Rabin exclaimed, unembarrassed by an angry glance from his foreign minister.

"It would have been more appropriate for the foreign minister to reply to the President's question," he would admit. "But when an ambassador is anxious about what his foreign minister is likely to say, he is well advised to get his answer in first."

"Good!" Nixon replied. "That was all I wanted to know."

However, he would still only replace worn-out weapons.

"If it were just a question of you and the Egyptians and the Syrians, I'd say, 'Let 'em have it! Let 'em have it! Hit 'em as hard as you can!' Every time I hear of you penetrating into their territory and hitting them hard, I get a feeling of satisfaction. I agree with you that the Soviets and the Egyptians are putting us both to the test. But it's not just a problem of Egypt and Syria. The other Arab states in the Middle East are watching us also. I don't have the slightest doubt of that. We don't have any choice. We have to play it so that we don't lose everything in the Middle East."

That was it! Nixon, Rabin apparently believed, was thinking of oil. In the final analysis, he would sacrifice Israel for oil.

But as if guessing what his visitors were thinking, Nixon said, in what seemed a sudden dramatic turnaround, "Damn the oil! We can get it from other sources. We have to stand beside the decent nations in the Middle East. We will back you militarily, but the military escalation can't be allowed to go on endlessly. We must do something politically."

Just what Rabin wanted. Once more he glimpsed the mountain peak. But then he learned what Nixon meant by "something"— another Rogers Plan. Both sides would cease fire for at least ninety days while peace talks took place under a UN umbrella. The United Arab Republic (Egypt and Syria), Jordan, and Israel would acknowledge one another's sovereignty, territorial integrity, and political independence, and most importantly, Israel would withdraw from territories occupied in the Six-Day War.

Once again, Rabin and other Israeli leaders gasped. Israel was being asked to withdraw from the conquered lands without being offered any concrete peace treaty. But before the gasp became audible, the Americans urged the Israelis not to reject the plan, at least before Egypt and Jordan responded to it.

And if Israel responded negatively?

Well, Israel wanted arms, didn't it?

"Of course," Rabin would say, "I objected to the linkage between arms supplies and our agreeing to American political proposals . . . but my words made little impression."

Golda Meir was about to reject the plan unreservedly, but Rabin intervened.

She must tone down her response, he warned. Did she want Nixon to turn against Israel at this critical time?

How critical soon became apparent. The Soviet-Egyptian missile system had advanced to a line about thirty kilometers west of the canal, and some batteries had inched even closer. And the threat became terrifyingly real when missiles brought down several Phantoms. So real that Nixon felt compelled to warn Moscow that "the two Great Powers would have to be very careful in their action to prevent a confrontation which neither wants." World War III, it seemed, loomed just over the horizon.

"Israel was now in a terrible double bind," Rabin would muse. "On the one hand, the political text of the Rogers initiative was not acceptable to the prime minister [though Israel had yet to state so publicly]. At the same time, however, if the Egyptians rejected the cease-fire proposal, our planes were helpless against the missile system that had crept forward toward the canal."

Then, on July 22, 1970, Egypt unexpectedly accepted the new Rogers Plan, placing Israel on the spot. Nixon immediately sent a personal letter to Golda Meir, after Rabin and Sisco worked out the wording, urging Israel to follow suit. Rabin urged Meir to agree, for the President had made some remarkable promises to Israel.

The United States would not press Israel to accept the return of a massive number of Palestinian refugees, and "no Israeli soldier should be withdrawn from the present lines until a binding contractual peace agreement satisfactory to you has been achieved." But Rabin was not very hopeful that Meir would listen to him. On

July 25 he wrote to Leah, who was vacationing in Israel:

The problems are especially great since Egypt gave a positive answer to the American initiative. The fact that Egypt has agreed to this initiative has created quite a few substantive problems and PR concerns for us. There's no doubt that we now face not Arab but Soviet thinking, which is much more sober and at a world power level. . . . Israel has been able up to now to proclaim from the rooftops that we want peace, but the Arabs do not. Now it will be more difficult if the government of Israel decides to continue not deciding.

With growing pessimism, Rabin concluded:

In brief, decision is difficult given a badly composed government. It's much more noticeable that we lack a man like David Ben-Gurion, with vision on the one hand, and ability to maneuver despite internal opposition on the other. Without this capability, Israel has no chance in the present circumstances. This places me in an awkward situation. In practice there is no possibility to answer any questions. All the TV stations want to interview me, and I'm refusing.

Rabin's mood brightened, however, when the Israeli cabinet, to his surprise, finally took his advice: It backed the Rogers Plan, though Menachem Begin and his followers in the National Unity government then ruling Israel walked out in protest.

American leaders were now so eager to begin peace negotiations to start under the plan that they urged UN mediator Gunnar Jarring, the Swedish ambassador to Moscow, who was to arbitrate, to move ahead with his mission even before Israel formally accepted the plan.

When Meir learned of this she angrily phoned Sisco and charged that the United States had practically "forged" Israel's signature on the plan.

"What do you mean 'forged'?"

"You notified Jarring that we had accepted the initiative before we accepted it!" Meir cried. "That's what I mean by 'forged.' I reached an agreement with [U.S. Ambassador Walworth] Barbour, and the United States now denies that agreement. You cannot formulate answers on our behalf."

"You received the text of our initiative weeks ago," Sisco

rasped. "One page, one paper—that's the whole initiative. Did you accept it or didn't you?"

"What do you mean did we accept the initiative? Do we have to accept your formulation? We have a formulation of our own!"

Rabin, who listened in on the conversation, didn't know about any Israeli formulation. Meir simply told him afterward:

"We accept the initiative, but we want to put it in our own words."

Rabin went to see Kissinger, who railed: "I don't understand you people. The paper's been with you for six weeks! If you have any comments, complaints, demands—go ahead, talk! Speak! The Egyptians have accepted our initiative. Have you or haven't you? Let us know clearly!"

In confusion, Rabin replied: "On the basis of the President's letter to the prime minister we agreed to the initiative but not to the wording you submitted to Jarring."

What wording did Israel object to?

Rabin sheepishly replied: He wasn't quite sure.

But despite the chaos, the cease-fire held, even though Israel refused on September 6, 1970, to attend the Jarring talks after the Egyptians violated the truce by moving surface-to-air missiles into a fifty-kilometer standstill zone.

Still, Rabin was exasperated. With all the molehills blocking the path to peace, who needed a mountain?

Hardly had peace descended over the Suez Canal that same month when gunfire rattled across the Jordan River. Yasir Arafat's guerrillas had carved out a mini-state of their own in Jordan, threatening the rule of King Hussein, who, they correctly suspected, was secretly meeting with Israeli leaders. Fearful of a coup, especially after the guerrillas plotted to assassinate him, Hussein rained tank and artillery shells on the Palestinian refugee camps sheltering them. In the chaos, Syria saw an opportunity to move in and do what the Palestinians failed to do—oust Hussein and take over Jordan. And its tanks clattered across the northern Jordanian border.

Hussein was horrified. His forces were no match for Syria's Soviet tanks and planes. The Hashemite kingdom, it seemed, was doomed. He became so desperate that he looked to another enemy to save him—Israel.

One evening that September, Rabin was sitting with Prime Minister Meir at a United Jewish Appeal dinner at the New York Hilton when he was called to the phone. Meir was on her way home after a visit with President Nixon to discuss the cease-fire agreement with Egypt, and Rabin thought that someone must be calling to wish her Godspeed. But it was Henry Kissinger, and he was interested only in speed.

"King Hussein has approached us," he exclaimed, "describing the situation of his forces, and asked us to transmit his request that your air force attack the Syrians in northern Jordan. I need an immediate reply."

With good reason, Rabin realized when he had recovered from his shock. The collapse of Hussein, a pro-West moderate, could radicalize the entire Middle East. What an opportunity, he felt, to exact some vital concessions from the United States!

"I'm surprised to hear the United States passing on messages of this kind like some sort of mailman," Rabin replied. "I will not even submit the request to Mrs. Meir before I know what your government thinks. Are you recommending that we respond to the Jordanian request?"

"You place me in a difficult position," Kissinger replied. "I can't answer you on the spot. Perhaps in another half-hour."

While Rabin conferred with Meir, who then conferred with subordinates back home, Kissinger called back and reported: "The request is approved and supported by the United States government."

"Do you advise Israel to do it?" Rabin asked.

"Yes, subject to your own considerations."

That same night, Rabin flew back to Washington in a White House plane that had been sent for him. He was elated. Israel could now thwart Soviet-backed aggression against an Arab leader who was seeking a way to make peace with the Jewish state. At the same time, Washington would realize that Israel could be a valuable Cold War ally. Thus, on meeting with Kissinger and Sisco, Rabin demanded, and was given, a promise of more weapons and Sixth Fleet protection against renewed Egyptian aggression while Israeli forces were defending Jordan.

Shortly, Israeli troops were concentrated near the Syrian border and the Sixth Fleet's aircraft carriers were heading toward the area. But before a shot was fired, Syria, viewing the threat with alarm, ordered its three hundred tanks to turn around and crawl out of Jordan.

On September 25, Kissinger was on the phone with Rabin again.

"The President," he rhapsodized, "will never forget Israel's role in preventing the deterioration in Jordan and in blocking the attempt to overturn the regime there. He said that the United States is fortunate in having an ally like Israel in the Middle East. These events will be taken into account in all future developments."

Rabin was ecstatic. Once more the mountain seemed less formidable. And though he didn't quite realize it at the time, he had made another lifelong friend in the bargain—King Hussein, who would crush the guerrillas in what the Palestinians would bitterly call "Black September," and remain on the throne at least in part because of Rabin's influence.

Some time later, when Hussein was visiting in the United States, an American diplomat told Leah that he had been invited to a party honoring the king, who still could not socialize, or even talk publicly, with Israelis without being labeled a traitor by the Arab League. She replied:

"Please . . . give him my regards and say that we Israelis very much admire his courage and the determination that he showed in his struggle with the PLO."

The next morning, the diplomat phoned her: "Mrs. Rabin, . . . you made the man happy last night. He was so excited that, when I escorted him to his car, he repeated: 'Please don't forget to give them my heartfelt thanks and best wishes.'"

It was the beginning of a true friendship that would ultimately help to reshape the political landscape in the Middle East.

15

Moving the
Mountain

Anwar el-Sadat? Who was he? Even most Israelis did not know that he had been the vice president of Egypt under Nasser. Suddenly, on September 28, 1970, Nasser died of a heart attack, and Sadat became president. Egypt was now seen to have a weak, colorless "yes-man" at the helm. And there was no reason for Israel to rush into peace talks when it was just a matter of time until a new, Nasser-type leader emerged from the crowd. What ideas could an obscure caretaker leader bring to the peace table?

Sadat let the Israelis know a few months after taking office. If Israel withdrew to a line about twenty-five miles from the Suez Canal, Egypt would thin out its forces on the Egyptian side and reopen the canal. Rabin was stunned. This was the same idea Moshe Dayan had proposed months earlier! Egypt was finally serious about agreeing to a permanent cease-fire and a return to the situation before the War of Attrition.

Rabin excitedly called Kissinger. What did the President think of the proposal? he asked, aware that the Pentagon, ironically, preferred that the canal remain closed to prevent supplies getting through to the North Vietnamese.

The next day, Kissinger brought Nixon's answer: "From the viewpoint of our own interests, the United States prefers the canal closed. But the Jarring talks are stalled, and the situation in the Middle East could deteriorate and lead to a renewal of the fighting. Since our greatest interest is to prevent such a development, the United States favors discussions with Egypt about reopening the canal."

Rabin was delighted, but before Jerusalem could fashion a reply to Sadat, Jarring, apparently unaware of the Egyptian leader's initiative, intervened with one of his own. He addressed a simple question to the two parties:

He asked Egypt: Would it make peace with Israel in return for an Israeli withdrawal from the Sinai?

He asked Israel: Would it withdraw from the Sinai in return for peace with Egypt?

Rabin fumed at Jarring. He was supposed to promote talks, not impose an agreement!

And Sadat jumped at the chance to get far more than he had been willing to accept when he made his own offer. Why demand that the Israelis move twenty-five miles from the canal when he might sweep them out of all the occupied lands? Even if the price was real peace?

Egypt, Sadat replied to Jarring, would sign a peace agreement with Israel if it withdrew not only from the entire Sinai, but from the Gaza Strip and all other territories lost in the Six-Day War. In addition, Israel must solve the refugee problem.

Rabin was elated. Israel, he knew, could not agree to this proposal as framed; any withdrawal from occupied lands had to be negotiated and then implemented in steps to make sure the Arabs were sincere about peace. Israel, after all, would be exchanging something tangible for a piece of paper. But this was the first official proposal by an Arab state—the largest and most important one—for a peace agreement, not simply a cease-fire.

At last Rabin saw his dream taking shape. An Arab leader, whatever his terms, had said he was ready to live at peace with Israel. It might take time, perhaps years. But there would be peace. And he must be part of the process—to make sure it was rooted in security.

And because it had to be, Rabin agreed with his government that Israel must not be rushed into an agreement, even though the Americans, hoping to seize the opportunity, were pressing for a quick accord.

"The Israeli government's desire to make peace," Sisco told Rabin, "will be put to a test by its attitude toward this document. You will have to reach some hard decisions."

Rabin was ready to. He recommended a reply expressing readiness to sign a peace agreement while stating Israel's stand on border and refugee issues. But Jerusalem responded with the same hard line that usually greeted less moderate Arab statements. As Rabin would describe the response with deep disappointment:

"The Israeli reply . . . turned out to be a rambling document whose long-windedness was exceeded only by its vagueness. Worst of all, it failed in its main task, presenting Israel's demands in return for peace."

Rabin was shocked. Didn't his government realize the significance of Sadat's proposal? Would history ever forget this mockery of peace? Would those who died in war ever forgive this betrayal of them? Rabin could only agree with his friend Joe Sisco, who said after seeing the Israeli reply: It would undermine America's standing in the Middle East and weaken those Arabs who would take risks for peace.

"For twenty years," Sisco lamented, "you have known no peace, and if you continue in this fashion, Israel will never experience peace."

Kissinger was more blunt, asking a question that seemed couched as a threat: "What would happen if the United States were to exert pressure upon you by cutting off military aid? Would Israel still stick by her position? . . . No one understands you. No one knows what you want. There is serious fear that all you really want is to evade any settlement that requires concessions on your part so that you can remain along the lines you hold at present!"

Rabin was forced to disagree with Sisco and Kissinger on a policy he actually supported, and, ironically, had his foe, Abba Eban, on his side. But how could he stand by and watch all his progress toward peace and security suddenly evaporate? Rogers convinced many senators that Israel was inflexible, and even some Jewish leaders quietly concurred. Rabin agreed that it would be premature for Israel to withdraw from the whole Sinai, but couldn't the government at least come up with counterproposals to Egypt's original proposal for a partial settlement? After all, that was Dayan's idea months ago. And Rabin found himself negotiating with his own government on the terms he would offer Egypt and the United States.

Should he resign from his post? he wondered.

Finally, under pressure from Golda Meir, he agreed to submit a plan virtually identical to those in the past, calling for Egypt to cease fire indefinitely and open the canal to Israel in exchange for a withdrawal of Israeli forces "a certain" unspecified distance from the canal. Kissinger's fury did not abate when Rabin presented the plan to him.

"What is this?" he demanded. "Where is the new line?"

As ordered, Rabin replied: "I have been instructed not to discuss the depth of our pullback in precise terms. But if Sadat is thinking in terms of a withdrawal of dozens of kilometers, his expectations do not coincide in any way with the thinking in Jerusalem."

"And you expect me to submit this proposal to the President?" Kissinger barked. "If that's your proposal, I don't want to have anything to do with it. Take it to Sisco. . . . I won't touch it! It indicates a fundamental misconception of both the basic problem and your standing in the United States. It will lead to stagnation and confrontation. So do whatever you want, but leave me alone!"

When Rabin reported to Jerusalem and asked what he should do, the answer was: "Submit the document to Sisco!"

When Sisco, too, refused to "touch" it, Rabin returned to Kissinger and asked him to reconsider his position.

"In every sphere of my activity regarding U.S. foreign policy," he replied, "including relations with China and the Soviet Union, I have developed a reputation for achieving my goals. I won't handle any matter that looks hopeless to me."

Rabin then decided to take a great risk. Without authority, he proposed terms he thought Kissinger might find acceptable: Israel would withdraw about twenty miles from the canal—if the United States continued to pour credit and guns into Israel and would not pressure the country to accept the Rogers Plan.

While Kissinger weighed the proposal, Rabin reported to Prime Minister Meir on the offer, and she was rabid. How dare he propose a plan without her approval! Tell Kissinger, she ordered, to regard the proposal as "null and void." At the same time, the Israeli media attacked Rabin for "toadying" to the Americans. He expressed his rage in a letter dated July 9, 1971, that he sent to Leah, who was visiting Israel.

> Pay no attention to the despicable reports in the papers! They're all envious of my success and they'll try any kind of smear. . . . The bottom line—I'm happy about my part in U.S.-Israeli relations so far. I was never convinced that, even when there are differences of opinion between friendly countries, like the U.S. and Israel, they should be reduced to the "witch hunt" dimension. True, we do have differences of opinion with the United States. And sometimes sharp differences.
>
> But at the same time there is no entity outside of Israel other than the United States, which helps with aid and armaments in unprecedented scope and quality, and with unprecedented financing. Despite all the uproar that we cause, no other country in the world is closer in political views to Israel than is the United States. I have no doubt that we must fight, and fight hard, with America on the subject of arms, aid and so forth, but there is no need to bring it public attention in a manner that presents the United States as the enemy of humankind. . . .

Rabin added with searing reproach, as he would twenty-five years later when he was under vicious attack:

> All these happenings trouble me more for their content than for the degree of my personal involvement. The newspaper attacks on me do not concern me at this stage. They have raised my status and prestige here in truly alarming terms. There have already been approaches in the name of the President and others to Golda to keep me here in this job out of consideration for United States–Israeli relations. Of course, I did not initiate them, and I gather that she is annoyed, as are her close associates.

Yet, at the same time, Rabin conceded that he would go home soon. In his letter to Leah, referring to Yuval's imminent return to Israel after the family's five-year tour in Washington, he wrote nostalgically:

> It all seems a bit strange: the family is beginning to retreat homeward. We have just finished packing (according to your instructions) and I have returned to the office. Yuval has gone for his last

spin in your car. . . . When we sat down to eat, he said: "It's strange to leave this house now and know that I won't return to it." All in all, it's a little sad, but what is there to do—we have to go home, to our real home. . . .

Actually, Meir had asked Rabin three times to come home and join her cabinet, but an enticing post was never available. In the fall of 1971, however, she promised he would be in the cabinet by about the end of 1972. Rabin did not mind the delays, for before leaving Washington he was determined to break the resistance of his own government to any risk for peace.

But the friction between the United States and Israel did not abate, even when Meir visited Washington and met with Nixon on March 1, 1972. Nixon's main reason for pushing Israel to reach an accord with Egypt on almost any possible terms was to avoid a dangerous confrontation with the Soviet Union. Yet here was the Israeli prime minister, and her ambassador, asking for arms while refusing to help defuse the threat.

Nixon was angered by what he felt was Israeli pressure on many senators to demand that Moscow let Soviet Jews leave the country. Senator Jackson was even campaigning to prevent the Soviet Union from acquiring most-favored-nation status.

"The problem is," Nixon told Meir and Rabin, "that the members of Congress say they are guided by the Jewish organizations here. The future of detente with the Soviet Union is liable to be foiled by the Congress. Personally, I can get better results for you."

Kissinger was less diplomatic: "Don't let the Jewish leadership here put pressure on the Congress."

"I cannot tell the Jews of the United States," Golda Meir replied, "not to concern themselves with their brethren in the Soviet Union!"

Kissinger shot back: "You don't have to tell them not to be concerned with their brethren. Just see to it that the senators get the hint regarding the Jackson amendment. That's sufficient."

Rabin would say of this demand: "Kissinger was asking the impossible of us, and especially of me personally. I could not go about undermining support for what was obviously a cardinal issue in the eyes of the Jews of America and Israel alike. Nor could I possibly take any step that would be interpreted as stabbing Senator Jackson in the back."

And he didn't.

Despite his problems with the Nixon Administration, Rabin was doubtful that any other President would serve Israel's interests any better. And he especially worried about Senator George McGovern, the presidential candidate of the Democratic Party in the 1972 election, who he felt tended to support the Palestinians and might cut aid to Israel if he won.

Rabin made his preference for Nixon clear in an Israeli radio broadcast. According to Rabin, he simply said that "never in America's history had any President gone so far in his pro-Israeli declarations or in expressing America's commitment to Israel's security as President Nixon had" in an address to Congress. Some American observers translated his remark to read: "While we appreciate the support in the form of words which we are getting from one camp, we must prefer the support in the form of deeds which we are getting from the other." In any case, the next day, June 15, 1972, the *Washington Post* published an editorial entitled "Israel's Undiplomatic Diplomat."

Jerusalem was outraged by Rabin's "involvement" in America's domestic politics and severely castigated him. But Rabin ignored the criticism. He wasn't taking sides, he insisted. He was simply stating the facts. And the facts showed that Nixon was more pro-Israel than any other President had been. True, most American Jews supported McGovern. But they were thinking of Vietnam and he was thinking of Israel.

Rabin now felt sure that Golda Meir would shortly whisk him back to Israel and cast him into oblivion. She was furious about his apparent involvement in American politics. Thus, on August 9, 1972, Rabin wrote to Leah, who was on a trip to Israel:

> . . . when I returned to New York after our parting at Kennedy, I had a strange premonition. I felt, as you put it—the beginning of the way back. I admit that, as has happened to me in the past, I am again leaving a job sadly. I have enjoyed it very much and, in my opinion, I have succeeded at it completely. It's always difficult to leave a job in which I have invested so much. This time the feeling is more tangible than when I left the post of chief of staff. At the end of that, I had the feeling that I had reached the end of a certain chapter. I had gotten there, as the saying goes, "in dignified old age"—in other words, in a state at which one can stop. In practice

that would also be true of my position in the United States. However, the great uncertainty about the future bothers me.

The prospect of returning home permanently sparked a surge of emotion in Rabin, who, though sensitive, normally did not reveal the depth of his feelings, even to his family. But on August 23 he wrote emotional letters to both Dahlia and Leah. In the one to Leah, he expressed the pride he felt in Dahlia for defending him so passionately in a letter she had written him:

> Her letter touched my heart. We always knew how she had stood— alone at first, then later with Yuval under her wing—in the face of the attacks on me and the hostile atmosphere. . . . To some extent she was the victim of our going to Washington. . . . Dahlia's letter . . . caused me deep emotion because of her common sense, sensitivity and fierce desire to make it easier for me . . .

Rabin then poured out his feelings for Leah herself, though he still found himself unable to use words of endearment like "love," "darling," or "dearest":

> When I look back over our 24 years of marriage, I am sure that despite all the little arguments that irritate as they happen, it would be diffi- cult to find among the couples that I know a better pair than us. . . . I am certain that there was great luck in my life when I married you, and you know how much I value that. I don't always manage to express it in the accepted conventional forms of daily life . . . . We have been through so much together, in times so critical for all of us, that it seems as if the content of our lives could fill the lives of scores of families. I'm referring to the positive aspects and the depth of the experiences that we have had together.

Over his signature, Rabin simply scrawled, "Kisses," perhaps because a more personal word had seldom been used in the hard- edged world of his childhood, which discouraged any expression of feeling.

To Rabin's satisfaction, Nixon won the election, but relations between the United States and Israel were still chilly. So in February 1973, Golda Meir visited the United States again in the desperate hope of warming the atmosphere. Perhaps she could still persuade Nixon to accept her views on peace and to pump more aid into the pipeline to Israel. Rabin thus found himself caught again in a vise between two unyielding forces and could only hope for a compromise that would relieve the pressure.

Before her talk with Nixon, Meir spoke with Kissinger, and he would conclude that "in the absence of any new ideas or proposals, there will be no progress."

Meir was piqued when she returned to Blair House, where she was staying.

"If what the President has in store for me resembles what I got from the people of his administration," she moaned to Rabin, "I'm better off packing my things and returning home before my meeting with him."

Rabin then went to the White House once again to see Kissinger, who suddenly came up with a "new idea." Israel would accept Egyptian sovereignty over the entire Sinai, but would keep military posts in some strategic positions. Of course, Kissinger said, dangling a carrot, Israel would in return be granted ample aid.

Rabin rushed back to Blair House and passed the idea to Meir, expecting another obstinate refusal. Giving sovereignty to Egypt in all the Sinai, leaving only a few patches of desert to Israeli control? Meir had rejected less painful solutions! But in her bleak vision of Israel's future, she was now ready, it seemed, to use Rabin's formula for brightening it.

With a shrug of resignation, she conceded: It could be a basis for negotiation.

But would Nixon embrace Kissinger's idea? After all, the secretary had proposed his plan to Rabin even before he conferred with Nixon.

"I watched the clock like a hawk," Rabin would say, "my nerves growing more and more taut, till finally, just a few minutes before the meeting with Nixon was scheduled to begin, the phone rang at Blair House. It was Kissinger. . . . "

Nixon, he reported, approved the plan.

Meir's glum expression vanished in a smile, and Rabin, who seldom smiled, managed to curl his lips into a crescent.

Shortly, the crescent stretched into a full grin when Nixon greeted Rabin with a cheery "Happy Birthday" and a boxful of souvenirs bearing the President's name; so tense had the last hours been that the ambassador had forgotten that he had turned fifty-one that day, March 1, 1973. Rabin was then given a more treasured birthday gift. The President confirmed what Kissinger had said, and promised Meir that she would get the aid she wanted.

Yes, a birthday to savor. Rabin had finally moved the mountain. He had persuaded the United States to turn its trickle of aid into a rushing stream; more than $500 million in arms would flow into Israel the next few years. He had set a precedent for Israel's access to the White House, where few of his predecessors had treaded very often. He had transformed Israel from a kind of national charity case into a strategic ally of the United States, virtually guaranteeing the future security of his country. And he had helped to pressure the Arabs and persuade his own government to move closer than ever before to a peace process that would finally end the bloodshed and redeem the promise he had made to those he had sent to their death.

But Rabin's smile soon melted into a flush of embarrassment when Nixon praised Rabin, who would soon be leaving Washington, and asked Meir what post he would get on his return home.

"That depends on how he behaves," the prime minister mischievously replied.

"Well," Nixon retorted, "if you don't need him in Israel, you're welcome to leave him here! I'll be glad to have him."

Despite the great successes he registered—*Newsweek* named him "one of the two most effective envoys in Washington"—Rabin, true to character, was uncertain that his own people would welcome him home. He had made many friends in Washington, but he had also occasionally offended and angered some people—Israeli and foreign journalists, Israeli cabinet members, foreign ministry officials, American Jewish leaders, Democratic Party bigwigs, and other diplomats.

They might wonder if he was suited for a high political position, perhaps forgetting his role in the Six-Day War or failing to understand his diplomatic successes. Nor, he learned, was there a job waiting for him despite Meir's promise of a cabinet post. He would have to wait until after the election, he was told.

"I had no more illusions," Rabin would say. "If I wanted to reach the cabinet, I would have to take the arduous path of politics and not rely on promises."

In a letter to Leah, he would glumly write:

I know for sure that the transition stage will not be easy. . . . Your assumption that my first public appearances will set the tone is not accurate. Public appearances have only limited effect. What matters is the real situation, where you are, and what is the real power that you hold in your hands. From that point of view, I will be in a less than easy situation for quite a long while. . . . However, I also know that I have no choice but to do it. It's not an ideal situation. It is the reality that has been forced on me. And now I must function within that reality.

There was a new mountain to move.

16

Odd Man In

Israel was not quite the same. When Rabin had left for the United States in 1968, it was still bubbling with the euphoria of conquest in the Six-Day War. Now, on his return five years later, the bubbles had dwindled to a mere froth as the nation settled into a complacent serenity induced by delusions of invincibility. Rabin himself, though often pessimistic, justified this attitude:

"The Israel I came home to had a self-confident, almost smug aura to it, as befits a country far removed from the possibility of war."

In a sense, he based this justification on his own triumphs.

As chief of staff, he had led the Israeli army to its great military victory. Then, as ambassador to the United States, he had solidified this victory, winning an American commitment to supply Israel with the arms it needed to remain militarily superior to the Arabs. Now, as the arms began to pour in, Israel had to absorb them into the army in a supreme effort to convince the Arabs, finally, that they could never defeat the Israelis and that peace was their only option.

And he made clear with a bold statement to reporters what he thought Israel should do to make this option possible: He would not mind visiting Kfar Etzion with a Jordanian visa.

Still, while Anwar Sadat had already hinted that he was prepared to recognize Israel under certain conditions, a final peace with the whole Arab world would take time, perhaps many years. As he would tell one Israeli audience, "Israelis must resign themselves—for the foreseeable future, at least—to a state of no peace, no normalization." But war was very unlikely.

Even so, Rabin could not avoid reminders that without real peace even a cease-fire did not guarantee a safe Israel. Shortly after returning home, he was being interviewed by Haim Shur, the editor of the daily newspaper *Al Hamishmar*, when the phone rang. Leah answered and a girl's voice asked:

"Is this the Rabin home?"

"Yes."

"Haim Shur is supposed to be there. Is he?"

"Yes, do you want me to call him to the phone?"

"No," the girl said in a broken voice, "I have to tell him that his son was killed last night in a raid on Beirut."

Stunned, Leah sputtered: "What do you want me to do?"

"Let me speak to Yitzhak Rabin."

As Leah, in tears, ran to the bedroom, her husband picked up the phone. There was silence for a few moments, then he said:

"Yes, I understand. Okay. Thank you. Shalom."

Rabin returned to the living room, hesitated, then said to Haim Shur: "I think we'll stop the interview. Your son was hit last night."

Shur turned pale. He knew what Rabin meant. He slowly rose and walked toward the door. Rabin offered to drive him to his office, but Shur declined with thanks. He could drive himself. And he left.

"I was devastated with sorrow and pain," Leah would say. "We had just returned home. We had left Israel after the Six-Day War with the hope that this might have been the last war, and that peace would follow. Now we were home again and peace was as far away as it had ever been. The war went on, and more young lives were cut down."

Rabin suppressed his tears, but his heart was breaking. All the pain of his past struggles for peace suddenly seemed compressed into the expression on Shur's face when the editor was told the news. Yet was this not simply an individual tragedy? War, he still believed, was unlikely. After the Six-Day War, the Arabs would not dare invade Israel. And in lectures and interviews, he voiced his views.

Once, at great political risk, he took issue with the stated view of Golda Meir and Moshe Dayan that the Palestinians had no right to determine their own destiny. They do have that right, Rabin said, sending a shock wave through many Israelis, who viewed almost all Palestinians as terrorists or their supporters. The right to national self-determination, he argued, "cannot be granted or taken away by outsiders. I would not presume to determine whether there is a Palestinian entity or not." But he added ambiguously that such an entity "cannot come at the expense of three million Jews."

Rabin failed to make clear whether he thought it would come at Jewish expense if the Palestinian "entity" agreed to live peacefully side by side with a Jewish state. Still, he was almost alone among Israeli leaders at that time to suggest, at least privately, that he would not rule out the creation of a Palestinian "entity," possibly a state.

Anyway, Rabin, while finding himself unemployed on his return from the United States, would likely have the chance to help in the final surge to peace, if in a minor way, after the next Knesset elections in October 1973. Happily, he found that the public still held him in high esteem in spite of the negative press coverage of his "undiplomatic" behavior in Washington. In fact, a poll taken in August 1973 showed that 61 percent of the people thought he deserved a cabinet post. And his American experience and ability now to speak English bolstered his confidence that he would serve well in a high political post.

But even if he was offered one, Rabin felt, it was unfortunate that he would become part of a political system corrupted by the ability of minority parties to blackmail the majority into supporting their petty goals. He dreamed of the day when an American-style political system would take root in Israel.

Labor Party leaders, for their part, were delighted when he finally joined the party that he had kept at bay until now, even while supporting its program. They assured him a seat in the 120-

member Knesset in which each party chose a list of candidates under a system of proportional representation.

If his election to the Knesset seemed assured, he was hopeful that he might at least be given a junior cabinet post. From there he might even rise to the top—if he had the same luck that had propelled him into the post of army chief of staff. Leah was more certain about his future.

"You will be prime minister one day," she said, generating in her husband a wary optimism.

While waiting for the election, Rabin traveled the country speaking to the people. A Labor Party victory, he assured them, would solidify the present cease-fire in the War of Attrition and give the country the breathing space to improve economic and social conditions at home. Rabin felt he had reason for hope. After all, Sadat, unlike Nasser, seemed like a moderate leader whom Israel could deal with, but could he make a final peace and survive politically? Was he smart enough to do this?

"Yuval Rabin's home?"

"Yes."

"May I speak to him? It's from his unit."

Leah was startled. Her son, who had just joined the army, had come home on leave that Friday, October 5, 1973, the eve of Yom Kippur, Judaism's holiest day. In the afternoon, Yuval went to his room for a nap, but hardly had he dozed off when a soldier came asking for him. What was so important? Leah wondered. Yuval had had a hard week of training. Why didn't they let him sleep?

Yuval went to the door. What was the message?

Report immediately to your unit, the soldier said.

And within minutes, Yuval was on his way.

Then, so was the Rabins' son-in-law, Avraham Ben Artzi, a tank commander who had recently married Dahlia, though he was due to enter the hospital the following day to be treated for a knee injury. Rabin and Leah, anxious and confused, realized that the call-up must be a sign of a serious emergency, and that night they could get little sleep.

At 8:30 A.M. on Saturday, the phone rang and Rabin groggily answered it. Yisrael Galili, a minister without portfolio who had headed the old Hagana, was calling.

All former chiefs of staff, Galili said, were to report to Defense Minister Dayan at 3 P.M.

Why?

He couldn't say.

"Calling such a meeting on a Saturday, our only day off in Israel," Rabin would later relate, "would have been strange enough. But that Saturday also happened to be Yom Kippur, . . . making such a summons downright bizarre."

Clearly, the IDF was on alert, but Rabin still did not suspect war.

But then, at 2 P.M., the air-raid sirens screamed, and Rabin finally realized that it was indeed war. The radio was shut down for Yom Kippur, but Rabin turned the knob anyway. If it was war, the radio would be back on the air. It was, and a voice confirmed the worst: The Egyptians had attacked across the Suez Canal. An hour later, as trucks and jeeps raced through streets that normally were free of traffic on the Sabbath and certainly on Yom Kippur, Rabin rushed to the defense ministry with the other former chiefs of staff.

They found Dayan pale and shaken. Only some weeks earlier, he had publicly stated that the Egyptians could never cross the canal. Now, describing the initial fighting, he confirmed that in the south the Egyptians were in fact crossing the canal, while in the north, the Syrians were massing on the Golan Heights. Jordan hadn't entered the war—yet. Should the Jordanians attack, few forces would be available to defend against them, for most were being rushed to the south and north. The former chiefs were told they would be contacted if their advice was needed.

"The faces around the room," Rabin would recall, "remained expressionless, concealing the stupefaction we all felt."

Rabin and the others then left and visited the command post in the defense ministry compound, where the developing tragedy struck home.

"I felt a strange sensation being there," Rabin would later say. "A tremendous battle was in the offing, and I was totally cut off from it. No one asked me for my advice; no one awaited my decisions."

Rabin's sensation appears to have stemmed in some degree from a sense of guilt and failure. He had led the army to victory six years earlier at a high cost in blood. And he had then gone to

Washington and won a long-term American commitment to supply Israel with the newest arms. But the Arabs had not yet been convinced that peace was their only option. Sadat, with his moderate stand, had in fact caught the Israelis off-guard in a life-and-death situation.

In view of Israel's unexpected vulnerability, would the Americans wonder whether the Jewish state, if it survived this war, was a reliable ally and ship it enough aid to avert still another disastrous conflict? Would it use Israel's predicament to try to impose a peace agreement on the country?

Rabin felt he had to play some role in the war. So he accompanied David "Dado" Elazar, who had become chief of staff, to the fronts as an informal adviser. Dayan had suggested that his forces in the Sinai retreat to the Mitla and Giddi passes, a natural defense line about eight miles east of the Suez Canal. But Golda Meir asked Elazar to visit the Israeli Sinai posts to examine the options and decide whether to order a withdrawal or a counterattack.

Thus, late on October 7, 1973, the second night of the war, Dado and his adviser, Rabin, visited Ariel Sharon at a divisional command post in the Sinai. Sharon, who had just come from the most forward tanks in his division, greeted the visitors with a somber assessment of what Israel was facing.

Thousands of Egyptian soldiers and hundreds of tanks had crossed the Suez Canal, he said, and they felt victorious, his own forces vanquished.

What was needed? Elazar asked.

Another division, Sharon replied, or the enemy could not be stopped.

"We can't do it," Elazar said. "Your division is the only force we have between here and Tel Aviv."

"The Egyptians aren't going to Tel Aviv," Sharon responded in frustration. "They're aiming at the Mitla and Giddi passes. We can perhaps stop them there."

When all agreed that a counterattack should be attempted, Rabin placed his hand on Sharon's shoulder and said:

"Arik, now everything depends on you."

Sharon recalled the night six years earlier just before the Six-Day War when Rabin, as chief of staff, together with then Prime Minister Eshkol, had visited his post. Then, too, Israel's very existence was at stake. But Rabin had maintained his usual reserve, showing no emotion, whatever he may have felt. Now, however, he appeared brimming with emotion, even placing his hand on Sharon's shoulder, though he normally never expressed himself in so personal a way.

Sharon was deeply moved, and even exhilarated. Yes, everything depended on him.

But Rabin was even more depressed than he had been before the Six-Day War. As Leah would say:

"For Yitzhak the Yom Kippur War was perhaps the toughest chapter of his life. The war was so terrible and threatening, and for the first time he was on the outside—with no job, no authority or opportunity to assist. . . . I remember him pacing the flat and muttering: 'If only Hussein doesn't join the war. If he does, our situation will be very critical since all our forces are in the Sinai and on the Golan.' The idea kept sleep from his eyes."

Who could have guessed after her husband's great victory in 1967 that Israel would be standing on the brink of catastrophe six years later, with all his peace efforts a shambles?

The next couple of days, Rabin, exasperated by his peripheral role in the war, spent much of his time at military headquarters just to be near the center of operations at this critical time. But he found it extremely uncomfortable sitting around waiting to be consulted by the younger men running the war, who largely ignored him. Their attitude, he felt, was understandable. Would he have liked it if some retired senior commander had looked over his shoulder when he was chief of staff? But Rabin was nevertheless hurt by the cool reception he received at headquarters.

After touring the fronts with his brother-in-law, Avraham Yoffe, a division commander in the Six-Day War, he suffered even greater depression; he found an army he didn't recognize. The men he loved were no longer high-spirited and confident but frightened and confused, their morale at rock-bottom. He tried to shake off nightmare visions of defeat while cursing his inability to affect their destiny.

Thus, when Finance Minister Pinhas Sapir asked him to head an emergency-loan campaign, Rabin readily agreed, if without enthusiasm. This was a good job for an ex-ambassador but not for an ex–chief of staff. Yet, as a fund-raiser, he could at least be useful.

The war was costing Israel untold millions, and when it was over, the nation could be destitute. It would need an infusion of about $250 million to barely survive economically. But as he traveled around soliciting funds, his thoughts remained with the bewildered boys he had met, with a loving but sinking heart.

Finally, on October 25, they could go home to nurse their wounds, psychological as well as physical. The war had ended. In the north, the Israelis had forced the Syrians to retreat from the Golan Heights. And in the south, Ariel Sharon, heeding Rabin's plea, blitzed with his task force across the Suez Canal, established a bridgehead on the Egyptian side, and advanced to within one hundred kilometers of Cairo—with the help of weaponry sent by Nixon and Kissinger.

Countering Soviet shipments to the Arabs, the United States flew 22,000 tons of equipment to Ben-Gurion Airport, from where it was rushed to the fronts. And Rabin could now ease his conscience with the knowledge that, as ambassador to the United States, he had laboriously laid the groundwork for this God-sent help.

The Russians, fearing their clients would suffer an even more ignominious defeat if the war raged on, reached an accord with Washington that led to UN Resolution 338, calling for a cease-fire. And three days later the cease-fire held.

Rabin could finally get a full night's sleep. His nightmare that Jordanian troops would smash into the center of Israel never became a reality. After being saved by Israeli intervention during Black September, Hussein was not inclined to help in the destruction of Israel, his ultimate protector from predatory Arab neighbors. Nor did Hussein forget that he had lost Jerusalem when he did leap into the abyss in the Six-Day War.

Unlike the victory in that war, this one brought no euphoric dancing in the street. The cafes were empty; the streets were abandoned; and smiles were rare in the funereal atmosphere. Another victory, yes, but a disastrous one. More than 2,500 Israelis were killed, and another 7,500 wounded. And the wreckage of more than one hundred Israeli planes and eight hundred tanks lay strewn across deserts and mountains.

With the country in mourning, a deep depression gripped the people, with faces, once aglow with optimism and self-confidence, now reflecting anger, agony, and fear. How close Israel had come to annihilation! Could they ever feel secure again?

Political wreckage followed in the next few months. On December 31, 1973, elections, which had been postponed for two months because of the war, were held in an atmosphere of despair and disillusion. Golda Meir's ruling Labor Party triumphed, though losing five seats, with Rabin winning one the first time he ran.

But Meir and the party were in trouble. For one thing, Moshe Dayan and Shimon Peres, both of the Rafi Party, refused to join a new cabinet since Dayan, reviled by the public for his role in the war, could no longer serve as defense minister. Yet Meir needed them to be able to form a stable coalition. She would have to bring the reluctant pair around, and to do so she would, with Machiavellian shrewdness, use Rabin as a convenient instrument.

How would he like to be defense minister? Meir asked him.

Rabin was stunned. He hoped to join the cabinet but never imagined that he would be offered the second most important cabinet position even though he had no political experience. But then it grew clear that he was offered such a plum only as a ruse to get Dayan and Peres to change their minds. The assumption was that they viewed Rabin's popularity and potential rise to power a threat to their own futures, especially their influence over the military.

At first the ruse didn't work. Dayan, apparently playing along with Meir—at Rabin's expense—phoned Rabin on the morning of March 5 to ask questions about the transition of power. And when Rabin replied that he wasn't defense minister yet, Dayan replied:

"Listen, I know politics. The central committee is going to approve the appointment of all the ministers today, and you are going to be defense minister." But it didn't happen. At the last minute, because many party members had wanted more changes in what was a largely discredited cabinet, Meir announced that she intended to resign. There would probably be new elections. Rabin now realized he had been duped. When his turn came to speak at the central committee meeting, it was already late afternoon, and the restless delegates, amid a buzz of conversation, were barely listening. But the buzz gradually faded as Rabin roared his anger:

"The Yom Kippur War was a shock, a shock that has raised questions about the leadership—not about this leader or that, but about the collective leadership of the party."

New elections were not the answer, he cried, for they would

only create new instability. "Elections are no game. If we want to halt the process of internal disintegration, we must form a cabinet!"

There was thunderous applause, and everyone knew that Rabin had emerged as an important party leader. Indeed, it appeared that Meir would have to change her mind about resigning. Actually, her threat to resign had simply been the final stage of her strategy to persuade Dayan and Peres to join her cabinet. And now it worked: The two Rafi men, who some say were worried by the threat Rabin now posed to their own careers, decided to join the cabinet after all.

There was a chance, they explained, that war might break out again in the wake of continued sporadic firing by Syria.

And now Rabin was tossed the crumb of the Labor Ministry.

Mortified by what he considered Meir's "trick," Rabin realized he had a lot to learn about the sleazy game of politics, which he despised. He only wished he could avoid the political gamesmanship usually needed to become a statesman.

"All my life," he told a reporter with a rare, somewhat cynical spark of humor, "I have been collecting ex's. I am an ex–chief of staff, an ex–ambassador to the United States, and now an ex–potential minister of defense."

Rabin's disappointment was especially painful since it followed on the heels of the personal disaster he suffered when he couldn't contribute much to the war. But now, with supreme irony, the larger disaster of the war would generate a political miracle.

The miracle began to unfold on April 11, little more than a month after the new government was formed. Meir resigned, bringing the cabinet down with her. Her decision was triggered by the report of the Agranat Commission, which had been set up to investigate the causes of Israel's near-collapse on Yom Kippur. David Elazar, the chief of staff, was alone blamed for intelligence failures that caught the army off-guard and unprepared, and for the slow pace of Israel's mobilization. He was forced to resign.

Golda Meir and Moshe Dayan were exonerated and no other civilian leaders were blamed—to the outrage of the public. Massive demonstrations rocked the country, especially against Dayan, who until the Yom Kippur War was regarded as the virtual reincarnation of the courageous, nearly flawless Maccabean warrior of biblical lore. And Rabin, more the general than the politician, agreed that in a democracy the leaders should share the blame.

Golda Meir also agreed, and thus resigned, ending her own political career and that of Dayan and most other cabinet members associated with the war. So now Rabin, who had wallowed in misery sitting out the war, suddenly found himself one of the few leaders "eligible" to play a top political role after the war.

Who would play the top role, the party chief who would become prime minister if Labor won the parliamentary elections? Finance Minister Pinhas Sapir, a longtime kingmaker, seemed the logical choice to Rabin and to most other Labor politicians. In fact, he was so powerful that few, including Rabin, would dare oppose his candidacy. But while Sapir was a master behind-the-scenes political manipulator, he had little stomach for the pressures at the summit.

No, Sapir asserted, he would not be a candidate.

Many people did not believe him, but influential Laborites nevertheless began shopping around for another candidate to support. Shimon Peres was one of those seeking their backing, and he sensed Rabin would be his main competitor. To set the rules for the prospective contest, Peres invited Rabin to lunch, where, according to Rabin, his host told him:

"In the final event, the two of us will find ourselves competing for the prime ministership. . . . Let's conclude a gentleman's agreement to hold a fair contest. Whoever loses will accept the decision in good spirit and be loyal to the winner."

Rabin would say later that he "was wary and my inclination was not to believe a word he said. Moreover, I was determined that if he became the next prime minister, I would not set foot in the cabinet. But I certainly had no objection to the terms he suggested, so I replied tersely, 'Agreed.'"

Actually, Rabin, it seems, was surprised by the assumption that he would be competing with Peres for party leadership. He hoped one day to be the prime minister, but who would support him before he served in lesser posts and gained some political experience? Peres, it seemed, was just covering all political bases. Anyway, Sapir might well change his mind about running.

But then Uzi Baram, who headed the Labor youth movement, called on him. One man, he said, was more qualified than any other to best salvage the tattered remains of the party—Yitzhak Rabin.

"Rabin didn't make an effort to win public sympathy," Baram told me, "but the public instinctively trusted him."

And the nation, he felt, needed someone they trusted unreservedly after the tragedy of the Yom Kippur War.

Would he agree to run for party leader? Baram asked Rabin.

Rabin was startled. Was Peres clairvoyant in predicting his candidacy? Or was he being set up for another disappointment? He could not forget that Meir had offered him the defense minister's post in her last cabinet without really intending to give him the job. Anyway, he had promised leaders of the old guard to support Sapir, and Sapir might still choose to run.

No, he would not betray him and his supporters.

Well, Baram suggested, why not speak with Sapir, and if he still refused to run, perhaps he would back Yitzhak Rabin.

Rabin thought it over and contacted Yossi Sarid, a young Labor powerhouse whom Sapir regarded almost as a son. Sapir, Sarid knew, did not like Rabin, whose introverted personality clashed with Sapir's extroverted temperament. But Sarid, like Baram, was convinced that if Sapir did not run, Rabin could best keep the party together.

According to Sarid, he "took Rabin by the hand" to see Sapir after he told the "kingmaker" why Rabin would make a good prime minister:

He was the only qualified party leader other than Sapir who was not involved in the Yom Kippur War or smeared by it. He was a good chief of staff and ambassador to the United States and was very popular. Why not select a popular candidate? Also, Rabin would have special appeal to the peace movement since he declared that he wouldn't mind going to Kfar Etzion with a Jordanian visa.

"All this adds up to a great combination," Sarid concluded.

But of course, he said, if Sapir decided to run, he, Sarid, would support him and not Rabin.

No, he would not be a candidate, Sapir said. He wasn't a glamorous general and didn't even come from the national security establishment. Moreover, as finance minister he had to push unpopular policies. He did not want to deal with the kinds of problems the unpopular Eshkol had to face.

Well, Rabin was a general and came from the national security establishment.

Sapir agreed. This was also true of Yigal Allon, who had been minister of education in the Meir cabinet as well as the prime minister's military adviser. However, he was too closely associated with decisions reached in the Yom Kippur War. Besides, many people resented him for staying abroad several years after the 1948 war instead of remaining in the army as Rabin did. And despite the greatness he displayed in that war, he was seen as a loser. He and Dayan had both run for party chief after the Six-Day War, canceling each other out and lifting Golda Meir into the job as a compromise candidate.

And the only other serious candidate was Shimon Peres, whom Sapir despised—apparently because he had abandoned the Mapai Party, the core of the umbrella Labor Party, to join Rafi. Also, he was linked too closely to Dayan, who was now political poison. Whatever his shortcomings, Rabin, Sapir concluded, was more acceptable than the others.

Yes, Sapir said, he would back Rabin.

Rabin was elated when Sapir told him of his decision, and after he visited Meir, she threw her support to him, too. She had a long memory, and she nursed a deep hostility toward Peres for having shut her out of the negotiations with the British and French for their collaboration in the 1956 Sinai War when she was foreign minister.

Sapir and Meir thus agreed: Peres must be beaten, and Rabin was the most likely available candidate to do it.

Now all he had to do was stop Peres, who, unlike Allon, was determined to run with or without Sapir's backing. And thus was launched the first of many bitter power struggles between Rabin and Peres that would stain Israel's political landscape during the next twenty years.

Characteristically, Rabin was not at all sure he would win this struggle—with good reason. Peres was campaigning vigorously, personally telephoning hundreds of members of the party's central committee who would vote. And he was popular in the committee, if less so in the country. Peres, members realized, had many achievements to his credit. As a disciple of David Ben-Gurion, he had played a major role in preparing Israel for the 1956 war and had built a nuclear industry in the Negev, among other successes.

"My supporters," Rabin would thus say, "were cautiously pessimistic, and I, too, had doubts about the chances of winning. It was only in January that I had entered the Knesset. I had assumed my first cabinet appointment in March. Now, in April, could I honestly expect the party to give me its full backing?"

On April 22, 1973, the eve of the vote by the party's central committee, the answer, it seemed, might well be "no."

"How are you, Yitzhak?"

Newsman Uri Dan was passing through a corridor in the Ministry of Labor, which Rabin headed at the time, at about 6 P.M. when he saw Rabin standing against the wall poring over some papers. He had apparently just come from a meeting of Golda Meir's caretaker government.

"Very bad," Rabin replied in a broken voice, but apparently grateful to see him.

"What's wrong?" Dan asked.

Rabin showed him the papers he had been reading—galleys of the next morning's *Ha'aretz* newspaper.

Dan glanced at the headline in dismay: "General Weizman: 'Rabin Collapsed on the Eve of the Six-Day War.'"

The collapse, Weizman claimed, disqualified Rabin for the job of prime minister.

What Rabin didn't know was that seven months after the Six-Day War, Defense Minister Dayan asked Weizman to prepare a secret memorandum detailing Rabin's seeming breakdown before the war, apparently for use at some future time. Weizman obliged, quoting Rabin as saying, "I must resign now; are you willing to take my place?" and concluding: "Throughout the entire war, our chief of staff, Rabin, was tense, anxious, tending to sweep into panic and unable to make decisions. This even caused us not to inform him of many problems we ran into."

As he drew from this secret report to Dayan, who happened to be a close associate of Peres, Weizman was making good on his reported warning to Rabin before he left for his post in Washington that the "collapse" would become public knowledge if he entered politics when he returned.

"This is going to be published tomorrow?!" Dan exclaimed.

"Yes, he wants Peres to win because I didn't recommend him to be chief of staff when I left."

Rabin, according to Uri Dan, paused, then asked: "Uri, do you think Arik can help me in this matter?"

Dan, Rabin knew, was a close friend and confidant of "Arik," Ariel Sharon. Rabin deplored Sharon's extreme, often undisciplined behavior on the battlefield that would finally lead to the cancellation of his commission as a division commander after the Yom Kippur War. And he disagreed with the man's support of a "Greater Israel." But he nevertheless respected Sharon's tactical talents and aggressive spirit. And he often held secret meetings with Sharon to talk about security concerns, though their personal relationship was limited and Sharon was never invited to a dinner party at the Rabin's.

"I would never go," Sharon told me. "Not after Leah called me a Jewish Hitler."

In any event, since Rabin found himself in a desperate situation, he felt compelled to draw on his friendly relationship with Sharon. After all, the man, he knew, harbored little affection for Shimon Peres. Rabin's political advisers had, in fact, warned their candidate to obtain "commendations" from at least three generals who had fought under him in the Six-Day War, including Sharon, and send them to *Ha'aretz* in time to appear in the morning papers alongside the charge. And though Rabin had seldom asked anyone for a favor before, he agreed to make a humiliating concession to political reality and ask Sharon and two other former subordinates to commend his professional behavior.

"I'm sure Arik will help you," Dan said.

But time was running out and Rabin had been unable to get in touch with Sharon. Nor would he feel comfortable asking Sharon directly for help. He thus asked Dan:

"Could you find him and ask for a statement refuting Weizman's accusation?"

"Sure."

Dan went to a phone and called Sharon at home, but he was not there. Where could he find him? Perhaps at a restaurant Sharon frequented. He drove to the restaurant and found Sharon dining there with his uncle.

"Sit down and eat something," Sharon greeted Dan.

"Thanks, but I have an urgent request from Rabin."

"What's the situation? Who's going to win?"

Dan told him about the Weizman document.

"What can I do?" Sharon asked.

"If you can say something positive about him, it will take the sting out of Weizman's accusation."

"This would help him tomorrow against Peres?"

"Yes."

"If I do it, will he remember it later, or behave as usual?"

Sharon felt that Rabin seldom showed his gratitude for support given him.

"The usual," Dan replied.

"It doesn't matter. He'll be a better prime minister than Peres."

Sharon removed a pen from his inside pocket and scribbled on a paper napkin: "Yitzhak Rabin was chief of staff of the IDF and in that job established the military force that enabled us to achieve victory in the Six-Day War."

Sharon and his two companions then drove to the nearby Tel Aviv Hilton from where the general personally phoned his comment to all the morning newspapers, though Weizman's accusation would appear in only one.

Meanwhile, Rabin obtained statements from the other two generals, Aharon Yariv and Israel Tal, and sent them to *Ha'aretz*, together with a medical report from the doctor who visited him during his brief breakdown, and a personal statement that read:

> I don't want to enter into a discussion of the motives of those who have seen fit to return to and publish, now of all times, an old story—and one man's version of it, at that. The facts are that I was absent from my post as chief of staff for 24 hours, from the evening of May 23 until the morning of May 25. On the evening of May 23 I called upon General Weizman and asked him to take my place in order to make it possible for me to rest after the draining preparation work for the war. On the morning of the 25th I returned to the command of the army and conducted the action on the eve of the Six-Day War and throughout the war until the victory.

Rabin suspected that Peres had conspired with Weizman to discredit him on the eve of the election, though Peres said he regretted publication of the charge. In any case, would the accusation work? On the evening of April 22, with headlines blaring the last-minute attack and denial, the central committee met to give the answer.

As the ballots were counted, Rabin sat in a room in the Ohel Theater adjoining the hall where the delegates were seated and nervously waited. The occasion seemed unreal. He was minutes away from possibly reaching the most powerful post in the government: the final step—once more in the wake of an unexpected, unlikely event, this time, regretfully, a nearly disastrous war. But though the polls made him a favorite, he was far from sure he would win, especially after the Weizman maneuver.

When the ballots had been counted, the result was announced to a cheering audience: Weizman's vengeful deed had failed. Rabin defeated Peres by a vote of 298 to 254 and would almost certainly be Israel's next prime minister, since the opposition Likud Party, which had never been in power, stood little chance of achieving it now.

17

Plotting a Delayed Peace

"**I** sat at home with friends, listening to the broadcast ... as they reported the vote and Yitzhak's victory," Leah would recall. "We raised a glass and drank a toast, and even dried a tear or two but I still hadn't grasped what had happened. After the vote, the house was flooded with phone calls, telegrams, and flowers. ... [I was] swept up in the joy around me, but not surrendering my own heart to it. Too many fears were with me that evening ... it was all so fast."

Fears of what? Leah wasn't sure. But was there some hidden meaning to her husband's swift rise to power when he had almost no political experience? Of course he would succeed, but the responsibility was so great. He would be more isolated, with more enemies and fewer friends. She would see him even less than she did when he was chief of staff. And the tremendously heavy burdens of his job could affect his health. Yes, there were many fears.

But joy overcame them when she heard her husband's sonorous voice proclaim that "the sons of the founding generations have come of age." A new generation had come to power, and he was, indeed, the first sabra to reach the political pinnacle. It was hard for Leah to imagine that the ginger-haired young man she had first glimpsed in an ice cream parlor thirty years earlier had actually become the most powerful person in Israel—even though she had predicted he would. Yet she seemed less perplexed than proud that her prediction had come true.

And she was euphoric when her husband shortly arrived home to a welcome of wild cheers, his cheeks flushed, his lips curled in a half-smile, his eyes agleam with wonder at the improbability of this moment. The improbability of a farm-trained boy eager to be a water engineer lurching from war to war and finally into the driver's seat—not of a tractor but of a country.

Thus Leah's fears dissipated in the prospect that she and Yitzhak would live happily ever after. Rabin, however, had little patience for fairy tales. He fed only on facts, and the central fact was that he wouldn't be prime minister if he couldn't form a government. And he wasn't sure he could.

"The wounds of the Israeli people were still fresh and painful after the recent war," Rabin would say of the country he now hoped to lead, "and deep fissures undermined its faith in its leaders and government."

Rabin realized he would not find it easy healing the wounds and the fissures. He found himself almost alone at the top, with his peers, even those who supported him, reluctant to help him form a government or show him the political ropes. The veterans who would normally wield the power were largely in disgrace because of the war and resented the inexperienced junior politician for sitting at the summit, even if they felt they had no other choice but to put him there. He was "better" than the other "pretender," Peres.

Golda Meir was especially bitter, feeling that Rabin, in a sense, was a usurper, and, though having voted for him, refused to support him after his victory. She even told Kissinger, in an obvious snipe at Rabin, that she admired President Sadat for admitting that his chief of staff had suffered a nervous collapse during the war.

Rabin urged Sapir to remain in the cabinet as his finance minister, but Sapir refused, preferring to head the Jewish Agency, which dealt with immigration.

Rabin's most agonizing problem was the choice of a minister of defense. He would have liked to be his own defense minister in view of his resolve to rebuild his demoralized army. But as a novice politician suddenly catapulted to the top by circumstance, he wondered whether he should divide his time between two full-time jobs.

Also, his old mentor, Yigal Allon, wanted this post, and he didn't wish to disappoint him, especially since Allon, as he knew from personal experience, was a great military strategist. But even more important, Allon's highly influential presence in the cabinet in the second most important post would strengthen Rabin's fragile government.

The problem was, however, that Shimon Peres coveted the job, too. And his Rafi Party, holding the balance of power in the umbrella Labor Party, made it clear that it wouldn't join the government if Peres was not offered it. Rabin was caught in an agonizing dilemma. He could not form a government without Rafi, since its votes were needed to give him a majority of the 120 Knesset seats. But he disdained Peres, in part because he was so closely associated with Moshe Dayan. Even before the 1948 war, the Rafi pair served David Ben-Gurion—who died in December 1973—as his most powerful and devoted disciples.

With Dayan now "in disgrace," at least temporarily, Peres had emerged as Rafi's leading candidate, but Dayan, Rabin suspected, would pull the strings in a Peres defense ministry. And this independent-minded warrior, he was sure, would never take orders from Yitzhak Rabin. Anyway, Peres at that time had hawkish views and might be an obstacle to a Middle East peace.

In desperation, Rabin urged the National Religious Party to join the government despite its initial refusal, even assuring it, with a rare lack of candor, that his statement about not caring if he visited Kfar Etzion with a Jordanian visa was a "slip of the tongue." But in the end he could not accept the party's demands for key political posts.

Thus, Rabin felt trapped, especially since Peres had received a very strong vote in the party election. With grave misgivings, he named his rival defense minister.

And now he would face one of the most traumatic moments of his life. He went to see Allon, who had always been a kind of father figure for him, and in a tense, dramatic midnight encounter, told him the news:

He was sorry, but he had to pick Peres. And he painfully described how political realism left him no choice. How would Allon like to be foreign minister?

Allon bristled, feeling betrayed. He remembered Rabin from the days he visited Kadouri Agricultural School and was honored as a hero. It was he who had urged Rabin to join the Hagana, and who, during the 1948 war, had molded him into a first-class commander. Although he was proud that his protégé had reached the top, should not the mentor be there instead?

Allon's pain was rooted in a history of misfortune. After he had emerged from the 1948 war as its greatest commander, Ben-Gurion had virtually forced him out of the army because he belonged to a competing political party. After years of self-exile in Europe, mostly England, he returned to Israel, worked his way into a top cabinet post, and finally sought to replace Eshkol as prime minister shortly after the 1967 war.

But Dayan had the same ambition, and when neither could win majority support in the Labor Party, Golda Meir became the compromise choice. Allon hoped to replace her after her term, but the Yom Kippur War intervened, and he, like the other veterans in the cabinet, was too politically sullied to run. And now the final blow: He would be deprived even of the second most important post—the defense ministry.

The foreign ministry? No, said Allon. The defense ministry or he would head for home in Kibbutz Ginossar.

Rabin pleaded with Allon to reconsider, not only because he needed Allon to strengthen his cabinet, but also, it seemed, because he hoped to ease his sense of guilt for choosing Peres over him, a feeling intensified by his special relationship with his old teacher. The two men talked for about three agonizing hours, but Allon wouldn't bend. At another meeting, however, Rabin offered to name Allon deputy prime minister as well as foreign minister, and Allon halfheartedly agreed.

Now there was Abba Eban to deal with. And Eban was not at all appreciative when Rabin informed him that Allon would be replacing him as foreign minister.

How would Eban like to be information minister?

Information minister? Eban felt humiliated. The foreign ministry or nothing!

He got nothing.

Finally, after a frantic effort with little help, Rabin managed to stitch together a cabinet commanding a bare sixty-one to fifty-nine Knesset majority when it was announced on June 3, 1974. It was the thinnest margin in Israel's history, but he was determined that it make its mark in history. He would say in his inaugural speech:

"I see it as the first duty of this government to explore every reasonable path [to peace], for I believe that even if we cannot achieve peace, the people must be convinced that we have done everything to avoid war. I want to look with a clear conscience into the eyes of fathers and mothers whose sons may fall."

But were his colleagues as passionate about pursuing this mission? Rabin, at fifty-two the youngest prime minister in Israel's history, took office barely on speaking terms with some of them.

On one occasion, even Rabin's son, Yuval, refused to speak with him, though not for reasons of policy or ego. The prime minister was visiting the West Bank when he learned that Yuval was in command of the security unit assigned to protect him. He happily exclaimed to his bodyguard:

"Yuval is here? Where is he? I'd like to speak with him."

Yuval appeared, and Rabin had barely greeted him when the youth cut him off: "Let's talk at home. I'm on a mission."

As the younger man strode away, Rabin glowed.

"He's my son," he said to his bodyguard. "A serious commander."

Still, Rabin was somewhat taken aback, though not surprised. Yuval was seldom talkative even at home, a bit intimidated, according to friends, by his powerful, famous father, however fond he was of him.

"I don't understand Yuval," the prime minister would tell one friend. "He doesn't talk very much. Where do you think he got that characteristic from?"

Well, perhaps the Americans would speak with him.

In an amazing political tightrope act, Henry Kissinger had managed to fashion separate military disengagement accords between Israel and its two enemies, Egypt in January and Syria in May. But these agreements, Kissinger felt, were too fragile to last more than a year and must therefore serve as a model for further peace negotiations.

And to press this view on the Israelis and Arabs, President Nixon flew to the Middle East personally less than two weeks after Rabin took office. Rabin realized that Nixon was at least partly motivated by the hope that new successes in the Middle East cauldron would boost his standing with the American people at a crucial moment: His presidency was tottering at the edge of an abyss known as Watergate. Rabin would write:

"I was glad of an opportunity to talk to the President about our readiness to continue the negotiating process and the need to ensure that the American commitments to Israel would be fulfilled in every sphere—above all in strengthening Israel's military power and her economy."

What a shame, Rabin thought, that the President, who had been doing just that, now seemed about to be banished from the White House. And at a moment when Israel so sorely needed American support to help it strengthen its armed forces, a buildup needed as a foundation for any future peace process. His view of how to pursue this process had crystallized almost into a magic formula since the Six-Day War. And he elaborated on this formula to Shlomo Avineri, director-general of the foreign ministry.

"Rabin was totally unprepared for the job," Avineri told me. "He could not communicate politically and had never made a political speech in the Knesset. He didn't know how to salve egos or to govern by political rules; he understood only the rules of the military and diplomacy. But on the strategic level, he was remarkably effective."

When Avineri first saw Rabin in his office to discuss his underlying peace policy, he was amazed by the sophisticated answers to his questions. He was committed, Rabin said, not to annex any of the occupied territories despite pressure from the rightist parties.

"In the long run," he explained, "we should not control the territories. There will be no way to reach an understanding with the Arabs if we do. However, the Yom Kippur War was a great setback. It diminished our military deterrent, for the Arabs succeeded in pushing us back. The army is demoralized, and the country is, too, feeling we've been weakened.

"So we can't make concessions at present because they would be made under duress and we are weak. We need three to five years to rebuild the army and the soldiers' morale. American aid jumped from a half-billion dollars in 1967 to 2 billion in 1973. Now we must make this permanent, guaranteed support. We must reestablish the balance of power that was shattered. After three to five years, the status quo will be set and the Arabs will realize that we are strong enough to defeat all of them together."

It was impossible, however, for Rabin to reveal this view to the public, which wasn't ready yet to hand the Arabs a sizable amount of territory. Nor would the United States look kindly on his plan to delay peace for three to five years, whatever his reasoning. To stay in power so he could achieve his peace aims eventually, he had to play a double role: appear dovish to the United States and hawkish to his people, though he was really a dove with pragmatic streaks.

Rabin admired Nixon for recognizing, too, that peace, whether in the Middle East or the Cold War context, could be negotiated only from a position of strength. But strength was relative, and the President was more impatient than he for a peace accord because of his own political needs. And Kissinger didn't want to tarnish his reputation for dynamism and success. Rabin would move forward, but slowly, while the flow of weaponry into Israel swelled into a flood and could be absorbed.

Nixon and Kissinger arrived in Israel on June 16, 1974, to the cheers of people crowding the sidewalks between the airport and Jerusalem. What a pleasure to hear cries of welcome instead of the shouts of "guilty" that brutally shook him in his own country.

"Thank you! Thank you!" Nixon called out. Then to his aides:

"They know what I've done for Israel."

Now he wanted Israel to do something for him: to make peace; a peace, he did not have to say, that would reverberate back home.

"Any further agreement that does not contain a meaningful political component," Rabin said, "will not be a further step toward peace." For every piece of territory, the Arabs must give a piece of peace.

His visit to Egypt on this trip, Nixon said, convinced him that Sadat wanted peace. But the PLO was growing in power and could threaten more violence in the region. Rabin, he said, could counter it by reaching an interim peace accord with Jordan's King Hussein like those already signed with Egypt and Syria. The Arab League recognized Jordan as the official representative of the Palestinians, but the PLO was winning ever-greater support among the 670,000 inhabitants in the West Bank and Gaza and could eventually win control of the area.

Rabin apparently didn't know that Hussein had been pleading with American officials to persuade Israel to agree to an interim agreement. He had said to the United States, according to Joseph Sisco:

"I'm your best friend. I've got to have a disengagement agreement like Egypt and Syria. Just five kilometers, anything to show we have one, too."

When Nixon now pressed Rabin to deal with Jordan, Rabin was reluctant. He despised the PLO as a "bunch of bloodthirsty terrorists," but he didn't feel they posed a serious threat to King Hussein's dominance in the West Bank.

"I need time to consolidate the agreements we have," he said. "We need time to digest them. I can't go ahead on the West Bank, which is a more serious matter than the other territories. I would be overturned as prime minister."

Besides, Jordan had not entered the Yom Kippur War as Egypt and Syria had, so why withdraw even an inch from the West Bank—at least until the king was ready for a final deal? In fact, Rabin had promised Golda Meir, and she had promised the National Religious Party, that before Israel withdrew from another inch of territory, the government would hold a referendum on the question or a new election. And he wasn't politically strong enough to risk such a test and perhaps his job. In fact, Rabin still hoped to reinforce his government by luring the National Religious Party into it—which he would in fact do in 1975. Anyway, Rabin thought, peace with Egypt, the largest and most powerful Arab state, was the key to an eventual overall peace and should be dealt with next.

Finally, however, he acquiesced to Nixon's pleas—hoping that Nixon would acquiesce to his. He needed weapons. But he knew in advance that he couldn't give up any land at this point.

Hussein had secretly met with many Israeli leaders, including Golda Meir, over the years, and Rabin knew that he had long desired peace, as had his grandfather, Abdullah, who was assassi-

nated by a Palestinian terrorist. But Hussein feared he might meet
his grandfather's fate if he was the first Arab leader to reach a full
accord. Rabin also knew that Hussein was beholden to him for
helping to save his throne when Syrian tanks threatened to grind
into Amman and overthrow him. Perhaps, Rabin thought, he
could at least set the stage for future peace with Jordan. And so
began in the summer of 1974, shortly after Nixon's visit, a series of
meetings with the king in Israel and Jordan that were shrouded in
secrecy.

"If you believe you can get a better deal with the PLO, good."
    King Hussein was driving a hard bargain. Accompanied by his
prime minister and military adjutant, he had flown in a military
helicopter to Atarot Airport in Jerusalem, where he met with
Amos Eiran, Rabin's deputy, who told me that he whisked the visitors into an Israeli military helicopter. Shortly, the helicopter
landed by an Israeli government guest house in a Tel Aviv suburb,
and there the guests were warmly greeted by Rabin, Peres, and
Allon. Remarkably, Hussein, trusting Rabin completely, had flown
into the enemy heartland and placed his life and throne in the
prime minister's hands.
    Over coffee, the negotiations began. When Hussein and Rabin
reached a deadlock, Hussein suggested somewhat caustically that
Israel try talking with the PLO.
    Israeli troops, Hussein insisted, should move back from the
border to a line to be negotiated.
    Israel, Rabin replied, could not agree to a unilateral pullback.
And he offered a broader plan that might appease Hussein without
requiring territorial sacrifice. Jordan would control the West Bank
administratively and share with the Israelis the responsibility for
its security and economic activity. Some Israeli troops would
remain in the area until a final peace agreement was reached.
    No, he could not accept this plan, Hussein responded. Not
unless he were given full responsibility for the West Bank and all
Israeli troops were withdrawn immediately.
    When Rabin rejected this idea, Hussein pointed out that he
was taking a great risk by meeting with the Israelis.
    "I'm being accused in the Arab world of joining in the wrong
war in 1967 and staying out of the right war in 1973," Hussein said.

There had even been attempts to assassinate him, he related.

Once, a motorcyclist fired at his car and wounded him in the hand, and another time his butler had poisoned his nose drops, though the poison was detected in time. Why didn't the Israelis take advantage of his willingness to take the risk and reach an agreement? Actually, the Israelis were aware of some of the attempts on Hussein's life, for the Mossad had "kept an eye" on him for years to help thwart any attempts on his life.

With the Arab League furtively watching his every move, Hussein needed an excuse to make a deal with Israel. And Kissinger came to his aid.

Give up Jericho, the secretary had suggested to Rabin. It was a small price to pay for a peace accord with Jordan.

Allon liked the idea, but Rabin rejected it. He hadn't forgotten his promise to Meir when she gave him her support: Don't give up an inch of land, surely not before holding an election. If he broke this promise, the National Religious Party would never join his fragile coalition. Nor was he inclined to violate his basic policy: No withdrawals until the IDF achieved unchallengeable military supremacy.

In his frustration, Hussein, according to Joseph Sisco, pleaded with American officials to convince Israel it should give him "just five kilometers—anything to show" he had gained some territory under a disengagement agreement with Israel. Anything to get the Arab League to let Jordan continue representing Palestinian interests.

Kissinger and Sisco pressed Rabin to heed this plea, but they were handicapped by Nixon's resignation in the wake of Watergate. Under this diminished pressure, Rabin bluntly responded:

"I can't go ahead on the West Bank. I need time to get my feet on the ground. I'd be thrown out as prime minister."

At one meeting with Rabin, Hussein acted like a child afraid that he would get fewer toys than his friends on a festival day.

"Are you going to reach an agreement with Sadat first?" he asked Rabin. "I know that's what you want."

Rabin remained silent. And the talks ended.

Nevertheless, the same figures met several more times, either at the same guest house or in desert trailers along the Jordan-Israel border in the south. But the stalemate continued, though their talks touched on other useful issues. For example, Hussein kept Rabin informed of Syria's plans, and Rabin made sure that Israeli planes stopped violating Jordanian air space.

Kissinger was furious when he visited Israel in October 1974 and found that the secret talks had collapsed. Blaming Rabin, he grumbled to Joseph Sisco:

"We are wracking our brains to find some formula, and there sits a prime minister shivering in fear every time I mention the word 'Jordan.' It's a lost cause."

And, in fact, it proved to be a lost cause. Later that month, Arab leaders meeting in Rabat, Morocco, shut out Hussein by giving the PLO the sole right to negotiate on behalf of the West Bank. Leading the move was Anwar Sadat, who feared the Israelis would not sign an accord with Jordan for months, delaying an agreement returning the Sinai to Egypt. Now Egypt would come first.

Hussein felt betrayed. His fellow Arab leaders had succeeded where his murderous butler had failed. Instead of using poison, they had used politics to destroy his power and influence in the Middle East. He was now completely isolated in the Arab world.

Kissinger was also shocked, and his earlier anger exploded into unrestrained rage at Rabin's "intransigence." The PLO had scored a huge victory, just as Nixon and he had warned Rabin, and its influence in the West Bank, and in the world, was bound to spread rapidly. Other Israeli officials agreed. The government, they felt, should have made a deal with Hussein when it had the chance.

"It was a bad miscalculation," Ambassador Simcha Dinitz, Rabin's successor in Washington, would say. "And it was our fault."

But while Rabin deplored the Arab summit decision and the likely spread of PLO influence in the West Bank, he felt he had had no choice but to stall off Hussein on any peace arrangement while one might have been possible. The fruit simply wasn't ripe.

Nevertheless, Rabin churned in turmoil, asking himself: Should he have relinquished some land in order to save Hussein's influence in the territories, even at the risk of his own government's demise and a weakening of his peace formula? Now that Hussein had been frozen out of the Palestinian picture, at least temporarily, Rabin would have to deal with the reality of the PLO's rising star. And his first encounter with this reality would come shortly after Rabat.

If Israel didn't obstruct the PLO leadership role in the West Bank and Gaza, the visitor said, the PLO would recognize Israel de facto.

Rabin found this hard to believe. But Uri Avnery, a Knesset deputy, newspaper publisher, and one of the country's leading doves, assured him that his PLO contact had suggested he relay this information to the prime minister.

Rabin considered the reported offer, his stare reflecting a familiar blend of skepticism and curiosity.

"No," he said, "if I take a first step, it could lead to a Palestinian state, and I don't want one."

He admitted, as few Israeli politicians would, that most Palestinians supported the PLO, and he would not try to set up a "Quisling leadership" on the West Bank. At the same time, he said wishfully, Hussein might make a comeback.

"We need him to sign a peace treaty," he said. "He will be the first Arab ruler to do this. What happens to him after that is not important."

"Let us assume," Avnery replied, "that King Hussein will indeed sign a peace treaty with you, and that you will give back to him the bulk of the West Bank . . . Hussein cannot possibly give up East Jerusalem or an inch of the West Bank, because he is so vulnerable to accusations that he is a Zionist imperialist stooge. Arafat can afford to be much more flexible than Hussein. . . . You yourself say that [Hussein] is likely to fall sooner or later. Let's say he is overthrown in five years. The new regime will probably be a radical Palestinian force, because the Palestinians will constitute three-quarters of the population of the kingdom. The new regime will denounce the king as a Zionist agent and abolish the peace treaty as an act of treason committed by him.

"In practice, therefore, you are going to have after five years a Palestinian state as your neighbor, but it will not be the Palestinian state which I propose. It will stretch from the outskirts of Netanya to the outskirts of Baghdad. It will have common borders with Syria, Iraq, and Saudi Arabia, and could become the staging point for four Arab armies. Its leadership will have no commitment at all to peace with Israel. On the contrary, it will be committed to the slogans of nonrecognition and war. What is the sense in that?"

Rabin ignored the question, and Avnery was disappointed. But he would say: "I was not in a bad mood. True, nothing had been achieved. Rabin had not budged an inch. But he had listened and argued, and perhaps some seeds had been planted in his mind. And no less important, I had full permission to continue my contacts with the PLO without being molested by the security services or the law enforcement agencies. This in itself could be construed as a significant gesture toward the PLO."

And while Rabin agreed to see Avnery when he had information, he asked him to come as a private citizen, not as a Knesset member. Even indirect government "contact" with the PLO, Rabin feared, could be politically explosive if it were known.

Some months later, in 1976, another peace activist, Colonel Meir Pa'il, a Knesset member, and several supporters went to see Rabin in the Knesset with similar information. The group had met in Paris with Dr. Isam Satawi, who had been sent by Arafat's top deputy, Abu Mazen. Satawi, Pa'il reported, said that PLO officials would like to talk with Israeli officials. Pa'il had seen Foreign Minister Allon and given him this message, but Allon had told him that he didn't "want to hear anything. You mustn't negotiate with them."

But Rabin carefully listened to Pa'il, as he had to Avnery.

Especially when he was told that Arafat actually asked for Israeli help in saving the PLO from a Syrian attack, arguing that it was trying to keep Damascus from taking over most of Lebanon. At one point, the prime minister leaned over and whispered to Pa'il that he should bring his information to two cabinet ministers who also had dovish inclinations.

"Rabin," Pa'il told me, "maintained an open ear to the possibility of peace. He said we were naive, but he wanted to hear everything."

Rabin was especially interested in reports from still another dove, Major General Matti Yahu Peled, who had helped lead Israel to victory in the Six-Day War and was a trusted friend of the prime minister. Peled, who was also in contact with PLO officials, told Rabin that in 1974 the PLO had decided that it was no longer feasible to seek Israel's annihilation and that it would henceforth push for a two-state solution to the conflict.

In fact, Abu Mazen confirmed to me that the conversion had indeed taken place, that Arafat realized in 1969 that the Arabs had to share Palestine with the Jews within a two-state formula, and in 1973, after the Yom Kippur War, that it was futile to continue the "armed struggle" even for half a loaf.

The conversion was first reflected publicly in November 1973, a month after the Yom Kippur War, in a startling commentary by Said Hammami, the PLO representative in London, that appeared in the *Times* of London. It read:

> Many Palestinians believe that a Palestinian state on the Gaza Strip and the West Bank . . . is a necessary part of any peace package. Such a Palestinian state would lead to the emptying and closing down of the refugee camps, thereby drawing out the poison at the heart of Arab-Israeli enmity. It is no small thing for a people who have been wronged as we have to take the first step toward reconciliation for the sake of a just peace that should satisfy all parties.

This initial hint that the PLO was changing its policy and tactics raised few eyebrows in Israel, appearing like just another verbal ruse. Nor did many Israelis, including Rabin at that time, want to believe that the devil could reform himself and force them to deal with him. For the first step toward conciliation could lead eventually to the feared Palestinian state.

But if the hint was vague and laced with the usual charges of "Zionist racism," et cetera, Arafat, who had approved the statement, apparently feared a direct turnabout could spark a violent reaction among his own people and the Arab countries. Nor did the Israelis offer any hint in reply that Israel might negotiate with the PLO. Even so, Abu Mazen told me, he sensed that Rabin had the courage and foresight to make peace when the time was ripe.

"Rabin was the man we were hoping to deal with from the time he became prime minister for the first time," Abu Mazen said.

But with Rabin hurdling over the old guard in Israel and Arafat anointed the sole leader of the Palestinians, the time was not yet ripe. Neither of the two men, though destined to be peace partners about two decades later, dared let his people think there was even the slightest contact between them.

18

A Dissipating Sandstorm

"**I**'m sorry, Mrs. Ford, but I simply don't know how to dance. Not a step. And I wouldn't dream of mauling your toes."

Rabin hadn't been as embarrassed since Ezer Weizman charged that he was unfit to be prime minister. And now he wondered whether Weizman wasn't perhaps right. Betty Ford, the wife of President Gerald Ford, the successor to Nixon in the White House, was asking him to dance during an official visit to Washington in September 1974, and he was unable to perform this essential social function.

The First Lady smiled and said: "Have no fear, Mr. Prime Minister. When I was a young woman, I used to teach dance, and I protected my toes from men far less skillful than you. Come along."

Rabin, his face more flushed than usual, tried his best, almost wishing he were back on the battlefield, where it was easier dodging artillery shells. Finally, Henry Kissinger, an expert in evading disasters, came to the rescue, cutting in, though he was no Fred Astaire himself.

"If he had never done anything else for Israel," Rabin would say, "I would still be eternally grateful to Kissinger for that small mercy."

Rabin would be grateful to Kissinger for a larger mercy, too. Playing a carrot-and-stick game with the prime minister, Kissinger persuaded President Ford to send Israel a $750 million arsenal that would help to save Israel in case another Middle East war erupted. And his success was all the more remarkable since Ford thought that Rabin was as rigidly inflexible on a Middle East peace accord as he was on the dance floor.

"He was . . . a tough negotiator," the President would write. "But toughness, I was convinced, was not the only ingredient needed to resolve the Middle East impasse. Flexibility—on both sides—was essential as well, and I wasn't sure how flexible Rabin could be. 'We have taken risks for peace,' he said, but he didn't spell out what those risks had been, and in toasting me at a state dinner . . . , he indicated that he wasn't going to make concessions readily."

If Rabin seemed inflexible, he was. But while Ford agreed to provide Israel with arms, he didn't know Rabin's rationale: Israel had to rebuild its battered army into an "invincible" force before he took the risk of returning land to the Arabs. And Rabin was not about to tell him and possibly jeopardize the whole aid program because of the delay. He pushed for even more aid than Ford agreed to give.

"What's the big deal?" he asked. "You agreed to that before."

According to one report, "there was total silence in the room. Ford looked embarrassed. Sisco's eyes wandered to the ceiling. Dinitz rubbed his hands nervously. Only Kissinger saw the humor in the situation and after a moment commented, 'Mr. President, I suggest that we go back to the Jordanian matter.'"

Ford, Rabin believed, gave Israel weapons not so much as insurance against catastrophe but as a kind of bribe to extract peace concessions from him. Nor, the prime minister felt, did Ford exhibit Nixon's passion for the concept of peace through strength; or harbor the ex-President's appreciation for Israel's courage and will to survive.

Ford was just as disappointed with Rabin and would respond to a question at a press conference: "There should be a continuation of talks between Israel and Egypt, and between Israel and Jordan or the PLO."

Rabin was taken aback. The President himself had suggested the possibility of talks with the PLO! Was this just an attempt to prod Israel into negotiations with Egypt? Or did he really mean what he said?

Just a "slip of the tongue," Kissinger would slyly explain.

But Ford and Kissinger kept turning the screw, and the President sent the secretary back to the Middle East in October "to see what he could do."

Kissinger soon found that he could do very little. But he tried his best, enthralling the Israeli negotiators with his charm, humor, and storytelling artistry in the large room adjoining the prime minister's office. Apparently for psychological reasons, he usually arrived late, when almost all the fruit, nuts, and cookies on the long negotiating table had already been consumed.

"He would invariably begin the first round of discussions," Shimon Peres would relate, "by reviewing the state of the world since his last visit, describing, in dire terms, how the situation had deteriorated and the dangers multiplied. Anti-Semitism was on the rise everywhere, he warned. The Arab world was restless and resentful; he had barely managed to retain its interest in the peace process. If we failed now, disaster would follow."

Kissinger would set the right mood for squeezing out concessions with his humorous stories. Describing his first visit to Saudi Arabia, he related how everyone in his party, including the Jewish journalists accompanying him, was given a personal gift—an embossed leather folder containing "The Protocols of the Elders of Zion," a viciously anti-Semitic forgery published at the turn of the century claiming that the Jews were plotting to dominate the world. And when King Faisal welcomed him "not as a Jew but as a human being who is U.S. secretary of state," Kissinger replied:

"Some of my best friends are human beings."

His audience howled and seemed softened up. Now, about that concession. Without it, Israel could be in dire danger!

Rabin's laughter did not come easily, though the prime minister fully appreciated Kissinger's humor; he would, in fact, tell a Hollywood audience, "In Secretary Kissinger you have lost a great comedian." But what he did not find funny was a remark that Kissinger had reportedly made before leaving for Israel: He was coming to "save Rabin from Peres."

The prime minister's secret policy was still to hold on to the occupied land until Israel could negotiate from a position of maximum strength. But under tremendous American pressure, he felt compelled to make an exception with Egypt. In bending to Kissinger's will, he rationalized that the Egyptian army's credible showing in the Yom Kippur War might have raised the nation's self-esteem sufficiently to permit Sadat to make at least an interim peace, perhaps a full one.

Thus, at one meeting Rabin told Kissinger privately—and later an interviewer publicly—that he would agree to a "far-reaching" withdrawal from the Sinai Peninsula, but only in return for a "termination of belligerency." When Sadat showed no interest, Rabin decided to take a dramatic gamble. If he had to give up land prematurely, he calculated, perhaps Israel would be safer giving up almost all of it in a final peace accord that required its demilitarization than giving up a smaller part of it in an interim agreement that permitted Egypt to improve its military position.

Please up the ante, he said to Kissinger, according to the Israeli officials. Offer Sadat virtually the entire Sinai for a full peace.

Kissinger, the Israelis said, was dismayed. Why make an offer that Sadat was certain to reject? Would he brazenly defy the Arab world at this point by making a separate peace? And indeed, the Egyptian leader was silent this time, too, though the Israelis suspected that Kissinger never communicated the offer to him. The secretary himself denied to me that Rabin had ever made such an offer. But if the Israelis are right, Kissinger, though having pressed Rabin relentlessly for weeks to be more flexible, now felt he was too flexible.

In any case, Rabin could not avoid going for an interim peace. But he and Sadat differed on how far Israeli troops must withdraw in the Sinai to achieve such a peace. And Rabin, bluntly undiplomatic as usual, had not helped his cause by suggesting in advance that he would meet all of Sadat's demands in exchange for a full peace, and most of them in return for a "termination of belligerency." Sadat now apparently surmised that if he held out long enough, he could get most or all of his land back without going "all the way" to peace as Rabin suggested.

Actually, the only substantial assets in the desert were the oil fields around Abu Rodeis near the Gulf of Suez in the west, which turned out 55 percent of Israel's oil, and the Giddi and Mitla passes, which were of vital strategic value, guarding the way from the Suez Canal to the heart of the Sinai and thence to Tel Aviv. Rabin now agreed to withdraw to a depth of twenty to thirty miles if the evacuated area was demilitarized, leaving it in Israeli hands. Sadat demanded that the Israelis withdraw to a point beyond the twin assets, which would revert to Egypt.

And Rabin was under particularly heavy pressure because the Arab summit leaders in Rabat, pressed by Syria, had declared that "there can be no separate peace agreement" and that talks with all the Arab states present should be conducted only in an international conference.

After several trips to Israel and Egypt, Kissinger, determined to succeed despite this declaration, embarked on a historic shuttle mission between Jerusalem and Cairo that would begin in March 1975 and stretch over half a year.

"Kissinger kept up his shuttle trips," Rabin would say, "forcing us to follow a strenuous regimen. No sooner had my own timetable been arranged than everything was disrupted by Kissinger's schedule. He would leave at abnormal hours, arrive at even more eccentric times, and often meet us for marathon talks that ignored the difference between day and night. No matter when he turned up, though, Kissinger always looked as if he had just had ten hours of sound sleep."

Once, after arriving in Israel from Egypt, Kissinger told Rabin that Sadat had asked him: "Does the Israeli government really want to achieve peace? Have the Israelis rid themselves of their security psychoses?"

He believed Israel really wanted peace, Kissinger answered Sadat, and now he asked Rabin to send Sadat a letter reassuring him. Rabin sent the letter with Kissinger, who was present when Sadat read it.

"He was deeply moved," Kissinger would say on his return to Israel.

Rabin never received a reply, but Kissinger's account of Sadat's reaction helped to dilute his unfavorable image of the Egyptian president, whom he felt could not be trusted. Had he not betrayed Hussein after promising to support him as the sole representative of the Palestinians? Had he not launched a surprise attack on Yom Kippur?

Rabin nevertheless realized that Sadat's moment of glory on the battlefield helped him, as he apparently had planned, to raise the self-esteem of his people and give them the impression he was negotiating with Israel from a position of strength. Rabin hoped that his "victory" would yet give him the courage to conclude a real peace with Israel eventually. And Sadat's reaction to his letter gave him hope.

But Kissinger felt it was mainly Rabin who was blocking the way to peace, though Rabin, under extreme pressure from the secretary of state, thought he had made important concessions to Sadat. In fact, the Egyptian leader was at least as immovable as he, convinced that the Israelis in the end would be forced to retreat totally from the passes.

Meanwhile, Rabin decided to pull back to the eastern part of the passes. He withdrew his demand for a "termination of belligerency" (embarrassing Allon, whom he had earlier instructed to insist on this term), while agreeing to the more limited term "nonuse of force." He offered to hand over the oil fields to the Egyptians. And he would let the Egyptian army occupy a buffer zone between the opposing forces and set up two forward posts at the western entrances to the passes.

Rabin, it appears, didn't expect Sadat to accept these concessions. And he wouldn't mind a rejection since the Israeli army, he felt, wasn't powerful enough yet to justify risking any concessions, though he was willing to mollify Kissinger with some. He actually hinted he planned to stall when he said at a press conference in December 1974, before the talks started, that Israel would seek to delay them until the U.S. elections in 1976.

Kissinger, who apparently had not been aware of Rabin's "peace formula," was aghast. "Why did he do it?" he asked. "Has Rabin gone mad?"

He now hoped to force Rabin's hand by encouraging the press to exert pressure on him. On a Friday, he told journalists that with Egyptian concessions, 80 percent of an agreement had already been reached. The report would thus suggest that if the accord fell through, Israel was to be blamed. And since the Sabbath would have started when the story was printed in the United States, Rabin would not be able to deny the report until Monday, making it appear in the United States and elsewhere that the story was true.

But Rabin's spokesman, Dan Pattir, learned about this "trick" and held a press conference before the Sabbath.

"The talks have unfortunately failed," he said.

At dinner that night, Kissinger pointed at Pattir and charged, "You ruined my mission!"

Rabin then retorted, also looking at Pattir: "Dan, you did a fine job."

Kissinger, according to Pattir, was furious. Pressed by his own political imperatives, he wasn't used to failure, which, after weeks of fruitless negotiation, seemed inevitable. Sadat was at least as intransigent as Rabin, since he was convinced that Israel would eventually withdraw almost completely from the passes as well as from the oil fields. But Israel, Kissinger insisted, should agree to Sadat's conditions. When Rabin refused, the secretary said plaintively:

"This will be a setback for me personally, certainly, but that's not the point. The main thing is how the President perceives it. The Soviets will be happy, and there will be an immediate Arab-Soviet demand to reconvene the Geneva Conference. Under the circumstances, I can't promise you anything about American policy."

Rabin was irate—and frightened—by this threat to cut off aid to Israel, and that evening he convened his cabinet to discuss the threat and Sadat's terms, even though the Sabbath had started. With peace at stake, this was an emergency. During the meeting, a message arrived from President Ford declaring what he himself would characterize as a "war of nerves":

> Kissinger has notified me of the forthcoming suspension of his mission. . . . Failure of the negotiations will have a far-reaching impact on the region and on our relations. I have given instructions for a reassessment of United States policy in the region, including our relations with Israel, with the aim of ensuring that overall American interests . . . are protected. You will be notified of our decision.

Ford was especially irritated by a letter signed by seventy-six senators urging him to "be responsive" to an Israeli request for $2.59 billion in military and economic aid. The American-Israel

Public Affairs Committee (AIPAC), Israel's lobbying group in Washington, had exhorted the senators to exert such pressure on the White House.

> The senators [Ford would write] claimed the letter was "spontaneous," but there was no doubt in my mind that it was inspired by Israel. . . . Because of the letter . . . the Israelis didn't want to budge. So confident were they that those 76 senators would support them no matter what they did, they refused to suggest any new ideas for peace. "Concessions will have to be made," they were saying in effect, "but we will make none of them. Sadat will have to make them all. And if Ford disagrees, we will show him who's boss." I thought they were overplaying their hand. For me, that kind of pressure has always been counterproductive. I was not going to capitulate to it.

Rabin, who was in fact counting on AIPAC—and the senators and congressmen it lobbied—to save Israel from a drastic cut in military aid, was devastated by the presidential message reflecting Ford's resentment. The prime minister's whole formula for peace was based on a continuing flow of arms from the United States. Rabin was alarmed by the prospect of a cool relationship with a country that Israel depended on for its well-being, and perhaps existence. But even if Israel survived, how many more of his soldiers would die in new fighting? How many more ghosts to haunt him? He met with Kissinger that evening and held "the most painful conversation we had ever had." Half in anger, half in anguish, he told the secretary:

"All of us have displayed considerable flexibility and goodwill to ensure the success of your mission. Under the circumstances, to accuse Israel of fostering expectations and then failing to live up to them, instead of laying the blame on Egypt's intransigence, is a distortion of the facts."

Rabin charged that Kissinger had asked Ford to write his bitter letter and may even have dictated it.

Kissinger looked shocked. He would never do such a thing! he exclaimed.

Slowly lighting up a cigarette, Rabin glowered at the secretary and snapped: "I don't believe you."

Kissinger stormed out of the room. Never had he been so insulted at a diplomatic meeting.

Had Kissinger, in fact, suggested the letter to Ford? Well, no, he told me, while conceding that Ford would not have sent it against his advice.

Now the secretary wondered if it was a mistake to send the letter. What if the cabinet was read the letter and reacted the same way? This could preclude any future progress. He called Ambassador Dinitz, who had arrived from Washington.

Would the ambassador please ask the prime minister not to read the cable to the cabinet? he urged.

It was too late. Rabin had just read it aloud.

Deeply depressed, Kissinger slumped into an armchair and awaited what he knew would be the bad news. When he was notified that the meeting was over, he drove to the prime minister's office. On arriving, he was not surprised. The cabinet had rejected virtually all of Sadat's terms. With his husky voice almost a whisper, Kissinger said:

"I am sorry to tell you that you will regret it. Your decision plays into the hands of your enemies in Europe and the whole world. I know quite a few people in Washington who will not regret the failure of the negotiations and not out of love for you. But I cannot tell you what to do."

He was sorry, Rabin said, but Israel would settle only for meaningful steps toward peace. And Sadat was offering none.

Kissinger stood up, utterly crushed, and strode out to telephone Cairo the news. And the next day the media announced that Henry Kissinger's mission had failed. Who was at fault? Israel, Sadat exclaimed at a preemptive press conference in Cairo. In Israel there was no press conference, for Kissinger had requested that Rabin wait a while before he commented. The same request was apparently not made of Sadat—or was ignored.

Headlines in Israel hailed Rabin as a national hero for the second time. In 1967 he had stood up to an enemy bent on annihilating Israel. Today he had stood up to a rich uncle who found it politically profitable to give the enemy a second chance. What would happen now? Perhaps war, the commentators cried. And Rabin feared they might be right. He urged Kissinger to continue his mission, but to no avail. The secretary was adamant; he was going home.

In quiet despair, Rabin accompanied Kissinger to the airport, and there, in a conference room, he poured out his heart to his friend and tormentor as he almost never did to anyone before:

"I am fully aware that the situation is fraught with danger. And that it is not just a political problem for me. I regard every IDF soldier as my responsibility—almost as if he were my son. You know that my own son is in command of a tank platoon on the front line in the Sinai. My daughter's husband commands a tank battalion there. In the event of war, I know what their fate might be. But Israel is unable to accept the agreement on the present terms, and there is nothing I can do but carry that heavy burden of responsibility—the national as well as the personal."

Rabin couldn't recall ever seeing Kissinger so moved. His voice "cracked with emotion" as he tried to reply, his eyes glassy with tears. And still with stuttering difficulty, he praised Rabin at an airport ceremony.

"In addition to this upset over the failure of his mission," Rabin would recall in contemplating his love-hate relationship with the man, "I could see his inner turmoil as a Jew and as an American."

As for his own sentiment toward Kissinger, Rabin would say: "Though personal feelings are not preferred tools for managing an international negotiation that is both rigid and demanding, I still had a special regard for this unusual man. He felt that he was working for the benefit of Israel, even when we had doubts about it."

And then Kissinger boarded his plane, while Rabin stood watching it like some forlorn lover "until it became a tiny speck against the sky." But he soon returned to earth. Had he missed the opportunity to make the peace he had been seeking so ardently for so long?

Aboard the plane, Kissinger's tears soon dried and he found it less difficult to speak. With a touch of anguish in his voice, he explained to newsmen why his mission had failed: No attribution, please, but Rabin, a newsman would quote the secretary as saying, was "a small man, whose only concern was what Peres might say of him."

Rabin proved to be a less fickle, or at least a less gossipy, lover than Kissinger. This seemed clear one day when the prime minister summoned his ministers to an urgent secret meeting and instructed them to come in taxis rather than in their official cars so no one would suspect a crisis was brewing.

What had happened? the ministers nervously wondered. Had war broken out? Rabin greeted them with icy stares that spoke of disaster. Yes, Egypt must be attacking Israel! There was a moment of terrible tension ... No, Matti Golan was attacking Henry Kissinger. Rabin seemed almost angrier now with Golan, the diplomatic correspondent of *Ha'aretz*, than he had been with Kissinger when he had threatened to cut off aid if Israel didn't agree to a perilous peace formula.

Golan, he charged, had submitted a book manuscript to the censor based on secret documents revealing the conversations between Kissinger and the Israeli negotiating team on the disengagement talks with Egypt and Syria. And Kissinger emerged in the book as a heartless, deceptive dictator.

If the book was published, Rabin warned, the secretary might be forced to resign. Relations with the United States could crumble, and the arms flow might dry up. What he didn't say was that Kissinger, for all his threats and bombast, was a dear colleague with a challenging mind, a man he could not easily live without. The person who leaked to Golan, Rabin promised, would be found and put on trial.

The cabinet, still recovering from the shock that Israel might be under attack, uttered "amen," in effect. And Matti Golan was forced to revise his book, sanitizing Kissinger to the required degree.

After all, where could Israel, or Yitzhak Rabin, find a better friend than Henry?

In June 1975, Rabin would have another opportunity to spar with his friend when he was invited to Washington for talks in the White House. With Kissinger at his side, Rabin entered the Oval Office with trepidation, feeling that the fate of Israel was at stake.

He had been looking forward to this meeting, Ford said, greeting Rabin with a smile that seemed to mask impending trouble.

"Our reassessment was not intended to penalize Israel," he said. "Yet after the United States had made a supreme effort to achieve an agreement in the Middle East and failed to do so, we had to reconsider our policies. I have reached my conclusions, but I thought it would not be fair to finalize them before giving you a chance to offer your opinion. I tend toward favoring an overall Middle East settlement to be achieved at the Geneva Conference. It would comprise a peace between Israel and her neighbors, and the final borders would be guaranteed by the powers concerned."

Rabin realized that Ford was simply twisting his arm, having stressed many times that the Arabs would never make peace as a group and that the Soviet Union would participate in such a conference. But he would not be blackmailed.

"We must have defensible borders," he said, "and those are not the same as the June 4 lines. And we will defend this position at Geneva, if the conference is convened. Let there be no doubt about that."

When Rabin and Kissinger left the Oval Office, they continued the talks with even more acrimonious overtones. Clearly, Kissinger was still smarting from one of his few failures.

"Your insistence on holding on to the eastern parts of the passes," he snapped, "prevents any continuation of the diplomatic process. As a result, the Geneva Conference will become inevitable, and I don't know what position the United States will adopt there!"

"This is no way to conduct negotiations," Rabin replied acidly. "We will not bow to Egypt's demands! And please don't threaten me with the Geneva Conference. There, too, we will resist any step that endangers our security, and it cannot be assumed that decisions will be reached by a majority vote!"

With the conversation getting out of hand, Joseph Sisco, who was present, suggested: "I have the feeling that we're all tired, and that doesn't improve the standard of discussion. Let's go to bed and meet again tomorrow."

And both antagonists agreed.

But the next day, the argument raged on until Rabin, his finger tracing a line along the Sinai passes on a map, agreed to move his forces a little bit more to the east. Kissinger, in frustration, groaned that he would convey the proposal to Cairo, but that "we shall have to go to Geneva."

"Very well," Rabin retorted, calling Kissinger's bluff, "let's go to Geneva!"

Rabin then flew home, drew up a map with the suggested new lines, and sent it to Washington to be forwarded to Sadat. The Egyptian leader rejected it.

Defense Minister Peres now came up with an idea. He would place a joint American-Soviet force in a newly created neutral zone embracing the eastern and western parts of the passes. Rabin declared that he was "flabbergasted," charging that Peres's "political thinking had soared to unforeseen heights." Invite Soviet troops into the Sinai? He didn't even want American troops brought in.

Peres argued that a small group of unarmed Soviet technicians would be harmless. But his idea came to naught, while giving Rabin new fuel for his distrust of Peres, professional as well as personal.

Rabin now realized, however, that he had no choice but to bend more in the negotiations, especially after Ford actually suspended new arms shipments to Israel. He ordered his general staff to work out a more extensive plan for withdrawal from the passes, and a new map was drawn up. No formal Israeli force would occupy the eastern entrances, though Israeli technicians would retain control of them. Also, Americans would operate all the early-warning installations in the area on behalf of both Israel and Egypt.

Ford was not ecstatic about Rabin's new plan, for he was reluctant to send American troops into the Sinai, especially with the specter of Vietnam still traumatizing the United States. But Kissinger, sensing that this plan might salvage the peace process—as well as his reputation—persuaded the President to support the idea after Rabin agreed to what he thought was an American plan, though it was actually Sadat's brainchild.

About two hundred American civilian technicians would be sent to the sands of the Sinai to monitor enemy troop movements and warn either side of an impending attack. But Israelis and Egyptians would man the large early-warning stations, while a few Americans would construct and man four smaller early-warning stations.

When Rabin agreed to an Egyptian demand that the Israelis give up control of the eastern entrances, Israel and Egypt were finally at peace—at least temporarily.

Ford and Kissinger were elated, but Rabin harbored mixed feelings. Maneuvered into a corner by the United States, he had reluctantly agreed to an interim accord that called for a weakened

Sinai defense line, though he had desired an end to belligerency. At the same time, according to Israeli intelligence, Egypt would be ready to go to war again in a year, while Israel, needing more arms, would take much longer. Israeli vulnerability thus could tempt Sadat to launch another surprise war. And the danger was all the greater since the Sinai had not been demilitarized as Israel had demanded. Rabin could only hope this interim accord would mature into full peace.

For most Israelis, the agreement offered the relief of a violent sand-storm dissipating into a tranquil desert wind. But right-wing extremists, especially members of Gush Emunim, an extremist religious group, were outraged by the accord. When Kissinger had earlier visited Israel, members "horrified" Rabin and other Israelis by crying anti-Semitic epithets such as "Jew-boy," while one rabbi referred to Kissinger as "the husband of a gentile woman." They demonstrated before the Knesset, and one rightist journalist wrote that the secretary deserved the fate of UN mediator Count Folke Bernadotte, who was assassinated during the 1948 war. Rabin would later rail:

"I felt so thoroughly shocked and ashamed before Kissinger—indeed, before the whole world—that there were no words to express my anguish. I doubt I shall ever witness more deplorable or misguided behavior on the part of my countrymen."

He was wrong, of course.

A billion-dollar spy satellite system? Rabin claimed to be dumb-founded. He had come to Washington again in late January 1976 to seek escalation of the arms flow that had been reduced to a trickle before he signed the agreement with Egypt. Also, to confer on the possibilities for new peace talks with the Arab states, which the United States was now demanding. In the next step, he would hold out for a "termination of belligerency" with any country sitting at the negotiating table.

The arms question, however, would still hold the key to Israel's flexibility. How strong would the IDF have to be for Rabin to make the necessary concessions for peace? It needed shiploads of conventional arms, but not, Rabin felt, sophisticated Cold War items like a spy satellite system. Hawkish Defense Minister Peres,

however, thought in maximal terms. He had visited the United
States a month earlier and unrolled a shopping list at the State
Department that included a spy satellite system.

Why not? Peres argued. At America's urging, Israel had made
dangerous concessions to Egypt to conclude an interim peace, and
the United States now owed Israel something special. Besides, ask
for the stars and settle for the moon. Rabin, who had not reviewed
Peres's shopping list carefully, was furious. Israel, he fumed, didn't
need this "outlandish," prohibitively expensive item. Since the
stars were out of reach, he felt, ask for the moon and fight vigorously to get it. No tricks, no exaggerations, just plain logic reached
by objective analysis. And he blamed Peres for being subjected, on
his arrival in Washington, "to some very embarrassing questions
by various congressional committees."

"Any hint of demands based on the assumption that the
American taxpayer would foot the bill," he would later say, "could
undermine the quality of American-Israeli relations. The list we
submitted in December 1975 was frivolous and unworthy of serious consideration."

But Rabin's attack on Peres backfired. At a cabinet meeting
after Rabin had returned to Israel, Peres charged:

"You are as responsible for the lists as I am."

Rabin paused, apparently dissecting his own role in the matter.

"I don't deny it," Rabin replied, "but I think we made a mistake and that we should learn from it."

With reason suddenly conquering rage, Rabin even agreed to
state in writing that he hadn't intended to criticize Peres, and confirmed that he had been a full partner in preparing the arms lists,
even though he might not have read them carefully. But Rabin's
angry original statements were still another manifestation of the
insecurity that, fed by dread of Peres's ambition, sometimes
tainted his perceptions and, ironically, solidified sympathy for
Peres among party kingmakers.

The political damage Rabin inflicted on himself was apparent
when the sensational headlines his accusatory statements generated in Israel blurred the great successes he had scored in
Washington. President Ford, this time with a genuine smile, had
handed Rabin a list of weapons he had approved for delivery.

Israel would receive arms worth $500 million more than what the National Security Council proposed, and they would be shipped with a priority second only to that given the U.S. armed forces. Rabin himself would lament:

"When I returned to Israel, I found that the principal topic of interest was not the concrete results of my Washington talks—the political and supply decisions that would shape Israel's immediate future—but the arms list!"

However, if the public did not realize the importance of the "concrete results," Rabin did: When the shipments arrived and were absorbed, he would finally have enough military muscle to transform the IDF into an "invincible" force. He could then push for full peace with the Arabs as the Americans were demanding.

But geopolitical chaos in the Middle East was not conducive to peace negotiations in 1976. Sadat was busy consolidating his gains from the interim agreement; Hussein, with or without jurisdiction on the West Bank, was too fearful to be the first Arab nation to make a full peace with Israel; and Syria was embroiled in the turmoil that was wracking Lebanon. The Christian Phalangists were fighting the PLO guerrillas, who, chased out of Jordan, had set up a state within a state in southern Lebanon. When the Palestinians grew too powerful, Syria, which wanted to rule Lebanon, joined the Christians in battle, and the country, it seemed, floundered in agony.

While Rabin feared that Syrian tanks might grind to the Israeli border, he wasn't too upset by the hiatus in peace-table talks, for he could meanwhile absorb the arms that were now streaming in and be all the stronger when the talks began again. Besides, with new elections on the horizon for 1977, he could focus for a while on domestic matters and plan his election strategy.

Although Rabin's trump card in the elections would be his reconstruction of the IDF and the interim peace accord with Egypt, he had done a good job domestically despite his political inexperience and preoccupation with his peace formulas. Since Rabin rose to power in 1974, he had pushed down inflation from 60 percent to almost 20 percent; changed the taxation and welfare systems for the better; and guided a law through Congress for the direct election of mayors.

But despite his achievements, Rabin still faced, in his emotionally charged view, one unrelenting threat—Shimon Peres.

Labor was in fact split over the two men, and Rabin regarded the nightmarish possibility of a Peres victory as only too real. Fiercely criticizing his defense minister at every opportunity, he accused Peres of leaking government secrets, and felt vindicated when the defense minister refused to take a lie-detector test together with Allon and himself. And he described Peres's demand for an increased military budget as "subversion" of his regime, though Peres would point out that it wasn't unusual for a defense minister to ask for more money.

The two men also clashed when, in December 1975, Gush Emunim settled in Sebastia near a Palestinian-populated area in the West Bank that Rabin did not deem necessary for security purposes. He wanted to evict them immediately, but Peres, backing "settlement everywhere" in this period and apparently trying to show that Rabin was incapable of handling the situation, arranged for them to move, but to another forbidden zone. They later moved to a third prohibited area, and lived there without being harassed by the succeeding government of Menachem Begin.

Rabin's opposition to "political" settlements, so evident in the Oslo years, was equally strong in his early years as a politician, while Peres only later supported this view.

Apparently to limit Peres's power and influence, Rabin appointed Ariel Sharon, Israel's bull-like Patton, as his special adviser on military affairs, though Sharon had joined Likud and was rigidly opposed to the prime minister's land-for-peace policies.

Peres, a hard-liner at that time, must be stopped, Rabin felt, even if he had to use a harder-liner to do it. What would happen to his peace plans if Peres replaced him? What would happen to Yitzhak Rabin?

19

An Incredible
Rescue

Occasionally, the shrill epithets hurled at each other by political leaders yielded to the thunder of exploding bombs as Palestinian terrorists infiltrated into the towns and took hostages, hoping to trade them for some of their own imprisoned comrades. Rabin would send a special force to free the hostages, even though some might die during the rescue attempt. Israel's enemies would have to learn they could not gain their objectives with force or terror. In the long run, he and most of his colleagues calculated, this policy would discourage deadly violence and save lives.

But Rabin was too pragmatic—and humane—to rule out exceptions when required by circumstances. Thus, if a plane was hijacked, he was prepared, as a last resort, to trade prisoners for hostages, for sometimes the risk of rescuing passengers was too great to justify a commando raid. On June 27, 1976, he would be faced with making this judgment.

Rabin was conducting the regular Sunday cabinet meeting when a military aide rushed into the room and handed him a message. The prime minister turned pale. An Air France plane, Flight 139 from Tel Aviv to Paris, had been hijacked after taking off from Athens. Shortly, other reports streamed in. There were 230 passengers on board, 83 of them Israelis. The plane had landed in Benghazi, Libya. Where was it going from there? Perhaps to Israel? No one knew.

Rabin called Peres, Allon, Transport Minister Gad Yaacobi, and Justice Minister Haim Zadok aside for consultations. They made three decisions:

- To make an intensive effort to identify the hijackers.

- To order a state of emergency at Lod Airport in case the hijackers decided to land the plane in Israel.

- To issue an immediate statement saying that since Air France was a national carrier, Israel considered France responsible for the safety of the passengers.

But could Israel depend on another country to save Israeli lives? Rabin hadn't felt such pressure since the Six-Day War.

Finally, the next morning, June 28, more news. The Sudanese had refused to let the plane land in Khartoum, but it came down in Entebbe, Uganda. Rabin felt relieved. At least it hadn't landed in an Arab country. He knew about the idiosyncrasies of Idi Amin Dada, the Ugandan leader, but the man had been trained as a paratrooper in Israel and had had Israeli advisers. He didn't seem to be an enemy.

At about 2 o'clock on June 29, the radio announced the terrorists' terms for releasing the hostages: fifty-three of their cohorts incarcerated in five countries, including Israel, had to be released within forty-eight hours and brought to Entebbe. It became clear that the hijackers were a mixed group of Arab and European terrorists. Rabin called a meeting of his ministerial team and asked the chief of staff, Motta Gur, who attended:

"Does the IDF have any possible way of rescuing the hostages by a military operation? If you do, that is our first preference. If not, we shall consider negotiating with the hijackers."

If Amin would cooperate with an Israeli rescue operation, Gur replied, such an operation might be feasible.

Rabin insisted that any operation had "to provide for a way to bring back the hostages. It won't be good enough if we just kill the terrorists. We must be able to fly our people out of there."

At this moment, when crisis might have brought the bitterest foes together, the deep hostility between Rabin and Peres flared with unseemly passion. Rabin would quote Peres about the defense ministry's plans for a rescue effort:

"The defense minister did not conceal his surprise at the query. 'There has been no consideration of the matter in the defense establishment,' he said. 'I haven't discussed it with the chief of staff yet.'. . . Peres was speaking the truth—and a deplorable truth it was. Fifty-three hours after we learned of the hijacking, he had yet to consult the chief of staff on possible military means of releasing the hostages."

Peres explained: "As minister of defense, I had to remain cautious and reserved. I said there was no operational proposal, as yet, that had been thoroughly checked out. We would be able to submit such a proposal only after meticulous examination. . . . "

It soon became clear from Ugandan radio that Amin, eager to enhance his standing with the Arabs, was cooperating with the terrorists—though he persuaded them to release the non-Jewish hostages. (More than twenty of the passengers were non-Israeli Jews.) And all doubt evaporated when a former IDF adviser to Idi Amin, Colonel Baruch Bar-Lev, whose daughter was a hostage, managed to reach Idi Amin on the phone.

Sounding pleased to hear from his old friend, the Ugandan dictator said the plane and the whole airport had been booby-trapped by the seven to twenty hijackers. He had visited the hostages and they were all in good health. They asked him to tell Israel to urgently accept the hijackers' demands.

Bar-Lev replied that Amin might receive the Nobel Peace Prize if he protected the hostages.

Amin said the leading hijacker, who was apparently standing next to him, had warned that Israel must release forty prisoners immediately. His sympathies were clear.

Meanwhile, the general staff came up with three possible operations:

- Launch a seaborne attack on the airport from
  Lake Victoria.

- Induce the hijackers to transact an exchange
  arrangement in Israel and then jump them.
- Drop parachutists to take over Entebbe with
  its harbor and airport.

The ministerial committee met again late that night to discuss these options, and Rabin found none of them feasible. So when the cabinet met the next morning, Rabin, convinced that no military operation would save the hostages, could, as he would later put it, "only propose that we negotiate with the hijackers on their terms. The reasoning was simple: We had had no right to abandon the hostages. If we were unable to rescue them by force, we must exchange them for terrorists held in our country. The negotiations were not meant as a tactical ruse to gain time. We would negotiate in earnest, and Israel would keep her side of any bargain."

When Peres delivered "a pathetic address on the implications of capitulation to terrorist blackmail," Rabin would sourly recall, he "required a considerable measure of patience to keep from interrupting him. Finally, when he had said his piece, I observed: 'Our problem at the moment is not rhetoric. If you have a better proposal, go ahead! What do you suggest?' The defense minister maintained a dignified silence."

Rabin then asked for a vote and was gratified when the ministers unanimously agreed to negotiate for the release of the hostages through the French government, while keeping the military option open. But even as he won, Rabin, again showing signs of insecurity, was not sure he had done the right thing. His humanity pressed him to sacrifice the basic security principle that had been drilled into him since he first learned how to fire a gun: Don't give an inch to the terrorist, whatever the cost.

As a young officer in the 1948 war, Rabin had agonizingly suppressed this humanity with an exaggerated show of toughness and arrogance that earned the hostility of many of his men.

So many died, never knowing that he loved them. He had then sent more to their death in the Six-Day War. And now there might be still more.

Rabin could not forget the anguished faces of the people who had broken into the compound housing his office in Tel Aviv hours earlier and demanded that Israel release terrorists to save the lives of their loved ones. He could still hear his friend, Yoske Tulipman, whose daughter was one of the hostages, desperately pleading over the phone:

"Yitzhak, you know that I'm an out-and-out hawk, but when it comes to my own daughter, my own flesh and blood, you start to see things in a different light. Do everything to release them!"

Nor could Rabin erase from his mind the plea of another man whose son, daughter-in-law, and their two children were in Entebbe:

"You agreed to every price demanded of you for the return of coffins after the Yom Kippur War. You released thousands of prisoners of war in order to get bodies. Are you waiting now for them to be returned in coffins? Save them while they're still alive! At any price for the lives of our children!"

Yes, he must save them.

"'We have no other option,'" Peres would quote Rabin as saying, "glancing at me each time. . . . I argued quietly that we had never agreed in the past to free prisoners who had killed innocent civilians. . . . Rabin countered that the relatives of the hostages were saying that Israel had freed terrorists after the 1973 war in exchange for the bodies of dead soldiers—so how could it now refuse to free terrorists in return for living people whose lives were in terrible danger?"

And Rabin was not impressed by Peres's argument that "if we give in to the hijackers' demands and release terrorists, everyone will understand us but no one will respect us. If, on the other hand, we conduct a military operation to free the hostages, it is possible that no one will understand us—but everyone will respect us, depending, of course, on the outcome of the operation."

That was the rub, Rabin felt—the possible outcome. To win some fleeting respect from the world, should the lives of all those innocents be put at such grave risk? What about respecting those lives? But if he agonized over the conflict between principle and humanity, he was relieved when Menachem Begin, who had once been accused of terrorism himself, told him:

"This is not a matter for debate between the coalition and the opposition. It is a national issue of the first order. We support the government's position, and we'll make our position known."

Rabin would react with gratitude: "To tell the truth, I was moved by Begin's support. I myself was less than content about our decision to negotiate with the blackmailers, and this backing from the opposition provided me with a certain measure of relief."

Rabin informed Peres of Begin's statement and would report in his memoirs: "Peres looked surprised. Evidently the opposition's display of national responsibility had descended on him like a cold shower, cooling his demagogy."

The prime minister was apparently trying to justify his decision, to dispel the doubt and even guilt he felt for violating an ingrained Israeli military code. But what would he feel if his two friends lost their children? Could he live with that? As in the period preceding the Six-Day War, he was torn between the demand of a survival culture that placed nation above individual and the dictum of a tormented conscience that he risk lives only in operations with a reasonable chance to succeed.

"It had been a very hard week for him," Leah would recall, "full of a tension that he had never experienced during his years of service as a soldier and diplomat [she may have momentarily forgotten the Six-Day War]. The terrible dilemma, the conflicting interests of the relatives of the hostages and those who ... screamed 'release them at all costs' and the wider public and politicians who insisted, 'We shall not compromise with terror! You cannot give in to the pressures of the families.'"

Yet, even as Rabin writhed in indecision over the hostage crime, he struggled with a more personal dilemma. He had been looking forward to attending Dahlia's graduation from law school, and it would take place in the midst of the crisis.

"Daddy, you don't have to come," Dahlia told him.

She didn't want to burden him at that critical time. Also, she would be somewhat embarrassed having the prime minister at the ceremony—especially when people expected him to be working to save other parents' children.

"But Dahlia," he replied, "I want to be there."

And he came. When he grew very restless listening to the long speeches and kept glancing at his watch, Leah whispered: "Remember, you were not forced to come. Find the patience, even if it's hard."

It was hard indeed, though he was thrilled to see his daughter receive her law degree.

When the terrorists announced they were extending their deadline to Sunday, July 4, Rabin thought that maybe now he would have enough time to find a way to honor the military code without dooming the hostages.

He wanted a military plan immediately, he told Peres. Especially after hearing a report that the terrorists had separated the Israelis from the other hostages and were releasing the non-Israelis. What would this mean for his countrymen? Shortly a plan appeared on his desk: Moshe Dayan, who knew Idi Amin well, should go to Uganda and talk with him.

"My reaction bordered on disbelief," Rabin would say. "Placing a famous and important individual like Moshe Dayan in the hands of Uganda's unpredictable tyrant?"

Bring another plan!

And Peres did. A military force would land at Entebbe in four planes. Although some members of the general staff harbored doubts about the plan, Peres told Rabin:

"At this moment, speaking personally rather than officially, I am convinced that we have a real military option available."

Rabin was cool to the idea. If it failed, he said, the IDF and Israel itself would suffer a great blow. Also, what if the terrorists attacked the first plane before the other two could land? If they had antiaircraft, how many men would die? The Hercules was, after all, a lumbering, unprotected aircraft. And of course, the terrorists had warned that the terminal housing the hostages was booby-trapped, though Rabin calculated this wasn't true since Ugandan troops were quartered on the second floor, just over the victims.

"Anyway," Rabin said, according to Peres, "I'm bound by the cabinet's decision."

Peres, however, was sure that Rabin was still wavering and lobbied the other ministers to prod him. Later that day, Saturday, July 3, the two men met with military leaders and dissected the plan. But Rabin was still worried about some of the gaps in intelligence. With so many lives at stake, the plan had to be perfect.

"The intelligence information we have," he lamented, "is far from adequate. ... I am in favor of all the preparations going ahead, but I propose we still see this thing as subsidiary to the negotiations. If only I could get them to release the women and children . . . that would change the whole picture."

On Saturday morning, July 3, Peres met in Chief of Staff Gur's office with the generals and other senior officers involved in the operation.

"After attending last night's exercise," Gur reported, "I can recommend that the cabinet approve the plan."

He then traced every stage of the plan. Four Hercules would soar into the skies from Sharm el-Sheikh at about 4 P.M. and land at Entebbe at 11 P.M. The first plane would halt at the end of the runway, and several jeeps and a Mercedes intended to deceive the enemy into thinking it was carrying Idi Amin would be unloaded, all bulging with soldiers. They would race to the terminal building and take it over. Meanwhile, the other three planes would land, protected by the soldiers already on the ground, and disgorge armored cars, to be used if the Ugandan troops resisted. The first plane would taxi to the terminal building and pick up the hostages. And no, there weren't any antiaircraft guns at the airport.

Satisfied with the final plan, Peres now had to win the support of Rabin and the cabinet—and he had little more than about an hour to do it, since, under the plan, the planes were to leave Ben-Gurion Airport for Sharm el-Sheikh at 11:30 A.M. He would meet with the prime minister and the ministerial committee just a half-hour before takeoff. If Rabin gave the go-ahead, the planes would leave on time and a cabinet meeting to bestow the final blessing would be held while they were airborne. But if the cabinet rejected the action—and Peres couldn't imagine it would at this stage—the aircraft could always be called back in mid-flight.

The meeting with Rabin and the ministerial committee was tense, with the fate of the hostages at stake. Peres would later write he told the prime minister:

"The prospects for a successful rescue operation were better now than they had ever been. The chief of staff was now totally in favor of the operation. Allon had said earlier that he supported it, and there was no reason to think he had changed his mind. Now it was up to him to take a final position."

The intelligence information they had, Rabin conceded, was twenty-four hours old; things on the ground might have changed since then. He asked questions with machine-gun rapidity.

"Clearly, he was still undecided," Peres would say of Rabin, though Rabin would claim he was cautious because he wanted to make absolutely sure there would be no hitch in the plan.

Anyway, Peres was taking no chances; he continued to pressure Rabin unremittingly: "We had lectured the world against giving in to terrorism. If we gave in now, our prestige would suffer greatly. . . . The hijackers had conducted a 'selection' [a reminder of the Holocaust], separating the Jews from the others aboard the plane. If the proposed operation succeeded, the mood of the entire country would improve suddenly and dramatically. Certainly, the operation would put our finest soldiers at risk. But we had always been ready to risk lives to save a larger number of lives by using our own forces, without recourse to outside assistance."

There was a chilling silence. Time had run out; it was either yes or no. History would remember this moment.

But Rabin needed no prodding. He would be influenced only by the facts. As one officer who was present would say:

"Rabin was a realist. He had to know every risk. Not many could absorb so many details and yet simultaneously see the whole picture."

And it all boiled down to the likelihood that at least ten to twenty hostages would be killed even if the mission succeeded. There was a pause, and then Rabin asked:

"When does the takeoff order have to be given?"

Peres would later say: "This was the first indication that he was coming around."

Indeed, after summing up in his mind the details of the plan, Rabin was at last satisfied that it could work—even if Peres happened to agree.

At a cabinet meeting held at 3 P.M., after the planes had already departed, Rabin explained in a firm, reassuring voice: "We have a military option. It has been thoroughly examined and recommended by the chief of staff. As long as we had none, I was in favor of conducting serious negotiations with the hijackers. Now the situation has changed. I believe that the rescue operation will entail casualties—among the hostages as well as among the rescuers. I don't know how many. But even if we have fifteen or twenty dead—and we can all see what a heavy blow that would be—I am in favor of the operation. If we have a military option, we must take it up—even if the price is heavy—rather than give in to the terrorists."

When one cabinet member complained that Rabin had placed the cabinet under pressure by letting the planes take off, the prime minister replied that "the ultimatum would run out the following day; and since such an operation could not be launched by daylight, this was the last opportunity."

The cabinet approved the operation unanimously.

After the meeting, Rabin drove home, he would say, "feeling calm for the first time in a week. Every detail, every phase of the operation was etched in my brain like an iron casting."

But if the prime minister now felt calm, Leah was not after her husband finally told her of the secret rescue mission.

"From that moment on," she would say, "I couldn't relax. What trepidation, what emotions, what prayers!"

Rabin took a short nap, his first real sleep in days, and got ready to leave for the defense ministry, where a loudspeaker linkup to GHQ had been installed so he and his colleagues could follow reports from the troops at Entebbe. The phone then rang. It was Major General Rehavam Ze'evi, who had gone to Paris to negotiate with the hijackers through French mediation. Rabin did not reveal the IDF rescue plan to him, feeling Ze'evi could more easily keep the terrorists preoccupied if he thought the negotiations were serious. Rabin talked about terms calmly, without a hint that their whole discussion was irrelevant.

After the conversation, Rabin would tell his wife: "Tomorrow Israel's prestige will be sky-high, or I'll be hanging from a lamppost in front of the town hall."

But even if he wasn't, he would resign if the operation failed.

"Everything is all right. Will report later."

A surge of excitement relieved the anxiety as Rabin and his aides, Transportation Minister Yaacobi, and the Mossad chief sat restlessly with Peres in his office listening to these first words from the Entebbe force at 11:10 P.M. And the excitement grew as other messages followed:

11:18 P.M.—"Shefel"—The other planes had landed.

11:20 P.M.—"Everything is going well. You will soon receive a full report." Then: "Falastin"—The attack on the terminal had begun.

11:32 P.M.—"Jefferson"—Evacuation of the hostages was under way.

11:33 P.M.—"Moving everything to 'Galila'"—Hostages were being taken to the plane.

Rabin and his colleagues were thrilled. Was it possible? No casualties? No surprises?

Then, at 11:50 P.M.: "There two Ekaterina"—two casualties.

Finally, at 11:51 P.M.: "Carmel"—The planes were all in the air.

"Our hearts leaped with joy," Peres would recall.

And cognac spilled down eager throats, some of it deepening the flush in Rabin's cheeks.

Meanwhile, Leah lay in bed trying to read an article in *Time* magazine while waiting for a phone call from her husband. But she couldn't concentrate. Even the drone of her neighbor's air conditioner disturbed her. Perhaps because it reminded her of an airplane engine. Would the hostages be saved? She prayed for them as she paused in her reading. She also prayed for her husband. Yes, they would hang him if the operation failed. And even if they didn't, he would view himself as the killer of Tulipman's daughter and the other hostages. In war, soldiers inevitably died. But these were civilians. It seemed so important: Tulipman would never forgive him.

At 12:30, the telephone rang. It was her sister, Aviva.

"They're safe!" she cried. "They're on their way home!"

How did she know? Leah was too excited to ask.

At army headquarters, Colonel Bar-Lev called Idi Amin once more to learn whether the dictator had heard yet of the mass escape:

Amin: President Amin speaking.

Bar-Lev: Thank you, sir. I want to thank you for your cooperation. Thank you very much, sir.

Amin: You know you did not succeed . . .

Bar-Lev: Thank you for your cooperation, sir. The cooperation did not succeed? Why?

Amin: What has happened? Can you tell me?

Bar-Lev: No, I don't know. I was asked just to thank you for your cooperation. My friends, who have close connections with the government, asked me to say that to you.

And Bar-Lev hung up.

At 2 A.M., Rabin was at the airport greeting the passengers—one hundred and four. As they stumbled out of the planes, his aides suggested that he deliver a welcoming speech. But after learning of the casualties, he was in no mood to speak. Three of the hostages and the leader of the force, Yonatan Netanyahu (elder brother of Benjamin), were killed, one woman was missing (she was murdered in a hospital), and three more hostages and five Israeli soldiers were wounded.

Fewer casualties than Rabin had expected, yet still a terrible blow. He was gratified that all the terrorists had been killed.

"I want to thank you for your efforts, and welcome you back home," he said. "Excuse me if I don't say more."

The minister of transport, Gad Yaacobi, who was at his side, would explain to me: "He had seen so many men die. He had been to so many funerals. . . . "

On returning home later in the morning, Rabin toppled into bed, exhausted and heartbroken, yet elated about the success of the rescue operation. Meanwhile, Israel and the world rejoiced over one of the most daring rescue operations in history. Even King Hussein sent a message lauding him for his courage in the struggle against terrorism (though his UN representative, unaware of the king's message, would bitterly attack Israel in a General Assembly debate the following day).

But when Rabin awoke, his euphoria was still dimmed by thoughts of the dead—and a newsman's query: Was it true that he had consistently opposed any military action, and that Peres had "forced" him to consent to it?

Rabin was livid. He was forced to consent? A lie! He had agreed on military action when he finally had a plan he thought had a chance to succeed.

"The story," he would claim, "was obviously a fabrication—neither the first nor the last to be disseminated by rivals within my own party in order to undermine my standing and advance their own ambitions."

"I'm going to fire Shimon," Rabin snapped to Gad Yaacobi. "I have no alternative. But I hope you'll stay in the cabinet. It's especially important since you're close to him."

"It would be a mistake to fire him," Yaacobi replied. "You

would simply bring the party and the government to a crisis. Instead, talk with Shimon and ask for an apology."

Rabin reluctantly agreed and met with Peres, who argued that his remarks to the press had been misinterpreted. Rabin would not accept this explanation, but simply warned Peres to stop making such statements. He realized Yaacobi was right; he didn't need a party crisis.

The acrimonious charges and countercharges between the two men over their respective roles in the Entebbe drama were symptomatic of their abrasive relationship. Not only were they competitors for political power, but their methods of solving problems were poles apart. Peres, in seeking to save lives in Entebbe, wanted to act swiftly, and was willing to take risks that Rabin did not find acceptable, at least before he thoroughly analyzed the plan, calculated the chances for its success, and then made the proper adjustments.

With this conflict exacerbating the political rivalry of the two men, once more Rabin, even at the height of his glory, could not hide his insecurity or the suspicion it bred—ironically, suspicion that, when applied to military planning, induced the skepticism and demand for virtual perfection that led to the operation's success.

And now Rabin could visit Tulipman and listen to his hawkish views with a smile.

20

Trapped in a
Nightmare

Rabin was sitting atop the world in mid-1976. Once more, he was a national hero, the man who had not only saved over one hundred lives, but had propelled Israel, it seemed, into a stratosphere exclusively reserved for supermen. He had, with one incredible operation, turned the lingering gloom from the Yom Kippur War into a renewed optimism rooted in a feeling that Israel was again plucky, proud, and powerful.

And this perception seemed valid. The economy had improved; though inflation was 38 percent annually and labor problems persisted, exports were rising and imports, as well as income tax rates, were falling, while unemployment was stable.

Moreover, peace was holding, at least temporarily, with Israel having reached an interim agreement with Egypt and Syria, and Lebanon hopelessly mired in civil war. And a secret meeting in Switzerland between Rabin and President Felix Houphouet-Boigny of the Ivory Coast heralded a gradual resumption of friendly relations with the African nations, which had severed them during the Yom Kippur War.

With a semblance of peace, Israel was acquiring a huge arsenal of American arms, which, with the deliveries up to mid-1977, would double the military strength that had shielded Israel from annihilation after the Yom Kippur War: 30 percent more planes, including F-15 fighter-bombers, the best in the world; 50 percent more tanks; 100 percent more mobile artillery; and 700 percent more armored troop carriers.

Rabin felt a rare surge of optimism; he had built, it seemed, the foundation he needed for full peace with the Arab countries. Now they would know there was no alternative to such a peace; now they would ask, why fight an invincible foe? He would no longer stall. It was time to strike a bargain with them, and he would start with Egypt.

Actually, Rabin had little choice. Jordan was out, for King Hussein would not dare be the first to make a separate final peace. And as he no longer represented the Palestinians, he could not negotiate their future. Unless this situation changed, Rabin knew, he might have to deal directly with non-PLO Palestinians. And he didn't rule out a deal with the PLO as a last resort if it really had changed its philosophy and tactics as his "leftist" informants believed.

As for Syria, it was still busy fighting the PLO forces based in Lebanon—curiously raising the possibility that if these forces were crushed, Jordan might once again be able to fill the power vacuum in the West Bank. Moreover, Syria insisted that Israel negotiate peace with the Arab nations as a group, a one-against-many framework that Israel would not accept. Nor would Israel find it easy abandoning the Golan Heights from either a security or a political point of view.

It would be relatively easy, on the other hand, for Israel to withdraw from the Sinai, which was not as sensitive an issue. So now ready and eager to make a final and real peace with Egypt, Rabin calculated that it could only come in four stages: disengagement (which had already been achieved); diffusion (human contact between the two peoples through tourism and cultural relations); increasing trust; and, finally, full peace.

The most immediate problem was how to approach Sadat again. The Americans, it was clear, felt that a full peace was premature and would not push for it. So Rabin sent Peres to Austria to see Karl Kahana, a friend of Chancellor Bruno Kreisky, who wanted to promote the peace process. Kahana promised to seek a meeting between Peres and Hassan Tohami, the Egyptian ambassador to Austria, who, it was hoped, would pave the way to an Israeli-Egyptian summit. But the plan died.

Then a political adviser of Rumanian President Nicolae Ceausescu was welcomed to Israel and returned to Rumania with an agreement that Ceausescu would also try to arrange a meeting at the top or even at a lower level. But again the effort fell through.

Rabin now decided on a daring new plan. He contacted King Hassan of Morocco, who had long been in secret communication with Israeli leaders, and startled the monarch with a proposal that Rabin personally come to Rabat to discuss a peace plan with him. Hassan agreed.

The Mossad, which had an agent in Rabat, arranged for the trip, and toward the end of 1976, Rabin flew to Morocco. On landing in Rabat, he emerged from the plane as a Moslem, disguised with a mustache, heavy glasses, and flowing robe. After being warmly greeted by Hassan in the royal quarters of a mosque, Rabin wasted no words: Could His Majesty arrange a face-to-face meeting with Sadat in Cairo?

Hassan was surprised but glad to cooperate. He would contact Sadat and suggest a meeting, he promised.

And after several hours of conversation about peace prospects, Rabin departed, carrying with him a valuable gift—an ancient Torah inscribed on deerskin, which he would donate to an Israeli museum with the source designated as an "unknown donor."

Rabin was excited by the vision of crowning his regime with a final Egyptian peace treaty, especially with an election looming in autumn 1977. He might be an amateur politician, and, indeed, he had a hard time juggling the demands of the politicians. But even if he didn't achieve any final peace accord soon, he was proud of his record so far. And symbolizing his success was the arrival of the first F-15s on December 10, 1976, shortly after he returned from Morocco—a timely event that could prod Sadat toward full peace.

Ironically, the event also symbolized the beginning of the disaster awaiting him just over the political horizon—a disaster sparked by a religious misdeed. The welcome ceremony took place just before sundown on a Friday afternoon, and continued into the Sabbath. Rabin would recall:

"As the chief of staff noted so aptly at that ceremony, with the arrival of the first F–15s Israel would not be the same as she had been before. He was quite right about that, but for more reasons than he imagined."

The reasons were rooted in the outrage of the religious parties at the desecration of the Sabbath. They pressured the cabinet to vote no-confidence in the government, but it merely expressed regret. In the Knesset, however, religious members abstained in a vote on the matter.

Rabin was shocked, or at least tried to give this impression. An abstention, he said, was the equivalent of a no-confidence vote. How could the public have faith in a government that even some of its members rejected? He asked for the resignation of the religious ministers and then submitted his own, becoming head of a caretaker government. New elections, scheduled for autumn 1977, were advanced to May.

Political upheaval was accompanied by upheaval in Rabin's personal life. With Dahlia pregnant, her husband was severely wounded in a jeep accident in November 1976. He remained unconscious for a month, and it appeared that he had sustained a permanent brain injury (though he would eventually recover to a large degree). So Dahlia had moved in with her parents to await the birth of her second child.

But on the job, Rabin wasn't too disturbed by the prospect of a new election, since his renewed popularity, the long period of peace he had brought, and the country's stable unemployment rate would give him, he felt, a stronger government in a new election than the compromise regime he now headed. Some politicians, in fact, accused him of deliberately fomenting a crisis for this purpose. In any event, he now started campaigning in earnest, and his Labor Party was favored to win.

Still, the euphoria of Entebbe had faded, and there was good reason to worry. A new third political party, the Democratic Movement for Change, founded by Yigael Yadin, the archaeologist and former chief of staff, promised a more democratic political system. It threatened to drain off many Labor supporters, to the benefit of Menachem Begin's rightist Likud Party, which was nipping at Labor's heels.

At the same time, if Rabin was a good prime minister, he was

far less successful as party leader. Thus, the party was torn by internal strife, especially with Shimon Peres announcing he would fight
Rabin for Labor's nomination for prime minister. Rabin expected
the challenge, believing that Peres had been planning to run
against him since the day he lost the last election. But he was nevertheless enraged. Never before in Israel's history had the prime
minister of the Labor Party been challenged by another member.

"If a party discredited its own prime minister, as Peres was
asking the Labor Party to do," he would snap, "how could it rea-
sonably expect the electorate to place any confidence in its next
candidate for the post? . . . No one seemed to be able to make Peres
see that challenging the incumbent prime minister was a formula
for political disaster."

And it almost was—for Rabin. On February 22, 1977, he won
the nomination, but by only 41 votes out of 2,800 cast at the Labor
Party convention. While Rabin was popular with rank-and-file
members, as he was with the population as a whole, many Labor
delegates preferred the traditional kind of politician they felt more
at ease with.

Indeed, even some members of his cabinet, as well as some of
his deputies, resented Rabin personally for his often arrogant,
high-handed manner of dealing with them, as symbolized by the
characteristic backhanded jolt of his arm dismissing the unfortunate mortal who tested his patience or the brave one who dared
disagree with him.

Rabin's principal victim was probably Foreign Minister Allon,
who alternately expressed to his colleagues pride that his former
pupil had reached the top—ahead of the teacher—and regret that his
former subordinate didn't quite have the experience for the post.
Rabin, for his part, seemed to show even less patience with his old
benefactor than he did with his other ministers (Peres excepted),
apparently reluctant to feel gratitude to him as he succumbed to the
tension of giving orders to a revered onetime superior.

According to one minister, Rabin didn't seem to "have a very
high opinion of Allon's performance as foreign minister." Nor did
the prime minister think that post itself was of great importance
since he was personally dealing with important foreign affairs.

This was symptomatic of the schism splitting the Labor Party.
But this was the least of the party's problems. After almost thirty

years of holding power, Labor was even more endangered by the moral decay that was contaminating its soul. Rabin's personal popularity with the public and his economic and diplomatic successes had helped to conceal this weakness. But scandals involving some of the most important politicians in Israel exposed the rot at the party's core.

In autumn 1976, Rabin nominated Asher Yadlin, head of the Kupat Cholim, the Histadrut trade union's giant health maintenance organization, to be governor of the Bank of Israel. But he soon had to withdraw the nomination when Yadlin was charged with taking bribes and kickbacks from public institutions and private companies to finance the party election campaign. Convicted and sentenced to five years in prison, Yadlin claimed he acted at the behest of some of the top party leaders, though not Rabin.

A short time earlier, headlines had trumpeted that Housing Minister Avraham Ofer, a close friend of Rabin, was being investigated for allegedly embezzling funds, also for use in the Labor campaign. Rabin, who had known Ofer for years, was dismayed and couldn't believe he was capable of such a crime. When Ofer went to see him in late December 1977, after months of investigation, the visitor pleaded:

"Yitzhak, believe me—I am not guilty of any transgression."

"I wholly trust in your innocence," Rabin replied.

A few days later, Ofer committed suicide.

Rabin was shattered and blamed the media for sensationalizing the case.

"His death broke my heart," he would tell his boyhood friend Haim Gurie.

It was the first time Gurie ever heard him say that his heart had been broken.

"Will this tragedy serve to shock people into learning to think twice about what they utter or print," Rabin would bitterly ask, "to treat their fellow man's reputation with respect, and not to pass judgment on anyone before he has had his day in court?"

Rabin would see to it that other government figures suspected of corruption had their day in court, whether he personally believed them guilty or not. Paradoxically, the major political and business scandals came to light while Rabin was prime minister, but this happened precisely because Rabin ended the policy of covering up scandals. The question was, could Rabin, even with his own clean reputation, make the electorate understand this paradox?

Hoping to counter any negative public reaction to the accusatory tabloid headlines, Rabin decided to play to one of his strongest suits, foreign affairs. But there was one trip abroad he would make that had to remain secret—a visit to Iran. Shah Pavlevi was in power then, but only precariously, for mobs loyal to Ayatollah Khomeini were demonstrating in the streets. A limousine carrying Rabin, a bodyguard, and a military aide from Teheran airport toward the royal palace had to thread its way through hundreds of shouting, wild-eyed Iranians who tried to stop the vehicle but finally let it through, unaware that the prime minister of Israel was among the passengers. When a rock broke one of the windows, Rabin wondered if he would survive. But he did and soon found himself in the palace shaking hands with the shah.

Rabin discussed the sale of Israeli arms to him in the face of the fundamentalist threat, ultimately a threat to Israel as well as to Iran. But Rabin worried about a more immediate threat—Leah.

"Don't tell my wife about the demonstration," he told his bodyguard, Amos Goren, as they feasted on eggs and salad they prepared themselves in the palace kitchen at about 3 A.M. "She would kill me for coming here."

"She'd kill me, too," Goren replied. "She ordered me to take good care of you."

And he did. But the risky trip proved futile. Shortly, the fundamentalists ousted the shah. And now Rabin was more determined than ever to forge a peace with Israel's neighbors that would help to counter the growing threat.

Back in Israel, Rabin saw an opportunity to make another trip, this one public and likely to win him many votes. Jimmy Carter had defeated Gerald Ford in the 1976 U.S. presidential election, and Rabin would now seek an invitation to the White House. But the election results disappointed him, for Ford, though hard on Israel at first, had come through with the massive aid he needed. Nor would Rabin have Kissinger around any more to blame for every negotiating failure—and to praise for every success. How could he get along without him?

On the other hand, he was wary of Carter as his advisers and the press described him. The new President, he understood, "had visions of curing all the ills of the American people and restoring its faith in the presidency. He was imbued with profound religious conviction and believed that the American electorate had charged him with the mission of carrying through a great metamorphosis in substance as well as in style."

A metamorphosis? That isn't what Rabin wanted. United States–Israel relations were just fine, with arms pouring in and the two countries virtually bound together in a strategic alliance, as he had planned.

Yet Rabin saw in the election of a new U.S. President—just months before Israel itself went to the polls—a chance to remind the voters it was he who had paved the way for shipments of guns and economic goodies that clogged the pipeline from America. And he could lay the groundwork for a productive summit when he was reelected, as he expected to be.

Hardly had Rabin sat down in the White House for a talk with Carter early in March 1977 when a surge of optimism swept away the skeptic in him. The President's opening words were "music to my ears." The United States, Carter said, was deeply committed to Israel and would not impose on it any peace accord. In fact, the U.S. commitment to Israel's security "took precedence over any other interest in the area."

Rabin was overwhelmed. He couldn't imagine a more pro-Israel stance.

"Do you agree," Carter went on, "that 1977 is a good year for a concentrated effort to achieve peace? If so, when shall we convene the Geneva Conference? Who should attend it? How can the question of Palestinian representation be resolved?"

Rabin's optimism began to fade. Geneva Conference? He would never agree to negotiate with all the Arab states as a unit. And why bring up the Palestinians, especially before the election?

"Let us understand what we mean by the word 'peace,'" the prime minister replied. "We maintain that peace comprises two elements: elimination of the state of war, and the building of concrete relations that establish new realities for everyday life. That is the difference between President Sadat and my government. He is prepared to terminate the state of war in return for a complete

Israeli withdrawal; but he is not willing to enter into a peace that means open borders for the movement of people and goods, cultural exchange, and diplomatic relations."

Carter's secretary of state, Cyrus Vance, who had just visited the Middle East, broke in: "All the Arab leaders told me that the nature of peace is their own sovereign problem. Whether or not they maintain trade relations with Israel, set up diplomatic relations, open up borders for tourists, and so forth, is their affair. As they see it, the first step is terminating the state of war, and that is all they are prepared to discuss."

Rabin was relieved. Vance did not have Kissinger's powerful personality, nor his passion and humor, but he seemed to support the Israeli view. Then, with the subtlety of exploding dynamite, President Carter asked:

"Would you object to a single united Arab delegation to the Geneva Conference, which would include a Palestinian delegation?"

Rabin paused, taken aback. All right, the Geneva Conference, if that's what the President wanted. But only under certain conditions.

"We have no objection to Palestinians being included in the Jordanian delegation, but we want to negotiate with sovereign states. It is not our business if the Arab states coordinate their policies at Geneva, as long as we negotiate with every one of our neighbors as a sovereign state."

"And if the Arabs insist on coming to Geneva as a single, united delegation?" Vance asked.

"We shall oppose such a proposal—for the sake of the conference. A joint Arab delegation to Geneva will go along with the extremist line of the Arab left—with Moscow's backing—and the outcome will be total failure."

It soon became clear to Rabin that what Carter wanted was an Israeli phased withdrawal from all the territory Israel conquered in the Six-Day War and the establishment of a Palestinian state in the West Bank and Gaza. Right after that war, Rabin might have agreed to the withdrawal (though not from Jerusalem) in return for real peace. But now he had significant conditions:

"Provided that the principles and borders of a real peace are agreed upon," he would say, "I see no difficulty in implementing the agreement by stages."

The peace he had in mind would be something comparable to the Allon Plan, with Israel in control of the Jordan Valley and King Hussein, not the PLO, entrenched in the West Bank.

Adding to his apprehension, at a White House stag dinner that night, House Speaker Thomas "Tip" O'Neill asked Rabin a question that "almost sounded like an accusation":

"Why don't you negotiate with the PLO? Why can't we ask you to do what we did? We talked with the Vietcong, not just with the North Vietnamese. If that's what we did, as representatives of a great power, why can't you do the same? Why could the French negotiate with the Algerian FLN and conclude an agreement with them? Why were the British able to negotiate with underground movements all over the world—yours included—while you are unable to negotiate with the PLO?"

"Did the Vietcong refuse to recognize the existence of the United States and call for its annihilation?" Rabin asked O'Neill. "Was their basic program a 'Vietcong Covenant' whereby the United States was to be replaced by a Vietnamese state? How can you compare the two situations? Did the FLN plan to annihilate France? Did the underground organizations in Israel and elsewhere challenge the existence of Great Britain? What basis is there for negotiations with the PLO, whose avowed raison d'être is to destroy Israel and replace her with a Palestinian state?"

Rabin did not mention to either Carter or O'Neill that he was secretly keeping indirect channels open to the PLO through several of his "leftist" friends; that with the future of the Middle East so uncertain, he was not ruling out any long-range peace option.

In any case, Rabin was in a curdled mood, especially after dinner when Carter invited him to the presidential quarters upstairs for a private face-to-face talk.

Now, what did the prime minister really think about peace terms? he asked.

Rabin was stunned. What did he really think? Did he ever say what he didn't think?

He had already explained what he really thought, he replied. He had no other policy.

With "his expectations dashed," Carter's face took on an "expression of annoyance."

Rabin was more than annoyed. It was when they rejoined the

other guests that Rabin tartly declined Carter's invitation to listen to his daughter, Amy, play the piano.

At another meeting, Carter persisted: "There were precedents for negotiations between states and organizations of this nature [the PLO]. I see no evidence of Palestinian leaders other than the PLO leadership. We might be able to find some compromise whereby the PLO leaders join an Arab delegation. I hope that you will be able to accept some such formula after the elections in Israel."

Rabin again rejected the idea. And he would not reply when he was asked whether Israel might change its view if the PLO changed its philosophy and policy, calling the question "hypothetical." And he was furious when Carter said that if the PLO did change and Israel still refused to sit down with its leaders there would be a "sharp reaction on the part of the American people."

Was Carter threatening to turn the American people against Israel? But then the President, apparently realizing that he had irritated his guest, returned to the music that so pleased Rabin:

"Israel's views coincide with those of the United States. I have undertaken the difficult task of bringing a permanent peace to your region. That means that Israel will enjoy peace, open commerce, and freedom of navigation in the Suez Canal. It will be possible for Israel to receive the energy she requires from the oil-producing countries. And Israel will receive massive aid from the United States. Let no one doubt that our countries are friends and allies. Your hopes with regard to the nature of peace are justified, and we shall support them. . . . Our job now is to examine whether there is any basis to assume that it is feasible to advance toward an overall agreement."

Before leaving Washington, Rabin was promised that their conversations would not be leaked to the press. Rabin was worried that the President's views on dealing with the PLO could encourage Arab intransigence and sabotage the chances for peace, while influencing Israelis to vote for the hard-line Likud in the election to preclude a deal with Yasir Arafat. He mustn't be seen as a dove. But then, at a press conference, the President, replying to a question, said there was need for a "Palestinian homeland."

Rabin was chagrined. His visit to Washington was ending on a sour note that did not seem to bode well for Israel. As for Carter's view, Secretary Vance would observe:

"The Carter-Rabin talks . . . went badly. The chemistry between

[them] was poor and the two appeared to grate on each other's nerves. By the end of the visit the President was angry at Rabin, regarding him as stubborn and unimaginative and unwilling to take positive steps or risks to achieve peace."

Nor was the chemistry between Leah and Rosalynn Carter much better. "I had been with Mrs. Carter three times [on one particular day]," Leah would say, "but by the end of it [Mrs. Carter] still remained an enigma. She was difficult to talk to. I asked her all sorts of questions, but she asked me none—not about my family, not about Israel, nothing! . . . I put a lot of my lack of rapport with [her] down to her newness in the role—one to which she and her husband had come from a totally different environment."

Rabin and his wife thus left Washington feeling nostalgic for their previous visits. The prime minister mused that "Israel would have to pay part of the tuition for the new administration's education in the finer points of foreign policy." And with an election looming, Labor might be stuck with the bill.

Yet, in weighing Carter's views, Rabin would conclude that "alongside his disappointing utterances on the Palestinian issue, the President expressed the most favorable views on the nature of peace that we had ever heard." A peace, though, that might now be more elusive than ever.

Rabin could only hope that his other achievements and his reputation for flawless integrity would outweigh the scandals and now this "failure" in the electorate's mind. A disaster was not impossible. Actually, it was more possible than he could imagine.

En route to Israel, Rabin stopped over in New York to deliver a farewell speech and in the evening went to a reception arranged by the Israeli consul general there. One of the guests sipping wine was Dan Margolit, the Washington correspondent for the Israeli newspaper *Ha'aretz*. While walking to the reception with Yehuda Avner, a Rabin aide, he had asked Avner a delicate question. So delicate that Avner replied:

"Leave me out of this. See Dan Pattir."

Now, at the reception, Margolit chatted with Pattir, Rabin's spokesman, who invited him to come to his room in the Waldorf-Astoria when the party was over to listen to a recording of the speech Rabin had made, since Margolit had missed it.

The reporter gladly accepted. It would be a good time to ask Pattir the question Avner had refused to answer. As with Avner, he felt almost too embarrassed to ask.

That morning Margolit had received a phone call from his wife in Israel, and she had related to him a strange story. The previous evening she had attended a reception in Tel Aviv, and another guest had told her about something that happened in Washington four years earlier, in 1973, when Rabin was ambassador to the United States. Three people from the Israeli embassy had gone to the Dupont Circle branch of the National Bank, and a clerk had told them proudly:

"You know, the wife of the prime minister also has an account in this bank."

Dan Margolit smelled a story. It was against Israeli law for an Israeli to have a bank account in a foreign bank—a law intended to keep black marketeers from depositing their ill-gotten earnings abroad to avoid paying taxes in Israel. Now its violation could politically damage, or perhaps even topple, a prime minister—perhaps the cleanest one in Israel's history.

Margolit went to Pattir's room after the reception for Rabin and told him what he had heard. Did the prime minister have a bank account in Washington?

"If he issues a flat denial," Margolit said, "I won't dig under his skin unless I can prove he lied."

This was almost an invitation to deny the story, Margolit told me.

He would check it out, Pattir said, surprised by the question.

Pattir rushed to Rabin's room in the hotel and said that *Ha'aretz* might publish the story of the bank account. Was it true?

Rabin hesitated for an agonizing moment, then conceded it was.

What should he tell Margolit? Pattir asked.

"Come back in an hour and I'll tell you," Rabin said, obviously perturbed.

This wasn't the first time an adviser had warned him about the bank account. Sometime earlier, an aide, Dov Tsamir, had visited a friend who had just returned from Washington. While in the Israeli embassy, the host said, he had overheard a secretary say that when Leah was about to return with her husband to Israel in 1973 she had gone to a bank to withdraw money.

"Do you know if she did?" Tsamir's friend asked.

Tsamir didn't know, but he went to Rabin and hesitantly began: "My friend, I have heard an unpleasant story. . . ." And he recounted the report about the bank account, eliciting no reaction (thought Rabin would then apparently tell Leah to close it).

Rabin would not discuss it with Tsamir, any more than he would now with Dan Pattir. When Pattir returned to his room, the prime minister snapped: "Leave it alone! Don't say anything!"

Pattir was a veteran reporter and knew that silence would be taken to mean he was trying to hide the truth.

"It would be a mistake to remain silent," he said.

Perhaps. But Leah had kept the account and was in jeopardy.

The following day, Margolit tried to call Pattir but wasn't able to locate him, and that night Rabin and his party left for Israel. Margolit then flew back to Washington, not sure that he could prove the charge. But at a party given by the Israeli air attaché, someone else told the newsman that Rabin had an account in the Dupont Circle branch of the National Bank, appearing to confirm the information from Tel Aviv.

Margolit went to the bank the next morning, March 14, and told a clerk: "I owe the Rabins $50 and wish to deposit it in their account, but I don't know the number."

"Okay," the clerk replied, "I'll take the check."

Margolit gave it to her and noted the account number she wrote on it, repeating it over and over in his mind until he could write it down. He went to his office and filed the story: The prime minister and his wife had opened a bank account in the Dupont Circle branch of the National Bank in Washington when he was ambassador and they never closed it.

A great story, Margolit thought, though not expecting it to have historic repercussions. He was furious when, on the following morning, March 15, it appeared at the bottom instead of at the top of the front page.

"Someone," he would grouse, "doesn't like me."

Whatever the reason, the story did not generate an explosive reaction.

Sometime later, he would meet Rabin in Israel and said: "You know, I told Pattir that if you denied the story I wouldn't pursue it."

Rabin stared at Margolit and in a tense voice replied: "What did you want me to do—lie?"

By remaining silent, Rabin didn't lie, even though a lie might have saved him from disaster. During his ambassadorial days, Leah had actually opened two accounts—a savings account and a checking account—jointly with him. A total of $21,121, including interest, had been in the two accounts during the period since the Rabins left Washington in March 1973. From this sum, Leah withdrew $10,618 in the next four years on several visits to the United States. After the trip to see Carter, about $2,000 remained, and would eventually be contributed to Leah's autistic charity.

She had intended to close the accounts before leaving Washington in March 1977, Leah told me, but she was in a great hurry because her husband was shortly to be given an honorary doctorate at American University, and a limousine was waiting outside the bank to whisk her there in time. Even so, she did have time to close the savings account, though she simply transferred the money to the checking account, planning, she said, to take it when she visited Washington again.

"Looking back," Leah would later say, "I now know that I wasn't aware enough of the gravity of my transgression. I looked at it much like I would going through a traffic light when it was amber in the hope of crossing the street before the light turned red. I knew I had to close the account, and I had every intention of doing so during that visit, but the technical obstacle of a timetable simply got in the way.

"And then—the bomb went off!"

Actually, it seemed to fizzle out at first. Typically, the *Jerusalem Post* editorialized:

"Mrs. Rabin should admit her error, the treasury should impound the money, and the press and politicians should get back to important matters—and everyone, hopefully, will have learned a good lesson."

After all, many Israelis felt, the Rabins had made only a technical error, and the prime minister never used either account, bearing responsibility only as a cosigner for them. But Rabin, according to friends, was furious at Leah, even as he stated that "there could be no question that morally and formally we shared responsibility equally."

"Yitzhak," one close friend of the prime minister told me, "was too busy working for Israel to pay attention to such mundane matters as family finances. He simply left it all to Leah and let her satisfy her whims."

Rabin now went to see Minister Without Portfolio Yisrael Galili, long a close adviser. He was ready, he said, to step down from his candidacy for prime minister if any members judged him a liability to the party.

No, he should wait, Galili said, until they knew the results of an inquiry that would be carried out.

Others close to Rabin also urged him not to step down. Leah would later say: "They insisted that it would be unconscionable to trample underfoot all those long years of outstanding service to the IDF and the country because of one small mistake."

It seemed ironic. At the height of their suffering, the Rabins were blessed with one of the happiest moments of their life. Dahlia gave birth to a girl, Noa. Was this new life a sign of new life for them, too?

A committee serving under Attorney General Aharon Barak investigated the matter and made a recommendation on April 5, 1977: The Rabins should simply have to pay a fine. It seemed the prime minister wouldn't have to quit the electoral race after all. He was greatly relieved, but still wasn't sure whether to quit. Anyway, the decision could have been worse.

Shortly before the Labor Party convention, Rabin was invited to speak at Kibbutz Ein Gev, but felt too embarrassed by the bank account charges to accept. Leah, who wanted him to go, called Dov Goldstein, the newspaper editor, and asked him to persuade her husband to change his mind.

He would be glad to, Goldstein responded, and he suggested that he and his wife accompany Rabin and Leah to the kibbutz. He then phoned Rabin, who finally agreed to go. And a little later, the foursome drove to an airport and took a helicopter to the kibbutz.

Warmly received there, Rabin managed to overcome his embarrassment and seemed in a good mood when the four boarded the helicopter for the return home. As they listened to the radio, there was suddenly a news flash: The attorney general had rejected his committee's recommendation. The prime minister would simply be fined 15,000 Israeli pounds ($1,600) for his passive role in the crime. Leah, however, would stand trial before a district court for her active role. She could go to jail.

There was a chilling silence aboard the helicopter. Leah suddenly rose from her seat and strode to the door.

"I'm going to jump!" she cried.

Rabin rushed to her and, tenderly taking her in his arms, brought her sobbing back to her seat.

"Leah," he pleaded, "please stop it. We're in this together and we'll fight it together. We'll overcome it together."

Leah wept all the way back to Tel Aviv. Had she really intended to jump? Those familiar with her steely character, including members of her family, say she never would have done it, that any such threat could only be a desperate momentary reaction to the disaster that had befallen her husband and herself.

"I would do everything possible to share full responsibility with my wife," Rabin vowed.

Though treasury officials felt a trial was unwarranted, Barak would not change his mind. The Rabins were especially resentful because a short time before, Barak had merely fined another high official who was found to keep a large sum in an American bank—after the official reportedly threatened suicide if he was tried.

Rabin felt trapped in a nightmare from which he would never wake. Yes, he had committed an offense and he deeply regretted it. But let them punish him, not just his wife. His career seemed over anyway, and he could no longer lead the fight for peace. Nor was his pain eased by the thought that his disgrace stemmed from money matters when he had been raised to scorn material values. He would not concede, at least in public, that while he was preoccupied with peace and other vital issues, Leah had kindled the nightmare.

"It was horrible watching this very private man suffering as he chivalrously stood by Leah," Yehuda Avner told me. "He felt a sense of loyalty that reflected a deep inner-family bond."

Rabin now made his decision: "I felt that I had to render my own personal and private account, which demanded consistency and courage. Friends tried to dissuade me from taking any fateful steps, but a man is always truly alone at such times. And alone, my conscience and I came to three interconnected decisions. I would withdraw my nomination as the candidate for prime minister. I would share full responsibility with Leah, and I would try to resign my post as prime minister, so that the Labor Party's nominee could fill the post up to the elections."

"Yehezkel," Rabin confided to his driver before telling anyone else, "I'm going to quit."

Sharabi felt he "was about to have a heart attack." He slammed down the brakes and the car ground to a halt.

"Don't you dare quit!" he exclaimed.

"Yehezkel," Rabin replied, "it's my wife. I'm not going to leave Leah. I'm not going to walk out on her. I owe it to her."

And shortly, the prime minister confronted Dan Pattir at the office: "Dan," he revealed once again, "I've decided to resign and withdraw my candidacy for the nomination."

Pattir had thought this might happen, but he was somehow shocked to hear the words, blunt and definite, unvarnished with any sign of hesitancy on this fateful day of April 7, 1977.

Was this really necessary? Pattir asked. Perhaps he should think it over.

He had made up his mind, Rabin replied. "Tell the radio and television reporters to expect an announcement at seven this evening in Tel Aviv."

But that would be only two and a half hours before the basketball game, Pattir pointed out. Maccabi Tel Aviv would be playing the Italian team, Mobilgirgi Varese, that evening in Belgrade for the European Basketball Championship. And all that most Israelis could talk and think about was the game. Perhaps, he could wait another day to make the announcement.

Rabin would not wait. He wanted to leave office immediately. Typically, he reached a decision only after agonizingly analyzing the facts, but he felt compelled to act on it without delay. Friends soon made it clear, however, that he couldn't simply walk away. By law his government was required to remain in power as a caretaker regime until a new government was formed.

He wanted to resign from the Knesset, too, but again he was frustrated. He would have to wait until he resigned from the premiership; the prime minister had to be a member of that body.

There were no loopholes in the law?

There was one, it seemed. He could claim that he was temporarily "unable to fulfill his duties" because the foreign currency affair had impaired his moral authority to serve.

Rabin declined—apparently because he didn't believe this was true and he would virtually be abandoning his political career, an unthinkable prospect.

He would make the announcement that night—after the game, which would end about midnight. He would not sour the festive, exciting atmosphere before or during the contest. Anyway, not even the resignation of a prime minister could compete for popular interest with a European championship game.

And that evening, Rabin, his aides, and Leah gloomily sat around a table watching the game on television in the prime minister's office, counting not the points but the minutes until Rabin would shake the nation out of its merrymaking mood, or intensify its melancholia, depending on the outcome of the contest. Israel took the lead, and the crowd at the game was shouting and cheering, together with all of Israel.

The time ticked on amid a cacophony of sounds that grated on minds throbbing with anguish—the roars from Belgrade, the cries of the guards gathered around a TV set downstairs, the soft sobbing of Leah Rabin, and, late in the evening, Rabin's own voice as he taped a resignation speech for Israel Radio that would be broadcast after the game.

Finally, at about 11 P.M., the chaos on the screen signaled the end of the game. Israel was the European champion, beating the Italians by one point. Almost immediately, cries and cheers rose from the street. It was time to go to the television studio some distance away. Rabin and his party walked downstairs and entered a number of limousines parked outside. The vehicles were soon crawling through celebrating crowds, held up by cars draped in Israeli flags, their horns honking jubilantly. At one crossroads, Rabin bent forward and told his driver to pull up to the side of the road until it was clear. Let the people enjoy themselves before they learned the nation was in crisis.

He hadn't seen such elation since the rescue of the Entebbe hostages. This was only a game, but the victory of tiny Israel over the powers of Europe struck a sensitive nationalistic chord. What a pleasure just to see their joy. If only he could feel it.

After Entebbe, the people adored their leader. Now, months later, they were about to learn that he was leaving in disgrace. The cries, the laughing, the honking. Were they already mocking him?

When the celebration had begun to peter out, Rabin's party

continued on to the studio. Stepping out of the car, the prime minister seemed calm, even while churning with despair.

And in minutes he was staring into the camera, as if into space, and explaining to the people why his career was coming to an end. He was forfeiting his nomination, he said, and seeking ways of resigning his post as prime minister.

If Rabin seemed cool and controlled, Leah, as she watched, sought to hide her anguish behind smiles and an almost cheerful air. He would be back. Yes, he would be back.

After admitting that he and his wife had made a mistake, Rabin told his people, suddenly deflating their jubilation: "The treasury appointed a committee. They recommended a monetary penalty. To my great sorrow, during the past twenty-four hours the attorney general did not accept this recommendation, at least with respect to my wife."

If Barak had accepted it, apparently, Rabin would not be resigning. And while most Israelis seemed to sympathize with him, some were disturbed by this implication, feeling that he should quit his post regardless as a matter of principle.

Fifteen minutes after Rabin had finished his announcement, a studio official told him: "Mr. Prime Minister, you must remember that you still have friends."

"I know," Rabin softly replied.

And years later, he would comment on that moment: "I immediately felt the kind of relief that can only be entertained by a man who knows he has been honest with himself and true to his own conscience."

On April 17, 1977, Leah Rabin, dressed in a dark blue suit and wearing sunglasses, walked grim-faced into the heavily guarded courthouse and, with Dahlia beside her, maneuvered her way through the crowds of curious people who packed the corridors, entered the courtroom, and stepped into the defendant's dock. Nervous at first but gradually relaxed, she wished her husband, who had driven her to the courthouse, had not left, but she understood that his presence would only turn the trial into a bigger circus than it already was. Anyway, he didn't want it to influence the court.

When the judge had pounded his gavel, the prosecutor stood up and asked the court not to impose a prison sentence. This was the accused's first offense, she pointed out, the money was obtained legally, and there was no evidence that Ms. Rabin had smuggled it into the country or had engaged in any illegal transactions.

Nevertheless, the prosecutor continued, the accused could not claim that she "simply neglected" to close one of her accounts. Moreover, she had made eight withdrawals between her departure from Washington in March 1973 and her most recent visit in March 1977. Also, the offense was brought to light not at Ms. Rabin's initiative, but rather as the result of a newspaper exposé.

"The incident has caused considerable public damage," the prosecutor added, "since the accused is the wife of the prime minister, who is in charge of the government's economic policy. A person in this position should have served as an example to the public."

The defense attorney then rose to plead that his client be treated leniently. He noted that she had admitted her guilt, had cooperated with the police, and had expressed her contrition for her "negligence and mistake."

Did the accused have anything to add?

"No, I have nothing to add," Leah replied to the judge.

The judge then recessed for about ninety minutes and, when he returned, looked at Leah and said: "One expects a public figure to observe the law more carefully, and we are all the more disappointed when we find this is not the case." But he wouldn't send her to prison. She had suffered enough "in her downfall from a position of importance to the benches of the courtroom."

Leah would have to pay a fine of 250,000 Israeli pounds ($27,000)—or she could go to jail for a year.

"I was there, yet absent," Leah would later say, "as though, at the press of a button, a partition had slid into place between me and my immediate environment. Nevertheless, when I heard the judge's ruling, I was in shock. He was far more severe than any of the experts had foreseen—and that included our own lawyer."

Yes, a large sum. The family was not rich. But a year in jail? How would she be able to groom Yitzhak for the struggle to the top again?

She would pay.

21

The Remnants of Disgrace

Did Henry Kissinger and his bride, Nancy, really love each other? This was the question that preoccupied Yitzhak Rabin and Moshe Dayan when they met at the chief of staff's reception for senior IDF officers on the eve of Israel's Independence Day, 1977. It was difficult for Rabin to shed his embarrassment completely and engage in serious conversation with his former colleagues after his disgrace. And so he found himself resorting to small talk, though he had never been able to tolerate such meaningless babble. As Leah would say:

"It was a baptism of fire for we knew that our presence would arouse comments and create waves."

Shortly after his resignation, Rabin had attended a soccer game at Tel Aviv's Bloomfield Stadium and was greeted with a standing ovation from the crowd. He was thrilled. Perhaps the people had not entirely abandoned him. Or were they simply honoring him for his past glories? Would they take him back—eventually?

Despite that brief moment of gratification, it was difficult for

Rabin to fit into a world in which he had little to say and in which, he suspected, most people had little to say to him—at least compared to the past. Because of what he regarded as a minor infraction of the law by Leah, he had been thrust into a limbo of loneliness and boredom.

After Leah's trial, Rabin took his leave of absence and went with his wife on vacation in Sharm el-Sheikh, leaving government affairs to Shimon Peres, who would replace him as Labor candidate for prime minister in the coming elections. To Peres's shock, Rabin had actually supported him as a replacement candidate, perhaps bowing to the inevitable and wishing to appear magnanimous in his lame-duck days in office. But Rabin could find no peace. For the more he relaxed, the more time he had to dwell on his downfall, on Leah's ordeal, on a future that seemed as bleak as the desert around him.

Even after they returned to Tel Aviv, he tried to avoid friends, colleagues, newsmen. Nor did the flood of some 2,000 letters and hundreds of phone calls from well-wishers cheer him, though Leah, who replied to every one, saw this outpouring of goodwill, like the one in the soccer stadium, as evidence that he would make a comeback. Her husband was not so sure; no Labor members were among the well-wishers. In fact, the only political colleague who wrote was a Likud Knesset member. It was thus with heavy heart that just before the election on May 17, Rabin made some speeches, feeling obligated to his party, which he still led, if without any real power. And his suffering was not diminished by the thought of helping Peres to succeed him in power.

He need not have worried, for Labor, though favored in the election, lost to the right-wing Likud, which won forty-three Knesset seats to Labor's thirty-two, with Rabin himself winning a seat. He had considered withdrawing from the Knesset race, worried how his colleagues would accept him. But Leah and some of his friends urged him to run, or else he might find himself frozen out of politics for good. And Leah, in particular, would not countenance that. He thus ran—and won.

Yigael Yadin's Democratic Movement for Change harvested fifteen seats, enough to rob Labor of victory. The scandals, including the forced resignation of the prime minister, took their toll. Rabin, like other Labor leaders, despaired at his party's first electoral loss since the birth of the state, though he found a measure of satisfaction in Peres's rebuff.

It seemed hard to believe—Menachem Begin would be prime minister. In recent years, Rabin had gotten along with Begin, and he was grateful for the Likud leader's crucial backing during the Entebbe crisis. But Begin was also the man whose supporters had exchanged fire with Rabin's Palmach fighters during the *Altalena* episode in 1948; the Irgun leader he had been ready to kill in the service of the state. Now he would have to work with him as a member of the Knesset—in the service of the state.

It would not be easy, especially since the two most important posts in Begin's cabinet would go to the two men who had sought so avidly to impede Rabin's political ascent. Ezer Weizman, Likud's campaign chairman, would be defense minister, and Moshe Dayan, abandoning Labor, foreign minister. These reputed hawks, in Rabin's view, were not apt to support the sacrifices necessary for peace.

Begin, Rabin felt, had mellowed since his fiery Irgun days. But Weizman had not in his contempt for Rabin. He seemed to derive a certain satisfaction in avenging Rabin's failure to support his candidacy for chief of staff after the Six-Day War. Now he was defense minister and Rabin was out of a cabinet job. Samuel Lewis, who had just come to Israel as the U.S. ambassador, would recall a meeting of the two men at a dinner in Dayan's home:

"We witnessed an extraordinary political tableau. Ezer Weizman . . . , now flush with Begin's and Likud's electoral triumph, for which he, as the Likud campaign manager, took full credit, heckled and needled Yitzhak across the table about Labor's debacle. There were few holds barred in Ezer's insults and condescension. The dignity with which Yitzhak withstood and quietly responded to Ezer's barbs has remained with me ever since. It is in adversity that a person's true character shines most clearly."

Weizman's insults did not stop there. On another social occasion at which he was apparently inebriated, he asked Leah to dance, and when she refused, he exploded in anger and described her husband in lewd, unprintable terms.

Despite all the taunting and disappointment, Rabin remained coolly contained, at least outwardly. Lewis would relate:

"Inevitably, the atmosphere in his office was sad, the conversation both philosophical and, at times, plaintive. Yet, even at such a bitter moment, I saw a man demonstrating the self-control, honesty, analytical rigor, and quiet determination that were hallmarks of Yitzhak's nature."

The irony of events was that the IDF was now strong enough to exchange more land for more peace with Egypt and then to make similar agreements with other Arab foes. And Sadat, it seemed, was ripe for a deal. Rabin was sure that if he had returned to power he would be cashing in on his secret trip to Morocco, perhaps haggling over the final touches to a Sinai accord. Full peace with Egypt, he realized, meant giving him back all or almost all of the Sinai, and Begin would never agree to that. Peres, he had to concede, would have been preferable.

And as Rabin passed the torch to Begin in the prime minister's office on June 22, the two men lifted a glass and toasted each other—"L'Haim" ("To life"). But what would life be like, Rabin wondered, listening to endless speeches, taking orders from party leaders, fantasizing about what might have been. Yet he found at least one advantage in his role as a backbencher.

"Being on the 'outside,'" he would say, "allows a political leader to view events from a different and sometimes broader perspective."

It was better, however, to be on the inside. Rabin was used to working under pressure, to never having the time to suffer boredom or dwell on unsolvable problems. But now there was less incentive to drive himself. There were no aides rushing in and out with vital documents for him to read or sign, or secretaries to take instant dictation. Some of the time, he stayed home writing his memoirs in collaboration with his friend, Dov Goldstein, the *Ma'ariv* columnist and editor.

He also spent time traveling. When the newspaper *Yediot Aharonot* suggested that he journey around the world with Eitan Haber interviewing world leaders for publication in the paper and for a book, he readily agreed. And for several weeks the two men flew from country to country on the assignment. Rabin was especially pleased to visit his old friend, President Nixon, in San Clemente following Watergate and his resignation. But he asked few questions, for he burned with anger at Haber for having asked Nixon on their arrival:

"Can I use my tape recorder—or is it still too dangerous?"

Nixon laughed at this reference to the notorious Watergate

tapes that indicated he had obstructed justice and replied: "There is no problem now."

But Rabin's face turned red and his eyes bore through Haber. Nixon was a good friend. He had supported Israel and provided arms that guaranteed its survival. It was shameful to treat the man's fate as a joke. Had he himself not experienced a similar fate, having also been forced to resign from the top post? He commiserated with Nixon, whom he knew was suffering. When the two visitors departed, Rabin snapped at Haber:

"How did you dare ask that question?"

It was like someone asking him if he still had a bank account.

On Saturdays, Rabin and his wife could still be found at the tennis court, where the speed of the ball was often seen as reflecting their mood. The harder they hit the ball, it seemed, the more determined they were to bounce back from adversity. Leah, in particular, was "a tiger at the net," according to Ambassador Lewis, who, with his wife, Sallie, often played doubles with them. Nor did she change her stripes in responding to someone who might criticize her husband's play.

"One time," Lewis would recall, "[Sallie] said joshingly to Leah that Yitzhak [their opponent] had foot faulted repeatedly in the last game. Leah, never ready to admit that Yitzhak could be wrong about anything, angrily cried: 'Yitzhak never foot faults, never!'"

And she would make sure that he wouldn't foot fault in his climb to the top again.

When in Jerusalem, Rabin spent considerable time looking over papers in the Knesset members' dining room, where, as prime minister, he had seldom been seen. Now, a reporter would observe, he would enter "unobtrusively, carrying a small black briefcase with his initials in gilded letters in the bottom right-hand corner. In the past he was never seen carrying anything bigger than a plastic case for his glasses."

In Tel Aviv, Rabin would work out of the small office in the defense ministry complex that he had been given as a former prime minister. One day, he found a young college graduate waiting for him. Introducing himself as a research assistant at Hebrew University, the youth inquired brazenly:

"Could you use me as a part-time parliamentary assistant?"

"I'm sorry," Rabin said, "but I'm not sure I need a parliamentary assistant."

"It wouldn't be a Catholic marriage—for life. Let me try for a while and then we can see how things develop."

Rabin liked the visitor's logic and enthusiasm. "Okay," he said without embellishment.

His new assistant soon became indispensable, preparing papers, researching background for laws—and simply keeping him company. Rabin easily grew bored by visitors, screened less carefully now, who didn't zoom to the point. When they asked him questions, his answers would gradually dwindle until finally he might simply stand up and stalk out of the room. With boredom came loneliness, and that is where his aide filled the vacuum.

Rabin would call him in and over tea inquire about his family, his ambitions, his philosophy. The aide would then ask Rabin questions, and found him only too eager to answer. He would reminisce about his childhood, discuss his practical nature, express his feelings about the influence of scholarly works on political decisions. Suddenly, the quiet, introverted Knesset member became almost loquacious as a stream of consciousness flowed forth with an uninhibited, rambling release that would have surprised even those who knew him best.

No longer under pressure from the ponderous problems at the top, from the challenges of those who wanted to replace him, he could now afford the time to dwell on who he was, where he came from, and where he was going. And it was somehow easier to use a virtual stranger as a listening device than a family member or close friend from whom he had for so long, through habit, hidden his innermost feelings. Besides, talking and remembering helped to relieve his loneliness.

If his aide helped Rabin build a psychological bridge to the future, the young man was repaid with the caring and kindness that the former prime minister lavished on those who managed to earn his trust. When he learned that the youth's father was dying of cancer, Rabin constantly showed his concern.

"I saw his human face," the aide would tell me. "I didn't think he would be that moved. He was delighted when I took Father to the Knesset to meet him. It was a dream come true for Father—to meet the hero of the Six-Day War. And Rabin treated him with such warmth. I was really grateful to him for making it possible for my father to die after realizing his dream."

Rabin himself had a dream—full peace with Egypt. But he was doubtful it would be realized soon. Not with Begin in power. Indeed, Begin, in his view, was rendering the dream impossible; first, by refusing to coordinate Israeli peacemaking positions with those of the United States, and second, by backing President Carter's proposal for reconvening a Geneva Conference in which Israel would face a single, unified Arab delegation. Such a conference could not possibly yield peace, Rabin was convinced, since the moderate states would lack the courage or ability to resist the demands of the radical countries.

Sadat agreed with Rabin and opposed being part of a unified delegation because he now needed peace with Israel. He had broken out of the Soviet orbit and, without new shipments of Russian arms, could not afford another war, even a war of attrition, especially since Rabin had persuaded the United States to flood Israel with arms. How could he risk losing the gains he had scored with the interim agreement? So the only long-term alternative to war, it seemed, was a full and final peace.

But while Rabin was still determined to make peace country by country, Washington and the Arab states other than Egypt insisted on a Geneva Conference. Sadat finally agreed to one— until President Carter joined with the Soviet Union in calling for it. Carter hoped that Moscow would press Syria, which depended on it for arms, to accept a reasonable peace in Geneva and persuade the other Arab countries to follow suit.

But Sadat, Rabin concluded, felt that the Soviets had become involved with "one thing in mind: to undermine his regime" in pursuit of their own global interests. In Geneva, Egypt would be forced to accept the dictates of the Soviets and Syria. Feeling trapped, Sadat presumably saw only one way out. He would not go to a Geneva Conference; instead he would make a separate peace with Israel before anyone could stop him.

Actually, the framework for such a move already existed, since the two countries had only to build on their interim agreement reached under Rabin's rule, and on the secret conversations that Rabin had had with Morocco's King Hassan, who told Sadat of the

Israeli leader's desire to sit down with the Egyptian leader at a summit meeting to hammer out a final peace. When Moshe Dayan became Begin's foreign minister, he learned how far Rabin had taken his peace initiative and convinced Begin that Israel couldn't afford to pass up this extraordinary opportunity to end the threat from Egypt.

And so events in the Middle East, Washington, and Moscow converged into a historic mission of peace that, while sparked by Rabin, would ironically transpire during the regime of an Israeli leader who had vowed not to give up a single inch of land.

He would go "to the ends of the earth, even to Jerusalem," in pursuit of peace.

Rabin, who was visiting Washington in early November 1977 to discuss his peace plans, could hardly believe what he heard over the radio: Sadat had actually told the Egyptian parliament that? He excitedly went to the State Department to see Secretary of State Vance and his advisers.

How had Egypt reacted to the American-Soviet agreement on holding a Geneva Conference? Rabin probed, testing their knowledge.

Quite positively, Vance replied.

Rabin was stunned. Positively? "I was amazed," he would later say, "to see to what extent they misinterpreted the true state of affairs."

And now the key question: What were "the chances that a meeting would actually take place between Begin and Sadat?"

"About fifty–fifty."

A few hours after Rabin saw Vance, Walter Cronkite interviewed Begin and Sadat on the evening news. That "barely probable" meeting in Jerusalem would take place.

Rabin rushed back to Israel and arrived on November 18, a day before Sadat would make his momentous journey. He was thrilled. How many months and years he had been working for this miracle? He would have chosen to give up territory chunk by chunk to test Arab behavior and intentions, as he would later deal with the Palestinians in Oslo. Still, his work was coming to fruition—even if history would credit his successor.

"There could be no doubt," he would say, "that Sadat's decision had opened a new chapter in the relations between the Arab countries. . . . His move was both a courageous and a desperate one. Courageous, because until then such a step had been absolutely unthinkable—and still was unthinkable in most of the countries in the Arab world.

"Desperate, because Sadat realized that if the policies of the United States were allowed to develop along the lines favored by the Carter Administration, they would bring about the destruction of almost four years of dogged efforts that had been conducted in a very cautious, low-key manner but had produced, for the first time, after a generation of hostility and stalemate, both negotiations and the signing of an agreement between Egypt and Israel.

"Thus, I believe that Sadat came to Israel with a twofold purpose in mind: to open up new opportunities by bringing down the walls of suspicion and eliminating the deeply rooted psychological barriers that existed in Israel vis-à-vis his intentions, and to force the United States to revise its policy on the Middle East."

Since his youth, Rabin had always viewed the Egyptians as the enemy. He had fought them in the 1948 war and opposed them in Rhodes, where he helped negotiate an end to that war. He remembered them from the 1956 Sinai War, the Six-Day War, the War of Attrition, and the Yom Kippur War. Now, as he waited for Sadat's plane to land in Israel on November 19, he "was possessed by a strange feeling."

"It was a uniquely electric moment for us all," Rabin would recall, "one of those moments that remain etched in our memory forever, the kind that people call upon to date a generation. Yet, for me, that 'moment' seemed to stretch on and on."

And when the plane landed and Sadat appeared in the doorway, "our emotion peaked in a way I hadn't thought possible." Yet his emotion soared even higher as the Egyptian leader reviewed the honor guard of the IDF, the army that had so bitterly fought his troops only a few years earlier.

"I felt that I was caught up in a dream," Rabin would exult in a manner that seemed as incredibly out of character as was this display of courage by an Arab leader. "Despite the evidence of my own eyes and ears, what was happening around me seemed quite unbelievable."

As Sadat moved along the receiving line, Rabin had a chance

only to exchange pleasantries, but he was "enormously impressed" by Sadat's poise and his talent for saying "just the right thing at the right time." And he was even more impressed by Sadat's oratory in the Knesset the following afternoon, November 20.

The Egyptian leader stressed that he was prepared to make a full, final peace with Israel if it accepted President Carter's proposals: a withdrawal from the territories conquered in the Six-Day War and the establishment of an independent Palestinian entity. In fact, if Israel accepted these proposals, Sadat indicated, he would conclude a peace agreement without waiting for approval from the other Arab states.

"Our archenemy," Rabin would marvel, "came to Israel and offered us terms that were even more forthcoming than what our best friend in the world, the United States, was prepared to extend."

And the final incredible surprise was Sadat's statement that while Israel must give up land, a way must be found to meet Israel's need for security. This concern was "absolutely revolutionary." And this revolutionary remark was especially poignant to Rabin, whose whole adult life had been devoted to assuring Israel's security. And this was the leader of Egypt speaking.

"The key to the future relations between the Arab states and Israel," Rabin would maintain, "lies in Israel's relationship with Egypt. Egypt led the Arab countries into every war with Israel; it was always the first country to halt the fighting by agreeing to a cease-fire; and it has always been the first of the Arab countries to conclude agreements with Israel. From the armistice agreements of 1949 onward, no accord has ever been concluded between Israel and any Arab state without Egypt's signing it first and alone."

And now there would be peace with Egypt, and surely the other Arab states would eventually follow. His plan, it seemed to him, had worked. Sadat had been faced with the choice of either war or peace. And because he realized that Israel had grown too powerful to beat, or to threaten seriously, as in the Yom Kippur War, he chose peace. Even at the risk of isolation from his fellow Arabs.

At a Labor Party meeting with Sadat, Rabin would tell him:

"Your courageous and daring coming over has created, I hope, a new era. I believe that you have removed the barriers that obscured in the past the relations between our two countries."

At the same time, it appeared, Rabin had in effect made it impossible for Begin to turn off the road that his predecessor had paved. Sadat was offering a peace that he could not reject without enraging the world and most of his own people. His ideology had not allowed for this and, however painfully, he had to adjust to reality.

But the road was still strewn with obstacles. While Begin was ready to give back the whole Sinai for real peace, Sadat, hoping to pacify the other Arabs, demanded after returning home that Israel also withdraw from all occupied territories as the price of full peace with Egypt. After several months of deadlock, Rabin pleaded in an Israeli newspaper for a summit meeting—"otherwise the game was up." A few days later, Begin and Sadat met with Carter at Camp David, the President's mountain refuge, to work out a final blueprint for peace.

Finally, after thirteen days of shouting, pleading, and conceding, a historic agreement was hammered out.

- Israel would forfeit the whole Sinai and evacuate every Israeli living there. But Israeli forces would remain in the southern area comprising about 40 percent of the Sinai for three years following the ratification of a peace treaty.
- Discussion of the most difficult issues involving the other Arab countries, such as the future of Jerusalem, the Palestinian problem, and the Israeli settlement controversy, would be delayed for a few years.
- During a transitional stage of five years, the Arab inhabitants of the West Bank and the Gaza Strip would enjoy autonomy. Within a year, Israel and Egypt would negotiate an agreement on the holding of elections for the self-governing authority in the two occupied areas. Not later than three years after the election, Israel and this authority would begin negotiating a final settlement, to be concluded before the end of the transitional period.

The Knesset approved the Camp David accords by a vote of eighty-four to nineteen, with Rabin voting in favor after praising their stage-by-stage structure, which would test the goodwill and sincerity of the peace partner as progress was made. He would later explain:

"Had peace been linked conditionally to solving the more complex issues we face . . . , without first giving Egypt and Israel the chance to experience living together and realizing that we can live in peace and create an atmosphere of mutual confidence, I don't think we would ever have moved an inch closer to a solution to the broader conflict."

The structure of the Egyptian peace would also shape the Oslo peace almost twenty years later. But Rabin could not foresee the future, declaring that "the beginning of the peace [with Egypt] marks the end of the heroic period of the Zionist movement." He could not know that he would initiate another.

As Rabin edged his way toward new glory, his sullen voice echoed through packed halls on both sides of the ocean. In the United States, he lectured to Jewish groups for $5,000 a talk in order to earn back the money he had borrowed from friends and relatives to pay the penalties imposed in the bank account case. How else could he clear away the remnants of disgrace that could threaten his resurrection? Nor did he agree with those who said it was unethical to charge people for listening to a talk on behalf of a government. After all, didn't Moshe Dayan earn double his fee?

In Israel, Rabin spoke to Labor Party forums, as well as on television and radio, though for political, not monetary, gain. When a radio interviewer asked if he intended to come back, he replied:

"I am still very much involved in politics."

This was not a happy harbinger for Shimon Peres, who was now the Labor Party leader and hoped to be prime minister after the next election without having to fight Rabin again. Peres was gratified, however, when party officials arranged for the two men to meet in October 1978, the first meeting since before the May 1977 election. The meeting was cordial, and it appeared that there might at last be a rapprochement between the two old rivals. Rabin, many believed, would not dare try to challenge Peres so soon after resigning in disgrace.

"There seems to be no groundswell of support for him," one pundit would write. "No one appears to have come forward spontaneously to propose his candidature [for party leader]. If he has heard a call, it appears to have come not from within the party, but from the depths of his troubled soul."

Rabin, in fact, had heard the call, wherever it came from, and he was determined to amplify it into a roar. How could he make the people quickly forget the bank account incident? He had to exploit his reputation as a conquering warrior and tough, almost inflexible peace negotiator. He must make them believe that he could assure their security better than anyone else.

Israelis knew that Rabin, like most Laborites, supported the land-for-peace principle, but since he had been reluctant to implement this policy until the IDF was "invincible," few people realized he was really a dove in hawk's feathers who was ready to give up more territory to the Arabs than were most party members.

Still, Rabin was considered less hawkish at that time than Peres, who until the mid-1970s favored widespread settlement in the West Bank, with the Arab inhabitants permitted to enjoy only "functional autonomy" under Israeli rule. Peres, it seems, had been influenced by Moshe Dayan, his political mentor in the hawkish Rafi group within Labor. But after Dayan was forced out as defense minister and then, to Peres's shock, joined the Likud government, Peres reexamined his perspective and had a change of heart. In fact, there was now little to distinguish his stated views on peace from those of Rabin, except that Rabin seemed more rigidly dedicated to the principle of peace through military strength.

But Rabin's distrust of Peres ran too deep for him to believe the change was more than political opportunism. While Peres turned dovish—a sincere turn, events proved—Rabin sought to appear more hawkish, and would indeed earn the popular title of "Mr. Security." The central committee, he felt, might back him for party chief again, even though preferring Peres, if national polls showed that he, but not Peres, was more popular than Begin and would more likely lead Labor to victory in the general election.

Thus, in May 1979, Rabin criticized Peres for suggesting that Israel be ready to negotiate with any Palestinians who recognized Israel. He also vowed four "no's": no withdrawal to the 1967 lines; no negotiation with the PLO; no Palestinian state; no division of Jerusalem. He kept moving farther to the right.

In a party debate on how to counter Likud charges that a Labor government would sell out to the PLO, he blamed Peres for giving Likud propaganda ammunition, contemptuously calling his once-hawkish foe a "left-wing intellectual." Rabin, it seemed, was trying to emphasize an ideological distinction between Peres and himself, though the only real distinctions were in personality and their tactical approach to problems. While Peres was a poetic dreamer with a pragmatic political sense, Rabin was a politically awkward general pragmatically pursuing a dream. Whatever his public pronouncements, Rabin kept listening to the super-doves who were secretly feeding him information about their unlawful talks with PLO officials.

In July 1979, Rabin went on television and announced that "there will be more than one candidate for the party leadership, and there may well be more than one challenger."

Was he referring to himself and Yigal Allon as challenging Peres? he was asked.

"You said it," Rabin replied.

But wouldn't this shake party unity?

"Three years ago," Rabin bitterly responded, "those who so loudly proclaimed the virtues of competition for the party leadership, although there was a Labor prime minister at the time, are precisely those who say today that this process is unacceptable."

Rabin was alluding to the preelection period in 1977 when Shimon Peres challenged him for the premiership. Now it was payback time. Rabin was determined to block Peres's path to the top. And in early 1979, his resolve, feeding his need for a catharsis, exploded into flaming print with the publication of his memoirs, which he had been writing with journalist Dov Goldstein for two years, three times a week for seven or eight hours each session.

Rabin told a shocked nation that Peres was unfit to be prime minister, describing Peres as an "inveterate schemer" who was "constantly and tirelessly attempting political subversion. He felt that all means were justified in his pursuit of winning the premiership. . . . He not only tried to undermine me but the entire government, trusting in the old Bolshevik maxim that 'the worse the situation, the better for Peres.' He spread lies and untruths and wrecked the Labor Party, thereby crowning himself as leader of the opposition."

When Peres lost in his bid for the premiership in 1974, Rabin charged, he "decided that he and the office of prime minister were made for each other, and that all he need do was kick me out of the way." Peres, he claimed, kept leaking information to the press, giving the impression that the prime minister was not functioning properly, and that only the defense minister was in full control.

Furthermore, Peres never served in the IDF, Rabin stressed, and was therefore not qualified to serve as defense minister—an argument that David Ben-Gurion and Golda Meir, among other defense ministers without IDF experience, might have disputed. In any event, Rabin said, he would never serve in a Peres government.

While Rabin, the straightforward iconoclast, struck with an emotional thunderbolt, Peres, the polished politician, replied with cool contempt: "His charges are very general in nature, and reflect more his problems than mine. . . . The book will cause very great harm to its author. There are standards even in political life, and we will have to take the damage which Rabin did to the party into account."

Many politicians and pundits agreed. A writer for the Labor-oriented *Jerusalem Post* wrote typically: "There is a view within the Labor party that Rabin's animosity toward Peres has gone well beyond the bounds of rationality, and that Rabin and his friends would prefer to see Labor lose the elections than Peres achieve power."

No one was more delighted by the chaos in Labor than the Likud, especially since it had just dropped below Labor in the polls. And jokes abounded that Defense Minister Ezer Weizman might sue Rabin for plagiarism; Rabin had stolen Weizman's charge, hurled before the 1974 election, that *Rabin* was unfit to be prime minister.

At a Labor Party meeting, leaders replied to the charges in the book by registering overwhelming confidence in the stewardship of Peres. Chain-smoking, Rabin sat through successive condemnations. Haim Zadok, who had been justice minister in Rabin's government, glared at him and railed:

"This debate is less about the book than about you, as you emerge from it." Looking away, he added that the book "damaged Rabin's credibility, and [belief in] his balanced judgment, and showed how personal enmity could affect an author's senses."

Later, even David Hacohen, Rabin's octogenarian uncle, who had helped spawn the Labor Party, would lament: "I am speaking with an aching heart. Never in all my years in politics have I seen such mud-slinging. . . . Let him keep a diary, or pour his heart out to his wife, but not write himself off politically."

Rabin defiantly replied to these angry comments: "I will not take back a single word I wrote about Shimon Peres and I stand by every one of those words. . . . I don't believe in insinuating and leaking. What I did in my book was to put things squarely on the table."

Rabin's aim in portraying Peres so brutally was to turn the people against the man, and he succeeded in a considerable degree. Peres would forever be stamped as a devious intriguer in the public's mind—an image that would play havoc with his career. But the charges bore no fruit among the party faithful, who viewed them as threatening ruin to the party.

Moreover, most members of the party's central committee, while resenting Peres for having abandoned the mainstream Mapai segment of Labor to help form Rafi before the two parties united, respected him for his intellect and political savvy. In fact, he had been amply demonstrating these qualities as Rabin's successor in the party saddle, leading the party out of the political wilderness. Besides, weren't most politicians, including themselves, devious intriguers? How else could anything get done in this country?

However Rabin's book played with the party, the people, while pondering the attacks on Peres, gave little weight to internal party quarrels, which were endemic in Israel. What they cared about was their security, and Rabin had led the nation to victory in the Six-Day War and taken a tough stand against the Palestinians. He was a "hawk," like most of them.

The polls thus showed a steady rise in his popularity, and, by October 1980, he was supported for the premiership by 34 percent of the populace, as compared to 23 percent for Begin and 12 percent for Peres. And while he was prepared to support Yigal Allon against Peres for party leader at the next Labor convention, destiny dictated otherwise. Allon died of a heart ailment before he could announce that he would run.

The way was now clear for Rabin to face Peres in another momentous clash. Allon had touched off Rabin's career as a soldier when Yitzhak was still a schoolboy. Now, in death, the hero of the 1948 war had opened the way for Rabin to return from political oblivion. And in early October 1980, Rabin formally announced he was out to win Labor's nomination for the premiership.

He didn't get much support from his colleagues. Indeed, Haim Bar-Lev, then Labor's leader, even refused his request for an office at party headquarters. And at one party meeting, no chair was reserved for him—deliberately, it seemed. There was one member, however, who vigorously backed him. Niva Lanir, a reporter for the Labor newspaper *Davar*, had been a New Left leader in college, where she had organized demonstrations for the "legitimate rights" of the Palestinians. Now Niva, an attractive, willowy brunette, was determined to help the Labor Party return to power, and not simply as a journalist. Ever since she had observed the emotional demonstration for Rabin at the soccer match he attended after his resignation, she "knew" he was the only man who could lead Labor to victory and peace.

"I realized," Niva told me, "that there was something in his character that made people trust him no matter what he did."

So now that Rabin had decided to challenge Peres for the party leadership, she asked to see him and he readily agreed, thinking she simply wanted to interview him for *Davar*. He soon learned that she wanted something more.

Now that Yigal Allon had died, Niva said, Rabin was pretty much alone and she wanted to help him become prime minister again.

Why? Rabin asked.

"Because you're the only one who can bring Labor back to power," Niva replied. "And then you will make a deal with Arafat—after you study all the facts in detail."

Rabin looked startled. On his round-the-globe tour to speak with world leaders, Anwar Sadat had edged him toward the view that he could solve the Palestinian problem only with the Palestinians and not through Jordan. But Rabin was thinking of eventual talks with local Palestinians, when and if he could find non-PLO leaders with sufficient authority to negotiate. Hadn't he publicly stated many times that he would not sit down with Arafat? It appeared that Niva's questioning of his intentions could bring an abrupt end to the "interview." Instead, without disputing the remark—after all, how could he foresee what future circumstances might demand?—he asked:

"Would you like to be my campaign manager?"

Niva quit her reporting job and immediately went to work for Rabin and the peace she was sure he would bring.

"It was a tough job," Niva told me. "The party tried to keep him from campaigning around the country and almost no one wanted to help us."

Niva's almost fanatical dedication to Rabin's restoration, "the only way to achieve peace," won her the affection of both Rabin and Leah, who came to regard her as almost a member of their family. When, in 1986, she suffered a heart attack, Rabin, though then defense minister, visited her in the hospital every day for about half an hour despite the heavy demands of his office—pragmatically asking the doctor to conduct tests on him so the time wouldn't be entirely lost. Leah, laden with food, pastry, and flowers, spent hours with Niva every day.

Though the efforts of Niva and other aides helped boost Rabin's poll figures, the mistakes in his past continued to haunt him. Shortly before Labor Party elections in December, the bank account was back on the front page. A French weekly, *L'Express*, claimed that Bezalel Mizrahi, an Israeli businessman, had paid the $27,000 Leah Rabin had been fined at her trial.

"Shimon Peres," the magazine said, "has a secret weapon against Rabin, a check for $27,000 that served to pay the fine."

The check, the story alleged, was in the hands of Peres.

Another "dirty trick" by Peres. Rabin was livid. Learning that *L'Express* intended to publish the story some days later and that the Israeli media knew about it, he warned the magazine and the press in general: Report it, and he would slap on them the biggest libel suit in history.

The threat gave the Israeli press pause, but the French weekly came out with the story and was sued for $270,000. Rabin furiously demanded that Peres deny in court that he had the alleged check, and Peres readily agreed, saying he knew nothing about such a payment. Finally, Rabin offered proof that a wealthy American friend and an Israeli cousin of Leah had provided the funds, and *L'Express* retracted the charge and paid the Rabins' legal expenses.

It was never determined whether those who provided the magazine with the false charge were really "Peres men," perhaps supporters who acted without Peres's knowledge. But despite the lack of evidence and Peres's denial, Rabin suspected that his rival was behind the effort. In any event, though the Rabins cleared themselves, the headlines had reminded the public—and Labor's central committee—of their transgression in Washington, virtually on the eve of the party convention.

Did the reminder make a difference? It is unclear, but Rabin would have another rancorous chapter to write in his memoirs. For at the convention on December 11, 1980, Peres won by a landslide—70 percent of the vote to Rabin's 29 percent. Rabin was devastated as he sat stone-faced listening to the results, and to Peres's victory speech:

"I have always believed in daring dreams. I do not fear so-called realistic men of little faith who tell us: Don't dream, don't dare, don't promise."

Rabin clearly resented what he thought was an allusion to him. Yes, he was realistic. And he would bring a realistic peace to Israel. He respected the decision, he told the convention, and the party would now be "united and whole." But he did not congratulate Peres. And when Rabin did not move to shake hands with Peres, the winner saw the chance for a grand gesture; he asked the delegates for "permission to go shake Yitzhak Rabin's hand." He walked over to the loser and, as the auditorium erupted in applause and cheers, reached out his hand to Rabin, who glumly shook it. Peres then asked each delegate who had voted for Rabin "to regard his own hand shaken personally by me as well."

"Cheap showmanship!" Rabin supporters charged.

The headline in the *Jerusalem Post* cried, "Disintegration of Rabin Camp Seems Certain," over a story reporting that "insiders of all factions agree that Rabin went for the jackpot—and lost everything."

Not quite. Shortly before the national elections, Begin came to his aid. Far behind in the polls at the time of Peres's Labor Party nomination, Begin began moving up swiftly after a sensational move. On June 7, 1981, three weeks before the elections, Begin sent off eight F-16s to Iraq, where they bombed the country's nuclear reactor so it could not be used to produce nuclear weapons. The nation—and the world—gasped in admiration, even if some condemned this bold action as unnecessarily provocative.

Immediately, the Labor lead vanished and one poll placed it twenty seats behind Likud. Peres was shocked when a Labor official gave him the news.

Could the situation be saved?

Only if Yitzhak Rabin were the candidate. The gap would then close. The people instinctively trusted "Mr. Security."

Would Peres do the truly grand gesture and let Rabin lead the party?

Peres found himself impaled on the horns of his greatest political dilemma. After all the sweat, the struggle, the humiliation, could he give up his dream and turn it over to his bitterest foe? Did not the party come first?

The next day, the phone rang, and Peres suddenly broke into a smile. Another poll showed he was now only six seats behind. He was catching up to Begin.

But Labor's victory was no longer assured. Peres thus decided to remain the party head but to make the next most difficult move. He would ask Rabin to be his defense minister even though he had already named Chaim Bar-Lev to this post.

Rabin had publicly vowed not to accept a post in a Peres government, but he decided to make an equally difficult move. Yes, he would be Peres's defense minister. It was, after all, only one step away from the top. And in this post, he could still pursue his dream of peace. However much he despised Peres, Begin had to be beaten or there would never be peace. For while Begin would grant the Palestinians a large degree of internal autonomy, as required by the Camp David accords, he would go no further.

To Rabin, this would be only the first stage. Ultimately, he felt, the Palestinians would come under Jordanian rule, as they had been before the Six-Day War, though perhaps this time within a federated state. Or if this proved impossible, he might make a deal for some form of semi-independent Palestinian "entity," which he was loath to describe as a "state."

But in the elections on June 30, Rabin's worst fear was realized. Likud beat Labor by a single vote, forty-eight to forty-seven. One vote away from an opportunity to end the cycle of death. And with three small parties, Begin managed to form a coalition government with a one-member majority.

The dream must wait. First would come the nightmare.

22

A Bloody
Adventure

Rabin was dismayed to hear Menachem Begin and Ariel Sharon talk of war. Israel's security lay in peace, not war. But the two Likud leaders were adamant as they briefed Laborites Rabin, Peres, and Bar-Lev in May 1982 on their plan to invade southern Lebanon and destroy the PLO forces entrenched there. The next terrorist act against Israel would trigger the plan.

The IDF, Begin explained, would clear the PLO out of a twenty-five-mile zone along the Lebanese border so Israeli villages would be out of range of enemy artillery.

It seemed clear that Begin and Sharon were simply waiting for a pretext to launch the attack. Yet Rabin, as well as the general staff, was convinced that Yasir Arafat did not wish to provoke Israel into massive retaliation and would probably avoid violence. About a year earlier, U.S. officials had mediated a truce between the PLO and Israel after some shells had rained on Israeli villages. And since then about the only sounds heard in the border area were the rustle of leaves and the grinding sound of tractors plowing the rocky earth.

Besides, Rabin was realistic; he "never believed that Arab terrorism can be eliminated by war. It can be contained but never uprooted."

Nor was Rabin confident that Sharon would stop after advancing twenty-five miles into Lebanon. If the very presence of PLO forces based so near was a source of fear for the Israeli frontier villages, it could mean an opportunity to Sharon. Seeking more precise information, Rabin asked Sharon if his troops would advance as far as the town of Sidon, at the far edge of the twenty-five-mile zone.

"I'm not sure," Sharon replied. And he got up and went to the door, saying: "I'll check it out on the maps."

After a few minutes, he returned with the news that Sidon was within the twenty-five-mile zone. But since he had not been sure, some colleagues suspected that he hadn't bothered to check earlier because he actually intended to race on to Beirut.

The Labor leaders were wary, anyway. For several days earlier, on May 8, Peres had convened a meeting with Rabin and other Labor leaders and told them he had heard of a far more ambitious plan drawn up by Sharon, though apparently opposed by Begin. And Sharon was not known as a stickler for discipline. The plan, Peres said, would "change the map of power and authority in the Middle East by creating a new political order."

Under this plan, the Israelis would push the PLO guerrillas into Jordan, where they could join the Palestinians already living there and, if they wished, overthrow King Hussein. They could even turn Jordan into a Palestinian state, as long as it didn't embrace the occupied territories. The IDF would also force the Syrians who had been fighting the Palestinians back into Syria, and then impose a peace treaty on a puppet Phalangist Christian government in Beirut.

Rabin reluctantly decided he would accept the twenty-five-mile plan—if a new mini-war of attrition threatened to break out on Israel's northern border. But he deplored the idea of full-scale military action to bring about a new Lebanese political order, to drive the Syrian army out of Lebanon, or to destroy the PLO entirely. Israel, he felt, should avoid initiating any war that did not threaten the nation's life. Should more mothers lose their sons in a war fought on foreign soil not for survival, but for political advantage?

Anyway, such a war could turn into an Israeli Vietnam and bring Israel back to square one. It might nullify all his efforts to resurrect a powerful army in the wake of the Yom Kippur disaster. Control Lebanese policy? Impossible. He had learned from personal experience that the Maronite Christian Phalangists, who were split into many feuding groups, no longer had the strength to dominate the country, even if backed by Israel. They had been uneasily sharing power with the Moslems since 1944.

In 1976, when he was prime minister, Rabin had met secretly with Phalangist leaders, who pleaded for arms to save them from annihilation by the Moslems. But he was not impressed with their sudden desire for Israel's "friendship." Meeting offshore in a missile boat with Pierre Gemayel, the veteran leader of a Phalangist group, Rabin stretched out his hand but found his guest reluctant to clasp it.

"I want to walk in Lebanon with my head held high as a Christian and as an Arab," Gemayel growled. "I have been forced to turn to you, but I am filled with shame and dismay."

Adding to the tension, Gemayel's son, Bashir, who had accompanied his father, grew seasick and vomited at the table where the negotiators were sitting. Rabin managed a smile of understanding, something he could not do in the future when Bashir, Sharon's malleable candidate for Lebanon's president, would prove to be as ruthless a warrior as his Israeli mentor.

But despite this disagreeable meeting, Rabin remained the pragmatist. The Christians, mainly Syrian-rooted Maronites, were the enemy of Israel's enemy. And soon arms were flowing into Christian arsenals—though, it turned out, with little effect against a stronger foe. It would be catastrophic now, Rabin thought, for Israel to get mired in Lebanese politics.

Sharon, however, was thinking in regional geopolitical terms, and U.S. Secretary of State Alexander Haig had hinted to him that the United States wouldn't mind if Israel responded vigorously to an indisputable PLO terrorist provocation. To Sharon, this could be interpreted as an American green light for his grand design. He had one problem, however; he needed an indisputable provocation. And he got one.

On June 3, 1982, Shlomo Argov, Israel's ambassador to Britain, was critically wounded when a Palestinian terrorist shot him in the head. Rabin was shattered by the news; Argov had been his deputy in Washington and was a dear friend. Surgery would save Argov's life, but his brain had been severely damaged. When Leonard Garment, a White House adviser, met with Rabin and asked about Argov, Rabin "didn't speak. His face flushed, his eyes filled with tears, and he bent his head, trying to gain control of himself. It was the most open display of emotion I had ever seen in him. After some seconds, he was again the matter-of-fact soldier. 'Those British surgeons,' he said with his characteristic shrug, 'did not do Shlomo any favor.'"

But Rabin was shaken not only for personal reasons. As he had feared, the attack would trigger a wider tragedy.

Actually, the assailant belonged to a radical Palestinian group that had threatened to kill Yasir Arafat for agreeing to a cease-fire with Israel. But to Sharon, he had the pretext he needed to launch Operation Peace for Galilee—and Begin agreed, though apparently in the belief that the Israelis would not advance farther than twenty-five miles into Lebanon.

Israel first bombed PLO ammunition dumps, provoking the PLO, as expected, to shell Israeli border towns in retaliation. Now it was time to move. On June 6, 1982, six Israeli divisions smashed into Lebanon. In a few days, Begin's trust in Sharon, it seems, proved to be misplaced. For Sharon, eagerly supported by Chief of Staff Rafael Eitan, pushed his troops to the outskirts of Beirut on the heels of fleeing PLO forces. Dodging artillery shells, these forces scrambled into the city to join a panicky civilian population bloodied with casualties.

Sharon then invited Rabin to join him at the front, since Rabin was a member of the Knesset's security and foreign affairs committee, and Sharon needed his support.

"If you were in my position," Sharon asked him, "what would you do now?"

Rabin noted that Sharon was surrounded by his commanders, who were listening intently for the answer. After all, Rabin had been chief of staff and led Israel to victory in the Six-Day War; his advice was important to them. Rabin was uneasy. He thought the drive toward Beirut was a mistake and might lead to disaster. But he was a soldier first. How could he tell these officers at the front that they were fighting the wrong war? He had to forget the geopolitics and think only of the tactics. The one question now was how to win this battle—without suffering the tremendous casualties that a direct assault on the city would produce.

"Since the population is sheltering the terrorists," Rabin said, "I would tighten the siege of the city and turn off the water supply."

When Rabin spoke later with his assistant, Niva Lanir, she couldn't believe what she heard.

"You went to Beirut with Sharon?" she exclaimed.

"Well, Sharon wanted to explain the situation to me."

"Why did you give him advice?"

"He asked me for it and I couldn't refuse in front of all those officers."

Niva was shocked. "You let Sharon manipulate you!" she exclaimed.

Rabin didn't reply. Only a commander would understand the need to support his men in battle whatever the justice of the cause. And only a political figure obsessively dedicated to the peace process would curry public support with a hawkish image if necessary.

Rabin had still another reason for offering his advice to Sharon. He hoped that tough measures would ferret out the terrorists from their hiding places and enable the IDF to make a swift exit from Beirut and Lebanon. But he grew agitated when newsmen focused on his trip to Beirut, perhaps feeling a sense of guilt for seeming to contradict his sentiment about the war.

"I repeat," Rabin would snap after the war, "I regarded the war as a national tragedy, and did my utmost to prevent it. . . . I strongly opposed the barbaric bombing of Beirut."

Not surprisingly, then, Rabin was sympathetic to a brigade commander who came to him and said that he had been ordered to take his men into Beirut but that he couldn't obey in good conscience.

"Hundreds of Israelis and thousands of civilians will die," the commander said.

Still the consummate soldier, Rabin advised the man: "You can't refuse a command—not without resigning from the service."

The officer then went to Begin and resigned.

With good reason, it seemed. As Abba Eban would describe the barbarity of this war after six weeks of battle: "The shattered bodies in the Beirut hospitals, the buildings fallen on scores of mangled civilian corpses, the piled-up garbage breeding rats, the children with amputated limbs, above all the Israeli soldiers on their endless stretchers and funeral biers. These six weeks have been a dark age in the moral history of the Jewish people."

Horrified by these scenes, Rabin now charged that Sharon had "failed to reach any of his goals" even after such cost.

The Syrian army, though dealt a serious blow, still had strong forces based in the Baka'a region of Lebanon. And while the PLO's South Lebanese infrastructure had been demolished, Arafat still held Beirut and had men and arsenals in Tripoli and north Lebanon. Moreover, Israel now faced a new and even more dangerous enemy on its northern border—the Shi'ite Moslems, who, with their PLO enemies in flight, now turned their guns on the Israelis for pulverizing their villages while triggering the flight. Finally, Lebanon still lacked a stable central government, and was unlikely ever to have one that would take orders from Israel in defiance of the whole Arab world.

Ironically, the United States, which had been encouraging the attempt to enthrone the Christians, suddenly turned against Sharon's enterprise when it viewed the tragic results. Rabin was alarmed by the reaction during a visit to the United States.

"Israel," he told the Israeli press, "is no longer seen as an underdog but as a giant crushing a dwarf with American weapons." The ultimate disaster, Rabin felt, would be a decision by Washington to cut off military aid to Israel if the killing didn't stop. It didn't. As he had feared, Israel remained bogged down in Lebanon, and army morale plummeted. Unless Washington replenished the dwindling arms supply, his peace plans, based on Israeli military power, could crumble into dust.

However, even as Rabin condemned Sharon's objectives and recoiled in horror at reports that thousands of Lebanese civilians and hundreds of Israeli soldiers had been killed, he had only praise for his beloved army, especially its "discipline and battle morality." Speaking of attacks on towns like Tyre and Sidon, which suffered heavy casualties, he said:

"Anyone . . . can see that the scenes of destruction were restricted to those areas where fighting took place with the terrorists. I hope it is realized that the IDF even extended the length of

the battle for this humane purpose. . . . I can say without any hesitation that when the army was ordered to take over these cities, it
did its utmost to preserve its humanity and morality, which are
supreme values for it and for the people of Israel."

He had to make it clear that the soldiers were trying to make
the best of a war that repelled him—a war, he would tell a Hebrew
University audience in January 1983, that the government should
admit was a mistake. Israel's armed might should not be used to
impose a formal peace agreement on Lebanon. Such an agreement,
he said, could evaporate with the slightest Arab pressure on
Beirut. Israel should seek to secure only its minimal needs in the
Israel-Lebanon border area.

"Some people," he went on, clearly referring to Sharon, "need
to prove that there is something to salvage from the political illusion behind the war, even if it amounts to an insignificant gain."

The government, Rabin added, should simply declare that a
state of war no longer existed between Israel and Lebanon.
Prolonging the conflict would prevent Egypt from continuing the
Camp David peace process, and the PLO from letting Jordan represent it in future West Bank–Gaza peace talks, as Washington had
suggested as a means of achieving an Israeli-Jordanian agreement.

Later summing up his view to a reporter, Rabin said: "I wouldn't
fire another shot to shape the future of Lebanon or thwart the creation of a Greater Syria. There is only one reason to justify making
war: to ensure the existence of my country."

But how could the IDF extricate itself from the Lebanese quagmire? How could he play a role in the effort?

The quagmire deepened when eight hundred Moslem civilians
were massacred by the Phalangists allied with Israel. According to
an investigative commission, Ariel Sharon had failed to prevent the
slaughter.

"In our view," the commission concluded, "[the] responsibility
is to be imputed to the minister of defense for having disregarded
the prospect of acts of vengeance by the Phalangists against the
refugee camps and for having failed to take this danger into
account when he decided to have the Phalangists enter the camps."

Sharon was a frustrated man. Not only was his army mired in
the Lebanese swamp, but Bashir Gemayel, who was to become the

country's president under his tutelage, had been assassinated by a pro-Syrian foe, throwing Sharon's plan into disarray. And a force led by Bashir's brother had taken its revenge in the refugee camps.

The commission said that if Sharon didn't "draw the appropriate personal conclusions," Prime Minister Begin should "consider exercising his authority" and remove him from office.

But Sharon would not draw the "appropriate personal conclusions" and Begin, as two Israeli reporters would write, "could not summon up the political and personal fortitude to fire him."

Begin was a tormented man. He felt that Sharon had deceived him, assuring him that his troops would not advance more than twenty-five miles into Lebanon, then thrusting toward Beirut without bothering to request permission. Begin had led the Irgun Zvi Leumi resistance to British rule; he had created the nationalist political force that would eventually come to power; he had made peace with Egypt.

And then he had turned over the IDF to a man who would lead it into a death trap. Whatever the responsibility of Sharon, Begin apparently felt, the blood of about five hundred Israeli soldiers, not to mention thousands of Lebanese civilians, was on his own hands. And now there were another eight hundred civilians brutally massacred by men who could have been stopped. And what had Israel gained from all this devastation?

And so Menachem Begin, conscience-stricken and broken in spirit, did not order his defense minister to resign, but simply persuaded him to become a less powerful minister without portfolio. It was Begin who resigned; he stepped down in September 1983 and lived like a recluse in his apartment, where he would brood over the tragedy he had presided over until his death in 1992.

Replacing Begin was Yitzhak Shamir, a more rigid hard-liner than his predecessor. He had been a leader of the Stern Gang before and during the 1948 war, having broken away from Begin's Irgun because he considered it too moderate. A secretive and taciturn but affable man, he once calmly explained to me how he had helped to plot the assassination of Count Folke Bernadotte, the United Nations mediator who, at Israel's birth, had drawn up a partition plan that the Sternists thought unfair. For many years after independence, he worked for the Mossad, then entered politics, moving from Knesset speaker to foreign minister.

Shamir, like Begin, would not accept the advice of Rabin, Peres, and many military leaders that Israeli troops withdraw from Lebanon.

Surrender? Yitzhak Shamir should surrender?

And so the war went on, with little chance of it ending until the next Israeli election in July 1984, when, Rabin hoped, Labor would slide into power again—with himself at the helm. But would he be there? In the previous election, Peres had beaten him handily in the central committee even though national polls had shown an opposite trend. And there was no reason to think the committee would shift its vote to Rabin in the coming contest.

Actually, members dreaded the prospect of another bitter, name-calling campaign and were not unhappy when a third candidate popped up—Yitzhak Navon, who had recently served as Israel's president. And since he was popular and noncontroversial, he was given a good chance to defeat both his competitors.

What if Navon won? He would, it seemed, serve as his own defense minister or choose Peres for the post, since the two men were close, both having been worshipful disciples of David Ben-Gurion. But if Peres won, he would have to appoint Rabin as his defense minister or find it almost impossible to form a government, the same situation in reverse that Peres was in during Rabin's regime.

Wouldn't it be better, Rabin wondered—if Labor won the election—to be assured the defense ministry than to risk being left out of the security loop altogether? Even if he couldn't be prime minister immediately, as defense minister he could still end the Lebanese war and move closer toward a general Middle East peace. His title was less important than his goal. And however distasteful it might be working under Peres, the man's views on the peace process basically dovetailed with his own.

Actually, since the start of the Lebanese war, the two men had improved their personal relationship, in large measure due to the secret mediation of Giora Eini, the union lawyer who had won the trust of both men. Eini went to both and asked the same question:

"Would you want me to serve as a go-between so you can find a way to work together?"

They both agreed, though expressing doubt that his effort would succeed. Eini then spoke with each man separately and drew up a list of problem-solving methods, which both endorsed.

One item called for each man to come to him and not to the press with any problem he might have.

The two leaders then met together with Eini in Peres's office—though only after hurdling a new obstacle. The meeting was so secret that Peres's daily schedule had Eini's name but not Rabin's written in. So when Rabin arrived, Peres's secretary wouldn't let him enter. Finally, with Eini's intervention, he was shown the way in.

Their unease by no means diminished by this embarrassing start, the rivals greeted each other with nervous smiles, as if they were strangers. Nor could they bring themselves to shake hands. They hadn't met for months, though they were the two chief figures in the party. Then, as Rabin sat down, silence. Finally, Eini commented dryly:

"The only thing that I'm not going to tell you is what one told me about the other."

Peres and Rabin laughed.

"This was the turning point," Eini would tell me. "From this moment, there was a new style of relationship between the two of them, and they began to work together on party problems."

It took some time before they felt comfortable enough with each other to meet without Eini present. But for the next fourteen years they would meet about once a week, calling in Eini when they needed him to prevent an explosion.

So now, in 1983, Rabin went to Peres and said what he had never dreamed he could say: He would support him for the premiership, but he wanted to be defense minister.

The two men shook hands, and the deal was made. Navon now bowed out of the race and Labor began planning a campaign most members felt they must win or see Israel sink deeper into despair over the war raging in Lebanon and the inflation raging at home. The Laborites were now buoyed by a sense of unity they hadn't felt for years.

And Labor, though starting out far ahead in the polls, won the election by only three seats—forty-four to forty-one for Likud. Thus, neither party was able to form a majority coalition and had to enter into a national unity government. The two parties would rotate: Peres would serve as prime minister for the first two years, and Shamir, the next two. Each would be foreign minister under the other.

Rabin was alarmed. With Likud in the government, how could peace be achieved in Lebanon and with the other Arab states? As defense minister, he must somehow steer history to this end. But he needed all four years in the post. He urged Peres to press for this arrangement, and felt relief when Likud agreed. Even Shamir saw Rabin as a tough hawk, despite his talk of peace. Rabin's hawkish image was paying off.

And on September 14, 1984, Rabin, together with other members of Peres's cabinet, was sworn in after a tumultuous debate in the Knesset, attended by Leah and other members of his family. As the Rabins went out into the night, they saw Yehezkel Sharabi, the new defense minister's old driver, who was in "seventh heaven" as he waited beside the car assigned to his revered boss.

But as Rabin climbed into the backseat, he complained that there was little room for his legs. The car was smaller than the one he had been given as prime minister. He would have to either curl up uncomfortably in this miniature limousine—or get back the prime minister's car.

Leah Rabin was deliriously happy when she entered the defense ministry compound escorted by motorcycle outriders and watched her husband stand with the chief of staff and listen to the national anthem, then inspect the guard of honor.

"Yitzhak had returned to the defense establishment as though coming home after a prolonged absence," Leah Rabin would recall. "Seventeen years had passed, his hair had turned gray, and he was wearing a suit in place of a uniform. Yet he strode like a soldier, as in the past, his face not revealing his inner feelings."

Actually, his feelings were not too hard to fathom. There were those glorious yet grievous days when he had sent doomed young men into battle while saving their families from annihilation; those agonizing days when a misused bank account had thrust him out of the highest office in the land. Leah, of course, shared in these feelings. She still had nightmares about sitting in court like a common criminal. Hadn't she assured him that he would come back, that there was no reason to doubt it? He was within sight of his old job.

And Leah returned home "to be flooded with congratulatory messages and flower deliveries. . . . I was exhausted from arranging vases and placing flower pots." An impromptu party followed and "the atmosphere was gay—exactly what was needed after a nerve-wracking week and on the verge of a new era."

After his years as a chief of staff, a diplomat, and a political leader, Rabin realized on entering the new era how vital the media were in helping him win popular support—and elections. He had thus been cultivating a hawkish image while waiting for an opportunity to act on his dovish intentions.

But as sensitive as he was to public opinion, Rabin would not sacrifice principle to avoid criticism.

This quality was tested when the mother of a soldier who had been killed in a training accident wrote a book censuring the army and demanding changes in its training methods. She came to the army publishing branch, Ma'arachot, and insisted that it publish the book. Uri Dromi, the editor, supported her request but was virtually certain his superiors would not agree. An army publication blaming the army for the death of a soldier? However, he called an aide to Rabin and requested approval.

"Are you crazy?" the aide exclaimed. "Do you want to open a can of worms?"

Worms that could undermine Rabin's chance for a full comeback.

Dromi then spoke with Rabin, who supported his aide.

"I think we should publish the book," Dromi persisted. "We'll show our sensitivity to our children. We're strong enough to do it."

Rabin considered the plea. What would the people think of their defense minister if the army published a book condemning it for killing one of their children? But he replied matter-of-factly, to the shock of his staff:

"All right, we'll publish."

And Rabin's popularity did not dip in the polls. What other defense minister, people asked, would admit to such a scandal? Despite the accident, they could trust him with their children. Even so, he felt he needed a more intensive and better organized campaign if he was to sit again in the prime minister's chair.

Until then, he had had few close advisers, thinking like a general. He might listen to aides but he would give credence only to his own views, based on intricate analysis. If he needed background information, why not simply ask the appropriate minister for it? Wasn't the cabinet like the general staff?

"Rabin felt he didn't really need us to prepare him" for meetings with important persons, one aide told me. "His general attitude was: 'Wait, don't do anything. I'll deal with it.' He had iron nerves."

But Rabin decided now that he needed specialized help—especially in promoting his image. And so he turned to an old disciple, Eitan Haber, an editor and correspondent for the newspaper *Yediot Aharonot*. The two men had first met in 1958 when Haber, only eighteen, was sent to cover the northern command and its commander, Rabin. And he covered Rabin's military career from then on until Rabin resigned as chief of staff, revering him like a father.

Now Rabin went to his "son" and asked him to be his media adviser.

No, responded Haber, a stocky, sensitive, somewhat cynical poet by heart. He wasn't a politician. He was a newsman. Besides, he didn't want to lose his pension.

Well, then, try it for one year.

Finally, Haber agreed. He came to work for Rabin—and served as one of his most trusted and devoted aides until the day of his boss's death. In his youth, Haber, a product of religious schools, had supported Likud. But he had come to believe that Rabin was right in pressing for peace and using hawkish tactics to achieve it.

"He understood," Haber would tell me, "that he must be hawkish in his speeches, his articles, and his image, but with the vision of peace before him and a readiness to make major concessions. People trusted Yitzhak because he was hawkish. When peace could become a reality, he would make concessions from strength."

Rabin also needed a political expert who could help him win the support of the agricultural and industrial sectors. And so he chose Shimon Sheves, a handsome, charismatic, trimly bearded kibbutz leader who had supported Yigal Allon until he died in 1980. Introduced to Rabin by campaign chairman Niva Lanir, Sheves then vigorously backed Rabin, who assigned him to deal with settlements, industry, and development areas.

Unlike Haber, whose desk, in the artistic tradition, was often in disarray, Sheves, no poet, was neat and well organized. He was a brilliant administrator and a tough farm-bred politician, the ideal counterpart to Rabin, who had neither the time nor the talent to deal with the prosaic aspects of governance. Sheves, according to some who knew him, was prone to temper tantrums, and could be ruthlessly demanding of his underlings. Once, he saw several women staffers idling on a sofa in an anteroom of Rabin's office and exclaimed:

"My God, this place looks like a whorehouse."

He apparently did not hear the reply of one of the women: "There is no whorehouse without a pimp."

But Sheves was masterfully efficient when serving Rabin and keeping the rabble at bay. In a sense, Rabin used him as his chief of staff in charge of an armylike bureaucracy, with departments organized in concentric rings. Rabin was still the general, lonely at the pinnacle.

After Rabin's death, Sheves would emotionally recall:

"He was everything to me. He was a good friend, a fatherly figure, and a guide. My life was related to him twenty-four hours a day. He became an essential part of my life. I spent half of my adult life with him. I spent my life with him as naturally as people are used to eating, drinking, and sleeping. I learned a great deal from him, too."

What did he learn?

"The most important thing ... was probably distinguishing between important issues and irrelevant matters. We both tended to pay attention to tiny details. ... Yet he knew how to separate, isolate, and create a list of priorities. He was well known as a smart man with an analytical brain, but he actually operated like a computer, too. I mean, he was fluent in any subject he came across and studied, as though he had been an expert in it for years. It was amazing."

An inspiring example for a man with political ambition.

Sheves and Haber would become Rabin's most influential aides and would often vie for his favor and attention, with Sheves stronger on domestic issues and Haber on international matters.

Rabin needed all the help he could get in dealing with his most immediate problem—extricating Israel from the catastrophic Lebanese war. As the days passed, he grew almost desperate as he pursued this effort. During one appearance before the Knesset foreign affairs and defense committee, an aide rushed in and handed him a slip of paper: A helicopter had crashed in Lebanon. After hesitating, he continued to offer testimony, only to be interrupted once more by the aide. A second note indicated that several soldiers had been killed. He looked up with glistening eyes and stammered:

"Okay, that's too much for me. I have to bring the meeting to an end."

Another time, to obtain the release of three Israeli soldiers captured in Lebanon by an extremist Palestinian group, he supported a move to release 1,150 Palestinian suspected terrorists, feeling, as he did while agonizing over options during the Entebbe crisis, that "when there is no military option . . . and after all the possibilities have been thoroughly examined, there is no alternative but to enter into negotiations and pay a price." Almost any price to save a soldier and ease his mother's distress.

But in seeking a peace solution in Lebanon, Rabin found himself caught between the demands of Shamir and Peres. Shamir wanted the IDF to withdraw only after border security arrangements were in place, which could take months. And Peres wanted it to withdraw immediately. Rabin, melding his security concerns with his peace aspirations, insisted on a three-stage withdrawal starting immediately. The last few hundred soldiers would hold on to a security zone along the border. It was the several-stage operation that Rabin would demand when negotiating for Palestinian autonomy ten years later.

"I don't want to be the policeman of Lebanon," Rabin would tell a newsman. "It's not the business of Israel. . . . We made it clear we don't link our unilateral decision to anything the Syrians do. They want to stay in Lebanon, let them stay. I know that whoever sets his foot in Lebanon has sunk into the Lebanese [swamp]."

Finally, in June 1985, Rabin, with Peres's help, began to pull the Israelis out of the swamp, agonizing over the results of this unnecessary war. Sharon had hoped to smash the PLO and the nationalist movement it represented in one massive blow, and in fact Arafat and his followers were driven out of Lebanon. But instead of the secular, pragmatic PLO, which had already realized that terrorism would have to give way to a two-state solution, Israel would now have to fight the previously passive fundamentalist Shi'ites led by the fanatical Hezbollah Party, which was driven by "orders" from God. At the same time, Sharon's plot to set up a puppet Christian government in Beirut collapsed with the decimation of the

Christian forces, while his plan to push the Syrians out of Lebanon also failed; they were still there. In trying to realize these aims, the IDF suffered more than seven hundred dead and thousands of wounded.

As a top leader in the postwar era, Rabin would have to help heal the moral wounds inflicted on his people in a needless war that cruelly claimed so many of their children. But he would also have to ease the economic disaster that threatened Israel's future security and his plan for peace that, he hoped, would underpin it. With inflation raging, Rabin slashed his defense ministry budget by at least 20 percent, releasing in the process 7,000 career soldiers. But he found himself trapped in a quandary as he pondered whether to back a project that could help lead Israel either to recovery or to further ruin.

Israel had been building the Lavi fighter-bomber in a fifteen-year project that would cost from $6 billion to $10 billion. But there was no certainty that aid would continue to flow from the United States over so long a period, and Israel could be left with a huge white elephant.

Rabin originally opposed the deal when he was simply a Knesset member, but as defense minister, after careful analysis, he changed his mind. With cancellation, he now argued, 3,000 workers would lose their jobs on a project that had already cost almost a billion dollars. In 1987, however, his generals, who felt that Israel needed other military equipment more than the super-expensive Lavi, pushed for cancellation. Rabin listened to their arguments and, after considering them in the light of the latest relevant facts, decided he could not gamble on a project that might jeopardize the economic underpinning of Israel's security. Better that Israel buy planes from the United States and build new "strategic concepts" that would make up for any of the lost advantages of the Lavi. He thus changed his mind again.

"Applying innovative concepts is difficult for politicians because of the uncertainty inevitably involved in changes," the *Jerusalem Post* would comment. "Overcoming that difficulty in the process of changing one's own previous commitment needs civic courage and leadership abilities—qualities with which Rabin is blessed."

As the war was ending, Rabin vowed to strengthen these qualities and to avoid in the future the mistakes he had made when he was prime minister in the 1970s. He would seek to bring greater unity to his party and would appear more hawkish until peace seemed possible.

Typifying this hard-line strategy was an incident described by Thomas L. Friedman in his keenly perceptive book *From Beirut to Jerusalem*. At a dinner party several months after the election, Rabin was called to the phone and, upon returning to the table, told his dinner partners that Ezer Weizman, the former defense minister, had called. Weizman had expelled the former mayor of Hebron after the murder of a settler, and the exiled man had then himself been mysteriously killed in Amman. Would Rabin agree to the plea of the dead man's family that the body be returned to his hometown? Weizman asked.

"So what did you tell him?" someone asked Rabin.

"I told him no," he replied, with a flick of his wrist. "I don't want any demonstrations."

Rabin didn't want another martyr's grave that could spark Arab violence—and an Israeli electoral backlash. There was no room for compassion if it hurt his chances of regaining power and pursuing peace as he saw fit. Didn't peacemaking reflect the greater compassion?

This time, unlike the last, he would not do anything "stupid" enough to jeopardize his position. In the view of some, however, he soon broke his vow.

According to a report by the 1987 U.S. Tower Commission investigating the Iran-Contra scandal, Israel, with Rabin in the vanguard, assisted the United States in selling arms to Iran in the summer of 1985 for use in its war with Iraq, and diverted profits from these sales to the Contra rebels in Nicaragua.

In addition to the money, Rabin was said to have sent a military aide to Washington to meet with Lieutenant Colonel Oliver North of the National Security Council and offer him military specialists as well in the struggle against the Nicaraguan leftist government:

> The Israelis would be willing [the report said] to put 20–50 Spanish-speaking military trainers/advisers into the DRF [Democratic Resistance Front—the Contras] if we want this to happen. They

would do this in concert with an Israeli plan to sell the Kfir fighter to Honduras as a replacement for the 28-year-old [Super Mystere] which the Hondurans want to replace."

North, in this report, said that Rabin wanted to meet privately with him "in New York to discuss details. My impression is that they are prepared to move quickly on this if we so desire."

Rabin, as well as Peres and Shamir, apparently saw an opportunity to tighten strategic ties with Washington, while making sure that Iraq, which then had the upper hand, would not win the war with Iran—a war that Israel hoped would continue and exhaust both sides. So, with its own interests in mind, Israel would, in effect, bribe the Iranians to order the release of American hostages being held in Lebanon by the Iranian-backed Hezbollah, and perhaps strengthen the hand of "moderate" elements in the Iranian regime.

It was not surprising that Rabin, who had sometimes pushed peace policies behind the backs of his colleagues, would agree to help an American administration that supported these policies. It seemed the pragmatic thing to do. And if U.S. leaders didn't worry about congressional reaction to this violation of American law, which banned aid to the Contras, why should Israel?

The problem was that Congress, which held the key to the arsenal feeding Israel the arms required to nail down a peace, found out about this brazen defiance of its will. And it was furious with Israel for its role in the affair. So, to save what he could of the congressional security lifeline, Rabin apparently felt he had no choice; he had to deny his, and Israel's, role in the deception, even though it wasn't in his character to lie.

However, few people in or out of Congress believed him, and the resentment toward Israel was apparently all the greater since its defense minister was reputed as one of the most trustworthy political leaders in the world.

"Israel's credibility has been shot," one pro-Israeli lawmaker said after Rabin's denial. "How can we believe anything they say anymore?"

Yet most congressmen and other Washington officials soon forgot this singular example of dishonesty, understanding Rabin's strategic life-or-death objective. In the final analysis, whom could they trust more than him?

Even so, hardly had the arms flow into Iran tapered off when Rabin found himself involved again in clandestine action that would fray relations with the United States, though he was apparently ignorant of this intrigue. As Rabin was meeting with fellow Labor Party members in his hotel room during a visit to New York one afternoon in December 1985, a military aide, Chagai Regev, burst in and handed him a note. Rabin read it, and his face turned even redder than usual. He was once more guilty of a "stupidity" that could imperil his position—failing to take preventive action on a vital security matter.

Who gave him the information? Rabin asked Regev.

A justice ministry official had called him and said: "Chagai, the FBI has arrested an American who was trying to enter our embassy to seek asylum."

The man had been accused of spying for Israel.

Cheeks still aflame, Rabin stared at Regev in disbelief. Two hours later, Rabin was aboard a plane headed back to Israel, where, on his arrival, he urgently met with Peres and Shamir. So far it was known that the arrested American was a U.S. Navy employee, Jonathan Pollard, and that he had confessed he had sold to Israel intelligence secrets involving the Middle East.

Jonathan Pollard? Who was he? The three men claimed they had never heard of him. And with the United States demanding to know who was responsible for the "Pollard affair," an investigation was launched. It uncovered a so-called Scientific Liaison Unit, which had directed Pollard's espionage mission. The mission, Rabin and his colleagues claimed, was kept secret even from them by the unit's leader, former Mossad chief Rafael Eitan, a protégé of Ariel Sharon. Actually, Pollard had begun spying for Israel under Shamir's regime when Moshe Arens was defense minister, but Arens was also apparently unaware of Pollard's existence.

Regardless, Rabin was so preoccupied with pulling his troops out of the quagmire in Lebanon and preparing for a wider peace that he apparently did not keep close enough watch over the military intelligence system. A report by Abba Eban's subcommittee of the foreign affairs and defense committee on intelligence and security services was critical of Rabin in the affair:

> [Rabin] had ample opportunity to take note of phenomena which
> should have caused him concern. . . . Rabin evinced no effort to

maintain procedures of scrutiny or to tighten control, as he was duty-bound to do. During his term of office, the Pollard affair became a protracted phenomenon without Rabin being aware that the source was Pollard. . . . The burden of ministerial responsibility devolving on him is beyond any doubt.

Rabin was furious, suspecting that Eban was simply seeking revenge for past grievances against him. And he was fearful, too. Yes, his failure to know about Pollard was "stupid." And he had jeopardized his job once more. But this time, he would fight any attempt to force him out of office.

He bore no special responsibility for the Pollard spy scandal, he told the press. A minister was not required to draw any "personal conclusions about an affair he had been unaware of."

The following day, however, Rabin backtracked on this statement, telling his party's central committee that he agreed to share with Arens the responsibility for the Pollard affair. Laughter erupted when he added that "avoiding pregnancy cannot be done in the sixth month." Pragmatism thus dictated his admission.

In the end, however, only Eitan and his contact man with Pollard were officially blamed for the spy mission, suffering temporary setbacks in their careers, while Pollard himself was sentenced in the United States to life imprisonment, and his wife, an accomplice, to five years.

Still, Rabin, it seemed, was disturbed. He had not been entirely true to himself. He had always accepted responsibility for his mistakes, but he so feared that he might be forced to resign that he had been reluctant to concede the obvious: He should have checked his intelligence system more carefully.

But he soon drove this episode from his mind. It was time to move toward peace with the local Palestinians now that Yasir Arafat and his PLO, having been ejected from Lebanon, might be too weak to control them.

In July 1985, about a month after the Lebanon War, Hana Siniora, the publisher and editor of the Jerusalem-based Palestinian newspaper *al-Fajr*, received a message from Yasir Arafat, who was now headquartered in Tunis: He must come to see him immediately.

Siniora rushed to Tunis and found the same pragmatic leader he had known for many years. Arafat's PLO forces in Lebanon had been shattered but he had not given up the fight for a Palestinian state. He had decided after the 1973 war that terrorism was counterproductive, though some extreme factions in the PLO still favored this kind of struggle. As Rabin felt he had to appear hawkish to win the support of his people, so Arafat felt he had to keep secret his desire for a deal with Israel to avoid charges of treason by his people.

But Arafat trusted Siniora. And so, in his desperation, he sent him on an ultra-secret mission.

Go see Rabin, he told the newsman, and make him understand that the PLO wants to open a channel with Israel. And then go to Washington to see Secretary of State George Shultz and tell him that the PLO wants to make a deal. He gave the same instructions to several other agents, according to Siniora, hoping someone would succeed.

Siniora and the others agreed, and the publisher first tried to see Rabin through Knesset members he knew. But Rabin refused to receive him. What would people think if they learned he had met with a PLO envoy, especially so soon after the bloody fighting in Lebanon? At the same time, Rabin's vision of a peace accord with local Palestinian leaders suddenly dimmed. For if Siniora, an influential Palestinian known for his moderate views, still took orders from the PLO, it would remain almost impossible to find any non-PLO Palestinians Israel could deal with.

But later in 1985, Siniora told me, he did get to see Peres, who apparently persuaded Rabin that Arafat had been so weakened by the Lebanon War that he might really want peace now. Why not secretly explore the possibilities of opening direct talks with the PLO? Rabin had been doing that indirectly for years through his leftist friends as well as a Labor Knesset member, Rafi Edri, who was meeting with PLO officials in Morocco. But doing it on a more official basis was another matter. He still wasn't sure the time was ripe, especially with the raw wounds of the Lebanon War still unhealed. Nor was it easy to forget the horrific images of terrorism and the tears it wrought.

Pragmatism, however, finally triumphed. With Rabin's support, Peres appointed Yossi Ginosar, a former Shin Bet official, to head the first direct—and ultra-secret—contacts with the PLO. Shamir, then foreign minister, knew of these contacts but was told their only purpose was to arrange the return of Israeli prisoners of war.

Thus, early in 1986, Ginosar, a shrewd, Arabic-speaking secret agent, was meeting with PLO officials in New York, London, Paris, and Brussels, and rather enjoying the unofficial title jocularly conferred on him by Rabin and the handful of others who knew of his role: Israel's "ambassador to Arafat."

In a meeting with one official, Hani el-Hassan, Ginosar told me, the Palestinian suggested that Israel grant autonomy to the Gaza Strip in the first stage of a peace deal. When Ginosar reminded him that the Palestinians had rejected the autonomy idea when it was proposed in the Camp David accords, Hassan replied:

"Chairman Arafat invites you to visit him and he will confirm that we are serious."

Ginosar reported the proposal to Peres, but Shamir, who would shortly take over as prime minister, rejected the idea. In any case, Shimon Sheves, Rabin's aide, who favored opening channels to the PLO, told me:

"Ginosar's objective in the 1980s was to understand PLO thinking and not to negotiate peace. Rabin felt he might have to deal with the PLO one day, but not then."

Meanwhile, in February 1986, Siniora and a Palestinian colleague managed to get an appointment with President Ronald Reagan's secretary of state, George Shultz, at the State Department and delivered Arafat's conciliatory message to him.

Before the meeting, a Shamir aide warned Shultz that his decision to meet the pair amounted to "a decision to negotiate with the PLO."

"I did not want to put the two on the spot," Shultz would later say, "so I stayed away from discussing the substance of my initiative," simply telling them that the United States could not negotiate with the PLO until it accepted Israel's right to exist and Resolution 242, and until it renounced terrorism.

According to Siniora, "Shultz wavered on how to move forward with the peace process."

He didn't waver, however, when in April 1987 he received another visitor, Yossi Beilin, the aide to Peres, who had exchanged posts with Shamir and was now foreign minister. Shultz was pleasantly shocked on being told that an agreement similar to one he had been pushing had been reached between Peres and King Hussein when they met at the home of a common friend in London. It called for an international peace conference, with Israel negotiating separately with Jordan, Syria, and Lebanon. The Palestinians would be part of a joint delegation from Jordan, and Arafat would presumably be frozen out.

But if Peres and Shultz, as well as Rabin, saw this accord as a major step toward an overall Middle Eastern peace, Shamir viewed it as an anti-Israel trap and vetoed it.

"We all paid a heavy price for the destruction of my milestone agreement with King Hussein," Peres would say later.

Perhaps not, for as two Israeli experts would write, "The king might just as well have sold Peres the Brooklyn Bridge." Hussein, after all, had long since been excluded from the Palestinian peace process by the other Arab states. And the king, now realizing that the time for a deal was past, declared flatly that he would not take responsibility for the fate of the Palestinian people.

But if the accord might not have generated peace, its stillbirth, together with the failure of the PLO overtures, helped to guarantee the emergence of a new, especially virulent form of violence that would turn Rabin down a new road and change the face of the Middle East.

23

Sticks, Stones, and Broken Bones

"**D**on't worry, it'll be quashed in a few days."

Rabin was assuring his host at a Washington dinner party that riots in Gaza that had erupted two days earlier, on December 8, 1987, were not really very serious. No more so than previous incidents of sporadic violence. Otherwise, would he have left Israel?

Rabin's confidence seemed justified. Israel once again had a powerful army that could beat all the Arab armies combined. Riots by a few unarmed, stone-throwing Palestinians, he felt, did not pose a great problem. In fact, the day after the eruption, his aides had agreed that he should go to Washington in spite of the unrest. Prime Minister Shamir could take over the defense ministry while he was gone and would be advised by Chief of Staff Dan Shomron. And of course, Rabin could always be reached by phone.

In fact, hardly had he arrived in Washington later that day when he received a call from his military aide, Chagai Regev.

The situation was swiftly deteriorating, Regev said, and he should return home immediately.

But Rabin remained convinced that the rioting would soon fizzle out. Anyway, if he rushed home precipitously, people would get the false impression that the violence had gotten out of hand, further inflaming the situation.

Besides, he was just starting on a mission more vital to Israel's security than any attempt by him to control a local riot. He was to sign a memorandum of understanding on the sale of Israeli goods to the United States and negotiate the price of seventy F-16 fighter planes. He would also visit several military installations and speak at an Israel bond rally.

No, he was not about to pack his bags and hurry home.

What had triggered the sudden, and surely short-lived, surge of violence was a typical Palestinian pretext, probably hatched, Rabin surmised, by Iran or Syria. On December 8, an Israeli truck struck a car entering Israel from the Gaza Strip and killed four Palestinian laborers. A common accident. But the Palestinians viewed the killings as murder. Two days earlier, an Israeli had been stabbed to death in a Gaza market, and the Arabic newspaper al-Fajr, charged that a relative of the victim deliberately ran into the four Palestinians in revenge.

After attending their funeral, hundreds of mourners crying "Jihad! Jihad!" ("Holy war! Holy war!") attacked an Israeli army post outside Jebalya, the largest refugee camp in the Gaza Strip, hurling stones and bottles.

"Send for reinforcements!" an officer belatedly called to the sector commander after several hours of rioting as the burst of fury was dissipating near midnight.

"Nothing's going to happen!" the commander replied. "You don't know these people. They'll go to sleep now and leave for work first thing in the morning, as usual. You'll see."

What Israel would see was chilling. The next morning, a jeep followed by two armored personnel carriers approached Jebalya intending to break through the roadblocks of rocks and pieces of furniture that the inhabitants had piled up during the night. A show of strength, the Israelis calculated, would end the troubles once and for all, as in the past. But the thousands of Palestinians lining the streets and standing on the roofs of dilapidated huts were not intimidated this time, and the soldiers were greeted by a barrage of stones and even a Molotov cocktail. Several young Arabs tried to climb into the vehicles and take control, forcing the drivers to zigzag in order to shake them off. Ze'ev Schiff and Ehud Ya'ari would report in their book *Intifada*:

> On one of these zigzags a machine gun and its tripod fell off an APC [armored personnel carrier], and a number of people rushed forward to snatch it. It took a burst of gunfire, while the vehicle was traveling in reverse, to stop them from getting to the weapon, but two of the Palestinians did manage to run off with the ammunition belt. The rioters were not daunted by the shots fired in the air. On the contrary, again and again the soldiers were confronted by frenzied people taunting them in Hebrew and daring them to shoot while they stood rooted to the spot in defiance.

The patrol, barely able to extricate itself from the mob, returned to its base.

This incident was to symbolize the start of a new relationship between Israel and the Palestinians, one that would be forged during three years of a stone-throwing rebellion of rage throughout Gaza and the West Bank that could not be stamped out.

As Schiff and Ya'ari would describe the phenomenon:

> The Intifada was an assertion of defiance that bubbled up from below, a statement by the legions of Palestinian youth who felt bereft of a future; the high school and university students doomed to choose between indignity and exile; the tens of thousands of laborers who made their living in Israel but were expected to remain invisible; the veterans of Israeli prisons who were more convinced than ever of the justice of their cause but saw their people sinking deeper and deeper into hopelessness. In short, it was the work of the Palestinian masses.

And in a sense, it was Gandhi-like work. Hana Siniora, editor of *al-Fajr*, told me:

"I was instrumental at the beginning of the Intifada in calling for a campaign of civil disobedience—resistance for the first time without major violence. We wanted to show that the Israelis must deal with us in seeking peace."

In the Middle East context, where blood has flowed so freely for decades, rock-throwing, indeed, amounted to comparatively light resistance—not provocative enough to yield massive deadly retaliation, but enough to keep Israel in perpetual turmoil. Beatings and bone-breaking? A bearable price in the struggle for independence.

As Rabin sat in his Washington hotel room watching television, scenes of carnage in Israel flashed on the screen, jolting him, but not enough to shorten his schedule. Eitan Haber, his aide, however, grew anxious. Perhaps, he thought, Rabin should skip the Israel bond rally talk after all and head home. But Rabin would not disappoint the thousands of Holocaust survivors who had come to Miami to hear him. And so it was not until December 21, after almost two weeks of rioting, that Rabin finally set foot in Israel again.

Who was behind the troubles? a reporter asked him at an airport press conference.

Iran and Syria, Rabin responded.

Israeli intelligence had indicated that the PLO had not fomented the riots but had simply tagged along. In fact, Yasir Arafat was as skeptical as Rabin about the revolutionary nature of the Intifada. In 1967, shortly after the Six-Day War, he had tried to foment a popular uprising in the territories captured by Israel, but it had failed, and he did not believe one could succeed. And he did not even consider the possibility of an unarmed mass rebellion, feeling that "the solution will come through the barrel of a gun."

As Schiff and Ya'ari would point out:

> Ever since 1967 [PLO leaders] had operated on the assumption that the inhabitants of the territories, loath to endanger themselves in a serious confrontation with the Israeli authorities, were unlikely to spearhead the Palestinian national struggle. It took time for them to absorb the enormity of their mistake.

It took time for Rabin, too. If the PLO hadn't sparked the violence, who else but the Syrians or Iranians might have? Rabin reasoned. He couldn't believe that this was a new phenomenon, a spontaneous, grass-roots revolt by the entire Palestinian population—men, women, and children.

Ever since he had led Israel to victory in the 1967 war, Rabin had viewed the Palestinians as potential wards of Jordan, as reflected in his secret conversations with King Hussein in the mid-1970s. Despite long-standing Arab League objections, that country, he still hoped, would ultimately swallow the occupied territories to form a Jordanian-Palestinian federation based on the principles of the land-sharing Allon Plan. After all, most inhabitants of Jordan were Palestinians anyway.

Meanwhile, though Rabin tried harder than most Israeli leaders to improve economic and social conditions in the territories, these areas had largely become Israeli colonies since they were seized in 1967—a market for Israeli goods and a source of cheap labor in the Jewish state, with little encouragement given to local enterprise and industry. Let Jordan make the necessary changes when it took over.

But just in case it couldn't, Rabin continued to keep secret direct channels open to the PLO, while trying to find local Palestinian leaders with whom he could negotiate. This wasn't easy, for until recently the Israelis had jailed or deported many potential leaders over the years. The irony was that the Palestinians were thus left to depend on Arafat for leadership, and he would settle for nothing less than a fully independent Palestinian state.

Rabin's fear of such a state was not the only reason he favored the "Jordan option." He questioned whether the Palestinians had the nationalist credentials deserving of a state with its own flag. Many Palestinians supported nationalistic terrorist groups like the PLO or Hamas, but, it seemed, largely because these organizations threatened those who refused to do so. Few of them demonstrated the fierce sense of national destiny that had driven the Zionist pioneers. They rioted occasionally, as they were doing now, but the riots were easily put down. What they principally wanted, Rabin felt, was to end the occupation, whatever the alternative might be. And he supported this aspiration. But he would never let them achieve it by force. They would never agree to make real peace if they thought they could achieve more by violence.

At the airport press conference, he warned: "They won't obtain a single thing via the threat of war, terrorism, or violent disturbances. Therefore, the main problem at present is to enforce order, with all the sorrow and pain over loss of life on the Arab side. Whoever goes to violent demonstrations is placing himself in grave danger."

But this, Rabin would soon learn, was precisely what the Palestinians wanted. Maybe some of them would fall, but television cameramen would record young boys being mowed down with stones gripped in hand. The whole world would be with them. And the world was. With rubber bullets in short supply, live ones were fired and viewers everywhere cringed, among them

American Jews who felt their own name was being besmirched. Jews didn't act like that!

Rabin himself was disturbed by the mounting Palestinian deaths, though he understood that Israeli units facing thousands of young stone throwers fired in fear for their lives. But they had to be more disciplined, especially since the world was watching them. So he issued clubs to his men and ordered them to take action that generated a new storm of criticism, with many believing the order was to "break their bones!" Rabin would later tell the Knesset:

"To the best of my recollection, at no time and in no place did I ever say 'break bones.'"

He had simply ordered in so many words: Beat them but don't kill them. Yes, the stone throwers had to be severely punished, but, he claimed, he was trying to save their lives. Anyway, whatever his exact words, "break their bones" was, in fact, an idiomatic military expression and did not literally mean to take such extreme action.

But many soldiers, humiliated by taunting youngsters, took the expression literally, and many bones were broken, to the horror of TV viewers in America and elsewhere, who seemed to regard the beatings even more barbaric than the shootings.

Rabin apparently had mixed feelings: He was dismayed by the flurry of charges that stamped him as a monster and would taint his reputation. But he had to make sure that counterviolence would convince the Arabs that their rebellion would not be rewarded. And he had to impress his people, who were demanding strong measures against the rioters and would remember that he was still "Mr. Security" when they went to the polls. He would tell Gad Yaacobi, the minister of economy and planning:

"My role as minister of defense must be detached from my concept of ultimate peace. My first duty is to protect our people. Besides, if we didn't take strong action, the enemy would consider us weak and it would be impossible to conduct political negotiations."

When Yaacobi suggested that Israeli troops simply withdraw from the occupied areas, Rabin replied: "Gad, what you are proposing is that we run away. This might be perceived as such. And so they'll feel they can expel us. We must stick to our targets."

Thus defying world opinion, Rabin stuck to his targets, issuing plastic bullets to his men and telling the press:

"I am not worried by the increased number of people who got

wounded, as long as they were wounded as a result of being involved actively, by instigating, organizing, and taking part in violent activities. The rioters are suffering more casualties. That is precisely our aim."

Yet after several days at home, Rabin began to realize that this was no ordinary surge of violence but a full-blown popular uprising and finally concluded that it could not be quelled by force—not with guns, clubs, curfews, or deportations of suspected riot leaders. In fact, the riots grew more violent as PLO representatives gradually assumed leadership. Perhaps tank assaults or air strafings might work, but, ignoring the demands of some rightists, Rabin refused to trigger a massacre. He reproached himself. Why had he not seen the Intifada coming? Why had his intelligence apparatus failed him?

With the riots spreading, Rabin told a group of party comrades on February 21, 1988: "I've learned something in the past two and a half months. Among other things, that you can't rule by force over one and a half million Palestinians."

What should be done? Annex the territories?

Never!

Transfer them elsewhere?

"Transfer so far has only been done to Jews, we should not forget that."

Make them Israeli citizens?

"They will have twenty-five to thirty seats in the Knesset. . . . We shall be a biracist state, not a Jewish one."

Rabin, who had always felt the urgency of making peace with the Arab states because their armies threatened Israel's existence, now fully recognized for the first time that Israel was locked in a struggle with another people fighting for its existence. Not with an organization or a minority group, but with a legitimate nation bearing a soul rooted in the same soil that nourished the Jews.

Rabin would tell Israel Television on March 9: "After three months we are facing a problem like none in our previous experience. It is the problem of violence committed outside the framework of terrorism by a large population under our control. . . . It is far easier to solve classic military problems. It is far more difficult to contend with 1.4 million Palestinians . . . who are employing . . . systematic violence without weapons, and who do not want our rule. Moreover, we are handicapped because we cannot use the

IDF's principal weapons. . . . There are 450 villages in [the West Bank], and the IDF cannot be everywhere at once. . . . Our objective [therefore] is to bring about a calming, not a solution."

In clarifying what Rabin said, his aide Niva Lanir told me: "Yitzhak understood the curse as well as the blessing of the Six-Day War, that it was wrong for Israel to rule another people," whatever the security considerations.

Only one solution seemed possible now—a political one. But Rabin tried not to shock his people too precipitously, especially since his tough, hawkish image had driven up his approval rating at home from a little more than 50 percent when the Intifada started in December 1987 to about 58 percent in March 1988— while Peres's support was dwindling.

Rabin kept repeating his mantra that he supported the Jordan option and still wouldn't negotiate with the PLO. But on a trip to the United States in the spring of 1988, he told reporters that if the PLO renounced the Palestinian covenant calling for Israel's destruction, accepted UN Resolutions 242 and 338, and stopped violence, he would talk with them—a revolutionary assertion at that time.

"As defense minister," he conceded, "it took me time until I understood the Intifada as a phenomenon and the willingness of Palestinians to persist with it. Until the Intifada broke out, Israel had not experienced such a comprehensive case of authentic popular uprising."

And so, in 1988, Rabin told Yossi Ginosar, his "ambassador to Arafat" who had regularly met with PLO officials two years earlier: "I want the Israeli government to reach a solution of the Palestinian problem."

Ginosar was now convinced, he said to me, that "Rabin realized he would probably have to talk directly with the PLO."

For one thing, Rabin could not ignore Washington's ground-breaking agreement in December 1988 to open low-level talks with the PLO. These talks would presumably lay the groundwork for an international peace conference if Arafat issued a statement renouncing all forms of terrorism and supporting "the right of all parties concerned in the Middle East conflict to exist in peace and security, . . . including the state of Palestine, Israel and other neighbors according to the resolution 242 and 338."

Furthermore, Rabin was now more persuaded than ever that the key to peace with the Palestinians was "separation." Israel vitally needed such a solution from a moral, an economic, and especially a security point of view. Separation was not a new concept for him, but he had always viewed it in the context of Jordanian rule in the territories, or some kind of autonomy under Israeli rule. He now recognized for the first time that neither the Jordan option nor a large degree of autonomy was feasible any longer. There had to be an independent Palestinian entity approaching a state.

The Palestinians themselves nailed down this conclusion. Rabin had tried by every rational means to crush the rebellion, but ironically, it was violence, sustained month after month, that swept away all his doubts. They had simply proved to Rabin that they deserved their own homeland. To his shock and admiration, they had acted like the Zionist pioneers, refusing to bend before impossible odds.

At the same time, on November 15, 1988, the Palestinian National Council (PNC), meeting in Algiers, proclaimed a Palestinian state in the West Bank and Gaza and thus implicitly recognized the existence of the state of Israel for the first time. Three weeks later, on December 7, Arafat met with prominent American Jews in Stockholm and confirmed the PLO's decision to grant such recognition. And the following week, he reiterated his pledge to the UN General Assembly meeting in Geneva—after the United States, citing his terrorist background, refused to let him into the country to speak.

And so Rabin, seeing a window of opportunity, drew up a plan reflecting his new pragmatic perspective on the Palestinian problem. The question was, could he induce Prime Minister Shamir to reward the Palestinians for their courage and dedication in their struggle against the Israeli forces?

Where would the plan lead? Abdulwahab Darawshe asked excitedly. To a Palestinian state?

Rabin was consulting with Darawshe, an Arab Knesset member, on his plan that could lead toward "separation." The plan called for a six-month moratorium on the Intifada, considerable autonomy, and general elections, with the winners to negotiate peace with the Israelis.

The Palestinians were free to demand a state, Rabin said, but he couldn't assure them one.

Darawshe was thrilled. Rabin appeared to be saying that he might support a state when the conditions were ripe. The deputy, though, was not too surprised. For one thing, the Israeli Arabs were conducting a mini-Intifada of their own. For another, Darawshe trusted Rabin. In 1985, Rabin declared that Israel would not initiate development in the territories or grant licenses for industrial or agricultural projects that could "compete with the State of Israel." But later he shifted his view and also tried more than other leaders to ease the discrimination against the Israeli Arabs in education, housing, and other fields.

Could he show the final version to Arafat? Darawshe asked.

After a pause, Rabin replied with a verbal wink: "You are a member of the Knesset, aren't you? You can do what you wish."

Darawshe flew to Tunis and met with Arafat, who approved the plan. On his return to Israel, the Knesset deputy told me, the police investigated him. They also "tried to investigate Rabin, but he threw them out of his office."

Shamir, it appears, had learned of Darawshe's visit with Arafat, a violation of Israeli law, and was behind this effort to thwart Rabin's plan. But Rabin was not discouraged. Nor was Peres, who, for all the friction with Rabin, supported his views on peace. After a new election in November 1988, in which Likud had defeated Labor by one vote, Shamir remained prime minister in a new national unity government; the Likud's Moshe Arens took over the foreign ministry; Peres became deputy prime minister and finance minister; and Rabin continued as defense minister.

Three months later, in February 1989, the PLO initiated a meeting in Holland with Abba Eban, who was no longer in the government, and the group of doves led by Meir Pa'il, who first tried to arrange talks between Rabin and PLO officials in 1976. At the meeting, Pa'il asked the PLO participants:

"Am I to understand your acceptance of Israel means you accept the partition of the country into two independent states?"

"Yes," chief PLO spokesman Bassam Abu Sharif replied.

After the meeting, Eban and Pa'il went to the Israeli embassy, and were invited by the ambassador to discuss the PLO talks at lunch. But he had to withdraw the invitation on orders from the foreign ministry in Jerusalem. And so the two Israelis returned to Israel, and Pa'il went to see Rabin.

"Rabin listened very politely," Pa'il related to me. "He listened to every word and syllable. But when I told him that the Palestinians seemed sincere, he replied, 'You're naive.'"

The prime minister didn't dare reveal that he was, in fact, already dealing with the PLO.

Rabin and Peres now confronted Shamir, who was preparing to visit Washington in April 1989 to see newly inaugurated President George Bush. Bush's secretary of state, James A. Baker, had already made clear he would press for an end to the Intifada and for the granting of autonomy to the Palestinians.

Shamir could not go the United States empty-handed, Rabin and Peres argued. He couldn't simply defy the new President.

Shamir finally relented, and Rabin helped him to draw up a four-point peace plan that was a watered-down version of the Rabin plan he had spurned; too watered down, Rabin felt, to be acceptable to the Palestinians. But it was better than nothing.

The Shamir Plan called for the people in the West Bank and Gaza to go to the polls and choose non-PLO Palestinians, who would then sit down with Israel and hammer out an interim agreement on autonomy as called for by the Camp David accords. But the restrictions sounded like the rules of an exclusive country club. No PLO members could be consulted or take part in the talks, nor could anyone living in East Jerusalem, since that could open the door to Palestinian claims to that area.

With the plan stuffed into his briefcase, Shamir left for Washington, where he was greeted by a man who was determined to penetrate his iron barrier of skepticism by establishing "a personal bond of trust"—Secretary Baker.

"Mr. Prime Minister," Baker said, "you've been described to me as a man of principle who is incapable of being practical. I've probably been described to you as a man totally lacking in principle who cares only about being practical. Let me tell you, like you, I'm very much a man who believes in principle, but I also think you have to be practical if you're going to realize your principles. . . . I think that you and I may be able to surprise some people by working together. . . . We want to take what you have and market it with the Arabs, but you have to give us something."

Shamir gave him his plan.

Baker perused it. Well, it was better than nothing.

The Palestinians disagreed.

With the opportunity for peace slipping away, Rabin and Baker collaborated in seeking to finesse compromises out of Shamir. Rabin realized it was unusual for a government official to conspire with a foreign power to shape the policy of his superior. But the Intifada was raging, and a solution, Rabin felt, had to be found before Israel sank deeper into quicksand.

Baker would later write of Rabin's role:

"We'd been working quietly with Rabin for months—so quietly that my staff and I referred to him in all our conversations as 'the man who smokes' to disguise our 'back-channel' conversations with the chain-smoking defense minister."

While many Israelis distrusted Baker for his sometimes cavalier preaching to Israel, Rabin grew fond of him. Both men found that they shared some distinctive qualities. They were pragmatic problem solvers and were suspicious of grand strategies. And they basically agreed on the direction that the peace process should take.

In July 1989, President Hosni Mubarak of Egypt drew up a ten-point peace program of his own, which he would submit to President Bush. Rabin, who was apparently in direct contact with Mubarak, was informed of the proposal, and he and Peres, as well as PLO officials, contributed suggestions. Shamir, however, was not informed of the plan for fear that he would kill it before it left the ground. Under this plan, elections would be held when Israel agreed to the land-for-peace formula, stopped building settlements, and permitted Palestinians from East Jerusalem and outside the territories to take part in the talks.

According to Chaim Asa, a national security adviser to Rabin, the defense minister told him with pragmatic frankness: "I don't believe Arafat. I don't believe the PLO. They are liars and bastards. But I'm sure Mubarak can control them. He's the only one who can. He is the key to arranging some kind of peace process with the PLO."

Rabin rushed to Washington to discuss Mubarak's plan with Baker, and on his return finally reported to Shamir on the draft and his conversation with Baker, apparently indicating that he had learned of the scheme not directly from Mubarak but from Baker. Afterward, Shamir called in Foreign Minister Moshe Arens, and both men expressed their rage.

> No notes had been taken at the meeting [Arens would later write], nor had Shamir or I been informed that it would take place. It was very strange. Why should Israel's minister of defense hold one-on-one unscheduled, unrecorded talks with the U.S. secretary of state behind the backs of Israel's prime minister and foreign minister?
>
> The answer was hard to believe but inescapable. Mubarak had transmitted his proposals to Bush, who had passed them on to Baker, who in turn had chosen to transmit them not to me but to Rabin for what could only be political reasons. It was neither the first nor the last time that Labor ministers tried to subvert a government in which they served, but it was certainly the first time that any U.S. Administration had directly intervened in Israeli internal affairs to further a policy of its own.

The following day, Shamir, Arens, Peres, and Rabin met, and Rabin, according to Arens, demanded that the government agree to Mubarak's plan.

What plan? Arens asked. They had seen nothing in writing. In any case, there was no hurry, he said, since he would be seeing Mubarak and Baker soon.

"An answer has to be given at once," Rabin insisted, his face reddening, or he would give his opinions to the media. He must know in a day or two.

Arens wondered whether Rabin had also been dealing with the Egyptians "behind our backs."

The next day, Baker phoned Arens. Before Rabin had arrived in Washington, he said, President Bush had received "this letter" from Mubarak.

"I would, of course, have conveyed the message to you," Baker said, "but since Rabin happened to be here, I gave it to him."

He would ask Mubarak for permission to send Shamir a copy of his letter. He hoped he "had not caused any complications."

His hopes were not met. Rabin and Peres "flew into a rage" when Arens repeated that he would delay the government's reply to Mubarak until he saw his letter to Bush.

No need to wait, they said. "Why is it so important to see the words 'Dear Mr. President' on top of a letter?"

But Shamir and Arens held their ground. "Subsequently," Arens would recall, "I saw the contents of the Mubarak letter to Bush. It included references to members of the Israeli cabinet who were in contact with the PLO—at the time this was illegal—and who were likely therefore to support the Egyptian points, and in retrospect partially explained Rabin and Peres's extraordinary behavior."

Arens would add: "How could it be that Baker did not understand . . . that the Mubarak proposal was unacceptable to the government of Israel? In Israel, Rabin lauded the Mubarak plan as a 'great and important step' in furthering the peace process, brushing aside charges that agreeing to the Cairo talks was tantamount to negotiating with the PLO."

In September 1989, Baker, apparently with Rabin's help, drew up a five-point "Baker Plan," which attempted to bridge the gap between Shamir's four points and Mubarak's ten.

- Israelis and Palestinians would negotiate in Cairo.
- Egypt would act as an intermediary with the Palestinians.
- Israel would have the right to approve a list of non-PLO Palestinians.
- Both sides would accept Shamir's plan as the basis for talks, but the Palestinians could present their own views on elections and the subjects to be negotiated.
- The foreign ministers of Israel and Egypt would meet with Baker in Washington within two weeks to facilitate the process.

Foreign Minister Arens met with Baker to discuss this new plan and was disturbed when the secretary "again brought up Rabin. He knew, as well as I, that there was little justification for substantive relations between the defense minister of Israel and the U.S. secretary of state. Perhaps he sensed that I suspected such a relationship had already been established."

"I haven't talked to Rabin. Would you object if I talked to him, if I let the Labor Party see the draft?" Baker asked.

"I don't think you ought to do that," Arens replied. "As you know, once the Likud agrees, Labor will automatically agree. If it now gets into the hands of Labor it will just cause complications."

Later, Arens met with Rabin and told him he "thought we were in the middle of a PLO offensive aimed at active participation in the peace process, attending the dialogue, and then holding forth not about elections or the peace initiative but about a Palestinian state and the 'right of return' [of the Palestinian refugees]. It was up to us to see to it that this did not happen and that Israel did not find itself trapped in some form of negotiation with the PLO.

"What made this all the harder," Arens said, "was the subversive behavior of people in his party, notably Peres and his young disciples, who were assiduously operating behind the government's back, whether in talks with Egyptians, contacts with the PLO, or the continued leaking of classified documents in the media."

"It has to be stopped," Arens said.

Rabin didn't argue.

Shamir now made it clear that he would not compromise with the Palestinians even if his government collapsed and relations with the United States crumbled. And they began to crumble in October 1989 when President Bush himself telephoned the prime minister and huffed:

"There is a perception that Israel is moving away from your own position. . . . We've invested a lot in this initiative."

"We are not pulling away from our initiative," Shamir replied, "but we will not meet with the PLO."

"That's fine," Bush responded with growing irritation, "because I've just read the wire story quoting you about a confrontation with the United States. If you want that—fine."

Rabin, seeing the Israeli-American alliance he had so carefully nurtured over the years about to disintegrate, rushed off to Washington to plot with Baker means of persuading Shamir to accept the five-point plan. Actually, he told Baker, he had floated a couple of ideas to Shamir and Shamir seemed to agree in principle. But he needed a little prodding. One idea was to choose a Palestinian representative who lived in the territories but kept a second residence in East Jerusalem. Another representative could be a deported Palestinian who would return to the territories and join his delegation.

"Ingenious!" Baker thought.

Arens thought so, too. On January 31, Baker called him "with the information that there had been this 'very positive' response from the Egyptians: They were ready to have two Palestinian 'deportees' in the delegation who could return to wherever they lived, or to the territories, once they had been named to the delegation."

"Is this the answer to a question that Rabin asked you when he was in Washington?" Arens wanted to know.

"You could say that," Baker replied.

The secretary went on to say that he had gotten a "positive response" from the Egyptians on the issue of Arabs with dual residences serving on the Palestinian delegation.

"Had Rabin brought that up, too?" Arens asked.

Baker indicated Rabin had.

The next morning, Arens reported on the conversation to Shamir. "So we had been wrong about our great hope for holding the coalition together," he said.

And later Arens would bitterly comment: "It took months for the truth to emerge. Rabin had not just entered into discussions with Baker, but had entered into a secret agreement with him about the composition of the Palestinian delegation, even picking by name the Palestinians he thought should serve on it, making as sure as he could that the real nature of his visit to Washington was not revealed to Shamir or to me. Had Rabin thought that his deception would remain secret?"

The persistence and secret maneuvering of Baker and Rabin appeared to be paying off, especially after Rabin—and Peres— threatened to bring the government down if Shamir didn't accept the Baker Plan. Shamir, according to Arens, had "made every effort to placate Rabin, hoping that Rabin's aversion to Peres becoming prime minister would set the basis for an alliance that could keep the coalition on an even keel."

Actually, Rabin mainly feared that Likud in the opposition could more easily sabotage peace efforts than it could as part of the national unity government. But he also thought such a government "constituted Israel's best alternative" because Peres, as party leader, would head a Labor government if one were formed. Rabin would thus charge in March 1990, clearly referring to Peres, that there were "some in Labor who seem to be in a great rush [to bring the government down], and it isn't the peace process which is their principal priority, but something quite different."

However, it seemed now, Arens would write, that Shamir's "strategy [of placating Rabin] had been exhausted." It became clear that if Likud didn't agree to the Baker Plan, Rabin would feel he had no choice but to seek a Labor government, even with Peres at the helm. Peres was Rabin's personal devil, tricky, backstabbing, and opportunistic in his view; in short, a threat to Rabin's own power, and thus to Israel's ability to achieve peace. But Peres was nevertheless on the peace track. Shamir, on the other hand, seemed to be Israel's devil, defiantly uncompromising with mind closed and sword unsheathed.

Still, Shamir, however rigid his philosophy, hinted he might support the Baker Plan with certain changes. And Rabin was now hopeful. The peace express could be revving up again.

Then, once more, the train crashed—when, ironically, the Americans inadvertently helped derail it. On March 1, 1990, Baker told a House appropriations subcommittee that the United States would grant Israel a $400 million loan guarantee to build housing for Soviet Jewish immigrants only if it agreed to stop building new settlements in the territories. President Bush then reiterated at a news conference that "the foreign policy of the United States says that we do not believe there should be new settlements."

Shamir had just the excuse he needed to reject the Baker Plan.

He would never submit to American pressure! Shamir grunted. The United States could not be objective as a mediator.

And he called a meeting of his ministers to decide on whether to accept the dual-residence compromise on Palestinian representation in the projected peace conference, the key stumbling block to the Baker Plan. Certainly, he felt, most of them would oppose it after the Washington insults. But he was wrong. Most listened to Rabin's bristling arguments for approval and backed the plan. Shamir, however, refused compromise to the end.

On March 13, Shamir called the Likud ministers to a final consultation before the full cabinet was to meet and perhaps end its existence. Arens "tried to suggest that there seemed a good chance of coming to an agreement with Rabin, who could probably get the Labor Party to go along." But Shamir "cut me [Arens] off." Shamir was in a quandary. What should he do—dismiss Peres from his twin posts of deputy prime minister and finance minister, or dismiss all the Labor ministers?

Shortly, at the government meeting, Shamir accused Peres of having "plotted the downfall of the government." Peres, Rabin, and the other Labor ministers handed Shamir a prepared collective letter of resignation. Then they rose and walked out of the room.

"In an instant, everything had shifted," Arens would recall.

"Shamir had cut loose from an association he loathed but which he himself had created and for years had tolerated. Peres was only a step away from trying to assemble the alternate government he had striven so long to establish."

But the step was steep and slippery, especially because of the fickleness of the religious parties. One of them, Shas, at first agreed to support Peres, but then changed its mind under pressure from Eliezer Menachem Schach, an influential religious leader.

Nevertheless, after several weeks of desperate bargaining, Peres laboriously pasted together a coalition with political bribes and grandiose financial promises, and managed to corral one religious party and even a disgruntled member of the Likud. Success at last, and the Knesset was finally called into session for the swearing-in ceremony. The gallery was packed with supporters ready to explode into celebration, and Peres's wife, Sonya, never seemed more radiant. But the glow soon paled.

At the last minute, two members of the seduced ultra-religious Agudat Yisrael bolted from the projected cabinet, leaving Peres two votes short of a majority. Peres scrambled to fill the gap, and finally one of the bolters returned to the fold. Now Peres needed one more vote. Two possibilities remained—the second bolter or a second Likud member who was leaning toward Labor. The Likud man finally chose his old party, and the bolter decided to refer to a higher authority. He telephoned his mentor, white-bearded Rabbi Menachem Schneerson, who headed the ultra-Orthodox Lubavitch movement in Brooklyn, and was revered by his followers as the "Messiah."

Should he join the Peres cabinet? the Likudnik asked.

No, Schneerson replied, thereby determining the direction of Israeli history, though he had never set foot in Israel.

Thus, Peres lost his majority and could not form a government, while the Likud could, after offering even greater bribes and promises and winning the belated backing of Shas and Agudat Yisrael. Shamir now returned to power—as the prime minister of a rigidly hard-line rightist regime.

Peres was devastated. It seemed unimaginable; his destiny had been decided by a Messiah living in Brooklyn! And Rabin lamented that the peace process would surely remain paralyzed as long as Shamir headed a Likud-dominated government.

"We have done everything to formulate the issues in such a way that Shamir could give a positive response," he told reporters. "The responsibility for the collapse of the government rests on Shamir's shoulders."

But Rabin was less devastated than Peres. He had worked with Peres without friction in the national unity government, and had even campaigned hard for him. But now that Peres had failed to form a government, the way was open for Yitzhak Rabin to replace him as Labor Party chief. He had already suggested his intention when he said shortly before Peres's failure:

"When the time comes, Labor's institutions will have to take steps to ensure that . . . a narrow rightist coalition is not established."

The time had already passed, but now steps must be taken to knock Shamir's narrow rightist coalition out of power. And the first step should be to replace Peres with someone who could win. Someone like Yitzhak Rabin.

Would anyone, he asked, vote for a man who resorted to "stinking maneuvers" in trying to patch together a cabinet?

Peres retorted that Rabin wouldn't have minded the odor so much if the maneuvers had succeeded.

In any event, the odor was not about to drift away.

24

The Showdown

"**W**e have no choice. Yitzhak must challenge Shimon now because he can win the next election and Shimon can't."

Uzi Baram, a leading Laborite, was addressing a group of party colleagues shortly after Shamir was thrust into power again, hoping to drum up a bandwagon for a Rabin run for the premiership. Baram's voice resonated for he had long been a left-leaning backer of Peres. Peres would make the better prime minister, Baram felt, but he couldn't win and Rabin could.

Rabin was grateful for the support of Baram and others, and he wanted to be prime minister again. But how intensely? According to Shimon Sheves, who vigorously pressed him to run, Rabin told him:

"The premiership for me is an option, not an obsession. I have done everything and have had jobs that people only dream of. I don't need the honor of being prime minister again. But I think I can bring peace to Israel and a change in priorities. The money we spend building settlements in the West Bank should be used for education, building industries, providing jobs, absorbing newcomers."

Rabin's chief objective was peace with Israel's moderate and less fanatical Middle Eastern neighbors, especially since extremist foes like Iraq, Iran, and Islamic fundamentalist groups throughout the area could, armed with unconventional weapons, pose a mortal threat to the Jewish state in ten or fifteen years. Rabin thus regarded peace with the Palestinians, Jordan, Lebanon, and even hardline Syria as a strategic necessity; serving as buffers of power and influence, they could prevent another Holocaust. And he didn't trust anyone but himself to pursue this supreme goal. Nor, for personal reasons, could he bear the thought of Peres in the driver's seat, though Peres largely shared his own peace aspirations. In any case, few took seriously Rabin's claim that he viewed the premiership as simply an option. His passion for the job was almost transparent.

But Rabin was not at all confident he could beat Peres in the race for party leader. According to Chaim Asa, who had become one of his political strategists, Rabin asked him:

"Would I stand a chance if I ran?"

"I don't know, but I'll check" was the reply.

Asa checked, he told me, and found that Rabin would have trouble winning a majority of the party's central committee, which chose the party leader. But he could win if Labor had an American-style primary system, since he was popular with the rank-and-file of the party, as with the country at large. He should first test his strength with the central committee, Asa advised, and if he failed, push for primaries.

Uneasily, Rabin decided to take the advice.

Actually, a trickle of party members, including leaders like Baram, were already switching their allegiance from Peres to Rabin, feeling that only he could lead Labor to triumph over Likud. True, some wished both Peres and Rabin would retire in favor of a younger, less controversial leader, for as one Labor chief put it, they were "tearing the party apart." And one politician quipped that "50 percent in the Labor Party want Peres, 50 percent want Rabin, and 100 percent don't want either." But all Laborites agreed that as long as the two men were around, no one else stood a chance. And between the two, as Baram pointed out, Rabin was a far more popular figure nationally.

In fact, according to the polls, he was the most popular politician in the country, especially after solving so many recent crises.

In the Lebanese war, he had made tough statements in support of the army, and then extracted it from a disastrous stalemate. And during the Intifada, which had dissipated into sporadic armed attacks by PLO-led activists, he struck back with an iron hand, and was now seeking to melt the iron in a crucible of peace. He seemed the ideal amalgam of security and conciliation.

But despite Rabin's high countrywide approval rating and the rush of party officials to the challenger's side, the majority of Labor leaders still favored Peres. Thus, in what amounted to an unofficial popularity contest held by the 1,450-member central committee, Peres, with his usual verve and active pursuit of votes, beat the more reticent Rabin by a vote of 582 to 504.

Though disappointed, Rabin was philosophical. The battle was just beginning. As Leah would say of his arrival home after the results were in:

"I vividly remember the moment he walked into the house. He had enormous composure. He made us relax and gradually cheered us up. 'This isn't the end of the world,' he said. He approached his political renewal much the same way he approached the peace process, step by step. A word he always used was 'patience.' I lack it. Savlanoot—'patience'—was such a pivotal word in his vernacular, such a crucial trait of his character."

Yet Rabin's patience was not without limit. It was time to end the "buddy system" and let the great mass of rank-and-file Laborites throughout Israel choose the party leader.

With General Secretary Micha Harish—another convert to Rabin's side—galvanizing forces for a changeover to the primary system and Knesset member Binyamin Ben-Eliezer directing a membership drive, more than 150,000 people would join the party from November 1990 to election time in February 1992. So overwhelming was the tide that even Peres, fearing to defy the public mood, reluctantly supported the reform, though he knew it was intended to kill his dream.

How could he work his charm on tens of thousands of people? Peres wondered. How many hands could he shake? How many phone calls could he make? Television was somehow unkind to him. He appeared too stiff, too dreamy and humorless. And he could not shed the image of the slippery, untrustworthy manipulator fostered by Rabin. Indeed, how could he get the people to know the real Shimon Peres, the warm, thoughtful, sensitive man so admired, respected, and even loved by many of his colleagues?

If Rabin won the race for Labor leader, the party, it appeared, would stand a good chance of beating Likud in the next election, especially with tens of thousands of Jews arriving from the Soviet Union, which had suddenly opened its gates and let them stream out. As wave after wave washed over Israel, housing and jobs for them grew increasingly scarce, and a whole new segment of Israeli society, impoverished and often discriminated against, threatened to vote against the ruling rightists.

But the Persian Gulf War in January 1991 seemed to turn things around. Shamir, at American bidding, had kept Israel out of the conflict and Iraqi Scuds exploding in the country caused few casualties. People simply suffered the inconvenience of spending much of their time in sealed shelters wearing gas masks. How wonderful to win a war without having to send sons and husbands into battle.

But as the glory faded, so once more did support for the Likud. Twenty percent inflation eroded living standards, and with the steady Soviet influx, unemployment continued to soar. Moreover, the peace process, as Rabin had expected, had sputtered to a halt. Yet, in his ideological zeal, Shamir was reluctant to grab on to a lifesaver tossed to him—by James Baker.

President Bush and Baker saw the Persian Gulf victory as blowing open the door to a new peace initiative, this time involving not just the Palestinians but also Syria, Jordan, and Lebanon. After all, several Arab countries, including Syria, had fought alongside the United States. The mood seemed right for peace among those who sided against a common enemy, incredibly an Arab country this time, not Israel.

Baker once more embarked on the tortuous process of edging Shamir to the peace table, visiting Israel many times and never failing to spend time with Rabin, who again quietly gave him advice. It is clear what advice he gave.

"Israel should try again to make peace first with the Palestinians," Rabin told me in early 1991. "The Gulf War has brought down their expectations, and I'm sure an agreement could be reached with them. Then Jordan should be next, and finally Syria, the hardest nut to crack. A multination conference would be dominated by the most intransigent countries, and it would be almost impossible to reach agreement with anyone. If I become prime minister again, we will have peace in the region after nine months."

But finally, the most Baker could wring from Shamir was an agreement to hold a multination conference in Madrid, with the Soviet Union and the United States sitting at the table as cosponsors. The Palestinians, supposedly unaffiliated with the PLO, would be part of a joint Palestinian-Jordanian delegation. Rabin proved to be right. Shamir and other Middle East leaders acidly pontificated on their well-known viewpoints, but reached no agreements, except to meet again soon in Washington.

Yet, psychologically, there was a surge toward peace. Improbably, Palestinians who had cheered while Scuds whistled over Israel during the Gulf War now tossed flowers rather than grenades at Israeli soldiers. And the sweet-smelling atmosphere did wonders for Shamir's electoral chances. Suddenly seen as a party of peace, Likud jumped into a lead over Labor in the polls.

Shamir hoped to consolidate his lead by luring to Likud's side the disgruntled Soviet immigrants, who could tip the election. And he counted on the United States to help him. After all, hadn't Israel agreed to stay out of the Gulf War at Washington's request in order not to antagonize the anti-Iraqi Arabs? In fact, six days after the war started, Shamir's finance minister had asked Bush for a $10 billion loan guarantee to enable Israel to build housing and create jobs for the new immigrants.

But Bush was infuriated by what he saw as a brazen demand for a "payoff" while his troops were still stuck in the sands of the Persian Gulf, and he delayed a reply. A year later, in January 1992, the United States agreed to give the guarantee if Israel stopped building settlements in the occupied territories.

Why, Bush asked, should the United States grant Israel such a guarantee when Israel had enough money to build these obstacles to peace?

There could be no linkage between the settlements and the guarantee, Shamir snapped. He would not submit to American pressure. And all of Israel would support him.

Actually, not all. Many Israelis were dismayed by Shamir's defiance of the United States, understanding that Bush had no wish to provide the prime minister with the means to build unnecessary settlements. Secretary Baker would later muse:

"Likud's failure to secure the loan guarantees from Israel's closest ally undercut it. The chill in relations with the United States as a result of an intransigent settlements policy cost Likud dearly, because proper management of the U.S. relationship is a must for any Israeli government to succeed. In retrospect, I believe the Shamir government could have been sufficiently flexible to obtain the loan guarantees without compromising its principles."

The deep freeze in Israeli-U.S. relations could not have come at a more propitious time for Rabin. Ironically, the leaders of three small right-wing parties within Sharon's coalition quit, largely because they feared Shamir would bend under American pressure and give the Palestinians limited autonomy. Shamir lost his majority, and early elections would have to be held.

Meanwhile, the Labor Party contestants—Rabin, Peres, and two others with little chance of winning—launched their campaigns for the party leadership. Rabin stormed from town to town, village to village, crying the same theme: Only he could lead Labor to victory. And the crowds roared their approval. Was he not the hero of the Six-Day War? Hadn't he been the iron-fisted defense minister during the worst period of the Intifada? Was he not demanding peace, but peace through strength? What if he didn't kiss babies, or ever smile? Who could trust a smiling politician? Suddenly, a disaster. He began to lose his voice. Obeying the doctor, he made the supreme sacrifice: He temporarily gave up smoking.

Rabin did not have to mention Peres's "shortcomings." Peres was seen as a dove; he did not speak hawkishly as Rabin did and had not been in a position, as Rabin was, to take a tough stand against the Intifada rioters. And the public, understandably plagued with a Masada complex, trusted hawks more than doves, even while pining for peace.

The trickle of Peres followers into the Rabin camp began turning into a flood as they smelled victory over the Likud with Rabin. The vivacious Rahama Hermon, who had served as an aide to Rabin from his days as deputy chief of staff through his ambassadorship, found herself in a painful predicament. As she was a devoted friend of both Rabin and Peres, she would go abroad during previous party elections so she wouldn't have to choose between the two men. But this time, many of Peres's longtime supporters were deserting him and she could not leave him feeling so abandoned. She had to support him.

Would he understand? Rahama asked Rabin.

Rabin smiled, perhaps hiding hurt. Yes, of course he understood. He understood that the Peres campaign was being fleeced to the bone. Let him have her vote.

And Peres needed every one, and fought for every one, rushing from one rally to another, reminding listeners that even his enemies had to admit he had been a good prime minister in the mid-1980s when he headed a national unity government; denying a charge by Rabin that only Rabin could win over the undecided and right-wing voters in the general election; charging Rabin with character assassination by declaring him obsessed with his own ambitions.

Rabin retorted that "playing the abject victim is no substitute for leadership." But Peres was undaunted and his passion and energy stimulated his audiences, who noted that, unlike Rabin, he seemed to enjoy the exercise in self-salesmanship. The gap between the two men began to close.

Finally, the day of the momentous clash came. On the morning of February 19, 1992, Rabin awoke worrying about the tightening race and hoping there would be a big turnout, since he was the favorite with the general population. He needed at least 40 percent of the vote to avoid a runoff race between the two contestants with the highest percentage.

After voting in mid-afternoon, Rabin went to party headquarters, then home to watch the election returns on television. At party headquarters, a rumor had Peres overtaking Rabin, and Rabin's advisers grew so nervous that Shimon Sheves removed a bottle of champagne from the refrigerator, to be used in a victory celebration, and hurled it out the window because it might bring "bad luck." But as the reports trickled in, it grew clear that Rabin was winning. And finally, victory—with 40.59 percent of the vote compared to 34.80 percent for Peres—just enough to avoid a runoff vote, and to get Sheves to kick himself for throwing out the champagne.

Rabin was aglow as his family embraced him. He was finally on the brink of a comeback that he had thought impossible fifteen years earlier when, in humiliation, he had submitted his resignation as prime minister. Only Leah didn't seem surprised.

She had assured him he would be back. In less than two weeks, her husband would be seventy. What a birthday party they would give him. It would be better than those wonderful parties in Washington.

Peres was crushed and was barely able to mumble congratulations to Rabin in a phone call heard nationwide. Why had so many people betrayed him? After all he had given to his country and his party. Through a leading newsman, Yeshaya Ben-Porat, Peres called in Chaim Asa, who had once worked for him.

And there took place a conversation that would plumb the emotional depths of the rancorous relationship between victor and vanquished; between two of Israel's greatest leaders, whom history had brutally linked together in a hybrid of mutual hate and need.

"Why did you help Rabin against me?" Peres asked bluntly, according to Asa.

"Look, Mr. Peres," Asa replied, "I like you very much. But you can't defeat the Likud. You talk about peace, but if we don't beat the Likud, there will be no peace. And the only one who can beat the Likud is Rabin. So if you want the peace process, you must help Rabin win."

"I could beat Shamir," Peres answered. "There was no need to change the leadership. Rabin is always hounding me, all my life, for twenty years."

"I'm a young man. I believe in peace, and I think the only chance for peace is Rabin and not you. I have nothing against you."

"You don't know what you're talking about. What have you got against me?"

"Nothing. I admire you, but you can't beat Shamir. Besides, I don't believe the peace process is your main thrust. Your main thrust is to be number one."

"Nonsense! It is Rabin who has always wanted to be number one. I've never had one minute of peace from him."

"If you were a young man like me who wanted peace very much, what would you do, help Rabin or Peres?"

Peres looked to Ben-Porat, who had accompanied Asa for support, but the reporter simply said that Asa was entitled to his view.

Rabin chats with President Jimmy Carter. There was no chemistry between the two men, and they showed little trust in each other.

Rabin visits Egyptian president Hosni Mubarak in his palace, where the two men devised plans for peace with the Palestinians.

Rabin meets with French
president François Mitterand.
Unlike Shimon Peres, a
Francophile, Rabin never
developed close relations
with France, believing that
Israel should be oriented
toward the United States.

Rabin is honored by Nancy Reagan during a trip to Washington, D.C.

Secretary of State James Baker discusses a document with Rabin as President George Bush *(right)* looks on. While he was defense minister under Likud prime minister Yitzhak Shamir, Rabin often met secretly with Baker to plot peace moves without Shamir's knowledge.

Rabin and Yitzhak Shamir toast each other as Rabin takes over the premiership in 1992.

Prime Minister Rabin confers with Israeli president Ezer Weizman, who briefly took over as chief of staff before the Six-Day War when Rabin suffered a one-day breakdown. Weizman never forgave Rabin for not supporting him as his successor.

Rabin meets with President Bill Clinton. The prime minister
had supported George Bush in the 1992 election, believing
Clinton knew little about foreign affairs and should not have
avoided duty in Vietnam. But he soon realized that Clinton
was the best friend Israel ever had in the White House.

Rabin visits Russian president Boris Yeltsin, hoping to develop trade ties.

Rabin is kissed by his granddaughter, Noa, whom he thought of as a daughter. *Courtesy of Ruth Goldmuntz*

Rabin and his son, Yuval, who became a tank commander in his father's army but refused to meet with the general while on duty. *Courtesy of Ruth Goldmuntz*

Rabin took up tennis while serving as ambassador to the United States and played almost every Saturday from then on when he was not traveling.

Rabin flanked by his friends Richard Dreyfuss and Barbra Streisand.

Rabin dines with writer Elie Weisel.

Rabin visits the troops. He loved his soldiers and felt responsible for every casualty.

Mr. Prime Minister,

The signing of the Declaration of Principles marks a new era
in the history of the Middle East. In firm conviction thereof,
I would like to confirm the following PLO commitments:

The PLO recognizes the right of the State of Israel to exist
in peace and security.

The PLO accepts United Nations Security Council Resolutions
242 and 338.

The PLO commits itself to the Middle East peace process, and
to a peaceful resolution of the conflict between the two sides
and declares that all outstanding issues relating to permanent
status will be resolved through negotiations.

The PLO considers that the signing of the Declaration of
Principles constitutes a historic event, inaugurating a new
epoch of peaceful coexistence, free from violence and all
other acts which endanger peace and stability. Accordingly,
the PLO renounces the use of terrorism and other acts of
violence and will assume responsibility over all PLO elements
and personnel in order to assure their compliance, prevent
violations and discipline violators.

In view of the promise of a new era and the signing of the
Declaration of Principles and based on Palestinian acceptance
of Security Council Resolutions 242 and 338, the PLO affirms
that those articles of the Palestinian Covenant which deny
Israel's right to exist, and the provisions of the Covenant
which are inconsistent with the commitments of this letter are
now inoperative and no longer valid. Consequently, the PLO
undertakes to submit to the Palestinian National Council for
formal approval the necessary changes in regard to the
Palestinian Covenant.

Sincerely,

Yasser Arafat
Chairman
The Palestine Liberation Organization

9 9 93

Yitzhak Rabin
Prime Minister of Israel

Palestine Liberation Organization (PLO) leader Yasir Arafat
responds to Rabin's conditions for Israeli recognition of the PLO.

September 9, 1993

Mr. Chairman,

In response to your letter of September 9, 1993, I wish to confirm to you that, in light of the PLO commitments included in your letter, the Government of Israel has decided to recognize the PLO as the representative of the Palestinian people and commence negotiations with the PLO within the Middle East peace process.

Sincerely,

Y. Rabin
Yitzhak Rabin
Prime Minister of Israel

10.9.93

Yasser Arafat
Chairman
The Palestinian Liberation Organization

Rabin agrees to recognize the PLO after agonizing over his decision.

Rabin and Yasir Arafat, prompted by President Clinton, shake hands in a momentous ceremony on September 13, 1993, signifying the success of the Oslo peace talks.

The two sides try to iron out last-minute differences at a ceremony launching Oslo 2.

Shimon Peres, Yasir Arafat, and Rabin discuss their peace plans.

Rabin and Jordan's King Hussein, who were close friends, celebrate at a ceremony honoring an Israel-Jordan peace accord.

First Lady
Hillary Rodham
Clinton, Jordan
Queen Noor
al-Hussein, and
Leah Rabin meet
at the Jordan-
Israel peace
ceremony.

Leah Rabin, surrounded by her family and friends,
mourns the death of the prime minister at his funeral.

President Clinton, with his hand covering his face, weeps at Rabin's funeral. Shimon Peres and Egyptian President Mubarak are to his right.

Young Israelis light memorial candles as they mourn the death of Rabin.

And the meeting ended. But Peres was soon talking again—telling crowds of people they should vote for Labor. He managed not to say, "despite Rabin's leadership role."

"Israel is waiting for Rabin."

This was one slogan plastered on the walls of almost every town and village as Rabin embarked on his campaign to unseat Shamir. It was a reminder of the battle cry, "Nasser is waiting for Rabin," that encouraged the Israelis to overwhelm the enemy in 1967. And with Shimon Sheves orchestrating his campaign, Rabin and his Labor troops were using the same strategy in seeking to overwhelm Likud in 1992.

In a sense, the campaign was unique, for the emphasis was not on the party now but on its leader, as if he were running in an American presidential race. Supporters shouted "Labor with Rabin," and posters with his image appeared everywhere. The party became almost insignificant amid the sea of personality propaganda.

And like the military commander he had been, Rabin now dictated orders to Chaim Asa, his campaign strategist. According to Asa, Rabin made starkly clear his demands:

"I'm telling you, and it's a command. I want a peace bloc. This is my only criterion for winning an election. If there is none, I'm going home. I want sixty-one peace mandates [a Knesset majority]."

Asa was "shocked." Rabin, he knew, figured that even with the smallest majority he could prevent the Likud from forming a coalition. But he wasn't at all sure that Rabin would win, much less win with a peace bloc alone. His calculations showed that the whole bloc might command only fifty-two to fifty-four seats.

"It's a dream," he said. "But I'll try my best."

Rabin, however, would have to capture the center as well, Asa added, and thus sharpen the contrast with Shamir's ideological rigidity. He must deny that he was the candidate of any particular wing and entice lukewarm Likudniks to vote for Labor. He should simply be "Mr. Security." But of course, he would also have to give the people hope, to stress that he would stop investing in settlement building and use the funds for education, infrastructure, and other public causes in Israel proper.

Rabin pragmatically agreed, according to Asa, and he was off on the campaign trail, leaving behind everywhere clouds of cigarette smoke, the scent of beer, which was sometimes all he had for lunch, and the feeling that this was a man who could be trusted. He promised to make peace with the Arabs within nine months and stop building "political" settlements, while strengthening the army he had built and led to victory. At the same time, when he wasn't speaking at balloon-festooned rallies, he was endlessly giving interviews to television and newspaper reporters.

"I am unwilling to give up a single inch of Israel's security," he told the *Jerusalem Post*, "but I am willing to give up many inches of settlements and territories—as well as 1,700,000 Arab inhabitants—for the sake of peace. That is the whole doctrine in a nutshell. We seek a territorial compromise which will bring peace and security. A lot of security."

The public was impressed. There was nothing wrong with giving up land if this policy brought security and a better life. Rabin was greeted by cheers even in normally Likud strongholds.

And feeding the rising Labor tide was the almost reckless behavior of Likud. Unlike Labor, it held no primaries, and so the party power structure, divorced from the people, remained the same. Shamir would again lead the party but his main competitors—Foreign Minister David Levy, Housing Minister Ariel Sharon, and Defense Minister Moshe Arens—were constantly challenging him on matters of power and policy. Levy even threatened to leave the cabinet when Shamir refused to give him certain additional responsibilities. Nor could Likud evade charges that it had mishandled the economy and the absorption of Russian immigrants, and that it was holding up the peace process it had initiated under American pressure.

With Rabin creeping ahead in the polls, the Likud sought to counter Labor's personality campaign with one of its own—not glorifying Shamir, who lacked the charisma and heroic persona for such an effort, but maligning Rabin. Had he not suffered a nervous breakdown just before the Six-Day War? In case anyone forgot, balloons floating overhead announced the "25th Anniversary of the Collapse." Though he had served as prime minister and in other government jobs in the twenty-five years since then, he was declared, as Ezer Weizman had claimed, unfit to govern.

Rabin was not only a psychiatric case, the Likud charged, but an incurable alcoholic, which presumably made him doubly unfit to govern. Did the people want a drunk giving orders in time of emergency? In fact, Rabin did enjoy drinking, but while wine, beer, or Scotch might yield a smile and induce him to view his glass as half-full, not half-empty, no one ever saw him intoxicated or in any way less intellectually nimble than he was when he abstained from alcohol.

And he was nimble indeed when he faced Shamir in a television debate, though, needing reassurance, he phoned Leah and asked her how he did.

"You were wonderful," she said.

But, she would later write, "he was still unsure he could win."

Even on election day, June 23, 1992, Rabin lacked confidence in his chances, though the polls had Labor far ahead of Likud. He was too nervous to permit even his best friends to join him and his family in his home to watch the returns as they were announced on television. What if he lost? How would he be able to face them in his misery? Who would want to drink champagne? As he sat in his library surrounded by his family amid subdued chatter that sounded more like prayer, he nervously drummed his fingers on his desk.

The time ticked on, and finally a hush. It was 10 P.M., time for a report on the exit polls. Anchorman Haim Yavin's image flashed on the screen.

"We have the exit poll results and they tell of an upheaval."

Labor was winning forty-seven Knesset seats to thirty-three for Likud. Together with the thirteen seats won by the Meretz Party, a strongly pro-peace party, Labor could control sixty seats, just short of a majority. He needed only to entice into a coalition one member of another party to form a government. Rabin had virtually achieved the dream team he had commanded his strategist, Chaim Asa, to assemble, though the actual results would give Labor and Meretz fifty-six rather than sixty seats, still guaranteeing a peace coalition.

"Pandemonium broke out in our apartment as visitors streamed in," Leah would later write, "but it was dwarfed by the roar throughout the neighborhood that was rushing in through our open windows. . . . Our eyes and ears flashed between the dramatic live coverage on television and the real-life celebration echoing all around us. It was as if the most crucial goal had been scored in the most important soccer match imaginable. . . . I was stunned and moved, crying my heart out."

But her husband was calm. The actual results were not yet in.

"Let's wait and see," Rabin said coolly, even as his family hugged and kissed him and friends continued to crowd in and choke the apartment with flowers.

It was hard to believe. If the first reports held up, he would be returning to the job he had left in disgrace fifteen years earlier. Fifteen years. How many years ago might Israel have found peace, his supporters asked, if only he had remained in power? How many young people who had fallen might be alive today?

At about 1 A.M., the results were confirmed. Rabin was prime minister. A faint smile at last. And now he and his family jubilantly went to Labor headquarters in the Dan Hotel, where he was greeted by ecstatic supporters whose cries of "Rabin! Rabin!" almost drowned out the catchy strains of the campaign jingle that filled the hall like heavenly music. When the cheers finally faded into silence, Rabin delivered a short, matter-of-fact acceptance speech, dominated by a succinct promise:

"I will lead the coalition negotiations, and I will appoint the cabinet ministers."

Applause echoed through the hall, but there was concern on many faces, especially on Peres's. No one doubted that Rabin's vow was intended to warn his rival: You'd better not try to usurp my power this time around.

During the campaign, Peres had faithfully pleaded at rallies for a Labor victory; earlier in the evening he told the crowd that there must be party unity; and now he sat listening to the man who had been "hounding" him for years, the man who now seemed to be sending him a threatening message. Yet Peres, twirling a red flower with nervous fingers, was not entirely surprised. He had tried to shake Rabin's hand before the speech, but Rabin had sneeringly ignored him. Would Rabin never forget the past?

Giora Eini, the secret mediator between the two men, noted Peres's pain and went over to him:

"Don't be hurt, Shimon," he said. "I'll ask Yitzhak what he meant."

When he asked Rabin this question, the new prime minister angrily replied: "Someone" had told him that Peres had uttered some unkind words about him. Peres, he felt, still hoped to drive him out of office. And clearly, he hoped to avoid the need to appoint Peres his foreign minister, as he had reluctantly done on becoming prime minister the first time.

Eini returned to Peres and told him what Rabin charged, and Peres denied he had made the alleged statement. Later that night, Eini went to see Rabin at home.

There had simply been a misunderstanding, Eini argued, and Rabin, after some hesitation, agreed this was possible.

Who was the "someone" who had reported to him that Peres had made the critical remarks? It is not clear, but Peres would tell me that the "people around Yitzhak," apparently referring to Sheves and Haber, were constantly seeking to turn their boss against him.

A few days after the election, Eini visited Peres and found him distraught.

He would accompany him to Rabin's apartment, Eini said, and the two rivals could discuss his appointment as foreign minister, since it was evident that without Peres and his supporters, Rabin could not form a government.

But Peres was reluctant to go. How could he visit the home of a man who had snubbed him?

"I could feel the tension," Eini told me. "Peres wasn't sure Rabin would offer him the job. . . . Maybe he didn't want to be in his government."

Eini finally persuaded Peres to go, however, and the pair walked to Rabin's abode, where Rabin finally reached out his hand. After a terse conversation, Rabin agreed to name Peres his foreign minister. And the tension broke.

Peres was almost seventy, a few months younger than Rabin. He had accomplished much in his life, and had been prime minister himself. And now he was tired, terribly tired. So he wouldn't be number one. Perhaps two old men together could make the peace they both so yearned for.

25

"Enough of Blood and Tears"

"**N**o longer is it true that the whole world is against us. We must overcome the sense of isolation that has held us in its thrall for almost half a century. We must join the international movement toward peace, reconciliation, and cooperation that is spreading over the entire globe these days—lest we be the last to remain, all alone, in the station."

The words reverberated powerfully through the Knesset on July 13, 1992, as its members, either elated or deeply concerned, listened to Rabin stress the central aim of his second premiership. He was finally in a position to seek a final peace with Israel's neighbors, no longer inhibited, as he had been in his earlier term, by a relatively weak military machine and unrelenting Arab hostility. And now the Knesset approved his cabinet.

Keeping the defense ministry for himself, Rabin had the peace government he wanted: Labor; the ultra-dovish, anticlerical Meretz; and the Orthodox but pragmatic Shas formed a mosaic of sixty-one seats to give Rabin a Knesset majority. In addition, the five Arab Knesset deputies would support him. Rabin had offered a cabinet post to Rafael Eitan, head of the rightist Tsomet, hoping to strengthen his government, but Eitan had declined to serve as a token cabinet dissenter.

And so did leaders of the ultra-religious United Torah Judaism Front, especially after Rabin chose Shulamit Aloni, the staunchly anticlerical leader of Meretz, as minister of education. She was anathema to them. They compared her appointment to the destruction of the million and a half Jewish children slaughtered in the Holocaust.

An outrage! Rabin exclaimed. Aloni stays! He could get along without religious extremists. In the end, he felt, they would simply cause him trouble.

Finally, Rabin needed only a minister of environment and turned to dovish Yossi Sarid, who had supported him for prime minister in 1974 but had since turned against him for his perceived hawkish views.

"What are you going to do to promote peace?" he asked, expecting Rabin to utter an evasive generalization.

"I am going to negotiate with the PLO," Rabin replied.

Sarid could hardly believe what he heard. This was apparently the first time Rabin abandoned his ambiguity and made this flat statement to anyone. Sarid not only joined the cabinet, but would become closer to the prime minister than any other member.

Rabin failed, however, to prevent the Knesset from selecting his old foe, Ezer Weizman, as president, and though he would be merely a figurehead, Rabin would now have to confer with him on policy despite his contempt for the man.

"How can I go to him on government decisions?" he asked friends.

But the two men forced themselves to have a civil relationship; Rabin wanted to prove, according to his ghostwriter, Dov Goldstein, "that his personal relations had nothing to do with politics."

With the cabinet complete, Eitan Haber drafted a blueprint of peace that seemed almost revolutionary by past standards. Both Rabins contributed their ideas, and the final draft asked the Israelis to shed their Masada complex and break out of their overprotective shell, to take risks that they had always seen as suicidal. The Arabs were admonished as well: Seize the moment!

"I am prepared to travel to Amman, Damascus, and Beirut today or tomorrow," Rabin told the Knesset. "For there is no greater victory than the victory of peace."

In a special message to the Palestinians, he pleaded with barely suppressed passion:

> We have been fated to live together on the same patch of land, in the same country. We lead our lives with you, beside you, and against you. You have failed in the war against us. One hundred years of your bloodshed and terror against us have brought you only suffering, humiliation, bereavement, and pain. You have lost thousands of your sons and daughters, and you are losing ground all the time.

> For 44 years now, you have been living under a delusion. Your leaders have led you through lies and deceit. They have missed every opportunity, rejected all our proposals for a settlement, and taken you from one tragedy to another. . . . You have never known a single day of freedom and joy in your lives. Listen to us, if only this once.

> We offer you the fairest and most viable proposal from our standpoint today—autonomy, with all its advantages and limitations. You will not get everything you want. Neither will we. So, once and for all, take your destiny in your hands. Don't lose this opportunity that may never return. Take our proposal seriously—to avoid further suffering, humiliation, and grief; to end the shedding of tears and of blood.

Amid the applause, Yitzhak Shamir's monotone voice cried:

"What we have heard today mostly resembles a nihilistic philosophy which will cost us dearly in the long run."

Shamir had not congratulated Rabin after the election, but on July 14, as Rabin took over his office, the outgoing prime minister expressed the hope that Defense Minister Rabin would influence Prime Minister Rabin not to make "too many unilateral excesses."

Shamir would make it clear to a reporter what he meant: Don't give up any land.

"I would have conducted negotiations on autonomy for ten years," he was quoted as saying, "and in the meantime we would have reached half a million people in Judea and Samaria [the West Bank]."

Though Shamir, after being charged with deception, claimed

he had been misquoted, few people believed him. Certainly not Yasir Arafat, who would jubilantly tell the press:

"Israelis have voted against the terrorism exercised by Yitzhak Shamir against the women and children of the Palestinian people. By making this choice, the Israeli people are pushing their government to act in the direction of peace."

President Bush was just as pleased. Come visit me at my summer home at Kennebunkport, Maine, he addressed Rabin. Meanwhile, he would send James Baker to the region to help infuse new life into the peace process.

Rabin was delighted, for relations with the United States, frozen under Shamir, would now heat up again. And this would mean weapon guarantees to reinforce any agreement; loan guarantees to help absorb the new immigrants and build the strong economy that was as essential as guns for Israel's long-term security; and American mediation that could make peace possible. He would now be dealing with his friend Jim Baker openly, not clandestinely as he had under the Shamir government.

Thus, in his first days in office, Rabin felt a current of optimism, which he shared with the public. The economy, stimulated by U.S. aid, would soon flourish with new jobs, and peace—real peace this time—seemed within reach. Peace with security; Rabin the "hawk" would see to that—even if his cabinet was a flock of doves.

Strengthening Rabin's resolve to achieve a peace that would finally end the shedding of Jewish blood was a trip he made to Auschwitz in April 1993. He took his granddaughter Noa with him, hoping she would leave the death camp with a feeling of triumph over the forces of hate, who, with all their gas chambers, were unable to exterminate the Jewish spirit that had spawned the Israel he now led. Accompanying them were survivors of the camp, guerrilla heroes, and successful people in many fields to further stress the point.

After observing the gas chambers and other installations of death and horror, the grandfather, it seemed, was as overwhelmed and traumatized as the granddaughter. Perhaps even more so than he was when he visited Bergen-Belsen in 1976 during his first premiership. There, uncharacteristically overcome by emotion, he had stumbled while reciting kaddish, the prayer for the dead, though the Holocaust, according to his aide Yehuda Avner, was never really an emotional component for him or for other native-born Israelis (sabras). But if the Holocaust was not deeply rooted in his psyche, now at Auschwitz it touched his soul once again.

"He suddenly changed," an IDF officer in the party told me. "He seldom expressed emotion, but now he looked as if he were carrying two tons of the weight of history on his shoulder. I could feel his trauma in the way he hugged and kissed Noa everywhere we went."

Yes, Noa was the symbol of the ultimate victory—the rebirth of her people. And they must live in peace.

So obsessed was Rabin with this objective that he neglected virtually all other aspects of government, leaving them largely to his ministers. He wanted to focus on strategic decisions, not on political ones. Aides Sheves and Asa failed to convince him that the prime minister's office should be strengthened rather than weakened. It had virtually no budget and did not implement policy but simply oversaw ministry activities without exercising real power. Only the prime minister himself had such power, and not everything could be referred to him.

At the same time, Asa drew up a plan for improving the educational system and using business as a tool for creating jobs, arguing that such projects directed from his office would make people trust the government enough to accept the sacrifices needed for peace. But Rabin was impatient; he didn't have time to deal with organizational reform or long-term projects. He wanted peace now. He even impeded the renovation of his office; what was wrong with its stained carpets, dark gray tiles, and doors needing paint? Why waste money? Why this frivolous distraction from what was really important—his peace effort?

The prime minister soon had the opportunity to show what a hawkish dove could do. Israeli soldiers surrounded An-Najah University in Nablus during student elections and demanded that the students leave the campus so the troops could enter and ferret out several terrorists thought to be lurking inside. When the students refused and the troops were poised to storm the university, Rabin acted quickly. He called the American consul in Jerusalem, and shortly the consul relayed Rabin's message to Faisal Husseini, the local Palestinian leader. Husseini told me:

"Rabin said he knew the crisis was not my fault or his, but the fault of the previous government. So we should solve the problem together."

They did. In a compromise arrangement, the terrorists were sent to Jordan and the troops were withdrawn. Thus, hardly had Rabin taken office when he diffused an explosive situation and set the tone for future relations between the two peoples.

The Palestinians were also impressed when, despite threats of violence by the settlers, Rabin ordered his housing minister, Binyamin Ben-Eliezer, to halt construction of new settlements in the territories.

And no less impressed was James Baker when he landed in Israel on July 19, 1992, and, he would later quip, "wasn't greeted by the opening of a new settlement," as he had been when Shamir was prime minister. Rabin welcomed him like an old friend and reported that he had already frozen contracts to build 7,000 new housing units in the territories and intended to cancel them. And he was also eliminating incentives and subsidies that had enticed people to settle there.

"For the sake of 3.9 million Israeli Jews and a million Israeli Arabs who should not have to mortgage their future because of the 100,000 settlers in the territories," Rabin told Baker, "I intend to persevere."

But Rabin thought that Baker, whose stern face, like his own, seldom reflected emotion, seemed skeptical. Somewhat hurt, Rabin approached Dennis Ross, the U.S. Special Middle East Coordinator, and lamented:

"Dennis, the secretary is treating me as if I'm the last Yitzhak [Shamir]. Tell him there is a different Yitzhak now."

Ross delivered the message to Baker, who, in fact, needed little convincing—especially after Rabin told him in a manner that the secretary found "poignant":

"We will do what we say and we will not lie to you."

Baker would write Bush on July 21: "I have just visited a different Israel. The mood is different and the atmosphere is one of hope. Rabin was open, direct, and very clear about his objectives. He is reordering Israel's priorities away from the territories and toward revitalizing Israel's economy."

Bush would confirm this appraisal on August 10 when Rabin and Leah flew into Kennebunkport, and the President and prime minister negotiated a settlement agreement until 4 o'clock the next morning. Rabin distinguished between strategic settlements, which could be "thickened" if necessary, and "political" settlements, which would be "frozen."

"We're reordering our priorities," Rabin asserted. No new settlements. No more expropriation of Arab lands. But of 16,500 housing units already being built, he could cancel only 6,500 because of legal obligations undertaken by the previous government. Still, any new money spent on settlements would be deducted against the loan guarantees. And on October 5, Congress approved $10 billion in these guarantees, sealing the new relationship between the two countries.

Now that Israel's needs had been met, however, many Israelis began questioning these ties. Like spoiled children, they could afford now to assert their independence from their patronizing elders. The newspaper *Ma'ariv*, noting the coming election in the United States, would editorialize:

"Bush's granting of the guarantees is purely a coldly calculated move to obtain Jewish votes and money. The next time Rabin comes to the U.S., Bush will be the president of a Texas university and Clinton will be in power. Rabin ought to heed this."

While on his trip to the United States, Rabin managed to upset another Jewish community as well—the American Jews. Meeting with leaders of AIPAC, the Jewish lobby group, he ripped into them for dealing with U.S. government officials without coordinating their efforts with the Israeli embassy. They had "antagonized" these officials, especially with their loan guarantee demands, and "did not manage to bring Israel one single cent."

Actually, it seems, Rabin suspected that AIPAC was still being influenced by the policies of the previous Likud government, and wasn't sure it fully supported his own.

"Rabin made it clear that AIPAC should 'butt out,'" one American Jewish activist told me. "That he didn't need them as a go-between with the U.S. He sent shock waves through the Jewish community."

At the urging of his aides, Rabin later said his remarks had been taken out of context and that, of course, he appreciated AIPAC's contribution to Israel's cause. But few doubted that he meant what he said the first time. He didn't quite trust AIPAC. Had it not supported Shamir when he was prime minister? The new prime minister wanted peace, and he had to be sure that American leaders knew it.

Even many Arab leaders knew it by now. Only a few days after taking office, Rabin visited President Mubarak in Egypt to mend fences that had all but collapsed under the Shamir regime. In fact, the Likud had virtually dismissed the Egyptian leader as a useful instrument in promoting a peace process. Yossi Ben-Aharon, the director-general of Shamir's office, had warned Rabin that Mubarak was a "leader without assets."

Now Rabin would reverse Israel's Egyptian policy. Israel, he understood, lived in a strategic environment, and it was geopolitically essential for him to work with the most powerful Arab country to achieve regional peace. As defense minister in the Shamir government, he had, in fact, dealt secretly with Mubarak as a go-between with the PLO and depended on him to help smooth the way toward peace. After meeting for almost two hours in the presidential palace in Cairo, the two men, sitting together on a sofa, met the press and praised each other's efforts to achieve this goal.

"It's a good step on the right track," Mubarak said of Rabin's plan to freeze settlements. "I know that [Mr. Rabin] generally supports peace."

"Egypt was in the spearhead of breaking historic walls and bringing a peace treaty between an Arab country and Israel," Rabin remarked, emphasizing the vital role that the country could again play in breaking down walls.

But the essence of this meeting between the two leaders lay in the feeling generated by their personal chemistry that the Middle East was poised on the edge of a new era. Here were two generals who had ordered the killing of each other's soldiers, who had seen the horrors of massacre, seeking together to make amends to those who lay buried in the sands of this inflammable region.

The question was, how could the amends be made? Since the Madrid peace conference, Israeli representatives had been meeting sporadically in Washington for peace talks with their Syrian,

Lebanese, Jordanian, and Palestinian counterparts. But while everybody talked, no one listened. The Syrians demanded an advance pledge that Israel would give them back all of the Golan Heights. The Lebanese would not dare undercut the Syrians. The Jordanians would not dare reach an accord before the Palestinians did. And the Palestinians would not budge without a go-ahead from the PLO leaders in Tunis.

Rabin told me some months before he became prime minister that he wished to fashion an autonomy agreement with the Palestinians first, for Jordan would quickly fall into line. He would then tackle Syria, the toughest nut of all. But Secretary Baker would convince him during his trip to Israel in July 1992 that he should give Syria priority. Baker told him that President Assad had assured Baker he was prepared to negotiate a final peace—provided Israel agreed to withdraw from the Golan Heights.

Rabin was hesitant, but the peace talks with the Palestinians in Washington were stalled, since they were referring all matters to Arafat. And he did have a certain respect for Assad, despite his ruthlessness, since the man had never violated previous agreements with Israel and was a stickler for details, as Rabin himself was. He therefore dangled pieces of the Golan Heights before the Syrian leader, but was offered little in return.

Rabin thus switched his focus back to the Palestinians, though he led the United States—which considered the Palestinian track almost hopeless—to believe that he was still giving Syria priority. No one had taken Rabin seriously when he promised in the election campaign to sign a peace accord with local Palestinian leaders within nine months, but this was still his intention.

If only he could woo them away from Yasir Arafat.

A deal with Arafat?

A deal could be made, Peres assured Rabin when they met on February 9, 1993. And he pulled out a draft of peace proposals drawn up by unofficial representatives of Israel and the PLO in Oslo.

Peres knew he was treading on shaky ground. For one thing, he wasn't supposed to be involved in bilateral peace talks with any Arab group. Rabin had reserved that job for himself, limiting Peres's role to mediating in multilateral talks about economic matters, the environment, the sharing of water, and other nonpolitical issues. Was Peres once more trying to usurp his powers, as Rabin had feared? Peres tried to convince him that he had just learned about the talks himself, and that he was seeking peace, not power.

Regardless, Rabin was not greatly surprised by the Oslo peace initiative that he suspected Peres had engineered. In fact, the prime minister's security forces had apparently penetrated Abu Mazen's office and had tapes that suggested there might be secret talks, however inconsequential. Furthermore, shortly after Rabin took office, Abu Mazen told me, he sent a letter to the new prime minister asking many questions, and Rabin answered all of them. The most important one concerned Rabin's attitude toward the future of Jerusalem, and Rabin replied that "'the Palestinians don't understand politics. They start with the hardest questions.' I was happy with this answer."

For the first time, it seemed to him, an Israeli leader had indicated that the future of Jerusalem was negotiable, that it was perhaps possible for the PLO to secure a foothold in the city. Thus, before the Oslo talks, Abu Mazen wrote Rabin again asking him if he would agree to establish a "back channel" for secret peace talks.

No, Rabin replied, he feared the Palestinians would leak such contacts after "one hour to one hundred people."

The prime minister, Abu Mazen realized, still hoped that the talks in Washington with Palestinians not directly linked to the PLO would succeed. But in view of Rabin's moderate answers to his questions, he felt that the prime minister would agree at a politically opportune moment.

Was the moment now opportune? Rabin asked himself. Shimon Sheves, as well as Yossi Ginosar, who had been in constant communication with PLO officials, were urging him to talk with Arafat, though Eitan Haber advised against it. Still, Rabin could not erase from his mind the vision of Israelis killed and maimed in Arafat's terrorist attacks. And as usual, he was cautious. A negative public reaction to official talks could kill the peace process. Perhaps it would be possible, he even suggested to Peres, to deal with the PLO without Arafat—though he apparently knew this was wishful thinking.

Impossible, Peres asserted. The Washington talks were fruitless because all questions were bounced back to Arafat. It was necessary to support him, because if he lost power Hamas would step in to fill the vacuum. Meanwhile, without their knowledge, Arafat would use the negotiators in Washington as a cover for his own secret role in Oslo.

Rabin was undecided as he perused the papers Peres had given him. Should he approve the secret talks? Could they by some miracle succeed?

Actually, there was no well-laid plan. It was more like serendipity, with a series of chance contacts between Israelis and Norwegians. One of the Norwegians was Terje Larsen, who directed a research organization called FAFO. While researching socioeconomic conditions in the territories in summer 1992, Larsen met Yossi Beilin, who would shortly become Foreign Minister Peres's deputy. In September, Norwegian Deputy Foreign Minister Jan Egeland visited Israel to inspect the FAFO project, and Larsen introduced him to Beilin.

Norway, Egeland told Beilin, would be glad to arrange a back channel between Israel and the PLO.

Egeland's offer was not the first Norwegian attempt at such mediation. Norway had had warm relations with both antagonists for some years. In the 1970s, its Labor government had knotted ties with the Israeli Labor Party through the Socialist International, and in 1982, Norwegian troops negotiated with the PLO as well as with Israel when they were sent to southern Lebanon to serve in a UN peacekeeping force.

In the early 1980s, Norwegian Foreign Minister Thorvald Stoltenberg had tried to arrange a meeting between the Israelis and a PLO representative, but the plan went awry when Palestinian extremists assassinated the PLO official. Now another Norwegian leader was trying to crack the ice.

But Beilin hesitated. Yes, he and some followers in the Knesset had been meeting with local Palestinian leaders, including Faisal Husseini and Hanan Ashrawi, and had been in indirect contact with the PLO since early 1989. But what if the public learned he was dealing directly with the PLO in violation of Israeli law? It would put the government up against the wall.

Nevertheless, Beilin decided, he would test the PLO temperature—unofficially. No one from the government could be involved, he told Egeland. But he knew two Israeli Middle East experts who shared his views and could play a role in back-channel talks—Professor Ya'ir Hirschfeld of Haifa University and Professor Ron Pundak of Hebrew University.

Larsen followed up. When Hirschfeld went to London in December 1992 to join the multilateral talks that were being held there, Larsen encouraged him to see Abu Ala, the PLO's "finance minister" who headed the PLO delegation and strongly supported peace with Israel. Hirschfeld and Abu Ala struck up a friendship and agreed to attend a seminar on human resources on January 20, 1993—deliberately one day after the Knesset was to lift the ban on contacts with the PLO—in the small town of Sarpsborg, south of Oslo. Larsen's FAFO would sponsor the seminar, which was actually a cover for peace talks.

Five men showed up for the conference—Hirschfeld, Pundak, Abu Ala, and two other Palestinians—and after two days managed to hammer out a proposed program for peace:

1. The Israelis would withdraw from the Gaza Strip within two or three years and the area would become a trusteeship under Egypt or the United Nations for a limited time. The two sides would meanwhile negotiate an autonomy plan for the West Bank.

2. The big industrial powers would draw up a plan for massive investment for the West Bank and Gaza.

3. Israel would cooperate in helping to build up the territories economically.

4. A declaration of principles on how to achieve peace would be announced and the Palestinians would assume autonomous powers on signing the agreement.

When the Israelis returned home, they submitted the so-called Sarpsborg document to Beilin, and he showed it to Peres, who until now had known nothing about the meetings in London and Oslo. Until they succeeded, Beilin didn't want to place Peres in the awkward position of having to confer with Rabin, who might have forbidden the talks for fear of political fallout. But with the draft a fait accompli, it was time to tell him.

Peres's eyes shown with delight as he perused the plan—an actual plan for peace with the PLO! He rejected out-of-hand the call for a trusteeship since it implied preparation for statehood. But the document could be, he felt, the kernel of a peace agreement.

"I've got to show this to Yitzhak," he said, uncertain how his old rival would react to negotiations he had not sanctioned.

And so Peres went to Rabin and showed him the plan, not daring to guess his reaction as the prime minister read it, his expression inscrutable. . . .

Well, Yitzhak?

Unacceptable.

But the talks could lead to something, Peres repeated.

Rabin pondered the logic once again. They could actually lead, if successful, to a peace treaty with Jordan, which he had sought for so long. King Hussein would no longer have to fear being charged with treason by fellow Arab leaders. And he remembered the rockets that had exploded in Israel during the Persian Gulf War. What if they had been armed with nuclear warheads? Should any chance for peace, however remote, be rejected?

Very well, he finally said. Continue the talks, though it was doubtful they would succeed.

Peres felt enormous relief. Was this the beginning of a new Middle East? His greater enthusiasm reflected the vast difference in the intellectual approach of the two men. The foreign minister grasped a principle and focused on it, while glossing over the details. But Rabin broke down the principle into minutiae and might reject the whole if a single detail was imperfect.

Meanwhile, that same month, Rabin flew to Washington on a vital mission—to reach a new strategic understanding with the new President, Bill Clinton. Martin Indyk, the U.S. ambassador to Israel, would explain:

"Rabin understood that the strategic environment had changed quite dramatically, and now the United States was the only superpower left in the world, and as a result of the end of the Cold War, Israel's Arab adversaries no longer had a superpower patron. And as a result of the Gulf War, Israel's Arab adversaries no longer had the potential for putting together an eastern front coalition against Israel. So there were now unique and new strategic circumstances which provided Yitzhak Rabin with the opportunity to make peace."

Visiting the Oval Office, Rabin told the President: "I have a mandate to take calculated risks for peace. I have been a warrior, a general for too long. I have seen too much bloodshed. It is time now to make peace."

"If you're going to do that," Clinton replied, "my role, the role of the United States, is not to tell you how to do it, or when to do it—my role is to minimize those risks."

And at that meeting a new strategic partnership was formed— one that was no longer, as in the Cold War period, in the defense of freedom, but in the pursuit of peace. The question now was, how was peace to be achieved?

At the suggestion of the Americans, Rabin agreed to bring Faisal Husseini, the most important local Palestinian leader, into the Washington talks, even though Shamir had kept him out because he resided in Jerusalem. But Rabin was pessimistic.

He had watched how Arafat had gained control of the Palestinian delegation, he said, and he didn't believe any longer that an independent local delegation could make peace.

Samuel Lewis, the ex-ambassador to Israel who now headed policy planning at the State Department, asked: "Well then, why don't you deal with Yasir Arafat?"

"Because," Rabin replied, somewhat taken aback, "I can't meet his requirements. His requirements are for an independent Palestinian state. His requirements are for Jerusalem as its capital, and I can't meet those requirements."

But the question, put by an American official and coming after Peres's plea, apparently did give Rabin pause. Politics, after all, was the art of the possible. And he had never ruled out an eventual deal with the PLO.

One important achievement on this trip was the start of a warm personal friendship between Rabin and Clinton that Rabin had not anticipated. He had hoped Bush would be reelected, for he was more in the mold of a man Rabin felt comfortable with—a military hero and intelligence expert who understood international affairs. Clinton, by contrast, knew little about the world, Rabin felt, and he had dodged the Vietnam draft. Rabin was not a general who sought the company of "draft-dodgers."

But on this trip Rabin found that Clinton was in fact very knowledgeable about world problems, especially those of Israel.

And Rabin appreciated his warmth and charm—which were especially evident at a White House dinner one evening when the President addressed Elyakim Rubinstein, a U.S. representative in the Washington peace talks:

"I heard you have a great sense of humor. Let both of us tell jokes and we'll see who's funnier."

The two men then recited their gems, and Rubinstein, one dinner guest told me, soon had the President "practically under the table."

"This is the first time anyone ever beat me," Clinton conceded.

And this was the first time many of the guests saw Rabin shake with laughter.

A most enjoyable evening—with a President who would help him realize his dream.

The unofficial Israeli and PLO teams, hoping to hammer out a declaration of principles, met again in February, March, and April, though the PLO delegation in Washington, which was not told of Oslo, walked out after Rabin deported four hundred Hamas members to Lebanon as punishment for a terrorist episode. The delegates, however, returned to the negotiating table—in dismay—after Arafat ordered them to, without telling them they were being used to cover up the real peace talks.

In mid-April, Rabin met with President Mubarak in Ismailia and learned something of Arafat's immediate ambitions. The Egyptian leader showed Rabin a map that Arafat had given him; Gaza and Jericho were circled. The PLO head wanted it made clear that "Gaza first" did not mean "Gaza only."

No, Israel would not give up Jericho, Rabin snapped. It was in a security zone close to the strategic Jordan Valley.

With PLO leaders now urging Israel to send officials to Oslo with the authority to make decisions, Peres asked Rabin for permission to go himself. But Rabin refused, since, he said, this would commit the cabinet to decisions even though it knew nothing about the talks. Peres then sent Uri Savir, the brilliant, forty-year-old director general of the foreign ministry, to Oslo, followed by Yoel Singer, a tough-minded attorney based in Washington who had close links with Rabin from his days as a colonel in the IDF.

"I want to hear from you that the PLO offer is real," Rabin told Singer, his skepticism still intact.

Singer, who was as obsessed with detail as Rabin, also had strong doubts after reading the Sarpsborg document, which he told me was "fuzzy" and "half-baked."

But the Palestinians knew now that Israel's willingness to consider their offer was real. For Rabin had made the talks "official." There was a surge of activity now, with Terje Larsen and Johan Jorgen Holst, the new Norwegian foreign minister, tossing ideas to the negotiators and shuttling between Oslo and Israel with messages and reports.

The Israelis were so afraid someone might suspect the peace plot that Peres would almost always meet at Rabin's home, furtively entering by the back door. And he avoided any contact with Larsen—until the Norwegian, on a visit to see a lesser official in the foreign ministry, approached the men's room as Peres was leaving it. Someone in the hall introduced them and Peres, in embarrassed silence, shook hands with Larsen, then raced off. At least he could deny that he had ever spoken with the visitor.

Actually, it appeared, there might not be a need to do so. As Abu Mazen would tell PLO officials in Tunis:

"This is the critical moment. When the Israelis hear what Singer has to say, they will either break negotiations or go on to conclude an agreement. If they come back to us after this session we will go right to the end. If not we'll just have to forget it."

They wouldn't have to forget it. Singer presented the Palestinians with more than two hundred questions, and from the answers extracted over two days, he concluded they were indeed serious. Now Rabin, for the first time, realized that the Oslo talks might just possibly yield peace.

At the same time, Yasir Arafat now began to reach the same conclusion, recognizing that the precise, detailed questions asked by Singer flowed from the computerlike mind of Rabin. And indeed, Rabin still had questions he wanted answered.

Ahmad Tibi, a gynecologist in East Jerusalem, was puzzled when his friend Histadrut leader Chaim Ramon asked him one day in early July 1993 to see Yasir Arafat in Tunis. Ramon, a close ally of Rabin, handed Tibi a list of the toughest questions the prime minister wanted Arafat to answer, concerning settlements, Arab refugees, and the future of Jerusalem.

Were Rabin and Arafat conducting secret talks? Tibi had never heard of any, and Ramon apparently hadn't either. But clearly something was going on.

Yes, of course he would deliver the message, replied Tibi, who knew Arafat well.

Shortly, on July 17, Tibi was seated in Arafat's office watching curiously as his host perused the message with a sour expression. Arafat suddenly asked:

"Ahmad, Rabin has offered to give me Gaza, but do you think he would give me Jericho, too?"

Arafat feared that a Gaza-only solution would give his people the impression that they wouldn't get the West Bank, or most of it.

Tibi, who claims he didn't even know about Gaza, now realized that secret talks were indeed going on. But he acted as if he were in on the secret, replying:

"It is possible. Let me check."

"Go now and talk with Abu Mazen," Arafat said. "He'll answer these questions."

Abu Mazen, Arafat's most trusted lieutenant, glanced at the questions and said he would have answers the following day. And when Tibi returned, Abu Mazen handed him the answers, all positive. Arafat had apparently been hesitant, but Abu Mazen convinced him to agree to a two-phased solution to peace, with all the subjects broached by Rabin to be discussed in the delayed final phase.

"Ahmad," Abu Mazen said, "go back to Rabin and tell him we won't agree to any changes in this. This is final. And tell him that if no progress is made in the talks, I shall resign my position."

Abu Mazen knew that the Israelis were aware he was a key figure in the Oslo talks, and that without him Oslo might collapse, threatening the Rabin government.

As Tibi departed, Arafat said: "God bless you."

His visitor then rushed back to Israel and met with Ramon, and shortly was told that Rabin was satisfied with the answers. The prime minister regarded it as a "breakthrough," and, despite earlier objections, even agreed to appease Arafat with Jericho. Passing the news on to Tunis, Tibi was thrilled by his role as a messenger of peace. He had been blessed indeed by God. And Abu Mazen, who had been born in Safed, Israel, would tell his sons and grandchildren that Safed was "no longer our city. Our home is in Ramallah."

After days of sometimes bitter haggling over every detail, the Israeli negotiators sent Rabin and Peres several peace alternatives. One called for Gaza and Jericho—as Arafat wished—to become the building blocks of an autonomous Palestinian interim authority, with the IDF remaining in some parts of the Gaza Strip to protect Jewish settlements there. This Gaza-Jericho formula became the basic structure of the proposed declaration of principles, though Rabin insisted that Israel alone must decide how troops would be deployed in any of the territories. He threatened at one point to call off the talks over the security issue, but Peres's pleading and Tibi's report on his trip to Tunis finally pacified him.

In fact, both sides were now so committed to an agreement that even as missiles flew between Moslem guerrillas and Israeli troops in southern Lebanon, negotiators bickered over every detail of peace. With the talks in Washington at an impasse, Rabin now knew that the local Palestinians were powerless to make peace. Arafat was his only option.

Arafat, however, wasn't so sure he was; for he knew that the United States was pressing Rabin to make a deal with Syria first. And if Rabin agreed, the present talks could collapse or prove too costly. For Arafat, Rabin was his only option.

Rabin was adamant. The accord must be reached during Peres's official tour of the Scandinavian countries. Peres concurred and flew to Sweden on the first leg of his journey. Arriving on the morning of August 17, 1993, he telephoned Terje Larsen in Norway and said:

"You must bring the foreign minister to Stockholm tonight."

He wanted "to wrap it up now," while he was in Scandinavia.

Rabin and Peres were in a hurry, fearing that they "may end up with a peace treaty but no government to sign it." The Israeli Supreme Court had ruled that a member of Rabin's cabinet accused of financial wrongdoing must give up his cabinet seat and the government might shortly fall. Rabin was also worried that the negotiations would be leaked before they were concluded, and a public uproar could preclude any accord. What a tragedy if this happened when Israel was on the verge of signing this historic agreement.

"This was the only time Rabin made a decision in an incautious way," Chaim Asa, his security aide, told me. "I warned him that Hamas terrorism might greatly increase if an agreement was reached and turn the people against it. But he was ready to gamble, though this wasn't his style. He understood that time was working against him and wanted to take advantage of this small window of opportunity. With this decision, Oslo became the project of his life and he neglected everything else and let nothing stand in his way."

After Terje Larsen told Swedish officials that Foreign Minister Holst had to see Peres on some urgent trade matter, the two Norwegians flew to Stockholm. They were soon at the Haga Palace, where Peres was staying, and were greeted by their Israeli friend.

At 1 A.M., Larsen was on the phone with Abu Ala. "I've got the two fathers here with me, he said, referring to the two foreign ministers. "My father wants to talk to you."

Holst took the phone and read the paragraphs that Peres wanted changed.

Abu Ala said he was "with my father [Arafat], and we need ninety minutes alone together before we get back to you."

After five more calls, the last at 4:20 A.M., agreement was finally reached. It called for:

- The withdrawal of Israeli troops from Gaza and Jericho by April 1994.
- Israeli-Palestinian economic cooperation.
- Regional economic development.
- Elections in the territories for a Palestinian executive council in July 1994, with East Jerusalem Arabs allowed to vote.
- Council responsibility for all government functions except defense and foreign affairs, while settlements would be under Israeli control.
- Negotiations on the final status of the territories involving Jerusalem, the settlements, water distribution, and final borders to begin by the end of 1995 and to continue for five years.

- Further negotiations for implementing the
  Declaration of Principles to be concluded
  before the end of 1993.

After the last phone conversation, Peres would say, "The excitement in Arafat's office was discernible over the line. When the last point was declared settled, we could hear them cheering and weeping, and we knew that they were hugging one another. . . . How strange it is, I found myself thinking, that we Israelis are now the ones granting the Palestinians what the British granted us more than seventy years ago, a 'homeland in Palestine,' in the words of the Balfour Declaration of November 1917."

"Hey, I'm from a kibbutz! You mustn't serve me."

Peres was admonishing Secretary of State Warren Christopher, who kept pouring drinks for the Israeli and Norwegian peace delegates; they had flown into Point Mugu, a naval base in California where the secretary was vacationing. Everyone, it seemed, needed a few drinks—especially Christopher and Dennis Ross, his Middle East adviser. They could hardly believe it. A deal with the PLO?

The Israelis and Norwegians had occasionally mentioned to U.S. officials that the Oslo talks were taking place.

Great! the Americans replied. Keep us posted.

But they never took the contacts seriously. And they were still hoping that the sterile talks in Washington would miraculously turn fertile and bear fruit. And Rabin, well aware of Washington's desire for Syria-first negotiations, told Peres:

"We don't want the Americans involved at this stage, as the talks are going well with the Norwegians. If they don't call, don't say anything."

They didn't call.

But now, to assure American support for the agreement, Peres suggested that the United States "adopt" it as its own initiative and submit it to the delegates in the Washington talks. Christopher recoiled at the suggestion:

"No, we can't do that because the truth is bound to surface and that would damage everything."

Peres then summarized the results of the Oslo talks as Christopher and Ross listened, mesmerized. When Peres had finished, the secretary asked Ross:

"Dennis, what do you think?"

"I think it's great," Ross replied.

Christopher remarked to his guests: "I'd like to thank you for what you've done. You have changed the world."

Hardly had the secretary uttered this remark when the world learned that it had changed. Someone had leaked the news to the press. Peres and the other guests learned this when frantic phone calls from Jerusalem disturbed their peace as they relaxed at a beach bar.

The Israeli public was stunned. Arafat the terrorist was now Israel's peace partner! Among the shocked were the Israeli military leaders, who had always been consulted before security policies were determined. Why was this necessary? Rabin asked. Wasn't he a military man himself? He was sorry that some were unhappy, but he knew best.

Most shocked of all were the Israeli and Palestinian delegates to the Washington peace talks—who for months had been unwittingly engaged in sham debate while the real negotiations were taking place under Norwegian skies. One of the Israelis feeling betrayed was Elyakim Rubinstein, who had been talking with the Palestinians since the Madrid conference.

"I didn't hear about the Oslo channel until the agreement had been cooked," Rubinstein told me. "Rabin called me in and said, 'Look, here's the text.' I read it and found that the agreement called for fulfillment of only about 60 percent of what we were demanding in Washington. I was angry, but he apologized for not confiding in me, and I was going to leave Washington, but Yitzhak finally persuaded me to continue talking with the Jordanian negotiators."

On the Palestinian side, Faisal Husseini and Hanan Ashrawi were even angrier when they learned of Oslo in Abu Mazen's office in Tunis. Her first reaction, Ashrawi would say, was one of dismay.

"It's clear," she told Abu Mazen, "that the ones who initialed this agreement have not lived under occupation. You postponed the settlement issue and Jerusalem without even getting guarantees that Israel would not continue to create facts on the ground that would preempt and prejudge the final outcome. And what about human rights? . . . And the transfer of authority is purely functional. . . . "

But finally accepting the fait accompli, Ashrawi groaned: "It's too late now; let's see what we can do with what you got us."

Meanwhile, in stormy Knesset sessions and demonstrations, the Likud, religious parties, settlers, and other right-wing groups accused Rabin of selling out Israel.

Yet polls showed that the majority of Israelis supported Oslo. They could trust "Mr. Security"—the real payoff for his sustained effort over the years to create a hawkish image. And the majority of Arafat's followers were even more enthusiastic, waving flags and holding up photos of their leader, though Hamas leaders threatened to kill the peace process with their bombs.

Actually, the negotiations had not yet ended. The Declaration of Principles generally outlined the relationship between the Israelis and the Palestinians, but mentioned nothing about mutual recognition. This matter would be dealt with in a separate letter. Rabin gagged at the thought that he must recognize the PLO as the sole legitimate representative of the Palestinians. He had known for years that this moment might come, and had been preparing for it by maintaining contact with the organization.

Nothing could stand in the way of peace—especially with the burning need to isolate the Iraqis, Iranians, and terrorist groups before they had the means to annihilate Israel. But he would exact a stiff price from Arafat.

The PLO had to refrain from all forms of terror; call on all Palestinians to stop violence and prevent it with force if necessary; recognize Israel's right to exist; and delete clauses in the Palestinian Covenant calling for Israel's destruction.

No, Arafat responded, he could not use force against his people to snuff out the violence of the still smoldering Intifada. He could not appear to them as a traitor. But he accepted the other demands.

Rabin would not compromise. All violence had to stop or there would be no accord. Finally, he agreed that Arafat's commitment on this point could be given in a separate letter to Holst.

And so, on September 10, 1993, Rabin sat at his desk with the look of a defeated general about to sign a document of surrender. The letter before him, which greeted the addressee simply as "Mr. Chairman," stated with stark coldness that Israel recognized the

PLO, no other promises. Rabin stared at the letter with anguished eyes as if willing the words to go away.

And there were some peace supporters who would later say they had the same wish. Professor Ariel Merari, an expert in terrorism at Tel Aviv University, told me:

"Rabin was too pragmatic. He bargained as if in a bazaar, arguing, for example, about how many personnel carriers the Palestinians could have. He should have laid out a broad plan. After the Intifada, the people wanted peace based on separation, but Rabin did not offer them a clear vision of the future. And so they would be confused."

To Rabin, the future would care for itself. He wanted to start down the road to peace now, and then move forward step by step as circumstances permitted. It was hard enough taking this first step. His aides sat around chatting, but he wasn't listening, except perhaps to the wails of the bomb victims and the cries of crazed men with bloody hands. But suddenly there was silence, and with an inexpensive pen Rabin scratched his name on the letter of peace. Was there another way to contain a simmering national rage before it exploded into a nihilistic storm?

The following day, September 11, Rabin's agony did not diminish. For President Clinton had telephoned to congratulate him and said he would like to host a ceremonial signing of the Declaration of Principles on September 13. Rabin was not cheered by this proposal, favoring a low-key signing. A highly publicized Washington ceremony that Arafat might attend could arouse public resistance at home. He therefore asked Peres to represent him at the ceremony, but then Secretary Christopher called:

Please attend personally, he said.

Rabin thought it over but could not overcome his reluctance. He asked the Americans, Dennis Ross told me, "to discourage Arafat from going so that he himself wouldn't have to go." Ross disagreed, feeling that if Arafat personally committed himself to the peace plan before the world, he would have a hard time backing out. But other State Department officials hoped that Arafat would choose to stay home and send a representative instead.

Rabin was especially concerned that the two leaders would have to shake hands. Shake hands with that terrorist? Even worse, what if Arafat, who often hugged and kissed Arab colleagues, tried to hug or, God forbid, kiss him? Pragmatism had forced him to reach an agreement with the man, but that didn't mean he had to have physical contact with him. He seldom touched even his friends. Besides, what would the public think? If Peres went, his counterpart would be the less tainted Abu Mazen.

That evening and the next day, Rabin spent hours speaking on the phone pressing advisers and colleagues for their opinion. Should he go or should he send Peres? Almost all the Israelis advised him to send Peres. It was too soon for Rabin to meet with Arafat, they argued, reinforcing his own view. The people wouldn't understand. Perhaps later the time would be ripe for such a meeting.

But Shimon Sheves and Niva Lanir, his aide during the 1980s, disagreed and would not get off the phone, insisting that without the prime minister there could be no agreement.

"You are the bridge for peace with the Arabs," Sheves told me he said. "You must attend personally or the people will not support or accept the agreement. A handshake will symbolize your identity with the agreement."

Rabin feverishly debated with himself. Once more, he had visions of dead children, of mutilated bodies, of bloodthirsty men of the night searching for innocent victims. And for one of the first times, emotionalism triumphed over pragmatism. He would stay home.

President Clinton was worried when he heard that Rabin might not appear for the ceremony, for he understood the political gravity of the event. The United States had little or nothing to do with the agreement, but why not give the impression that it was involved? He called Martin Indyk, his ambassador to Israel, and ordered him:

"Make sure he comes!"

Indyk phoned Eitan Haber, who opposed the trip, and asked him to convince the prime minister, but Haber would not do so, nor would many of the people he sounded out. Thus, Sheves and Lanir felt they were pleading to the deaf. Even Leah, who wanted Rabin to go, could not move him. If he stayed home, he felt, Arafat would follow suit. And Rabin had the impression from talking with Clinton that he didn't relish the prospect of welcoming Arafat to the White House, especially since the United States had always viewed Arafat as an outlaw. Understandably, Rabin felt. Why give respectability to a terrorist even if circumstances made him a peace partner now? Why force the prime minister of Israel to shake a hand stained with the blood of Israel's victims?

At about midnight, however, Rabin learned the worst. The United States had delivered an invitation to the "PLO," rather than to any individual member, and Arafat himself chose to come. And the United States, to Rabin's surprise, was glad—if only because Rabin would now have to come.

Indeed, he had no choice. How could he let Arafat radiate alone in the glow of peace before the whole world? He muttered to Leah:

"We're going to Washington."

But there was a problem Rabin wanted solved first. Arafat, he told the American ambassador, could not carry a gun or wear a uniform at the ceremony. The PLO leader agreed not to bring a gun, Rabin was assured, but he insisted on wearing his traditional army garb.

Well, Indyk suggested, why not call it a "safari suit"?

Okay, as long as he didn't call it a uniform.

The last problem, it seemed, had been solved—except for one matter. Though Rabin had solicited the views of perhaps a dozen aides and friends, he neglected to consult with the man who had urged him to support the Oslo peace process in the first place. Shimon Peres once again felt like an outsider. How could Rabin bask alone in the White House ceremony when he, Shimon Peres, had done the tough negotiating? In his hurt, he let friends know that he intended to resign his post as foreign minister.

When the Peres camp notified Rabin aides of his intention, Rabin was thunderstruck. Yes, he had ignored Peres. He was simply not accustomed to debating Peres on peripheral matters. He did what he had done since his army days—confer with the small group of trusted insiders fiercely loyal to him. And Peres was not among them, though he had earned Rabin's rather grudging respect for his work on Oslo. But how, Rabin asked, could Peres threaten political calamity on the eve of one of the most momentous events in Israel's history?

It was time for Giora Eini to work his magic once more. He shuttled between the homes of the two men, with Rabin anxiously watching through the window each time he approached with a message from Peres. A compromise was finally reached: Both Rabin and Peres would attend the ceremony and speak.

Giora was drained. The two leaders had together produced one of the most important documents in Israel's history. Peres had pressed for the Oslo agreement and helped shape it; and Rabin had made sure the security aspects were airtight and was probably the only man who could persuade the people to support the accord.

Yet even at the moment of shared glory, their long feud still simmered. What a shame, Eini felt, that he was still needed to mediate between them. But at least now both would stand before the world as giants of their time.

The butterflies in Rabin's stomach were, it seemed, appropriately oversized. On the eve of his departure for Washington, he told Clyde Haberman of the *New York Times* as he churned his hands around his stomach:

"The idea that I'll meet Arafat . . . still creates certain feelings of rejection. How will I explain it to those who were killed and wounded, to the soldiers I commanded and fought with, who fought the PLO terror groups and lost their lives?"

After a pause, he answered himself: "I will tell them that whatever happened was painful, but let's make it different in the future. Or at least let's take a chance, a possibility that it will be different. I'm an old guy. I served twenty-seven years in the military. My son served. Now, my grandson serves. Let's give a hope that at least my grandson will not need to fight if there will be a need. I'm sure that a fourth generation also will do it. But I feel a responsibility to give a chance that it will not happen."

And then Rabin expanded on his theory of risk: "Once the Jewish people decided that, here in the Land of Israel, we have to establish a Jewish state, we decided also who will be our neighbors—the Arab countries, the Moslem world, hundreds of millions. And there are two ways to deal with this reality: a prolonged war of violence and terror, or to live in peace. There is no third choice. In wars we took risks. I believe that for peace, we should take calculated risks."

Rabin could almost imagine the day, it seemed, when the only butterflies around were flitting in the tranquillity of his garden.

Everything had to be perfect. It was Monday, September 13, 1993, a day that history—and America's voters—would remember. And so President Clinton spent a restless night, waking at about 3 A.M. as if from a nightmare. What if something went wrong? His speech—there was something missing. He got out of bed, put on a blue jogging suit, and went to his study, where he picked up a Bible. He leafed through the Book of Joshua until he found the passage telling how trumpets had brought down the walls of Jericho. The ideal symbol for his speech to contrast the victories of war and peace. In fact, why just talk about trumpets; he would wear them, too. He had a blue and yellow tie with little trumpets on it. It was still dark when he put down the Bible and walked to the kitchen; he made himself a cup of coffee, then slouched in a chair by a window and waited for the dawn.

Everything now seemed perfect—though Clinton was a little edgy about having Yasir Arafat in the White House. A month earlier, he wouldn't have let him in the country, for one of Clinton's most publicized policies was his struggle against terrorism. And Arafat, some felt, was the father of terrorism.

By contrast, the young, newly inaugurated President regarded Rabin with a certain awe. Rabin had visited him several months earlier, in March, and made a powerful impression on him, almost as a father figure. Here was a military hero who lobbied ferociously for U.S. aid to help him build the conditions for peace. Rabin was one of the few political leaders he had ever met who spoke his mind without deviating one iota from the purpose of his mission, a man he almost instantly respected and knew he could trust. And also one whose ideas for peace in the Middle East basically coincided with Clinton's own.

While the President waited for the trumpets to blow and the walls to fall, other sounds, loud and bitter, suddenly echoed through the White House in the hours before the ceremony. Everything was perfect—except that the whole affair almost crumbled like a burnt pita. Arafat insisted that the reference to "Palestinians" in the agreement be changed to "Palestine Liberation Organization" to avoid an interpretation that the Palestinians were part of a Jordanian delegation. He warned that he would leave for home if Rabin didn't agree.

Just twenty-four minutes before the ceremony was to start, as the unwitting guests waited in the Rose Garden, Peres and Singer convinced Rabin that he must yield on this point or risk a monumental political disaster. The prime minister finally agreed. It was his last surrender to reality.

Finally, the moment came for the trumpets to sound, though the walls remained sturdy until the last minute. With the last problems solved, representatives of the two sides gathered in the Blue Room for coffee and orange juice, with each group clustering at opposite ends of the room, where they were joined by U.S. leaders and diplomats from Russia and Norway.

When all dignitaries except Clinton, Rabin, and Arafat had headed for the garden to be introduced, the Israeli and Palestinian exchanged their first words.

"You know, we have a lot of work to do," Rabin said gravely.

"I know, and I am prepared to do my part," Arafat replied with a smile that reflected his joy at suddenly emerging from the political wilderness to be welcomed at the White House like a chief of state.

And the three leaders, with the President in the center, walked briskly to the podium, where they signed the agreement. Afterward, Rabin, fidgeting and obviously uncomfortable, found himself sandwiched between Peres, his political nemesis, and Arafat, his "terrorist" enemy, while the world looked on incredulously.

But no one was more incredulous than Rabin. Yet it somehow made sense. He had devoted his whole adult life, fighting on the battlefield and in the political arena, for the security of the Jewish state and the peace necessary to make it secure. And now all his efforts, saturated with the blood of the dead and the tears of heartbreak and failure, had finally yielded this moment of victory. Yet a terrifying moment as he viewed from a corner of his eye a man he would have shot on sight only very recently.

And then came a metaphoric moment that history would never forget—or perhaps even believe. Arafat extended his hand toward Rabin, and the prime minister, nudged slightly by Clinton, slowly, tentatively, reached out and limply took it, a pained grimace on his face. He was paying, it seemed, the ultimate price of peace. Arafat then reached toward Peres, and Rabin whispered to him, as if to suggest to his old political rival that he was deserving of the dubious honor:

"Now it's your turn."

The President delivered his introductory speech, praising Rabin and Arafat for their "brave gamble that the future can be better than the past." And then Rabin's turn came again to express with heartfelt words the extraordinary change that had overtaken old feuds in the Middle East. Stepping to the rostrum he intoned with cadenced, raspy emphasis:

> Let me say to you, the Palestinians, we are destined to live together on the same soil in the same land. We, the soldiers who have returned from battles stained with blood; we who have seen our relatives and friends killed before our eyes; we who have attended their funerals and cannot look in the eyes of their parents; we who have come from a land where parents bury their children; we who have fought against you, the Palestinians—we say to you today, in a loud and a clear voice: enough of blood and tears. Enough.

And Arafat, relishing his few moments in the sun, replied: "Our two peoples are awaiting today this historic hope, and they want to give peace a real chance."

But not all of the people did.

26

Rivers of Hate,
Reservoirs of Hope

L ess than two weeks after the cries of peace echoed around the world, a terrorist's knife claimed the first Israeli casualty. As the days passed, other victims were found in bloody pools. And within three months almost twenty more were buried to the sounds of grief uttered by loved ones. What kind of peace was this, this peace of the dead? And most Israelis who had supported the peace process by the end of 1993 told pollsters that the process should stop.

Stop? And give in to the murderers?

"We will fight terror as if there are no peace talks," Rabin roared, "and we will conduct peace talks as if there is no terror."

Ironically, much of the terror was inadvertently spawned by the Israelis themselves. For the Hamas sprang from a fundamentalist movement that was nurtured in the 1980s by Israeli staff officers who viewed fundamentalism as a tool they could use to help fight the PLO. These officers had allowed Moslem extremists to gain control of the religious institutions and encouraged them to build their own clinics, schools, and other social projects aimed at luring the populace away from the secular PLO. A religious force, it was believed, would confine itself to spreading the faith and bend politically to a patronizing Israel while fighting Arafat's secularism. PLO nationalism, the Israelis thought, was more threatening than Moslem fundamentalism.

Only during the Intifada did Israel awaken to its momentous error. For while the IDF pushed the PLO forces into exile during the Lebanon War, the Hamas and a smaller fundamentalist group, Islamic Jihad, were enticing many Palestinians into their camp with their extremist views.

Gradually aware of this growing menace, Rabin realized, after some nudging by Peres, that he might have to deal directly with the PLO soon after he took office in 1992. The nation, it seemed, needed the PLO to neutralize the power of the fundamentalists. Israel had helped to create a Frankenstein monster that, after acting as a proxy in weakening the PLO, turned on its benefactor with a vengeance exceeding that of the PLO.

This Islamic vengeance escalated to a peak in the aftermath of the Washington ceremony. And adding to the tension was the violent anti-Oslo rhetoric of the right-wing Israeli extremists. While the Palestinian extremists feared Oslo would lead to a Palestinian state that did not embrace all of Israel, the Israeli extremists feared it would lead to a Palestinian state and smash their dream of a Greater Israel.

Only months before the handshake, Rabin, while pragmatically seeking a deal with Arafat, had doubted that one could be reached. But, characteristically, now that he had concluded a deal, he pushed ahead relentlessly, and would not be intimidated either by the right-wingers at home or by the terrorists in the territories. Especially after viewing Arafat for the first time as a human being and not as the evil ghost who had been haunting him for years.

After the reluctant handshake, Rabin began to develop a certain respect for the man. According to Leah, he "wondered how Arafat had been able to survive all those years. He asked what made him so popular with his people, and said there had to be something authentic and very tough about him. Yitzhak appreciated toughness." And when he met with him in Cairo only months later, his instincts told him that perhaps the PLO leader had really changed. Peace no longer seemed an illusion; the knives flashed and the bullets sang precisely because the murderers knew that peace was becoming a reality.

Yet, with each flash, each shot, and each howl from the Israeli right, the public doubt grew, and by December even Rabin began to wonder if Arafat was really doing his best to prevent the violence. The prime minister had to know how far he could go in defying the popular will. If he was convinced that Arafat was sincere, nothing would turn him from the road that ran from Oslo. Otherwise, he might have to slow down the process.

Israeli intelligence was feeding Rabin information on Arafat from Tunis, but he wanted a direct pipeline to him to better judge his intentions. And so he called in Yossi Ginosar, who had been his personal emissary to the PLO as far back as 1986. Arafat at that time had invited Ginosar to meet with him, but Shamir replaced Peres as prime minister and relations with the PLO were cut.

In 1988, Ginosar told me, he advised Rabin that he "should negotiate with Arafat eventually, and Rabin did not argue. I knew then that he would do this when the public atmosphere was right."

Now, in 1993, the time seemed ripe, Rabin felt, and he asked Ginosar, who had been in constant contact with the PLO, to accept Arafat's old invitation. The prime minister wanted a back channel to the PLO leader, and it must be kept secret—even from Peres.

Thus, Ginosar, called "Joe" by PLO leaders, went to see Arafat in October 1993, and would continue his secret talks at the same time the Israelis and Palestinians were openly implementing the Oslo agreement. The talks were so secret that, Ginosar told me, Peres would only learn of them a year after they began, in October 1994.

Simultaneously, the minister of housing, Binyamin Ben-Eliezer, who originally proposed a "Gaza-first" peace solution in 1988, now suggested that he visit Arafat to explore his thoughts, and Rabin, who trusted his judgment implicitly, agreed. A portly, shrewd, tenacious politician, Ben-Eliezer knew the Palestinians well. He had served as military governor of the West Bank in the 1970s and 1980s. Now he would go to Tunis, the first Israeli minister to visit there, and have a heart-to-heart talk with Arafat. But his heart nearly stopped when he saw the men who greeted him on arrival on December 19, 1993. He had imprisoned or deported them during his rule in the West Bank!

"Abrach!" ("God help me!") he exclaimed to himself.

And God did. His hosts welcomed him like an old friend. Soon he was sitting with Arafat, and over a sumptuous lunch and then dinner, the two men talked for hours.

Rabin could trust him, Arafat said. He wanted to close the door on the past. He realized that the two people had parallel destinies, while none of the Arab leaders came to his help.

"They don't give a damn about us," he asserted.

As for the violence, "tell the prime minister to ease the way for me. Tell him I am facing internal problems, that I have more enemies than supporters."

"Listen, Mr. Arafat," Ben-Eliezer replied. "I know you very well. Once you decide to put an end to any activity, you succeed."

"Yes, yes, you are right."

"No one can convince me you can't."

"You must understand that I am the leader not only of the PLO, but of the Palestinian people, and they include the opposition. You can't expect me to massacre them all. That would mean civil war. That is not my aim. I want to find a way to govern them. Time is in our favor, time to convince them that we are acting for the benefit of all Palestinians and to make their dreams come true. We need more talks, not a greater split. No matter what they think, they are still Palestinians."

Ben-Eliezer returned to Israel and reported to Rabin, who understood Arafat's internal problem because he had one himself with the settlers and other right-wingers. He, too, was reluctant to take drastic measures against these extremists, even though they had attacked Palestinians a dozen times in their own rage over Oslo.

Regardless, Rabin said, Israel must pressure Arafat relentlessly to end the violence, though he realized that the PLO leader could not assert his authority over all the extremists overnight. But since it seemed clear that Arafat really had changed, Rabin would move full-speed ahead with the peace process, however great the political peril.

"I'm fed up," he said. "It's time to bring something new to our children. We belong to a generation that has had to fight. And though there is a deeply held feeling that this is Israel's fate, I must try to change it. We must either close the door to this feeling or close the door to the whole world, for the whole world supports the peace process."

Baruch Goldstein, an American-born physician who had settled in Kiryat Arba, a religious community near Hebron, disagreed—violently. Early on the morning of February 25, 1994, Goldstein, wearing his army uniform and a skullcap, barged into the mosque in Hebron after knocking down the guard with his assault rifle. He approached a group of men kneeling at prayer on this first day of Ramadan, and sprayed them with bullets, killing thirty Palestinians before he himself was shot dead by a guard. He became an instant martyr to many of the settlers, who would visit his grave and bless his memory.

Horrified, Rabin phoned Arafat an apology, but the peace process was quickly grinding to a halt. With a curious irony, the prime minister had threatened Arafat with such a halt after a number of Hamas terrorist attacks, and now an Israeli had committed this horrendous crime. Arafat currently held the high ground, at least psychologically, and Rabin would have a harder time forcing a crackdown on Arab killings. He would now gain a better understanding of the difficulties Arafat faced trying to stop Hamas murders.

Like Arafat, Rabin hesitated to take drastic measures against his own terrorists and their supporters, and for the same reason. He feared he might trigger a rightist revolt, perhaps even civil war. But his cabinet wanted him to evacuate the settlers in Hebron, and he began to wonder whether he should, in order to preclude new massacres that could wreck the peace process. Professor Ehud Sprinzak of Hebrew University, who sometimes advised Rabin on matters of right-wing extremism, now helped him make up his mind. He phoned Eitan Haber and said:

"I could complete a study of the Hebron situation and report to the prime minister in a couple of days."

A good idea, Haber replied.

Sprinzak rushed to speak with the settlers in Hebron and found them in a "desperate mood." Especially alarming was the extremism of a group of seven families who lived in mobile homes in Tel Rumeida, perched on a hill in the center of Hebron. Sprinzak heard that some residents of this area might blow themselves up if they were ordered to move. And on March 30, 1994, he wrote Rabin that suicides were "highly probable" should an evacuation be ordered, and that this could lead to massive violence and the fall of the government.

Sprinzak's advice apparently tipped the scales against uprooting the settlers. But this decision did not relieve the tension between Rabin and the Hebron rightists, or between the settlers in general and the Palestinians. The question was how to start up the peace process again. About two weeks after the massacre, the answer came.

Rabin's secretary, Marit, rushed into the office of an aide, Jacques Neriya, and said: "There is somebody on the phone who claims he is Arafat."

Neriya took the phone. "Who is this?" he asked.

"This is Yasir Arafat," a voice replied, confirming Marit's report. "I'm calling from Tunis."

Neriya recognized the voice. It was Arafat. The aide was startled that the PLO leader himself would call Rabin.

"How can I help you, Mr. Chairman," he asked. "Do you wish to speak to the prime minister?"

"Yes."

"I'm sorry, but he's busy meeting with his cabinet."

"Well, tell him that I'm traveling to Egypt. Please have him call me at 5 P.M. [He gave his phone number.] And ask him meanwhile to send someone to Cairo as soon as possible."

When Neriya brought the message to Rabin, the prime minister was furious.

"Why didn't you transfer the call to the meeting?" he asked. "Don't you understand how important that call was?"

"Yes," Neriya replied in embarrassment. "It's the first contact since the massacre."

"Now I may have to call him," Rabin said ruefully. He would lose the psychological advantage.

"Don't worry, he'll call you at 5 o'clock."

But 5 o'clock passed and there was no call. Neriya was worried. He had blundered and must find a way out. He finally thought of a way—and conspired with Marit. The secretary dialed Arafat in a room next to Rabin's office, then opened the door to the office and announced:

"Arafat is calling."

Rabin quickly picked up the phone. And shortly, Neriya was on his way to Cairo to confer with Arafat. He returned to Israel with welcome news:

"We're resuming negotiations."

The muscles in Rabin's tense face appeared to loosen. A good thing that Arafat called again.

Despite the resumption of talks, Goldstein's massacre had lit a fuse that would have explosive consequences. In April 1994, less than two months after the killing orgy, Arafat would be apologizing to Rabin. Hamas, seeking to match the intensity of violence achieved by Goldstein, initiated a new and equally deadly form of terrorism. A suicide bomber blew up a bus in the northern town of Afula, killing seven Israelis, followed by another such tragedy in Hadera, near Tel Aviv. Israeli and Palestinian terrorists and their sympathizers were now reinforcing each other in an unholy conspiracy of murder to destroy the peace process in the name of God.

Many Israelis had stoically borne the terrorism in the settlements, but with the suicide attacks in their cities, much closer to home, their support for Rabin dropped dramatically, though he still remained ahead of Likud leader Benjamin Netanyahu in the polls. At the same time, Arafat's popularity among his people dipped with each apology he made. But neither man would bow to extremist pressure. Arafat, having pragmatically abandoned his previous all-or-nothing stance, wanted a Palestinian state now in whatever territory he could get.

And while many Israelis, though favoring Oslo, thought that a slower pace might reduce the terrorism, Rabin and Peres viewed the deadly resistance through a more coldly realistic prism. They interpreted it as a tragic but inevitable by-product of the process and as evidence that it was working, since the aim of the terrorists was to kill it. To save the Jewish state from a possible nuclear holocaust in the future, Rabin and Peres felt they had to make peace with its neighbors even if a relatively small number of Israelis were victimized by fanatical gangs opposed to their own government. After all, it took only one madman with a hidden bomb to mount a bus and blow it up, taking the lives of many passengers, including the terrorist. Should Israel's destiny, the two leaders asked, be hostage to a few madmen?

In the last analysis, Rabin and Peres felt, security could only grow out of peace. For the more the Palestinians experienced its political, economic, and social benefits, the more the fanatics among them would find themselves isolated and discredited. On the other hand, failure of the peace process would produce ever more bombers with a supporting infrastructure embracing almost the whole population—a powderkeg situation that, in this nuclear age, could even threaten Israel's existence.

On May 4, Rabin and Arafat met again in Cairo to convert words into action. In a ceremony reminiscent of the Washington signing, the two men sat at a table holding pens that would scribble into reality the Declaration of Principles. Rabin could only feel relief as Arafat signed this implementation accord without any last-minute delay as at the previous event. Then, as he himself was about to sign, he scanned the documents, which included six maps, and abruptly lifted his pen.

Arafat had not signed the maps, Rabin mumbled to his aides. Unless the PLO leader signed the maps, he wouldn't sign anything.

But Arafat wanted the Jericho area earmarked for the Palestinians to be open to future revision, and the maps showed the exact borders of the areas to be turned over.

Suddenly, the stage seethed with chaotic movement as dignitaries, including Peres, U.S. Secretary of State Christopher, Egyptian President Mubarak, and Russian Foreign Minister Andre Kozyrev, rushed from one knot of delegates to another, arguing how to break the impasse. A huge worldwide television audience watched in wonder as the peace process seemed about to disintegrate before their eyes.

All those involved disappeared offstage for several minutes and tried desperately to keep the process alive, returning after several minutes with weary smiles. Rabin had agreed to guarantee in writing that the Jericho boundaries would be flexible. And the show resumed. Rabin was determined; with peace in hand he would not let it slide past. Besides, as Oded Ben-Ami, Rabin's spokesman, would observe:

"For Rabin, seeing Arafat was like going to the dentist. The anxiety before was much worse than the treatment."

And so, amid the taunts of wildly celebrating Palestinians, Israeli tanks and trucks loaded with troops began snaking out of the Jericho area and most of the Gaza Strip. Some 3,000 Palestinian policemen recruited and trained in other Arab countries would fill the vacuum. A Palestinian Authority, an autonomous government with full responsibility for civilian affairs, had begun to replace the Israeli occupation in the first stage of a peace process that even Rabin apparently realized would inevitably yield a Palestinian state. If this was the ultimate price of peace, so be it.

Meanwhile, peace became more bearable when, on May 25, 1994, it paid a handsome dividend. King Hussein and Rabin met in Washington in another dramatic encounter on the White House lawn to proclaim before a beaming President Clinton that the state of war between Jordan and Israel was over. A treaty would now solidify their joint effort to fight terrorist infiltration from Jordan into the West Bank.

Once the Palestinians made peace with Israel, Hussein, who had long been meeting with Israeli leaders in secrecy, now felt he could do what he had always wanted to do. And he was particularly happy to shake the hand of Rabin, who more than twenty years earlier had helped to save his throne after an attack by PLO forces. Indeed, Hussein would later tell Danny Yatom, Rabin's military adviser:

"I have met many leaders in my life, but Prime Minister Rabin has been my closest and best friend."

But not everyone at the ceremony was happy—especially not Shimon Peres. After one meeting with the king, Peres elatedly told reporters, hinting at an accord with Jordan:

"Put November 3 in your calendars as a historic date. All that's needed is a pen to sign it."

Hussein, who had insisted on secrecy, was furious, and so was Rabin, who conducted subsequent talks without Peres and even decided not to have Peres at the ceremony. But the foreign minister once more used his political clout to prevail and he came. But he enjoyed little glory; he had no speaking role and was hardly mentioned in the press. At a party afterward, while others drank, chatted, and joined in the merriment, reporters found him sitting alone sullenly pondering the fate of dreamers left to dream.

Rabin still believed that Peres intended to challenge him for leadership of the Labor Party and had little wish to suggest publicly that he was a coengineer of this great political coup. He acknowledged that Peres deserved some credit for the Oslo accord, though it was Yitzhak Rabin who had checked every detail and made sure that

Israel would be secure with it. He surely didn't need Peres, he felt, to deal with King Hussein when he himself was so close a friend.

Yet Rabin's frigid attitude toward Peres showed signs of thawing in the following months, perhaps because his rival's hurt, compounded so many times, had aroused a sense of guilt or compassion. At any rate, on October 26, 1994, three months after the Washington event, Peres stood in the sweltering desert sun with Rabin, King Hussein, and other leaders and reveled in the ceremony commemorating the signing of a formal peace treaty with Jordan in the Arava desert on the Israeli-Jordanian border.

Even so, Peres told me, Rabin had tried to exclude him from the picture and changed his mind only at the last moment, agreeing that they were partners. With little time to prepare a speech, Peres had to speak extemporaneously at the ceremony, which took place, appropriately enough, on an asphalt strip that covered an old minefield. But he had little to do with the treaty negotiations. They had been conducted in the royal palace in Amman, with Rabin himself negotiating the most difficult points with the king.

When the treaty had earlier been wrapped up, Eitan Haber, one of Rabin's negotiators, suggested that the two leaders call President Clinton, and they woke him in the middle of the night as he was flying in Air Force One. After all, they reasoned, he was awakened when there was bad news. Why not awaken him with good news?

Would the President consider attending the signing ceremony in Arava?

Yes, he would consider it, Clinton mumbled—and he came.

It was a joyous moment for Rabin when he reached agreement on the final point of contention—this time with a good friend he was certain he could trust. Nor did he mind demonstrating this trust when, to Arafat's rage, he agreed to give Hussein special rights to manage Moslem and Christian holy places in Jerusalem. Arafat would not be invited to the ceremony.

The final day of talks ended with a dinner in the palace, and a memorable surprise. An old Jordanian soldier, called by the king, suddenly walked in—a colonel Rabin had known when they were both students at the Royal Staff College in Camberley. The two men, in joyous shock, embraced like brothers. At school, they had talked of peace between their countries. Who could have guessed that they would be celebrating it together after some forty years?

Several months later, when the colonel had a stroke, Rabin arranged for him to be helicoptered to a hospital in Israel, and went to visit him. The colonel cried in gratitude, whispering that he would "never forget what you have done for me."

It was a poignantly symbolic moment for Rabin. He had been trained to kill this colonel and his fellow Arabs. He had sent hundreds of his own men to kill them, or die trying. And now he was sitting at the bedside of this enemy officer, soothing him as if he were his own soldier. Seldom had the tragedy of war seemed more sharply in focus.

Now there remained Syria and Lebanon. Would Assad finally agree to a reasonable peace? So eager was Rabin to finish the job and end the recurring bloodshed along Israel's borders once and for all that he startled Secretary of State Christopher, who was to visit Syria, with a remarkable concession. If Syria agreed to "real peace" and strict security terms with Israel, he would consider relinquishing the whole of the Golan Heights and withdrawing to the line that divided the two countries before the Six-Day War.

Should he present this offer to Syria as Israel's negotiating position? the delighted secretary wanted to know.

No, he should present the idea hypothetically to test Assad's reaction.

But the Israeli negotiator, Itamar Rabinovich, ambassador to the United States, made little headway in his talks with the Syrians. Still, he would tell me, he would have continued giving Syria priority, for though Assad was a tough negotiator, "he could deliver" once a deal was reached.

The question was whether Yasir Arafat could deliver. He was apparently trying to carry out the Oslo accords, if only because failure could finally fling him into oblivion, and he managed to thwart a number of planned terrorist attacks in Israel that could have claimed many lives. But he couldn't fully control the Hamas and Islamic Jihad extremists, who were desperately seeking to sabotage the peace process, and the killing raged on. Why not a full-scale crackdown on the dissidents? Such action, Arafat continued to argue, could spark a civil war that would destroy him and catapult the Hamas into power—a warning that Rabin and Peres grimly agreed could not be ignored.

Politically imperiled by the Hamas campaign to discredit Oslo, Arafat often resorted to heady speeches about soon making Jerusalem the capital of a Palestinian state. For nothing won him more public support than this promise. Israeli rightists, on the other hand, viewed his bombast as a threat of violence. But it was tolerated by Rabin and Peres as unthreatening political demagoguery. When I asked Peres why, he replied with a shrug:

"One person can have a dream, but it takes two to have an agreement."

The announcement in December 1994 that Rabin, Peres, and Arafat had won the Nobel Peace Prize seemed to mock the reality on the ground. Rabin viewed the award as one of the highlights of his life. But with meticulous Middle Eastern timing, just a few days earlier, Hamas terrorists had kidnapped a soldier, Corporal Nachshon Wachsman, and were holding him hostage. They warned they would kill him if Israel did not release their jailed spiritual leader, Sheikh Ahmed Yassin, and two hundred other prisoners. And Rabin, who would not pay the ransom, feared that the terrorists would kill the young man.

He demanded that Arafat find Wachsman and free him, and Arafat rounded up hundreds of Hamas members and organized a huge dragnet—and apparently helped the Israelis locate the house where the youth was hidden. Just before the Hamas deadline, a commando force attacked the house and killed the terrorists, only to find Wachsman's body inside.

As the soldier's shattered father, Yehudah, would say: "Again and again, [Rabin] went over the considerations and the explanations of why there was no other way, other than the way it was done, to carry out the rescue operation. I was convinced that Yitzhak Rabin had done everything he could to save my son."

But Rabin could do little to ease his own pain as he set out for Stockholm to receive his award.

"Yitzhak assumed full responsibility for the failed effort," Leah would say. "This was an unbearably difficult moment for him. . . . I remember Yitzhak wearily rubbing his forehead with the tips of his fingers after learning of Wachsman's death. He said he would gladly have forgone the Nobel Prize if he could have exchanged it for Wachsman's life. His heart was bleeding."

It was also softening—at least toward Peres. Their sharing of the Nobel Prize, fittingly in Oslo, of all places, made him realize as never before how much they needed each other. Was their partnership not a truly effective symbiosis in the search for peace? Perhaps he needed a dreamer to provide the raw material for his pragmatism. Most important of all, Rabin had begun to believe that Peres's interest now lay simply in peace, not power. It seemed he would no longer have to fear or fight a challenge from Peres.

Rabin's new feeling was touchingly displayed one evening in Oslo when Peres slipped on the ice and fell on his face. Rabin learned about this when he arrived at an official dinner and was told about the accident. He rushed to Peres's table and was anguished on seeing his bandaged visage. Ya'acov Heifetz, a close friend of Rabin, turned to his wife and said:

"Naomi, it's hard to believe, but we've just seen true friendship."

Apparently even Leah was surprised. In keeping with the norm in Rabin-Peres relations, she had reportedly refused to ride in the same limousine with Peres's wife, Sonya.

On returning home, Rabin, who previously had dealt personally with the Americans and Norwegians when they asked important questions involving the peace talks, now referred them to Peres.

"This was the first evidence that Rabin was letting Peres deal alone with delicate matters," Dennis Ross told me.

The reverential magic of the Nobel Prize apparently generated a softer attitude by Rabin toward Arafat as well. Before and after the awards ceremony, Rabin locked himself in a room with the PLO leader and, in a warm encounter that contrasted sharply with the chill of their meeting in Washington, sat down to hammer out details for an expansion of territory under Palestinian rule. His conciliatory mood was reflected in his moving speech at the ceremony, which reached to the root of his long-held obsession with peace:

"As a military man, as a commander, as a minister of defense, I ordered the carrying out of many military operations. And together with the joy of victory and grief of bereavement, I shall always remember the moment just after taking such decisions; the hush as senior officers or cabinet ministers slowly rise from their seats; the sight of their receding backs; the sound of the closing door; and then the silence, in which I remain alone."

And it seemed to Rabin that he was almost alone as the terrorists, ever more desperate with each step of the peace process, struck again and again. In the first seven months of 1995, suicide bombers killed thirty-five people in various parts of Israel, and many others were wounded. Eli Landau, the mayor of Herzylia, typically cried:

"If the peace process is paved on the bodies of dead Jews, then I don't want it."

In fact, only 37 percent of Israelis in early 1995 wished to continue the peace talks, according to the newspaper *Ma'ariv*, a sharp drop since the handshake. And Rabin found himself for the first time falling behind Benjamin Netanyahu in the polls. But Rabin, who had always been sensitive to popular opinion, was now prepared to bull forward toward final peace regardless of the political consequences, hoping he could conclude at least the first stage of the process by the time election '96 rolled around.

And so, in the village of Taba on the Egyptian border, amid palm trees swaying in a balmy breeze that served as a perfect backdrop for peace talks, Peres and his delegation met with the Palestinians on September 23, 1995, and reached agreement on implementing Oslo. But Rabin's approval was needed. Peres came to the prime minister's office, and the two men, together with several military and political advisers, reviewed the accord point by point. But Rabin wanted further concessions, as did most of those in the room.

Peres was exasperated. He had wrung every possible concession out of Arafat! He warned:

"If I don't get a mandate, I am not going back to Arafat."

Rabin hesitated and took Peres aside. Fearing that rejection of the agreement could bring a halt to Oslo, Peres played his final card: If Rabin, he warned, did not accept the accord as written, he might challenge him in the next election for leadership of the party.

Rabin was dismayed. He could hardly imagine a greater nightmare. For whatever reason, Rabin approved the deal.

Oslo 2 thus burst into history with a concrete plan, to be fully implemented by March 30, 1996, transferring control of much of the West Bank to an elected eighty-two-member Palestinian council and chief executive, certain to be Arafat. Israel would control the borders and foreign affairs in an interim period, and a final settlement would be reached by May 1999.

In fact, elements of the final settlement were already being secretly discussed. Yossi Beilin and Abu Mazen were exchanging ideas on how to solve the thorniest problem—Jerusalem.

Perhaps the Palestinian capital could be located in an Arab village, Abu Dis, just across the municipal boundary of the city. Abu Dis would be called Al Quds, the Arabic name for Jerusalem. Each side would thus control a "Jerusalem" of its own—an ingenious compromise that could perhaps satisfy both.

Peace now seemed more than a distant vision.

On September 28, 1995, Rabin and Arafat sat under the gleaming lights of the White House East Room and signed the historic blue-bound Oslo 2 agreement. The President, as well as King Hussein and Egyptian President Mubarak, who had been invited to reflect the regional importance of the event, followed with their signatures as witnesses. Then, standing on either side of President Clinton as they had during the ceremony for Oslo 1, the Israeli and Palestinian chiefs shook hands to the sound of thunderous applause. And this time Rabin appeared relaxed and comfortable, and in stark contrast to the previous ceremony, seemed friendly to his peace partner.

In fact, after Arafat had spoken of his desire for peace, Rabin took the podium and remarked with a straight face that he wondered if the PLO leader had some Jewish blood. The PLO leader, the President, and the other guests roared. Arafat the terrorist—Jewish? Then, with the eloquence of a prophet and the voice of a man who could hardly believe the miracle he had wrought, Rabin declared:

"The sight you see . . . before you at this moment was impossible, was unthinkable just two years ago. Only poets dreamt of it. And in our great pain, soldiers and civilians went to their death to make this moment possible. Here we stand before you, men whom fate and history have sent on a mission of peace to end once and for all 100 years of bloodshed. . . .

"Yes, I know, our speeches are already repeating themselves. Perhaps this picture has already become routine. The handshakes no longer set your pulse racing. Your loving hearts no longer pound with emotion as they did then. . . . We have matured in the two years since we first shook hands here. . . . "

And then Rabin spoke of the terror bred by peace:

> The sounds of celebration here cannot drown out the cries of innocent
> citizens who traveled those buses to their death. . . . I want to say to
> you, Chairman Arafat, . . . together we should not let the land that
> flows with milk and honey become a land flowing with blood and
> tears. Don't let it happen. If all the partners to the peacemaking do not
> unite against the evil angels of death by terrorism, all that will remain
> of this ceremony are color snapshots, empty mementos. Rivers of
> hatred will overflow again and swamp the Middle East. . . .

Even as Rabin spoke, the rivers were rising in Israel and the
territories. Demonstrations wracked Hebron, and Rabbi Moshe
Levinger, a settler leader in that city, shouted that "abandoning
these places is treason and murder and the government is committing treason and murder."

Simultaneously, Hamas denounced Arafat as a "Palestinian
traitor" who had betrayed "his faith and his homeland."

But while Rabin was worried that an Arab terrorist would kill
Arafat, and the peace process with him, he could not imagine that
an Israeli terrorist would kill *his* own leader.

As the rivers of hate rose, so did the reservoirs of hope.

With Rabin in power for little more than three years, Israel had
surged from insolvency to a healthy economy with lightning
speed, largely propelled by the peace process. Traffic jams tied up
towns as cars clogged a network of magnificent roads criss-cross-
ing the cities and the country. Chic shoppers swarmed through
ultra-modern, labyrinth-style malls mushrooming everywhere,
with stores flaunting the finest Italian shoes and French fashions.
Heavily booked airplanes carried holiday-makers to the pleasure
spots of Europe, the United States, Africa, and even the Far East.

Oslo helped make possible this picture of prosperity by per-
mitting Israel to break the siege imposed on it by much of the
world. More than 150 countries now recognized Israel, double the
number twenty years earlier, with over 50 nations tying the diplomatic knot since the announcement of Oslo, and others queuing
up to open embassies.

Among the now-friendly nations were many Moslem countries, including Jordan, Morocco, Tunisia, Oman, Qatar, Bahrain,
and Indonesia. Some of them welcomed Israeli delegations and

even Rabin himself. An Arab boycott of companies investing in Israel had died, as demonstrated in October 1995 when Rabin and Peres, guests at an Amman Economic Conference, negotiated expansive trade deals and joint-venture development projects with many of Israel's former enemies, designed to pull the Middle East into the global market. These deals were concluded even though Israel was suspected of engineering the assassination of an Arab terrorist leader in Malta only days before the meeting. Earlier, in October 1993, Rabin had visited Indonesia, the world's largest Moslem country—though, to avoid provoking anti-Israel riots, he stayed in Jakarta only a few hours to speak with President Suharto.

China, which Rabin also visited in October 1993; Japan, which depended on Arab oil; and India tightened relations with Israel, and by the end of 1995 Israeli flags flew over diplomatic missions in all but five countries from Eastern Europe to Eastern Siberia. Also, many African nations that, under Arab pressure, had severed ties with Israel after the Six-Day War, resumed them, while the Vatican, which had snubbed Israel since its birth because of a conflict over the fate of Jerusalem, now recognized it. At the same time, halls at the United Nations and other international organizations no longer echoed with vicious diatribes against Israel.

These new links helped to yield remarkable economic results under Rabin, who, in a sense, was a socioeconomic chameleon. He gradually changed from a socialist to a social democrat, and finally, influenced by his ambassadorial days in the United States, to a capitalistic liberal, pursuing privatization but also protecting some industries. Rabin radically altered Israel's economic priorities—siphoning funds intended for West Bank settlement expansion into social fields such as education, increasing its budget by 70 percent, and boosting investment in infrastructure and research and development by 200 percent. He helped to turn Israel's potholed road system into a network of sleek highways.

In pursuing these goals, Rabin would not waste a minute on matters of little importance.

"When he wanted to postpone dealing with something," Shimon Sheves would explain, "he used to say, 'Why don't we do it on Thursday afternoon?' In time it became a kind of code name between us. Whenever he'd say, 'Thursday afternoon,' we both knew it would not be taken care of."

With Rabin's peace-oriented budget policies thus propelling Israel forward, the economy grew by 20 percent and living standards jumped 25 percent; per capita income reached $17,000, the twentieth highest in the world. Some international bankers predicted that Israel's economy would be the world's most successful by the end of the century, spurred in particular by its investment in high-technology industries and communication development, as well as education. A Middle East Silicon Valley was emerging.

And all this growth despite an influx of hundreds of thousands of immigrants, mainly from the former Soviet Union, in the last few years. Many musicians and engineers had to take menial jobs, but their children began developing high-tech and other skills.

Reflecting Israel's peace-driven prosperity, exports to Asia leaped from less than $2 billion in 1991 to more than $3 billion in 1994. And Rabin played a direct role in this boost. For example, when Kazakstan's prime minister visited Israel wishing help in setting up agricultural enterprises and a power plant, Rabin met him after reading volumes of material on these subjects, astonishing his guest with his newly acquired knowledge of the most technical details.

At the same time, direct foreign investment in Israel vaulted from $366 million in 1991 to nearly $1 billion in the first six months of 1995. Monthly tourism rose from about 80,000 in 1991 to 140,000 in 1995. And with peace so pervasive, defense spending in Israel dropped from 35 percent of the gross national product in 1975, one of the highest percentages in the world, to under 10 percent in 1995, about normal for many industrialized countries.

Rabin himself was sometimes astonished by manifestations of the spreading prosperity. Caught in a monumental traffic jam one day, he groused to his driver, Yehezkel Sharabi:

"Yehezkel, how could there be so many cars in so small a state?"

The territories were also profiting from peace, with returning Palestinians, for example, investing $500 million in the construction of seventy high-rise office and apartment buildings and hundreds of small enterprises in impoverished Gaza.

Jordan, too, was benefiting from peace as thousands of Israelis crowded into buses or mounted tired donkeys in the desert to visit the red-rock wonders of Petra.

Thus, Oslo, which could ultimately promote change throughout the impoverished Middle East, had already transformed Israel from a besieged, boycotted, debt-ridden, survival-obsessed country into a nation that, for the first time, was able to relax, enjoy a good life, and even display little shock when someone sought excuses for evading military duty so he could go into business and compete in the global economy. Even though shaken up by each exploding bomb, this was a new, happier, less militant Israel.

The product, according to some, of treason . . .

27

The Halo of Pinhas

Overthrow the "evil" government of Prime Minister Rabin and try him for treason if he doesn't abandon Oslo!

This advice was offered in a startling letter three prominent rabbis wrote in February 1995 to other members of the clergy, including chief rabbis Israel Lau and Eliahu Bakshi-Doron.

Israel's rabbis and opposition political leaders, the authors argued, "should warn the prime minister, as well as the other government ministers, that if they continue to submit the residents of Judea, Samaria, and the Gaza Strip to the care of the Palestinian Authority's murderers, then, according to the Jewish Halakah, we must put them on public trial and punish them according to the rules on dealing with *mosers*."

A *moser*, according to the Halakah (the body of Jewish law supplementing the Talmud, or scriptural law, especially its legal part), was someone who handed over responsibility for Jewish security or Jewish capital to non-Jews. And the penalty for this act, virtually ignored since biblical times, was usually death.

The signers of the letter, Rabbis Eliezer Melamed, Dov Lior, and Daniel Shiloh, even asked whether the army leaders who "took part in shaping the . . . agreement" should be considered "partners in this sin."

Action against these army leaders would almost certainly spark civil war, but this apparently did not occur to the three rabbis.

Nor did they feel that the forced ouster of the government would be undemocratic. For after the Shas, a small Jewish religious party, had quit the cabinet, Rabin, they argued, relied on Israeli Arab votes in the Knesset to achieve a majority. Why should Arab votes count? Didn't biblical law take precedence over secular law?

The three rabbis urged their fellows not to "tell us that we should not ask such indecent questions, for we can no longer mute them. We can no longer control these questions, since they come out of many Jewish hearts in this land as well as throughout the diaspora. Many of them discuss the matter very seriously. Our brothers' blood is calling to us from beneath this land. . . . We had better provide the cure before the blow."

These rabbis received only three replies. Two claimed that the problem could be solved only by the Messiah when he came, and that today's rabbis still didn't have the right to discuss it. The third rabbi responded that "no individual is allowed to accuse the government of handing over [Jewish land to the Arabs]." But if the public as a whole decided to put the government on trial, it could do so.

According to experts, an estimated twenty to thirty rabbis were contemplating a "cure," even if they were afraid to admit it in writing. Conversation about biblical passages that might justify murder was, in fact, fervent in the West Bank synagogues and schools. Paradoxically, these God-driven zealots ignored God's commandment, "Thou shalt not kill." The settlers, feeling cornered in a world crumbling around them, with their lives and homes endangered, their children risking death every minute, despaired, some, it seemed, to the point of madness. And they were willing to kill in order to thwart Oslo—in God's name.

As early as May 13, 1994, Aharon Dumb, spokesman for the West Bank settlers' council, warned Rabin in a letter:

> The fact that you and many other government officials don't identify with the suffering of Jews . . . gives many people in Israel a terrible feeling of alienation. Many people translate that feeling into

desperation. For a few of them that desperation may lead to taking radical steps. Unfortunately, I hear that the only solution to this problem is committing a political murder. Such a murder, God forbid, would be a terrible misdeed in every respect. . . . Still, I find it appropriate to warn you about it, for if you continue your current trend, you'll bear at least indirect responsibility for some individual's satanic action.

Thus, not surprisingly, Satan saw his opportunity a year later when a rash of demonstrations by religious groups erupted every day across the country, with Likud and other secular rightist forces playing a less prominent role in the streets. Some rabbis recited kaddish, the prayer for the dead, to express their wish for Rabin's death. And one rabbi organized an ancient Jewish ceremony, *Pulsa Denura*, to place a curse on the prime minister.

In the inflamed atmosphere, the nation's focus was now less on the political struggle than on two individuals—Rabin and Peres—who were supposedly responsible for killing Jews. The cries of "treason" and "murderer" rang in the ears of a young religious rightist, Yigal Amir, and fellow extremists; and posters caricaturing, in Nazi style, a hook-nosed Rabin with gnarled fingers dripping blood incited them further—though Amir needed little encouragement to play God's avenger.

Rabin was a *moser*, yes. But wasn't he also a *rodef*? This was a more efficient excuse for murder, for the victim wouldn't even have to be tried. According to the Book of Numbers, Chapter 25, Zimri, the head of the Tribe of Shimon, had sex with a daughter of a Moabite priest in front of Moses and other Israelite elders, possibly triggering a wave of assimilation with the Moabite idol worshippers in violation of God's will. Horrified, Pinhas, the grandson of the high priest of Aharon, the brother of Moses, ran toward the lovers and stabbed them to death. God was said to approve these murders because Pinhas was acting as a zealot, seeking in passion to prevent a crime against Him. And this approval would be interpreted by some rabbis to mean that a person could, without trial or approval by a rabbi, justifiably kill someone chasing an intended victim with a knife in hand.

Although this obscure biblical ruling had been collecting cobwebs for centuries, Yigal Amir dusted it off and revived it. But he twisted its meaning to apply to Rabin, whom he saw as the modern Zimri, supposedly responsible for killing Jews by pursuing the peace process. And he saw himself as a man wearing the halo of Pinhas. He thus had a God-given right to murder Rabin.

Amir, a deeply religious Yemenite Jew, began forging the halo after he witnessed the Rabin-Arafat handshake that stunned the world in late 1993. Ironically, he decided he might have to kill the man who had opened the way to Redemption in the 1967 war. Amir was born in 1970, only three years after Rabin had liberated Jerusalem and other holy territory. To commemorate that "miracle," his parents named the boy "Yigal," which means "he will redeem" in Hebrew. Had not God redeemed His nation—if with the help of Yitzhak Rabin? In fact, Rabin came to be seen by many religious Zionists as another Judas Maccabees, the Jewish patriot who led a revolt in 168 B.C. against Hellenism and Syrian rule. Some even wondered if he was another Joshua, who had led the Israelites into the Promised Land.

Thus, during the euphoric aftermath of that war, Rabin's secular Zionism, rooted in Theodor Herzl's dream, and the religious Zionist movement, founded by Rabbi Avraham Kook, merged into an umbrella nationalism with spiritual overtones that stirred even the unreligious chief of staff. Yet the 1967 war, together with the 1948 conflict, promised different destinies to Rabin and to Yigal Amir, who grew up in an atmosphere imbued with religious Zionism. To Rabin, these wars signified the beginning of modern Zionism, the building of a powerful, democratic, Western-oriented Jewish state that could protect world Jewry from the ravages of anti-Semitism while living in peace with its neighbors.

To Amir, the two wars signaled the beginning of the fulfillment of God's promise of redemption, the start of the messianic period, with the building of a Greater Israel to herald the coming of the Messiah. And as the Jews waited for him to come, they would protect the sacred land from the gentiles' grasp. For the Jews to voluntarily give up any of it was a crime deserving of death.

As Israeli philosopher David Hartman would tell me, Amir was "an outgrowth of a single-minded perception of Israel based on a single value—the Greater Land of Israel, the key to salvation. By giving back some of the land, the government was spitting in God's face."

Amir came from a traditionally ultra-Orthodox family, but he soon embraced Rabbi Kook's more modern, activist strain of Orthodoxy. The true ultra-Orthodox were not Zionists at all and were even excused from military service—the supreme duty of the Zionist—so they could sit in the yeshivas all day studying the Torah. In fact, they opposed the rebirth of a Jewish state until the Messiah came, since only then would the Jews, exiled for 2,000 years for their sins, be redeemed and permitted to live under their own rule. When Herzl first pushed for a Jewish state, many Orthodox argued that the Jews should meanwhile settle in Uganda.

Rabbi Kook, however, moved from Russia to Palestine in 1904, rationalizing his support of Zionism with a new movement merging Jewish mysticism with modern nationalism. This was justified, he argued, because the first trickle of European Jews to the Holy Land signaled the birth of the messianic period and was proof that a state could be built with God's approval. And Kook's religious Zionists were soon plowing the land alongside the socialist pioneers and forming their own kibbutzim, preparing to greet the Messiah with all the biblical land in their hands, some dreaming of the day when the Third Temple would rise over the ashes of the al-Aksa Mosque. And when the Jewish state was reborn in 1948, the Zionist rabbis, who would enter politics with a National Religious Party, called Israel "the first flowering of our Redemption."

After the second flowering of 1967, Amir, one of eight children, was brought up in an ambiance of Torah study in a poor neighborhood of Herzliya, near Tel Aviv. His father, Shlomo, a gentle, black-bearded Torah scribe, who had emigrated from Yemen, pored over the Torah through thick-lensed glasses and repaired damaged sacred scrolls. But Yigal's mother, Geula, earned most of the family income, running a nursery school at home while raising her own brood. Yigal was no problem; he would study beside his father while other children were outside playing soccer. He had more important things in mind.

"Even as a young child," Geula would say, "Yigal displayed an energy and drive that set him apart from other children. Whatever Yigal wanted, he found a way to get."

One thing her son wanted was to be admired as a great religious scholar. Narcissistic and schizoid "in some degree," according to psychiatrists, Amir, in his yeshiva high school, was especially driven by the desire to show the lighter-skinned, sometimes prejudiced students of European origin that a Yemenite could be smarter than they. He earned good if not outstanding grades in the yeshiva, but learned nothing of democracy, since this subject was not on the agenda in the religious schools. Later, he served as a model soldier in the elite Golani Brigade.

Shortly after the shock of the handshake, Amir enrolled in Bar-Ilan University, a prestigious religious institution, where he earned high grades in law, computer science, and especially Torah studies. According to his lawyer, Shmuel Fleishman, he held an exceptionally high IQ of 144, though, unfortunately, "he thought in black and white." He often missed classes, preferring to pore over books in the study room or at home under his own superior tutelage. Seeking to show off his knowledge, he claimed to know more than his teachers.

"I never had so stubborn a student," Rabbi Moshe Raziel, his mentor at Bar-Ilan, told me. "He asked questions and I answered, but he never accepted anything I said. He gave his own answers and never admitted he was wrong."

But Amir would argue, according to his friends: "What can the rabbis teach me? They bore me."

This egocentric attitude found an explosive outlet in the Oslo accords, symbolized by the handshake. Here was "treason," and who could better serve as God's agent in stopping it than Yigal Amir? And his rage over the subsequent bus bombings, with all the casualties they caused, further nurtured the vision of himself as the divinely appointed protector of his people, who could murder a *Zimri* with impunity.

Appropriately for a modern Pinhas, Amir would not suffer people who did not explicitly agree with his views on how to deal with the pernicious peace process.

"Yigal would not listen," a former friend of Amir told me, "when I tried to explain that many rabbis didn't think the *rodef* rule would justify murder today."

Din rodef, Amir vigorously insisted, was still a living concept, though it wasn't clear whether he considered this solution to the Rabin problem only in a theoretical sense. He argued that in biblical days someone could be executed for simply violating the Sabbath rule.

"Do you want to live the rest of your life in jail?" his friend asked.

"So what if I do?" Amir replied. "I'll read the Talmud in jail."

"You're crazy," his friend replied. And he added sarcastically: "Go and kill him."

Amir smiled.

To make sure his fellow students would not be swayed by soft-liners like his friend, Amir began to organize campus demonstrations against the government and arrange Sabbath weekend trips to the settlements and to various towns where sharp-tongued speakers would dwell on Rabin's sins.

At one demonstration, Amir for once dwelled on something other than these sins. Her name was Nava Holtzman. Amir, short, dark, and fragile-looking, had never shown much interest in girls, telling his friends that none he had ever met was good enough for him. She would have to be pretty, smart, and rich, he said. And Nava was all of these things.

Soon, Amir, after carefully researching her religious background and moral conduct, asked her to marry him, but she declined. The reason, some of his friends thought, was that members of her family objected to him because he was a Yemenite, a pejorative background for many Ashkenazis, Jews from Europe, who associated this Sephardic origin with dark skin and low social status. Shortly, Nava married—but not Amir; the groom was one of his best friends. Amir attended the wedding, apparently to show that he didn't really care.

"Actually," a former schoolmate of Amir told me, "he was shattered. Especially since he was very sensitive about his Yemenite origin and was always trying to prove he was smarter and better in everything than the Ashkenazis. And the one girl he wanted rejected him, he felt, because he was a Yemenite—and then married a close friend."

Like a burning match tossed into a barrel of nitroglycerin, the ingredient of bias-based rejection added to an already potent mixture of narcissism, ultra-nationalism, and religious fanaticism had an incendiary effect. Amir would have to prove in some way to Nava and all the others who had rejected him that he had the God-given courage, will, and ability to do things nobody else would dare do. God, he was sure, would help him to become a hero, a modern prophet, the savior of his people. He intensified his search for the answer to Rabin's "treason." And the answer ripened in his mind after his first personal encounter with the prime minister. As psychiatrists who later examined him would report:

> The idea to perpetrate [the murder of Rabin] . . . began to take form when he saw Mr. Rabin at the wedding of one of his friends to the daughter of Chief Rabbi [Israel] Lau. It was at this time that he saw the late prime minister for the first time as, in his words: "flesh and blood," and thought to himself: "Some day I will be sorry if I do not kill him."

"Peres and Rabin are snakes," Amir would tell several friends one day. "Cut off their heads, and the snake will lose its way. Poke out their eyes and they're in the dark. They must both be killed, because each eggs the other on. The state will be saved if someone gets up and eliminates them. There will be elections. Bibi [Netanyahu] will come to power."

When someone pointed out that only rabbis could give a ruling on this, he testily replied: "The rabbis are all cowards, all afraid to interpret Jewish law my way. They are no longer relevant."

Yigal's elder brother, Hagai, who seldom disagreed with his more assertive sibling, did not disagree. And a friend, Dror Adani, apparently didn't either. Adani learned of Yigal's "fantasy" when Yigal played cupid for his sister Vardit, even as he nursed his own heartbreak. Yigal brought Adani home as a potential suitor for Vardit, but while the young man was immediately attracted to her, the feeling was not reciprocated. Adani would not give up, however, and he joined her two brothers in plotting murder only as an excuse, he would claim, to come to the house so he could be with Vardit.

Adani, as well as several other friends who supported the plot, would insist they thought the plotting was theoretical and didn't believe that Amir would actually try to kill Rabin. In any case, Amir suggested some imaginative schemes. They could booby-trap Rabin's car; introduce nitroglycerin into his home through the water pipes of his apartment building; shoot at him through his apartment window when he came into sight; place a car bomb along the route traveled by the prime minister; or fire at him with a missile.

But after analyzing all possibilities, the plotters concluded that only one was feasible. The best way to kill Rabin was simply to fire at close range the 9-mm Beretta pistol Amir was licensed to possess.

Though Hagai had an arsenal of weapons at home that he had stolen while in the army, he would claim that he tried to dissuade his brother from committing the murder—from short range. Yigal's chances of survival, he argued, would be slim. Hagai proposed another, more practical plan in which Yigal would fire a rifle from a distance. But Yigal was immovable. To be sure of success, he had to fire from close range. Perhaps he would be killed himself, but just as likely he would be captured and sent to prison. It was the least sacrifice he could make in the service of God.

In fact, Amir would carry out his plan only when God provided the perfect opportunity. And obstacles in his path would be a sign from heaven that the time was not ripe. God surely understood that his "goal was not to murder him as a man. I gain nothing from the fact that he is dead. Were he to be paralyzed and stop functioning as prime minister, it would be the same as far as I am concerned."

But as determined as Amir was to carry out his mission, it would be nice, he felt, if a rabbi would confirm that the *din rodef* rule applied to Rabin. However, Adani told him he had asked his yeshiva rabbi, Moshe Tsuriel, about this, and the rabbi had replied that theoretically the rule would apply to the prime minister, but practically it would not, for Rabin represented half the people and his murder could spark a civil war that would endanger the nation more than Oslo would.

Amir ignored the advice. The rabbis were boring, as usual. Anyway, because he knew the intricacies of the Torah, he hardly needed rabbinical guidance. After all, Pinhas, acting as a zealot, attacked Zimri without consulting a rabbi, even though Moses himself, the greatest prophet, was present at the murder scene. Amir ignored the fact that Pinhas acted spontaneously out of passion, while he himself would act only after careful planning and cool analysis—a premeditated crime inconsistent with the concept of zealotry. There was no scriptural evidence strong enough to dissuade Amir from projecting himself for history as a prophetic link between biblical times and the coming of the Messiah; he would, with God's approval, murder a man to save the Jewish people.

Nor did Amir think killing the prime minister was likely to

ignite a civil war, as Adani's rabbi warned. Many people, spoiled by Western democratic norms, would surely deplore the action. But they would soon realize that he had saved the state and paved the way for final Redemption. Israel's soldiers wouldn't turn on each other. Meanwhile, ever greater numbers of religious Zionists were rising in the army hierarchy and would control dissenters. Further bolstering Amir's confidence in their power, Shlomo Goren, the chief military chaplain in the 1948 war and later chief rabbi of Israel, had issued a ruling in December 1993 requiring soldiers to ignore any orders to dismantle settlements.

Even as he plotted the murder, Amir continued to arrange virulent anti-government demonstrations in the settlements and elsewhere. And also to help in the building of new illegal settlements and in the struggle against army efforts to evacuate some. He had to generate a constantly escalating feeling of outrage that would spark such resistance to the peace process that the government would find it impossible to pursue it, at least after Rabin was out of the way.

But peace opponents, especially secular Israelis, turned out in rather sparse numbers at the right-wing rallies; the unreligious represented only about 20 percent of the demonstrators. Some secular right-wing leaders like Benjamin Netanyahu showed up at the big rallies; less, it seemed, to promote ideology than to harvest votes in the next election. Amir worked feverishly on the phone for hours, rounding up people to attend his meetings. Thus, he was helping mightily to fuel the flames that were, in turn, spurring him toward extreme violence.

In this effort, Amir had the full cooperation of a fellow student named Avishai Raviv, whose rightist activism made him the terror of the Bar-Ilan campus. Raviv, a good-looking youth with narrow eyes and curly hair, was a longtime member of the violent, extreme right-wing Kach movement founded by Rabbi Meir Kahane, which sought to establish a theocratic Greater Israel cleansed of Arabs. He had been expelled from Tel Aviv University for his troublemaking, but he carried on his activities at Bar-Ilan, ordering his gang, called Eyal, to beat up backers of the peace process and labeling his enemies "traitors."

Finally, Raviv was ousted from that school, too, when it was learned he was encouraging people to throw acid in the faces of Arabs. But though he was arrested many times for his violent activities, he was never detained for long. Why? Because he was on the payroll of Shin Bet, Israel's domestic security service, which had used him to penetrate right-wing groups and inform on their violent activities since 1987. He was also, apparently, an agent provocateur, perhaps self-appointed, whose aim was to incite prospective terrorists to some action that would make them liable to apprehension and punishment.

There is no question that Raviv was a spy for the Shin Bet, which ignored his own violent activities as long as he furnished it useful information. Carmi Gillon, who was the Shin Bet chief, would not deny to me that Raviv worked as an agency informer. And Raviv himself admitted as much when, despite public denials, he told me that he would not betray the organization by replying. The question was whether he was mainly interested in provoking violence for his own ideological ends, or was more interested in trapping his rightist comrades for monetary gain before they could act. How did he pay for his new Subaru car? He used money donated to his group, he claimed. But his assistant Nathan Levi would say:

"I never saw anybody donating money to our movement."

Shin Bet apparently believed that Raviv could be trusted—a possibly deadly error. In any case, the extremist groups suspected that any outsider contacting them was working for the agency, and it was hard for Shin Bet to recruit someone from within these groups. Raviv was thus a valuable intelligence asset. Minister of Police Moshe Shahal told me he asked agency leaders for information about Raviv's extremist movement, but received no cooperation. The group, Shin Bet simply said, was very small and ineffective.

"Yigal Amir or his brother," Shahal pointed out to me, "drove by Rabin's apartment building in an old Volkswagen almost every day for a year checking when he left, how many guards were around, etcetera. I never heard of Amir before the assassination. Protection of the prime minister was not the responsibility of the police, but of the Shin Bet. Why didn't they check who was in that car? Why didn't they investigate Amir?"

Perhaps because Raviv threw his patron, Shin Bet, off the track.

Shahal was utterly frustrated. In July 1995, he had sent two letters to the attorney general asking for an investigation of rabbis who advised soldiers to disobey any orders to evacuate settlers, and was told that their demand was not a crime. And shortly afterward, when he warned rightist Knesset members that their "very harsh" language against Rabin could incite some hothead to assassinate cabinet members, they ignored him. Now the Shin Bet was silent about Raviv's group.

Amir first met Raviv at Bar-Ilan in spring 1994 and was impressed by his new friend's bold activities. Raviv sponsored a paramilitary Eyal summer camp for young militants, and proudly showed reporters how he trained them in the use of automatic weapons, pistols, and knives. He plastered extremist posters on buildings all around the campus. He was, in short, doing what was necessary to stoke a revolutionary atmosphere in Israel.

But though Amir worked closely with Raviv in creating this atmosphere and, according to Amir's friends, often discussed his murderous intention with the man, as he did with them (though they would claim they didn't believe he was serious), Raviv offered Shin Bet no hint that Amir might spark a possible catastrophe.

Nor did Shin Bet readily act on hints it already had, including one dropped by a former Bar-Ilan student, Shlomo Halevy, who had heard Amir talk about the need to kill Rabin. Not wishing to inform on him by name, Halevy told a contact in army intelligence that he had overheard a conversation in a Tel Aviv public rest room in which an unknown person spoke of his plan to murder Rabin.

Soon summoned by the police at the request of Shin Bet, Halevy described the person—his features, size, clothes—and even said the man had indicated he was a Bar-Ilan student. And if the police had pressed him harder, Halevy would later say, he would have revealed that the man was Amir. But Shin Bet never took the hint. Even so, it was concerned enough about Amir to ask Raviv to check him out in August 1995. Raviv reported back that Amir had talked to him about killing Arabs, but not any Jew.

Carmi Gillon, the Shin Bet chief, was not sure whether this report was accurate, but he had heard rumors that some Israeli might be waiting for the proper moment to assassinate the prime minister, perhaps motivated by the demonstrations at which he was viciously accused of murder and treason. He went to Rabin and told him:

"I don't think the danger is from Likud members. All you need is one crazy guy with a gun who takes the slogans seriously."

Rabin shook his head and replied: "Impossible. I don't believe it."

Shin Bet was, of course, responsible to Rabin, and the prime minister could demand to see the Shin Bet's raw data and study every detail. But it isn't clear whether he saw the information on potential terrorists—like Amir and Raviv—thought dangerous to his own safety. In any case, he seldom if ever questioned its wisdom. Like most Israelis, he was conditioned by military training to put complete faith in the security system. Nor would stressing his personal safety be macho.

Besides, a Jew, he felt, would not kill a Jew. He preferred to ignore the Jewish civil war 2,000 years earlier in which thousands of Jews died at one another's hands; and even more to the point, the *Altalena* incident during the 1948 war, in which he himself exchanged fire with, and may have killed, supporters of Menachem Begin. Somehow, in this modern age in which Jews around the world were basically united in their support of the Jewish state against the anti-Zionist forces of the world, it didn't seem possible that one Jew would kill another, when every one was so precious in the struggle for survival.

But in fact, Amir was at this point thinking only about killing a Jew—the prime minister. And he was in a hurry because he feared that someone might preempt him and rob him of the glory he felt he deserved.

"I wanted a thinking person to do it," he would say. "I was afraid that an Arab would kill him. I wanted it to be seen from heaven that someone of the People has done it."

He was the thinker most qualified to commit the holy act, Amir was convinced—failing to explain how a well-thought-out murder could be justified under the *din rodef* rule.

"I was afraid that I would try and fail," he would admit. "This was my greatest fear—to throw away my life for nothing. I decided, therefore, that there is no such thing as failure. I will do it only if I'm sure I'll succeed. I am not willing to accept the possibility of failure."

Amir was cautious indeed. Carrying in a pocket of his trousers a pistol loaded with especially lethal dumdum bullets procured by his brother, he stalked Rabin three times in the first nine months of 1995. He was thwarted the first time in January when the prime minister failed to appear for a scheduled visit to the Yad Vashem Holocaust museum, ironically a memorial to millions of Jews who were also the targets of a madman. He failed the second time in April when he found Rabin too well guarded, and the third time in September when he arrived at a ceremony after his quarry had departed. Amir wasn't too disappointed. If God did not think the time was right, who was he to argue with Him? Soon, Amir was confident, God would give him the go-ahead signal.

On October 5, 1995, Raviv would do his best, it seemed, to nudge God's hand. At a huge demonstration of some 30,000 rightist party members in Jerusalem's Zion Square after the Knesset approved the second Oslo accord, Raviv and his supporters distributed and burned posters portraying Rabin in a Nazi uniform. Standing on a balcony overlooking the crowd, Benjamin Netanyahu delivered a speech blasting Rabin's policies while the prime minister watched the frenzy on television at home.

"Well, what can be done?" Rabin commented when his family expressed horror. "We are living in a democracy."

Netanyahu would claim later that he did not see the posters being held up and that he had admonished the audience to eschew violence and violent words, though others say his pleas were lukewarm. And he had tried, if unsuccessfully, to meet with Rabin to answer the prime minister's charges that he was inciting violence. Rabin was convinced Netanyahu did indeed support the incitement, and grew even more defiant.

Meanwhile, Amir joined with another extremist, Binyamin Elon, a Knesset deputy and member of the far-right Moledet Party, to organize a demonstration in Arab East Jerusalem.

"I am against Oslo," Elon, an affable, rotund, trim-bearded man, told me. "I don't want peace with the Palestinians, only with Syria, Jordan, and the other Arab states. The Palestinians should have civil rights, but the land is the land of Israel."

Elon saw nothing wrong in calling Rabin a "traitor," though conceding that the prime minister himself "didn't think he was a traitor." Crying "murderer," however, was going too far.

But not for the demonstrators that Elon, with Amir's help, had gathered. Amir had brought about 150 fellow students from Bar-Ilan University with him, and he had arranged for the speaker, Uri Milstein, a Bar-Ilan instructor on military and security matters who would eventually be fired for his extremism. Milstein was the author of books that viciously attacked Rabin as a cowardly, monstrous human being. Now he expounded on his obsession for more than ten hours, disturbing even Elon with his villainous portrait of Rabin—and the army he had served.

Amir rejoiced in Milstein's lecture, which had excited the audience and would help to make Rabin's murder seem justified. Teacher and student had a warm relationship. Amir greatly admired Milstein's books, especially one about the "dynamic philosophy" of Israel's security organizations, pointing out the holes in its operations. Amir studied these weaknesses zealously so he could exploit them when the time for action came.

Milstein regarded Amir, he told me, as one of his best students.

On October 10, another meeting of rightists was held in the Wingate Institute in Netanya, and both Rabin and Netanyahu were invited. To the surprise of many, the prime minister found the time to attend, while the Likud leader did not. Rabin was determined to show that he could not be intimidated, whatever the risk. And the risk was substantial.

Even before he started to speak, the audience, mainly right-wing Anglo-American immigrants, booed and heckled him venomously and would not cease even when his voice boomed through the microphone, drowning him out. Then a man rushed toward him with obviously hostile intentions, and was fortunately stopped by bodyguards. His face beet-red with anger and frustration, Rabin shouted at the audience, which was calling for an end to Oslo:

They were "racists," "Kahanists," "an embarrassment to Judaism."

Finally, after ten minutes, Rabin gave up, but he didn't run off. He joined the organizers for refreshments, acting as if nothing had happened. When one of them apologized and remarked in jest that if the audience had consisted of Kurds, for example, "this wouldn't have happened," Rabin replied:

"No, the Americans do this best."

Rabin greatly admired the United States and fondly remembered his ambassadorial days there, but he also remembered that President Johnson would not dare face the bitter "anti-Vietnam" crowds in his last months in office. Nor could Rabin forget the fate met by the Kennedys and Martin Luther King Jr. Rage could be uncontrollable in America. Not so in Israel. Yes, he could stand up to a little heckling.

Rabin was, in fact, less concerned about an assassin's bullet than about the prospect of losing supporters to the Likud. Throughout his political life, his game plan had been to convince a majority that they could trust whatever peace deal he might reach. Did the crowd's refusal even to let him speak suggest that, at the moment of truth, he was losing the game? In calling them names, he reacted much as he had as a child when he threw sand at girls who ridiculed him; it was his instant, automatic antidote to insecurity.

Even so, some observers thought Rabin actually welcomed the insult. The general public, hopefully the majority, would believe what he had been telling them: His attackers were extremists, even if they didn't attack with bullets. Moreover, he had demonstrated that he had the courage to face them.

The question was, in the minds of many people, even some of his supporters, should he have faced them with more tact and sensitivity? This would be difficult, of course, for someone being called a "traitor" and "murderer," especially for someone as thin-skinned as Rabin. But, it was pointed out, opponents of Menachem Begin had called the late Likud leader a "murderer," and yet he had met with them and shown understanding. Sometimes Rabin, too, would talk with protesters, asking his driver to stop his car when he saw them in the street. But he tended to lecture them rather than inquire about their problems.

A more sensitive response to the settlers' distress probably wouldn't have eased the hatred of the real extremists, but it might have softened the attitude of many anti-Oslo Israelis and prevented their radicalization to some degree. Professor Ehud Sprinzak of Hebrew University told me:

"Rabin didn't defuse the settlers' anger because he didn't make a distinction between the majority and the extremists. The hard-core and leadership is Orthodox, but 85 percent of the activists are pragmatic, and most are secular. He was simply unable to address himself to this matter."

Rabin might have told the settlers that while he disagreed with their views, he realized they were in pain and would do his best to minimize their sacrifices; in short, he should have convinced his foes he cared about them even as he pursued peace.

The prime minister was a paradox; the very straightforward- ness and honesty that had won the admiration of most Israelis and almost all foreigners he dealt with generated bitter hatred among his domestic foes. And Rabin's habit of dismissing someone's opposing view with a sharp jerk of his hand was reflected verbally in his sarcastic, sometimes brutal remarks.

Curiously, Peres, who was associated as closely with Oslo as Rabin, and indeed brought the idea to him, had never aroused the same enmity in the opposition.

"We don't agree with Peres," said one settler typically, "but he visited us and asked us about our problems. Rabin treated us as if we weren't even part of Israel."

This distinction, it seems, was due in part to expectations. Peres had for many years been viewed as a dove who would make peace even at a high cost to Israel, while Rabin was "Mr. Security"; he would never make a deal at Israel's expense. But the hawk had suddenly turned into a dove—though, in fact, the "hawk" had always been waiting for the appropriate moment to thrust toward peace. In the eyes of the settlers, he had betrayed them.

The depth of the opposition's rancor toward Rabin was poignantly, if subjectively, mirrored in the words of one member of the Anglo-American audience that hooted him off the platform:

> Did one support this spiteful, almost hateful, exhibition of derision of our highest office-bearer; or did one turn on one's heel and leave in disgust . . . ? However tempting it may have been, I couldn't boo Rabin for his politics. Though I believe that our prime minister has made a complete mockery of, and shown utter contempt for, the genuine ideals of both Judaism and Zionism, I do believe there is validity in the argument that political debate should not descend into verbal violence and abuse. . . .
>
> What I began to ponder was the man himself, and how Rabin's behavior has affected his office. I remembered his invective, his arrogance. I began to think about the kind of man he seems to have

become, how the trappings of statesmanship seem to have removed him from the day-to-day concerns of so many of the people he was elected to represent.

"I remembered his utterances, very many of them foul-mouthed, voiced from the insulation of the Knesset podium, or the comfort of television studios. Many of them were made against huge numbers of his own people, citizens whose feelings and legitimate concerns he has so blatantly ignored over the past months, people who have repeatedly asked for acknowledgment that he hears them. Sadly, our premier has made a point of not hearing them.

"Suddenly, . . . I didn't want to hear him either. I took a shallow, painful breath. And booed."

What this man, like most of the opposition, did not seem to realize was that while Rabin unreservedly spoke his mind, as he always did, whether as soldier, diplomat, or politician, and reacted acidly to the charges being hurled at him, he did indeed hear the settlers. In fact, while rejecting the concept of a Greater Israel, he had been fighting for the settlers' rights ever since the Oslo talks began. He thus envisaged a final plan that called for an exchange of land with the Palestinians that would incorporate about 90 percent of the West Bank settlements into Israel proper.

As one security official told me: "Rabin loved the people he ridiculed, though he condemned their behavior."

One West Bank settler who did realize that Rabin was a friend, not an enemy, of the settlements despite his caustic comments was Rabbi Yoel Ben-Nun, a red-bearded man of extraordinary courage who dared to confront his extremist colleagues despite threats to his life.

"I was frightened by all the talk of pseudo-Jewish law that was being applied in a political context," he told me. "I felt I must try to stop it, to change the atmosphere before it was too late."

Ben-Nun was especially concerned when several yeshiva students told him that some rabbis were calling for the punishment of the premier under the *din rodef* and *din moser* rules, possibly referring, among others, to the three who sent a letter to their colleagues with this suggestion. His fear growing, Ben-Nun urgently advised the two chief rabbis to choose three honored rabbis to hear evidence and take action against those using pseudo-Jewish law to inflame the atmosphere.

"They agreed," Ben-Nun would say, "but then they changed their mind. They were afraid of the results. They said the police should deal with the matter, though I knew that without direct evidence the police would do nothing and no court would touch the case."

In fact, some months later, Sephardic Chief Rabbi Eliahu Bakshi-Doron, though hesitant to check the *din rodef* rule as it applied to Rabin, did not hesitate to apply it to another perceived enemy. He accused the leadership of the Jewish Reform Movement that embraces many Jews in the United States and is making headway in Israel of being the modern *Zimri* out to destroy traditional Judaism—an allusion that, despite his denial to me, many Jews would interpret as meaning the Reform leaders should be tried as *rodefs* and perhaps condemned to death.

Rabbi Ben-Nun was desperate. He could see disaster ahead, fueled by pseudo-Jewish law and the public words of Rabin.

"Actually," he told me, "Rabin cared a great deal about the settlers. But he didn't make this clear in his speech and his mannerisms. And he was often misinterpreted. For example, he was said to have remarked that he didn't care what happened to the '2 percent' of Israelis who lived in the West Bank. But what he really said was that they would suffer great hardships living there. I'm sure I could have convinced my colleagues of his true intentions, but I would have had to spend an hour with each and I didn't have the time. In any case, everybody who wanted to know his view knew, but they were carried along by the poisoned atmosphere."

Ben-Nun went urgently to see Rabin and advised him to treat the settlers humanely and avoid the language of "delegitimatization."

"You know that I care about the settlers," the prime minister replied, "and that I don't intend to evacuate them."

Ben-Nun realized that Rabin was often rude in speech and manner even to his friends, but that these expressions of impatience or anger seldom reflected the feelings in his heart.

"Yes, I know," he said, "but that is not important. Thousands of people out there feel you don't care. This is very important."

Rabin was silent for a moment, then responded: "You're right. I won't make any inflammatory statements again."

"Well, will you retract what you have already said?"

No, he couldn't do that. How could he apologize to those who called him a "traitor" and a "murderer"?

But, urged by Eitan Haber, who was present, Rabin agreed to talk with several West Bank rabbis and explain his position.

On October 31, three bearded men sat with Rabin in his office.

One of them, Rabbi Melamed, had been a signer of the letter circulated among his colleagues suggesting that Rabin be tried as a *rodef*. Another was Rabbi Rabinovich, known for his extreme views. Some weeks earlier, Yitzhak Frankenthal, the father of a soldier who had been murdered by Hamas terrorists, warned him that he must do nothing to provoke a civil war, which would mean only more death. Rabinovich replied:

"You should know, Yitzhak, if the army gives an order to evacuate any settlement, we must do everything possible to prevent it—even lay land mines."

In shock, Frankenthal, who strongly supported Rabin and Oslo, responded: "I don't understand. You mean that people must kill our soldiers? My daughter and surviving son are in the army and they might have to carry out the order."

"If they do," Rabinovich retorted, "they should be careful because they would be considered evil. If Israelis carry out the order, they will be resisted as if they are soldiers of the Third Reich."

Now these godly men, who were prepared to use ungodly means to achieve their ends and might have been arrested in any other democratic country, sat sipping tea with Rabin, the "devil" himself. And Rabin, apparently unaware of their mortal threats to his soldiers and himself, seemed to be less evil than they had thought.

No Jewish settlements would be uprooted, the prime minister promised (though he had apparently been thinking about leaving some 10 percent of them in Palestinian territory). And he wanted to speak with the settlers so he could reassure them that the army would protect them.

When the rabbis had departed, Rabin remarked to Haber: "Look how pleasant they were. Rabinovich reminded me of a British noble."

Haber, who had arranged the meeting to reduce the friction with the religious right, realized that he had succeeded only too well, at least with Rabin. Ease the friction, yes, but utter pleasant words about people who wanted to destroy him?

"You don't really know them," Haber replied. "Yitzhak, you're naive."

The rabbis were surprised by Rabin's own pleasantness as they left, but they were skeptical. Even if Rabin didn't evacuate the settlements, he was still determined to give away Jewish land to the Palestinians. And that was a crime. Amir, of course, would agree, though, as he waited for the proper moment to strike with God's help, he didn't care what the rabbis thought. Did Pinhas?

On October 20, Rabin, with Leah, returned with a sense of relief to a country where he didn't have to listen constantly to hecklers spitting their venom outside his home—the United States. The trip was one grand love affair. At the United Nations, which once regarded Israel as a virtual pariah, about eighty heads of state who had gathered there eagerly sought appointments with him, though there was time for only forty. One of them, President Jiang Zemin of China, which had for so long shunned Israel, told Rabin, referring to the relative size of their two countries:

"To us, the quality and might of a nation is judged not by the size of its population, but by the culture and technological advancement of its people. By those standards, Israel is indeed a superpower."

In Washington, Rabin was treated every bit like the head of a superpower, with officials and members of Congress lining up to shake his hand. One particular scene was especially moving: When Rabin one evening had no time to change from a business suit to a tuxedo for an official black-tie function, President Clinton personally clasped a bow tie on him. Rabin was reminded how far he had come since the peace conference in Rhodes almost fifty years earlier, when someone had to show him how to put on his first tie.

Rabin—and Peres—had turned the world around.

But had they turned Israel around? Rabin was worried that his people might be losing their faith in him. The hate demonstrations were growing, and not many of his backers were showing their support openly. When Gad Yaacobi, then Israeli ambassador to the United Nations, returned home on a visit and told Rabin that he should take care of himself, the prime minister waxed philosophical about his longevity, startling Yaacobi with a rare effusion of wistful emotion:

"Most of my closest friends are no longer alive. They were killed in wars when they were young. I shall always remember them. I think I'm lucky to live long enough to be able to change the future of Israel in a very profound way."

None of the hate mongers could change his—or Israel's—destiny.

Still, supporters told him, a rally being planned for him on November 4 could prod Israel along. Rabin, however, was hesitant to appear personally. What if few people showed up? Yes, destiny would run its course regardless. But why risk humiliation? Still, he finally agreed to attend. But there were moments when the Rabins wished they were back in America—especially the night before the rally. Sitting at the dinner table with her husband, Yuval, and her son's girlfriend, Leah described the terror she felt during a demonstration that had taken place a little earlier outside the building as she arrived home. The protesters had cried:

"We will hang you and your husband from a lamppost in the square like they did to Mussolini and his mistress!"

Though Rabin was enraged by the curses constantly hurled at him, he was not greatly concerned about his own safety. But the mob had now threatened his wife as well, and *that* concerned him.

When Yuval's girlfriend whispered to the son that his father was not being guarded very well, Yuval replied:

"In our family, we don't discuss security."

Not to worry. The Shin Bet would protect him. Dad trusted it completely.

28

Flight to the Angels

As the euphoric crowds filed out of Malchei Yisrael (Kings of Israel) Square after the peace rally on the night of November 4, 1995, Tel Aviv police chief Gabriel Last could finally relax. He had never worked so hard to assure security at a political gathering. And he was pleased that the prime minister, Leah, and the Shin Bet mission commander, among others, had congratulated him for keeping perfect order. But he was exhausted. He couldn't remember a more hectic week.

It was, of course, the Shin Bet's job to protect the prime minister personally, but it was his job to make sure that no terrorist would interrupt the meeting with bomb or bullet. And the pressure had mounted when reports persisted that one or two Arabs would seek to infiltrate the meeting wearing explosive belts and blow themselves up.

Last would hear only later, he told me, that the Shin Bet had learned of a Jewish terrorist threat as well. Shin Bet officials, according to Last, had told his superior of this threat but, apparently finding the report unbelievable, said it was "only for your knowledge." And so Last, lacking this vital information, had not considered the possibility of a right-wing assassination attempt in his security plans.

In fact, by refusing to allow rightists to hold a meeting of their own across the street from the square, Last felt confident that he was preventing a Jewish attack. The extremists had hoped to set up a fifty-foot-high Arafat puppet as a reminder of Rabin's "treason."

To secure the area, Last had surrounded it with the five hundred buses that had brought many of the people to the rally from all over the country. He had cleared all adjacent streets of cars to preclude the parking of car bombs and had checked the credentials of the occupants of some five hundred apartments around the square. He had scattered about 1,000 security men in and out of uniform throughout the danger zone, including snipers who, in the bright lamplight illuminating the whole scene, peered with rifles poised from many roofs. And he had blocked off the narrow street where, just in front of the stairway leading to the speaker's platform, Rabin's car was parked. How could an Arab terrorist get anywhere near the prime minister? And none did.

But a Jewish terrorist had no obstacles. Yigal Amir looked for a signal from God as he stood waiting at the outer edge of the garage hollowed out of the Municipality Building just behind the staircase. Waiting for Rabin and Peres, who, he hoped, would come down together before heading for their respective cars. Then he could kill them both with a single burst of fire. But no such luck. Peres came down first, alone, thereby immunizing himself from death. Rabin, after all, was the head of the snake. It was God's decision; one *Zimri* was enough.

And God, Amir thought, might be giving the sign he had been waiting for. There were few policemen or guards around now, since they apparently believed the danger was over; so few that people had been able to break through the barriers blocking off the street to get near Rabin's car. No one was likely to question him now. Without his skullcap, he was just another secular dove.

Finally, Rabin appeared at the bottom of the stairs and, in keeping with the breakdown in security, was poorly guarded as he headed toward his Cadillac a few paces away amid a rumble of applause from the spectators. They were mockingly joined by a young man with fierce resolve in his eyes and a gun in his pocket.

Several Shin Bet men had gone ahead to the home where the Rabins were to appear at a party, and only four were now guarding the prime minister. A fifth had been sent to check on a suspicious box, while a Shin Bet commander replaced him and covered Rabin's rear. But when the prime minister asked the commander where Leah was, he left to look for her. Now there were only four men guarding Rabin, none to his rear. His back, unprotected, had thus become a perfect target as he approached the car and started to move toward the rear of the vehicle so he could go around it and wave to the cheering people just beyond.

Later, Rabin's former bodyguard, Amos Goren, would tell me that the Shin Bet security system in which he once served was inherently defective; it needed a more active system that would prevent disasters, not one that simply responded to them. Even so, Shin Bet had scored a major coup recently after it had received word that two brothers, Eitan and Yehoyada Kahalani, members of a fanatical settler group called the Revenge Underground Movement, were plotting to murder an Arab. It arranged for an agent to infiltrate the group and place blanks in the gun that would be used, and when it was fired, the two brothers were caught red-handed.

Now the Shin Bet's response to an assassination plot would be tested once again. . . .

So easy; he couldn't miss. . . . Amir felt God tapping him on the shoulder. Yes, the sacred signal. He took a few steps forward, removed a pistol from a pocket of his trousers, extended his arm until the weapon touched the center of Rabin's back, and fired two bullets into it. As the prime minister fell, a third bullet, misaimed, hit the agent beside him in the hand as he threw himself on the prime minister.

"It's a blank! It's a blank!," someone cried—apparently the shooter, hoping to avoid instant retaliation by confusing the guards.

Whatever his intention, the Shin Bet men did not fire back as they had been trained to do. Some Israelis wondered: Had someone, perhaps Raviv, with the killer's knowledge, double-crossed the agency and failed to replace the real bullets with blanks as he might have been ordered to do in a plot to trap a would-be assassin, as in the case of the Kahalanis?

"Are you in pain?" the wounded Shin Bet man, Yoram Rubin, asked Rabin, who lay in the back of the car as the driver, Menachem Damti, took off toward Ichilov Hospital, about five minutes away, with three of the doors still open. Damti didn't wait for a Shin Bet escort car parked behind him.

"Yes, in the back," Rabin murmured. "But it's not too bad. . . . "

Before he finished the sentence, his head suddenly tilted to the side and he fell unconscious due to a lack of oxygen to the brain.

"Give him artificial respiration!" Damti exclaimed to the Shin Bet man, pressing his foot more forcefully on the accelerator and turning on his siren as he wove recklessly through the traffic. Damti was desperate. Was his beloved boss dead? He pleaded with God to save him.

And his desperation grew when the guard cried: "Damti, I'm wounded, too!"

"Don't worry," Damti replied, believing the man's injury was greater than it was. "I'll be there in a few minutes."

"Well, please drive faster."

But the traffic grew heavier, and Damti stopped when he saw a policeman and asked him to get into the front seat and direct him along the least crowded streets.

"Why do you need my help?" the policeman asked, unaware of the assassination attempt.

"The man in the backseat is the prime minister!" Damti cried. "He's been shot!"

In shock, the policeman jumped in and remained in the car directing Damti until the traffic abated. And finally the vehicle careened into the hospital courtyard and screeched to a halt at the front door. Nobody was there to greet them, as news of the attack had not yet reached the hospital. So Damti leaped out of the car and cried:

"This is the prime minister! Bring a stretcher!"

A policeman rushed over and helped Damti and the security man carry Rabin from the car toward the door as two attendants came running toward them wheeling a stretcher. When the prime minister had been pulled into the trauma room, Damti, in tears, sobbed:

"Please take care of him."

* * *

About 10 P.M. Dr. Nir Cohen, the resident physician in Ichilov Hospital, was speaking with his wife over the phone.

"The rally is over," he said, "and there have been no problems."

His wife was furious with the hospital authorities. It seemed so unfair. This was her husband's birthday and she had long been planning to celebrate it with him. But his superiors insisted that he come to work on this particular evening because of the rally. Although violence seemed unlikely, the hospital had to be ready to receive any victims. So, many doctors and nurses were given extra duty. But why her husband? Didn't a birthday count for anything?

Suddenly, Cohen heard a siren that gradually grew louder and finally sounded right outside the building. Must be an ambulance.

"A trauma," he matter-of-factly told his wife. "Gotta go now. Bye."

Cohen was calm; he was used to these emergencies. He rushed to the intensive care room, put on his latex gloves, and waited. In a minute, stretcher bearers hurried through the door to the trauma area in the room. Cohen went to the patient, who was lying on his side, and saw an elderly, white-haired man dressed in an expensive suit with a gold pen protruding from the inside jacket pocket.

"It's a catastrophe!" Rabin's security guard, nursing his own wound, exclaimed.

Cohen could understand the man's hysteria. Of course, every accident was a tragedy. But how could he do his work if he himself regarded each one as a catastrophe? Then he placed a stethoscope to the patient's chest and, bending over him, saw the other side of the man's face.

"I thought I was hallucinating," he told me. "It was the prime minister! I couldn't speak or think. It can't be true! I told myself."

He had to try to keep the man alive, if he wasn't already dead, until the specialists arrived. Actually, Rabin was clinically dead. His heart had stopped and he had no blood pressure or pulse, but Cohen tried to restore breathing with an airbag. Within minutes, other doctors arrived, and they soon determined that Rabin had sustained bullet wounds in the spinal cord, lungs, spleen, and tissues surrounding the heart. Air had entered the blood vessels and had reached the heart and brain. The doctors managed to revive him slightly with a chest drain, and his pulse and blood pressure returned, just barely. Enough to justify an operation.

Ten minutes after his arrival, Rabin was rushed to the operating room, where at least six surgeons would try the impossible, for the internal injuries were devastating.

"There was a huge hole in each lung," Dr. Mordechai Gutman, a trauma surgeon, would say. "When we saw that, we knew there was no chance."

And even if the doctors could perform a miracle, what would he be like if he survived? They noted that his gaze deviated to the left, and this could only mean damage to the brain stem. Still, they would not give up. Tears soaked the masks of some as they worked frantically for more than an hour to reverse a lost cause. They gave him twenty-two pints of blood, removed the shattered spleen, controlled chest bleeding, applied medication, massaged the open heart. Nothing worked—or would work. But no one dared admit it.

To Dr. Gutman, more than a man he loved was dying. What would this mean for the peace process, the future of Israel and the Middle East? Rabin had had the courage to take calculated risks for peace, to fight for universal values. What would happen now? He didn't weep like some others. He was too focused on accomplishing a miracle up to the last second.

"During the operation," Gutman told me, "I hopelessly looked for something I could fix. As I massaged the heart, I felt total despair. I knew we were playing. But I didn't have the guts to say so and declare him dead."

Finally, just before 11 P.M., surgeon Yoram Kluger stammered, his tears dripping onto his surgical mask:

"We have to stop."

Amid the quiet hysteria, the hospital director, Dr. Gabi Barabash, who had arrived from the party that was to be held in Rabin's honor after the rally, asked Kluger if he was sure nothing else could be done.

Yes, Kluger murmured as he ripped off his mask.

Barabash dreaded the next moments. He had to go to the room where Leah was waiting and tell her the news. Leah, as she had headed toward the Cadillac, heard three firecrackerlike sounds and saw her husband drop to the ground with a security guard on top of him. But before she could find out what happened, other security agents whisked her into their car, which then tried to catch up with Damti's speeding vehicle but got lost in the traffic.

She was taken to Shin Bet headquarters, where she heard that her husband had been wounded, and had then been driven to the hospital. Shortly, the whole Rabin family was at her side, while Peres and other government leaders filled the corridors.

Barabash had earlier held out some hope to Leah, but now he didn't have to speak. His eyes spoke for him even before he muttered the words:

"He's no longer with us."

Sobbing uncontrollably, Leah cried:

"They should have shot me instead of Yitzhak."

Leah now knew from Shin Bet agents that a Jewish religious fanatic had fired the fatal shots, but "they" represented not only the trigger man, but all those with murder or malice in their hearts who had been demonstrating against him, and sometimes her, threatening death in the name of God, or standing by while the crime brewed.

Yigal Amir had been captured—and would, in fact, be tried and sentenced to life imprisonment, with his brother and Dror Adani receiving shorter terms. But they would live while their victim, she now learned, was dead—an agonizing reality that within minutes, at 11:15 P.M., would be reported first by Israeli TV anchorman Haim Yavin.

She must see him one more time, Leah said.

Barabash tried to discourage her, hoping to spare her emotionally. But he agreed, and other members of the family, as well as close friends and associates, filed into the room where Rabin lay, his mouth slightly open, his lips swollen, his face pale in death. Leah stood for a moment by her husband and kissed him on his forehead, which was creased with a red scar. So did a grieving Shimon Peres—a good-bye kiss for a once-bitter foe he now desperately needed. He had tried so hard to be prime minister again, and now his dream was materializing within a nightmare. Could he make peace without Yitzhak? Could he find peace without him?

Gradually, the visitors left for home and most of the doctors followed. But Dr. Kluger remained behind, sitting alone in the operating room and trying to make sense of his shattering failure, though only God could have saved Rabin.

"I thought of how we saved a drug dealer who should have died but didn't," Kluger told me, "and we couldn't save the leader of the nation."

He had literally held in his hand the heart of a man who had led his people through the wilderness of war, across deserts strewn with dead, to the edge of a new Promised Land. And he hadn't been able to make it throb again. Was there something else he might have done? He would, he knew, forever stoop under the crushing burden of this devastating tragedy . . . as would the nation Rabin was trying to save for posterity—and from itself.

Finally, at about 5 A.M., Kluger removed his surgical smock, strode into the cold dawn, and went home.

They swarmed into Israel on November 6, 1995, to honor Yitzhak Rabin—some eighty-five rulers from America to Armenia, Belgium to Belarus, Kenya to Kazakhstan, Singapore to Slovenia. Most important of all, they came from the Arab world—Egypt, Jordan, Morocco, Oman, Qatar. Among the mourners were twenty-two presidents, twenty-five prime ministers, fifteen foreign ministers, a king, a queen, a chancellor, and the heir apparent to the throne of England.

One leader was conspicuously absent—Yasir Arafat—but not because he didn't want to come. Edward Abington, the U.S. chief of mission in Jerusalem, called Arafat while the Palestinian leader was at dinner with a visiting dignitary and told him the news.

"There was a pause," Abington told me, "and he asked me three times in a choking voice if he had heard me correctly. I said yes, and he started weeping uncontrollably. 'I've lost my partner,' he sobbed. And then I said, 'Let me call you back in fifteen minutes so you can absorb the news.' He showed tremendous shock and grief. He was devastated."

Though Arafat wanted to attend the funeral, Peres feared the political fallout if he showed up in Jerusalem, where he had claims. Also, it would be difficult to guarantee his security. And so Arafat would stay home and watch the funeral on television. Some days later, however, the Israelis would steal him into Tel Aviv, where he visited Leah and her family, embracing them as if they were loved ones.

Others in Israel and around the world joined the family, the cabinet, the Knesset, the nation in bidding good-bye to Yitzhak Rabin, the murdered prime minister of an Israel that had been virtually ostracized in much of the world before he rose to power three years earlier. Now, many countries that had snubbed Israel were among those paying homage to a man who had revolutionized Israel's image. And they were not afraid to show their feelings at Rabin's extraordinary, internationally televised funeral in the cemetery on Mount Herzl, where many Israeli greats were buried. Representative leaders poured out their hearts at the ceremony.

"Every moment we shared was a joy," President Clinton said after the camera had caught him weeping, "because he was a good man and an inspiration, because he was also a great man. . . . Legend has it that in every generation of Jews from time immemorial, a just leader emerged to protect his people and show them the way to safety. Prime Minister Rabin was such a leader."

"He was a man of courage," King Hussein asserted, "a man of vision, and he was endowed with one of the greatest virtues that any man can have. He was endowed with humility. . . . I grieve the loss of a brother, a colleague, and a friend."

President Mubarak called Rabin "a fallen hero of peace" whose "earnest efforts to achieve peace in the Middle East are a testament to his vision."

Speeches by leaders from other countries struck a similar chord. But no words were more moving than those uttered by the Israelis themselves, speaking for a nation that agonized in its grief and disbelief. Thousands of people had gathered at Ichilov Hospital the night of the murder, lighting candles in his memory, and repeatedly singing the "Song for Peace" that Rabin had joined in minutes before his death. And thousands more soon kept similar vigils before the Rabin residences in Tel Aviv and Jerusalem and in other places.

Few people slept after the murder, digesting the horror, dreading the future, though some reveled in the crime. People attending a theatrical performance in the West Bank settlement of Ariel, for example, burst into applause when word of the assassination spread. Other extremists were silent, waiting anxiously for a sign from God that He approved the murder. Most Israelis, however, shared the sentiments expressed by countrymen called to the podium.

"We have come not to bury you," lamented Shimon Peres, Israel's most noted dreamer, "we have come to salute you, Yitzhak. To proudly salute you for who you were: a valiant fighter who brought victories to his people; a great dreamer who forged a new reality for our region."

Eitan Haber, Rabin's trusted aide, waved a bloody paper before the audience and roared: "Yitzhak, you know you had a thousand good qualities . . . , yet singing was not your strong point. You faked the words just a little bit during the song and . . . put it into your jacket pocket. . . . Now, I want to read some of the words from the paper, but it is difficult for me. Your blood, your blood, Yitzhak, covers the printed words. Your blood on the page of the 'Song for Peace' . . . "

And he recited the words.

Rabin's granddaughter Noa moved the world with her own words: "Excuse me for not talking about peace. . . . People talk about a national catastrophe, but how can you console a whole people or make them part of your own private sorrow when Grandmother never stops crying and we are mute, conscious of the huge emptiness left by your death?" She remembered his "meaningful half-smile, that which is no more, frozen with your death . . ." And she asked "the angels who are looking after you now" to "take good care of him."

Only President Ezer Weizman, despite his dovish views, spoke little of Rabin's achievements, ruminating casually about "the hour that we sat alone, ate some good food, drank some good drinks."

With the speeches over, the teary-eyed guests filed by Leah, who was clad in black, and her family, shaking her hand, though she was selective as she peered at each person through dark sunglasses. She refused to clasp the hand of Benjamin Netanyahu, who, she would charge, had done nothing to calm the murderous extremists.

With their power and importance submerged in the humility of mourning, the guests then moved to the grave site and watched in silence while Yitzhak Rabin was laid to rest, a martyr for peace.

Leah stared at the coffin, which was draped in the blue-and-white Israeli flag, as it was lowered into the grave, trying, it seemed, to pierce it for one last glimpse of her beloved Yitzhak. And when it was all over she didn't want to leave, but was finally coaxed by "Chich" Lahat to let her husband go. Speaking of the rally, he said soothingly to her:

"He enjoyed it so much. Suddenly he realized that they loved him. And then it was over."

But for one man it was not. Yehezkel Sharabi, Rabin's primary driver, sat by the graveside and cried. And he would not leave even when friends returned for him.

No, Sharabi sobbed, he could not leave his friend, his confidant, his prime minister. He loved him as much as any member of his family. How could he live without him? How could Israel?

"Yitzhak was everything to me," he sobbed. "He was part of my own body. If I had been next to him and had seen them shooting, I would have jumped in front of him without worrying about what might happen to me. I would gladly have died in his place."

Sharabi finally stood up and, helped by his friends, hobbled away—into a world diminished in grandeur, its covenant with God savagely violated.

Epilogue

As Yigal Amir had so confidently calculated, the bullets that killed Yitzhak Rabin would soon threaten to kill the Oslo peace process as well. Upon taking over as prime minister, Shimon Peres desperately sought to advance Oslo but, without the support of his inspirational partner, could not overcome the rightist-driven emotional backlash against Labor Party rule sparked by a succession of terrorist suicide attacks.

Actually, polls showed that a large majority of Israelis wanted to continue the process, but at a slower pace that might induce the bombers to halt their rush to paradise. Thus the combustible mixture of Palestinian terrorism and Israeli right-wing agitation brought to power in May 1996 a nationalist-theological government led by Likud chief Benjamin Netanyahu. He had bitterly opposed Oslo but, to lure voters into his camp, promised to implement that accord without leaving a trail of corpses. He would bring "peace with security" to Israel.

But the far-rightists and religious zealots dominating Netanyahu's cabinet, with their demands for more settlements and continued military occupation of most West Bank territory, have

517

blocked the road to both peace and security. After long hesitation, Netanyahu, pressed by Washington, finally shook hands with Yasir Arafat, but it was soon the earth that was shaking: Bulldozers were at work digging a controversial tunnel near Arab holy sites in Jerusalem and leveling rocky land in a disputed section of that city and in the West Bank to accommodate new Israeli housing.

Netanyahu did agree to relinquish most of Hebron to the Palestinians, as required by Oslo, but he has been reluctant to give up much additional land, demanding that Arafat must first try harder to squelch the terrorists, who were provoked now by the bulldozers as well as the peace moves.

In this heated atmosphere, devastating suicide attacks have continued to plague Israel, occurring periodically in cafes, in marketplaces, and on busy streets swarming with shoppers. Netanyahu has retaliated with drastic measures, at one point sealing the Palestinian borders so that workers could not enter Israel and withholding vital tax revenue due them under the Oslo accords. By the end of 1997, the Oslo peace process had broken down almost completely.

At the heart of the breakdown is a conflict of the dreams that drive Arafat and Netanyahu. Arafat is determined to lead a Palestinian state before he dies; Netanyahu is just as resolved to thwart this dream and pursue his own—Israeli settlement of much of East Jerusalem and most of the West Bank.

Both men, prodded by the United States, have compromised on occasion, but each finds himself a political prisoner. If Arafat cracks down too hard on the Moslem extremists, he risks being assassinated or forced to fight a civil war. If Netanyahu concedes more to the Palestinians, he risks triggering a far-right revolt that could collapse the government and perhaps catapult the Labor Party into power, paving the way to a Palestinian state.

Rabin was also faced with many risks. He had built a powerful army to buttress Israel against the dangers that could result from land transfer. But though the Yom Kippur War showed that sheer physical power could not ensure survival, Rabin, unlike Netanyahu, was willing to take calculated risks for peace. For without peace, he believed, Israel was taking the greatest risk of all—the risk of a new Holocaust perpetrated by fundamentalist and nationalist Arab forces possibly armed with nuclear weapons, germ bombs, and poison gas.

Moreover, although he pressed Arafat—who has prevented more than a dozen terrorist attacks—to crack down much further on the extremists, Rabin gradually came to understand the political problems of his peace partner, especially because they paralleled his own. As a pragmatist, he did not intend to scrap the Oslo agreement if Arafat failed to take draconian measures against the Moslem extremists that could, in the end, backfire and perhaps propel the Palestinian leader into oblivion. Should this happen, Rabin realized, Hamas might well fill the power vacuum, confronting Israel with a new Iran in its backyard.

Netanyahu, for his part, has been playing into the hands of the terrorists by weakening Arafat's authority with his provocations. His settlement and restrictive land-transfer policies render progress almost impossible—while swelling the ranks of Hamas and its suicide squads and bringing ever closer the nightmare that Rabin so feared. At the very least, Netanyahu may be defeating his principal declared aim: ending terrorism. At the same time, he has deeply antagonized the moderate Arab states that Rabin had won over to the cause of peace, while producing an atmosphere conducive once more to international isolation that could seriously affect Israel's future prosperity and well-being, as well as its security.

Still, one can hope that the peace process spawned by Rabin and Peres cannot be stopped permanently, despite all the setbacks. Even those blinded by ultra-nationalist and ultra-religious dreams must one day come to terms with the bottom-line reality: The only alternative to the peace process, whatever its defects, may ultimately be a catastrophic war.

Only the United States, it appears, has the power to pressure both sides to make the concessions and take the essential actions to put the process back on track, to pay meaningful homage to Yitzhak Rabin, who so firmly believed in America. And no electoral considerations can justify failure to exert the necessary pressure.

Even so, in the long run, people may be more important than pressure in making sure that Yigal Amir's bullets will not determine the destiny of Israel—and the entire Middle East, which is so strategically important to the United States and the rest of the world.

Both Israelis and Palestinians experienced, if for only a glittering moment in history, the rapture of peace as symbolized by the handshake on the White House lawn. They had savored the thought, however fleetingly, that they need never worry again that the next coffin carried on the shoulders of vengeance-seeking mourners might contain the body of a son, a daughter, a husband, a father.

That moment might recede to the back of the mind as the procession of death passes under one's window day after day, but it remains a seed of hope—hope that the flower of peace Yitzhak Rabin so painstakingly nurtured will not die. Even amid the wails and the weeping, the cries and the curses, the dramatic, cadenced plea of Rabin to his Palestinian partners at the memorable White House ceremony is likely to resonate through the ages in the soul of peace lovers everywhere:

"We, the soldiers who have returned from battles stained with blood; we who have seen our relatives and friends killed before our eyes; we who have attended their funerals and cannot look in the eyes of their parents; we who have come from a land where parents bury their children; we who have fought against you, the Palestinians—we say to you today, in a loud and a clear voice: enough of blood and tears. Enough."

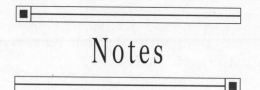

Notes

Interviewees ("Int.") are identified in the Acknowledgments. Full data on printed material can be found in the Bibliography. Page numbers of books published in Hebrew are not indicated.

Prologue

1   Rabin awakens: Int. Leah Rabin (including quotations).

3   Meeting with Eini: Int. Giora Eini.

4   *"Their offensive remarks . . . "*: Eli Landau, *Ma'ariv*, November 10, 1995.

4   Meeting with Ramon: Int. Chaim Ramon.

5   Lahat's role: Int. Shlomo "Chich" Lahat (including quotations).

5   Damti's role: Int. Menachem Damti (including quotations).

6   Gillon and Cadillac: Int. Carmi Gillon.

6   *"A Jew would not kill . . . "*: Ibid.

7   Rabin, Last, and Lahat: Int. Gabriel Last (including quotations).

8   Lahat greets Rabin: Int. Lahat (including quotations).

9   Aliza's role: Int. Aliza Goren (including quotations).

9   *"He always sang off-tune"*: Int. Hayim Hefer.

10   The crowd disperses: Int. L. Rabin (including quotations).

Chapter 1

16   *"ambassador"* to the *PLO*: Int. Yossi Ginosar.

17   *"The more you distrust . . . "*: Int. Amos Chorev.

17   *"Sometimes Yitzhak would show up . . . "*: Ehud Barak, *Ma'ariv*, November 10, 1995.

17   *"Yitzhak," Barak would relate . . .* : Ibid.

17   *as Haim Israeli . . .* : Haim Israeli, *Ma'ariv*, November 10, 1995.

19   *"Until I find a way . . . "*: Int. Chaim Asa.

19   *"Rabin possessed few of the attributes ..."*: Henry Kissinger, *White House Years.*

20   Rabin, Carter, and Amy: Int. Dan Pattir.

20   The diplomat's aunt: Int. Sol Linowitz (including quotations).

20   *Unsocial behavior*: Int. Dov Tsamir.

21   Rabin helps reporter impress editor: Int. L. Rabin.

23   Rabin and the two chief rabbis: Int. Eliahu Bakshi-Doron, Yisrael Lau.

23   Rabin and Navon: Int. Gad Navon.

26   *As a young military instructor ...*: Orit Harel, *Ma'ariv,* November 10, 1995 (including quotation "didn't dance to the music ... ").

26   Unit freed after three hours: Meir Pa'il, *Tzevet,* December 1955.

26   Rabin and "chicken dropouts": Int. Uri Dromi.

27   Sharabi worships Rabin: Int. Yehezkel Sharabi (including quotations).

28   Danon idolizes Rabin: Int. Marit Danon (including quotation).

28   Rabin never seen intoxicated: Int. Tsamir.

28   *"We keep no such beverages around"*: Int. Dov Goldstein.

29   *"Oh, I'm sorry ... "*: Int. Jacqueline Efrati.

29   *"He cared about everything ... "*: Shimon Sheves, *Ma'ariv,* December 10, 1995.

29   *"how to get the best out of people ... "*: Int. Niva Lanir.

29   *"Introduce Dromi!"*: Int. Dromi.

30   Rabin, Leah, and art: Int. L. Rabin (including quotation).

31   Coming home to Leah: Ibid.

32   *"Fortunately," Leah told a reporter ...*: Tsivia Cohen, *Na'amat,* September 1993.

32   *"She was with me ... "* (Naomi Heifetz): Debora Shapira, *Ma'ariv,* November 1995.

33   Leah protests to commentator: Int. L. Rabin.

33   Leah shuts door on husband's friend: Anonymity requested.

33   Rabin gathers with family: Int. L. Rabin, Dahlia Pelossof, Yuval Rabin.

34   Rabin proud of Dahlia: Int. Oded Ben-Ami (including quotation).

34   Rabin and grandchildren: Int. L. Rabin, D. Rabin, Goldstein; Goldstein, *Ma'ariv,* November 10, 1995 (including quotations regarding Jonathan); Dana Modan, *Ma'ariv,* November 10, 1995.

35   *"Rabin was in the army for thirty-five years ... "*: Int. Tsamir.

36   *"Yitzhak knew me since ... "*: Int. Eitan Haber.

36   Rabin reminisces with aide: Aide requests anonymity (including quotation).

Chapter 2

37–50 Rosa in Russia and Palestine, meets Nehemiah: Int. Rachel Rabin; Eliezer Smoli, *Rosa Cohen and Children of the First Rainfall* (Hebrew); Yitzhak

Rabin, *My Father's House* (Hebrew); Y. Rabin, "My Mother, Rosa Cohen," *Monitin*, April 1981, and reprinted in *Ma'ariv*, January 10, 1995 (including quotation "My mother was very radical"); Yossi Porat, "Moshe Netzer, Yitzhak Rabin's Friend for 68 Years," *Tzevet*, December 1995.

50   *"If Rosa would have found here . . . "*: Smoli.

Chapter 3

54   *"No, I was the cashier . . . "*: Int. R. Rabin.

54   *"This was simply the only opportunity . . . "*: Y. Rabin, *House*.

54   *"Whatever a person chooses . . . "*: Y. Rabin, "My Mother."

55   *"Just living by a synagogue . . . "*: Ibid.

55   Description of Rabin home: Int. R. Rabin, Aida Tamir.

55   *"How can we spend money . . . "*: Int. Avraham Shafir.

56   *"One did not work merely . . . "*: Y. Rabin, *The Rabin Memoirs*, p. 6.

56   Rosa pinned notes on dress: Smoli.

56   Parade by Jewish employers: Ibid.; int. Shafir (including quotation); Y. Rabin, *Monitin*, April 1981.

57   *"The way they respected our thoughts . . . "*: Y. Rabin, *House*.

58   *"Mother had no time . . . "*: Y. Rabin, *Memoirs*.

58   Yitzhak in school: Int. Tsuria Bin-Nun, Moshe Netzer; Y. Rabin, *House* and *Memoirs*; Smoli.

59   Smoli's influence: Int. T. Bin-Nun, Netzer; Y. Rabin, "I Was One of the Children of the First Rainfall," a Hebrew memoir on his school days (including quotations).

59   *"It was . . . sweltering hot . . . "*: Ibid.

61   Yitzhak and the donkey: Ibid.

61   Yitzhak's shyness: Int. T. Bin-Nun, Chana Gurie Rivlin.

62   *"It was the only way . . . "*: Int. Rivlin.

62   *"I generally maintained a close relationship"*: Y. Rabin, *House*.

62   Yitzhak smokes first cigarette: Int. Rivlin (including quotation).

63   Yitzhak's special status: Int. Rivka Kramer (including quotation).

63   Soccer and marbles: Int. Shafir.

63   *"We felt Moshe Netzer could be"*: Int. Kramer.

64   Home after school: Int. R. Rabin; Y. Rabin, *House* (including quotations).

64   Alone during the 1929 riots: Int. R. Rabin; Y. Rabin, *House*.

67   *"But you ate yours"*: Int. T. Bin-Nun.

67   *"I was dogged by the fear . . . "*: Y. Rabin, *Memoirs*, p. 7.

68   *"Her activity in the city . . . "*: Smoli.

Chapter 4

69   *"As a city boy . . . "*: Y. Rabin, *Memoirs*, p. 7.

69   Jokes about working ethic: Int. Haim Gurie.

70   Yitzhak a brilliant student: Int. Netzer.

70   *"He didn't show any signs . . . "*: Ibid.

70   Yitzhak builds radio: Int. Shafir (including quotations).

73   *"This shock of failing . . . "*: Assaffa Pelled, *Yediot Aharonot*, September 2, 1994.

73   *Suddenly he was "captivated . . . "*: Y. Rabin, *Memoirs*, p. 7.

73   Ari Kimmel's coach: Pelled, *Yediot Aharonot*, September 2, 1994.

74   Life at Kadouri: Ibid. (including quotations); Y. Rabin, *Memoirs*, p. 8; int. H. Gurie.

76   Rosa dies: Int. Rivlin (including quotation "We stood watching Yitzhak . . . ").

76   . . . *"that I would find my mother conscious . . . "*: Y. Rabin, *Memoirs*, p. 8.

77   *"After the seven days . . . "*: Y. Rabin, *Memoirs*, p. 8.

79   Wingate helps Jews: Christopher Sykes, *Orde Wingate* (including quotations); Leonard Mosley, *Gideon Goes to War*.

80   *"They taught us how to throw stones . . . "*: (Naor) Pelled, *Yediot Aharonot*, September 2, 1994.

82   *"I was fond of my companions . . . "*: Y. Rabin, *Memoirs*, p. 9.

Chapter 5

83   *"Do you know how to fire a rifle?"*: Robert Slater, *Rabin of Israel*.

86   Raid into Lebanon: Int. R. Rabin; Y. Rabin, *Memoirs*, pp. 10–12 (including quotations).

88   Should Palmach survive?: Int. Yigal Allon, Uzi Narkiss, R. Rabin, Zvi Zamir; Y. Rabin, *Memoirs*, pp. 12–13 (including quotation).

89   "Filching" a mortar shell: Y. Rabin, *Memoirs*, pp. 13–14 (including quotation).

90   Rabin and women: Int. Netzer, R. Rabin.

90   Leah meets Rabin: Int. L. Rabin; L. Rabin, *Cal Ha'zmon Ushto* (*"All the Time His Wife"*) (including quotations).

92   *"As my relationship with Yitzhak . . . "*: Ibid.

93   *"He had a special, persuasive voice . . . "*: Int. Yitzhak Hoffi.

93   Leah joins Palmach . . . : L. Rabin, *Wife*.

94   Ben-Gurion and Sonnenberg: Int. Sonnenberg (including quotation).

95   The Atlith operation: L. Rabin, *Wife*; Y. Rabin, *Memoirs*.

99   Rabin hit by truck: Ibid.

100   Black Saturday (general): Ibid.; int. R. Rabin, Zamir.

101   Leah arrested and released: L. Rabin, *Wife* (including quotations).

101   A kibbutz without menfolk: Ibid.

102   Rabin and father arrested: Y. Rabin, *Memoirs*, pp. 17–18 (including quotations).

104   Rabin chooses Palmach over college: Ibid, p. 19; int. R. Rabin.

105   Ben-Gurion warns of war, consults Allon: Int. David Ben-Gurion, Yigal Allon (including quotation).

106   Ben-Gurion and Laskov plan for war: Int. Laskov (including quotations).

107   *"My feelings about Ben-Gurion . . . "*: Y. Rabin, *Memoirs*, pp. 19–20.

107   *"Who is willing . . . "*: Michael Bar-Zohar, Ben-Gurion, p. 141.

108   Meir visits Abdullah: Int. Ezra Danin, Golda Meir.

108   Ben-Gurion learns of UN vote: Bar-Zohar, Ben-Gurion, p. 142; Larry Collins and Dominique LaPierre, *O Jerusalem*, pp. 35–36.

109   Rabin meets Leah but won't celebrate: L. Rabin, *Wife* (including quotation).

109   Rabin harbors "few illusions": Y. Rabin, *Memoirs*, pp. 20–21.

Chapter 6

111   Rabin can't give Narkiss arms: Int. Narkiss (including quotations).

112   Planning Operation Nachshon: Int. Allon, Ben-Gurion, Yigael Yadin; Chaim Herzog, *The Arab-Israeli Wars*, pp. 17–20.

113   The battle for Kastel: Int. Mordechai Gazit, Narkiss (including quotations); Herzog, pp. 18–19.

115   Trapped on the road: Int. Narkiss (including quotations); Y. Rabin, *Memoirs*, pp. 26–27.

116   Operation Jebusi launched: Int. David Shaltiel, Narkiss; Herzog, pp. 30–32.

119   *"The sheer stubbornness . . . "*: Y. Rabin, *Memoirs*, p. 27.

119   Rabin seals self in shell: Int. Narkiss (including quotations).

121   Council votes for state: Int. Israel Galili, Ben-Gurion, Meir, Moshe Sharett, Yadin; Ben-Gurion's diary; Bar-Zohar, *The Armed Prophet*; Zeev Sharef, *Three Days*.

121   *"Considering the mood . . . "*: Y. Rabin, *Memoirs*, p. 29.

122   Ben-Gurion proclaims state: Int. Moshe Brilliant; Sharef, pp. 281–82; Pinhas Yorman, *The First 32 Minutes*, pp. 26–32; Brilliant, *National Jewish Monthly*, March 1970; *Jerusalem Post*, April 30, 1968.

123   *"I was mute . . . "*: Y. Rabin, *Memoirs*, p. 29.

123   Shaltiel asks Rabin for help: Ibid., pp. 30–32; int. Shaltiel, Narkiss.

125   Narkiss demands replacements for attack on Zion Gate: Int. Shaltiel, Narkiss (including quotations).

125   Desperate messages from Jewish Quarter: Int. Shaltiel.

126   Israeli attack on Old City: Ibid.; int. Narkiss.

126   *"The Legion has entered the Old City . . . "*: Int. Shaltiel.

127   Rabin witnesses evacuation of Jewish Quarter: Y. Rabin, *Memoirs*, p. 32 (including quotations).

128   Rabin resented by some soldiers: Int. Narkiss.

Chapter 7

130–3   The attacks on Latrun: Int. Allon, Shimon Avidan, Ben-Gurion, Ya'akov Dori, Israel Galili, Zvi Gilat, Laskov, Ya'acov Prulov, Shlomo Shamir, Yadin; Israel Baer, *Carvor Latrun* (*"Battles of Latrun"*).

131   Chorev and the "Burma Road": Int. Chorev (including quotations).

132   Rabin "sells" Ben-Gurion on road: Y. Rabin, *Memoirs,* pp. 33–34 (including quotations).

133   Marcus insists Allon attack: Int. Allon (including quotations).

134–9   The *Altalena* incident: Int. Allon, Samuel Ariel, Menachem Begin, Ben-Gurion, Mulah Cohen, Richard Fallon, Monroe and Malka Fein, Galili, Hayim Hefer, Shmuel Katz, Moshe Kelman, Zvi Kraushar, Yaacov Meridor, Sam Merlin, Amihai Paglin, Israel Sheib; L. Rabin, *Rabin: Our Life, His Legacy*; Eliah Lankin, *Sipuru shel Mefaked* Altalena (*"The Story of the Commander of the Altalena"*); Begin, *The Revolt*; Katz, *Days of Fire*; Sheib, *The First Tithe*; Allon, *Battles of the Palmach*; Arthur Koestler, *Promise and Fulfillment.*

137   *"I occasionally wrote him short notes . . . "*: L. Rabin, *Rabin,* p. 80.

137   Rabin takes charge on beach: Ibid.; int. Allon, Hefer.

Chapter 8

140   Ben-Gurion's decision on Lydda-Ramle: Rabin quoted in *New York Times,* October 23, 1977.

141–5   Kelman captures Lydda: Int. Moshe Kelman (including quotations), Simon Garfeh.

143   Events in mosque and cemetery: Int. Kelman (including quotations).

144   Evacuation of Arabs from Lydda and Ramle: Ibid.; Y. Rabin in *New York Times,* October 23, 1977.

146   Rabin and Leah marry: L. Rabin, *Wife* (including quotations); Y. Rabin, *Memoirs,* p. 36.

147   Ben-Gurion dissolves Palmach: Int. Allon, Ben-Gurion, Yadin; Y. Rabin, *Memoirs,* p. 45 (including quotations); Ben-Gurion's diary.

148   Operation Ten Plagues: Int. Allon, Yeroham Cohen; Y. Rabin, *Memoirs,* p. 37 (including quotation).

149   Nasser and Taha: Gamal Abdel Nasser, *The Truth About the Palestine War* (pamphlet) (including quotation "How can I surrender . . . ").

150   Cohen reports to Allon: Ibid.; int. Cohen (including quotations).

151   Israelis meet Taha: Int. Cohen; Allon-Taha dialogue, provided by Cohen.

153   *"Gamal, we were guests . . . "*: Nasser.

Chapter 9

155   Operation Horev: Int. Allon, Cohen; Y. Rabin, *Memoirs,* pp. 38–39 (including quotations).

156–7   Allon confers with Ben-Gurion: Int. Allon (including quotations).

161–6   Rabin goes to Rhodes: Int. Walter Eytan; Eytan, *The First Ten Years* (including quotations not involving Rabin); Y. Rabin, *Memoirs* (including quotations involving himself), pp. 41–43.

167   *"I had been under arms.... ":* Y. Rabin, *Memoirs,* p. 4.

Chapter 10

168   *"Standing now at a crossroads ... ":* Y. Rabin, *Memoirs,* p. 45.

169   Rabin–Ben-Gurion conflict over Palmach: Ibid., pp. 46–48 (including quotations); int. Ben-Gurion.

171   Rabin transfers command to Dayan: Y. Rabin, *Memoirs,* p. 46 (including quotations).

172   Laskov offers Rabin training command: Ibid., p. 46; int. Laskov, Meir Amit.

172   Leah worried over Rabin court-martial: L. Rabin, *Wife* (including quotations).

174   *"I was thrust into the running ... ":* Ibid.

175   Rabin runs Holocaust refugee camps: Y. Rabin, *Memoirs,* pp. 48–49 (including quotations).

176   Rabins move into own home: Int. L. Rabin; L. Rabin, *Wife* (including quotation).

176–9   Rabins go to England: Ibid. (including quotations from *Wife);* Y. Rabin, *Memoirs* (including quotation by him); Robert Slater, *Rabin of Israel,* pp. 95–97.

177   *"I passed all seven stages ... ":* Y. Rabin, letter to Rachel, December 17, 1975.

177   *"Although the kindness of the English ... ":* Ibid.

179   Rabin and Dayan meet in London and Israel: Y. Rabin, *Memoirs,* p. 50 (including quotations).

179   *"I hope you won't take ... ":* Slater, p. 97.

180   *"In the early stages ... ":* L. Rabin, *Wife.*

180   *"I still shudder ... ":* Ibid.

180   *"That was a truly instructive ... ":* Y. Rabin, *Memoirs,* p. 51.

180   Rabin parachute jumps: Ibid.; Slater, p. 98 (including quotations).

181   *... Dayan "was reluctant to acknowledge ... ":* Shimon Peres, *Battling for Peace,* p. 144.

181   Rabin plays no role in Sinai War: L. Rabin, *Wife* (including quotations); Y. Rabin, *Memoirs,* p. 51.

182   *Border incidents "were Yitzhak's ... ":* L. Rabin, *Wife.*

184   Rabin rushes to hospital: Int. Dahlia Rabin.

184   *"When he raised my name ... ":* Y. Rabin, *Memoirs,* p. 52.

185   Rabin appointed chief of operations: Ibid., pp. 53–54 (including quotations).

187   *"We've been caught . . . "*: Y. Rabin, *Memoirs*, p. 56.

188   Leah quits her job: L. Rabin, *Wife* (including quotations).

189   Leah and the mouse: Ibid.

189   The children need their father: Ibid.

190   Ben-Gurion, Rabin, Zur controversy: Y. Rabin, *Memoirs*, pp. 57–58 (including quotations).

192   Rabin meets with Peres: Ibid., p. 60; Peres, *Battling*, p. 144.

193   Rabin urges Ben-Gurion not to resign: Int. Yitzhak Navon; Y. Rabin, *Memoirs*, pp. 60–61 (including quotations).

194   *"I remember my promise . . . "*: Y. Rabin, *Memoirs*, p. 61.

195   *"You know, when I finish . . . "*: L. Rabin, *Wife*.

195   *"The shock and mourning . . . "*: Ibid.

Chapter 11

196   *"Our neighbors were in a full-blown . . . "*: Y. Rabin, *Memoirs*, pp. 61–62.

197   Rabin's clandestine operations: Int. Ehud Barak.

197   *"Every time Yitzhak sent . . . "*: Int. Rahama Hermon.

198   *Israel should take measures . . .* : Ba'machane (Israeli army newspaper), April 1965; Abba Eban, *Personal Witness*, p. 354.

199   The U.S.-Israeli compromise on arms: Y. Rabin, *Memoirs*, pp. 64–66 (including quotations); Abba Eban, *An Autobiography*, p. 299.

201   *"Daddy," Dahlia screamed . . .* : L. Rabin, *Wife*.

201   Nasser's threat: Walter Laqueur, *The Road to Jerusalem*, p. 73.

203   *"Whether or not the Egyptians . . . "*: Y. Rabin, *Memoirs*, p. 71.

203   Rabin consults with Eban: Eban, *Witness*, p. 364.

203   *"Time. We need time . . . "*: Ibid., p. 364.

203   *"If Nasser should block . . . "*: Y. Rabin, *Memoirs*, p. 72.

203   *"An army," he would say . . .* : Ibid.

204   Sharon wants one swift strike: Int. Ariel Sharon; Sharon, *Warrior*, pp. 182–83 (including quotation).

205   *"Arik, what you are saying . . . "*: Ibid., p. 183.

205   *"There's only one element . . . "*: Sharon, p. 184.

206   *"You didn't tell me . . . "*: Int. Yuval Rabin.

207   Ben-Gurion recalls meeting with Rabin on Palmach: Y. Rabin, *Memoirs*, pp. 74–75.

208   Rabin receives advice from Ben-Gurion: Ibid., pp. 75–76 (including quotations).

208   *"When Yitzhak returned . . . "*: Int. Hermon.

209   Rabin meets with Dayan: Ibid., p. 76.

209   *"Yitzhak seemed not only tired . . . "*: Moshe Dayan, *Moshe Dayan: Story of My Life*, p. 319.

210   *"It's not just freedom . . . "*: Y. Rabin, *Memoirs*, p. 78.

211   Shapira opposes preemptive strike: Ibid, pp. 80–81.

212   Rabin goes home exhausted: Ibid., p. 81–82 (including quotations); L. Rabin, *Wife* (including quotations); int. L. Rabin.

213   Weizman visits Rabin: Ibid.; Ezer Weizman, *On Eagles' Wings*, pp. 190–191, 211–213 (including quotations); L. Rabin, *Wife*; Ronel Fischer, *Hadashot*, May 22, 1992; int. L. Rabin.

215   *"I felt he had acted rashly"*: Y. Rabin, *Memoirs*, p. 83.

215   *"I had to hold his balls"*: Source requests anonymity.

215   *"I had a personal problem . . . "*: Y. Rabin, *Memoirs*, p. 83.

216   Meeting with Eshkol and other officials: Ibid., pp. 86–87.

217   Rabin's family prepares for war: L. Rabin, *Wife* (including quotations); int. Dahlia Pelesoff, L. Rabin.

218   Dayan and the defense ministry: Y. Rabin, *Memoirs* (including Rabin quotations); Dayan, pp. 335–37 (including Dayan quotations).

220   Ben-Gurion urges Dayan to accept post: Int. Yigal Kimche.

221   *"Yitzhak wanted to see . . . "*: Int. David Ivry.

221   *"I felt calm and relaxed . . . "*: Y. Rabin, *Memoirs*, p. 99.

Chapter 12

222–8 The Israeli thrust: Dayan, pp. 361–365; Herzog, p. 161–163; Ze'ev Schiff, *A History of the Israeli Army*, pp. 131–137; int. Sharon, Israel Tal.

223   *"The night of June 5–6 . . . "*: Y. Rabin, *Memoirs*, p. 106.

223   Leah waits at home: Int. L. Rabin; L. Rabin, *Wife* (including quotations).

225   Fear of Soviet intervention: Y. Rabin, *Memoirs*, p. 107; int. Dayan, Sheldon Cohen.

225   U.S. ship *Liberty* attacked: Y. Rabin, *Memoirs*, pp. 108–111; Neff, pp. 254–259; Schiff, *Army*, pp. 141–142.

225   Capture of Jerusalem: Dayan, pp. 367–373; Y. Rabin, *Memoirs*, pp. 111–112 (including quotation "Its stones . . . "); int. Dayan, Narkiss (including quotation "I believe . . . "), Ya'acov Heifetz.

229   Discord over attack on Syria: Dayan, pp. 373–377; Y. Rabin, *Memoirs*, pp. 114–118 (including quotations).

Chapter 13

229   Dahlia laments injustice: L. Rabin, *Wife* (including quotations).

230   *"Our home," Leah would say . . .* : Ibid.

230   Dayan wants credit for victory: Slater, p. 150 (including quotation).

231   *"The Six-Day War . . . "*: Int. Israel Lau.

231   He *"felt far from certain . . . "*: L. Rabin, *Wife*.

232   *"If there can be any recompense . . . "*: Y. Rabin, *Memoirs*, p. 121.

233   *"A genuine agreement . . . "*: Ma'ariv, June 5, 1968.

234   Rabin wants ambassadorial post: Y. Rabin, *Memoirs* (including

dialogue with Eshkol); Eban, *Witness*, p. 478 (including Eban statement); int. Heifetz.

235 Rabin shakes bureaucracy: Y. Rabin, *Memoirs* (including quotations); int. Dinitz.

236 *"If you intend to return . . . "*: Int. Dov Goldstein.

236 Rabin at farewell party: Int. Menachem Brinker (including quotations).

238 *"I suppose they found it . . . "*: Y. Rabin, *Memoirs*, p. 126.

239 *"If that's the way . . . "*: Ibid., pp. 126–127.

239 *"He gave us some good advice . . . "*: Int. Joseph Sisco.

239 Rabin advises on carrier: Int. S. Cohen.

239 *"I watched people looting . . . "*: Slater, p. 157.

239 *"Suddenly I saw Haifa . . . "*: Ibid.

240 *"Soldiers don't bother me"*: Int. S. Cohen.

240 *"We are really going through . . . "*: Letter, Leah to Rachel, April 8, 1968.

240 *"Believe me . . . "*: ABC documentary, April 15, 1975.

240 *. . . he found "bitterness—the endless . . . "*: Slater, p. 158.

241 Rabin-Nixon meeting in Israel: Int. Dan Pattir; Y. Rabin, *Memoirs*, pp. 131–132 (including quotations).

242 Rabin–Nixon meeting in Washington: Ibid.

242 U.S. official warns Rabin regarding Nixon: Int. S. Cohen.

243 *"I continued to be dogged . . . "*: Y. Rabin, *Memoirs*, p. 150.

243 Rabin and Sisco on peace process: Ibid., p. 149 (including quotations starting, "Our interests in the Middle East . . . "); int. Sisco.

244 *Finally, on October 25, 1968 . . .* : Y. Rabin, *Memoirs*, p. 157.

245 *"In Israel I was regarded . . . "*: Ibid.

245 *"After a daring raid . . . "*: Eban, *Witness*, p. 567.

245 *"Rabin ventured to suggest . . . "*: Gideon Rafael, *Destination Peace*.

246 Rabin and Sisco on Rogers Plan: Int. Sisco.

246 Rabin, Nixon, and Kissinger on Rogers Plan: Y. Rabin, *Memoirs* (including quotations); int. Henry Kissinger.

248 *"From then on," Rabin would say . . .* : Y. Rabin, *Memoirs*, p. 165.

Chapter 14

249 *"Life in the U.S. . . . "*: Y. Rabin, letter to Rachel, February 22, 1968.

250 *"Whenever we encountered them . . . "*: L. Rabin, *Wife*.

252 Rabin and American sports: Int. S. Cohen (including quotations), Abe Pollin.

253 Rabin and Sisco: Int. Sisco.

254 Rabin and Kissinger: Int. Kissinger, Sisco.

254 Rabin most comfortable with gentiles: Int. Irene Pollin.

254 *. . . shared none of their "Yiddishkeit"*: Int. David Klayman.

255   Harriman and U.S. Jews: Int. S. Cohen.

255   Rabin and dietary laws: L. Rabin, *Wife*.

256   *"Following a deeply ingrained . . . "*: Y. Rabin, *Memoirs*, pp. 228–229.

256   *"Like most Jews . . . "*: L. Rabin, *Wife*.

256   *"My Jewish identity . . . "*: Farewell talk at synagogue.

257   Rabin disappointed in young protesters: Y. Rabin, *Memoirs*, pp. 224–226 (including quotations).

258   Rabin charges fee for lectures: *Jerusalem Post*, September 22, 1974.

258   *"During his service in Washington . . . "*: Eban, *Witness*, p. 567.

258   *In one of Rabin's cables*: Ibid., pp. 567–568.

259   Rabin's pink paper service: Int. Avner.

260   *"Golda didn't easily make concessions . . . "*: Int. Dinitz.

260   Golda cancels meeting with Katharine Graham: Ibid.

260   *"We have achieved a marked . . . "*: Y. Rabin, *Memoirs*, p. 167.

261   *"The Russians have promised . . . "*: Ibid., p. 170.

262   Rabin accompanies Eban to see Nixon: Ibid., p. 175 (including quotations); Eban, *Witness*, p. 488.

264   *"The problems are especially great . . . "*: Y. Rabin, letter to Leah, September 25, 1970.

264   Confusion over Rogers Plan: Y. Rabin, *Memoirs*, pp. 180–186 (including quotations); Kissinger, pp. 559–593; int. Kissinger, William P. Rogers, Sisco.

265   Rabin helps save Jordan from guerrillas: Y. Rabin, *Memoirs*, pp. 186–187 (including quotations); Kissinger, pp. 617–631; int. Dan Pattir.

265   Leah and the king: L. Rabin, *Wife* (including quotations).

Chapter 15

268   Rabin's reaction to Sadat offer: Y. Rabin, *Memoirs*, p. 191.

270   *"The Israeli government's desire . . . "*: Ibid., p. 193; int. Sisco.

270   *"The Israeli reply . . . "*: Y. Rabin, *Memoirs*, pp. 194–195.

270   Rabin, Kissinger, Sisco discuss peace terms: Ibid., pp. 195–206 (including quotations); Kissinger, pp. 1,280–1,283; int. Sisco.

272   *"Pay no attention . . . "*: Y. Rabin, letter to Leah, July 9, 1971.

273   Rabin and Golda meet Nixon and Kissinger: Y. Rabin, *Memoirs*, pp. 208–209 (including quotations); int. Amos Eiran.

274   Rabin "supports" Nixon: Y. Rabin, *Memoirs*, pp. 232–233; *Washington Post*, June 15, 1972.

274   *". . . when I returned to New York . . . "*: Y. Rabin, letter to Leah, August 9, 1972.

275   *"Her letter touched my heart"*: Y. Rabin, letter to Leah, August 23, 1972.

276   Golda agrees to peace approach: Y. Rabin, *Memoirs*, pp. 215–218 (including quotations); int. Eiran, Kissinger.

277   *"That depends on how he behaves . . . "*: Int. Eiran, Chaim Yavin.

278   *"I know for sure . . . "*: Y. Rabin, letter to Leah, August 23, 1972.

Chapter 16

279   *"The Israel I came home to . . . "*: Y. Rabin, *Memoirs*, p. 234.

280   *"Is this the Rabin home? . . . "*: L. Rabin, *Wife* (including quotations).

281   *Once, at great political risk*: *Jerusalem Post*, June 29, 1973.

281   61 percent want Rabin in cabinet: Ibid, August 20, 1973.

282   *"Yuval Rabin's home? . . . "*: L. Rabin, *Wife* (including quotations).

283   *"Calling such a meeting . . . "*: Y. Rabin, *Memoirs*, p. 235.

283   Ex-chiefs of staff briefed on war: Ibid. (including quotations).

284   Rabin visits Sharon at front: Int. Sharon (including quotation).

285   *"For Yitzhak the Yom Kippur War . . . "*: L. Rabin, *Wife*.

287   Golda's ruse: Y. Rabin, *Memoirs*, pp. 236–237 (including quotation).

Chapter 17

296   *"I sat at home with friends . . . "*: L. Rabin, *Wife*.

297   *"The wounds of the Israeli people . . . "*: Y. Rabin, *Memoirs*, p. 206.

297   Rabin struggles to form cabinet: Int. Sarid, Dov Tsamir.

299   Allon after 1948 war: Int. Chorev, Yaacobi.

299   Rabin tries to persuade Allon: Int. Tsamir.

300   Rabin "snubbed" by son: Int. Amos Goren (including quotations).

301   *"I was glad of an opportunity . . . "*: Y. Rabin, *Memoirs*, p. 243.

301   *"Rabin was totally unprepared . . . "*: Int. Shlomo Avineri.

302   Rabin meets with Nixon: Y. Rabin, *Memoirs*, pp. 243–245 (including quotations); int. Tsamir.

304   Rabin meets with Hussein: Int. Eiran (including quotations).

305   Hussein pleads with American officials: Int. Sisco.

305   *"Are you going to reach . . . "*: Int. Eiran.

306   Kissinger angered by failure of Hussein talks: Int. Kissinger.

306   *"It was a bad miscalculation . . . "*: Int. Dinitz.

307   Rabin hears Avnery report: Int. Uri Avnery; Avnery, *My Friendly Enemy*, pp. 79–88.

308   Rabin hears Pa'il report: Int. Pa'il.

308   Rabin opposes trying Matti Peled: Int. Menachem Brinker.

308   Abu Mazen confirms PLO conversion: Int. Abu Mazen.

309   *"Many Palestinians believe . . . "*: Said Hammami, *Times* (London), November 1973.

309   *"Rabin was the man . . . "*: Int. Abu Mazen.

Chapter 18

310   Rabin and Betty Ford: Y. Rabin, *Memoirs*, pp. 246–247 (including quotations); int. Avner.

311   *"He was . . . a tough negotiator . . . "*: Gerald Ford, *A Time to Heal*, p. 183.

311   Rabin's talk with Ford: Matti Golan, *The Secret Conversations of Henry Kissinger*, pp. 225–226 (including quotations); int. Avner, Kissinger.

311 *"There should be a continuation . . . "*: Golan, p. 227.

312 *A "slip of the tongue"*: Ibid., p. 228.

312 *"He would invariably begin . . . "*: Peres, *Battling*, p. 141.

314 *"Kissinger kept up his shuttle trips . . . "*: Y. Rabin, *Memoirs*, p. 254.

314 Sadat doubts Israel wants peace: Ibid. (including quotations).

315 *"Why did he do it?" . . .* : Golan, p. 229.

316 Kissinger's alleged "trick": Int. Dan Pattir (including quotations).

317 *"All of us have displayed . . . "*: Y. Rabin, *Memoirs*, p. 257.

317 *"I don't believe you"*: Golan, p. 237.

318 Kissinger waits for cabinet decision: Ibid., pp. 238–239 (including quotation).

319 Kissinger's dramatic farewell at airport: Ibid., p. 241; Y. Rabin, *Memoirs*, p. 258 (including quotations); int. Pattir.

319 *. . . Rabin . . . was "a small man . . . "*: Golan, p. 241.

320 Meeting on Golan's book: Ibid., pp. 11–13; int. Pattir.

320 Rabin, Ford, Kissinger, Sisco discuss peace: Y. Rabin, *Memoirs*, pp. 263–264 (including quotations); int. Sisco.

322 Peres proposes U.S.-Soviet force: Y. Rabin, *Memoirs*, p. 267; Peres, *Battling*, pp. 145–146.

323 *"I felt so thoroughly shocked . . . "*: Y. Rabin, *Memoirs*, p. 271.

323 *A billion-dollar spy satellite system?*: Ibid., pp. 277–278 (including quotations); reporters' briefing, February 6, 1976; *Jerusalem Post*, February 8 and 9, 1976.

326 Settlement in Sebastia: *Jerusalem Post*, May 10 and 11, 1976.

Chapter 19

327–37 Rescue at Entebbe: Y. Rabin, *Memoirs*, pp. 282–289 (including Rabin's quotations); Peres, *Battling*, pp. 152–169 (including Peres's quotations); *Jerusalem Post*, June 30, 1978, July 4, 5, and 7, 1976, December 12, 1976, August 19, 1979; int. Avner, Eiran, Mischa Harish, Chaga Regev, Gad Yaacobi.

Chapter 20

342 Rabin's secret visit to Morocco: Int. Eiran.

343 *"As the chief of staff noted . . . "*: Y. Rabin, *Memoirs*, p. 290.

344 *"If a party discredited . . . "*: Ibid., p. 309.

344 Rabin's relations with Allon: Int. Dinitz, Gurie, Goldstein, Yitzhak Hoffi, Harold Saunders, Tsamir, Haim Zadok.

345 The Yadlin scandal: *Jerusalem Post*, February 15 and 16, 1977.

345 The Ofer scandal: Ibid., January 6, 1977 (including quotations), January 4, 9, and 10, 1977.

346 Rabin visits shah: Int. Amos Goren (including quotations).

347 Rabin visits Carter: Y. Rabin, *Memoirs* (including Rabin-Carter dialogue); int. Pattir.

351   *"The Carter-Rabin talks ... went badly ... "*: Cyrus Vance, *Hard Choices*, p. 173.

351   *"I had been with Mrs. Carter ... "*: L. Rabin, *Wife*.

351   Margolit hears of Rabin bank account: Int. Avner, Dan Margolit (including dialogue involving Avner and Pattir), Pattir.

352   Pattir rushes to Rabin: Int. Pattir (including quotation).

352   Tsamir and the bank account: Int. Tsamir (including quotations).

353   Margolit finds bank account: Int. Margolit

353   Margolit meets Rabin: Ibid. (including quotations).

354   Details of the account: Int. L. Rabin; *Jerusalem Post*, April 15, 1977, also March 21, 1977, April 2, 8, 10, 11, 14, and 19, 1977.

354   *"Looking back ... "*: L. Rabin, *Wife*.

355   *"Yitzhak," one close friend ...* : Source requests anonymity.

355   Galili advises Rabin: Y. Rabin, *Memoirs*, p. 310.

355   *"They insisted that it would be ... "*: L. Rabin, *Wife*.

355   Leah threatens suicide: Int. Goldstein (including quotations).

356   *"It was horrible watching ... "*: Int. Avner.

356   *"I felt that I had to render ... "*: Y. Rabin, *Memoirs*, p. 312.

356   Rabin confides in Sherabi: Int. Sherabi (including quotations).

357   Rabin confronts Pattir: Int. Pattir (including quotations).

359   Rabin tells public his decision: Ibid.; int. L. Rabin.

359   *"I immediately felt the kind ... "*: Y. Rabin, *Memoirs*, p. 312.

359   Leah tried in court: *Jerusalem Post*, April 18, 1977.

360   *"I was there, yet absent ... "*: L. Rabin, *Wife*.

Chapter 21

361   *"It was a baptism of fire ... "*: L Rabin, *Wife*.

363   *"We witnessed an extraordinary ... "*: Samuel Lewis memoir, made available to me.

363   Weizman insults Rabins: Source requests anonymity.

363   *"Inevitably, the atmosphere ... "*: Int. Samuel Lewis.

364   *"Being on the 'outside'"* ... : Y. Rabin, *Memoirs*, p. 315.

364   Nixon and the tape recorder: Int. Eytan Haber (including quotations).

365   *"One time," Lewis would recall ...* : Int. Lewis.

365   Rabin hires assistant: Source requests anonymity.

368   Rabin visits Vance: Y. Rabin, *Memoirs*, p. 321 (including quotations).

368   Sadat comes to Israel: Ibid., pp. 321–324.

370   *"The key to the future relations ... "*: Ibid, pp. 328–329.

372   *"Had peace been linked ... "*: Ibid., p. 329.

372   *"There seems to be no groundswell ... "*: *Jerusalem Post*, July 12, 1978.

374   *"... there will be more than one candidate ... "*: Ibid., July 2, 1979.

375   *"His charges are very general . . . "*: Ibid., August 9, 1979.

375   *"This debate is less about the book . . . "*: Ibid., August 13, 1979.

375   *"I am speaking with an aching heart . . . "*: Ibid., August 10, 1979.

377   Niva Lanir works for Rabin: Int. Niva Lanir (including quotations).

378   Rabins visit Niva in hospital: Ibid.

378   Bank account back on front page: *Jerusalem Post,* November 23, 1980; int. L. Rabin.

379   Peres defeats Rabin: *Jerusalem Post,* December 19, 1980 (including quotations); int. Lanir.

379   The headline in the *Jerusalem Post . . .* : Ibid., December 22, 1980.

Chapter 22

381   Begin, Sharon inform Labor leaders: Int. Eiran; Schiff and Ya'ari, *Lebanon,* p. 60 (including quotations); *Jerusalem Post,* September 23, 1983.

383   Rabin's 1976 meeting with Phalangists: Schiff and Ya'ari, *Lebanon,* pp. 18–19.

383   Rabin shattered by Argov tragedy: Leonard Garment memoir.

384   Rabin visits Beirut front: Int. Eiran, Lanir (including quotations).

385   *"The shattered bodies . . . "*: Eban, *Witness,* p. 611.

387   *"Some people," he went on . . .* : *Jerusalem Post,* January 11, 1983.

389   Eini mediates between Rabin and Peres: Int. Eini (including quotations).

391   Sherabi waits for Rabin: L. Rabin, *Wife.*

391   *"Yitzhak had returned . . . "*: Ibid.

391   *And Leah returned home . . .* : Ibid.

392   Rabin publishes controversial book: Int. Uri Dromi.

393   *"Rabin felt he didn't really need . . . "*: Int. Chaim Asa.

393   Rabin hires Haber: Int. Haber.

393   *"He understood," Haber would tell me . . .* : Ibid.

393   Rabin hires Sheves: Int. Shimon Sheves.

394   *Once, he saw several women . . .* : Source requests anonymity.

394   *"He was everything to me . . . "*: Int. Sheves.

395   *"I don't want to be the policeman . . . "*: *Jerusalem Post,* February 3, 1985.

396   The Lavi project: Ibid., December 7, 1984, January 31, 1986, September 4, 1987 (including quotation); int. Y. Navon.

397   Rabin and Iran-Contra: Ibid., February 1, 1987 (including quotation); U.S. Senate Intelligence Committee report.

399   The Pollard scandal: Report, Subcommittee, Israel Foreign Affairs and Defense Committee on Intelligence and Security Services; Wolf Blitzer, *Territory of Lies,* p. 199; *Washington Post,* November 29, 1985, May 29, 1987; int. Eban, H. Regev.

400   Arafat summons Siniora: Int. Hana Siniora.

401 Ginosar meets PLO officials: Int. Yossi Ginosar.

401 *"Ginosar's objective . . . "*: Int. Sheves.

402 *"I did not want to put the two . . . "*: George Shultz, *Turmoil and Triumph,* p. 1,020.

402 *"Shultz wavered . . . "*: Int. Siniora.

403 *"We all paid a heavy price . . . "*: Peres, *Battling,* p. 270.

Chapter 23

404 *"Don't worry, it'll be quashed . . . "*: Int. Joseph Gildenhorn.

404 Situation in Israel deteriorating: Int. C. Regev.

405 Intifada starts after accident: Schiff and Ya'ari, *Intifada,* pp. 17–23 (including quotations); int. Amnon Lipkin-Shahak.

406 *"I was instrumental . . . "*: Int. Siniora.

407 *"Ever since 1967 . . . "*: Schiff and Ya'ari, *Intifada.*

409 Exchange between Yaacobi and Rabin: Int. Gad Yaacobi.

411 *"Yitzhak understood the curse . . . "*: Int. Lanir.

411 Rabin tells Ginosar he wants solution: Int. Ginosar.

412 Rabin sends Darawshe to Arafat: Int. Darawshe (including quotations).

413 Pa'il tells Rabin of PLO talk: Int. Pa'il (including quotations).

414 Shamir's peace plan: Moshe Arens, *Broken Covenant;* James A. Baker III, *The Politics of Diplomacy,* pp. 119–120; William B. Quandt, *Peace Process,* pp. 388–389; int. Baker.

415 Rabin–Baker relationship: Baker, p. 126 (including quotation); int. Baker.

415 Mubarak's peace plan: Baker, pp. 124–125 (including quotations); Arens, pp. 74–81, 83, 91.

415 *"I don't believe Arafat . . . "*: Int. Asa.

416 *"No notes had been taken . . . "*: Arens, p. 75.

417 Baker's plan: Ibid., pp. 89–111 (including quotations); Baker, pp. 124–130; int. Baker.

421 Peres fails to form government: *Jerusalem Post,* April 12–27, 1990; *Jerusalem Report* staff, *Yitzhak Rabin,* pp. 102–103; Slater, pp. 436–439; int. Uzi Baram, Shimon Sheves.

Chapter 24

423 *"We have no choice . . . "*: Int. Baram.

423 *"The premiership for me . . . "*: Int. Sheves.

424 Asa checks on Rabin's chances: Int. Asa (including quotations).

425 *"I vividly remember the moment . . . "*: L. Rabin, *Wife.*

426 *"Israel should try again . . . "*: Int. Y. Rabin.

428 *"Likud's failure to secure . . . "*: Baker, p. 555.

428 Rahama solves her problem: Int. Rahama Hermon.

431 *"I'm telling you . . . "*: Int. Asa.

433   *"You were wonderful . . . "*: L. Rabin, *Wife.*

433   *"Pandemonium broke out . . . "*: Ibid.

434   Eini mediates between Rabin and Peres: Int. Eini.

Chapter 25

437   Sarid shocked by Rabin vow: Int. Sarid (including quotations).

437   *Rabin wanted to prove . . .* : Int. Goldstein.

439   Visit to Auschwitz: Noa Ben Artzi-Pelossof, *In the Name of Sorrow and Hope* (large-print edition), pp. 116–135; int. Amos Gillad (including quotation).

439   Visit to Bergen-Belsen in 1976: Int. Avner.

440   Rabin refuses to strengthen his office: Int. Asa.

440   Rabin settles Arab university crisis: int. Faisal Husseini (including quotation).

441   Rabin halts building of settlements: Int. Binyamin Ben-Eliezer.

441   *"For the sake of 3.9 million Israeli Jews . . . "*: Baker, p. 556.

441   *"Dennis, the secretary is treating me . . . "*: Int. Dennis Ross.

441   *"We will do what we say . . . "*: Baker, p. 556.

441   *"I have just visited . . . "*: Ibid., p. 557.

442   *"We're reordering our priorities"*: Ibid.

442   *"Bush's granting of the guarantees . . . "*: Ma'ariv, August 11, 1992.

442   . . . *"did not manage to bring Israel . . . "*: Slater, p. 528.

442   *"Rabin made it clear . . . "*: Int. David Klayman.

444   Peres pushes for a deal with Arafat: Int. Shimon Peres.

445   Abu Mazen sends letter to Rabin: Int. Abu Mazen.

445   Rabin reluctant to deal with Arafat: Int. Peres.

446   Genesis of Oslo talks: Int. Yossi Beilin, Ya'ir Hirschfeld, Terje Larsen, Abu Mazen, Peres, Ron Pundak, Dennis Ross, Uri Savir, Yoel Singer; Jane Corbin, *The Norway Channel*; David Makovsky, *Making Peace with the PLO.*

448   Rabin flies to Washington: Int. Martin Indyk (including quotation).

448   Oval Office meeting: Samuel Lewis memoir (including quotations); int. Lewis.

449   Rabin favored Bush over Clinton: Int. A. Gillad.

449   White House dinner: Int. Elyakim Rubinstein (including quotations).

451   Tibi visits Arafat: Int. Ahmad Tibi (including quotations).

452   *"no longer our city"*: Int. Abu Mazen.

452   Closing the agreement: Int. Larsen, Peres, Ross; Corbin, pp. 148–177; Makovsky, pp. 70–79; Peres, pp. 298–306 (including quotations).

453   *"This was the only time . . . "*: Int. Asa.

455   *"Hey, I'm from a kibbutz"*: Peres, p. 303.

455   *"We don't want the Americans involved . . . "*: Int. Larsen (who quotes Peres).

455 Negotiators inform Christopher of deal: Ibid. (including quotations); Corbin, pp. 72–77; Peres, pp. 303–306.

456 Rubinstein angered at being used: Int. Elyakim Rubinstein (including quotation).

456 Husseini and Ashrawi even angrier: Int. Husseini; Hanan Ashrawi, *This Side of Peace*, pp. 260–261 (including quotations).

458 *"Rabin was too pragmatic . . . "*: Int. Ariel Merari.

458 Rabin agonizes over trip to Washington: Int. Haber, Indyk ("Make sure he comes"), Lanir, Peres, L. Rabin ("We're going to Washington"), Ross, Sheves.

460 Eini mediates between Rabin and Peres: Int. Eini.

461 *"The idea that I'll meet Arafat . . . "*: Clyde Haberman, *New York Times*, September 13, 1993.

461 *Everything had to be perfect*: Maureen Dowd, *New York Times*, September 14, 1993.

462 Clinton and Rabin grow close: Int. Gillad.

462 A hitch in the accord: Int. Singer, Tibi.

463 Rabin and Arafat exchange words: Thomas L. Friedman, *New York Times*, September 14, 1993.

463 *"Now it's your turn"*: Int. Peres.

Chapter 26

465 Israelis nurtured Hamas movement: Schiff and Ya'ari, *Intifada*, pp. 223–224; int. Jamil Hamami.

466 Rabin wondered how Arafat survived: Int. L. Rabin.

467 Ginosar's advice to Rabin in 1988: Int. Ginosar.

467 Ginosar conducts secret talks with PLO: Ibid.

467 Ben-Eliezer visits Arafat: Int. Ben-Eliezer (including quotations).

469 Sprinzak advises Rabin on Hebron massacre: Int. Sprinzak (including quotation).

470 Arafat phones Rabin: Int. Jacques Neriya (including quotations).

473 *"I have met many leaders . . . "*: Int. Danny Yatom.

473 Negotiating the treaty with Jordan: Int. Haber, Noah Kinarti, Israel Ben-Yaacov.

475 Little headway with Syria: Int. Itamar Rabinovich.

476 *"Yitzhak assumed full responsibility . . . "*: L. Rabin, *Wife*.

477 *"Naomi, it's hard to believe . . . "*: Int. Y. Heifetz.

478 *"If I don't get a mandate . . . "*: Int. Peres.

478 Peres plays his final card: Ibid.

479 A plan for Jerusalem: Int. Yossi Beilin.

481 *"When he wanted to postpone . . . "*: Sheves, *Ma'ariv*, November 10, 1995.

482 *"Yehezkel, how could there be . . . "*: Int. Sharabi.

Chapter 27

484 Rabbis seek punishment for Rabin: Letter sent to other rabbis, February 1995.

485 Warning to Rabin: Letter from Aharon Dumb, May 13, 1994.

486–91 Amir's background: Report, State Commission of Inquiry into the Murder of the Late Prime Minister Yitzhak Rabin; Summary of the Verdict in Severe Crime Case Number 498/95; *Jerusalem Report* staff, *Yitzhak Rabin*, pp. 183–194; Geula Amir, *George* magazine, March 1997; int. Meir Bar-Ilan, Shmuel Fleishman, Yehuda Friedlander, Menachem Friedman, Aharon Katz, Charles Liebman, Moshe Raziel, Avraham Rivlin, Ohad Skornick, Yehuda Skornick, Yehuda Stern.

490 *"Do you want to live the rest . . . "*: Source requests anonymity.

491 *"The idea to perpetrate . . . "*: Summary of the Verdict.

491 *"Peres and Rabin are snakes . . . "*: *Jerusalem Report* staff, p. 188.

491 *"The rabbis are all cowards . . . "*: Ibid.

491 Adani's role: Int. Tsion Amir.

493 Raviv ousted from Bar-Ilan: Int. Raziel.

493–5 Raviv's role: Report of the State Commission of Inquiry; G. Amir, *George*, March 1997; Zvi Zinger, series of articles in *Hadashot*, spring and summer 1996; int. Raziel.

494 *"Yigal Amir or his brother . . . "*: Int. Moshe Shahal.

495 *Shahal was utterly frustrated . . .* : Ibid.

495 Amir overheard plotting murder: *Jerusalem Report* staff, pp. 198–199.

496 Gillon warns Rabin of danger: Int. Carmi Gillon (including quotations).

496 *"I wanted a thinking person . . . "*: Summary of the Verdict.

496 *"I was afraid that I would try . . . "*: Ibid.

497 *"I am against Oslo . . . "*: Int. Binyamin Elon.

497 *Elon saw nothing wrong . . .* : Ibid.

498 Milstein lectures on Rabin: Ibid.; int. Uri Milstein.

498 Meeting in Netanya: Int. David Bar-Ilan (including quotation); *Jerusalem Post*, October 13, 15, and 18, 1995.

499 *"Rabin didn't defuse . . . "*: int. Ehud Sprinzak.

500 *"Did one support this spiteful . . . "*: Stephen Bloch (guest writer), *Jerusalem Post*, October 25, 1995.

501 *"I was frightened . . . "*: Int. Joel Ben-Nun.

502 *"They agreed," Ben-Nun would say . . .* : Ibid.

502 Bakshi-Doron and the *din rodef* rule: Broadcast from Tiferet Jerusalem synagogue, July 6, 1996; int. Bakshi-Doron.

502 *"Rabin cared a great deal . . . "*: Int. Ben-Nun.

502 Ben-Nun visits Rabin: Ibid. (including quotations).

503 Rabin meets three rabbis: Int. Haber (including quotations).

503   Nahum Rabinovich and Yitzhak Frankenthal: Int. N. Rabinovich, Frankenthal (including quotations).

504   *The rabbis were surprised . . .* : Int. N. Rabinovich.

504   Rabins visit the United States: L. Rabin, *Rabin: Our Life, His Legacy,* pp. 274–276; int. L. Rabin.

505   *"Most of my closest friends . . . "*: Int. Yaacobi.

505   Worry at the dinner table: Int. Yuval Rabin (including quotations).

Chapter 28

506   Last's role at rally: Int. Last.

508   Shin Bet a defective agency: Int. Amos Goren.

508   Amir shoots Rabin: Report of State Commission into the Murder; Summary of the Verdict; int. Avi Benayahu, Damti, Fleishman, Carmi Gillon, Aliza Goren, Last.

509   The drive to the hospital: Int. Damti (including quotations).

510   Cohen's role: Int. Dr. Nir Cohen (including quotations).

511   Gutman's role: Int. Dr. Mordechai Gutman (including quotations).

511   *"We have to stop"*: Int. Dr. Yoram Kluger.

511   Barabash's role: Int. Dr. Gabi Barabash.

511   Leah finally reaches hospital: Int. L. Rabin, *Rabin* (including quotations), pp. 11–15.

512   Kluger remains with corpse: Int. Kluger.

513   Arafat weeps when told of murder: Int. Edward Abington.

513   Arafat visits Leah: Int. L. Rabin, Abu Mazen.

515   *"He enjoyed it so much . . . "*: *Jerusalem Report* staff, p. 216.

516   *"Yitzhak was everything to me . . . "*: Int. Sharabi.

Bibliography

Books

Ambrose, Stephen E. *Nixon*, vol. 3. New York: Simon & Schuster, 1987.

Arens, Moshe. *Broken Covenant*. New York: Simon & Schuster, 1995.

Ashrawi, Hanan. *This Side of Peace*. New York: Simon & Schuster, 1995.

Baker, James A., III. *The Politics of Diplomacy*. New York: Putnam, 1995.

Beilin, Yossi. *Israel*. New York: St. Martin's, 1992.

Ben-Artzi-Pelossof, Noa. *In the Name of Sorrow and Hope*. New York: Knopf, 1996.

Bender, David, and Bruno Leone, eds. *Israel: Opposing Viewpoints*. San Diego: Greenhaven, 1982.

Ben-Sasson, H. H., ed. *A History of the Jewish People*. Cambridge, Mass.: Harvard University Press, 1988.

Benziman, Uzi. *Sharon: An Israeli Caesar*. New York: Adams, 1985.

Black, Ian. *Israel's Secret Wars*. New York: Grove Weidenfeld, 1991.

Brandon, Henry. *The Retreat of American Power*. Garden City, N.Y.: Doubleday, 1973.

Bush, Barbara. *Barbara Bush: A Memoir*. New York: Scribner's, 1994.

Carter, Jimmy. *Keeping Faith*. New York: Bantam, 1982.

Cockburn, Andrew, and Leslie Cockburn. *Dangerous Liaison*. New York: HarperCollins, 1991.

Corbin, Jane. *The Norway Channel*. New York: Atlantic, 1994.

Dayan, Moshe. *Moshe Dayan: Story of My Life*. New York: Morrow, 1976.

Eban, Abba. *An Autobiography*. New York: Random House, 1977.

———. *Personal Witness*. London: Jonathon Cape, 1993.

Elon, Amos. *The Israelis*. New York: Penguin, 1983.

Ford, Gerald R. *A Time to Heal*. New York: Harper & Row, 1979.

Friedman, Thomas L. *From Beirut to Jerusalem*. New York: Farrar Straus Giroux, 1989.

Golan, Matti. *The Road to Peace*. New York: Warner, 1989.

———. *The Secret Conversations of Henry Kissinger*. New York: Quandrangle, 1976.

Gordon, Haim. *Make Room for Dreams*. New York: Greenwood, 1989.

Haig, Alexander M., Jr. *Caveat*. New York: Macmillan, 1984.

———. *Inner Circles*. New York: Warner, 1984.

Halevy, David, and Neil C. Livingstone. *Inside the PLO*. New York: Morrow, 1980.

Harkabi, Yehoshafat. *Israel's Fateful Hour*. New York: Harper & Row, 1988.

Hersh, Seymour M. *The Price of Power*. New York: Summit, 1983.

Herzog, Chaim. *The Arab-Israeli Wars*. New York: Random House, 1982.

———. *The War of Atonement*. Boston: Little, Brown, 1975.

Hiltermann, Joost R. *Behind the Intifada*. Princeton, N.J.: Princeton University Press, 1991.

Hunter, Robert. *The Palestinian Uprising*. Berkeley: University of California Press, 1991.

Isaac, Rael Jean. *Israel Divided*. Baltimore: Johns Hopkins University Press, 1976.

Isaacson, Walter. *Kissinger*. New York: Simon & Schuster, 1992.

Jerusalem Report staff (David Horovitz, ed.). *Yitzhak Rabin*. London: Peter Halban, 1996.

Kahane, Meir. *They Must Go*. New York: Institute of the Jewish Idea, 1981.

Kalb, Bernard, and Marvin Kalb. *Kissinger*. London: Hutchinson, 1974.

Kissinger, Henry. *White House Years*. Boston: Little, Brown, 1979.

Kurzman, Dan. *Ben-Gurion: Prophet of Fire*. New York: Simon & Schuster, 1983.

———. *Genesis 1948: The First Arab-Israeli War*. New York: World, 1970 (reprint: New York: Da Capo, 1992).

Laqueur, Walter. *The Road to Jerusalem*. New York: Macmillan, 1968.

Leiter, Yehiel M. *Crisis in Israel*. New York: S.P.I.–Shapolsky, 1994.

Leshem, Moshe. *Israel Alone*. New York: Touchstone, 1989.

Lewis, William, and Phoebe Marr, eds. *Riding the Tiger*. Boulder, Col.: Westview, 1993.

Linowitz, Sol M. *The Making of a Public Man*. Boston: Little, Brown, 1985.

Makovsky, David. *Making Peace with the PLO*. Boulder, Co.: Westview, 1996.

McDowall, David. *Palestine and Israel*. Berkeley: University of California Press, 1989.

Meir, Golda. *My Life*. New York: Putnam, 1975.

Melman, Yossi. *The New Israelis*. New York: Simon & Schuster, 1995.

Milstein, Uri. *The Survival Principle*. Tel Aviv: Survival, 1991.

Morris, Roger. *Haig: The General's Progress*. New York: Playboy, 1982.

Moskin, J. Robert. *Among Lions*. New York: Arbor House, 1982.

Neff, Donald. *Warriors for Jerusalem.* New York: Linden/Simon & Schuster, 1984.

O'Brien, William V. *Law and Morality in Israel's War with the PLO.* New York: Routledge, 1991.

Organski, A. F. K. *The $36 Billion Bargain.* New York: Columbia University Press, 1990.

Peres, Shimon. *Battling for Peace.* New York: Random House, 1995.

————. *From These Men.* New York: Wyndham, 1979.

————. *The New Middle East.* New York: Henry Holt, 1993.

Perlmutter, Amos. *Military and Politics in Israel.* London: Praeger, 1969.

Perry, Mark. *A Fire in Zion.* New York: Morrow, 1994.

Quandt, William B. *Peace Process.* Washington, D.C.: Brookings Institution, 1993.

Rabin, Leah. *Rabin: Our Life, His Legacy.* New York: Putnam, 1997.

Rabin, Yitzhak. *The Rabin Memoirs.* Boston: Little, Brown, 1979.

Rabinovich, Itamar. *The Road Not Taken.* New York: Oxford University Press, 1991.

Randal, Jonathan C. *Going All the Way.* New York: Viking, 1984.

Reich, Walter. *A Stranger in My House.* New York: Holt, Rinehart and Winston, 1984.

Roth, Stephen J., ed. *The Impact of the Six-Day War.* New York: St. Martin's, 1988.

Sacher, Howard M. *A History of Israel,* vol. 2. New York: Oxford University Press, 1987.

Saunders, Harold H. *The Other Walls.* Princeton, N.J.: Princeton University Press, 1985.

Schiff, Ze'ev. *A History of the Israeli Army.* London: Sidgwich & Jackson, 1987.

Schiff, Ze'ev, and Ehud Ya'ari. *Intifada.* New York: Simon & Schuster, 1989.

————. *Israel's Lebanon War.* New York: Simon & Schuster, 1984.

Schulzinger, Robert D. *Henry Kissinger.* New York: Columbia University Press, 1989.

Sharon, Ariel. *Warrior.* New York: Simon & Schuster, 1989.

Shipler, David K. *Arab and Jew.* New York: Times Books, 1986.

Shultz, George P. *Turmoil and Triumph.* New York: Scribner's, 1993.

Slater, Robert. *The Life of Moshe Dayan.* New York: St. Martin's, 1991.

————. *Rabin of Israel.* London: Robson, 1996.

Smith, Charles D. *Palestine and the Arab-Israeli Conflict.* New York: St. Martin's, 1992.

Sohar, Ezra. *Israel's Dilemma.* New York: Shapolsky, 1989.

Teveth, Shabtai. *Moshe Dayan.* Boston: Houghton Mifflin, 1973.

Vance, Cyrus. *Hard Choices.* New York: Simon & Schuster, 1983.

Viorst, Milton. *Sands of Sorrow.* New York: Harper and Row, 1987.

Wallach, Janet, and John Wallach. *Arafat*. New York: Carol, 1990.
———. *The New Palestinians*. Rocklin, Calif.: Prima, 1992.
Weizman, Ezer. *On Eagles' Wings*. New York: Macmillan, 1976.
Yaniv, Avner. *Dilemmas of Security*. New York: Oxford, 1987.

Other Media

ABC Television Network (Bill Seamans, Rabin Biography, April 15, 1975).
al-Fajr (East Jerusalem)
George magazine
Ha'aretz (Israel)
Jerusalem Post
Jerusalem Report
Jewish Forward
Ma'ariv (Israel)
Monitin magazine (Israel)
Na'amat (Israel)
Newsweek
New York Times
Paris-Match
Time
Times (of London)
Tzevet (Israel)
Washington Post
Yediot Aharonot (Israel)

Index

About the Author

Dan Kurzman, a former foreign correspondent for the *Washington Post*, is the author of thirteen previous books, including the bestselling *Fatal Voyage: The Sinking of the USS Indianapolis*. He has won the National Jewish Book Award for *Ben-Gurion: Prophet of Fire*; the Overseas Press Club's Cornelius Ryan Award, twice, for the best book on foreign affairs—*Miracle of November: Madrid's Epic Stand, 1936* and *Subversion of the Innocents*; the George Polk Memorial Award for the articles that formed the basis of his book *Santo Domingo: Revolt of the Damned*; and the Newspaper Guild's Front Page Award for dispatches from Cuba.

Mr. Kurzman's book *Genesis 1948* was called by Roderick MacLeish in the *Washington Post* "the best thing on the 1948 [Arab-Israeli] war that this reviewer has ever read—or is likely to read." And the book was acclaimed as "almost [reaching] the panorama and intensity of *War and Peace*" by Jerry O'Connell in *Catholic World.* "Barbara Tuchman," the reviewer wrote, "is perhaps [Kurzman's] only peer." Meyer Levin described another Kurzman

About the Author

book, *The Bravest Battle*, as "monumental and awe-inspiring, . . . the definitive story of the Warsaw Ghetto revolt."

Kurzman has written or broadcast from most countries in the world. He has served as Paris correspondent for the International News Service, as Jerusalem correspondent for NBC News, and as Tokyo bureau chief of the McGraw-Hill News Service.